Slavery in
the Structure of
American Politics
1765-1820

A VOLUME IN THE SERIES

The Founding of the American Republic

Planned and initiated by CLINTON ROSSITER

Slavery in the Structure of American Politics 1765-1820

DONALD L. ROBINSON

Harcourt Brace Jovanovich, Inc.

New York

TO

My Father and Mother

It seemed now to be pretty well understood that the real difference of interests lay, not between the large and small but between the Northern and Southern states. The institution of slavery and its consequences formed the line of discrimination.

—*James Madison, at the Constitutional Convention, July 14, 1787*

The Almighty has His own purposes. "Woe unto the world because of offences! for it must needs be that offences come; but woe to that man by whom the offence cometh!"

—*Abraham Lincoln, Second Inaugural Address, March 4, 1865*

Contents

ix

Tables

Acknowledgments

THE idea of writing something about the black presence and its significance during the founding of the American political system was suggested to me six long years ago by the late Clinton Rossiter. His interest in this subject reflected a determination to temper his celebration of the American promise with a candid appraisal of the flaws in the American performance. I was blessed with the benefits of his counsel and encouragement through all stages in the preparation of this book. My sense of gratitude to him, not only in connection with this book, but also as my mentor and friend, is enormous.

The years of work on this book have been long not only in scholarly effort, but also in psychic time for the people of my generation. Ways of looking at the black presence in American history have changed rapidly and profoundly during these six years, and the result has been an equally profound change in ways of looking at the totality of the American experience. Besides Mr. Rossiter, many other friends and fellow scholars have tried to help me keep my bearings during these shifts. Among those who have contributed in personal ways, I would like to single out Vincent Harding, Stanley Elkins, David Brion Davis, Staughton Lynd, Robert F. Nichol, David X. Spencer, and Stephen C. Rose.

I would also like to acknowledge my debt to Smith College. The stimulation and encouragement of colleagues and students, the friendliness and skill of the administration, the efficiency and courtesy of the staff, and the pleasures of the academic, civic, and natural environment often helped to transform despair into hope and to bring renewal in moments of fatigue. Among col-

Acknowledgments

leagues, I would like especially to mention Peter Rowe, Thomas Jahnige, Cecelia Kenyon, and Leo Weinstein; among students, Jean Lamb, Lydia Weiss Jones, Susan Dunlay, Deborah Smith, and Pamela Chamberlain; among staff members, librarians Pat Delks, Regina Lapoint, Blanche Cooney, and Emma Kaplan, and typists Barbara Rowe, Norma Lepine, and Agnes Shannon; and in the administration, Thomas Mendenhall, Phyllis Lehmann, and Patricia Olmsted.

The purpose of this book is to record and to judge the ways in which the founders of the American political system dealt with the gravest problem that confronted them. My greatest debts remain to be acknowledged: to my parents, who taught me to love the United States, but who bred me also in the Christian tradition, which teaches that speaking the truth is part of love's service; to my parents-in-law, who contributed hospitality and encouragement along the way; and to my wife, Polly, and sons, John and David—but of my gratitude for their sacrifices, I shall not try to write in public.

Northampton, Massachusetts
August, 1970

Slavery in
the Structure of
American Politics
1765-1820

Introduction

THIS is a study of the impact of slavery on the founding of the United States as a national political community. It analyzes how the leading politicians of the founding period sought to deal, and to avoid dealing, with the issues raised by slavery, and by their own and their constituents' racial prejudice. It is an attempt to clarify and correct our "memory" about the role of slavery in the crisis of the founding.

A primary purpose is to correct the impression that slavery and racial prejudice did not become a problem for the American national government until the 1820's or 1830's. The traditional interpretation holds that the founders of the American republic believed that slavery was gradually disappearing, and that it was therefore both wise and possible to proceed in the task of founding national political institutions virtually as if slavery did not exist. It assumes that this strategy was upset by the unexpected invention of the cotton gin, which saved slavery from extinction and gave it new vitality and power to influence American affairs, forcing politicians in the second and third generations of national leadership to come to grips with a problem that could be safely sidestepped by the founding generation.

In contradicting this traditional interpretation, this work will show that slavery was not disappearing during the founding period in those regions where it was most intrinsically a part of the social, economic, and political fabric; that many of the founders, particularly those who had grown up where slavery was strongest, knew perfectly well that the institution was not dying. It will argue that the decision of the founders to try to ignore the challenge posed by slavery and racial prejudice was based, not on confidence that the institution was vanishing, but on the conviction that slavery was ungovernable.

The challenge of the founding of the United States was like the challenge of political foundings everywhere. The first necessity was to create a government with authority to manage the nation's affairs. Such authority is necessarily built on trust and confidence between those who join in creating the government. Americans then and since have made much of the cultural affinities of the British-American settlers in the thirteen colonies and of the similarities of their experience in North America. Indeed, it was on these likenesses, reinforced by complementary interests, that the possibility of federal union rested. But despite these unifying factors, there existed a "line of discrimination" through the middle of the union, drawn, as James Madison pointed out, by "slavery and its consequences." In its earliest form, this line lay between sections that differed in circumstances, rather than in moral principle. In the early national period, there were many opponents of slavery in the South, just as there were large numbers of apologists for it in the North. It was not moral principle, initially at least, that drew the line of discrimination. It was the fact that 90 per cent of the blacks in America lived in the five southernmost states, where they constituted about 30 per cent of the population of the region, and in some places outnumbered their white masters at ratios of over ten to one. In the North, blacks were dispersed among a more numerous and faster-growing white population and constituted only a small percentage of the total population.

The causes and consequences of these conditions will be traced in some detail. Suffice it here to say that these facts, coupled with a nearly universal racial prejudice on the part of white men throughout North America, produced very different social patterns and social possibilities on the northern and southern sides of Madison's line of discrimination. As a direct consequence of the distribution of blacks among the thirteen founding states, 95 per cent of the blacks in the South remained slaves, whereas in the North slavery was quickly and easily abolished in some states, and in the rest more gradually, by laws declaring that children born to slaves after a certain date would automatically become

4

free upon the attainment of maturity. These differences in social
pattern in turn produced tensions between the sections, which
manifested themselves in differences on public policies of taxation, tariffs, and subsidies, policies governing expansion on the
western frontier, attitudes toward foreign powers, and the style
and outlook of the leading officers of government.

But most of all, there were differences in attitude toward slavery itself. Northerners were free, as they saw fit, to pity Southerners for being saddled with a regrettable necessity or to hate them
for profiting from a vicious evil, and, alternately, to encourage
Southern development according to Southern lights or to bring
hostile pressure against the institution that lay at the root of
Southern society. In choosing between these courses, Northerners
might follow the strategy of their party, or respond to pressure
from abolitionists or slave merchants among their constituents, or
heed considerations of national interest in the field of foreign
affairs, or do whatever the political situation and their own judgment seemed to require. Southerners might choose to apologize
for slavery or to defend it for its advantages to whites and blacks,
community, state, and nation. But after 1790, they were not free
to favor public policies that seriously threatened slavery. And
whenever Northern politicians favored such policies, Southern
leaders almost universally regarded the stand as hostile to the
South and therefore hostile to the union.

Southerners were especially sensitive on this issue because they
knew that they were in a vulnerable position. The political
thought of the American Revolution, even as modified through
the framing of the Constitution and the mounting of a viable
central government, was ultimately irreconcilable with slavery.[1]

Southerners were vulnerable for another reason, too. Their
practical commitment to slavery set them at odds with the thrust
of modernity toward an increasing "equality of conditions," as
Tocqueville put it. While the North and Northwest pursued industrial and commercial development, the South was lashed to a
system that seemed to offer the greatest rewards, and the greatest
safety, for agricultural development. Population and prosperity
were going one way; slavery prevented the South from joining the

1. Notes are on pages 451–543.

5

line of march. Southerners blamed Northern avarice for their difficulties, but their own economic journals suggest that a basic reason for their failure to follow the urgings of modernity was their inability to convert slavery to the requirements of industrialization and urbanization.[2]

A full consideration of these matters would go far beyond the early national period. They are adumbrated here only to suggest the ways in which a difference in situation and circumstance gradually began to take on moral overtones. Northerners, who were initially nearly as ambivalent about slavery as Southerners, gradually realized that slavery inhibited development, that it was forcing Southern politicians to advocate public policies that impeded industrial and commercial development. Gradually, their sympathy turned into anger. For their part, Southerners, who were surrounded by menace, gradually laid aside their ambivalence toward slavery and became more candid in asserting its alleged advantages.

In tracing the development of thirteen colonies into independent nationhood, this book focuses upon slavery as an obstacle to "more perfect union." It seeks to show how the political processes of the young nation were perverted by the commitment to slavery, how white men, captives of their own racial prejudice, sought to evade the obligations of justice toward their black fellow countrymen. It seeks to draw up an account of the costs of this "white racism" in the founding period. This book is based on the assumption that, though there were certain points at which a keener moral sensitivity might have prevented certain specific injustices, slavery could not have been eliminated by political processes during the founding period, and consequently that the cataclysm of war between the states could not have been prevented by different decisions taken at the founding—except perhaps the decision not to attempt union at all. But that decision would have entailed costs of its own and would almost certainly not have relieved the suffering of Southern Negroes during the first half of the nineteenth century.

When this study began, six or seven years ago, I sought to analyze the role of black people in the founding of the United States.

As my research unfolded, I concentrated on the great events of the founding—the Stamp Act Congress, the First and Second Continental Congresses, the great battles of the Revolutionary War, the framing of the Constitution, Jay's Treaty, the Louisiana Purchase, the War of 1812, and the controversy over Missouri. I began by trying to get a general picture of these events, through secondary accounts and primary source materials, and I tried to develop an understanding of the way these events related as parts of the drama of emerging nationhood.

Clues to the role of blacks in helping to shape these events were found particularly in the accounts of Revolutionary War battles and in the *Annals* of Congress. In the *Annals*, direct evidence of black activity bearing on the conduct of American government came in two forms: petitions from black citizens against slavery and the slave trade, and accounts of slave revolts and rumors of slave revolts, particularly in the speeches of Congressmen from South Carolina and Georgia. The figure of Toussaint L'Ouverture, leader of a successful uprising by blacks against French colonial rule in Santo Domingo, haunted the American political imagination. There is no doubt that his activities worked an important effect on national policy in the United States, beginning in the early 1790's.

But most of the evidence pointed in a different direction. In national politics, black people were almost entirely mute, politically passive. Being victims of almost total human repression, they were restrained from all but indirect and nonpolitical expressions of their passions and resentments. No Frederick Douglass emerged to cry out their agony or call for resistance. No Nat Turner arose to organize a fight for liberation.[3] To be sure, Phyllis Wheatley was able on one occasion to read her brilliantly plaintive poems to George Washington, and many Negro soldiers performed with heroism during the War for Independence. No doubt these and other exposures to black humanity helped to complicate Washington's attitude toward slavery. It may also be supposed that the ministrations of Sally Hemings troubled the conscience of Thomas Jefferson more than he ever publicly admitted.[4]

As my research developed, it seemed that the search for black political activism would lead away from the great events of the founding. One might tell about Crispus Attucks, the first American to fall in the struggle for national independence, or Benjamin Banneker, the mathematician and architect who helped to develop plans for the new nation's capital in the District of Columbia. But however important these people might be to an understanding of the history of the black people in America, from the viewpoint of the central events of the founding, their activities were of marginal importance.

Far more important to over-all national development were the work, the suffering, and the incredible endurance of tens and hundreds of thousands of black men, women, and children who cleared the forests, cultivated the fields, and tended to the comforts of their masters. But these contributions, crucial though they were to the nation's development, were not central to political events. They are important aspects of social and economic history, but politically they were part of the background.

Gradually, the intention of my project was modified. Instead of studying the role of blacks in the founding, I began to concentrate on the performance of whites, as it was affected by the presence of blacks. For example, in studying the political ideas that lay behind the Revolution, what struck me was the ironic juxtaposition of ideology and social institutions. The dialectic of events drove the colonists to reliance upon the doctrines of equality and consent, but their environment made them masters over a slavery so egregious as to mock the application of the term "slavery" to their own situation with respect to Great Britain. The paradox reached its climax when Thomas Jefferson, himself the owner of many slaves, became the draftsman of the Declaration of Independence, the document that laid the commitment to liberty and equality in the cornerstone of the republic.

But that was only the beginning. To assert independence, the new nation had to fight a war. The fighting of that war—the circumstances of America's defense and the offensive strategies of the British—was heavily conditioned by the fact that slavery constituted the basis of Southern culture and economy and that slave owners feared their slaves. To establish independence, the new nation had to create a national government—to agree on a formula for distributing power among the various regions and to determine what powers should and could be assigned to the central government. Directly and indirectly, the pervasiveness of racial prejudice and the dependence of the South on slave labor helped to shape these acts of creation. To maintain independence, the new nation had to put the government into operation and make it work. Here again, at almost every point, the national politicians confronted problems that were rendered more difficult by slavery and by the attempt to ignore it whenever it seemed that the national government could proceed as if it did not exist.

What has emerged is a book, not about black people, but about white people.* It contributes almost nothing to the current search for knowledge about the role of black people in the American past. It makes no judgment, explicit or implied, about that search, except to say that I have found virtually no evidence at all in the public documents of the founding period of political action on the part of black Americans. No doubt there were black heroes in America between 1765 and 1820, but, so far as I have been able to tell, they did not assume explicitly political roles, at least on the national level.

Perhaps a word should be offered about the rationale for the particular focus and limits of this study. It focuses on the national political arena between 1765 and 1820. The years chosen constitute the founding period of the American political system. They are somewhat arbitrary. Scholars argue fervently about the starting point of the American Revolution. The roots of the revolutionary ideology in America can be traced back at least to the

---

* I must confess that I am uneasy about this aspect. Currently, there is much research into the role of blacks in the antebellum period. The fruits of this research cannot help but alter our ways of looking at the founding period. Intimations of what may be found, and of its significance, can be gleaned from the following statement by a member of Gabriel's "rebellion." "I have nothing more to offer than what General Washington would have had to offer, had he been taken by the British officers and put to trial by them. I have ventured my life in endeavoring to obtain the liberty of my countrymen, and am a willing sacrifice to their cause; and I beg, as a favor, that I may be immediately led to execution." [5] We would not have to find many statements like this one, or many examples of uprisings like Gabriel's, to force a substantial revision in our thinking about blacks as participants in the founding process.

beginning of the eighteenth century. The habit of regarding the thirteen mainland colonies as a distinct entity can be found nearly that far back, too. But I have preferred the more conventional date of 1765 as the beginning of the American revolutionary movement, for it was then that British imperial policy really began to chafe the American colonies, and then, too, that the relevance of the ideology of the Revolution to Negro slavery began to be noticed by prominent public men.

This book studies the process by which thirteen colonies gradually, very gradually, began to knit together into a "more perfect" federal union of states. The focus is on the politics of national integration, the attempt by countless different communities of men on the western shores of the Atlantic Ocean, between New Hampshire and Georgia, and later inland across the Appalachian Mountains to the Mississippi River, and then, after 1803, almost to the Rocky Mountains, to establish a central government. It argues that one feature distinguishing these communities was their differing situations and attitudes toward race relations and the institution of slavery, and that these differences constituted one of the greatest obstacles to national integration during the theme of this book.

The line of discrimination was not between the races, but between regions differently situated. The fact that this line could be traced on a map (that is, slavery was confined for the most part to a geographically distinct region) made the situation particularly dangerous, giving rise to the belief that the problem belonged basically to the South and could thus be dismissed from the national political arena. This erroneous assumption and its rationale, function, and calamitous consequences provide a central theme of this book.

This study ends with the crisis over the status of slavery in Missouri and the unsettled parts of the Louisiana Purchase. That controversy provides a kind of coda to the Constitutional Convention of 1787. The Convention sidestepped the question of slavery in the territories, relying on the forces of momentum and precedent to govern the matter. But the arrangement of 1787 did not apply to territory across the Mississippi River, and so, when the Louisiana Purchase added this vast, unanticipated region to the governance of Congress, the national government inherited a task that forced a confrontation between the sections over slavery. The inevitable clash took place in 1820, and though its outcome proved inconclusive, it provides a fitting close to a consideration of a founding process that never did succeed in conceiving a political solution to the nation's gravest and most persistent threat.

No reader will be as painfully aware as the author of the weaknesses and limits of an approach that concentrates almost exclusively on politics and the art of government. But the limits of time, space, and energy require that some focus be chosen. A study of the political arena at the founding illustrates particularly well the operation and costs of the American approach to race relations. As Max Weber has pointed out, decisions taken when a polity is young can have a powerful effect on the future development of the body.[6] This is certainly true with respect to the relationship between race relations and national integration in America. The founders followed a pattern that endured far into the nineteenth century and that had its effects on race relations in this country down to the present.

No doubt the political arena as an object of focus provides an imperfect mirror of attitudes and forces in the society at large. But politicians are responsive to their constituents. Their acts often give important clues to the condition and outlook of the people they govern. Richard N. Goodwin makes the point this way:

Of all human activities, politics—the process of acquiring and using governmental or official power—is among the most responsive to shifting values and situations, always reflecting the dominant and visible themes of the human turbulence which creates it and which it attempts to govern. . . . An artist may be an age ahead of his time. Even the greatest politician can only be a step or two ahead of his. . . . Actions and public words based on a more profound vision than this may suit a prophet, but not a politician. His material is the desires and attitudes of living people. . . .[7]

If we listen sensitively to the words and acts, especially the *public* words and acts, of politicians at the founding period, they can tell much about the "limits of the possible" at that time. And the limits of the possible for our own time may be stretched by assessing the costs of their attitudes and decisions. That, at any rate, is my hope.

1

The Establishment of Slavery

in America

ONE of the ironies of American history stems from the fact that communities which began as British colonies were rushed in their development toward democratic nationalism by an institution that represented the very antithesis of democratic values. With or without slavery, the thrust of European civilization into the New World would doubtless have begun during the seventeenth and eighteenth centuries, but without it, even the most mature colonies would probably not have taken sufficient shape by the third quarter of the eighteenth century to mount a drive for national independence.

Slavery played an important role in the development of every North American colony. In some colonies, slaves were used to clear forests and drain swamps, plant seeds and gather harvests. In others, they served primarily as domestic helpers, artisans, and sailors, and joined in the defense of settlements against Indian raids. Colonies that engaged in maritime commerce also owed much of their wealth to slavery, by virtue of the trade that brought slaves from Africa to the New World. In one way or another, every British-American colony was hurried along in its development by the availability of black slave laborers—and by the willingness of white settlers to import them and keep them enslaved.

To achieve a proper understanding of the role of slavery in the founding of the United States, it is necessary to go back to the beginnings of British colonization in America. By seeing how slavery was established in the first place, how it was abolished in certain states, and how it became embedded in the economic and social structure of the nation, a better understanding of the predicament that confronted the founders of the nation's political structure can be gained.

Slavery did not spring fully developed into the American colonies.[1] The massive enslavement of black men by white men was virtually without relevant precedent, and it seems to have developed by a series of "unthinking decisions," made in various circumstances by men of various temperaments and predispositions.[2] Yet, however various the circumstances of its origins in America, the institution tended to take on the same characteristics wherever it appeared: it was perpetual, and heritable; it was confined to black men; unlike other forms of servitude in America, it typically resulted in the total deprivation of civil, political, and social rights; and, unlike previous kinds of slavery in human history, its victims were denied all opportunity to improve themselves, and were thus stigmatized by virtually indelible "badges of inferiority" which pursued them even into emancipation.[3]

It all began in 1619 when a Dutch vessel sold twenty Negroes to settlers in Jamestown, Virginia. These were apparently the first black people to join any of the communities that were to declare their independence as "one people" a century and a half later. The fact that they were sold does not mean that they came as slaves, in the full sense of that term. A slave is a person who owes all the labor of his lifetime to another man, and whose children inherit the condition of their parents. Many servants were bought and sold who were not slaves in this sense, but who served their purchasers for a term of years and then went free. How long these twenty Negroes worked for their new owners or what happened to any children they might have had is not known. What is known is that by the mid-1640's there were Negroes in Virginia who were not slaves. In fact, one Negro, apparently a free man, himself owned a slave.[4]

Whether the first Negroes who came to America were slaves or not may never be known, but whatever their status, several factors were soon at work that made the eventual enslavement of Negroes all but inevitable. From the vantage point of two centuries of slavery, and an additional century of flagrant racial discrimination, during which white men have shown a frightful willingness to treat black men with brutality and utter disregard of feelings and dignity, it is difficult to recover the atmosphere in which slavery was born. Yet we must try to imagine the attitude of those who first laid eyes upon black men and wondered how these creatures might fit into the communities of the New World.

According to the Oxford Dictionary, the word "black" in the sixteenth century had the following connotations: "soiled, dirty. . . . Having dark or deadly purposes, malignant; pertaining to or involving death, deadly; baneful, disastrous, sinister. . . . Foul, iniquitous, atrocious, horrible, wicked. . . . Indicating disgrace, censure, liability to punishment. . . ." Thus, when the British who first came in contact with Africans adopted the Spanish term "Negro," meaning "black," the relationship between the two peoples took on a heavy burden. The Africans were varying shades of brown, not black, just as Englishmen were varying shades of pink and tan, not white. The important thing, however, was the way men looked to one another's eyes, and in this case, from the "white" side at least, the situation was conceived in terms of its polarities, much to the prejudice of the Africans.[5]

Furthermore, sub-Saharan Africa was un-Christian, at a time when humility was not the virtue most characteristic of communities that called themselves Christian. Many of the earliest settlers dedicated their lives in America to the evangelical imperative, and even those whose faith was coolest were proud to be the bearers of "Christian civilization" to the wilderness. Africans, on the other hand, came from a pagan civilization, a fact that individual baptisms alone could not eradicate. The evangelical thrust of British Christianity, spurred by the energetic Society for the Propagation of the Gospel in Foreign Parts, eventually reached the transplanted Africans, but the stigma of having come from a heathen culture seems to have lingered with the Africans long after their conversion to the Christian faith.[6]

There was a cultural dimension, too. Negroes were also different in their social habits. In their language, table manners, and "morals" (family units, codes of honesty, honor), the Africans seemed savage to white men—not just different, but wild, and

14

distinctly inferior. There may have been white men with rough tongues, crude manners, and loose morals, but there did not seem, to white men's eyes, to be Africans who were refined in these matters.[7]

Because of their reactions to black men, whites in America were willing within two or three decades of their first exposure to create a special status for their black neighbors. But this was only one element in the picture. The second was that Negroes were almost uniquely able to endure the rigors that slavery entailed. If Negroes had had less stamina, or if they had been more susceptible to white men's diseases (as were the native Hawaiians, for example),* the processes that led to slavery might have been discouraged from the start. If Negroes had been less amenable to the settled ways of agriculture, the yoke of slavery might have fit less easily onto their necks. But, in almost every respect, the Negro seemed capable of enduring the agony of slavery. No work was so difficult, no master or overseer so brutal, no environment so inhospitable to human habitation as to be beyond the endurance of black men. If their capacity for suffering, psychological as well as physical, knew any bounds compatible with their owners' advantage, white men never found them.

If white men were willing, and Negroes able, the situation was

---

* On this point, Philip D. Curtin has written an article relating the slave trade to epidemiology, the science that studies the incidence of epidemic diseases in specific geographical areas.[8] He begins by asking why Europeans interested in establishing plantation colonies in the tropics did not do so in Africa itself, rather than incur the expense of transporting the Africans all the way to the New World. Part of the answer, he suggests, lies in the susceptibility of white men to diseases indigenous to Africa. On the other hand, Africans seem to have been only slightly more susceptible to diseases in the New World than to those in Africa, and not greatly more so than were white men themselves. These facts made it feasible to establish plantations in the New World, and to bring black laborers from Africa to work on them. If the death rate among Africans in the New World had been higher, this feasibility would have vanished. Thus, by surviving in their new environment, the first African transplants encouraged the massive black migration to the New World.

It used to be said that differences in color indicated the design of Providence that the races of men belonged separate. But if this were so, Providence might have gone one step further and discouraged mixture by establishing different patterns of susceptibility to fatal diseases. Instead, it seems that black men and white are curiously similar, among the races of men, as far as immunities to disease are concerned.

15

certainly ready. A vast continent lay open to development, its present inhabitants unaware of the dangers posed by the intruders, or unable to resist them. Europeans, pursuing a destiny that lay utterly beyond their wildest imaginings, nevertheless realized that labor on a scale without precedent was needed to establish their enterprises on the west coast of the Atlantic Ocean. Strenuous efforts were made to recruit white workers. Their passage was given in exchange for a term of service in the New World, usually four to seven years. So desperate was the appetite for laborers that children were kidnapped and convicts transported, and the search was carried outside England, to Ireland, Scotland, Germany, and France.[9] But white workers could not sate the appetite, especially where the need for disciplined workers was greatest. For one thing, there was a limit to the amount of degradation that could be imposed on them.[10] For another, their term of service was too short. It seemed that they had barely learned the ropes when their term was up and off they went, demanding exorbitant wages or setting out to seek an independent fortune.

Waiting to fill the gap was one of the most remarkable growth industries of the era. Englishmen were latecomers to the slave trade, but during the seventeenth and eighteenth centuries, they entered with a vengeance. It is conservatively estimated that by 1715 nearly 30,000 Africans had been brought to the mainland British colonies.[11] During the ensuing century, the trade reached its zenith, bringing perhaps a half-million persons to labor as slaves in the British colonies of North America.

The slave trade constitutes one of the most ghastly episodes in human history. The traffic implicated nearly everyone involved in the European colonization of America in its guilt. The Crown and its ministers in London and their agents in Williamsburg and Boston, tribal chieftains and warriors in Africa, merchants in Liverpool and Newport, Rhode Island, traders in Charleston, planters at Monticello and on Nantucket Island, sailors from Salem and Philadelphia, clergymen who blessed it, lawyers and judges who certified it, agents who insured it—all these and many others were part of the network that brought Negroes to bondage in the New World.

Colonial legislatures, sometimes moved by moral qualms, but

more often by fear of slave insurrections or concern for the balance of payments, periodically sought to regulate the pace of the trade.[12] When these curbs took the form of revenue-producing taxes, they were often doubly effective. But when a desire to restrict the trade threatened the profits of merchants, the Crown intervened with its power of veto to counteract colonial squeamishness.

The character of slavery in America can be further illuminated by considering the failure of white men to enslave so-called "red men." By European standards, Indians were dark-complexioned, heathen, savage folk. Yet they were never successfully enslaved, at least not in British North America. There seem to have been several reasons. For one thing, Indians apparently lacked the Negro's capacity for suffering. Whereas Negroes seemed amenable to the settled ways of agriculture, savages out of the American wilderness seemed to languish and die rather than undergo the rigorous discipline of work on plantations. Another factor was the proximity of Indian nations to the scene of enslavement. Occasionally, an Indian would be sold by his tribe to white men as a form of punishment, but this source of recruitment was obviously inadequate to the needs of the white settlers. Indians who were enslaved *against* the wishes of their tribesmen could escape into the forest whenever the white man relaxed his vigilance, and reenter the society from which they were snatched. Furthermore, when Indians were taken forcibly, whites ran the risk of devastating reprisal. In time, white men would be able to carry out a policy of removal and systematic destruction of the aborigines, but they never did find a way to make Indians reliably useful to their purposes. As Tocqueville put it, Indians had no aptitude for slavery, and so they had to be destroyed.[13]

In searching for people whose servitude could be extended into slavery, the English inhabitants bypassed not only Indians, but also other whites. Here the primary factor seemed to be the unwillingness of English settlers to reduce fellow white men to slavery —however much they needed laborers and however deep their contempt for Irishmen and Scots and Germans.

This distinction between races is significant for the light it sheds on the rationale sometimes used to justify slavery. According to the Lockean tradition of English liberalism, slavery was justified only in cases where men taken captive in a just war were permitted to render themselves slaves rather than be executed. By becoming aggressors, men forfeited their right to life and liberty. Locke argued that, if they were defeated in warfare and taken captive, their captors could decide to spare their lives without restoring their liberty, and keep them in slavery.[14] This notion was often used to justify the slavery of Negroes, who were said to have been captured by other Africans in "just war," then sold by their captors to European merchants and transported to slavery in America. There were, of course, several flaws in this reasoning: Locke never argued that the condition of slavery was inheritable, or negotiable, and no one in America knew or cared whether the warfare between African tribes was "just" or not, by any standard. But the argument was nevertheless used—sometimes even to limit slavery, as when a court in colonial Massachusetts freed and ordered the repatriation of an African who had been taken captive by a European merchant against whom he had committed no offense, but in whose path he chanced to lie when the merchant was pursuing a slave-hunting mission into Africa.[15]

That the "just war" argument was a rationalization, rather than a reason, is indicated by the fact that other immigrants, even more plainly than the Africans, came to America as prisoners captured in a so-called "just war," and yet no attempt was made to hold these men to perpetual servitude. Scots, taken captive by Cromwell at the Battle of Dunbar, were transported to America, but assurances were immediately given that these white, Christian, English-speaking immigrants would not be bound to their masters forever.[16] The plain fact is that the spirit of the age ran against Locke's strange apology for slavery. The leading student of white servitude in America states that no white man was ever reduced to slavery in any British colony.[17] Perpetual bondage was a status specially fashioned for Negroes, and its origins had nothing to do with "just wars." [18]

During the course of the seventeenth century, slavery became the presumed status of Negroes throughout British America. In light of the lack of contact between the colonies, this is a remarkable fact. There was some interclonial migration. Planters from Barbados and from Providence Island, scene of a bloody insurrection of slaves in 1638, came to New England during the 1640's.[19] The colony of South Carolina was established during the 1660's by transplanters from the Caribbean. In addition, there was some commercial contact between the mainland colonies. Still, it is remarkable that in each of the colonies it came to be regarded as normal and correct that all Negroes be treated as property, not for a term, as with white servants, but perpetually.

By the end of the seventeenth century, Negro slavery was an established fact in each British colony on the North American mainland. At first, there was little difference between the colonies in their attitudes toward blacks or in their employment of black slave labor. Negroes did the same work that white servants did in New England as well as Virginia, New York as well as Maryland. Gradually, however, differences developed in the fundamental social and economic order of the colonies, and as they did, these differences were reflected in the proportion of slaves among the white population, and in the kinds of work these slaves did.

Negro slavery never took hold in New England. Towns there needed labor as much as communities elsewhere, but settlers there were thought of as workers *and* potential constituents. The "planters" of New England (the term was used of the founders of New England as well as of settlements farther south) thought of their townships as permanent little polities. Their sponsors in Great Britain might have had commercial motives in sending them forth into the wilderness,[20] but the settlers themselves had far broader purposes. To fulfill these, they needed inhabitants who could take a full and active part in the life of their communities. Many came as servants, of course, bound to their masters for a term of years; and many youngsters, sons of free men, bound themselves as apprentices for a term to a master. But the end of these contractual relationships was always in sight. They were thought of as preparation for full participation in the life and work of civilization-building in the wilderness.

New Englanders must have reacted to Negroes the same as did any son of old England. Most of them would have had difficulty seeing Negroes as full members of the communities they were building. They were surely tempted by the promises of slavery. Having found great wealth in carrying slaves to West Indian and Southern plantations and bearing off the produce of slave labor, they must have wondered whether slaves might not help them clear the stones from their craggy fields or build the ships that carried their commerce. Indeed, some Negroes were employed in these tasks. But mostly, New Englanders, governed by a proto-democratic image of communal development and by their prejudice against Africans, had little difficulty resisting the attractions of slavery.

The same prejudice worked an opposite effect in the Southern colonies. The longer growing season and richer soil, plus the tendency to divide the land into larger holdings, led them to develop the production of staple crops—tobacco in Maryland and Virginia, rice and indigo in the Carolinas and Georgia. The colonies of the South were conceived by their planters in a way more consistent with the image held by their sponsors in England, as producers of raw materials for emergent British capitalism. To make their plantations work, they needed laborers who could be counted upon to put in extremely long hours under trying conditions, immediately at the bidding of the plantation manager. Men who were able to resist the rigid disciplines of such work often did, and thereby rendered themselves a poor investment for the planters.[21] This left the Negroes.

In Virginia and Maryland, by this process of elimination under the stress created by the determination to produce a profit-making crop of tobacco, the plantation slavery of black men was born. In the Carolinas, the process was more deliberate. The charter and early prospectuses show that the founders of English colonization in the Carolinas, including the philosopher John Locke, intended that the enslavement of blacks be integral to the whole conception. The Carolinas were to be a mainland Barbados, in which rich soil, tropical climate, and black labor under white management would yield quick riches for a London-based company and its colonial agents in the New World.

The colonies of New York, New Jersey, and Pennsylvania were often called the "middle" colonies. They stood midway not only geographically, but also in respect to the tendency to import and enslave black men. Pennsylvania was most like New England in this respect. The notion that the communities on the western shores of the Atlantic would be entire unto themselves and ought to be developed with this purpose constantly in mind seems to have grown up quite early there. Not everyone could see as far into the future as Benjamin Franklin, or trace the influence of current practices on future developments as well as he, but there is little doubt that he articulated the instincts of his neighbors in 1755 when he warned against the importation of Africans and called for measures to encourage the immigration of settlers from Northern Europe.[22] In the colony of New York, on Long Island, and in the valley of the Hudson River, there developed some manorial estates of large acreage, on which Negro slaves were employed in fairly large gangs. On and around Manhattan Island, slaves were more numerous than in any other town north of Maryland. But in Northern towns, a kind of natural limit to the use of black labor was set by the competitive presence of white laborers, and by the difficulty of maintaining control over subject groups in an urban environment.[23] The full logic of this latter impediment to the development of slavery would not be apparent until cities began to emerge from the wilderness, but the same impulses and conditions that drove the North toward unbanity helped to discourage a reliance upon the labor of black slaves.

While the varying course of development in the colonies meant that the institution of slavery played differing roles, everywhere the institution itself took on the same basic aspect. Everywhere the distance between white indentured servants and black slaves increased. While servants achieved the recognition of certain rights, slaves suffered a gradual, persistent erosion of status. As slaves, they had no right to marry and rear a family, no right to own and accumulate property, however hard they might be willing to work, no right to bear arms or defend themselves against assault.[24] Their status was determined by the race of their mothers, which meant, in effect, that if children had any Negro blood at all, they were consigned to slavery.* From the first, codes ap-

* Presumably, the child of a black father and white mother would legally have been free, but there were apparently few such children. Most instances

plying to Negroes were patently discriminatory in their definitions of criminal behavior and in the penalties they assigned to such behavior.

Actual relations between white men and black men are no doubt imperfectly reflected in the slave codes.[26] In some cases, neighborhood opinion and the humanity of masters must have saved slaves from the full wrath of the law. The quite genuine concern of some masters for the well-being of their property may also have mitigated the harshness of the system, particularly in the case of slaves who did not strain against their bondage. But for the slave who resisted by rising up against white control or by trying to flee from it, the wrath of his owner, strongly reinforced by the opinion of the neighborhood, was seldom effectively restrained by public statutes aimed at protecting slaves from excessive cruelty.

The overriding concern in the process by which slavery was wrenched off the back of the Northern states, at the same time that it was fastened ever more firmly onto the Southern states, was the advantage of white men, rather than a sense of compassion or a commitment to justice for the Negro.

The institution of slavery enjoyed the protection of the law in each of the eight Northern states that joined in the Declaration of Independence. Negroes constituted about 4 per cent of the population throughout the North, but the proportion of Negroes among whites varied a good deal from place to place. In New Hampshire, for example, there were only about 600 Negroes, less than 1 per cent of the total population. In Pennsylvania, too, Negroes were sparsely scattered in a population drawn predominantly from England, Scotland, Ulster, and Germany. In New York, on the other hand, Negroes constituted over 10 per cent of the total population, and in New York City the proportion was even higher.

These bare statistics are reflected with remarkable accuracy in

---

of miscegenation were produced by a mating of white men and black slave women. Thus, the myth of the lascivious Negro male was the precise opposite of reality, produced, according to W. J. Cash, by the twisted, guilty imagination of white men.[25]

TABLE I. NEGROES AND SLAVERY IN THE NORTH, 1790–1820

REGION	NEGROES AS % OF TOTAL POPULATION	SLAVES AS % OF NEGROES
New England (New Hampshire, Massachusetts, Connecticut, Rhode Island, Vermont, Maine)		
1790	1.7%	22.2%
1800	1.5%	7.2%
1810	1.4%	2.1%
1820	1.3%	.7%
Mid-Atlantic States (New York, New Jersey, Pennsylvania)		
1790	5.3%	72.0%
1800	4.6%	54.0%
1810	4.1%	32.8%
1820	3.3%	19.9%

SELECTED STATES

Massachusetts		
1790	1.4%	0%
1800	1.5%	0%
1810	1.4%	0%
1820	1.3%	0%
New York State		
1790	7.6%	81.9%
1800	5.3%	66.7%
1810	4.2%	37.2%
1820	2.9%	25.6%

SOURCE: U.S. Bureau of the Census, *Negro Population, 1790–1915* (Washington: Government Printing Office, 1918), pp. 45, 51, 57.

the sequence by which the Northern states adopted laws abolishing slavery. New Hampshire and Massachusetts, which had the lowest proportion of Negroes among the American states, were the only states in which slavery was eliminated by judicial decrees that simply declared the bondsmen free and then virtually ignored their erstwhile masters' claims to compensation. Pennsylvania, Connecticut, and Rhode Island were next lowest in the percentage of Negroes, and these were the first three states to eliminate slavery by statute, each of them passing laws of gradual abolition in the immediate aftermath of the Declaration of Independence. New York and New Jersey had slightly more slaves, and it took them an additional decade to put slavery firmly on the road to extinction. Delaware, which had three times as many slaves as New York and New Jersey, proportionally, was one of the three jurisdictions in which slavery was still legal in 1865, when the Thirteenth Amendment went into effect.[27]

In each state, of course, the process of abolishing slavery was different, reflecting slightly different attitudes toward black men and toward the process of becoming communities in which black men were legally free, at least of the restraints of slavery.

The abolition of slavery in Massachusetts remains shrouded in mystery. The tradition is that slavery was ended in the early 1780's by a series of lawsuits between Nathaniel Jennison and his former slave Quock Walker. Walker sued Jennison for his freedom. Levi Lincoln, Walker's attorney, and later Jefferson's Attorney General, based his plea on the argument that slavery was contrary to natural law and Biblical teaching, unsupported by positive law, and in violation of the declaration of rights in the constitution of the Commonwealth of Massachusetts. The court granted Walker's plea for freedom, and once Jennison's claim to Walker had been denied, the chains fell from every slave in the commonwealth.

This is the tradition, and in broad outline it is true. A closer inspection of the facts, however, reveals certain significant difficulties. For one thing, scholars have found technical impediments in the cases themselves. The decision in Walker's original suit for freedom contains no judicial opinion. Since his attorney offered several possible bases for a decision in his client's favor, and since the court was not limited to Lincoln's arguments, the reasons for the court's ruling that Walker was a free man can only be guessed. In addition to the broad philosophical and constitutional arguments presented by Lincoln, there was the fact that Walker had been promised manumission by a previous master, a fact occasionally seized upon by courts in Massachusetts as a pretense for granting freedom.[28]

24

Two years later, in 1783, Jennison was brought to trial for assaulting Walker. He told the court that his attack was intended as correction for a runaway slave. In his charge, Chief Justice William Cushing instructed the jury that this argument should be ignored. Having been promised manumission, he said, Walker was a free man. But he went beyond this narrow ground, pointing out that, whereas slavery had once been permitted in Massachusetts, it was now undermined by a growing regard for the "natural rights of mankind." This new spirit, enshrined in the recently ratified state constitution, abolished slavery "as effectively . . . as it can be by the granting of rights and privileges wholly incompatible and repugnant to its existence.' [29]

No doubt Cushing's charge to the jury was a grave blow to slavery in Massachusetts.* Coming from the State's Chief Justice, a declaration that the courts regarded the constitution as having granted rights and privileges wholly incompatible with slavery rendered slavery an untenable institution. What is significant is that this decision was made by judges, and not by the elected representatives of the people.† The legislature had not simply been outhustled by the courts. There had been no race to see which branch could be the first to earn the gratitude of the people, and the applause of history, for this reform. On the contrary, the incident has all the aspects of a decision made almost furtively by the dominant element in the state's elite, over the objections of some from its own ranks, and despite the faintly hostile attitude of the people.

Note that the decision in the initial suit of 1781 was unexplained. Cushing's charge to the jury in 1783 implies that the decision in 1781 had been based on the narrowest possible grounds—the promise of a previous master to manumit Walker. It was clear that the courts had determined not to enforce slavery's claims, but it was also clear that the courts were reluctant to legislate slavery out of existence by judicial decree. Courts,

---

* It was apparently not immediately fatal, however, Evidence has been found that a slave was sold in Massachusetts in 1784.[30]

† A friend, speaking primarily of mid-twentieth-century America, once remarked that racial discrimination has been most effectively combated by generals, bishops, and judges—a sad commentary on the competence of democracy in this area.

particularly in a representative government, usually prefer to base their judgments on the narrowest grounds that will support a desired result. They eschew large reasons for their actions because their basic function is the interpretation and application of statutes rather than the achievement of far-reaching social purposes. The latter task, in the extent to which a democratic polity desires it, is usually best reserved for the legislative branch of government, which is directly accountable to the people who must carry out such broad reforms, and upon whose acceptance of them their success usually depends.

Thus, there may have been a trace of sarcasm in Cushing's charge to the jury when he said that slavery was "as effectively abolished as it can be by the granting of rights and privileges wholly incompatible and repugnant to its existence." Indeed, the Massachusetts legislature had had several opportunities over the years to consider abolition. At least once during the colonial period a bill to end slavery had been proposed in the Massachusetts Assembly, but it had failed to muster enough support to pass. In 1777, in the flush of excitement that attended the separation from Great Britain, abolitionists gathered considerable support for a bill to abolish slavery gradually by freeing all children born to slaves after a certain date. This time the effort was thwarted by a maneuver to refer the question to the national Congress, to inquire about the impact of such a move upon "our brethren in other colonies." John Adams, knowing well how the brethren in other colonies would react, succeeded in sidetracking the petition, and there the issue died.

The framing of a state constitution in 1778 provided still another opportunity to come to grips with slavery, but, instead, Article V of the proposed constitution contained a clause limiting the suffrage to "free inhabitants," which implied that some inhabitants were not free. This might have been the first recognition of slavery in the positive law of independent Massachusetts, but the constitution failed of ratification. The one submitted in its place, ratified in 1781, contained the declaration of rights upon which Lincoln's argument and Cushing's charge were based. There is no evidence, however, that the clause declaring all men "born free and equal" was intended to outlaw slavery. A

26

far stronger clause in the Bill of Rights of the Virginia constitution of 1776 had not affected the status of 200,000 slaves in that state. If the framers of the Massachusetts constitution of 1780 had really intended to abolish slavery, it would not have been difficult to say so explicitly.

In the same year that Cushing dealt slavery its mortal wound, the legislature was considering one of the most straightforward abolitionist bills ever proposed anywhere. The bill declared that slavery had never been legal in Massachusetts; it provided compensation for masters whose claims to property were undercut by the declaration against slavery; and it provided help for destitute Negroes unable to support themselves in their sudden exposure to liberty. The state had so few Negroes, not all of whom were slaves, that the plan might have been feasible economically. The bill passed the Assembly, but died when the Senate took no action.

Against this murky backdrop, Cushing's decree amounted to an announcement that although the legislature had failed to provide for the abolition of slavery, the courts would refuse to recognize its claims. Whenever the "rights and privileges" granted by the Massachusetts declaration of rights clashed with the alleged obligations of slavery, courts would honor the former at the expense of the latter. This declaration did not abolish slavery; it made it unenforceable in the courts. Courts had no machinery for going about the countryside separating slaves from masters. Cushing had simply put white men on notice that no pleas based on the claims of slavery would be recognized in the courts of Massachusetts.

Abolition failed in the representative branch of government for several reasons. No one but a few idealists, and of course the blacks themselves, cared about slavery. To those who thought about it at all, it must have appeared that its abolition would make little real difference. Where masters, like Jennison, were cruel, the courts were available to protect the abused black. Slavery's main function was to restrict the opportunities of Negroes by binding them to their owners, or to those who were willing and able to hire slaves. John Adams once attributed abolition in Massachusetts to the antipathy of white workers toward competition from black slaves. What white workers really wanted, however, was not the emancipation of the slaves, but their removal from the state. That alone would have eliminated their competition. A letter in the Massachusetts *Centinel,* December 18, 1784, deplored the migration of free Negroes to Boston, arguing that the influx of blacks (which could not have been great) made it hard for poor white people to make a living.[31] The abolition of slavery could not have made much difference to a man who saw the problem in these terms.

If the workers felt ambivalent, so did the elite. James Winthrop, descendant of the first Governor of Massachusetts Bay, Librarian of Harvard, and Chief Justice of the Court of Common Pleas in Middlesex County, complained sourly in 1795 that "by a misconstruction of our state constitution . . . a number of citizens have been deprived of property formerly acquired under the protection of law." The quick, quiet death of the bill of 1783 in the state Senate is further testimony to the opposition of leading citizens. A letter in the Boston *Evening-Post,* urging the defeat of members who had favored the bill, complained that it would commit the double error of depriving gentlemen of their property and turning a horde of black vagabonds loose on society.[32]

Massachusetts was the first of the original thirteen states to be rid of slavery. Its undermining there was thus a significant event. It made little immediate difference in the actual status of black people, but it did demonstrate that the "contagion of liberty," to use Bernard Bailyn's phrase, could reach the institution of Negro slavery when social and economic conditions, particularly relating to the number of blacks enslaved, were not prohibitory. Because it had so few Negroes, the commonwealth was able to include them in its constitutional declaration that all men were by nature free and equal. In time, this would be an important factor in the life of the state and the nation, requiring adjustments that were unanticipated by whites or blacks in the 1780's.

For the nation as a whole, the more significant meaning of the abolition of slavery in Massachusetts was the difficulty with which it was achieved. Although the people of Massachusetts were as deeply committed as any in America to the equalitarian ideals of the Revolution, and although Negroes constituted less than 2 per cent of their population, the decision to free slaves had to be made by men isolated from direct political accountability, and by a branch of the government unable to compensate masters for property purchased under the protection of the laws and unable to provide Negroes with support during the adjustment to life in freedom. Massachusetts was free of slavery by 1790, but its example was of little value to men for whom slavery was a pervasive feature of their social and economic lives.

Pennsylvania was the first state in America to pass a law for the abolition of slavery. The people there had been subjected by Anthony Benezet and other Quakers to a continual barrage of anti-slavery propaganda since mid-century, but, ironically, abolition was accomplished while Quaker politicians were in disgrace for their pacifism and other forms of nonco-operation with the independence movement. What needs explaining in Pennsylvania's case is how the state was able to summon the will to abolish slavery even while the most strenuous opponents of the institution were in exile from political power.

Quakers and wealthy merchants made Pennsylvania a most reluctant partner in the movement for independence. Thus, when separation from the British Empire finally came, radicals from Philadelphia, in alliance with Scotch-Irish frontiersmen from the western part of the state, were able to seize control of the government.[33] Abolitionists feared the worst, but canny old George Bryan, an Irish immigrant who had become a merchant in Philadelphia and a leader of the Constitutional, or Presbyterian, party, was a man whose notions about individual liberty ran deep. He was determined to show that the constitution framed by his party could work well, and he was particularly anxious that his party not be vulnerable to the charge of being less zealous for freedom than the opposition. Accordingly, in 1778, as soon as he became president of the state's Executive Council, he sent a message urging the legislature to abolish slavery. Two years later, the unicameral Assembly complied, making Presbyterian-governed Pennsylvania the first polity in the world to abolish Negro slavery by legislative act.

Bryan's bill provided for gradual emancipation, according to a scheme that would often be paid the tribute of imitation by other states anxious to reconcile the claims of property and the natural right to freedom.[34] The statute provided that in the future every child born to a slave would continue as the slave of his mother's master until his twenty-eighth birthday, and then go free. The purpose of this provision was to cover the master's costs of raising the child by granting him some benefit of the slave's service. The law specifically provided that slaves be entitled to all the privileges of indentured servants. A clause banning interracial marriages, upon pain of fine or imprisonment for the offending Negro, was stricken from the bill before it was passed, as was another clause that bound free Negroes to work for the benefit of the state if they failed to support themselves. The fact that the law was serious was indicated by a provision requiring all masters to register their slaves with the state by November 1780. Failure to comply would result in the immediate emancipation of any unregistered slave.[35]

It was this registration clause that became the main bone of contention in the first two years of gradual emancipation. Many slave owners failed to comply, some of them apparently out of contempt for the Presbyterian government. When the unregistered Negroes began to go free, a howl went up from their masters, who begged for an extension of the deadline. Elections had been held between the passage of the act and the deadline for registration. The Constitutional party had suffered an erosion of its domination of the legislature. At first it appeared that the new legislature was sympathetic to the request for crippling modifications of the act of 1780. A test vote early in the session showed surprising strength for the opponents of the law. But supporters of abolition quickly roused themselves and pointed out that an extension of the deadline would mean the return to slavery of men already growing accustomed to freedom. The original deadline had been widely publicized. An extension now, it was argued, would only justify and augment the contempt for decency and public order already shown by the haughty slave owners.

When the proposed extension came before the legislature in September 1781, it was easily defeated. Within a few months, the attempt to deflect abolition in Pennsylvania was ended.[36] Thus,

30

before the War for Independence was over, one state had discovered the political will to proceed against slavery.

Without detracting from this achievement, certain observations about it must be made. In the first place, it occurred in a state that was less than 2½-per-cent black. The importance of this fact must not be underestimated. Tocqueville argued that "gradual abolition," giving freedom at a certain age to Negroes born after a certain date, was impossible where Negroes were numerous enough to menace the white community.[37] In Pennsylvania, slaves were still reported in the census of 1840, which presumably meant that these blacks either were more than sixty years old or had been born since 1812 to women born before 1780. In either case it must have rankled in black breasts that slavery had lasted almost two generations beyond the date of its official sentence of death. But where Negroes constituted so small a proportion of the total population, there was little danger that this resentment would be expressed in forms dangerous to the white community.

The sparseness of blacks was important for another reason, too. It meant that whites had little to fear from the prospect of Negroes free from the restraints of slavery. The fact that Negroes were free meant that white men had to pay for their services, which put the competition between black and white laborers on a footing more favorable to white workers. This was the consideration that appears to have dominated the thinking of white workers in Massachusetts. But it also meant that Negroes might eventually begin to challenge the prerogatives of white men in other areas. For example, in a land that was reforming its suffrage in the direction of greater inclusiveness, the prospect of Negroes voting inevitably loomed.[38] Where Negroes constituted just 2 or 3 per cent of the population, this prospect of black mingling and participation in white society was not nearly so terrifying as where Negroes made up 30 or 40 or 50 per cent.

Yet even in Pennsylvania there was substantial resistance to the act for gradual abolition. The final vote in 1780 had shown thirty-four assemblymen in favor, twenty-one opposed. The losers, mostly from the western part of the state, issued an explanation of their opposition in which they argued that the act was an affront to the Southern states in the union and was particularly nettlesome coming, as it did, just when the scene of battle was shifting to the Southern states. They objected that the act opened the way to Negroes voting, holding public office, serving as witnesses, and marrying whites. These opinions, from sections of the state where Negroes were virtually unknown, were eloquent testimony to the fact that the fears and prejudices of white men needed little provocation.

New York, along with the eastern half of New Jersey, had always had the largest proportion of Negroes of any of the Northern states.[39] In Kings County (now Brooklyn, but then an area of broad, rich farms), fully one-third of the population consisted of black slaves throughout the second half of the eighteenth century. One hundred and sixty-nine families owned slaves; thirty-five had more than five slaves each. This meant that slaves were probably employed in large-scale farming. The system of slavery there seems to have had all the aspects of slavery in parts of the upper South: large holdings, commercial agriculture, a high proportion of blacks in the total population, and an affluent style among the owners.

In the Hudson Valley, a number of manorial estates employed black labor fruitfully and extensively. Lewis Morris, a signer of the Declaration of Independence, owned twenty-nine slaves on his estate in Ulster County (now the Bronx, but then a magnificent pastoral region quite a distance up the Hudson River from the settlement on the lower tip of Manhattan Island). Travelers upstate noted that black farm-laborers were encountered everywhere in the upper Hudson and Mohawk River valleys. According to the Federal Census of 1790, only one-fifth of the families in Albany, New York, lacked at least one slave.[40]

The history of slavery in New York was bloody and tense. In 1712, a group of Negroes in New York City had killed five whites and wounded six others while firing from ambush. From the point of view of the havoc wreaked upon the white community, it was one of the most successful uprisings in the history of slavery in the United States. White retribution, however, had been swift and extremely severe. Twenty-one Negroes, innocent and guilty alike, were subjected to the "most exemplary punishments" that man's lust for revenge could imagine.[41] Throughout the rest of the century, rumors of servile insurrection were frequently heard in New York. The memory of white men often ran back to that bloody April night in 1712, reminding them that the price of safety in the midst of enslaved Negroes was eternal vigilance.

In 1777 Gouverneur Morris, Lewis's younger half-brother, proposed that the new state constitution include a promise of emancipation as soon as it could be accomplished "consistent with the public safety and the private property of individuals." [42] The preamble to his resolution mentioned "the rights of human nature and the principles of our holy religion," but it also acknowledged that "it would at present be productive of great dangers to liberate the slaves within this state." At that time, New York, the last and most reluctant state to accede to the Declaration of Independence, was occupied by a strong British force. In the circumstances, the "great dangers" of abolition and the rights of private property were more than a match for the rights of human nature and the principles of holy religion. Morris's carefully qualified proposal was easily sidetracked by his older fellow delegates.

After the war ended, there was a brief flurry of activity on behalf of the enslaved blacks in New York. In January 1785 a group of luminaries, including John Jay, Alexander Hamilton, General Philip Schuyler, Melancton Smith, James Duane, and Chancellor Robert Livingston, joined in the formation of the New York Manumission Society. Shortly thereafter, the state legislature began wrestling, briefly and maladroitly, with a bill for gradual abolition. The bill was lost in a struggle over the rights that freed Negroes were to enjoy. The Assembly insisted on including a provision that Negroes be excluded from the suffrage, while the Council of Revision refused to pass a bill that denied Negroes the right to vote. The drive for abolition bogged down over this debate.

It might have been assumed that victory for the antislavery forces was just around the corner. But in 1788, instead of abolishing slavery, the legislature passed a new code regulating the treatment of slaves. Its significance lay not in its brutality; it was not much different from earlier codes in New York or in other states. What made it important was that it was the first explicit acknowledgment by the newly independent government of New York that slavery was a legal institution in the state. New York had seen to the effective management and control of slaves before it moved in the direction of abolition.

The New York legislature was not eloquent during this period on the reasons for its reluctance to decree an end to slavery. But a report issued by the legislature of New Jersey helps to explain why these two states were so loath to act. A committee of the Assembly of New Jersey, responding to a petition for gradual abolition in 1790, argued that it was "not necessary or expedient at this time to make any new law upon the subject." Negroes, it said, were protected by law from abuse by their masters and from export to places where slavery was more rigorous. Furthermore, voluntary manumissions were encouraged. "[F]rom the state of society among us . . . and progress of the principles of universal liberty, there is little reason to think that there will be any slaves at all among us 28 years hence." "Experience," concluded the committee, showed that "precipitation in the matter" of abolition did more harm than good, both for society and for the Negro.[43] The committee did not explain how a law for gradual emancipation would be precipitous in a community where slavery was dying anyway.

That the same pressures were abroad in New York was demonstrated during the gubernatorial campaign of John Jay in 1792. His opponents sought to make capital of his previous service as president of the Manumission Society. An owner of slaves,[44] as well as an experienced diplomat, he responded by asserting that he would always be "an advocate for the manumission of slaves in such way as may be consistent with the justice due to them, with the justice due to their master, and with regard due to the actual state of society." [45] There was not a man in South Carolina who could not have subscribed to the same statement.

But Jay was not a South Carolinian. Despite his smooth manner, or perhaps because of it, he was one of the canniest foes of slavery in the United States. Defeated in 1792, he ran for governor again, successfully, in 1795. A series of attempts began immediately in the legislature to pass a bill for gradual abolition. The main obstacle seemed to be the widespread concern for the property rights of slave owners. New Yorkers had such respect for private property that they hesitated to interfere with a master's right to the labor of his slave's children. It was widely accepted that a slave's issue belonged to his master and that it would be wrong to deprive an owner even of this aspect of his property without compensation.[46]

Proposals for compensation in the form of purchase by the state were easily defeated. But in 1798 it was proposed that owners who objected to the cost of raising children who would later be freed might "abandon" them to the care of the government. The government would then place the black children in homes and reimburse their new guardians for the cost of their care. In practice, the transaction was a paper one. Children were turned over to the state, then returned to the previous owner, who was paid a tidy fee to cover upkeep. Presumably the Negroes did not remain idle, and so the master benefited doubly until the time of emancipation at age twenty-eight. A bill including this provision for abandonment passed the New York legislature in 1799. All children born to slaves after July 4, 1799 were to be freed at age twenty-eight, after they had repaid their master for raising them by working seven years as adults.

The act for gradual abolition immediately undercut the value of blacks and posed the threat of racial amalgamation. The situation was grim, but not irremediable, from the slave owner's viewpoint. In the South and the West Indies, slavery was not threatened with extinction. Slaves were therefore easily marketable, if only one could get them delivered. New York had a law against selling slaves with the intent of exporting them from the state, but a law depending on proof of the vendor's intent was obviously a good deal harder to enforce than it was to frame. The export trade was illegal and covert, and so there are no reliable figures on the number of Negroes transported south after gradual abolition was decreed. Yet there are grounds for suspecting that such a trade in fact was carried on. Traders in New York had been making a solid profit since the 1780's on slaves transported to Southern markets. With the value of slaves to New Yorkers decreasing, and with the demand for slaves in the South increasing, it seems reasonable to suppose that this trade southward would continue to show enough profit to keep it going. Investigators for the Manumission Society were convinced that "the illegal transportation of slaves is . . . carried on to an alarming extent from this [state] to the southward, particularly to New Orleans." [47] Further evidence lies in the diminishing proportion of Negroes among the population at large. Part of this decrease was due to the immigration of white workers, which carried the population of New York to the front rank among the states by 1810. But part must also be attributed to the fact that the Negro population was growing at a rate substantially below normal. Whereas Negroes constituted a little over 10 per cent of the population of New York on the eve of the Revolution, the percentage fell to about 8 in 1786, 7.6 in 1790, 4.2 in 1810, and 2.9 in 1820. It seems not unreasonable to conclude that one factor helping to account for this diminishing proportion was the sale of slaves outside the state.

In 1817, under the leadership of Governor Daniel Tompkins, New York became the first state in the union to declare by statute that after a certain date (July 4, 1827) no citizen of the state could hold any other inhabitant of the state in slavery.*

Thus in the Northern states, in the face of profoundly held convictions about man's right to consent to the power by which he was governed, despite the persistent hostility of prophets like Anthony Benezet, despite the resentment of white workers toward the competition of slave labor, despite the kindly paternalism of men like William Cushing, George Bryan, and John Jay, despite the nasty arrogance often exhibited by slave owners as they defended their "property," and despite the marginality of the institution—despite all these opposing factors, slavery hung on far into the nineteenth century.

The two main obstacles to abolition in the North were the claims of slave owners that slaves, as property, should not be set free by a government devoted to the protection of private prop-

---

* It is difficult to make flat statements about slavery's demise during the early national period. One would like to say that in 1827 New York became the first state to make it illegal to hold slaves within the state. But that is not quite true. Until 1841, there was a law that permitted nonresidents to keep slaves in the state for a period up to nine months.[48]

erty; and the fear of white men, those who owned slaves and those
who did not, that free Negroes were a threat to the safety and an
offense to the sensibilities of white men. The first point was
finally overcome because slave owners, relatively few in number,
lacked political power to resist the drive toward abolition indefinitely. Nearly everyone respected the fact that owners of
slaves had bought their property under the protection of the law.
Even those who argued that the law ought not to recognize the
claim to property in another man's labor realized that, ought or
no, the law had permitted and protected the selling of slaves, and
that these rules could not now be changed without some general
sharing in the responsibility and cost of the transition. This attitude, coupled with the meagerness of public resources, was the
largest single obstacle to emancipation in regions where slaves
were relatively numerous and valuable, as in New York and New
Jersey during the eighteenth century. When owners argued that
the price of slaves included the expectation that the children of
slaves would serve their mother's master, an effort was at first
made to meet them part way with the abandonment scheme. But
in the end, owners were forced simply to sacrifice this part of their
property. Since many redeemed their investment by selling their
slaves to exporters, not much was lost. The outnumbered owners
could not resist the onslaught of abolition, but neither did they
suffer much from it.

As far as the fears of the white community were concerned, the
scope of the problem in the North minimized these, too. The
committee of the New Jersey legislature had remarked in 1790
that "experience" showed that the abolition of slavery would require difficult adjustments for blacks and whites alike, but the
committee was mistaken, and nearly everyone in the North knew
it. Leon Litwack, in his book *North of Slavery,* has told what
experience really showed—namely, that abolition meant little in
the actual status of Negroes among whites. Tocqueville, whose
notion of man's innate hunger for liberty and dignity was not
compromised by racial prejudice, could foresee the time when
freed Negroes would rise against the restraints imposed by the
white majority, but even the Frenchman expected this "civil war"
to break out in the South, where Negroes were numerous enough

37

to strike real terror into white hearts.[49] In the North during the early national period, Negroes constituted less than 5 per cent of the population, and they were poor, illiterate, constantly harried by the threat of kidnapping and re-enslavement, and deprived of almost every opportunity to associate together.[50] Such a group of people was simply incapable of provoking widespread disorder, and most whites knew it well.

In the national Congress, an abolitionist from Connecticut once called the fear of white Southerners a "bugbear." He was mistaken to ridicule the justifiable terror of South Carolinians and Georgians, but his jibe accurately reflected the seriousness of the danger of Negro uprisings in the North. The white community in the North had no good reason to fear freed Negroes, and it was not long before an awareness of this fact removed the last obstacle to abolition there.

In the South in the late colonial and early national period, Negroes constituted a substantial portion of the total population, almost all Negroes were slaves, and, though they were owned by a minority in the white community, their owners were in virtually complete control of life in the region. The Revolutionary ideology and the obligation to benevolence were sincerely affirmed in many parts of the South, and their relevance to Negro slavery uneasily suspected. Yet men there were firmly committed to the "resolve" that the United States "shall be and remain a white man's country." [51] Southern men could conceive only two ways to avoid the racial integration of their society: maintain slavery or remove the Negroes. Since removal was impossible, slavery had to be kept. This necessity never fully resolved the conflict in values, however, and many sensitive Southerners contemplated their predicament with dread and foreboding.

The South got into this position gradually and unthinkingly. Assuming that there is a statistical point beyond which people of British descent living in eighteenth-century America were unwilling for Negroes to move about free of the discipline of slavery, then, on the basis of the Northern experience, it seems evident that the level must lie considerably under 10 per cent. The resistance of New Yorkers to emancipation began to crumble as the percentage of Negroes in the state fell below 10 per cent, and thence toward the vanishing point. In the South, the opposite progression took place, with the opposite result.

But it happened gradually. When the first twenty blacks came to Jamestown in 1619, they came to a settlement that included over 2,000 whites. By 1630 Negroes constituted just 2 per cent of the total population of Virginia, 1.4 per cent in 1640, and just 3.5 by 1660. The figures for Massachusetts are comparable: 1.7 per cent in 1640, 2 per cent by 1660. The process of distinguishing the status of black and of white servants had clearly begun by 1640,

TABLE II. NEGROES AND SLAVERY IN THE SEABOARD SOUTH, 1790–1820

REGION	NEGROES AS % OF TOTAL POPULATION	SLAVES AS % OF NEGROES
Seaboard South (Delaware,* Maryland, District of Columbia, Virginia, North Carolina, South Carolina, Georgia)		
1790	36.4%	95.2%
1800	37.6%	93.0%
1810	40.4%	91.0%
1820	41.6%	90.8%
SELECTED STATES		
Virginia		
1790	40.9%	95.7%
1800	41.6%	94.5%
1810	43.4%	92.7%
1820	43.4%	92.0%
South Carolina		
1790	43.7%	98.3%
1800	43.2%	97.8%
1810	48.4%	97.7%
1820	52.8%	97.4%

* Delaware is grouped with the Southern states because in terms of both the proportion of blacks and the durability of slavery it was closer to the Southern than to the Northern states.

SOURCE: U.S. Bureau of the Census, *Negro Population, 1790–1915* (Washington: Government Printing Office, 1918), pp. 51, 57.

in both Virginia and Massachusetts. By 1660, slavery was a fully recognized institution for blacks, and confined exclusively to them.[52] The evolution of a distinct status—slavery—for blacks did not depend upon the proportion of blacks in the area, but upon the prejudice of whites.

Yet with the coming of the Revolution and independence, slavery was abolished in Massachusetts, but not in Virginia. If the proportion of Negroes in Virginia had remained where it stood in the middle of the seventeenth century, there is no reason to assume that Southerners would not have followed the same course as New Englanders, abolishing slavery in the wake of a revolution justified by the principle that "all men are created equal," a principle cast in unforgettable language, after all, by a Virginian.

What would have become of the South in the absence of the massive immigration of Africans is, of course, impossible to say. One close student of the section suggests that without slaves plantations could never have developed, and "the small farm unit would have prevailed." [53] In time, black servants might have followed white servants to the frontier, bought land when it was nearly free, and become small-farm operators. In this case, the South would never have developed toward the kind of affluence and ostentation made possible by large-scale commercial agriculture. It would have been virtually ignored by London and Liverpool, and its leading sons would not have studied law in the Inns of Court at London. It would not have had the fascination for New Englanders that it finally held. Its character would probably have been more like North Carolina's throughout the Revolutionary and early national periods—rebellious, "antifederalist," poor, proud, and prickly, whose people had a radical desire to be independent from those with whom they shared the American continent, as well as from the authorities across the sea.

But the massive importation of Africans did occur. Toward the end of the seventeenth century in Virginia, the proportion of Negroes broke through the 10-per-cent level. In 1680, Negroes constituted 7 per cent of the total population; in 1690, 18 per cent, and by 1700, 27 per cent. What happened, according to students of Southern agriculture, was that a way was found to cultivate a fine grade of tobacco on the soil of Virginia and Maryland.[54]

The cultivation of tobacco does not lead inevitably to large plantations, as the example of Cuba demonstrates.[55] But profits can be greatly increased where good land is plentiful, tractable labor readily available, and landholdings sufficiently large to encourage efficient production. Tobacco, as it happened, is well suited to slave labor. It consumes the energies of laborers nearly year round, which is an important factor where the investment in labor is fixed. The work is routine, requiring little initiative or skill, which is important where enslavement reduces a man's incentive to develop his skills. The operation was widely dispersed across great quantities of land, which isolated the laborers, thereby reducing the problems of control and discipline. Not all these things were fully understood in seventeenth-century Virginia, but as the cultivation of tobacco spread, the demand for laborers who were capable of extremely heavy work and could be made to do the bidding of managers and overseers grew steadily. The production of tobacco brought substantial rewards to planters who seized the opportunity.

Was it inevitable that the planters of Virginia turn to the massive use of Negro slave labor? As historian Kenneth Stampp has written, "Slaves were used in southern agriculture because men sought greater returns than they could obtain from their own labor alone. . . . Certainly no colonial . . . farmer could have hoped to reap such fruits from his own labor." [56] Virginia was established to make profits for a company based in London and for its agents in America. It proved impossible for these entrepreneurs to resist the temptation presented by the opportunity to import African slaves. Indeed, there is little evidence that the opportunity was seen as a temptation, or as a mixed blessing, until it was well on the way to institutional stability in the colonial South. In a sense, slavery was a "man-made institution," but it was made by men who never paused to consider that the logic of their course impelled them toward the conclusion that slavery must last forever.

In the case of the Carolinas, the commitment to slavery was much more deliberate. During the sixth decade of the seventeenth century, a group of eight distinguished proprietors, including an outstanding planter from the island of Barbados, was granted authority by the Crown to establish a colony south of Virginia. In 1669 the proprietors issued the Fundamental Constitutions of their enterprise. Prepared in part by Locke, the charter included the provision that "every freeman of Carolina shall have absolute power and authority over his negro slaves, of what opinion or religion soever." [57] This fantastic document, full of elaborate feudal remnants—landgraves and lords of manors and the like—was rudely rendered inoperable by conditions in the New World, but the determination of the planters to grow staples on large plantations with the use of black slave labor met a more encouraging reception.[58]

The purposes of the founders are reflected in the fact that the first population statistics for South Carolina, those for 1670, show thirty Negroes among 170 whites, already 15 per cent of the total. From there, the proportion grew rapidly. By 1710 Negroes constituted 40 per cent of the total population; by 1720, 70 per cent.

At this point, whites grew alarmed for their safety, and efforts were made to curb the slave trade and to encourage the immigration of white settlers. The result was that the Negro population continued to grow, but at a reduced rate, while the white population increased more rapidly. By 1770, around Charleston and in the tidewater region generally, Negroes were heavily concentrated, outnumbering whites in some counties by as much as ten or twelve to one, but in the colony as a whole, Negroes constituted about 60 per cent of the total population. By 1780 this proportion had fallen off to 54 per cent, and by 1790 it was under 50 per cent for the first time since 1720. South Carolinians had gotten the problem under control. Planters would still argue among themselves, and with the white settlers in the Piedmont and beyond, about the advisability of permitting further importations, and those who favored an opening of the slave trade would prevail for a time at the beginning of the nineteenth century. But, in general, South Carolinians appeared to believe that the ratio of blacks to whites established at the beginning of the national period was about right for their purposes. It gave the largest and most efficient planters an adequate labor force, and it permitted responsible white leaders to think that they were safe against "servile insurrections," most of the time, at least. Negroes could be usefully employed, and, at the same time, perfectly controlled by the white community. Doubts on the latter point frequently nagged the imagination of sensitive men, but conviction on the former point overwhelmed, even if it did not allay, the doubts.

Once the proportion of Negroes in the South rose above 20 or 30 per cent, the dominance of the plantation system was assured —at least until some outside force could alter the balance of the Southern mind. Once the South had been committed to the dominance of plantation agriculture manned by Negro slaves, a wedge was driven into the American union that could not be withdrawn by political processes.

The United States at the time of its birth was overwhelmingly agricultural. It is estimated that 90 per cent of the inhabitants, north, middle, and south, along the coast and inland to the frontier, were engaged in the business of farming.[59] In every section, and particularly along the coast, there were men engaged in nonagricultural pursuits. But the economic base was agriculture. America was predominantly a land of farmers.

The nature of farming varied greatly in different sections.[60] In the North, most men farmed to subsist. Enough men grew more than they needed so that a culture of lawyers and doctors and educators and merchants could be spared from direct participation in farm labor. But few men grew wealthy at farming. The soil was too poor, the climate too severe, landholdings too small, and labor too expensive. New England could not get rich until it learned to perform services for men who farmed in more hospitable climes.

In the mid-Atlantic states, the soil was more productive and the climate a little gentler. The products that grew best were foodstuffs. Farming was a better business there than in New England, and so these states had greater inherent wealth. But farming was not so productive that it completely pre-empted the attention of the ablest men in society. It was a fulfilling way of life for capable people, but there were opportunities in the cities, too—in the professions and in politics, in banking and trading, and in the tiny industrial enterprises that were beginning to emerge on the banks of the Delaware and Susquehanna rivers.

There were different nuances in the societies developing in New England and in the mid-Atlantic states, but in terms of political economy, and particularly in terms of demands upon government, the two sections were quite similar. In both, the tendency toward commercial development placed a premium upon settled foreign relations and economic stability. Some elements in each section favored easy credit and inflationary policies, but classes that pulled in the opposite direction dominated. Leading men in the mid-Atlantic states were more interested in the encouragement of manufacturing by bounties and "internal improvements" than were their counterparts in New England. New Englanders were more likely to place the emphasis of policy upon the securing of open markets abroad and the development of a naval capacity to protect American commerce. But these were questions of priority and emphasis, rather than antagonistic purposes.

The regions were similar, too, in their fears about what an overly powerful central government might attempt. Yankees, particularly, were concerned that they might have to pay more than their share of the costs of defending America from foreign exploitation or assault. New England counted itself tough, but poor, and sometimes wondered whether the cost of defending fellow Americans was justified by the tariff-free access to Southern staples that came with union. Men from the mid-Atlantic region, who counted themselves wealthy as well as tough, shared the fears of New Englanders that involvement in the union might cost them more than it was worth. The leading faction in New York politics was particularly inclined to feel the weight of this concern.

And there was a feeling, especially among New Englanders, that the spirit of their society, which they regarded as more sincerely equalitarian than that of other regions, might be contaminated by involvement with the Southern aristocracy. Leaders in New England feared that ordinary yeomen, seeing the grand manner of Southern visitors, but knowing little of the gruesome social conditions that produced their affluence, might grow contemptuous of their own plain but virtuous style of life. Leaders in the mid-Atlantic states tended to be less self-righteous and xenophobic, but they, too, were apprehensive about the influence of Southern aristocrats on American mores.

As far as the South was concerned, most men there, too, were farmers of one sort or another. The productivity of the soil and the length of the growing season, however, as well as the availability of large plots of land and the abundance of slave labor, impelled the region toward a system in which a relatively few men could make a great deal of money growing staples. By their wealth and its attendant prestige and power, these men were able to establish and maintain control over their social environment.

When these possibilities were first glimpsed, the plantations that grew up along the seaboard were conceived, like the islands of the Caribbean, as suppliers of products that could be exported at enormous profit. Economy dictated that investment be channeled where it would do the most good, without much concern for the social implications of the processes by which fortunes were being made. In its stress upon the values of egalitarianism, "mild" government, and vigorous enterprise, the development of the colonial South was typical of early capitalism.

But there was a flaw in the South that diverted it from the path of orthodox modern development. That flaw was race. When Southerners decided to rely upon black men to do their heaviest labor, they were angling for profits that no colonial farmer could have made by his own labors—and they were also setting their feet upon a path from which there would be no turning. They obtained a labor force that was capable of the work required on plantations, and many of them were able to reap the glorious profits that danced before their eyes when they contemplated an investment in plantation agriculture. But their own attitudes toward this labor force would soon transform the plantation system from a gaudy cloak into a merciless strait jacket.

The problem with the black laborers of the Old South was that they were constrained to farm laboring. Slavery gave Negroes little incentive to develop. The opinion that they could not work machinery, or care adequately for animals, or be trusted to live in towns, and therefore had to be kept to field labor and domestic work, became a self-fulfilling prophecy. Because most Negroes were withheld from these alternatives, they had little or no op-

45

portunity to develop and demonstrate aptitudes in these areas.*

Throughout the early national period, several leading Southerners saw the advantages of diversifying the economy of the region.[62] Anyone with an eye for economic development—and many Southerners had such an eye—could see that it cost the South a great deal to depend upon others to provide their tools, process their raw materials, and carry their produce. All that was needed was to turn capital, and labor, to the tasks themselves—or so it seemed to many analysts at the time, and since.

Why, then, did the South fail to move adequately in this direction?[63] There is no simple answer. Robert R. Russel has argued that the main factors were climate and geography: the enervation resulting from the heat, the lack of raw materials for industry, the absence of deep rivers and inviting roadbeds, and the great distances between centers of population.[64] By this analysis, the best analogies for the South would be southern Italy and Spain, which have lagged behind the rest of Europe since the Industrial Revolution for similar reasons.

The relevance of these factors cannot be doubted. Yet, however powerful they may have been, they do not complete the account. Southerners failed to move with the currents of the Industrial Revolution because the men who controlled the main resources of Southern society did not want to move in that direction. They resisted the pressures of economic modernization because they enjoyed their status and life as planters, and because they believed that their labor force might escape from its separate and subordinate status if it were released from the disciplines of agricultural slavery.

Thus, a society which began as an appendage to British capitalism ended as a rural aristocracy, striving for political and social independence while attempting to fit its economy into the pattern of eighteenth- and early-nineteenth-century Atlantic civilization. As soon as it was able, this Southern "fragment" of British liberal capitalism struck for independence.[65] Upon achieving independence, its leaders argued for a number of years among

---

* The problem of the development of aptitudes pursued Negroes into freedom. Tocqueville put the problem this way: "To induce the whites to abandon the opinion they have conceived of the moral and intellectual inferiority of their former slaves, the Negroes must change; but as long as this opinion persists, they cannot change."[61]

themselves about the proper course for future development. But before the end of the eighteenth century, and with increasing confidence and unanimity as the nineteenth century unfolded, these leading elements had determined that the nature of their laboring force constrained them to reserve their major investments for plantation agriculture, a destiny against which they were not disposed to struggle.

This decision, however necessary and desirable it may have seemed to the men who made it, had its drawbacks. It meant that the South faced a continual danger of insurrection. The Negroes were always an anomalous element in the social structure of the South. They did not quite fit the feudal model of the serf, who held a plainly and irrevocably inferior status in society, but also enjoyed certain rights that his master was bound to respect. Most important, both parties trusted one another to fulfill these obligations. But Negro slaves were not feudal serfs. They were human beings living in an age and in a society that never wearied of testifying to its belief in human equality. They were treated, in some respects, more like dumb animals than like human beings—like mules or horses or sheep, except, as Benjamin Franklin once pointed out, that there was a difference: sheep did not make insurrections. The South spared no efforts to purge from black people the desire to be free, but it never quite succeeded.[66]

So the whole social structure of the South was built on the nose of a volcano. The effect on the dominant social character of the region was tremendous. Throughout the union there were deeply conservative people who greatly feared the coming age of egalitarianism—"Federalists of the Old School," as David Fischer has called them.[67] But in the North, these men either reconciled themselves to the changing times or were gathered into the extreme wing of the Federalist party and gradually deprived of political power. In the South the determination of the planters to retain power was fortified by racial prejudice. By appealing to the popular fear of racial mixture, wealthy planters were able to divert the pressure for fundamental reform.[68] They ruled in a situation in which fundamental reform was impossible without running the risk of weakening the barriers that held the Negroes separate and subordinate.

Recent studies have emphasized that there were manufacturing establishments in the Old South and that slave labor was "almost exclusively" used in these establishments. But most of these "manufactories" were situated on plantations and used slave laborers owned by the plantation.[69] The development of manufacturing was confined, for the most part, within the structures of a plantation system fundamentally inimical to the demands of the Industrial Revolution. Industrial establishments that were dispersed as far afield as the plantations and used a labor force as fixed and frozen as slavery were bound to be inefficient and hamstrung in competition with establishments in other sections that were free of these handicaps.

The solution, of course, was to establish industrial centers— cities or towns where the various phases of a modern enterprise could be concentrated in one place and where workers with varying skills could be gathered together and encouraged to develop the flexibility demanded by modern industrial techniques. But this was where the plantation masters balked. To encourage the development of urban industrial centers would be to invite a Trojan horse within the gates. The problem of control forbade the experiment. Slavery "required a high degree of order, the careful regulation of Negro affairs, and a fixed status for bondsmen. On the other hand, the city demanded fluidity, a constant reallocation of human resources, and a large measure of social mobility." [70]

There were other aspects to the resistance of planters. They disliked the urban bourgeoisie and urban working classes, white as well as black. Thomas Jefferson's well-known animus against cities—cancers on the body politic, he called them—was widely shared among Southerners. The men who controlled the resources of the Southern economy had no intention of investing in industrial centers, and no intention of allowing themselves to be taxed to support "internal improvements" or pay the bounties demanded by modern industry. It seemed to most a far better scheme, even if it was more expensive, to allow others to do the dirty work while they remained close to Mother Earth.

And so the South was caught. Partly because of the image of itself as an agrarian paradise in a world racked by the agonies of industrialization, partly because of fear that any departure from

48

present patterns would release the demon of black revenge, the men who dominated the social and political structures of the South were compelled to preserve the *status quo*.

To be sure, there were dissenting voices. A deep impulse within the Southern breast called out for an end to the enslavement of human beings. Many Southerners were sincere in their affirmation of the Declaration of Independence and in their Christian faith, both of which told them that it was wrong to treat other men like animals.[71] Especially in the upper South and in the regions west of the Appalachians, men who caught the vision of a great democratic republic on the North American continent were deeply troubled by the attempt to found such an enterprise on the labor of slaves. These misgivings led to demands that manumission be encouraged, and finally to pressures for full emancipation. These pressures should not be discounted. In Virginia alone, it is estimated, 10,000 Negroes were emancipated during the 1780's, which is more than were freed in all of New England during that decade, and nearly as many as existed altogether in the State of Pennsylvania.[72]

But these facts, suggestive as they are of a real strain of Southern thinking about slavery, can be more misleading than instructive. They need to be balanced with the following considerations: that the wave of manumissions in Virginia ended around 1790, primarily because of white reaction to the release of blacks from the disciplines of slavery; that Virginia enacted a law in 1806 requiring all freed Negroes to leave the state within one year of manumission or else surrender their freedom and be sold at public auction; that all the writhings of conscience and all the abolition societies in the South never produced a single plan for abolition that had the slightest appeal in a Southern legislature, or indeed the slightest chance of constituting a realistic assault upon the institution of black slavery.[73]

There were two insuperable obstacles to abolition in the South by political processes. The first was the fact that plans for abolition were invariably tied to schemes for the removal of blacks from the vicinity of their enslavement.[74] But the removal of the Negroes was utterly impossible. Men who did not care about the feelings of blacks still had to confront the cost of such a migration. Jefferson, who estimated that it would cost $300 million to establish the Negroes in independence somewhere, suggested that the transplantation might be subsidized by the federal government. But that would cost $10 million a year for thirty years, at a time when federal budgets *in toto* often ran to less than that annually.[75]

The second obstacle to general emancipation was the value of slaves held in the South. Southerners, no less than men in other parts of the country, believed that governments were instituted to protect property. In a state like Massachusetts, a clever lawyer might argue that slavery had never been legally established, and the outnumbered and disgraced slave owners were unable to make effective reply. But no such fiction could ever stand in the South. Almost all Southern fortunes were based on the labor of slaves, and the cleverest lawyers were employed by masters of these slaves. Besides, of what avail was cleverness in trying to convince George Washington or Charles Cotesworth Pinckney that they had no valid claim to their slaves? If these men had valid title to their property, there was no way in a polity trained in Lockean principles to deprive them of their property without compensation. Individuals might free their slaves; the wealthy Quaker Robert Pleasants released eighty-eight blacks in 1786. But men of such grand philanthropy are rare in any society. Ordinary men could not be expected to divest themselves voluntarily of property worth $60 million. This was what the slaves in Virginia were worth in 1790, at the rate of $200 apiece.

Nor could the state be expected to shoulder the bill. The government of Virginia was answerable both to planters who relied on the labor of slaves and to nonslaveholding whites who already complained that most of the benefits of government went to the planters. In such a situation the state could not spend a great proportion of its wealth to buy freedom for men whose slavery was deemed essential to the safety and well-being of the state in the first place.

With these considerations in mind, the contention, sometimes advanced, that slavery, being an unprofitable institution, was doomed to extinction before the invention of the cotton gin can be dismissed.[76] Slavery functioned in the South not only as an economic institution, but also as a system of social control. What killed the manumission movement in Virginia was the growing fear of freed Negroes—the fear that they would degenerate in liberty, or rise up against their oppressors, or refuse to do the work upon which the economy of the South was based. So long as white men harbored these fears, large-scale emancipation was unthinkable. A way simply had to be found to make slavery pay.

But no one in the South seriously doubted that slavery could be made to pay. Men who tried to eke out a profit growing tobacco on the tired soil of eastern Virginia had hard times throughout the antebellum period, but there was always better land to the west. The rice and sugar planters in the Deep South and in the lower Mississippi Valley never doubted their prospects, despite occasional depressions caused by overproduction or the inflationary aftermath of war. When the Industrial Revolution in Great Britain created a tremendous demand for raw cotton, Southerners quickly saw the opportunity. All they had to do was to find a way to separate the seed from the fiber. A problem of this kind could not baffle people as enterprising as the planters for long. Eli Whitney's "improvements" on the cotton gin should not be seen as a fortuitous event that burst upon the surprised slave owners of the South and retrieved the institution of slavery from extinction.[77] It was one step in a process to which slave owners were totally committed: the continuing effort to make a necessary institution profitable.

Because of their commitment to slavery, the South gradually became the object of opprobrium among men whose ancestors had played leading roles in saddling the institution upon the South, by bringing the Africans in the first place, and by carrying the products of slavery without the slightest compunction about the plight of the laborers who produced it. By committing themselves to agriculture, Southerners became "overseers" for the merchants and credit makers and industrialists of the world. But they had no choice. So long as they refused to integrate with their black neighbors, they were forced to hold them in utter debasement. The only way to do that was to keep them lashed to the plantation. Few white men in the eighteenth and nineteenth centuries could accept, or even imagine, the only realistic alternative: a racially integrated society.

. . .

By the middle of the eighteenth century, Negroes constituted a larger proportion of the nonaboriginal population—about 30 per cent—than at any other time in American history. Men of British descent, who dominated the colonial settlements along the coast, came almost unanimously to the conclusion that Negroes belonged in chains. Thus, during the eighteenth century—the age of enlightenment, the century that led to the democratic revolutions—slavery became fastened to America.

Rousseau once suggested that political institutions are conceived in irony. "Men run headlong to their chains," he wrote, "in hopes of securing their liberty; [they have] just wit enough to perceive the advantages . . . without experience enough to enable them to foresee the dangers." [78] To create an asylum for liberty and to facilitate their enjoyment of it, Americans imported great numbers of black laborers from Africa. Southern planters produced staples by the labor of these slaves, brought to them by merchants of the North. Slavery helped to make both sections prosperous.

But prosperity was part of the seduction. Circumstances dictated that slavery settle mostly on the South. When the idea dawned that chattel slavery was wrong in a nation committed to the proposition that "all men are created equal," only half the union was able to follow this idea to its natural conclusion. For the rest, no political process could induce white men to liberate the blacks, who composed so substantial a proportion of the total population.

It is ironic that the birth and early beginnings of the American experiment should have rested so heavily on the labor of slaves. But the irony does not end here. Tocqueville pointed out that the modern drive toward equality and democracy is served alike by its sympathizers and by its foes.[79] The great transplantation of blacks was certainly not engineered by conscious servants of equality. Yet by the slave trade the destinies of the two races became "indissolubly linked together," as Justice John M. Harlan told a disbelieving Supreme Court in 1896. It may be that, in the document that committed the United States to equality, "Jefferson did not mean to include slaves as men." [80] Yet the sponsors of the Declaration could not fence off its promises, any more than the framers of the Constitution were able to create a permanent niche for slavery in an otherwise free land.

Try as men would to evade the logic of their predicament, the presence of black men in a white man's country drove a reluctant nation to an ever-deeper confrontation with the meaning of its promise.

2

"Slavery" in the Ideology of the American Revolution

IT is difficult, in reflecting on the American Revolution, to know which is more remarkable: that a nation whose population included hundreds of thousands of slaves and whose leadership included many slave owners could have chosen to found its claim to independent nationhood on the proposition that all men are created equal, or that a nation conceived in liberty and dedicated to the proposition that all men are created equal could have permitted the institution of Negro slavery to endure in its midst throughout the Revolutionary period, and far beyond.

The age of the American Revolution was a time of rampant, almost boundless idealism. The founders are often pictured as practical men, anxious to conduct their affairs with prudence and restraint, to see that resistance to tyranny was not made the occasion or excuse for reckless upheaval or wanton violence. Yet even the most careful men among the Revolutionary leaders were not averse to speculating about the meaning of America, and expressing their visions in the most exalted terms. John Adams exhibited this impulse when he wrote, "I always consider the settlement of America with reverence and wonder, as the opening of a grand scheme and design in Providence for the illumination and emancipation of the slavish part of mankind all over the earth." [1]

One of the surprising things about this idealism was its indifference to the institution of Negro slavery. The same John Adams, as Vice-President of the young republic, could write in 1795 that he had never given much thought to the problem of Negro slavery.[2] Nor was he at all unique in this respect. For all the dreaming and reforming and rebuilding that was going on in America between 1765 and 1780,[3] no leading politician was brooding much about Negro slavery, or seriously at work on plans to loosen its hold on the nation's life.*

From the earliest settlements, slavery had been, as David Brion Davis has said, an "intrinsic part of American development."[4] Negroes were among the first immigrants to the New World, and their labors played a vital role in clearing the wilderness and making it fruitful.

By the mid-eighteenth century, Negro slaves were an established part of colonial society. In the colonies most valued by Europeans—those in the West Indies and the mainland South— slaves performed the labor that made the production of staple commodities possible. The supply of provisions to these plantation colonies provided a vital market for the commercial farms and craft industries of Pennsylvania, New York, and New England. And it was the trade that carried away the products of the plantations, bore provisions from the mainland colonies to the West Indies, and furnished a continual supply of new slaves from Africa that gave New England its opportunity to escape from the confines of subsistence farming.[5]

Though every colony was dependent upon slavery in one way or another, they varied in the nature of their involvement with the institution. In Georgia and South Carolina, the choicest lands

---

* It is true that during the 1780's slavery was undercut by judicial decree in Massachusetts and New Hampshire and by acts of gradual abolition in Pennsylvania, Connecticut, and Rhode Island. These events are indeed traceable in large part to the ideology of the Revolution. The point here, however, is that no important political leader with a national, or "continental," outlook expressed or exerted himself publicly against *chattel* slavery at a time when concern about *political* slavery was at white heat. The acts of the 1780's on the state level, as well as others adopted in the aftermath of the Treaty of Paris, left chattel slavery virtually untouched in its citadel, the five southernmost colonies. Interest in what Arthur Zilversmit calls "The First Emancipation" (the abolition of slavery in the North) must not obscure this fact. Despite the gradual elimination of slavery from Northern states, the economy and culture of the young republic continued to depend, to a considerable degree, on "slavery and its consequences." The Revolutionary ideology, despite its obvious relevance, brought little relief to the half-million blacks enslaved at the time of the Revolution.

were devoted to the production of rice and fibers. The work was performed by slaves and managed, for the most part, by hired overseers, whose assignment was simple: maximize profits by driving the blacks to the limits of their endurance. The result was that South Carolina was the richest colony on the mainland, and slavery there the harshest. The prevailing attitude toward slavery in South Carolina is indicated by the fact that Henry Laurens, a leader in the colony who was beginning to have scruples about the slave trade, which had made him a rich man, was forced to deny publicly that he had abandoned the trade from "goodness of heart," insisting instead that his motives were economic.[6]

Society in Virginia also lay on a broad foundation of Negro slave labor, but slavery there was a different institution from that practiced on the huge plantations of South Carolina and the West Indies. As Daniel Boorstin has remarked, the effort of Virginians to emulate English country living cast Negroes in the role of English peasants, at least to some extent.[7] The result was that slavery there was not as harsh as in other planting areas. Despite its modified severity, however, slavery pervaded the atmosphere. Political and social power was exercised by a small group of families, almost all of whom possessed large numbers of slaves, and this elite was responsible to an electorate, two-thirds of whom owned slaves.[8]

The hold that slavery had on life in Virginia, as well as the bad conscience of many sensitive men, is well reflected in a letter written in 1757 by an Anglican pastor named Peter Fontaine, serving in tidewater Virginia, to his brother back in England. "[T]o live in Virginia without slaves," he wrote, "is morally impossible." Because plantations were largely self-sufficient, there was no steady market where one could buy basic foodstuffs and supplies. A man had either to cut his own firewood and hoe his own garden or else to hire a servant or buy a slave. Unless he was exceedingly robust, Fontaine wrote, a man could not fend for himself while carrying on the duties of a pastorate, teaching school, or practicing law. White servants were notoriously lazy, despising to do a slave's work, and exorbitantly expensive. One had to pay about twenty pounds per year plus "diet and lodging" for a "lazy fellow to get wood and water . . . ; add to this seven or eight pounds more and you have a slave for life." "This of course draws us all into the original sin and curse . . . of purchasing slaves," he concluded, "and this is the reason we have no merchants, traders, or artificers of any sort but what become planters in a short time." [9]

In the middle colonies, there were slaves working in agriculture, especially in Delaware and on the manorial estates along the Hudson River. For the most part, though, climate and land policies were unsuited to the production of staples, to which slave labor was most adaptable. Instead, the industrious farmers there produced wheat, corn, peas, beans, oats, and hogs, and exported large quantities from their surplus to the West Indies and to the Deep South. As they developed, the economies of these colonies became heavily dependent on profits from this commerce.[10]

Similarly, in New England the involvement in slavery was mainly indirect. Some Negroes did live there (about 1,000 in Boston, 5,700 in Connecticut), and most of them were still enslaved on the eve of the Revolution.[11] Boston newspapers in the early 1760's were full of matter-of-fact advertisements dealing with slavery—asking for the return of runaways, telling of the arrival of a shipment of slaves from Africa, announcing an auction for their sale.[12] More significantly, however, New England was involved in slavery through its participation in the triangular trade that bore the products of slavery—molasses, mainly—away from the West Indies to Newport or Boston, where it was distilled into rum; carried the rum and other products of New England to Africa and exchanged them for slaves, which were then transported to the American colonies.[13] The trade had other channels as well, such as carrying provisions (fish, lumber, grain, horses, nails) from the mainland to the West Indies; taking staples from the mainland South to Great Britain for manufacturing; plying up and down the coast on errands of delivery and supply. This commerce supported a growing number of bankers, creditors, and insurance agents; and the rum distilleries employed a surprising number in Rhode Island.

The centrality of this trade is reflected in the protests directed by New Englanders against the Sugar Act of 1764. The main purpose of the act was to confine the triangular trade to the British

West Indies, despite the colonial preference for the French islands, particularly Santo Domingo, where molasses was more plentiful, of higher quality, and cheaper. An anonymous pamphlet, abundantly entitled "Considerations upon the [Sugar] Act . . . Showing Some of the Many Inconveniences Necessarily Resulting from the Operation of the Said Act, Not Only to those [Mainland] Colonies, but also to the British Sugar Islands, and Finally to Great Britain," noted that the act, by disrupting the triangular trade in general, would deprive the British sugar islands of New England's fish, thus raising the cost of maintaining slaves; and by forcing colonial ships out of the trade, would raise the price of new slaves from Africa. Governor Stephen Hopkins, of Rhode Island, in another pamphlet, added that the act, by confining trade to the British islands, would "ruin" the Northern colonies because the British islands by themselves were incapable of absorbing "our exportation of lumber, horses, flour, and fish." [14]

Whether a quarantine from the slave trade and from commerce in the products of slavery would have "ruined" New England or not, there can be no doubt that life as it was lived in late colonial New England was deeply implicated in slavery. New Englanders who knew the true state of affairs in their section should not have been ignorant of the fact that they depended ultimately on slave labor for the margin that supported civilized life.

It is clear, then, that the American economy, in all sections, rested substantially on slavery and its fruits. Yet it is also clear that the tenets of the Revolutionary ideology were widely held and deeply felt by colonial leaders. To penetrate this irony, the "public philosophy" [15] of the Revolutionary generation must be studied.

The ideology of the American Revolution is often identified as "constitutional liberalism," and its adherents as Whigs. Its most appropriate slogan was "Liberty and Property." [16] The slogan was popularized by the Sons of Liberty, an organization of mechanics and artisans that seems to have centered in New York City. But it would have been equally acceptable to the planters of South Carolina and Virginia, the merchants of Philadelphia and New York, and the lawyers and doctors of Boston.[17]

The theory begins with the notion that all men have a right to be free, to improve themselves and their environs without interference from other men. All men are born with this right: it exists "before" men enter into societies. All men retain this right: it is inalienable, even after men form communities.[18]

In the beginning, men found themselves in a universe aching to be developed. Industrious men began to exercise their freedom to the fullest, ordering nature by the exercise of intelligence and by hard work. Soon, however, conflicts arose. Sometimes the natural order was disrupted by evil men who refused to work for their own provisions and who begged or stole from others; sometimes it was disrupted by good men who pursued revenge too far when they were wronged, or who were negligent and unconcerned when they inadvertently harmed others.[19]

The need for established rules, and for arbiters of their meaning and agents to insure their application, became apparent. And so men agreed to a covenant, in which they promised to respect one another's property (those parts of the universe that a man had improved through his own work), and to form a government to see that this respect was maintained. It was not necessary for man's basic liberty to be sacrificed or fundamentally compromised by this covenant. Certainly the government would have to interfere to some extent with men's property—to raise taxes to maintain itself, for example, and to impose regulations in the general interest on the use of certain kinds of property. But a just government would impose taxes and regulations only when the public good required it, and then on all members equally, without fear or favor toward any person. The government would be held to these standards of justice by the fact that it was accountable to the people it served. Governments answerable to the people—if those people remained alert for their liberties—would always be just and good governments.

Though all men have had the right to government based on these principles, few, in the opinion of the colonists, had ever enjoyed it.[20] Almost alone, the English people emerged from the mists of prehistory with their liberty intact. Uniquely, they had beaten back a series of challenges to their freedom, instigated by foreign invaders or by the ambition of kings. In each case, though imperiled for a time, English liberty had survived and had been strengthened by the encounter, because the English people had cherished their freedom, knowing its requisites and preferring death to its loss. Now the colonists, inheritors of this tradition by the grace of being English, found themselves free; and, by the works of vigilance, they were determined to remain free.

Though theoretically liberty could be enjoyed under many different forms of government, most American colonists in the middle of the eighteenth century believed that the British constitution was the best that had evolved in the experience of men. Its greatest feature was the way in which it balanced the elements of which British society was composed, providing the Crown, the aristocracy, and the commons each with the means to perform its services and advance its legitimate interests. The idea of the "separation of powers" was not well developed at this time, but there was a feeling that the Crown was responsible for protecting the realm, symbolizing its unity, and administering public policy. The function of the commons, through its representatives, was to make laws and to grant "supplies" and support to the Crown. The aristocracy, about whom most colonists knew little and cared less,[21] was to assist the Crown, to review the legislation of the commons, and to serve as judges. These constitutional arrangements were reflected in the colonial governments, where the governors served as agents of the Crown, the governors' councils and justices of the peace performed the functions of aristocracy, and the assemblies operated as local houses of parliament.

If liberty was the Promised Land for the chosen few in human history, slavery was the Hell in which most of mankind had always wallowed. The close juxtaposition of these concepts in the thought of the Whigs was reflected in the opening lines of a pamphlet written during the controversy over the Sugar Act of 1764 by Stephen Hopkins. "Liberty," he wrote, "is the greatest blessing that men enjoy, and slavery the heaviest curse that human nature is capable of." [22]

Whenever the colonists felt that an established and familiar pattern of governance was being disturbed, the cry of "slavery" rose almost automatically to their lips. These men, so apprehensive of the tendency of free states to evolve into tyrannies, interpreted every departure from precedent as a menacing effort to slip the shackles of slavery onto free men. "Slavery" was defined as the condition of being under the control of someone else's will.[23] For an individual, it meant that one's life and labor were at the disposal of another man, to do with as he pleased. For a community, it meant that the lives and properties of its members were controlled by laws and lawmakers over whom they had no certain influence.

As a concept in political theory, slavery had two important associates: property and consent. The slave was the man, or community, whose possessions could be taken without consent.[24] The slave was thus without "property," in the strict sense of the term, since property in a thing, by definition, involved an exclusive right to possess, enjoy, and dispose of it.

Whigs made no bones about their commitment to the inviolability of property.[25] They were convinced that the prosperity of the community and the happiness of all its members depended on respect for property rights, especially by public authorities. This faith was not limited to men of great wealth. Artisans and mechanics, for example, had shared in the general suffering in 1765 when the Stamp Act led to a boycott of legal papers by American merchants and a consequent slowdown in business and a period of unemployment.[26] The Sons of Liberty, no less than the heirs of great wealth, had reason and disposition to fear the interference in American property by an English legislature.

If the concept of property seemed clear, the concept of consent was susceptible to many different interpretations. One of the roots of tension between Britons and Americans in the decade before 1776 was the divergence in understanding of this central concept. Locke himself had been vague on the subject. He had left the impression that consent could be tacit, and that it influenced the conduct of government decisively only when a long train of abuses drove the people to withdraw their consent from one regime and replace it with another.[27]

British constitutional theory in the mid-eighteenth century was both more generous and more specific concerning the role given to consent. Parliament, representing the common people of Britain, considered the program of the Crown's ministers, and either gave consent or refused it on behalf of the people. If consent was refused, either the ministry had to alter its program to meet Parliament's objections or Crown and Parliament had to appeal to the nation for a mandate. The search for a mandate was conducted in the form of elections in which the common people of Britain chose a new Parliament. Once chosen, members of this body, in a new dialogue with the Crown, framed policy for the nation.

Members of Parliament were chosen from "constituencies," or districts, which had evolved over the years. The evolution had been *away* from the principle of "one man, one vote." [28] By the mid-eighteenth century in Britain, the representational system was a patchwork of rotten boroughs and unrepresented urban masses. Though the system was under pressure, it was justified by the notion that the duty of every member of Parliament was to join in a common effort to discover the best policy for the nation as a whole, to represent all the common people of the realm, rather than stand as "attorney" or delegate for a given region.[29] It was this understanding that stood behind the doctrine of "virtual representation"—that "every member of Parliament sits in the House not as representative of his own constituents but as one of that august assembly by which all the commons of Great Britain are represented." [30] Parliament regarded itself, not as a brokerage house, but as the corporate legislature of a great empire, representing all His Majesty's subjects equally.

To most colonists, this theory was obnoxious. It consisted, said Daniel Dulany, of Maryland, "of facts not true and of conclusions inadmissible." [31] As far as the colonists were concerned, men who were under constant pressure from their neighbors and who had never seen America could not humanly have the same regard for American interests as for English, and would not know how to serve those interests if they did. Just representation could only be given by a man chosen by the people he intended to represent, preferably from among their midst. This was the kind of representation to which the colonists had grown accustomed in their own assemblies,[32] and it seemed to them the only kind of representation that could give real meaning to the doctrine of consent.

A community governed by a legislature in which it was not represented, in this full and literal sense, was a community enslaved. When that legislature sought to take property from the community, it imposed slavery of the most bitter sort. As John Dickinson wrote in the seventh of his "Letters from a Farmer in Pennsylvania," *"Those who are taxed without their own consent expressed by themselves or their representatives, are slaves. We are taxed without our consent. . . . We are therefore—SLAVES."* [33]

The Assembly of the colony of New York, in a petition to the House of Commons protesting the passage of the Sugar Act of 1764, warned against "certain designs . . . to impose taxes upon the subjects here, by laws to be passed there." Such a program, they argued, would violate "the grand principle of every free state," that citizens should be exempt from "ungranted, involuntary taxes." "In fidelity to their constituents," they added, in pointed reference to their standing as "actual" representatives of the New Yorkers, they asked Parliament to "leave it to the legislative power of the colony, to impose [taxes] upon its own people." [34]

Daniel Dulany agreed that the problem of taxation lay close to the heart of the matter. If Parliament succeeded in stripping the colonies of their "right of exemption from all taxes *without their consent,*" they would "at the same time deprive [them] of every privilege distinguishing freemen from slaves." [35]

Taxation was not the only issue. A decade of wrangling between colonists and imperial authorities taught colonial leaders that the attempt to "enslave" the colonies could take many forms. John Dickinson warned William Pitt in 1765 that the colonies would think themselves in "a state of slavery" if Parliament interfered in any way with their "internal government." [36] By the end of the decade, Dulany's "privilege distinguishing freemen from slaves" had been broadened. James Duane, a most reluctant rebel from New York, who is credited with having toned down the Declaration of Colonial Rights and Grievances in 1774, wrote that "liberty" could be enjoyed only by the man "bound by no laws to which he does not assent by himself or his representative, a privilege which forms the distinction between freemen and slaves. . . ." [37]

The chains of slavery were not always fashioned in Great Britain. The Regulators of North and South Carolina thought the main danger lay in the colonial capitals. For the Regulators of Anson County, North Carolina, it came in the form of judges and other public officials, "extortionists" who forced poor farmers to yield themselves "slaves to remorseless oppression." [38] For some South Carolinians, the complaint was not that the government oppressed them, but that it ignored them. Woefully underrepresented in the colonial assembly (partly because formulas of representation were based on total population, including slaves, and the farmers in the "back country" had fewer slaves than the planters around Charleston), these farmers were unable to secure the services of judges or police. As a result, their property was insecure, and if they were charged with crime, they were tried in Charleston, where trial by a jury of their neighbors was impossible. The whole development of the region was being retarded by the lack of law enforcement. Whenever they saved enough to buy slaves, the money was stolen. Nor could they hire slaves to clear their land; planters in Charleston were afraid to lend their property for fear it would be stolen or escape into the forest and never be recovered. "We are free men," complained these frontiersmen, "British subjects, not born slaves." As free Britons, they claimed that they were entitled to the protections and services of the government. [39]

Slavery always stalked the unwary. It was unsuspected but hidden, according to John Dickinson, in the attempt by Benjamin Franklin and the Quakers to change Pennsylvania from a proprietary to a royal colony. [40] It lurked in the possibility that authorities in London would veto Virginia's Two-Penny Act, which lowered the compensation due to clergymen of the established church. Richard Bland, a leading planter and legislator in the Old Dominion, warned in 1764 that if the act was not allowed to stand, Virginians would be no better off than "galley slaves in Turkey or Israelites under an Egyptian bondage." [41] When Parliament interfered with trial by jury by removing certain types of cases to the Courts of Vice-Admiralty, or abused the right to petition by ignoring all colonial protests against the policy of taxation, [42] again the cry of "slavery" was heard throughout the land.

When Parliament showed a disposition to enforce its new policies by stationing troops in Boston and New York and quartering them in the homes of the colonists, fears were intensified. What could be the purpose of these troops? Some claimed they were intended to protect the colonies from the French and the Indians, but the colonists were confident of their own defenses against these foes. The troops could only be meant to guarantee the submission of the colonies to the acts of Parliament. But if those acts were just, surely the colonists could be trusted to obey them without a show of military force. There must be something ominous about policies that had to be imposed on men of British stock by force. As the decade wore on, the troops were a constant reminder that the colonies were being forced to obey laws to which they had not consented.

Was slavery ever justified? On this point, there was a subtle but significant difference among colonial theorists. Locke had taught that slavery could be the just condition of the victim of conquest. If I invoke a state of war by committing "some act that deserves death" against you, you may rightfully respond by attacking me. If you succeed in bringing me under your power, you may choose to spare my life and make me a slave. The state of war continues until I am forgiven—or I may commit suicide if I prefer death to slavery. But if I choose to live, according to Locke, you have just claim to my slave labor.[43]

Richard Bland seemed to accept this line of reasoning. Chief Justice Sir John Holt, of Great Britain, had ruled in 1707 that, since Virginia was "a conquered country," the laws and liberties of England did not extend there. Bland could have argued that even conquered men have rights, but he did not. Instead, he replied that Virginia was in no sense a conquered country. It was populated by Britons who retained their British liberties when they migrated to America. Virginians had worked hard to extend Britain's authority, and had had to repulse the Indians to do so. But it was absurd to argue that "by making conquests, [Virginians had] become slaves."[44]

James Otis, on the other hand, met the Lockean argument head on. "A state has no right to make slaves of the conquered," he wrote. Citing Vattel rather than Locke, he argued that the rights of the conqueror were limited by reason and humanity. "After satisfaction and security is obtained . . . and examples are made of so many . . . as the ends of government require, the rest are to be restored to all the essential rights of men and of citizens." [45]

The significance of the difference between Otis and Bland on this point is clear. Otis was one of the most outspoken opponents of Negro slavery in the colonies at the time. His pamphlet "The Rights of the British Colonies Asserted and Proved" contains the most memorable critique of slavery in the entire polemical literature of the American Revolution. Bland, on the other hand, was a slave owner and a prominent political leader in a colony that numbered nearly 200,000 Negro slaves among its population. While the Virginians yielded to no one in their devotion to the principles of republican government, they had to be careful that their theories left room for the justification of Negro slavery. On this point, Bland's discussion of the argument for slavery by conquest was wrought with full prudence.

If the colonists differed subtly in their formulations of the concept of slavery, they were absolutely unanimous as to the appropriate response if an attempt was made on their liberties. Beginning with Jonathan Mayhew's famous sermon "Concerning Unlimited Submission and Non-Resistance to the Higher Powers" in 1750, and with gathering intensity as the Revolution neared, the colonists showed they were convinced of their right, indeed their obligation, to resist slavery by every available means. In Mayhew's opinion, the doctrine of passive obedience and nonresistance was itself "slavish." As his fellow Bostonian the Reverend Andrew Eliot put it, when tyranny is abroad, "submission . . . is a crime." [46]

Mayhew's critics responded that such advice from the pulpit would encourage the weak to engage in reckless acts of violence, and thus pave the way, through licentiousness, to the imposition of greater authority, and finally to slavery.[47] But by the mid-1760's, determination of the appropriate response to Parliamentary abuse was no longer a matter between learned clergymen and Tory letter writers. During the winter of 1765–1766, Sons of Liberty throughout the colonies were passing resolutions terming the Stamp Act a plot to enslave Americans and calling for opposition by force if necessary. Mob violence, or the threat of it, forced the resignation of every stamp agent named by imperial authority. Similar responses greeted the passage of each of the revenue acts of the pre-Revolutionary decade. In justifying their threat of violence to the pilot of a vessel bearing tea to Philadelphia in October 1773, a group of Pennsylvanians acted angrily that the stated purpose of the duties on tea was to pay the costs of government in the colonies, and that the tendency of such a tax was to render the colonial assemblies "useless and to introduce arbitrary government and slavery." Under such circumstances, they concluded, "a virtuous and steady opposition . . . is absolutely necessary to preserve even the shadow of liberty." With that, they set out to the dock to intercept the hated herb and to tar and feather the captain of the ship that bore it if he would not consent to remove it from the harbor.[48]

Joseph Warren, a leading physician in Boston who established a reputation for fiery oratory and became a favorite speaker at patriotic ceremonies, chose the occasion of the second anniversary of the Boston Massacre[49] to spur the zeal of his audience to resist British oppression. "None but those who set a just value upon the blessings of liberty are worthy to enjoy her," he warned. Liberty was like a virgin. Dirty men were always trying to ravish her by force, or steal her virtue by flattery and fraud. She had been protected from these attempts of old by the sturdy hands of their ancestors, and he hoped that the present generation would be worthy of its forebears.

The voice of your father's blood cries to you from the ground, *my sons scorn to be slaves!* . . . We bled in vain, if you, our offspring, want valour to repel the assaults of her invaders! . . . [I]f you, from your souls, despise the most gaudy dress that slavery can wear; if you really prefer the lonely cottage (whilst blest with liberty) to gilded palaces surrounded with the ensigns of slavery . . . tyranny, with her whole accursed train, will hide their hideous heads in confusion, shame, and despair.[50]

A more stately expression of the same sentiment appears in the Declaration of the Causes and Necessity for Taking Up Arms, adopted by the Continental Congress on July 6, 1775. Parliament, said the delegates, "by an inordinant passion for . . . power" had tried for a decade to convert the colonies into the "absolute property" of Great Britain. When the colonies protested and refused to pay the taxes imposed on them without their consent, troops had been dispatched to try to enslave them by violence. Now they were "reduced to the alternative of choosing an unconditional surrender to the tyranny of irritated ministers, or resistance by force." Because "nothing is so dreadful as voluntary slavery," they said, "the latter is our choice." They could not "endure the infamy and guilt of resigning succeeding generations to that wretchedness which inevitably awaits them, if we basely entail hereditary bondage upon them." Consequently, they were "resolved to die freemen rather than live slaves." [51]

In summary, the concept of "slavery" in colonial political theory held the following: for a community to be enslaved meant that the members of the community had no control over the government. It meant that political practices could never be firmly established, that they were continually subject to modification or suspension at the will or whim of the rulers. It meant that property holdings were insecure, held only at the pleasure of the rulers, subject to confiscation or taxation without consultation or consideration of the good of the subjects. Whether the rulers were benevolent or not was irrelevant. Those who were bound to obey the will of another over whom they had no control were slaves, whether their master was good or evil.[52] In theory, slavery was justifiable, if at all, only as a consequence of war between individuals or communities that existed in a state of nature toward one another. But in fact, in human history, slavery was the normal condition of mankind. It ensnared all who lacked vigilance and courage in the defense of their liberties, or who accepted favors from those in power without being mindful of the precedents that were being established.

The curious thing about the doctrines of the colonists was that, by their own definitions, they had been slaves to Great Britain since their settlement in America. To be sure, the yoke of Parliament had been easy and the burdens of mercantilism light. Nevertheless, the attitude of most Britons toward the colonies was exploitative, to say the least. It had been fairly summarized by William Pitt, properly regarded by Americans as one of their best friends in Parliament. In supporting repeal of the Stamp Act in 1766, Pitt urged at the same time that "the sovereign authority of [Great Britain] over the colonies be asserted in as strong terms as can be devised, and be made to extend to every point of legislation whatsoever. That we may bind their trade, confine their manufactures, and exercise every power whatsoever, except that of taking their money out of their pockets without their consent." [53]

Though the exception that Pitt suggested was not included in the final version of the Declaratory Act of 1766, his speech did accurately reflect the design of the empire before 1764, and therein lay the slavery, from the American point of view. Parliament's authority had been exercised in various ways, most notably in the series of Navigation Acts. These acts confined colonial trade to English or colonial ships, required all colonial imports from Europe, with a few exceptions, to pass through England, and directed that colonial products on an "enumerated" list (which included such items as tobacco, sugar, rice, indigo, naval stores, and hides) be exported only to Great Britain, Ireland or other English colonies.[54] These acts were not, in fact, all bad from the colonial viewpoint. Britain, being the queen of the seas, would in any case have carried most of the colonial trade, and, being the most advanced nation in the world, would have been a natural market for colonial staples, even without the laws. Furthermore, Britain provided invaluable services to the colonies, including protection from the French and others on the high seas, and the steadying influence of association with an ancient political system. Still, the wages of mercantilism had to be paid, and by the third quarter of the eighteenth century they had become steep and immensely irritating to a burgeoning colonial economy.[55]

Around 1765 [56] tensions between Great Britain and its colonies on the North American mainland began to force themselves to the attention of statesmen. They were a product of two divergent evolutions.

In Parliament, in the aftermath of the "Great War for the Empire," [57] the guiding vision called for closer integration of the elements of the British Empire, a tightening of imperial reins, and more active governance from the center. To maximize the value of the North American colonies, British troops would have to protect them from the conniving French and Spaniards, and more care would have to be taken that imperial specie was not drained off in trade between British and foreign colonies. To support these administrative reforms, and generally to enrich the Crown's coffers and help to defray the costs of the war, Parliament sought to lay taxes on the colonists.

Unfortunately for the British Empire, Parliament's program of imperial reform and taxation coincided with the other evolution, that of the mainland colonies in America toward economic, social, and political maturity. There was at this time, among the inhabitants of the thirteen colonies, an emerging sense of American "nationality"—that is, a developing awareness that Americans constituted one people and that this people wanted to control its own affairs.[58] Until the mid-eighteenth century, most colonists were sincere in their expressions of loyalty to the empire, proud to be Englishmen and inheritors of Magna Charta and the Glorious Revolution. Some of the imperial regulations—the acts to hinder the manufacture of hats or woolen cloth or iron products—had been nettlesome, but they had inspired no thoughts of outright resistance. Until the crisis of 1764–1765, imperial arrangements, though in conflict at many points with Whig doctrines, were accepted, even celebrated, because they provided a loose and expansive framework that encouraged the growth of the colonies. The reins of empire, however firmly in Parliament's hand, were loose on the backs of the colonists.[59]

But as the colonies matured—as their economies diversified and prospered, as they gained confidence and strength in the exercise of internal government, as they came to have increasing contact with one another, and to knit together along the Atlantic seaboard [60]—directives and interferences from London came to be resented more and more.[61] Now was the time, thought the colonists, not to be laying new restraints, but to be lifting old ones, giving the colonies their head to develop as nature intended.

And so the outlooks in Parliament and in the colonies began to diverge ominously. The developing controversy assumed a rhythm of its own: an intermittent counterpoint of imperial regulation and colonial disobedience, of guarded imperial retreat and unguarded colonial celebration, of new imperial taxation and renewed colonial resistance, culminating in the King's "Proclamation for Suppressing Rebellion and Sedition" of August 23, 1775 and in the American Declaration of Independence.[62]

From the colonial viewpoint, it appeared that Parliament was attempting to "enslave" them—that is, to regulate and tax their property without their consent, and then, when they resisted, to quell their objections by applying military force. As avid students of history, concerned colonial leaders thought they saw a familiar pattern: the imperial capital grown rich and fat, drunk with overweening power, in its debauchery losing its virtue, its sense of measure, its self-restraint, trying to feed its gluttony by robbing its colonies.

The "Turks," the "sooty" and "tawny" races, all "the slavish part of mankind all over the earth," indeed most of mankind throughout the ages, might wallow in slavery. The English people themselves might be dragged down into bondage. But not their American cousins. Dickinson, quoting Montesquieu, had warned that "SLAVERY IS EVER PRECEDED BY SLEEP";[63] those who watched over America were determined not to be caught slumbering. Having been posited by their ancestors on the pinnacle of liberty, they would resist the tidal waves of tyranny with their lives, their fortunes, and their sacred honor.

David Brion Davis has pointed out that the "American colonists were not the first to combine a love of political liberty with an acceptance of chattel slavery." [64] Locke, for example, found a way to justify slavery in a political theory based on a covenant among equals. Yet the American case seems unique nonetheless. Never was a people more thoroughly or knowledgeably committed to liberty, or more acutely aware of the contaminating power of slavery. Yet rarely, if ever in human history, has the institution of slavery formed so fundamental and so pervasive a part of a political community.

There is no question that the atmosphere surrounding the institution of Negro slavery was profoundly changed by the intense reflection on the question of human rights that occurred in the Western world in the mid-eighteenth century. Montesquieu, a philosopher much read and admired in America, had included an ironic, if easily misinterpreted, critique of slavery in the eleventh book of his *Spirit of the Laws.* Other leaders of the French Enlightenment, after some ambivalence, had finally concluded that slavery was economically burdensome and violated the natural rights of Negroes without justification. Several Scottish moral philosophers—most notably, Francis Hutcheson—had been unmistakably blunt in their criticism of Negro slavery, and their influence had been widely felt by colonial leaders who had studied in Scotland or in American colleges where Scottish educators held sway. Anthony Benezet, the diligent Quaker publicist of Philadelphia, had seen to it that the writings of these European critics of slavery got wide distribution in the colonies.[65]

Colonial writers gradually began to contribute to this slowly mounting critique of Negro slavery. Before 1750, writings against slavery were like fireflies in the night: a lonely resolution by a group of Germantown Friends, whose conscience cried, "Repent!" but whose influence was weak; an awkward little tract by a judge in Massachusetts whose timid excursion against the slave trade was quickly overwhelmed by heavier guns; a nasty pamphlet by an irascible Quaker named Benjamin Lay, whose vinegary prose attracted few followers.[66]

During the third quarter of the eighteenth century, colonial writers were beginning to shed a pale moon of illumination on the institution and its moral and social weaknesses. Benjamin Franklin, for example, in his "Observations Concerning the Increase of Mankind" (1751), produced calculations to show that slavery was uneconomical. When one compared the costs of slave labor (purchase price, insurance or risk, upkeep, the cost of overseers, plus the fact that slaves "from the nature of slavery" work badly, and steal from their masters) with the wages of a free laborer, no one could doubt that the latter was cheaper. Furthermore, he argued, slavery discouraged the growth of population. White immigrants, unwilling and unable to compete with slave labor, were driven to other regions. Whites who owned slaves, meanwhile, "became proud, disgusted with labor, and . . . educated in idleness."[67]

Franklin's arguments were addressed to leaders in Philadelphia, where there were still few slaves, and where policy makers had real options about the make-up of the immigrant laboring class. The same arguments had a different cast, however, in the eyes of those already surrounded by slaves. Since, as Patrick Henry once remarked, it was "impracticable" to export slaves once they were here, what Southerners wanted to know was not whether Negro slaves were as good as free white workers, but how best to use the Negro laborers they had. That the working force might be racially integrated was as far from Franklin's imagination in 1751 as it was from Patrick Henry's in 1773.[68] Still, if Franklin's arguments were largely irrelevant to the Southern colonies, they did reinforce the determination of Pennsylvanians not to allow slavery to pollute their commonwealth, and gave a strong impetus to studies, particularly by the Physiocrats in France, into the economics of slavery, studies that later became powerful weapons in the arsenal of antislavery forces.[69]

Thirteen years passed between the publication of Franklin's brief "observations" and the next important public assault on slavery. In 1764, James Otis published his pamphlet "The Rights of the British Colonies Asserted and Proved," in which Negro slavery was explicitly arraigned before the bar of natural rights. The pamphlet became instantly famous and was read throughout the colonies. In discussing the scope of the powers of Parliament, Otis took the argument back to first principles.

In order to form an idea of the natural rights of the colonists, I presume it will be granted that they are men, the common children of the same Creator with their brethren of Great Britain. Nature has placed all such in a state of equality and perfect freedom to act within the bounds of the laws of nature and reason. . . .

Having established these familiar points, he then launched into the kind of gratuitous digression that soon had him in deep trouble with his fellow colonists, as well as with British authorities. "The colonists are by the law of nature freeborn," he began, "as indeed all men are, white or black." Citing Montesquieu, he went on to warn that the "cruel slavery exercised over the poor Ethiopians . . . threatens one day to reduce both Europe and America to the ignorance and barbarity of the darkest ages." Not content to let the aspersion against slave owners and slave traders remain in any way implicit, he pressed on.

> Does it follow that 'tis right to enslave a man because he is black? Will short curled hair like wool, instead of Christian hair, as 'tis called by those whose hearts are as hard as the nether millstone, help the argument? Can any logical inference in favor of slavery be drawn from a flat nose, a long or a short face? Nothing better can be said in favor of a trade that is the most shocking violation of the law of nature, has a direct tendency to diminish the idea of the inestimable value of liberty, and makes every dealer in it a tyrant, from the director of an African company to the petty chapman in needles and pins on the unhappy coast.[70]

At first "universally approved" in the colonies,[71] Otis's pamphlet was soon challenged from all sides. Critics, both loyalist and patriot, accused him of inconsistency in acknowledging the absolute sovereignty of Parliament while arguing that Parliament was not free to be arbitrary in its enactments. In a frantic attempt to explain himself, Otis published in the following year a "Vindication of the British Colonies" and of himself, but to no avail for either. His critics persisted, and Parliament, despite his arguments, passed the Stamp Act. Otis, enraged beyond control, poured his feelings into yet another pamphlet, in which he dubbed his opponents a "little, dirty, drinking, drabbing, contaminated knot of thieves, beggars, and transports." Such outbursts revealed a mind losing its balance, and his authority and usefulness to the patriotic cause were soon exhausted.[72] Yet his original pamphlet, which taught that Negro slavery violated the rights of man, was at least widely read, if not "universally approved."

As the pre-Revolutionary decade proceeded, the assault on slavery slowly mounted. The Quakers continued their pressure, mostly within the Society of Friends, although through the publications of Benezet and others, Quaker feelings of revulsion against the suffering of slaves began slowly to disseminate.[73] Clergymen in New England now added their voices. The Reverend Nathaniel Niles in 1774 preached a sermon in Newbury, Massachusetts, in which the enslavement of Africans was related to the climaxing struggle with Great Britain: "Would we enjoy liberty?

Then we must grant it to others. For shame, let us either cease to enslave our fellow-men, or else let us cease to complain of those that would enslave us." [74]

Another indication that some colonists were beginning to see slavery and natural rights as incompatible came at the Harvard University commencement exercises of July 21, 1773. As part of the program, two graduates presented a "forensic dispute" on the question whether slavery, "to which Africans are in this province, by permission of the law, subjected," be agreeable to "the law of nature." The debate makes fascinating reading, foreshadowing as it did so many of the themes that became familiar in the national debate over slavery during the following century. The young man who took the position that slavery violated the law of nature began confidently, scolding his audience for giving so little attention to "the case of these unhappy Africans," and expressing dismay that "those, who are so readily disposed to urge the principles of natural equality in defense of their own liberties should, with so little reluctance, continue to exert a power, by the operation of which they are so flagrantly contradicted." His tone and the straightforward march of his argument indicated his assurance that his audience was with him in seeing the incompatibility of natural rights and slavery, and in deploring the latter. His opponent, however, was not shaken. Shifting the ground of the argument, he began to talk about "the state of society," where "the greatest good of the whole" required that some men exercise authority and impose discipline, and that others accept subordination. Just as men were properly subordinate to God, and children to parents, so ought slaves to be subordinate to masters. Whether Negroes were inferior to whites for want of education or were different in capacity or potential for improvement, he would not presume to say. The fact was that they were inferior, and that the good of the whole required that they be kept in subordination. Nor, he argued, could the doctrine of consent affect the case. The consent of the governed should be sought only when the greatest good for the community as a whole was in danger of neglect without it. The typical African, he noted, is part idiot, part madman, and part child. No one asks the consent of these types before exercising authority over them.

Not once during his argument did this young man apologize for the enslavement of Africans by Americans. On the contrary, he called their transplantation to America "a great blessing" for them. In Africa, where the character of men was not tempered by Christianity and slavery was unregulated by law, life was miserable for everyone. In Massachusetts, however, as everyone in Harvard Yard knew, things were different. Slavery was "limited" by law, and Africans were treated well. Why, he asked, interfere with a stable and beneficent social order, just to pursue some mythical primeval equality?

The advocate of natural rights was duly horrified by this parade of precedent and prescription. Just as his opponent had anticipated some of the arguments of the "positive good" school of apology for slavery, so this young man now foreshadowed some of Abraham Lincoln's arguments, if not his rhetoric. If slavery was to be justified by the Africans' kinky hair, woe then to anyone whose hair had an unusual wave in it. He disputed the analogy between the authority of God and parents and that of masters. God was infinitely wise, and parents were bound to children by affection, but slaves were in no similar way protected from abuse by their owners. The main burden of his rebuttal consisted of an appeal to facts and to the compassion of his audience. Citing the large and growing body of literature on life in the West Indies, much of it critical, he urged his audience not to confine its view to Massachusetts. Slavery was not everywhere the benign institution it appeared to be in Boston. He "acknowledged" that Negroes appeared ignorant, impolite, strangers to science and philosophy, and utterly lacking in urbanity. But he argued that it was slavery that had reduced them to this condition, and he disputed the logic that justified an institution by calling attention to the wrecks it had produced. Nor would he allow that Africans were certainly better off here than in their homeland. If they were, slavery might be justified, he acknowledged. But he cited the work of Anthony Benezet on life in "Guinea" to show that Africans in their native land were people of charm, who lived a pleasant, if primitive, existence. He concluded by appealing to his audience for compassion toward "those ignorant wretches."

His opponent's rebuttal was brief, but devastating. If they

agreed to rest the argument on matters of fact, he commented, then his opponent had yielded on the matter in dispute. As for facts, he concluded, he would leave them to the judgment of others. And there the matter closed.[75]

There could hardly be a more instructive episode in the colonial corpus. The debate began with a simple, almost simple-minded, juxtaposition of natural rights and slavery, to the disgrace of the latter. But the debate at this point was arid, a game of words and pure concepts. The other young man brought it directly down to earth, drawing attention to things as they were, encouraging his audience to take comfort in familiar surroundings. Negroes were better off here than in wild Africa. Consent applies only where those under authority are chafing, where the greatest good is obviously being neglected. The only reply to this argument was to draw attention to places where slavery was harsher, and to insist that Africa had been caricatured in the popular imagination. The "forensic dispute" was an unequal struggle on these grounds. Boston was at hand: Guinea and Barbados were vague and distant.

The ideology of natural rights was a formidable weapon in the hands of people who were hurting and who sought to understand and explain their hurt. But it seemed to have little capacity to propel the imagination, to induce men to care about or to feel the slavery of others. There is no doubt that chattel slavery is incompatible with the doctrine of natural rights. But it is also true that slavery, especially where it was deeply entrenched, faced a more serious challenge in the nineteenth century, when a public philosophy that gave a larger place to human compassion began to have its sway.[76]

One man who seemed to sense that the heart as well as the mind should play a role in the assault on slavery was the Reverend Samuel Hopkins, a former student of Jonathan Edwards, now pastor to the slave traders of Newport, Rhode Island. In 1776 he dispatched a pamphlet to the "Honorable Continental Congress" entitled "A Dialogue, Concerning the Slavery of the Africans." Already, in the early 1770's, he had delivered several sermons declaring the incompatibility of Christianity and the slave trade to a congregation that included many prominent slave merchants. His "Dialogue" was written in the form of an exchange between an apologist for slavery and the slave trade and a respondent who demolishes the apologies one by one. He sought to make his reader—including, so he hoped, the delegates to the Continental Congress, to whom the pamphlet was dedicated—feel what the slave felt. Thus he described the agonies of the slave who overhears his master saying that "slavery is more to be dreaded than death."

. . . [W]hen they observe all this cry and struggle for liberty for ourselves and children, and see themselves and their children wholly overlooked by us, and behold the sons of liberty oppressing and tyrannizing over many thousands of poor blacks who have as good claim to liberty as themselves, they are shocked with the glaring inconsistence. . . .

He warned that Britain, in the military struggle that had already begun to rage around the colonies, would try to persuade slaves to take up arms against their masters; he urged the members of Congress to forestall the British policy, to free the slaves "by some public acts and laws, and then give them encouragement to labor, or take arms in the defense of the American cause, as they choose." [77]

It is clear, then, that by the mid-1770's, particularly in New England and Pennsylvania, Negro slavery was under attack as an uneconomical, un-Christian, cruel, and dangerous institution, an institution at war, in its principles, with the ideas upon which the colonial struggle against British "tyranny" was based.

Yet this attack was a by-product of the main business of the Revolution. Of the thirteen colonies, the only legislature even to consider an act for emancipation between 1765 and 1780 was Pennsylvania's, and even there, the scene of much of Benezet's activity and blessed with the capable and persistent leadership of George Bryan, the opponents of slavery could not achieve an act of gradual abolition until 1780.[78] Some colonies did enact prohibitions against the slave trade, but similar acts had been passed earlier in the eighteenth century, and seem to have been produced more by fear of slave insurrections and by the desire not to discourage white immigration than by genuine antipathy toward slavery.[79] Besides, these acts were regularly vetoed by authorities in London, and in the context of pre-Revolutionary hassles it seems likely that acts against the slave trade were adopted by colonial assemblies at least partly to court an annoying veto from the royal governor.[80]

The slave trade was also specifically proscribed in various non-importation agreements used by the colonists in an attempt to pressure Parliament into repealing "ungranted" taxes. The language used in some of these, particularly in the Association of the First Continental Congress of 1774, suggests that genuine revulsion against the trade did play a part in the decision to suspend it. The second article of the Association of 1774, for example, read, "We will neither import, nor purchase any slave imported after the first day of December next; after which time, we will wholly discontinue the slave trade, and will neither be concerned in it ourselves, nor will we hire our vessels, nor sell our commodities or manufactures to those who are concerned in it." [81] This language went significantly beyond a mere prohibition of the importation of slaves.

The resolutions adopted by certain counties in Virginia prior to the convening of the First Continental Congress were even more emphatic. The Fairfax County resolves, written by George Mason and adopted at a meeting presided over by George Washington, urged that the slave trade be suspended "during our present difficulties and distress," and added, "We take this opportunity of declaring our most earnest wishes to see an entire stop forever put to such a wicked, cruel, and unnatural trade.' The resolutions of Prince George County were less moral and more pragmatic, but no less total in their indictment of the trade. "The African trade," they contended, "is injurious to this colony, obstructs the population of it by freemen, prevents manufacturers and other useful immigrants from Europe from settling amongst us, and occasions an annual increase of the balance of trade against this colony." [82]

Yet it would be a mistake to assume that these agreements to suspend the slave trade represent the triumph of moral principle over desire and interest. The desire for slaves was qualified by fear that the ratio of white masters to black slaves was becoming dangerously low; interest in the trade from Africa and the British West Indies was at least temporarily weakened by dislocations in Southern agriculture and by economic disruptions occasioned by the discord with Britain. Furthermore, simply in terms of the logic of the nonimportation movement, it would have made no sense to exempt one of the most important elements in the empire's commercial system. The decision to include slaves among the items proscribed by the Association could not have been avoided, regardless of differing views on the morality or expediency of that trade.

And since the trade was to be stopped for the duration, why not clothe the decision in moral dress? Slavery, and especially the slave trade, had long been the taunt of loyalist critics at home[83] and abroad (recall, for example, Samuel Johnson's remark "How is it that we hear the loudest *yelps* for liberty among the drivers of negroes?" [84]). It gave great satisfaction to be able to quit the trade for a time, and it was an even greater delight for those who had genuinely hated it for many years to assign large reasons for their action.[85]

If these resolutions against the slave trade can be fairly discounted as reflections of the Revolutionary ideology, then it is accurate to say that the institution of Negro slavery survived the Revolutionary period essentially untouched by the clamor for liberty and equality that echoed throughout the colonies. Few colonial leaders called public notice to the connection between political slavery and chattel slavery.[86] James Otis and Benjamin Rush did, but both were erratic personalities and were dismissed as political leaders not long after their emergence into public view.[87] Benjamin Franklin, under the influence of the Physiocrats, was developing during this period into a deep critic of slavery, but he spent the decade abroad.[88]

Others apparently saw the anomaly and regretted it, but withheld their opinions from public view. Such a man was Patrick Henry. He confessed "an abhorrence of [Negro] slavery," and expressed amazement that slavery flourished "in a country, above all others, fond of liberty"; but, so far as is known, he confined the expression of these opinions to a private letter to a Quaker, Robert Pleasants, who had sent him a copy of a book by Benezet.[89]

Another prominent Southerner who shared Henry's profound uneasiness was Henry Laurens. He made his confession in a letter to his son, written in 1776. He informed him that he was watchful for an opportunity to free his slaves, but knew that the time was not yet ripe, and that he would be identified as "a promoter not only of strange, but of dangerous doctrines" if his neighbors ever discovered his true feelings toward slavery.[90]

The fact that Samuel Adams made no public record on the subject of slavery may have been due more to personal style than to political judgment about this specific issue. Though naturally a voluble man, he rarely talked for the record. He preferred to move behind the scenes. During the early 1770's, a series of petitions from Negroes was received by the Massachusetts General Court, pointing out that Negroes had, "in common with other men, a natural right to be free and without molestation to enjoy such property as they may acquire by their industry." The petitioners said that they expected "great things . . . from men who have made such a noble stand against the designs of their fellow-men to enslave them." [91] Adams was undoubtedly interested in these petitions and was rightly regarded by the Negroes as their champion in the corridors of the legislature, and he served on the committee to which these petitions were referred.[92] But although he is said to have discussed slavery often with his friends in Boston, and although there is no doubt that he hated the institution thoroughly, contemporaries reported that he never, by word or deed, sought to interfere with it elsewhere in the country, because he believed that if he did, he would jeopardize the unity of the colonies, which was essential to the achievement of his primary goal for them—namely, independence.[93]

The only political leader of consequence in Revolutionary America who moved openly against Negro slavery was the slave-owning Virginian Thomas Jefferson. During his first term in the Virginia House of Burgesses, he made "one effort" to change the law of manumission so that it would be easier for a master to free his slaves. The effort was abortive; in fact, it left no trace in the official *Journal* of the Burgesses.[94] If this effort rubbed conservatives the wrong way, they could charge it to inexperience and youthful indiscretion; Jefferson was twenty-six at the time.

Seven years later, Jefferson again struck a glancing blow at slavery, then quickly retreated in the face of resistance from bolder slave owners. In his masterly draft of the Declaration of Independence, which laid the principles of liberty and equality in the cornerstone of the republic, he included a clause on slavery and the slave trade in the list of counts against King George.

He has waged cruel war against human nature itself, violating its most sacred rights of life and liberty in the persons of a distant people who never offended him, captivating and carrying them into slavery in another hemisphere, or to incur miserable death in their transportation thither. This piratical warfare, the opprobrium of *infidel* powers, is the warfare of the *Christian* king of Great Britain. Determined to keep open a market where MEN should be bought and sold, he has prostituted his negative for suppressing every legislative attempt to prohibit or to restrain this execrable commerce; and that this assemblage of horrors might want no fact of distinguished die, he is now exciting these very people to rise in arms among us, and to purchase that liberty of which *he* deprived them, by murdering the people upon whom *he* also intruded them; thus paying off former crimes committed against the *liberties* of one people, with crimes which he urges them to commit against the *lives* of another.[95]

This clause, called a "vehement philippic against negro slavery" by John Adams,[96] was obviously wrought with great care. The idealistic Jefferson may have imagined that he had succeeded in meeting the objections that many colonists might have had against an antislavery proposition. For one thing, Britain was made to bear all the blame for the slave trade, despite the fact that the involvement of colonial ships must have been well known to everyone in the Congress. Thus did he seek to avoid offending the slave dealers of Newport, Boston, New York, and Charleston. But at the same time, his indictment of the slave trade, though directed solely at the King, was general enough to constitute a serious obstacle for those who looked forward to reopening the slave trade after the attainment of independence.

Jefferson's double motives are also evident in the peroration of the clause. He blames the King for "crimes" against the liberty of Negroes, but also for inciting the Negroes to insurrection. Again he is trying to push in the direction of emancipation but to control the process, and, above all, to avoid saying anything that would commit the signers, so many of whom held slaves themselves, to abolition.

But his craft was in vain. John Adams, who read the draft before it was submitted to Congress, later claimed that he knew the South Carolinians and Georgians would never accept it,[97] and indeed they would not. There is no record of the debates in Congress, but Jefferson tells us that the clause against slavery was stricken from the final draft at the insistence of the Deep Southerners.[98]

These references—a sermon here, a pamphlet there, a college commencement debate, and a handful of petitions to the Massachusetts legislature—in the context of the swirl of events and flood of publications that heralded the American Revolution, show the marginal consideration given to Negro slavery by a people who thought of little else, publicly, but the political slavery that threatened to engulf them. How could these men, many of whom were honorable and sensitive people, filled with idealism for their country and regard for their fellow man, have continued to hold slaves themselves, and to traffic in them, while conducting a struggle for their own liberty? Several explanations can be offered.

The leaders of the Revolution were inheritors of habits and attitudes that made it easy to ignore their black neighbors. The habit of regarding Negroes as a thing apart from the constituent elements of colonial society is frequently reflected in the pamphlets of the period. Dulany, the vain Marylander who never forgot that he had been educated in London, wrote that his English readers would be surprised to learn that there were North Americans who were "neither black nor tawny," who spoke the English language and who seemed "in other respects . . . for all the world, like one of them!" [99] Even James Otis, author of the sternest rebuke of slaveholding in the entire polemical literature of the pre-Revolutionary period, exposed his prejudice in a passage in which he scolded "the common people of England" for their misconceptions of America. The continental colonies, he pointed out, were settled, not with "a compound mixture of English, Indian, and Negro, but with free-born British white subjects." [100]

Politically, Negroes were virtually invisible.[101] The best illustration came in Virginia. The same convention that instructed Richard Henry Lee to move in the Continental Congress for a resolution and declaration of independence also called for a new constitution for the Old Dominion, one that would "secure substantial and equal liberty to the people." A debate soon developed over the proposed preamble to the constitution, drafted by George Mason, a wealthy planter from the tidewater region who played a large role throughout this constitution-making period. In his draft, he had written that "all men are by nature equally free and independent." Many planters objected, calling the clause a "forerunner of civil convulsion," a standing invitation to Negroes to claim their freedom from the necessary discipline of their masters. Defenders of Mason's language replied that the clause could not have this effect because it did not apply to Negroes, since Negroes were not "constituent members" of the society being formed. With a sense of relief, though not without misgivings, the convention proceeded to adopt Mason's language.[102]

There were nearly as many Negroes as whites in Virginia, more than in any other colony in America. No one explained how the theory of constitutional liberalism, upon which Virginia's constitution was based, could be interpreted to justify the framing of a social contract for just half of the population of a given territory. The need for such an explanation was apparently not felt. Negroes were simply not perceived as active political agents.[103]

One might suppose that the Revolutionary situation would have forced a reconsideration and revision of these inherited attitudes and social patterns. J. Franklin Jameson has shown that the American Revolution did touch off a "social movement" of significant proportions.[104] Yet in light of the evidence, the fact that Negro slaves benefited far less from this development than many of their white brethren must be accounted for.

One clue comes from a theme that was central to the Revolutionary ideology. Repeatedly, colonial Whigs, who regarded liberty as a rare thing in human history, told one another that he who would be worthy of it must be willing to fight for it.[105] Parliamentary enactments that struck the colonists as oppressive were seen as "an important trial of our virtue" by the Sons of Liberty in New York.[106] In this spirit, an anonymous pamphlet published

in 1774 exhorted Americans to honor and obey the resolutions of
the newly convened Continental Congress. Anyone who failed to
do so, cried the author, was "a slave," and he recommended the
following punishment: "Expose him for sale at a public vendue.
Send him to plant sugar with his fellow slaves in Jamaica."[107]
Through all these pronouncements ran the notion that liberty
was something that had to be fought for, and that he who submitted to slavery in some measure deserved it. The keynote had
been struck by Jonathan Mayhew, who taught that resistance to
slavery was the duty of those threatened by it, and that those who
failed to resist "conspired" in their own slavery.[108]

Though this point was not ever explicitly applied to Negroes,
it does help to explain the colonial attitude toward slavery. The
prevailing perspective was defensive. Colonial political leaders
stressed those qualities needed to resist enslavement. Meanwhile,
with the air full of bombastic assertions of the determination to
fight for liberty, Negro protests against bondage were isolated,
sporadic, and for the most part inarticulate. Thus, Negroes could
be an object of compassion, and were,[109] but they did not command respect, and their plight did not command much attention.

The mood of the leaders of the Revolution was belligerent
and aggressive, rather than benevolent, analytical, or self-critical.
Those who urged the Revolution forward most strenuously, who
stated its justification in the boldest terms, looked around them,
not for American practices that needed reform, but for imperial
intrusions and disruptions that invited resentment. It is no accident that the one aspect of the system of Negro slavery genuinely
deplored by colonial leaders was the slave trade, for the slave
trade had been conducted in large part by British vessels, and
had been protected against colonial regulation by imperial authority. When the gentry in Virginia cast about them for grievances against the Crown, it was natural that they should seize on
the trade that had brought their problem to them, and virtually
ignore slavery itself, in which they were deeply implicated.

Furthermore, the ideology of the American Revolution, for all
its emphasis on natural equality and human liberty, was not egalitarian. David Brion Davis has commented on "the ambivalence
of rationalism": its tendency to search for social equilibrium, its

respect for the evolution of institutions, its conviction that ethical principles arise out of environment and must be shown to be practical and useful.[110] These ideas heavily qualified the reforming thrust of the Enlightenment. The feeling seemed to be that if absolute equality were decreed today, for white men and for blacks, tomorrow there would be chaos, and the day after that men would be pleading for security, even if it entailed bondage.

The Revolutionary effort against Great Britain consumed the energies of most colonial leaders, leaving them little time or emotion to pursue internal reforms. Slavery was an extremely complicated institution, raising difficult theoretical problems. Few men, then or later, dared to confront it directly. Slaves were persons, but they were also property, which meant that a Negro's right to liberty conflicted with his master's right to property. In the colonial ideology, the right of property was central. The slave owner's right to property in slaves had been sanctioned by long prescription and was woven deeply into colonial law. Under these circumstances, there was hardly a man in all the colonies who would not have seen a serious problem in calling for an end to property in slaves without consent or compensation.[111]

There were also enormous practical problems. Compensation at full market value was utterly beyond the capacity of colonial public economies, especially in a colony like Virginia. Even the citizens of Massachusetts would have objected to being taxed to pay wealthy men for freeing their black slaves. And what was to be done with freed slaves? Should they be returned to Africa, colonized somewhere on the frontier, or mixed in with white neighbors? If the latter, how would they be prepared for their new independence? How would white workers react to their competition? Few colonists got as far as these problems in their thinking, but those who did must have been intimidated by their enormity and complexity. It is not surprising that responsible men would have been intimidated by the thought of coming to grips with these problems in the midst of the nation's birth pangs.

Colonial leaders exempted chattel slavery from their critique of political slavery because the movement for independence, which was their primary concern, required it. John Adams once said that the biggest problem that confronted colonial leaders in 1776 was to get thirteen clocks to strike at once.[112] If Adams and his fellow Northerners had expressed criticism or misgivings about slavery in the Southern colonies, the alarm of Revolution might never have gone off at all.

What some of them might otherwise have said is indicated by passages directed against the planters of the "sugar islands' in the Caribbean. John Dickinson, for example, in his analysis of the importance of the American colonies in the British imperial system, found occasion to express contempt for the British islands, where "a few lords with despotic power over myriads of vassals" lived in luxurious comfort, supported by their slaves.[113] James Otis showed the same tendency to vent his spleen against slavery by excoriating the West Indian planters. He cast the following aspersion on them:

It is a clear truth that those who every day barter away other men's liberty will soon care little for their own. To this case must be imputed that ferocity, cruelty, and brutal barbarity that has long marked the general character of the sugar islanders. They can in general form no idea of government but that which in person or by an overseer . . . is exercised over ten thousand of their fellow men, born with the same right to freedom and the sweet enjoyments of liberty and life as their unrelenting taskmasters, the overseers and planters.[114]

Otis was typical of many New Englanders who regarded the island planters with a mixture of jealousy and contempt, and frequently indulged these feelings by expressing them.[115]

Evidences of tension between the mainland colonies are abundant in the Revolutionary period. Many of the disputes had nothing to do with slavery, of course. There were conflicts over border claims and claims to territory west of the Appalachians. There was an inevitable jockeying for advantage among merchants in the several colonies, both in invoking and in suspending the nonimportation agreements of 1769–1770. These tensions persisted right up to the eve of the Declaration of Independence —so much so that John Dickinson, in explaining why he could not support a resolution of independence on July 1, 1776, predicted that "A partition of these colonies will take place if Great Britain can't conquer us." [116] The co-operation of the colonies against Britain's changing imperial policy was an uncertain thing from start to finish, something that contemporaries could never take for granted. From this point of view, it is probably fortunate that abolitionism as a movement of consequence in America was still far in the future, for if Samuel Adams and John Jay and Benjamin Franklin and other Northern politicians had forthrightly criticized Negro slavery in the early 1770's, American history would have developed far differently. To begin with, there would have been no Association of twelve colonies in 1774,[117] and certainly no "Unanimous Declaration of the Thirteen United States of America" in 1776.

The course of the struggle between Revolutionary ideas and slavery in the years immediately following the War for American Independence is best shown by analyzing one man's thought. Thomas Jefferson, perhaps the outstanding spokesman of Revolutionary ideas, was keenly aware of the tension between the ideals of his country and the brutal presence of slavery. Yet he lived in a region where slavery was a pervasive feature of social and economic life. In his *Notes on the State of Virginia,* and in his painful attempts to control its dissemination, the explosive relationship between slavery and the ideological patterns of the American Revolution stands starkly exposed.

The *Notes* were prepared in response to queries sent to each of the state governors by the Secretary of the French legation in New York, the Marquis de Barbé-Marbois, asking for an account of affairs and conditions in each state. Jefferson, as Governor of Virginia, received the queries in 1780, but did not have time to concentrate on his response until after he had retired from public office in June 1781. During the late summer of that year he spent several weeks assembling his replies from memorandums on Virginia that he had made over many years. On December 20, 1781, he sent a copy to Marbois, but did not publish his work. Intermittently during the ensuing two years, at home in Monticello and while serving in Congress, he revised it. When, in 1785, he finally arranged for a private printing, the work was three times as long as the manuscript submitted to Marbois.[118]

Jefferson's remarks about slavery in Virginia came in two striking passages. The first was an extended digression in his answer to Query XIV, which concerned the "administration of justice and the description of the laws." Having devoted the previous section to a critique of Virginia's constitution, he described, in reply to this query, the report of a state legislative committee that had prepared revisions of the code of the State of Virginia. The revisions were intended to purge the code of "principles inconsistent with republicanism."

He listed "the most remarkable alterations proposed," among them, the following: "to emancipate all slaves born after the passing the act." [119] The bill, he wrote, directs that slaves born after a certain date continue with their parents until adulthood, being trained at public expense in farming, arts, and sciences, "according to their geniuses"; that they then be "colonized to such place as the circumstances of the time should render most proper," equipped with arms, tools, seeds, domestic animals, and other necessities, declared "a free and independent people," and offered alliance and protection "till they have acquired strength"; and that Virginia "send vessels at the same time to other parts of the world for an equal number of white inhabitants" to replace the black laborers.[120] Here was the outline of a solution to the problem of slavery in Virginia (and, incidentally, a good indication of the difficulty of framing political solutions to the problem).

Like the Declaration of Independence, the *Notes* were written, not only for domestic consumption, but for "a candid world." Having described this plan, Jefferson recognized that Frenchmen, at least, might want some explanation for its rather awkward provisions. "It will probably be asked," he acknowledged, "Why not retain and incorporate the blacks into the state, and thus save the expense of supplying, by importation of white settlers, the vacancies they will leave [not to mention the incalculably greater expense of colonizing the blacks]?" His answer to this pertinent question, one almost never directly faced, much less answered, by the founding generation, consumes the next seven pages of his text.

The first element in this answer was that there were profound political obstacles to the "incorporation" of blacks into Virginian society. "Deep-rooted prejudices entertained by the whites; ten thousand recollections, by the blacks, of the injuries they have sustained; new provocations; the real distinctions which nature has made; and many other circumstances" had produced profound alienation between whites and blacks. If the legal barriers between the races were torn down, but no provision made for their separation, "convulsions" would ensue, which would "probably never end but in the extermination of the one or the other race."

But Jefferson was not content to rest the case on "political" considerations alone. The "prejudices" of whites had to be justified somehow; else how could the author of the Declaration of Independence tolerate his own, and his neighbors', involvement in slavery even for a moment. There were, he contended, "physical and moral" reasons for opposing racial integration. With "diffidence," he presented the fruit of his own observations regarding the physical attributes of black people. Blacks are less beautiful than whites, give off "a very strong and disagreeable odor," are "more tolerant of heat," and "seem to require less sleep" than whites. Their senses are keener, but their imagination "dull, tasteless and anomalous." Consequently, "they are more ardent after their female; but love seems with them to be more an eager desire, than a tender, delicate mixture of sentiment and sensation."

In assessing these differences, wrote Jefferson, one needs "to make great allowances for the difference of condition, of education, of conversation, of the sphere in which they move." But, even so, the performance of blacks gives no substantial basis for qualifying the judgment. Suffering and love, he noted, have often produced exalted poetry; yet blacks have suffered grievously, and their love is ardent, but still they produce no poetry. By contrast, from among the white slaves of Rome several distinguished poets and scientists emerged, though Roman slavery on the whole was no less severe than American. "It is not their condition, then, but nature which has produced the distinction" between the races in intellect and imagination.[121]

As for moral considerations, Jefferson saw more reason to grant the influence of extenuating circumstances. It is sometimes held that slaves are more prone to theft, he wrote, but may not man "justifiably take a little from one who has taken all from him . . . ?" Just laws "must give a reciprocation of right." "The man in whose favor no laws of property exist, probably feels himself less bound to respect those made in favor of others." Furthermore, notwithstanding their unfavorable circumstances, "we find among them numerous instances of the most rigid integrity . . . of benevolence, gratitude, and unshaken fidelity." [22]

At this point, the mood of the analysis shifts significantly. In light of the moral stature of some slaves, he seemed to want to qualify almost everything he had said.

The opinion that they are inferior in the faculties of reason and imagination must be hazarded with great diffidence. To justify a general conclusion requires many observations . . . [particularly] where it is a faculty, not a substance, we are examining, where it eludes the research of all the senses . . . [and] where our conclusion would degrade a whole race of men. . . . I advance it therefore as a suspicion only, that the blacks . . . are inferior to the whites in the endowments both of body and mind.

But immediately upon offering this qualification, he returned to his initial proposition. In a way, it was finally irrelevant whether the "prejudices" of whites were rooted in historical circumstances or in the natural aptitudes of blacks. Whether the blacks were "originally" a distinct race or had been made so "by time and circumstance," they were in fact distinct by nature. Consequently, among the advocates of emancipation, those who were concerned to preserve the "dignity and beauty" of the human race were led always to couple their advocacy of liberty for the blacks with the demand that blacks, "when freed . . . be removed beyond the reach of mixture" with whites. [23]

The closer this discussion is examined, the more puzzling it seems. It purports to explain a scheme for emancipation, but it ends by providing a virtually impregnable argument for the necessity of slavery in a racially balanced society. If the best available evidence of natural science drove toward the conclusion that blacks are inferior in mental and imaginative endowments, but lighthearted and capable of hard labor in hot climates, then perhaps slavery was not such a vicious system after all. Perhaps the only thing wrong with it was the bad conscience of white men and the resentment of blacks. But if science could show that these sentiments were unjustified, it might be that the institution could yet be stabilized. All that was required was for people to accept the conclusion that blacks did not belong in the same phylogenetic category as whites. Jefferson's generation was not prepared to go all the way to this conclusion, but there was a clear invitation in this passage of the *Notes* to accept such a resolution of the issue.

The other passage in the *Notes* that deals with slavery, the answer to Query XVIII, carries a far different tone and reaches a dramatically different conclusion. Unlike Query XIV, where the categories of analysis are relatively static and scientific, those in Query XVIII are dynamic and moral. Marbois had asked about "particular customs and manners that may happen to be received in that state." Jefferson's answer was brief, concentrating on just one "unhappy influence on the manners of our people"—slavery. Slavery, he said, involved "a perpetual exercise of the most boisterous passions, the most unremitting despotism on the one part, and degrading submissions on the other." And because man is "an imitative animal," slavery's effect on the development of children was pernicious. Watching their parents discipline slaves, children got the clue that their own most aggressive instincts could be vented on slave children. They were "thus nursed, educated, and daily exercised in tyranny." Slaves themselves suffered, too, of course, particularly in the erosion of their *"amor patriae."* "For if a slave can have a country in this world, it must be any other in preference to that in which he is born to live and labor for another; in which he must lock up the faculties of his nature. . . ." But the worst effect of all was that slavery tended to undermine the "only firm basis" of liberty, the conviction in the minds of the people that liberty is "the gift of God."

Indeed I tremble for my country when I reflect that God is just; that his justice cannot sleep forever; that considering numbers, nature and natural means only, a revolution of the wheel of fortune, an exchange of situation, is among possible events; that it may become probable by supernatural interference! The Almighty has no attribute which can take side with us in such a contest.[124]

Whereas the answer to Query XIV had ended at least superficially on a note of hope and possibility, that to Query XVIII veered toward total despair. But it was not Jefferson's disposition in the early 1780's to yield to despair, however overpowering the evidence against optimism might be. In the pitifully candid concluding passage, he admitted that the problem of slavery was too portentous for cool analysis.

[I]t is impossible to be temperate and to pursue this subject through the various considerations of policy, of morals, of history natural and civil. We must be content to hope they will force their way into everyone's mind.

But was there any basis for hope? Jefferson thought there was. "The spirit of the master is abating, that of the slave rising from the dust, his condition mollifying, the way I hope preparing, under the auspices of heaven, for a total emancipation. . . ." But how this could be, given "the unhappy influence" of slavery on the manners and morals of man, the "imitative animal," and given the "deep-rooted prejudices" of the whites, the injured memories of the blacks, and "the racial distinctions which nature has made," Jefferson did not explain.

Jefferson's words may have been guarded, but he knew they were full of potential offense, to slave owners and to opponents of slavery alike. The latter jumped in outrage on the passages that discussed the capacities of blacks in terms of "the gradations in all the races of animals," as perceived by what Jefferson called "the eye of philosophy." Reacting to the passage in the *Notes* on the ability of blacks to write poetry, one Northern political opponent declared that "one would have thought that modern philosophy herself could not have the face to declare that the wretch who is driven out to labor at the dawn of day, and who toils until evening with the whip flourishing over his head, ought to be a poet." [125]

But it was the reaction of Southerners that Jefferson most feared. He was apprehensive, for one thing, that his neighbors might take offense at his suggestion that the question of the capacities of blacks cried out for analysis and research. Unless such research could be guaranteed in advance to justify the deep-rooted prejudice of whites, whites in the South could regard it only with foreboding.

Another aspect offensive to many Southerners was the broaching of the question of emancipation. Among certain circles in Virginia it was still admissible, even fashionable, to speculate about schemes of emancipation, provided that one was careful to avoid the suspicion of sympathy with integration.[126] But even in Virginia, not to mention the Deep South, there were people who reacted sharply to any suggestion of emancipation, however well guarded. Whether they regarded colonization as a fantasy or slavery itself as an indispensable tool for the cultivation of the South, they were convinced that it was dangerous and foolish to allow the idea of emancipation to gain currency. To talk as if emancipation was possible raised hopes in both whites and blacks that would certainly, in the view of these critics, eventually have to be crushed. It was thus better for everyone not to encourage such dangerous speculations.

Sensitive to these inevitable reactions, Jefferson was extremely reluctant to release his work to the general public. There were probably both personal and public reasons for this hesitancy. Jefferson was an extremely irenic man, who cringed before the prospect (if not the actual fact) of political conflict. He was also a man ambitious to influence the course of political events. He believed deeply in eventual progress, in the gradual enlightenment of man, and his reaction to the French Revolution demonstrates that he did not always insist upon tidiness or nonviolence. But he believed that progress, especially moral progress, would not come quickly, and would not come at all until the public mind was ready.[127]

Regarding slavery specifically, he knew in 1785 that the public mind was a long way from readiness to affirm a feasible plan for abolition. The primary obstacle was racial prejudice, which meant that emancipation on a broad scale could be countenanced only if it was linked to some scheme for the removal of blacks. Furthermore, it was all but impossible to imagine a nation like the United States at the end of the eighteenth century—humane in ideals, weakly integrated in social structure, poor in economic resources, and primitive in administrative machinery—accomplishing the herculean feat of colonization. If these enormous obstacles were to be surmounted, a "reformation" of the public mind would have to prepare the way. What worried Jefferson was whether his *Notes*, by raising hard and unfamiliar questions, would help to stimulate this reformation or whether, conversely, "these strictures might produce an irritation which would indispose the people towards . . . the emancipation of their slaves. . . ." [128]

Because of these uncertainties, compounded by his own timidity, he approached the question of publication and distribution with extreme caution. While serving in Congress in New York City during 1783–1784, he had a few copies made for distribution to intimate friends. Not until he went to Paris on a diplomatic mission did he have as many as 200 copies printed. Even then, he tried to retain close control over the dissemination of his ideas. In May 1785, he sent a copy by personal messenger to James Madison, with the message that he was sending another to James Monroe, and asking their advice, "and . . . nobody's else," on whether he should distribute his remaining copies to students at his alma mater, William and Mary College, an institution "where are collected together all the young men of Virginia under preparation for public life." [129] Madison urged the proposed limited distribution, and it was apparently undertaken.

In addition, Jefferson sent a copy to some "estimable characters" in France and Great Britain, among them the distinguished historian and theologian Dr. Richard Price, whose history of the American Revolution, while sympathetic to the United States, contained trenchant criticism of slavery as inconsistent with the ideals of the Revolution. Jefferson's inscription in Price's copy reflects the mood with which he hazarded even the limited distribution of his work: "Unwilling to expose them to the public eye, he asks the favor of Doctor Price to put them into the hands of no person on whose care and fidelity he cannot rely to guard them against publication." [130]

Despite his care, however, a copy soon fell into the hands of an unscrupulous Parisian bookseller, who straightway began to prepare a French translation. Realizing that his hope of controlling the distribution was ended, Jefferson quickly prepared an authorized version, and made arrangements for it to be printed in London by John Stockdale. In 1787, an edition bearing Jefferson's name on the title page was finally published.[131] He was then able to follow, not without anguish, the effect of his ideas on the thoughts of Americans about slavery.

Jefferson's words fell on the South at a time when it was fast adjusting to the continuing presence of slavery. His openness to evidence that the "prejudices" of whites were insupportable, his trembling over slavery in the presence of a just God, and his "hope . . . for a total emancipation" gave his political opponents, especially those in the Deep South, an issue with which to stir up feeling against him. During his campaign for the Presidency in 1796, an anonymous "Southern planter" quoted the passage on emancipation and added, "If this wild project succeeds . . . and *three hundred thousand* slaves are set free in Virginia, farewell to the safety, prosperity, the importance, perhaps the very existence of the Southern states." [132] A leading Federalist from South Carolina, citing not only the *Notes,* but also Jefferson's courteous letter to Benjamin Banneker thanking him for a copy of his *Almanac,* asked in a pamphlet of 1796, "What shall we think of a *secretary of state* thus fraternizing with negroes, writing them complimentary epistles . . . congratulating them on the evidences of their *genius,* and assuring them of his good wishes for their speedy emancipation?" [133] Jefferson lost the votes of South Carolina and the election by narrow margins. His unreliability on the subject of slavery may have had something to do with his difficulty in gathering support in the Deep South. In any case, he and his managers were taking no chances four years later. During the campaign of 1800, Charles Pinckney announced that Jefferson had

authorized his friends to declare as his assertion: "That the Constitution has not empowered the federal legislature to touch in the remotest degree the question respecting the condition or property of slaves in any of the states, and that any attempt of that sort would be unconstitutional and a usurpation of rights Congress do not possess." [134]

There is no evidence in this pronouncement that Jefferson had resolved his own profound doubts about the justice of slavery or its baneful effects on morality and manners in America. But he was apparently prepared to promise that he would not use his national office as a forum for attacking slavery or seeking to work for its abolition.

By 1800 he had apparently concluded that the work of emancipation would not be accomplished by his generation.[135] More than that, he gradually became fatalistic, even apocalyptic, in his attitude toward the future of America with slavery. In a letter of August 1797 to St. George Tucker, he related the uprising of slaves in Santo Domingo to the revolutionary currents in Europe, and concluded that "if something is not done, and soon done," to begin the work of emancipation and colonization, "we shall be the murderers of our own children." He went on to confess his suspicion that it was already too late.[136] Virginians and Southerners generally were unwilling and probably unable to fashion any plan for emancipation. The passage of time only made the reform seem more remote. The movement away from a political solution to the problem of slavery culminated for Jefferson in the Missouri crisis, when he told friends they were hearing the knell of union.[137]

In 1785 Jefferson had permitted himself to hope that the way was preparing, "under the auspices of heaven, for a total emancipation." By 1820, convinced that the way was preparing for civil war over slavery, his hope was that he might not live long enough to witness the awful climax of his country's struggle with slavery and its consequences.[138] Thus did the author of the Declaration— the one leader of the Revolutionary generation bold enough to stare slavery in the face—end his days, surrounded by scores of his own slaves, still believing that the "expatriation" of the blacks was feasible, but increasingly convinced that the avarice of slave owners and the ignorant fanaticism of the abolitionists were driving the union toward disaster.

3

Slavery and Strategy in the War
for American Independence

WHEN the war of words between England and its North American colonies turned into a struggle between armed men, the population of the thirteen colonies stood at about 2½ million people. About one-fifth were Negroes. Throughout the conflict, as well as in the ensuing peace talks, both sides had to decide how to relate to these anomalous persons.

The basic strategic facts were these: 90 per cent of America's Negroes lived in the five southernmost colonies, where 95 per cent of them were held in slavery. In Virginia the population of a half-million was 40 per cent black. In the colony of South Carolina, Negroes and whites were about equal in number, but in the districts nearest the ocean, those most vulnerable to assault from the sea, Negroes outnumbered whites by as much as ten or twelve to one.[1] No one knew how these people would react to the coming of war to their neighborhood, but everyone knew that the outcome might depend on the answer.

The war began in New England. The American headquarters of the British Army was at Boston in 1775, and it was near Boston that the American resistance movement first resorted to arms. By March 1776, the British had been forced to evacuate Boston, and, rather than fight their way back, they decided to move their headquarters to New York City. They needed a more central location, and they expected to be waging a war in which the British Navy would play a large role. New York's superb harbor, midway between Boston and Chesapeake Bay, and within easy reach of Charleston, met the specifications perfectly.

Slavery and Strategy in the War for Independence

During the first winter of the war, the British undertook their first foray into the South, an operation based on the expectation that loyal colonial government could be restored in Georgia and the Carolinas by a single vigorous assault. Their strategy was based on the assumption that most Southerners were still loyal to the King, and that the British Army had merely to make a strong show of force to embolden these loyalists to seize power and exercise it in obedience to the British Crown.

A message from Lord North, the British wartime Prime Minister, to King George III, written in October 1775, summarized the reasoning behind this proposed move. North reminded the King of several reports submitted by royal governors of the Southern colonies. Governor Josiah Martin, of North Carolina, for example, had reported that Britain had many friends in his colony and could rely on sympathy and support, especially from inhabitants of the back country. He added that the British Army need not fear the leaders of the rebellion in North Carolina, most of whom lived on plantations in the Tidewater. The latter, he wrote, were outnumbered by their slaves and were thus effectively neutralized.[2] Citing Martin's report, as well as others, from Virginia and South Carolina, to the same effect, North added the following comment:

The accounts we have received from these provinces are the more to be credited, as we all know the perilous situation of three of them from the great number of their Negro slaves, and the small proportion of white inhabitants, and the exceeding want of European commodities, which must soon prevail in them all. Lord North looks upon it, therefore, as certain, that a very considerable number of the people in those provinces wish for a speedy accommodation of the disputes with Great Britain. . . .[3]

Because the South seemed so vulnerable, and because the British forces lacked employment for the winter of 1775–1776, he urged the King to authorize a sharp blow at the South, delivered "with vigor and éclat." Once a beachhead was established there, the rebellion might quickly collapse. The desertion of the planting colonies would tip the balance in the middle colonies in favor of those loyal to the Crown. As for the colonies in New England, fear and distress would soon recall them to a sense of their duty. Even if the Southern colonies could not be pacified entirely, much could be accomplished by a Southern expedition, he felt. Supplies for the British Army could be taken, rebel provisions and powder magazines destroyed, ringleaders seized, and the friends of the British government armed and organized.

With the understanding that all this might be accomplished in time for the expeditionary force to rejoin the rest of the army in New York by the early summer of 1776, a British force assembled off the coast of North Carolina and proceeded, after some delay, to the harbor of Charleston. There ensued the "most egregious fiasco" of the war, from the British viewpoint. After wasting several weeks in extensive reconnoitering, British gunboats made a belated assault right into the teeth of the American defenses. That by itself would not have spelled disaster had not the British and Americans alike been surprised by the remarkable resiliency of palmetto wood, of which the defenses at Charleston had been hastily constructed while the British forces loitered at sea. The palmetto logs absorbed cannon balls like a blotter daubing ink blots. Meanwhile, guns inside the American fort sent carefully aimed fire into the anchored British ships.

In a few hours, it was all over. The ships retreated weakly out to sea, leaving the loyalists, many of whom had declared themselves in expectation of a decisive British victory, exposed to the revenge of their neighbors. The rebels took hope from their surprising success, and used the respite mainly to pacify Indians on the frontier.[4]

With the exception of this abortive lunge at Charleston, the war centered around New York during most of 1776 and 1777. Britain's basic plan was to isolate New England by cutting the colonies in two, up the Hudson River valley. In response, American troops under George Washington sallied back and forth across New Jersey and around Philadelphia, until an American force at Saratoga ruined the British plan by capturing a large army trying to descend through the Hudson valley from Canada. The British defeat at Saratoga led to a reappraisal of strategy in London.

The result was a decision to maintain the base at New York, but to concentrate offensive efforts, for the time being, in the South. This decision represented a triumph for those British policy makers and advisers who had from the beginning urged such a course. Prominent among these advisers was William Knox, agent of the colony of Georgia, owner of a plantation there, and wartime Under-Secretary of State for the American Colonies. He had been arguing since 1775 that, instead of fighting in the North, the army should begin its assault in the South, secure the royal government in Georgia, then take the Carolinas in succession, and move on to subdue Virginia.

After Saratoga, Knox, whose influence was probably not great, was joined by a more formidable official, Charles Jenkinson, of the Treasury, whose argument was both bolder and more comprehensive. He suggested that the Hudson River be accepted as the new boundary of the empire in America. New England, populous and stubborn, would be costly to discipline and hardly worth the effort. It produced little of value to the home country, and its purchases of British manufactures would continue in any case. New England, he said, "could be cast out of the empire without damage to Britain's wealth or security." [5] These arguments were added to the old ones: that the South was shot through with loyalists, weakened by the danger of slave insurrections from within and Indian attacks from without, and dependent on maritime trade that could easily be blockaded.

The Southern states suffered terribly from the resulting British invasion, which began at Savannah early in 1779 and tore northward through the region for most of the next two years. Separated by barriers of racial caste and social class, the people in the South were unable to pull together in common defense. Off on the fringes crouched the Indians.[6] It never occurred to most whites that they might become an integral part of their communities, and there is no evidence that the Indians coveted such a relationship. Both races clung to what they had and tried to snatch what the other held. For the Indians, the war provided new opportunities to disrupt and harass the settlements that penetrated ever deeper into their midst. Only rarely did they fight alongside their American neighbors, and such temporary alliances were always delicate affairs, subject to reversal without notice.

Within the white population, there were deep social cleavages. The settlers in the hills resented the wealth of the planters and felt, deep within their proud Scotch-Irish bones, the snubs directed at them by the gentry on the coast. One source of grievance was the use of black laborers by planters in the low country. Because they could not compete with the slaves, whites who owned few slaves or none were forced to settle in the hills, away from the land engrossed by planters for their mammoth operations. The government of the Southern colonies naturally centered in the low country. The back-country settlers hated public officials, who would not extend their services to the hills, nearly as much as they despised these same officials when they did come to the back country to collect taxes and impose civil discipline. Many dwellers in the hills sided with the British during the war, mainly on the theory that any enemy of their enemy must be a friend of theirs.[7]

The main impulse for rebellion in the South came from the planters. It was they whose transactions had been most heavily burdened by the stamp tax, they who jostled with British "placemen" for the control of affairs, they who had been in most intimate contact with the rebels to the north, they who had written most of the pamphlets and adopted most of the resolves that led to the break with Great Britain. Yet they, too, were divided. Some had developed strong ties with the Mother Country during their studies abroad. Others doubted whether they could keep control over affairs in their colonies if the steadying hand of Britain were withdrawn. Jonathan Boucher was not the only planter to wonder, in 1774, whether those who called for independence had calculated the dangers. With Indians at their backs and slaves ever ready to break loose and turn on them, he advised that the prudent course for Southerners was to seek accommodation within the framework of the empire.[8]

Most of the leading planters, some boldly, others reluctantly, rejected this advice. The boldest, of whom Richard Henry Lee was exemplary, were right in step with the most militant New Englanders, outraged by Britain's "unconstitutional" legislation for America, eager to assert American independence. The reluctant ones, including Peyton Randolph, of Virginia, and John Rutledge, of South Carolina, tried hard to prevent the ultimate rupture. Only gradually were they persuaded that the course settled upon by the British government was incompatible with their habitual notion that the American legislative assemblies were masters of their own house, at least internally.

The event that did most to open the breach between planters and the Crown, even to sap the will to span it, was a proclamation issued in November 1775 by Lord Dunmore, Governor of Virginia, promising freedom to slaves who would repair to the King's standard and "bear arms" against the rebels.[9] Dunmore confined his offer of emancipation to slaves "appertaining to rebels," but the alarm among slave owners in Virginia and throughout the colonies was general. Slave owners knew, even if Dunmore did not, that such a proclamation would plant dangerous notions in the heart of every black man who heard about it. John Rutledge's brother, Edward, sent to the Continental Congress to thwart the drift toward independence, reported that Dunmore's proclamation had done more "to work an eternal separation between Great Britain and the colonies, than any other expedient which could possibly have been thought of." [10]

The other main part of Southern society was, of course, the slaves. Almost totally illiterate, they left no reliable record of their sympathies in the War for American Independence. It may be surmised, however, that, like the other groups in the South, they were divided in their loyalties. Some must have sought opportunities to aid their masters' foes, but since the planters themselves were divided, this would have put Negroes on both sides of the struggle. Others, out of affection or habit, or ignorance of what was going on, must have willingly served their masters.

Those few slaves who understood the real issues of the war must have been divided, too. There was always the possibility that Britain after the war would be different from Britain before the war. Perhaps the wartime proclamation of emancipation was a genuine earnest. On the other hand, there was little likelihood that the British, if they won, would entirely displace the planters from control over Southern society. Slaves who angered the planters were taking an awful chance. Probably only the boldest and most desperate willingly opposed their owners' wishes.

This divisive situation set the stage for civil war in the South of almost unimaginable savagery and brutality, one which raged with special intensity whenever British forces approached. But there were other factors besides internal divisions that made the South particularly tempting to the invader and weak before his assaults. One was its geography. Deeply penetrated by rivers and bays, the area was an especially inviting target for an amphibious attacker. Geared to producing staples for markets across the seas, most of the population in the Tidewater had arranged itself as close as possible to these waterways.[11]

The staple-producing economy contributed in other ways to the South's weakness. It relied on New and old England for many essential supplies, and on the middle colonies of Pennsylvania, New Jersey, and New York for food. When these supplies were diminished or cut off, it was in a perilous condition. The scarcity of food and supplies, compounded by the expanse of the South, made the problem of logistics a grave one. One American general, whose soldiers had existed for weeks on green corn and unripe peaches, complained that his army was "like a dead whale upon a sea shore—a monstrous carcass without life or motion." [12]

Furthermore, the economy of the South was based on credit, and depended on sales in the markets of Europe and England. When these sales were suspended or interrupted, the economy collapsed. When Britain set out in earnest to subdue the South in 1779 and blockaded the export of commodities, America was deprived of its best source of specie, derived until then from the sale of staples on the European continent.[13]

After all these physical and economic factors are given due weight, however, the impression persists that it was the social structure of the South that contributed most essentially to its vulnerability. Dominating this structure were the low-country planters. They had led their colonies throughout the pre-Revolutionary agitations. Many of them had tried to avoid a split with Great Britain, but leadership remained in their hands when war broke out, and continued there. Slave owning had been an important element in building the character of these men. It had made them watchful and zealous to retain control over their affairs. As Edmund Burke noted, men who own slaves are particularly conscious of the distinction between freedom and bondage, and extremely jealous of their own liberty.[14] This intense love of liberty made them extremely difficult subjects for the Crown, but it also prevented them from co-operating fully in the effort against Great Britain. As Jefferson discovered when Virginia was under assault in 1781, slave owners would sometimes refuse to allow their slaves to be used even in building fortifications. He had to explain to an impatient German officer in charge of building defenses that the governor of Virginia had no authority to direct the use of slaves for this purpose against the "consent" of their masters.[15]

Early in the war, the American strategy in the South had been badly handicapped by the effort of slave owners to protect their property. A delegate to Congress from Georgia told John Adams in 1775 that the British could subdue Georgia and South Carolina in a fortnight, with a mere thousand regular troops, simply by promising freedom to the Negroes there. Twenty thousand Negroes would flock to the British standard in response to such a declaration. The only thing that prevented the British from taking such a course, he said, was that loyalists, too, had Negro slaves, and would surely disapprove of such a policy, since it would be impossible to confine the disruption to the rebels.[16] The slaves were the great unknown quantity in the military balance. Men on both sides owned large numbers of them. If either side had been prepared to pronounce a general emancipation, it might immediately have had a large number of black men available for military duty.

But each side was restrained from pursuing such a course. The British were trying, not to institute a revolution, but to end a rebellion. *Status quo ante bellum* was their basic policy. Furthermore, they had at least as many inhibitions against inducting raw black recruits as did the Americans. The general staff was never able to integrate loyalist recruits into its professional army; how much more difficult it would have been to alter their traditional thinking enough to use Negro soldiers effectively. There was also the political dimension within England. Parliamentary critics of the war in America had already scolded Lord North's ministry for using Indians against the Americans.[17] No one in the government wanted to face the wrath that would greet the announcement of a decision to free black slaves en masse and draft them into His

Majesty's Army, for the purpose of disciplining British subjects.[18]

On the American side, many of the same inhibitions were at work. The Americans were no more interested in social revolution than were the British. They hoped to emerge from the war with their social system intact, and to proceed in the future as they had in the past, only without disruptions from across the sea. Nor would they have known any better than the British how to use a large number of black recruits. Effective military action requires discipline and coherent deployment of forces in pursuit of a plan. Not many American commanders were prepared psychologically to think in terms of shaping large numbers of Negroes into an effective fighting force.

The political problem, too, was an insurmountable obstacle. For most slave owners in the Deep South, the abolition of slavery was unthinkable. A modern Georgian accurately represents the thinking of his forebears when he writes, "Without slaves, plantations could produce nothing." [19] Whatever some people in other parts of the country might have been thinking by 1780, most Deep Southerners had no intention of remodeling their society after the war. On the contrary, they intended to wage war so as to disrupt it as little as possible.

The Southerners were not alone in these opinions. Many Northerners, even those who hated slavery, were embarrassed when confronted by reports that Negroes were fighting alongside white Americans. Early in the war, they had been stung deeply by such jingles as the following:

> *The rebel clowns, oh! what a sight*
> *Too awkward was their figure*
> *'Twas yonder stood a pious white*
> *And here and there a nigger.*[20]

Because of these inhibitions, both sides in the Southern theater were reluctant to open Pandora's box by being the first to employ Negroes in combat. With the Negroes thus neutralized, the military balance in the South lay with the British, whenever they chose to take the offensive, for they relied mainly on regular forces brought from overseas, which left loyalist planters free to

safeguard their property, whereas the rebels had to rely on men
who could be spared from their usual occupation of managing
slave laborers.

The second British assault on the South, larger in scope and
more ambitious in purpose than the first, began in 1779. The
campaign started confidently and well from the British viewpoint. Savannah was quickly subdued, almost without resistance,
and a subsequent siege by American land forces in combination
with the French Navy was soon abandoned.

From there, the British moved northward into South Carolina.
After failing to take Charleston by invasion from the land, they
planned, and this time neatly executed, a siege, almost without
having to resort to combat. At Charleston, in May of 1780, the
American forces suffered their worst losses of men and matériel of
the entire war.

One modern student of the war wonders whether the American
cause there was abandoned before all hope for escape or resistance had been exhausted, out of reluctance to see the city wrecked
by battle.[21] But if South Carolina suffered less than it might have
at Charleston, its cup of woe was drained to the dregs during the
ensuing campaign. The British thought they had virtually won
the war in the South when Charleston fell. Their commander in
chief, Sir Henry Clinton, departed for New York City leaving
Lord Cornwallis in charge of what he expected would be a mop-
ping-up operation. But the men of the South, who might mad-
deningly withhold their support when the battle seemed remote,
showed that they could fight with desperate courage and resourcefulness when they were directly threatened. Guerrilla bands operating outside Charleston soon persuaded the British that there
would be more resistance in the South than they had anticipated.

An overwhelming British victory at Camden, South Carolina,
in August 1780, encouraged the British to think that their momentum had not been stopped. But at this point, physical factors
began to turn against them. Distances in the South were greater
than elsewhere in the war theater. This complicated their effort
in two ways. First, territory, once subdued, had to be held. In a
compact area, a few soldiers might pacify a great number of resi-

dents. Where distances were greater, a far larger force could be pinned down by a determined band of guerrillas.[22] Second, as the British Army moved from its base at Charleston, the problems of logistics grew serious. When Cornwallis's forces pursued the Americans inland, they ranged far from their naval suppliers along the coast. The heat wore them out, the scarcity of food weakened them, and the necessity of trekking hundreds of miles through guerrilla-infested territory sapped their will to fight.[23]

As the military situation worsened for the British, their political position also weakened. There was nothing that planters of the Deep South loathed so much as disruption. When the British took Savannah and Charleston, many of these men decided to submit to British rule, in the interest of stability and order. But soon the loyalists among them, heartened by the presence of His Majesty's army of occupation, began to take revenge on the Whigs who had harried them during the four years between attacks on Charleston. British authorities were unable to stop the civil war, and by midsummer of 1780 guerrilla bands, led by diehard planters Francis Marion, Andrew Pickens, and Thomas Sumter, were marauding through the countryside, inflicting terrible punishment on British sympathizers.[24] Soon those who longed for a return to order began to realize that their best hope lay in driving the British out of America entirely.

Meanwhile, Lord Cornwallis, outrunning his lines of supply, but encouraged by his victory at Camden, urged his troops forward to a decisive confrontation with the new American commander in the Southern theater, Nathanael Greene. Boldly, Greene authorized the division of his small force, with General Daniel Morgan in charge of the detachment deployed to the west. Cornwallis, thinking he saw a chance to end the war in the South, sent his brilliant cavalry commander Banastre Tarleton to demolish Morgan's army. The test came at Cowpens, in western South Carolina. In one of the most heartening engagements of the war from an American point of view, militia forces and Continental regulars co-operated to annihilate Tarleton's army.

Greene then undertook a deadly game of cat-and-mouse with the main British force in the central region of the Carolinas. The Americans were constantly on the run and never won an important battle, but the drain on the stamina of the British was tremendous. Early in 1781, Cornwallis decided to disengage from Greene and move on into Virginia. But by now the British were too weak to resist or escape when American and French forces tightened the noose at Yorktown.

With the capitulation of Cornwallis, the British effort in America was effectively finished. The war dragged on for several months, mostly in the West and the South, where civil authorities had a difficult time ending these savage and brutal engagements. The last land action on the seaboard was a skirmish between loyalists and a patriot force under Colonel John Laurens at Combahee River, South Carolina, on August 27, 1782. The battle came six months to the day after a vote in the British House of Commons against further prosecution of the war in America.

Why was Britain, the most powerful nation in the world at the time, unable to suppress the rebellion in the American colonies? The answers are complex, to be sure. Not least among them was that the American war was only one of several concerns of the British in the late eighteenth century. Perhaps because of this preoccupation, policy makers consistently underestimated the difficulty of suppressing the rebellion in America.

Having committed themselves to war, the British were victims of irresolution in their own strategic thinking. Many of their calculations were based primarily on hope. As historian Paul Smith has shown, their policy toward the loyalists demonstrated this weakness. Time and again, a campaign would be undertaken in the belief that persons loyal to the Crown would desert the American cause and rally to the support of the Mother Country. Indeed, there were many people in the colonies anxious to do just that. But once they had declared themselves in response to British proclamations, British commanders were uncertain how to use these recruits in the context of a regular army. Then, before the problem could be solved, the exigencies of war would draw the British force away, leaving the loyalists exposed to the wrath of their neighbors.[25]

The British attitude toward Negroes in America showed the same irresolution. Frequently, in planning or advising on a campaign, especially in the South, British policy makers would mention that the slaves contributed greatly to the vulnerability of the region. Indeed they did. But to capitalize on the weakness, certain changes in attitude were required. The British had to overcome their own squeamishness about the place of Negroes in His Majesty's Army. They had to bring themselves to the point where they could convince skeptical Negroes that they would be safe in British arms, that they would not be sent off to a harsher slavery in the West Indies once their military service was done.

Most important, the British had to decide what they intended for the future in America, and how Negro slavery fit into that future. Many who urged an assault on the South, and who pointed to the presence of slaves as a factor comtributing to the weakness of the area, were planters themselves—including the royal Governor of Georgia, James Wright, and colonial agent William Knox. To these men, the strategic importance of slaves lay in the fact that they made planters who might have been tempted to rebellion long for the return of stability and order. These men had no intention of using the war effort to "reform" Southern society or abolish slavery. Yet if Britain were to capitalize fully on the opportunity presented by the bondage of Negroes, it would have to accept a revolution in the Southern social system. This, in the last quarter of the eighteenth century, it was simply not prepared to do.

As a result, the approach to the problem was fitful and vacillating. On one side were men like Lord Dunmore, whose proclamation of 1775 was the product of frenzy and fear rather than part of a complete scheme for using slaves against their masters. He persisted to the end in his belief that the war could be won if Britain would arm Negroes against the Americans.[26] At the other extreme were men who regarded the Negroes as forbidden fruit. Such a man was Edmund Burke. Speaking in March 1775 in favor of conciliation with the colonies, he took note of the proposal to tame the "high aristocratic spirit of Virginia and the southern colonies . . . by declaring a general emancipation of their slaves." Against this proposal, he offered three main arguments: that the slaves might not accept the offer ("It is sometimes as hard to persuade slaves to be free as it is to compel freemen to be slaves; and in this auspicious scheme we should have both these pleasing tasks on our hands at once"); that the Americans might respond with a counteroffer, thereby nullifying the military advantage to Great Britain; and that the offer would expose Britain to ridicule.

> Slaves as these unfortunate black people are, and dull as all men are from slavery, must they not a little suspect the offer of freedom from that very nation which has sold them to their present masters—from that nation, one of whose causes of quarrel with those masters is their refusal to deal any more in that inhuman traffic? An offer of freedom from England would come rather oddly, shipped to them in an African vessel, which is refused an entry into the ports of Virginia or Carolina, with a cargo of three hundred Angola Negroes. It would be curious to see the Guinea captain attempting at the same instant to publish his proclamation of liberty and to advertise his sale of slaves.[27]

Since London failed to devise a general policy toward the Negroes, it fell to commanders in the field to make *ad hoc* decisions on the question. A typical predicament confronted Clinton after the fall of Charleston. A great number of Negroes fled behind British lines, and he was asked to give directions as to their disposal. For several days he procrastinated, torn between his desire to use the Negroes to the best advantage and his intention to restore stable royal government to South Carolina as quickly as possible. On June 3, 1780, he issued his proclamation. Slaves fugitive from loyalist masters were to be returned to those masters who would promise not to punish them for their flight. But slaves who had run away from rebels now belonged "to the public." If they served faithfully for the duration of the war, they would be set free at the war's end. For the present, 5,000 of them were to be put to work under a commissioner who, with a staff of a hundred overseers, was assigned to restore the plantations around Charleston to working order.[28]

Clinton's compromise was a failure in its principal purpose: restoring discipline and stability in South Carolina. It infuriated the patriots without satisfying the loyalists. Both groups, insofar as they looked forward to a future in South Carolina, were appalled at the thought of rewarding fugitives by granting them freedom. The reappearance of serious armed resistance in South Carolina, in the form of planter-led bands of guerrillas, came shortly after the issuance of the proclamation.

In the face of Britain's desultory effort to exploit the weakness produced by slavery, Americans offered a variety of responses, combining the carrot and the stick. The carrots offered to the slaves were small and slippery. A letter published at Williamsburg in response to Dunmore's proclamation noted that American efforts to stem the slave trade had been frustrated by British merchants. The British would send fugitives to slavery in the West Indies, warned the correspondent, whereas the Americans, "were it in their power, or were they permitted, [would] not only prevent any more Negroes from losing their freedom, but restore it to such as have already lost it. . . ." One planter in South Carolina instructed his overseer to watch his tongue in disciplining the slaves, lest they take offense and run to the British lines.[29]

The greater reliance was on the stick. Several of the states authorized augmented patrols to pick up fugitives and return them to their masters. Georgia directed that one-third of the troops raised in each county should stay where they were, to guard against servile uprisings and mass flights. Slave owners in Virginia and North Carolina locked up their small boats, to prevent slaves from stealing off down the river at night. Others removed their slaves from the coastal areas and set them to work in the lead mines and elsewhere in the back country, far from British lines. Showcase executions were staged to frighten other slaves who might be tempted to flee. In South Carolina, one free Negro was hanged and then burned in August 1775, despite the protest of the Governor, because he was allegedly arming slaves and urging them to flee to the British.[30]

Though all these modes of discipline played a role in reducing the flight of slaves, the ablest strategists knew that there was no substitute for the demonstration that Americans were going to win the war. Without such a demonstration, it would simply be impossible to maintain discipline across the expanses of the South. Washington was one who sensed this fact. When he heard, at Cambridge, of Dunmore's proclamation, he wrote that the Virginians ought to crush him "instantly," lest large numbers of Negroes be tempted to join him. Later he wrote to Richard Henry

Lee that unless Dunmore was captured or killed "before Spring," he would become "the most formidable enemy America has." General Charles Lee, writing to Richard Henry Lee in early April 1776, saw the Southern campaign of 1776–1777 entirely in this context. "Your dominion over the blacks is founded on opinion; if this opinion fails, your authority is lost." [31] From the point of view of masters trying to prevent the flight of their slaves, the most felicitous developments of the entire war were the rout of Dunmore's "Ethiopian Regiment" at Great Bridge, Virginia, in December 1775 and the successful defense of Charleston in June 1776.

Like the British, the Americans, too, had a "Negro problem." In waging war against the most powerful nation on earth, Americans could not indefinitely ignore the resource represented by one-fifth of their population. Yet they were unable to decide how to use it.

There were, of course, some colonial precedents. As a rule, after 1693 slaves had been legally excluded from serving in colonial militias. The law in Connecticut was typical. It had been passed in 1660, three years after an uprising against the white settlement at Hartford, and it barred all Negroes and Indians from service with the militia. Under the pressures of war, however, these laws were often ignored. There is considerable evidence that Negroes served with both armies and navies. In 1713 the legislature of New Hampshire compensated a master who loaned his slave to fight at Fort Henry, in New York. During the war against the French and Indians, 1756 to 1763, many towns were unable to meet their militia quotas by using only white men, so they admitted Negroes, both bond and free. The town of Deerfield, for example, had to enlist four Negroes to meet its quota.[32]

For the most part, colonial precedents—proscriptions against military service for Negroes, loosely enforced—were followed in New England during the War for American Independence. At the beginning of the war, Negroes seemed to be accepted as part of the militia, at least in Massachusetts. There were Negroes on the green at Lexington in April 1775, and in the army over which Washington assumed command at Cambridge in July.

The situation was soon complicated by the fact that the soldiers of New England were now part of a nationwide effort. In September, South Carolinian Edward Rutledge moved in Congress that all Negroes, slave and free, be dismissed from the American Army. Although "strongly supported by many of the Southern Delegates," he was "powerfully opposed" (on what grounds is not known), and his motion was defeated.[33]

On October 8 the question was brought before a council of general officers at Cambridge. This group was composed of three men from Virginia, including Washington, and seven from New England. Unanimously, they decided against the enlistment of slaves and, by a great majority, "to reject Negroes altogether," bond or free. Their determination was reinforced by an official delegation from Congress which met with Washington later in the month. The group from Congress, composed of a South Carolinian, a Virginian, and Benjamin Franklin, met with civilian authorities from Massachusetts, Connecticut, and Rhode Island, and reached the conclusion that Negroes, bond or free, should be "rejected altogether" from military service.[34]

Apparently this policy stirred rumblings among Negroes who had served outside Boston, and their reaction was sufficiently menacing to force a slight but significant revision in policy. On the last day of 1775, Washington wrote to the President of Congress:

It has been represented to me that the free Negroes who have served in this Army are very much dissatisfied at being discarded. As it is to be apprehended that they may seek employment in the Ministerial Army, I have presumed to depart from the resolution respecting them, and have given license for their being enlisted. If this is disapproved by Congress, I shall put a stop to it.

Congress did not disapprove. Persuaded of the danger, they resolved "That the free Negroes who have served faithfully in the army at Cambridge may be re-enlisted therein, but no others." [35] With this exception granted, the question was apparently settled for the time being. The states that might have been most inclined to recruit Negroes (those north of the Mason-Dixon Line) complied with national policy by passing legislation exempting non-whites from the draft.[36]

Slavery and Strategy in the War for Independence

It is important to distinguish the reasons behind New England's acquiescence in this policy from those operating in other sections. The motives primary in other sections—the fear that armed Negroes would pose a danger to the native white population and the concern that releasing some Negroes to military service would corrupt the discipline of those who remained behind to work the plantations—were far less important in New England. No doubt many New Englanders were not convinced that Negroes would make good soldiers, and those who owned slaves were reluctant to expose their property to the dangers of warfare. But the primary factor behind the reluctance of New Englanders to draft Negroes was the effect that such a policy would have in other colonies. Victory in the War for Independence depended upon a united effort by the thirteen colonies. What dictated the policy of men like John Adams and Benjamin Franklin was not an animus against Negroes, but a desire for strong national union in the effort against England.

Increasingly, though, the lack of available manpower plagued the American effort. Men were reluctant to sign up for extended service. When Roger Sherman contended that long enlistments were "slavery," he spoke the mind of many Americans. During the winter at Valley Forge, the situation grew particularly acute. Riddled by disease and riven by desertions, unpaid, underclothed, and undernourished, Washington's army seemed on the point of complete dissolution.

At this critical juncture, General James Varnum, of Rhode Island, approached Washington with a suggestion. If military service seemed like slavery to white men, perhaps it would have a different aspect to men who were slaves to begin with. He suggested that the two Continental battalions from Rhode Island, both badly depleted, be combined, and that the set of officers thus relieved from command be sent back to Rhode Island to recruit a new battalion, composed of Negroes. Washington forwarded Varnum's memorandum to the Governor of Rhode Island, with a covering note urging only that his state do everything within its power to meet the quota of troops set by Congress.[37]

The situation in Rhode Island was, if anything, worse than that at Valley Forge. The British occupied two-thirds of it, including the capital city of Newport. The extensive coastline had been thoroughly ravished; seagoing trade, upon which the economy of the state depended, was at a standstill; farms had been destroyed; and the public treasury was exhausted. Varnum's suggestion apparently offered the only recourse.

Yet opposition was not wanting. While the proposal, having passed the Assembly, lay before the upper house of the legislature, six members of the Assembly submitted a petition outlining the reasons for their dissenting votes. They doubted, they wrote, that there were enough Negroes in the state to fill a battalion. They warned that such a move would have an adverse effect on public opinion. The British would return the ridicule heaped on them at the time of Dunmore's proclamation; neighboring states would regard these troops with contempt and would object when Rhode Island sought to list these black troops against quotas set by Congress. "The world" would decry the purchase of a "band of slaves to be employed in the defense of the rights and liberties of our country [as] wholly inconsistent with those principles of liberty and constitutional government, for which we are so ardently contending. . . ." And, finally, the petitioners warned that the expense would be too great, and that masters would be dissatisfied with the prices allowed.[38]

Despite these arguments, the act was passed, in February 1778. It provided that "such slaves as should be willing to enter into the service" might enlist in the Continental Army for the duration of the war with Britain. ". . . [A]nd whereas history affords us frequent precedents of the wisest, the freest, and bravest nations having liberated their slaves, and enlisted them as soldiers to fight in defense of their country," every slave, upon passing muster, would be set free, and his owner compensated for his full value up to $400. The resulting "black battalion," the only all-black unit to fight in the American Revolution, joined for five long years in the struggle for American independence, fighting with courage and skill on battlefields ranging from upstate New York to Yorktown, Virginia.[39]

Rhode Island was not the only state to permit the enlistment of Negroes. After Congress began to impose quotas on the states in 1777, slaves were frequently accepted as substitutes for masters who preferred not to serve in the field.[40] What made the Rhode Island enactment particularly significant was the fact that it authorized the formation of a "black battalion," and promised freedom to its members immediately upon enlistment. In each of these respects, the law was a product uniquely of New England, where fear of the Negro was not deep-seated and slave owning was a marginal feature in the economy and the social structure. No doubt, too, the dawning opinion in the North that slavery was morally wrong contributed to the feeling that Negroes ought to share in the defense of America and gave encouragement to governors and legislatures who were forced by events to consider the use of black troops.[41]

Once Northerners had decided to use Negro soldiers, they found many advantages in the practice. Negroes were less reluctant than whites to sign up for long enlistments, and readier to go wherever their commanders ordered them. Typically, they had fewer reasons for clinging to civilian life and were thus less likely to desert their regiments to go home. Thus they made better Continental soldiers. Furthermore, when blacks served in Continental regiments, whites could be given shorter enlistments and be saved for local defense.

Therefore, where slaves were few in number and the services they performed in civilian life could be obtained without their being held in slavery, as was the case in most of New England and the mid-Atlantic states, they were recruited without too much hesitation, even though they had to be promised that they could go free when the war was over.

In the South, though the situation was no less desperate, the balance of factors affecting the use of Negroes leaned the other way. For one thing, the feelings of slave owners counted more heavily. These men were greater in number, weightier in prestige, and far more determined in defense of slavery and its essential disciplines than their Northern counterparts. No one could tell the Pinckney brothers of South Carolina, as slave owners to the North were told, that their fears of armed Negroes were "bugbears of their own creation." [42] No one could tell them that the labor performed by Negroes was marginal, or that the danger of enemy retaliation was unimportant. In the North, it might be conceivable to arm all Negroes who might otherwise be tempted to flee to the enemy. In the South, Negroes were needed on the plantations if any semblance of normal life was to be maintained.

Even if guarantees could be given that black soldiers would be disarmed and returned to their masters at the end of the war, slave owners had also to fear that the British would retaliate by forming black battalions of their own. These apprehensions, bolstering a more general social conservatism, enabled Southerners to fend off the proposal for black troops throughout the darkest days of the conflict. Negroes did serve in the South as spies and messengers, as laborers in the building of fortifications, and in the "navy" as pilots and dock laborers. But they never served as combat troops.[43]

There were, however, several notable efforts to overcome the opposition to black soldiers in the South. Throughout the last three years of the war, the South lay virtually naked before the despoiling hand of the invader and his American sympathizers. British units roamed across the countryside, and native whites waged civil war with one another. In these circumstances, Governor John Rutledge, himself fleeing before the British Army, early in 1779 dispatched an emissary to Congress to plead for help. A committee appointed to receive his agent listened in astonishment as he requested Congress to authorize the enlistment and arming of Negro slaves in the two southernmost states.

The idea had been in the mind of twenty-five-year-old Colonel John Laurens, of South Carolina, for some time. The son of Henry Laurens, a former President of Congress and one of the wealthiest and most influential men in South Carolina, young Laurens was a man of "zeal, intelligence, [and] enterprise," in the opinion of Alexander Hamilton, who served with him on Washington's staff. During the winter of 1778, at Valley Forge, Laurens had first conceived the idea of raising a corps of Negro troops in the Deep South. His father at first discouraged him from publicizing his idea, for fear of his ruining his reputation in a lost cause. But in mid-March of 1779, when it looked as if the British were about to turn southward, Henry finally yielded to his son and wrote to Washington that, "had we arms for three thousand such black men as I could select in Carolina, I should have no doubt of success in driving the British out of Georgia and subduing East Florida before the end of July."

With his fellow delegate from South Carolina, William Henry Drayton, he joined Rutledge's emissary in testimony before the committee. According to them, their state was unable to defend itself with its own militia "by reason of the great proportion of citizens necessary to remain at home to prevent insurrection among the Negroes and to prevent the desertion of them to the enemy." They suggested that the emergency be met by raising a force of Negroes, which "would not only be formidable to the enemy from their numbers . . . but would also lessen the danger from revolts and desertions by detaching the most vigorous and enterprising from among the Negroes." Finally, they urged that, "as this measure may involve inconveniences peculiarly affecting the states of South Carolina and Georgia," it be submitted in the form of a recommendation to the "governing powers" of those states, along with an offer that the United States would defray the expenses of the project.[44]

This testimony, as remarkable in its candor as it was surprising in its implications, was enough to persuade Congress to adopt the extraordinary proposal. At the end of March it unanimously recommended that South Carolina and Georgia "immediately" raise 3,000 Negro troops and form them into separate battalions, commanded by white officers. (Colonel Laurens, who had already left for the South, would be in charge.) Congress was to compensate the masters, up to $1,000, for each Negro who passed muster. The black soldiers themselves were to receive no pay, but each one who served "well and faithfully . . . to the end of the present war, and shall then return his arms," was to be emancipated and receive fifty dollars.[45]

Colonel Laurens was full of hope as he headed south, but the remaining hurdle—obtaining the consent of the legislatures of South Carolina and Georgia—proved insurmountable, despite repeated attempts. On the first try, in May 1779, Rutledge was rebuffed by his own Council. In September the Assembly rejected the proposal. Apparently there was some support—around twelve or thirteen votes, according to one report[46]—but the main effect of the project, despite the role of Rutledge and of Henry Laurens in it, was to alienate the Deep South from the central government. Many planters took serious umbrage, feeling themselves "mocked and insulted" that their request to Congress for aid against the British had been answered in such "contemptuous" fashion.[47]

There were two ways of looking upon this project: as a move in the direction of the abolition of slavery or as a measure dictated by military necessity. Colonel Laurens liked it from both points of view. The raising of a Negro battalion, he wrote, would advance the lot of "those who are unjustly deprived of the rights of mankind," [48] and would reinforce "the defenders of liberty with a number of gallant soldiers." [49] But for most planters in South Carolina, the project was anathema from both points of view. If military affairs in South Carolina could not be advanced in any other way, most of these men were ready to abandon the war. It was "unjust," in their view, to require planters to bear a disproportionate share of the burden of defense, sacrificing their property for the safety of the whole.[50] Government under the British could not be worse than having to rely on Negroes for defense. That was not independence; it was a new and portentous kind of dependency.

But the worse part of the project, as far as the planters were concerned, was its tendency to open the question of emancipation. The proposal was not unguarded. It left in the hands of white men the decision whether the Negroes had served "well and faithfully," before they could be freed at the end of the war, and it specifically required that they be disarmed. Furthermore, free Negroes were not unknown in Charleston before the war. The project under consideration would augment their numbers by only 3,000, in a total Negro population of 97,000.[51] Still, the project had ominous implications, from the planters' viewpoint. It would release these 3,000 able-bodied Negro men from the disciplines of slavery and provide them with training and experience in military conflict. It would deprive masters of some of their most valuable laborers and compensate them with money that was not worth a Continental, as the saying went. It would provoke restlessness among those slaves who remained behind. And it would give a powerful argument to those who might later contend that Negroes should share in the blessings of liberty in a land they had helped to defend.

Colonel Laurens, in a letter to Washington, ascribed the defeat of the proposal to the "howlings of a triple-headed monster, in which prejudice, avarice and pusillanimity were united." Washington agreed. In a letter of consolation to his young friend, he noted that the "spirit of freedom," which had been ready for every sacrifice in 1776, had lately been overwhelmed by "selfish passion." "It is not the public," he continued, "but the private interest which influences the generality of mankind, nor can the Americans any longer boast an exception. . . ." [52]

Washington's attitude toward slavery was undergoing a slow metamorphosis at this time. As early as 1778 he had written to tell the manager of his plantation that every day he wished more and more "to get quit of Negroes." In February 1779 he wrote another long letter to his manager, instructing him to investigate the possibilities of selling his slaves: what the highest price he could get was; where, and in what manner, it would be best to sell them; how he could best insure that families of Negroes not be separated. In early 1781, when Benedict Arnold and his raiders were softening Virginia for the imminent invasion of Cornwallis, Washington's plantation was pillaged and seventeen of his slaves carried off. [53]

He was concerned about the problem, not just as a planter, but as a military commander. Northern states kept sending him Negro troops, [54] and the presence of these in camp sometimes had a corrosive effect on the morale and effectiveness of the other troops. Yet despite these difficulties, he was willing to accept Negroes into the Continental Army. Furthermore, he surrounded himself with young men, John Laurens and Alexander Hamilton in particular, who were eager to use Negro troops. Occasionally he urged his field commanders to employ the Negro manpower that surrounded them. When he did so, he was not loath to face the consequences. It was foolish, he thought, to assign a slave to guard the supply wagons. The man would only desert to the enemy to obtain his freedom and, in order to court a favorable reception by the British, take the wagon and wagon horses with him. If the Americans were going to use Negroes in the army, he believed that they had to set them free. [55]

Washington seems to have been genuinely dismayed at the failure of Laurens's mission. Laurens kept his proposal before the legislature of South Carolina throughout the rest of the war. After the fall of Charleston and the disaster at Camden, General Nathanael Greene, the prestigious and able new commander of

Continental forces in the South, lent his weight to the idea, but to no avail. The South Carolinians were determined not to arm the blacks, however helpless they might be without them.

After Yorktown, when treaty negotiations seemed in prospect, Greene warned Rutledge of the consequences of South Carolina's refusal to adopt the measure. Britain, he said, might try to grant independence on the basis of *uti possidetis* (in this case, yielding territory which the Americans then controlled, but no other).[56] The only way to counteract such a scheme was to retake Charleston, he said, a project in which Americans could have no hope of success except by the use of Negro soldiers. This time the project got twice as many votes as it had in 1779, but still it failed decisively. In place of Laurens's plan, the legislature of South Carolina sought to spur white enlistments by promising a slave as bounty to each new recruit.[57]

In June 1782 Colonel Laurens set out for Georgia, for one last effort to persuade that state to adopt the project. Before the Georgians had rendered their decision—which was, of course, negative—Laurens left with a detachment of militia to disperse a band of loyalists that continued to wreak havoc near the Combahee River. He lost his life during the skirmish, the last engagement of the Revolutionary War to take place along the seaboard. His father, who was in London negotiating the treaty that would end the war, was consoled in his grief by John Adams, who flatly declared that the country had lost its most promising character.[58] Certainly South Carolina lost a man who would have added an otherwise missing element to its political life in the years that followed—an element of vision and courage, where slavery was concerned, backed by high reputation.

As the war drew to a close, many Americans, especially planters in the South whose way of life depended on the labor of slaves, became anxious to recover slaves who had fled behind British lines during the conflict.[59] Once it became clear that Cornwallis faced disaster, the attempt began in earnest. For Washington, who had assumed command at Yorktown, the problem soon became an enormous headache. As the allied noose tightened, many Negroes fell into French and American hands—so many, in fact, that he issued orders that all Negroes in the vicinity who could not prove that they were free should be delivered to the guard-house at Yorktown or Gloucester to await further disposition. Officers were forbidden to seize these Negroes for their own uses.

The moment Cornwallis surrendered, Washington ordered sentinels to be stationed along the beach to prevent Negroes from stowing away aboard British vessels. Then he appointed a commissioner to see that Negroes were sent back to their rightful owners (many had apparently come from New York City with the British Army and belonged to Americans in the North), and that they were put to work in the meantime to earn their food and clothes.[60]

The surrender at Yorktown put an end to British hopes of subduing America. When the news arrived in London, Parliament quickly decided to repudiate the policy of Lord North's ministry, and authorized the Crown to make peace with the Americans. Congress was eager to meet this overture, and an American delegation was soon chosen. It included two "ambassadors" already serving in Europe, John Adams and Benjamin Franklin; the Secretary for Foreign Affairs, John Jay; and two delegates to Congress, Thomas Jefferson (who never served) and Henry Laurens, who had been captured by the British on his way to Holland for secret talks and was a prisoner in the Tower of London.

The composition of this delegation reflected sectional considerations. Though the five members—from Massachusetts, Pennsylvania, New York, Virginia, and South Carolina, respectively—were equally committed to American independence, each represented a part of the country that had interests, as far as the specific stipulations of the treaty were concerned, that differed from those of other regions. New England, for example, wanted an explicit recognition of the right of Americans to fish in the coastal waters of Newfoundland. For Southerners, the most important features would be generous boundaries to the west and a recognition of American rights to navigate the Mississippi River. For the commercial elements of the mid-Atlantic states, no specific consideration was as important as the early restoration of normal trade with Great Britain and the rest of Europe. The treaty delegation was fashioned to reflect, as far as possible, each of these points of view.[61]

As it turned out, the captivity of Laurens and his subsequent illness, plus Jefferson's failure to go to Europe, resulted in an American delegation that lacked a Southerner until the eve of the signing of the preliminary articles, when Laurens was finally able to attend. Thus it was left to the diplomatic skill of Franklin and his colleagues, and their great sensitivity to the political realities of the American union, to produce a treaty generally acceptable to Americans.

The talks went on through the summer of 1782, conducted mainly by Franklin and Jay for the Americans. By late November a "provisional treaty" had been drawn up. At this moment Laurens, suffering from gout aggravated by his stay in the Tower and grieving for the loss of his son, dragged himself to Paris, just in time to read over the text and find in it one important omission. Though no lover of slavery, and having been out of the country for over two years, he knew his neighbors well enough to realize that they would search the treaty carefully to see that it showed a proper regard for their special interests. The treaty asserted American rights to fish off Newfoundland, which was New England's favorite prerogative, but it made no mention of American rights to navigate the full length of the Mississippi River, which was the prime concern of many Southerners. Laurens was astute enough to know that a specific mention of American "rights" to recover fugitive slaves would go a long way toward appeasing those who would notice these other factors.

And so, at the last moment, he persuaded his fellow negotiators to seek an addendum to Article VII, to guarantee that the British Army would leave the United States without "carrying away any Negroes or other property" belonging to Americans. The British agreed, and Adams, who had joined the negotiating team in October, saluted his friend for a shrewd contribution to the final text.[62] As it turned out, however, these apparently straightforward words failed to resolve an extremely bitter controversy already brewing over the removal of slaves from America during the British evacuation.

Even before the treaty was signed, there had been trouble over the disposition of slaves in the wake of the departing British.[63] The trouble began at Charleston. The British general in charge of the evacuation there agreed with the Governor of South Carolina that he would try to arrange for the return of slaves stolen from Americans. (He refused to return Negroes who had been promised their freedom by the British or who had rendered themselves "obnoxious" to the Americans by military service with the British.) But the arrangement broke down in a swirl of mutual recriminations and charges of bad faith, and the British had left Charleston in December 1782 with over 5,000 slaves, bound for British ports in the Caribbean and elsewhere.[64]

In this episode all the seeds of the future controversy were apparent. The Americans were perfectly clear about their rights as they conceived them. Justice required that slaves who had been plundered from their plantations or who had fled to British lines be returned to their owners. The British had had no right to them in the first place. Now that the war was over, they should be returned to their rightful owners. For a mixture of reasons, the British felt otherwise. Loyalists who had been plundered themselves by raiders as well as by men acting under confiscation laws were eager to recoup their losses, as far as possible, by taking slaves to their new homes in East Florida or the West Indies. Some British officers expected to reap a nice profit from the sale of slaves in the West Indies and elsewhere.[65] There were also considerations of national policy involved. The British had issued promises of emancipation to which many of these slaves had responded. The question now was whether Britain could and would keep its word.[66] And there were difficulties in distinguishing Negroes who were plundered from those who had reached British lines under their own power.

Slave owners who hoped that the treaty's provisions would prevent a re-enactment of the scene at Charleston soon met with bitter disillusionment. The first real test came at New York. The British commander in charge of this final evacuation was Sir Guy Carleton. In April 1783 he had posted a warning to his officers not to breech the articles of the treaty. He specifically mentioned the article affecting the removal of Negroes who were the property of Americans. But Negroes were still slipping away from New York City. Lacking the full co-operation of the British, Washington soon realized that he had little hope of recovering many of the Negroes who were with the British there.[67] He was determined, however, to try to implement the treaty as the Americans understood it, if only to make a case for future negotiations. He requested a personal meeting with Carleton to discuss the "delivery" of the Negroes, as well as the exchange of prisoners and the disposition of military posts. A conference was scheduled for May 6, 1783.

Washington opened the meeting by noting the provisions of the treaty and expressing his concern that the Negroes in New York be prevented from departing, so that their masters might reclaim them. Carleton responded by saying that certain Negroes who had rendered themselves obnoxious to the Americans were being permitted to leave the country along with other refugees. Washington interrupted to say that he was surprised that the British intended to violate the treaty. Not at all, replied Carleton. The Negroes who were shipping out with the British were no longer American property, having joined the British under their own power, in response to promises of emancipation. Great Britain must not violate its faith to these people. If his interpretation of the treaty was later deemed an infraction, Britain would pay compensation. He had ordered that ledgers be kept, recording the age, name, and occupation of each Negro who left. Washington responded coldly that the British were violating the letter and spirit of the treaty. And the prospect of compensation did not relieve the violation. No such facts as the British were recording could form the basis for a fair determination of the value of slaves, and it was foolish to rely on fugitive slaves to tell the truth about themselves. Carleton was calmly adamant. He reminded Washington that the British had agreed, not to deliver the Negroes to the Americans, but simply not to carry them off. But if the British simply let them go, out of control, the Negroes would steal aboard their ships or flee to the north. By his method slave owners had at least a chance for compensation. In any case, it was best to leave such disputed matters to the determination of commissioners at a later date, after the facts had been fairly settled.[68]

Washington knew the significance of this conversation. That evening, he wrote to Governor Benjamin Harrison, of Virginia, telling him of Carleton's interpretation of the treaty and of the departure of large numbers of Negroes from New York. The Negroes, he concluded, "will never be restored." [69]

The removal of slaves by the British was a vitally important issue for Southerners. Southern planters had suffered heavy losses during the war. Estimates vary, of course, and none are completely reliable, but Jefferson once reported that Virginians had lost 30,000 slaves during the war, and a leading South Carolinan, David Ramsay, stated that losses in that state amounted to 25,000.[70] Many of these losses were beyond recovery; some Negroes had died of fever or been killed.[71] But these losses only increased the desire to recover the Negroes who had survived.

An indication of the concern that many Southerners felt came during the debate in Congress over the disbanding of the Continental Army. It was expensive to keep an army in the field, and the government's financial crisis was growing more and more acute. Yet several Southerners insisted that the army be held together until the Negroes were secure in American hands. So strong was the feeling on this issue that John Rutledge, the former Governor of South Carolina, declared that he "almost" regretted an earlier decision by Congress to release the British prisoners of war.[72]

Reluctantly, Congress faced the fact that it was dangerous to keep in the field an army that was near the point of open mutiny. A pair of angry addresses, belaboring Congress for "coldness and severity" and threatening defiance if their claims to back pay and lifelong pensions were not met, had been delivered in March by officers encamped near Newburgh. A brilliant speech by Washington, affirming his confidence in Congress and advising the officers to be patient, had succeeded in diverting the movement for the time being, but no one was sure how long he could keep matters under control. And so, on May 26, Congress adopted a compromise whereby most of the army was to be furloughed, rather than kept together or disbanded, until the Americans were convinced that the British intended to abide by the Treaty of Paris.

The compromise was a poor expedient. It obliged Congress to continue the charade of seeming to pay the troops, though everyone knew that the Continental certificates were almost worthless. And it accomplished little in the way of providing a military force to coerce the British to leave the slaves behind. Congress voted to give certificates for three months' pay to the furloughed troops, but the soldiers signaled their contempt by leaving camp in June 1783 without waiting for these papers to arrive.

It was apparent that the planters were going to have to rely on argument alone to get their slaves back or to win compensation for their losses. As it turned out, argument was of little avail. Throughout the 1780's, Congress instructed its ministers abroad to "remonstrate" against the removal of "Negroes and other American property," and to require "with firmness and decision, full satisfaction for all slaves and other property." [73] But the British, without ever stating their position explicitly, seemed to abide by Carleton's interpretation, which was that Negroes who had joined the British before the signing of the preliminary articles of peace in November 1782 were subject to the authority of Great Britain, whereas those who had entered the British lines after that date could be recovered by the Americans. Under this interpretation, Carleton had actually released a few Negroes to the commissioners appointed by Washington to watch over American interests during the embarkation. Those who were sick, or old, or otherwise helpless were also left behind by the departing British, and some were sold to Americans by departing loyalists.[74]

But the great majority of able-bodied Negroes who had disappeared behind British lines during the conflict was set beyond the reach of American hands by Carleton's rule. The result was the creation of an issue that contributed greatly to the alienation of many planters from Britain and from those Americans who were anxious to accommodate the differences between Britain and the United States.

The main impact of the war on American attitudes was to increase tensions between sections of the country. Southerners were miffed because when the war shifted south, the Continental Army remained in the North. From a thoroughly national point of view, this decision made sense. Clinton's headquarters were still in New York, and Washington and his main army could not afford to leave the nation's midsection bare before the enemy's main thrust. Nevertheless, many Southerners believed that the effort of the central government in their defense had been defective.[75]

Southerners also believed, with some justification, that the two generals who had preceded Nathanael Greene in charge of the Southern Department, Benjamin Lincoln and Horatio Gates, were incompetent in their command. Even Greene, though an able commander, seemed not to understand or have full sympathy for the agonies of those he was sent to protect. As a result, the richest and most vulnerable territory in America had been plundered and pillaged by the enemy almost at will. As Southerners saw it, only the paramilitary operations of Francis Marion, Thomas Sumter, and Andrew Pickens had given South Carolina a measure of revenge. Nothing that the "continent" had done for them had been of any avail.

Northerners, for their part, were equally critical. As they saw it, New England and New Jersey had been defended in large part by farmers-turned-militiamen, who had armed themselves and sniped at the enemy's flanks and rear until he withdrew to cover in his sanctuary at New York. Then the British had turned south for easier pickings.

Northerners had been alarmed at the South's weakness. The British had cut through the lowland there like a hot knife through butter. Yet the South, even in its extremity, had refused to adopt the "obvious" expedient of arming its Negroes, though this course had been urged on Congress by the Governor of South Carolina himself, and though a brilliant South Carolinian had volunteered to take charge of the operation. The South might boast of its wealth, but, as far as many Northerners were concerned, it was a house built on sand.

The Virginians were caught in the middle of this dispute, a position that was to prove painful ideologically, but politically strategic. With the New Englanders, they saw the weakness of a society based on slavery, and they deplored it. But with the Deep Southerners, they knew the difficulties of extricating themselves from it. Washington was a typical Virginian in this respect. He was sufficiently persuaded of the impolicy of slavery to be willing to discuss Lafayette's "wild scheme"—the term was Lafayette's—of buying a small tract somewhere in western Virginia and encouraging freed slaves to settle on it as tenant farmers.[76] Yet he was unwilling to free his own slaves on the ground that such indi-

129

vidual acts were unavailing against the system as a whole and of dubious benefit to the Negroes, who would become, in Ulrich B. Phillips's phrase, a "third element in a system planned for two." [77]

In the end, Southerners insisted that slavery had not rendered the South indefensible during the War for Independence. Certainly the South had paid a terrific cost for its attachment to slavery. But it was two factors indigenous to the area that had forced the British to abandon their plan of separating it from the rest of the union. One was the exertion of the frontiersmen, led by a relatively few planters, who fought with extraordinary courage and resourcefulness when their backs were to the wall. The other was the geography of the South: its expanse, which stretched British supply lines past their limits; and its climate, to which the Americans were more accustomed than their British cousins.

Might a more ruthless and resourceful foe have succeeded where Britain failed? Might a Napoleon, lacking the concern of the British for the future of America, and less prejudiced toward Negroes, have inflicted even greater punishment on the South? Perhaps so. Certainly the British did not exhaust the possibilities for shedding blood in America. Yet the unleashing of full-scale racial warfare would not have led to success, as the British conceived it. No one who planned to reconstruct a society after the war that looked anything like society before the war would have wanted to turn a half-million Negroes on their white masters, nor could he have done so if he had wanted to. As far as slavery was concerned, the British had not fallen far short of using the advantages available to them. Slavery raised the cost of war for the Americans, but it did not make the country indefensible, at least not in the last quarter of the eighteenth century.

4

Slavery under the Articles

of Confederation

HAVING determined upon independence, and having committed the American people to that course, the leaders of the Revolution confronted the task of instituting a new government according to the promise of their Declaration of Independence. The task of governing the people of America was not entirely new to these men, of course. Britain's "policy" of "salutary neglect" before 1763 and, more recently, the struggle against the royal governors and the enactments of Parliament had given them considerable opportunity to develop political skills and a sense of common purpose.

Nevertheless, two aspects of the situation after 1776 were unprecedented for the leaders. First, they now had ultimate responsibility. No more could they complain that their good impulses were thwarted by the vetoes of the royal brute in London. No more could they count on the fleets and foot soldiers of the Crown to defend them against the French and Indians. No more could they look to London for help in resolving disputes among themselves. Second, these men, each of whom had developed as a political leader in a single colony, were now undertaking to govern an entire nation. Their first act on behalf of this new nation was to commit their people to resist the will of the most powerful nation on earth. Many among them believed that their first act should have been to discover and establish a basis for co-operation, a constitution, before entering the test of strength with Britain.[1] These cautious souls were overruled, however. The business of agreeing upon modes of co-operation was postponed until after the challenge had been dropped at the King's feet.

Ultimately, this problem had to be faced. The prospect made wise politicians tremble. Their job was to establish institutions and rules for ordering the affairs of people who hardly knew one another, and whose communities, despite some similarities, varied greatly in tone, temper, and circumstance. Furthermore, these people had shown themselves extremely sensitive to political halters. Their first instinct for many years had been to mistrust public authority.[2] Thus, among the many critical problems facing the leaders, the most fundamental was that of drawing the constituent elements of the population toward a sense of common nationality. This sense of "belonging together" is the essence of modern nationhood, the rock upon which all other political development rests.[3] It does not necessarily presume the doctrine or condition of equality among the component elements, although in the American case, over time, the doctrine of equality did gradually assume a central position in the public philosophy. What it does require is the development of common, or at least compatible, notions of the function of public authority, and the willingness to trust those who hold authority to abide by these notions. It requires that unacceptable distinctions between people be swept away, that enduring distinctions be accepted, and that processes be established by which the latter can become the former without violence or other disruption.

To later generations, it would seem that the founders of the United States had many advantages in this work. They operated at a time when social patterns were flexible. It is undoubtedly an exaggeration to say that Americans then, even white Americans, were "born equal."[4] Yet the drive toward independence did have the effect of disrupting settled social hierarchies. Many loyalists, people of considerable wealth and social standing, were disgraced, divested of their property, and exiled. American merchants, artisans, and farmers rose to new importance in a society that was determined to count no longer on the services and supplies of foreigners. And warfare, with its voracious appetite for infantrymen, introduced many poor farm boys to a broader world and forced many officers from relatively aristocratic backgrounds to realize that the society that was emerging on the western shores of the Atlantic Ocean would be more "level" than the European models to which some of them aspired.

Furthermore, the "mind" of the American Revolution was favorable to social reform in an egalitarian direction. The Declaration of Independence, "an expression of the American mind," had been couched in the language of Locke's doctrine of political equality, because these concepts seemed to most Americans to express "the common sense of the subject." [5] This is not to say that Americans in 1776 were committed to a program of social equalization. Yet most Americans *were* profoundly republican, wedded to the principle that the government was answerable to the people. Although few of them understood the social implications of this essentially political principle, their commitment to it helped to render all distinctions of caste and class forever precarious on this soil.

The American Revolution was a decisive moment in the movement of the Western world toward democracy. And the significance of this fact was not lost on the erstwhile colonists. They seemed to realize, and to glory in the realization, that their new nation was to serve as a kind of laboratory in which the world would develop methods for integrating diverse elements of a population into a single "people." Toward this end, they abolished the feudal remnants that encumbered much of the land holdings. They removed many qualifications from the right to vote and resisted the imposition of other qualifications. They began the movement to disestablish the Protestant churches. They devised plans for systems of public education, developed "immigrant aid societies," revised criminal codes, and sought to improve conditions in the jails. They adopted public policies to encourage the development of the economy and to create opportunities for artisans, merchants, and farmers.[6] All of these policies were consciously intended to encourage broader and fuller participation in the life of the community. All were animated by a spirit of adventure in innovation, of reform in the direction of humanitarianism, and of a more inclusive view of the constituent elements of a polity.

Yet despite the evident flexibility in the American social structure, despite the impetus of the Revolutionary ideology, despite the spirit of reform abroad in the country, the institution of slavery survived under the Articles of Confederation virtually unaffected in its citadel, and few Negroes in any part of the country, whether slave or free, experienced a change in status cr circumstance as an immediate consequence of American independence.

During the Confederation period, slavery was put on the road to extinction in Pennsylvania and New England. In Virginia, the laws affecting manumission were liberalized to permit an owner to free his slave by deed or will. Most of the states forbade the importation of slaves from Africa or the West Indies. And, particularly in Virginia, a spirit of guarded hostility toward the institution was widespread among prominent men. Yet in the Deep South, the commitment of society and economy to slavery was unshaken, and even in Virginia, the critics of slavery were prevented by racial prejudice, their own or their neighbors', from fashioning realistic programs for abolition.[7] Already, it seemed, the states where slavery was strongest were caught. If the incubus of slavery was to be overthrown, the leverage would have to come from the national government.

But it is hardly an exaggeration to say that during the first decade of American independence the United States had no national government. The uneven distribution of slavery throughout the union was partly to blame for the reluctance of politicians to build a viable national government. The resulting weakness in the middle of the political system in turn made effective legislation on slavery impossible.

Political authority is sometimes defined as the power to direct the allocation of values. According to the liberal tradition, this power is posited voluntarily by the people and must therefore rise on a foundation of public confidence. The people must trust that their property, what they value, is safe in the hands of those exercising authority.

This formula, so widely approved by Americans in the eighteenth century, begged a crucial question. Who was to be included among the constituent elements of the new nation, those to whom the new governments were to be held responsible? The question had a territorial dimension in the 1770's and 1780's, as the letters and addresses to the inhabitants of Quebec, Nova Scotia, and Florida bear witness.[8] But the most important aspect of the problem of inclusiveness was not territorial. It had to do with elements of population. Several incidents suggested that the right to citizenship was to be opened to all white people who were willing to identify with the struggle against the King. One such incident involved the new national seal. A committee consisting of Benjamin Franklin, John Adams, and Thomas Jefferson was appointed by Congress to devise the seal. In August 1776 they proposed that the seal contain representations of England, Scotland, Ireland, France, Germany, and Holland, 'the countries from which these states have been peopled." [9] Apparently neither the Africans nor the Indians were thought, even by this cosmopolitan committee, worthy of representation; nor was any thought given to the possibility that future generations of Americans might include other stock. Americans were already beginning to think of their country as an "asylum" for oppressed people, but their experience directed them to think almost exclusively in the context of the civilization of the North Atlantic world.

Another illuminating incident involved a set of "proposals" to the Hessian mercenaries who had been drafted into the British Army. Drawn into a strange and distant conflict by the lingering dynastic politics of European royalty, these hapless young men looked like fruit ripe for the picking from Britain's rotten vine, especially to a nation hungering for laborers and soldiers and stirred by an image of itself as the best hope of oppressed people everywhere. "We now address you as part of the great family of mankind, whose freedom and happiness we most earnestly wish to promote and establish," declared the Congress. Providence surely intended to "establish perfect freedom in this new world, for those who are borne down by the oppression and tyranny of the old." Promising land and livestock to those who deserted to the American side, together with a chance to re-enlist for service in a "detached corps" of native Germans, Congress exhorted the Hessians to

Disdain, then, to continue the instruments of frantic ambition and lawless power. Feel the dignity and importance of your nature. Rise to the rank of free citizens of free states. . . . [A]ccept from our munificence what can never be obtained from our fears. We are willing to receive you with open arms into the bosom of our country.[10]

Another episode shows Congress wrestling with the issue of inclusiveness as it related to the Indians. In 1784 a committee of delegates from the Southern states, including Jefferson, submitted a report containing instructions for commissioners who were to arrange a treaty with Indians in the southern part of the country. As a condition for negotiations, the report directed that the Indians yield up all prisoners and "all fugitive and other slaves." After that, the commissioners might try to persuade them that "their true interest and safety . . . depend upon our friendship," and that the Americans were "disposed to be kind to them, to supply their wants. . . ." The commissioners were instructed to use arguments "most likely to prevail with the Indians to enter into the society of the citizens of the United States," and to acquaint them with state laws intended to encourage new settlers. The report concluded by advising Congress to urge the states to make it easy for Indians to become citizens.[11]

This report was tabled in May and not revived further that year. The next year, it was reported again, but directly sent to a new committee, which soon returned a far different report. The new instructions referred to the Indians, not as potential citizens, but as possible allies.[12] These instructions were quickly adopted, commissioners were appointed and straightway dispatched. The swift action represented the triumph of realism over the posture of magnanimity. It also helped to clear the air, enabling men to sharpen and clarify their mental image of the United States as a country for white men; for however ambivalent some Congressmen might have felt toward their red neighbors, most men on the frontier regarded Indians as their enemy and were in a better position than Congressmen to give effect to their views.

These episodes all suggest that the "one people," to whom Jefferson referred in the opening paragraph of the Declaration of Independence, were the white people of the thirteen colonies, gathered into thirteen political entities that fancied themselves somehow "sovereign, free and independent," yet bound together in a firm and perpetual "league of friendship."

In the Declaration on Taking up Arms (July 1775), Congress announced to the world that the union of the colonies was "perfect." Many Americans were not so sure. Carter Braxton, a wealthy planter and leader of the aristocracy of Virginia, predicted that a separation from Britain would produce "intestine wars and convulsions," mainly over conflicting land claims. Joseph Galloway, of Philadelphia, agreed. Self-appointed spokesman for the "propertied classes," he opposed independence because the colonies were full of the seeds of discord and ripe for civil war. An Englishman, James Anderson, returned to Great Britain following a tour of the colonies and published a pamphlet offering his "Free Thoughts on the American Contest." He believed that the economies of the Northern and Southern colonies were fundamentally incompatible, that, freed from the disciplines of the empire, the North would inevitably dominate, that the South would be driven to arms to defend itself, but that the South, with fewer numbers and enervated by its climate, would certainly be crushed and its people reduced to the status of exploited subjects.[13]

These forebodings should not be dismissed as loyalist propaganda. The writings of John Dickinson, John Adams, and Edward Rutledge from the early years of American independence also reflect deep concern about the future of the union.[14] The vision of union proclaimed by Congress in 1775 and 1776 was heady but insubstantial, born more of hope and of fear than of calm judgment. Its essential ingredient was the fact that the colonies needed one another if they were to have any chance of separating from Great Britain. Old Benjamin Franklin put the point graphically when he said that the revolutionaries must "hang together, or they would surely hang separately." What has since become a glib wisecrack may have been literally true for the men who signed the Revolutionary declarations.

The problem with fear as a cement of union was that once the Redcoats were withdrawn this factor would weaken considerably in force. It would not evaporate, for there would always be foreign dangers which could be used to build support for the union. But just as the neutralization of the French and Indian threat loosened the British Empire in North America following 1763, so the gradual evacuation of British forces in the 1780's stripped away an iron band from the barrel of union.

Another subtle force at work in the union was the growth of a sense of being "American" in the colonies-become-states during the last half of the eighteenth century. Some interesting attempts to measure this phenomenon have been made by Richard Merritt. He has applied the techniques of "content-analysis" to the colonial press in the cities of Boston, New York, Philadelphia, Williamsburg, and Charleston to see whether the language used in newspapers reflected an emerging consciousness of things American—the extent to which they focused on events in America rather than events in Great Britain, the extent to which they informed their readers of events taking place in other colonies, and when they began to refer to the colonists as "American" rather than "British." The study shows that interest in things American rose rather markedly after 1763.[15] As for references to other colonies, the papers of Boston were most self-centered, those of the middle colonies most "pluralistic" (referring to other colonies individually), while those in the South were most "collective" (referring most frequently to events involving the colonies as a whole). In all sections, however, an interest in American affairs was plainly increasing throughout the period under analysis.[16]

Yet the evidence does not all point in the same direction. Gilbert Chinard has called Jefferson a "prophet of Americanism" in large part because of his vision of the Americans united into a continental empire. He points out, however, that Jefferson, when forced in September 1776 to choose whether to accept appointment as an American commissioner to the Court of France or to stay in Virginia to join in framing a constitution for his native "country," chose the latter, regretting that he could not serve the union at this crucial hour, but not hesitating as to his primary obligation and interest, to see that Virginia was safely launched toward republicanism.[17] Not until after Virginia had emerged from the war did Jefferson feel able to accept a "Continental" diplomatic appointment and thereby satisfy his urge to visit the Old World.

Jefferson's choice of priorities suggests how tenuous a hold the union had on the American imagination in the last quarter of the eighteenth century. There was undoubtedly a growing sense of nationalism in America at this time, but the object of this powerful feeling was not yet clearly perceived. Delegates from the colonies had been meeting together at least since the Albany conference of 1754, and with increasing frequency in the decade preceding the Declaration of Independence.[18] Men in the colonies, as well as aides in the colonial offices in London, had been busying themselves for decades devising schemes for intercolonial coordination,[19] but these gestures had been motivated primarily by a concern for problems of mutual defense—against the Indians and the French, and finally against the British. Occasionally, someone would invoke the vision of an American Empire on the North American continent. But it was not until fighting had actually broken out between Great Britain and the Continental Army that the possibility of a nation of united states began to excite the imagination of any but the most far-seeing prophets. As Edmund Morgan has put it, American nationalism was the child, not the father, of the American Revolution.[20] It took a number of years, and many traumatic adjustments, before the idea of national union could ripen into maturity and develop a vitality of its own sufficient to counteract the loyalties that pulled and animosities that pushed in other directions.

In the excitement of taking on the British, the colonists experienced a warm glow of sentimental oneness. As long as the contact was at long range, through committees of correspondence between like-minded leaders, the colonists believed they had much in common. They all used the language of the liberal Whig tradition, and they had no reason to suppose that the words had different nuances in different social contexts. Thus, when the counties of Virginia resolved in 1775 that Britain's "mercenary forces" were "dangerous to the liberties of the people," and that a militia composed of "gentlemen and yeomen" would be necessary to "secure our inestimable rights and liberties," [21] Sam Adams, in Boston, had no disposition and little reason to note that 40 per cent of the human population of Virginia was systematically deprived of its "inestimable rights and liberties" by these very "gentlemen" who now resolved to challenge the "tyranny" of Britain. And when the leaders of South Carolina heard in 1774 that the port of Boston had been sealed shut by act of Parliament, their minds conjured up an image of Charleston besieged, and they straightway dispatched a shipment of rice to their stricken brothers.[22] What the Bostonians thought when they received this gift is not known. No doubt they were grateful—having no conception of the circumstances under which the rice had been grown and no accurate mental picture of the men by whose generosity they had been favored.

When these distant contacts turned into firsthand confrontations, some rude adjustments in mental image were required. Reporting on his first trip to a "foreign country," to attend the Stamp Act Congress in New York City, John Rutledge* described the experience in a letter to his mother that plainly revealed the shock and disgust aroused in this aloof and arrogant man when he viewed the bustling port city of the North for the first time.[23] No doubt there was much to arouse disgust in a sensitive nose. New York was not a large city at that time, having a population of about 20,000, but it was surely a dirty one and one whose vitality has always seemed to defy the principles of order and cleanliness. Compared with Charleston, a town about half as large as New York City in those days,[24] New York simply lacked the fine opulence and the disciplined behavior among the "lower orders" of men, white and black, that characterized the Southern metropolis.

This reaction was reciprocated by Josiah Quincy, a leader of the Revolutionary effort in Boston. He went to Charleston in 1773 to seek relief from symptoms of tuberculosis. What he saw there distressed him deeply. "The inhabitants," he confided to his diary, were "divided into opulent and lordly planters, poor and spiritless peasants and vile slaves." The planters were in complete control. "Cards, dice, the bottle and horses" were their main diversions. The topics of serious conversation, when these games did not interfere, were Negroes and the price of indigo and rice. He noted the influence of slavery on life in Charleston.

The brutality used toward the slaves has a very bad tendency with reference to the manners of the people. . . . They will plead . . . "this severity is necessary." But whence did or does this necessity arise? From *the necessity* of having vast multitudes sunk in barbarism, ignorance and the basest and most servile employ.

---

* Rutledge had studied law at the Middle Temple in London five years earlier. It is not known whether this reference to New York as his first "foreign country" was facetious or whether, in his shock at seeing the city, he actually forgot his earlier travels.

He also found "a general doubt of the firmness and integrity of the Northern colonies" as the final breach with Great Britain approached. The differences in "manners and religious tenets and notions" between himself and his hosts seemed to him to lie at the root of the "envy and jealousy" felt between the sections.[25]

When the Continental Congress began to meet, men did not have to travel further to experience the social tensions within the union. Confrontations between men bred in different sections were often quite dramatic. Many Yankees were simply awed by the plantation masters of the Deep South. When Silas Deane, a delegate from Connecticut, prepared biographical sketches of the other members during the early days of the Second Continental Congress, he began with the South Carolinians, who obviously fascinated him most, and spent several days describing them. To his bedazzled eye, the Southerners "appeared like men of importance."

At first, John Adams was impressed, too, especially by the Virginians and by the head of the delegation from South Carolina, Thomas Lynch. But it was not long before profound differences in temperament and experience began to dissolve these initial impressions into more stable reactions. About a month and a half after their first meeting, Adams entered his estimate of Edward Rutledge, a leading planter and later Governor of South Carolina, in his diary: "a perfect Bob-o-Lincoln . . . excessively vain, excessively weak, and excessively variable and unsteady; jejune. inane, and puerile." [26] Adams is famous for his harsh judgments of political opponents. Rutledge at that time was dragging his feet on the road to independence. But the fireworks that flew when the elites of the various states began to jostle in Congress are accurately reflected in Adams's comment.

The question whether or not to declare independence before they had reached agreement on modes of co-operating in the effort against Britain brought these tensions to a head. No prominent leader of the Revolution really opposed the establishment of some kind of American union.[27] After the disappointing experience with retaliation by nonimportation, most colonial leaders felt that a continental authority was necessary if the "tyranny" of the British was to be successfully resisted.[28] The central constitutional question was on what basis this central authority ought to rest. The general impression in the Second Continental Congress was that the delegates from New England, especially those from Massachusetts, led the way in wanting to declare independence sooner than the other colonies, to establish a government with a generous grant of power to act for the union, and to base this government on "republican principles." On each of these heads, there was enthusiastic support from some of the Virginians, especially Richard Henry Lee, but opposition from the men of the mid-Atlantic and, especially, from the Deep Southerners.

As far as John Adams could tell, the main obstacle to declaring independence in early 1776 was "the reluctance of southern colonies to republican government." Unity could be achieved, he thought, "only on popular principles," and these principles were "abhorrent to the inclinations of the barons of the South and the proprietary interests in the middle colonies." [29] In accounting for this difference between New England and the Deep South, he spoke of the fact that South Carolina was dominated by "large plantations of slaves," which gave to the planters "a higher notion of themselves, and the distinction between them and the common people," than was found among most New Englanders. Yet despite his critical attitude toward the South, he knew that unless the delegates approached one another with forbearance and "mutual condescension," their differences would undermine and betray the strike for independence.

So acutely did he feel the need for sensitivity that, in 1777, he derailed a move in the Massachusetts legislature to ask Congress whether it would be all right to "prevent" slavery. It is unclear what was behind the move in Massachusetts. The appeal to Congress may well have been a tactic to stall or divert a drive for abolition. At any rate, Adams believed that the referral would create "jealousy, discord and division" among the states.[30]

Students of the Revolution have learned to regard Adams's jeremiads with a certain skepticism, but in this case his forebodings of intersectional tension were reciprocated by testimony from the other side of the divide. A week before independence was finally declared, Edward Rutledge dispatched an urgent appeal to John Jay, a New Yorker about on a par with the Rutledges in wealth and social position. Hurry to Congress, he begged Jay, and join other men of property in opposition to the "low cunning" and "levelling principles" being advanced by the "government of the Eastern provinces." In the interest of "what they call the good of the whole," these "men without character and without fortune" were trying to establish a central government with full powers to assume direction of the war for independence. In the process, they threatened to "destroy all provincial distinctions" and to provoke "such a fluctuation of property as to introduce the greatest disorder." In order "to keep the staff in our own hands," he urged Jay to lend his stabilizing presence to the proceedings in Congress.[31]

The lines of cleavage did not pit one end of the coast against the other. Accidents of election provided that the Virginia delegation was headed in 1776 by two men most compatible with the New Englanders, Richard Henry Lee and Thomas Jefferson. The result was that the drive for independence was led by Massachusetts and Virginia, despite the fact that there were important elements in both colonies that favored a more cautious course.

Meanwhile, men from the middle colonies and from the Deep South had to be "lugged" toward the break with Great Britain. These men, who had accumulated substantial property under the government of the Crown, were naturally loath to embark on uncharted seas in the company of navigators who struck them as impetuous. As far as the Morrises and Rutledges were concerned, the Virginians, with their enormous debts they were so anxious to repudiate, and the Yankees, with their pinched, unproductive farms, had so little valuable property at stake in the contest that they could not be trusted to behave responsibly, either in the effort against Great Britain or in the reconstitution of society should the drive for independence by some miracle succeed. So these men wanted keenly to force their excitable colleagues to establish the terms of union before the ship set out to sea.

The delegates from the middle colonies held out longest from the vote for independence. New York abstained from the vote on July 2, and did not agree to endorse the Declaration of Independence until July 9. The real leaders of South Carolina—John Rutledge, Henry Laurens, William Henry Drayton, and Christopher Gadsden, among others—were as determined as the Adams cousins to break with the British Empire, and those who held the greatest amounts of property in land and slaves were confident that they could defend themselves against an attempt to take their property without consent. Yet they wanted to reach agreement on terms of co-operation against Britain before declaring independence, and their dogged insistence on this point led Jefferson to observe that the colonies were still "perfectly independent" of one another, in spirit as well as in law, on the eve of the break with Britain.[32]

Despite the reluctance of the conservatives, however, independence was declared about sixteen months before Congress was ready to submit the Articles of Confederation to the states for ratification. A committee to draft such articles had been appointed on June 12, 1776, and had submitted its draft, in John Dickinson's handwriting, exactly one month later. For several weeks, in the midst of feverish preparations for war, Congress debated the articles, but then the press of other business distracted them completely.

In April 1777 Congress once again took up the problem of confederation. Throughout the summer, constitution making was sandwiched in among other work, but gradually it became apparent that "the very salvation of these states" and the successful assertion of independence depended upon the completion of the articles. "None of the European powers will publicly acknowledge [us] free and independent, until [we] are confederated," wrote Thomas Burke, a delegate from North Carolina, to his Governor.[33] Thus spurred on, Congress finished its task in November 1777, and asked each state to complete its ratification by March of the following year.[34]

There were three issues that made the framing of Articles of Confederation difficult: the basis of representation; the basis for taxation; and the extent of national control over western territories. On each issue, important interests collided, while accepted political principles offered conflicting guidance. Each issue threatened to shatter the fragile union of the fledgling nation into two, three, or thirteen pieces, or perhaps whirl them back into the British Empire. In each case, accommodation was reached by accepting solutions that could not be permanent, because they served the principles of state sovereignty at the cost of viable national union.

On the question of the basis of representation, inertia suggested that each state should have one vote in the councils of the nation, and inertia in the end prevailed. That was the way it had been in the early councils of union, at the Stamp Act Congress and in the First Continental Congress. In these earlier meetings, most men were not thinking about forming a new nation. They were merely trying to find ways to demonstrate resistance to the enactments of Parliament, in the hopes of changing those enactments. Besides, time was short and communications extremely primitive, which made it impossible to gather data for determining the comparative weight of the colonies.

When the Second Continental Congress convened, Benjamin Franklin, realizing that a new situation obtained, proposed that representation now be apportioned according to population, and that affirmation by a majority of the delegates present, each voting as an individual, be required for the passage of laws and resolutions.[35] Two hundred years later, the nation has still not moved that far in the direction of pure representational democracy, even with the aid of modern Supreme Court rulings on redistricting. In 1775 Franklin's proposal was almost eccentric, and certainly doomed to rejection by the "small states."

Instead, Dickinson's draft provided that each state have one vote on all questions. The delegates from the populous states of Pennsylvania and Virginia, as well as some delegates from the Carolinas, who expected that population trends would favor their states in the years to come, proposed various ways of proportioning representation to population. Benjamin Rush, the enthusiastic but politically naïve physician from Philadelphia, thought the question of representation afforded a fine opportunity to strike a blow against slavery. He proposed apportionment according to the number of free inhabitants. This, he said, would have at least "one excellent effect, that of inducing the colonies to discourage slavery and to encourage the increase of their free inhabitants." [36] Other delegates kept insisting that America was now "one large state," "one common mass," but nothing could have been better calculated to put that vision beyond reach than Rush's remark.

The Virginians made an effort to save part of the principle of government by popular majorities. Earlier, it had been agreed that certain important questions before Congress would not be decided affirmatively until the assent of nine of the thirteen states had been obtained. Now the Virginians pleaded for an amendment stipulating that the nine states agreeing to a measure contain a majority of the people of the United States, excluding Negroes and Indians.[37] From Virginia's viewpoint, this was a generous proposal. By excluding Negroes from the formula, the Virginians were "giving away" about 200,000 inhabitants, nearly 40 per cent of their total population. The proposal was a measure of their desire for some acceptance of the principle of proportional representation.

But these arguments were to no avail. Most of the delegates regarded themselves as agents of full-fledged "states,' who were met together to find ways of co-operating in foreign affairs and common defense. In this business, each state was to be a discrete entity, fully sovereign, participating only of its own free will.

Once this decision had been made, the Articles were doomed to a short and turbulent life. Men would not voluntarily commit their happiness, their blood and treasure to a government in which the strength of their voice was determined not by their stake in its proceedings, but by the accident of their location with respect to state boundary lines. So long as the war continued, and all patriotic Americans had an obvious stake in its successful conclusion, the hoop of union would hold of its own accord. Once the centrifugal forces began to have their sway, however, an alliance of sovereign states could not hope to govern America's 3 million inhabitants.

Because the apportionment of representation was determined to rest on the principle of state sovereignty, it became necessary to establish a principle for apportioning taxes in the Articles themselves rather than by statute. If men had been satisfied that their property would be represented fairly in Congress, they might have trusted Congress to apportion taxes. But the factors that dictated that representation be based on unrepublican principles (wariness, mistrust, a narrow, tentative, guarded commitment to the union) necessitated agreement before ratification on a formula for apportioning taxes.

Dickinson's draft provided that "All . . . expenses . . . shall be defrayed out of a common treasury, which shall be supplied by the several colonies in proportion to the number of inhabitants of every age, sex and quality, excepting Indians not paying taxes." [33] This proposal followed the resolution of Congress adopted July 29, 1775, which had provided that each colony's proportion of the bills emitted by Congress should be determined according to the total population, including Negroes. [39]

These schemes were unacceptable to the Southern states. Southerners were in perfect agreement with the general opinion that the fundamental purpose of government was the protection of property. Like all Whigs, they recognized that property often had to be sacrificed in order to protect property, and that it was therefore just that the burden of taxes ought to be apportioned to wealth. A dispute arose, however, over the appropriate way to measure wealth. Most men agreed that population reflected wealth. [40] People tended to drift toward the economic action and to enhance that action by their presence—their labor and their purchases. But Southerners argued that not all men labored and consumed with equal vigor. Negroes, they insisted, contributed less to the wealth of their neighborhood than whites did. Many Northerners agreed.

The first move against Dickinson's formula was a proposal by the Maryland delegation that taxes be apportioned according to the number of white inhabitants only. Negroes, argued Samuel Chase, were property, and ought no more to be considered members of the state than the horses and cattle owned by farmers in other sections of the country.* 'They have no more interest in it," he said. Therefore, unless Congress intended to include the cattle of New England in the basis for taxation, they ought not to include the Negroes of the South.

John Adams disagreed. Whether laborers were slaves or free

---

* Throughout his remarks, as recorded by both Jefferson and Adams, Chase represented all Negroes as "property." Neither in his amendment nor in his argument did he make any distinction between slaves and free Negroes.

did not matter, he said. They were considering persons as indicators of wealth, not constituent elements of a polity. Obviously Negroes, slave or free, contributed to the wealth of the state. Since it was agreed that population was a satisfactory index of wealth, Negroes ought to be included as well as whites.

James Wilson, of Pennsylvania, an immigrant from Scotland who often showed more of his native land's penchant for logic than sensitivity to his adopted land's fixed irrationalities, suggested that if slaves were less productive than free men, perhaps the slaves ought to be freed. Immediately Thomas Lynch jumped to his feet to assert that if gentlemen insisted on debating whether or not slaves were property, the confederation was finished. Lynch was an intimidating man, but he did not frighten the seventy-year-old Franklin. Lynch had asked, that since slaves were "our property, why should they be taxed more than the land, sheep, cattle, horses, etc." The reason, said Franklin, was that slaves weakened a state and contributed to the burden of defending it. They were different from sheep, for example, in that "sheep will never make any insurrections." But if slaves added to the nation's wealth, countered Rutledge, "Eastern" merchants would benefit, and draw some of the wealth back to New England.

The problem was obviously complicated, as tax legislation always is. As a means of compromising the differences, Benjamin Harrison proposed that two slaves be counted as one free man—although he doubted, he said, that two slaves actually did the work of a single free man. But the vote was taken on Chase's amendment, and it produced a straight sectional alignment. The four New England states, New York, New Jersey, and Pennsylvania voted against it; Delaware, Maryland, Virginia, and the Carolinas were in favor; Georgia's vote was divided.[41] Thus slavery was already producing an ominous "line of discrimination" through the middle of the union's political arena.

This left Congress with Dickinson's draft, which apportioned taxes to total population. There the matter lay through the long and chastening winter of 1776–1777. During the summer of 1777, while Congress completed most of the rest of the Articles, the formula for apportioning taxes was occasionally debated. It was not

until October that this vexing problem was given serious attention. By then it was apparent that only the New Englanders
found justice in Dickinson's formula. And so it was moved that
the expenses of government be apportioned according to the
"value of all land within each state," including any buildings or
other improvements thereon, as estimated according to a mode to
be directed by Congress. The motion carried by five states to four,
with the Carolinas, Virginia, Maryland, and New Jersey voting
favorably, New York and Pennsylvania divided, and New England unanimously opposed. To the delegates from New England,
the clause seemed unfair, because their land was more valuable
than land in the South, and because the formula left what one
delegate, Nathaniel Folsom, from New Hampshire, calculated as
one-third of the Southern wealth, consisting of Negro slaves, out
of account.[42]

Adding further to their grievance was the fact that another
clause in the Articles directed that troops for the Continental
Line be drawn from states in accordance with the total *white* population. Yet laws in the Southern states required that patrols of
white men, who might otherwise have been available for military
service, be maintained there to prevent fugitive slaves from escaping and to protect white homes against servile insurrections. It
was therefore difficult for Southerners to comply with the requirement that troop requisitions be based on the free white population. New Englanders accepted this necessity, if not always with
complete grace, with the understanding that New England contributed "strength" to the union, while Southerners contributed
wealth. Now, however, the formula for apportioning taxes rested
on the understanding that taxes ought to be proportioned only
according to those forms of wealth held by all Americans, ignoring a form of wealth owned predominantly in the South. Thus
the wealthiest section was to be the one least burdened by taxes
for the common treasury.

If New Englanders had dreamed that the formula for apportioning taxes was practicable, they would surely have opposed it
more strenuously than they did. But canny old Roger Sherman
correctly predicted in November 1777, the month it was adopted,
that the formula would never work, that Congress could never

agree on a mode for comparing the value of land in different states.[43] Congress was already falling into the egregious habit of adopting legislation that could not be obeyed or enforced.

In many respects, Dickinson's draft moved timidly in granting powers of government to the national Congress. On the question of national authority to control territory in the West, however, the draft upon which Congress began work in July 1776 must have seemed breath-taking to the representatives from states with large claims there—particularly Virginia. In this respect, Dickinson was a true son of Pennsylvania—a state that one historian has described as "landless" in 1776.[44]

The draft gave Congress power to set limits on colonies whose claims ran to the "South Sea," and to ascertain the boundaries of those colonies that "appear to be indeterminate." It gave Congress the power to lay out new colonies in any territory thereafter obtained by the United States, and to dispose of land in such territories "for the general benefit of all the United Colonies." Finally, it indicated, though in the passive voice and thus without a direct grant of power, that "forms of government are to be established [in these new colonies] on the principles of liberty." The assignment of an agent for this task, as well as an operational definition of the "principles of liberty," were not yet settled eighty years later, when Abraham Lincoln and Stephen Douglas debated the question across the length and breadth of Illinois.

Dickinson's draft was wholly unacceptable to the Virginians, and, since ratification had to be unanimous, it was clear that the Old Dominion had to be accommodated. Nor was Virginia alone. Other states—the Carolinas, Georgia, New York, Connecticut, and Massachusetts—had claims to western lands, and they were supported by the prevailing notion that the national Congress ought not to have power or resources to coerce its constituent states. The accession of large amounts of land, to be disposed of at profit and to be governed in the meantime according to undefined "principles of liberty," would surely deliver vast powers to the central authority.

But if Virginia and its allies had the power to veto the whole of the Articles on this question, so did Maryland and its "landless" allies. Maryland was afraid that Virginia would liquidate its wartime debts by the sale of western lands, thereby avoiding internal taxes. This would give Virginia an almost irresistible lure. Emigration would soon leave Maryland depopulated and bankrupt. Besides, many non-Virginians had bought land in the West from the Indians. The legislature of Virginia would never recognize these purchases as valid, conflicting as they often did with purchases made by Virginians from the state legislature. Earlier, these speculators had looked to the imperial authority for succor against the Virginians; now they hoped that Congress would intervene to support their claims.

Also at stake was a conflict about the future status of the West in the American union. In a rare and impressive instance of the force of principle in political calculation, Virginians gradually persuaded themselves that Montesquieu and others had been right about the optimum extent of republics. With its vast western holdings, Virginia might be too big to be a republic. Marylanders must have been astonished as this argument gained power over minds in Virginia. But at the same time, Virginians had a strong conviction that all men, or at least all white men, were capable of self-government and had a right to it. On this point, many leading men in Maryland and elsewhere along the middle coast were firmly opposed. What the former seem to have intended was that the West be ceded to the national government, then parceled out to land companies and operated under their guidance and for their profit. In other words, the West was to be America's colonial empire, and operators in the East were to take the roles performed in the British Empire by the East India Tea Company, the Royal African Company, and the Virginia Company.[45]

Because of the need to obtain unanimous ratification, and because men were not yet convinced of the necessity for a competent national government, Congress in 1777 was utterly unable to adjust or integrate these competing interests and visions. After fifteen months of aimless debate, all the powers suggested by Dickinson had been eliminated, and, in their stead, a wholly unworkable machinery of adjudication for conflicting claims was adopted. Congress was made the "last resort on appeal" in all disputes between two or more states over boundaries, jurisdiction, "or any other cause whatever."

In the contest between Maryland and Virginia, Virginia had

won a victory of sorts: Congress had no power to draw a western boundary for the Old Dominion, and was forbidden from taking a single acre of land "for the benefit of the United States." But Maryland, of course, had the last word: its ratification was essential. The result was that Virginia was finally induced by desire t complete the Articles and by Maryland's stubbornness to cede its western holdings north of the Ohio River, provided that all claims to purchases from the Indians be declared void, and provided further that the territory be laid out into states, which would eventually be accepted into the union as equals.[46] By this cession Virginia neutralized, rather than yielded to, Maryland's demands. Eastern Maryland's speculators were deprived of claims based on purchases from the Indians, and coastal aristocrats were forced to accept the prospect of many new states developing in the West.

Yet, since Maryland's refusal to ratify the Articles had ostensibly been based on Virginia's greed and supposed advantage, there were no longer any grounds for delay. Thus, out of the struggle of interest and speculation, the foundation of a national domain was begun. Soon a gigantic battle over this vast wilderness started, and the nation was drawn into controversies that could not be settled without civil war.

In November 1777 the Articles of Confederation were completed by Congress. A letter, dispatched from York, Pennsylvania, whither Congress had fled before the advance of the British Army, urged the states to empower their delegates to ratify the Articles by March of the following year. Noting the difficulty of reconciling "so many sovereign and independent communities," the letter called the Articles "essential to our very existence as a free people." Without them, the union might as well bid "adieu to independence, to liberty and safety." [47]

Despite these pleas, it was not until the following June that Congress was able to consider the responses of the states. By that time, twelve states (all but Delaware) had responded, and ten (all but Delaware, New Jersey, and Maryland) had been empowered by their state legislatures to ratify the Articles. Eight of the states, however, asked Congress to consider amendments before declaring the Articles in force.

In late June Congress addressed itself to these amendments, many of which stand as symbols of the tensions that were to wrack the union until they were resolved by war fourscore and three years later. Most of the fire from New England and the mid-Atlantic states was directed at the articles apportioning troop requisitions to the white population and taxes to land values. Connecticut asked Congress to reconsider the suggestion that taxes be apportioned among the states according to the total number of inhabitants of all descriptions, but the request was defeated, by 3 to 9.

From Massachusetts, Pennsylvania, and New Jersey came a request to revise the clause apportioning troop requisitions by striking the word "white," thereby assigning quotas on the basis of the total population. In presenting this request, New Jersey made curious use of the national commitment to equality written in the Declaration of Independence. This commitment meant, the argument went, that all must contribute equally to the nation's defense. Though "necessity or expediency" might justify some states in refusing the liberty to bear arms to certain kinds of inhabitants, there should be no exemptions from the numbers of inhabitants from which each state should draw its contributions to the army. But the promise of the Declaration, whatever its future power might be, was confined in 1776 to white men. This was a "white man's country," and white men must shoulder the burden of asserting its independence, or else reconstitute their self-conception. The proposed amendment was defeated, gaining the support of only three states.

From the other end of the union came a different sort of objection. South Carolina was most disturbed by the clause guaranteeing to "the free inhabitants of each of these states . . . all privileges and immunities of free citizens in the several states." Although by 1778 not a single state had abolished slavery, and nowhere was there any substantial number of free blacks, and although South Carolina could not be considered an attractive or likely haven for free blacks seeking larger opportunities, the legislature of that state nevertheless asked Congress to insert the word "white" in this clause. Their proposal gained the support of one other state, doubtless Georgia, but was rejected by the votes of eight states, less from a desire to safeguard the rights of free Negroes than to finish the ratification of the Articles withcut having to submit them once again, as amended, to the states.[48]

Having quickly and rather summarily disposed of these requests for amendment,[49] Congress invited delegates to sign the Articles as passed in November 1777. Ten states did so in July 1778; New Jersey, in November 1778; and Delaware, in 1779. Maryland's holdout was finally ended in 1781 by Virginia's cession of the Old Northwest. And in March 1781, the first constitution of the United States of America was officially launched.

So far as is known, no jubilant celebrations attended the event. The ratification merely gave *de jure* sanction to arrangements that had obtained *de facto* for nearly six years. The Articles of Confederation added no powers to Congress; they merely "described" the union.[50] By the time they were ratified, the chaos in national finances made it obvious that they were wholly inadequate to the purpose for which they had been framed—"for their common defense, the security of their liberties and their mutual and general welfare," in the words of Article III. The war with Britain was nearly over, but the army was still in the field, and increasingly mutinous, out of resentment over lack of pay. But Congress, sensitive as it was to the justice of the soldiers' claims and the good policy of satisfying them, was powerless to do its plain duty. It had no revenue.

As nearly everyone knew by then, Article VIII, distributing taxes among the states according to land values, would not work. The distribution was to be based on a census of land values, but no census had ever been taken. Men throughout the union, except possibly in South Carolina, were beginning to realize that there simply was no fair way to compare land values in South Carolina with those in Massachusetts, though the South Carolinians, whose land had been ravaged by war and was thus at a low value, still hoped somehow that a way could be found.[51]

Yet Congress had to raise revenue. "Our very existence as a people" was at stake, as Congress itself acknowledged.[52] Accordingly, in 1781 the states were asked for authority to lay an impost of 5 per cent on all foreign goods, with the exception of arms, clothing, and salt, imported into the United States. The request, in the form of an amendment to the Articles, needed the approval of all thirteen states, and was doomed by the refusal of Rhode Island to ratify it. Rhode Island explained its veto on the grounds that imposts were a mode of taxation unfair to commercial states, that federal revenue collectors would be beyond the discipline of states, and that the revenue yielded by the impost was to be "unrestricted" and would give Congress resources to make it independent of the states that gave it being. The proposed impost was therefore repugnant to American liberty.[53]

But the pretensions of Congress were not the only threat to American liberty. The army was seething over politicians who made lavish promises and exacted enormous sacrifices while the British were still in the land, but who now refused to deliver. A group of officers stationed at Newburgh, New York, communicated this impatience to Congress early in 1783. These restless veterans, verging on mutiny, were becalmed by the only man in America who could have done it: the American Cincinnatus, George Washington.[54] The officers' warnings of feelings among the soldiers at Newburgh were referred for study to a committee of Congressmen most notorious for their reluctance to yield to the demand for an adequate means to raise national revenues.[55]

Meanwhile, Congress as a whole was addressing its ponderous self to these matters. In February a committee chaired by John Rutledge had offered a resolution "requiring" each state to authorize that a census be taken by the "principal freeholders" and delivered to Congress by January 1784. The Deep Southerners, who apparently knew what the term "principal freeholders" meant, favored the proposal, but it was defeated by the opposition of men, led by James Madison, Alexander Hamilton, and James Wilson, who favored more decisive moves toward nationalism.[56]

What these young nationalists had in mind was to revise the article entirely, in the direction of an apportionment related, not to land values, but to population figures. As the crisis mounted, the question of "restoring public credit and obtaining funds" was referred to a new committee, chaired by Nathaniel Gorham, and including Hamilton, Madison, and Rutledge among its members. Rutledge, of course, had been a strong supporter of apportionment geared to land values, but the others on the committee were

convinced that "the value of land could never be justly or satisfactorily obtained, that it would ever be a source of contentions
among the states." [57] Hamilton and Madison, particularly, were
convinced that Congress needed an independent revenue if ever
there was to be a national government capable of defending
American liberty and promoting prosperity. Accordingly, in mid-
March of 1783, the committee submitted two major proposals. To
raise revenues immediately and for the next twenty-five years,
they advised an impost on a list of enumerated articles, plus a
straight 5-per-cent impost on all other articles; and, to provide a
permanent income, they suggested that the Articles be amended
to base the distribution of the tax burden on a census of population rather than land values.

It was during the consideration of this report that the so-called
"federal ratio"—calculating the value of a slave at three-fifths the
value of a free man—first gained a footing in American law. As
Wilson recalled during the debate on the Gorham Committee report, the original attempt to apportion revenues according to
population had foundered when Northerners and Southerners
were unable to agree on the value of slaves in calculating a state's
capacity to pay taxes. Back in 1777, Benjamin Harrison had proposed that slaves be calculated at half the value of free men, but
New Englanders refused to concur, insisting that slaves should be
counted at full value.

It should be noted that humanitarian regard for the Negro as a
person was not the motive of Northerners who insisted that slaves
should be counted as equal in value to free men. What was at
stake was not the dignity of individuals—or even, by this time,
their capacity to produce wealth. What was at stake was the distribution of the tax burden between Northern and Southern
states.

Using the figure sought in the requisitions of 1785, around $3
million, and the population estimates generally given for the year
1780, which approximate the figures Congress would have used, if
slaves were calculated at one for one with free men, the tax burden per individual would have been about $1.08. This would
have meant that Massachusetts would have owed the national
treasury $343,000, and South Carolina $194,000, to take two states

differently situated with regard to the proportion of slaves in the general population. But if slaves were calculated at the ratio of three for every single free man, which was the proportion suggested by John Rutledge, the tax burden per full individual would have been $1.25, and Massachusetts would have owed $396,000, while South Carolina owed $154,000. With five slaves valued equally with three free men, the ratio finally agreed upon, the rate per individual would have stood at $1.17, and Massachusetts would have owed $373,000, and South Carolina $165,000.*

New Englanders argued that all the advantages lay with the South. Slaves might produce somewhat less than a man who was responsible for his own upkeep, but the difference was more than compensated for by the cost of supplying a free man's maintenance. Furthermore, the warmer climate in the South contributed to productivity, and made more of what the South produced suitable for export.[58] Southerners responded by arguing that slaves were generally not put to work as young as free men and having no direct interest in their labor, were typically lazy and stupid. And if Southern exports were greater than New England's, so were imports. In fact, argued the Southerners, the balance of trade was distinctly unfavorable to the South.

A vote was finally taken on a motion that the report be amended to weigh three slaves as the equivalent of two free men. The motion needed a majority of the thirteen states, but it got only five, being opposed solidly by the four southernmost states. A vote was then taken on Madison's compromise proposal of five for three, and barely carried. But before adjournment, a final vote was taken on the clause as a whole, and the motion received only six votes. The delegations from Virginia and South Carolina were still insisting that the method of apportionment according to land values, as outlined in the Articles, be tried before being replaced.[59]

Four days later, Gorham announced that unless Congress

---

* It is important to remember that in 1783, when the three-fifths ratio was first agreed upon, it measured the burden of taxation, and it was therefore to the advantage of New England to see that slaves were raised as near to equality with free men as possible. In 1787, at the Federal Convention, the ratio was used to measure the right to representation, and then it was the turn of the Southerners to see slaves as equivalent to free men.

adopted a reasonable and workable plan for establishing public revenues, the "eastern states" would have to call a convention of their own to see what could be done to raise money to pay public debts. The spectacle of states jockeying for the last ounce of advantage while a mutinous army cried out for justice was too degrading to be endured any further. Despite the complaints of delegates still determined to attempt a census of land values, the motion to adopt the Gorham report now passed.[60]

In submitting the proposal to the states for ratification, which would have to be unanimous, an "Address" by Congress noted that the existing provision for apportioning taxes according to land values was inadequate, and that the only alternative was to base taxation on a census of population. The problem with the latter scheme had been to arrive at a fair and acceptable way to compare the difference in value "between the labor and industry of free inhabitants and of all other inhabitants." The ratio agreed on had been the result of "mutual concessions." The address concluded with a strong peroration, urging a quick and affirmative response from the state legislatures. "It has ever been the pride and boast of America, that the rights for which she contended were the rights of human nature." Now the fate of America, with its "unadulterated forms of republican government," hung in the balance. If Americans valued their newly won liberty, they would not fail to provide Congress with the money needed.[61] With this address, Congress sent to each state a number of enclosures, including a copy of the Officers' Petition from Newburgh, which had entreated Congress "to convince the army and the world that the independence of America shall not be placed on the ruin of any particular class of her citizens." [62] The officers were referring, of course, to the soldiers. The irony of all this rhetoric from the viewpoint of the blacks apparently went unnoticed.

Despite these appeals, and the obvious necessity of amending Article VIII, the reforms of 1783 were doomed. It was not the three-fifths provision to which the states objected. By 1786 the four states failing to comply were divided equally between New England (New Hampshire and Rhode Island) and the Deep South (South Carolina and Georgia), and a Congressional committee indicated that the main opposition to the three-fifths rule came from Northern states that had already agreed to the amendment.[63] Instead, the effort to amend Article VIII was lost in a welter of counterproposals, timidity, paranoia, and a growing sense of futility about the government of the Confederation as a whole.

In urging prompt fulfillment of the requisition of 1786, the Board of the Treasury argued that the existing constitutions, state and federal, had been established by the free consent of the people, and that they firmly supported "the civil and religious rights of all who live under the shadow of their influence"—a situation that would continue only so long as these governments were able to pay for the defense of their liberty.[64] Throughout this period of crisis for the Confederation, the issue was conceived in the same terms. Together, the states had established their independence from the British Empire. With British authority overthrown, they had moved to re-establish government by consent of the governed in America. It was believed almost universally that matters of "internal police"—all public responsibility for domestic law and order—belonged to the state governments. But the assertion and defense of the right of the states to perform these functions of government was the business of Congress. Thus, the chief purpose of the government of the union was the defense of internal government by consent in the states.

But to defend the states from foreign meddling or conquest was no easy or simple task. It meant managing the military effort undertaken by the erstwhile colonies, raising and supplying an army and launching a navy; it meant conducting diplomacy with foreign nations, arranging alliances, identifying and stating vital interests, giving warnings to enemies, and negotiating treaties; it meant encouraging and regulating a national economy by establishing a national currency, arranging credit, maintaining postal service, lowering tariff barriers between the states, and co-ordinating the use of imposts against unwanted foreign competition; it meant managing conflicts between the states over disputed boundaries and competing land claims west of the Alleghenies. It meant, in short, accomplishing those basic tasks without which there would have been no union at all.

No serious politician during the period of the Confederation proposed that each of the thirteen states should go its own way. But if union was necessary to protect American liberty, then a viable system of federal taxation was likewise a minimal necessity. As Benjamin Franklin remarked, "It is absurd the pretending to be lovers of liberty while they grudge paying for the defense of it." [65]

Some men, including Hamilton and James Wilson and Robert Morris, were dreaming dreams of national grandeur during the 1780's. Many other men were deeply frightened by the implications of these dreams, fearing the sacrifice of local autonomy and particularity. The debate between these nationalizers and localists had one unfortunate effect from the standpoint of the localists: it tended to make them resist any and all efforts to provide the government of the union with a viable income. They meant to prevent the accretion of additional powers to the national government; they wanted to confine it to diplomacy and defense. But in the end, by opposing all attempts to give Congress a limited but stable income, they pushed affairs to the crisis of 1787, when a pitiful and abortive uprising of farmers in western Massachusetts brought widespread popular support for an effort to replace the frail government of the Confederation with a sturdy structure.

The proposal of 1783 was not the only attempt to gain an adequate revenue for Congress. Hamilton and Madison were rotated out of Congress in 1784 by the rule that a delegate could serve only three years at a stretch. But in their places, James Monroe, Charles Pinckney, and Rufus King, the second string of the gathering forces of nationalism, took up the quest for viable reforms. Despairing of obtaining the necessary perfect consensus on a formula for apportioning domestic taxes, they sought instead to gain from the states the power to levy tariffs on foreign commerce.

Inevitably, of course, the power to levy these imposts carried with it the power to affect domestic affairs, however well guarded the power might be. And well guarded these proposals were: the imposts were to be collected by agents appointed by and accountable to the states, the revenues were to be turned over to the states for use at their direction, and the grant of power was limited to a period of twenty-five years—that is, until the war debt was paid off.[66]

Yet even these proposals failed to gain the necessary support. The proposal of 1783, for authority to lay an impost for twenty-five years, foundered on Rhode Island's acute fear of the development of a national bureaucracy of customs officials. The proposal of 1784, for authority to prohibit imports from nations with which the United States had no commercial treaty, died from a myriad qualifications, including Georgia's proviso that no prohibition by Congress could be "construed" to extend to the slave trade.[67]

The proposal of 1785 was the most carefully guarded of all. It would have given Congress perpetual authority to regulate foreign and interstate trade by prohibitions and taxation, with the provisos that states could prohibit trade to their ports in any item, that customs officials would be state officers, and that revenues would go to the states that collected them. In short, the power proposed was not a source of revenue at all, but a way of establishing uniform trade policies throughout the union, to be implemented by the states. This time the proposal never got past Congress. The Southerners objected to "navigation acts" on the ground that they threatened to deprive the staple-producing states of a choice of markets and of carriers.[68] In submitting the proposal, James Monroe, twenty-seven years old and serving his first term in Congress, had noted, "happily," that "no measure can be taken to promote the interests of [any single state or section], which will not equally promote that of the whole." [69] But in the President's chair was another Virginian, dour old Richard Henry Lee, who, as the years wore on, grew more and more skeptical of co-ordinating the interests of the differing sections. In the Congressional politics of 1785, Monroe was no match for the prestigious and skillful Lee. But once again, by diverting reform, Lee and his friends took the union closer to a constitutional revolution.

The drama of the Confederation was not played out entirely between those who liked the Articles and those who were straining toward a stronger central government. The idea of separating into multiple confederacies was also current among leading politicians. When controversies between the sections paralyzed Congress, the "spirit of mutual forbearance," for which nationalists like James Madison and John Adams often pleaded, failed in certain men. It happened to Nathaniel Gorham, the nationalist merchant from Boston who was an important figure at the Convention of 1787 and a leader in the development of central New York State, who threatened in 1783 that the "Eastern states" would confederate by themselves unless Congress could agree on a revenue plan. And in 1785, as Monroe's attempt to give Congress power to pass "navigation acts" moved inexorably toward failure, young Rufus King wrote to John Adams that it was time for the eight Eastern states to think about forming a "subconfederacy" with power to regulate foreign commerce. These states "have common interests, are under similar embarrassments," and would therefore be driven to act separately unless the Southern states would agree to vest Congress with the necessary power.[70] In August of the following year, Monroe told a correspondent that the Yankees were openly talking of forming a separate union.[71]

Merrill Jensen has warned that the incapacity of public authority under the Articles of Confederation must not be overestimated. The fledgling nation inherited enormous problems following the war with Great Britain, but the remarkable thing, to his way of thinking, is the vigor with which these problems were assaulted. States jostled over conflicting territorial claims and navigational rights, but in many cases these dangerous disputes were resolved by negotiation and mediation between the contending parties.* Congress lacked power to undertake "inter-

---

* Among the achievements of the Confederation, Jensen lays heavy emphasis on "the creation of the national domain," beginning with the cessions of territory by the states to the federal government, and culminating in the Northwest Ordinance of 1787.[72] While the establishment of the principle of federal responsibility for superintendence over territorial development was a noteworthy precedent, Congress under the Confederation was a relatively passive factor in the process. It received the cessions and provided the arena within which Maryland and Virginia and the land speculators carried out their struggle. But Congress during the 1780's was merely one place—along with state legislatures, the meeting rooms of Eastern speculators, and, perhaps most crucially, the frontier itself—where the forces seeking to determine the course of territorial development confronted one another. As for Congress, it had no independent power to enforce the decisions recorded in its ordinances, should the parties involved fail to accept them. It was not until the Constitution of 1787 was ratified that the Northwest Ordinance of 1787 became an effective piece of legislation.

nal improvements," but this did not prevent the development of interstate facilities. Jensen offers, as evidence of this potential, the co-operation of Pennsylvania, Maryland, and Virginia in the building of a road to the West. As far as tariffs were concerned, he argues that trade regulations were "reciprocal," and that most state laws on this subject exempted American-made goods.[73]

Jensen does a service to understanding of the period by emphasizing that the United States was not a whale on the beach during the 1780's. It was a nation full of enterprise and hope. If the period was "critical," it was not empty of achievement. Unoccupied places between settlements, along the coast and in the interior, were filling up. Interstate travel and commerce were increasing, and postal services were improving. Leading men were becoming better acquainted and learning to respect one another's abilities, feelings, and interests. Americans were already taking the first crucial steps along the road to regarding the territory in the West, not as a colonial empire, but as a region of potential states that would one day take their place in the union alongside the original thirteen.

But before these achievements, contacts, and commitments could become the basis for truly national development, the elements of the union would have to agree on the formation of an agent of integration, a government with power to reconcile and adjust the elements and develop common policies to fit a diverse, but unifying, community. Before agreement could be reached on the establishment of a government with this kind of power, the elements themselves would have to begin to integrate, to find bases for common policies and complementary development.

The process of national development involves an interaction between society and government. The integration of economy and society gives birth to confidence, upon which government can be built. The establishment of common government in turn creates an agency to aid in the integration of a national society. If the process is to begin, if a nation is to be founded, founders must work acts of statesmanship on the elements at hand.

For all the development to which Jensen so astutely calls attention, the nation had no national government under the Articles of Confederation, and, as Alexander Hamilton wrote in number 85 of *The Federalist,* "A nation, without a national government, is . . . an awful spectacle." The urgent need to gain for this nation that "equal station" among nations to which nature and nature's God entitled it, the opportunity to draw the area west of the Appalachian Mountains into a continental union with the region along the Atlantic Coast, the drive to achieve the destiny that beckoned, to establish self-government, government by consent of all the governed, to test whether popular government could exist in a vast, continental nation—all this awaited the framing of a truly national government.

There were many reasons for the failure to abolish slavery throughout the United States during the eighteenth century, reasons having to do with the attitude of white men toward blacks and with the weakness of men's moral imagination and the terrible ease with which men justify the oppression of others. But the reason highlighted here is the stage of political development attained in America by the 1780's. Analysts of the emerging nations often speak of "the sovereignty of politics" in the developmental process.[74] Speaking mainly of the new nations of Africa, Asia, and Latin America, they argue that the need to accumulate capital for investment, to overcome illiteracy, superstition, and fear of change in the masses, and to eliminate resistance by privileged minorities—and to do all these things quickly, under the goad of hostile neighbors and impatient rivals—often requires that public authority be centralized and exercised in an authoritarian, sometimes even totalitarian manner. Sometimes it is noted that the case of the United States was different from contemporary examples.[75] The American people, it is said, were not afraid of change—quite the contrary. "Privileged minorities" in America were less rigid and diehard than their counterparts in contemporary developing areas, owing not so much to their superior moral character or insight, as to their inability to protect their privileges in a continent full of opportunity for all classes of men. And the pace of development in the United States was less forced. Neighboring Indian tribes may in some instances have been hostile, but their menace was felt only intermittently in the seats of government and never seemed beyond the capacity of militia forces to contain. The challenge from across the seas was more serious, but after 1781 it was more often economic than military. After the Treaty of Paris, Americans rarely imagined that hostile armies threatened their territory or political independence.[76]

The nation born in 1776 felt the need for centralized political direction less strongly than its modern counterparts—and certainly had far less disposition to resort to it. According to prevailing opinion, the task of statesmen was "to make the exercise of power difficult, dangerous and unprofitable."[77] Hannah Arendt has argued that the Revolution of 1776 was a political revolution par excellence. While its leaders speculated endlessly about the proper principles of political arrangement, by comparison they gave hardly a thought to the need for social reform.[78] It was not that they were oblivious to social realities. In the Aristotelian manner, they gave considerable attention to the relevance of prevailing social patterns for the politics of their republic, and took keen interest in the social implications of political decisions. But the guiding principle seems to have been that politics ought not to be an agency of social reform, but, instead, a means of smoothing the channel for natural social development. Governments should reflect social reality, not shape it.

So development in the United States was different from development in the Soviet Union, or Cuba, or India. In the United States, it proceeded rapidly, but with only the mildest political direction. Conditions seemed to be such that stronger leadership, greater political co-ordination, and tighter integration of the elements of the nation were not necessary. Nature had been abundant, social patterns were flexible, and the American people had inherited an animus against public authority and the habit of developing their environment by voluntary associations.

The emergence of a national bureaucracy is one sign of the extent of political management. If the government undertakes much, it needs many agents to perform its tasks. Under the Articles, the United States saw the beginnings of federal bureaucracy, but the size of those beginnings is a measure of the ambition of the federal government. For several years, the execution of public policy—the drafting and dispatching of diplomatic correspondence, the direction of the military effort, the letting of contracts for supplies and postal services, supervision over the printing of money and deposits and withdrawals of public funds—was handled by delegates to Congress, operating as committees. Gradually the task grew, and by 1780, it was patently beyond the capacity of men whose primary job was the consideration and adoption of policy. Accordingly, a beginning was made by appointing "secretaries" to manage specific responsibilities.

The precedent had been set in 1775, when Congress had appointed Benjamin Franklin Postmaster. By 1782, his successor had charge of twenty-six mail carriers, a small staff of officials in Philadelphia, and a number of deputy postmasters throughout the states. The War Department was authorized in 1781, but it was not until 1785 that its duties were made clear: to keep track of military supplies, to dispose of continental troops, stationed for the most part on the western frontier, and to administer military-bounty lands. To perform these tasks, Secretary Henry Knox in 1788 had the assistance of three clerks and a messenger, and an army of 679 men and officers. Two other departments, Foreign Affairs and the Treasury, were also established. Both were capably, sometimes very well, administered, but starved for funds and woefully understaffed.[79]

A government this size could not make much of an impact. It was not intended to. Most Americans were not ambitious for radical changes in their society, and almost no one, with the possible exception of Alexander Hamilton in the mood that later produced the Report on Manufactures, turned to government, especially federal government, for an agency to promote development. Under the Articles, the call in the Report on Manufactures for vigorous national encouragement for industrial development would have been quite precisely unthinkable.[80]

This line of argument is familiar. Americans avoided peasant revolts and the slaughter of the kulaks, the agonies of land reform and the terror of counterrevolution, because they were "born free." Determined to remain so, they could and did resist the siren call of progress through centralized government.

But why were they unable to eliminate human slavery, the quintessence of all they abhorred and sought to avoid in the innocence of the New World? It has been suggested that slavery was more vulnerable between 1776 and 1790 than it ever was again.[81]

If this is so, and if a more vigorous government might have directed its energies toward an assault on chattel slavery, then it must be acknowledged that the nation paid a high price for the slowness with which it mounted a real national government.

5

Slavery and the Constitutional Revolution: The Debate over Representation

IN the preamble to the Declaration of Independence, the Congress of the United States declared that it had become necessary for the Americans—"one people"—to separate themselves from the British Empire. The Americans argued that their inclusion in the British Empire had repeatedly, and with increasing frequency and mounting pain, entailed a denial of justice, and that they now intended to terminate this relationship through an appeal to arms. Five years of deliberate, violent resistance to British authority ensued, at the end of which 2½ million erstwhile colonists at last succeeded in establishing their legal and political independence.

Even while the War for Independence was in progress, it became clear that there was another aspect to the successful assertion that Americans were "one people." The American nation needed to be defined as distinct from Great Britain; but it needed also to develop an internal rationale and meaning. The nation was born in a violent assertion of its independence; but it could grow only through the development of political and social forms that fostered and exhibited the unity invoked by the Declaration. Thus, the definition of America involved two quite distinct acts of creation: the assertion of independence from foreign domination, and the establishment of free government at home.[1]

It is sometimes said that the former aspect was substantially achieved by 1783, being officially recognized by Britain in the Treaty of Paris that ended the War for American Independence, and that it is the latter task that has given enduring purpose to the American nation. Leaders in the founding generation might have taken issue with the first part of this statement. The struggle over Jay's Treaty in 1795 and the War of 1812 are only the most dramatic illustrations that the substance of American independence was often threatened by the overbearing presence of European nations, especially Great Britain.

Yet if the establishment of national independence provided a continuing challenge to the young nation's diplomats, it was the task of building the foundations of political freedom at home that absorbed its politicians. Perhaps if foreign dangers had been more imminent, or more perpetual, the nation's commitment to corporate unity—and to equality—could have been more readily ignored. Perhaps the demands of national security might have seemed to justify the preservation of existing social hierarchies and the repudiation of the doctrine of equality as utopian and foolish. But America's relative isolation from Europe's entanglements and the inability of foes on its own continent (Indian, Spanish, and French) to mount a serious threat to its existence make an observation by Abraham Lincoln relevant to the founding period: if Americans ever lost their liberty, the culprit would be a failure of national virtue, rather than the hostility of foreign foes.[2]

Even before political independence had been certified by the Treaty of Paris, the nation turned—gradually, hesitantly, often reluctantly—to the other, more fundamental, part of its task: laying the foundations of internal freedom. The effort began with an instrument fashioned under the guns of the Revolutionary War. The Articles of Confederation gave the nation a government that might have been appropriate if corporate unity had already been a reality in the 1780's—which is nearly the same as saying, as Madison wrote in number 51 of *The Federalist*, "If men were angels, no government would be necessary." Confining the national government to certain carefully prescribed functions, the Articles required special majorities for the performance even of these minimal tasks, and required unanimity among the states for conferring additional powers, since such an augmentation of authority could be accomplished only through the amendment of the Articles. While the energies of patriotic Americans were devoted to a task that enjoyed enthusiastic support among the elements that controlled political affairs, as during the early stages of the War for Independence, the defects of government under the Articles were obscured. But as the passion for the struggle against Great Britain cooled, as the costs of that struggle began to mount, and as the states, one after another, in accumulating precedents, defaulted on their support of the national treasury, it became clear that the foundations laid in the Articles were wholly inadequate to support the "separate and equal" nationhood that had been the boast and promise of the Declaration.

The fact that the Articles were inadequate, however, did not make the Constitution of 1787, or any viable national constitution, inevitable. The period of the late 1780's saw a genuine crisis in American affairs,[3] and the fact that the framing and ratification of the Constitution was so hazardous helps to explain the effect of the deliberations of the Constitutional Convention on slavery.

There were at least three basic outlooks among politically active people on the problem of national governmental structure. Men of one persuasion, of whom Richard Henry Lee and George Clinton were perhaps most notable, believed that the Articles of Confederation, properly amended, could provide an adequate frame of government. They tended to disparage the sense of crisis that gripped other men.[4] They wanted to amend the Articles to give Congress real, if severely limited and temporary, powers to raise revenues and regulate trade, powers that would not be quite so dependent upon the voluntary acquiescence of the states. But they rejected the notion that a centralized government could be a fit agency of America's destiny, and they were suspicious of the motives of those who wanted to call separate conventions to consider the question of constitutional reform. This group was probably numerically dominant in the mid-1780's, and was in control of Congress in 1785 and 1786. Though no polls were taken, it is safe to surmise that the normal inertia of public opinion would have induced most people to prefer the tolerable present under the Articles to an uncertain future under either of the two possibilities that suggested themselves to most minds: a powerful national government or multiple confederacies. What Jefferson had written in the Declaration of Independence remained true in 1787: ". . . mankind are more disposed to suffer, while evils are sufferable, than to right themselves by abolishing the forms to which they are accustomed."

But despite this consensus, there were some who were beginning to doubt that the American union could ever be made to work. On the eve of the Federal Convention, James Madison noted that the idea of "partition of the union into three more practicable and energetic governments" was beginning to appear in newspapers.[5] One who did not regard the notion of separation as unthinkable was Theodore Sedgwick, the spirited and influential legislator from western Massachusetts who suggested in a letter to Caleb Strong, later a delegate to the Federal Convention, that "an attempt to perpetuate our connection with [the Southern states] . . . will sacrifice everything to a meer chimera . . . It becomes us," he concluded, "seriously to contemplate a substitute." [6]

A third group believed that fundamental constitutional reforms were both necessary and possible. Even in the spring and summer of 1787, this group probably constituted a small minority of the total population, a minority, perhaps, even among the politically active. And although several leaders of this group (Madison, Hamilton, Dickinson, Mason, Washington) had been working together, both informally, through correspondence and visits in one another's homes, and formally, in Congress and at the Annapolis Convention of 1786, it would be wrong to assume that their ideas, their models of a reformed constitution, had reached a mature form even in their own minds. What drove them toward wanting to reform the national constitution was not so much a compelling vision of national grandeur, as their conviction that the alternatives were unacceptable. Efforts to amend the Articles of Confederation, they were convinced, were vain because the Articles were fundamentally defective. So long as Delaware and Virginia, Rhode Island and Massachusetts had equal weight in the decisions of the union, powerful men in the larger states would be understandably reluctant to commit their resources to the governance of the Confederation. If the government was to have real power to regulate commerce and manage foreign affairs (including tariff policy and the decision to go to war or make peace), a revision in the basis of representation was a primary necessity. Only then would the wealthier, more populous states and regions be willing to grant adequate powers to a national government.

This was half of the "necessity" for a wholly new constitution. The other half came into view when contemplating the leading alternative: partition into multiple (most likely two or three) confederacies. Clinton Rossiter has written, of the reason this idea was rejected by most American politicians of the founding generation:

> The trouble with this possibility . . . was that the jealousy and inertia that made it so difficult to form a "more perfect union" in 1787 would have still been present in 1790 or 1800 to make it almost as difficult to form three more perfect unions in New England, the Middle States, and the South. It is hard to imagine South Carolina knuckling under to Virginia, or Rhode Island to Massachusetts, hard to guess in which direction Maryland or New York would finally have decided to move, not at all ridiculous to conceive of New York City trying to have the best of all possible worlds as a "free city" like Bremen or Lübeck. It is very easy to imagine a condition of continuing instability within each of these clusters of states and, thanks to the rise of new states in the West, of growing hostility between the Middle States and the cluster on either side—all of which may help to explain the sense of urgency that propelled nation-minded men to Philadelphia in 1787.[7]

Perhaps even more than the prospect of internal instability, the thing that made this Balkanization frightening was the invitation it offered to foreign intrigue. The animus against "foreign meddling," reinforced by the conviction that America was blessed by its isolation from Europe's squalid politics, was a powerful feeling in most Americans, and the nationalizers played on it skillfully.[8] In fact, the fear of foreign meddling was probably stronger at this time than the patriotic commitment to the unity of the American nation, and thus a more effective appeal.

So from the nationalist point of view, constitutional reform was necessary. But the *possibility* of such reform, if it existed, lay in the nation's social and economic conditions and in the skill of its leading politicians, particularly in their capacity to fashion governmental forms appropriate to the conditions and attitudes of the country.

American unity was encouraged by a common cultural heritage among the dominant white population. Of that population, over 60 per cent were of English descent; nearly 20 per cent were either Scotch, Irish, or some combination of the two; and most of the remaining 20 per cent were either German or Dutch, the former heavily concentrated in Pennsylvania, the latter in New York and New Jersey. Most of these Americans were middle-class farmers, and almost all who cared or knew anything about politics subscribed to the tradition of political ideas loosely called Lockean liberalism, in which the fundamental notions of private property and "republican government" were embedded beyond controversy.

Two other factors nourished the drive toward national integration. One was the shared memory of the Revolutionary War. Politicians who were close to the management of this war knew that it had not always been a glorious undertaking, that patriotic commitment had been an occasional thing for almost everyone involved, and that the frailty of the bonds of union had been brutally exposed, time and again. Still, independence had been successfully asserted against the most powerful nation on earth, and there were not many breasts in America so cold as not to be stirred by that achievement. The second factor was the belief that the American states complemented one another. Some observers might regard the differing interests of the states as a sign of certain trouble ahead. Josiah Tucker, a British clergyman, after analyzing the different habits and "clashing" interests of the various regions of the country, concluded that the "fate [of the Americans] seems to be—a DISUNITED PEOPLE, till the end of time." [9] But most Americans drew another lesson from the plain and incontrovertible facts of diversity. The words of George Washington, written with the help of Madison and Hamilton, the leading nationalists of 1787, illustrate this:

. . . every portion of our country finds the most commanding motives for carefully guarding and preserving the union of the whole.

The *North* . . . finds in the production of [the *South*], great additional resources of maritime and commercial enterprise and precious materials of manufacturing industry. The *South* . . . benefitting by the agency of the *North,* sees its agriculture grow and its commerce expand. . . . The *East,* in a like intercourse with the *West,* already finds, and in the progressive improvement of interior communications, by land and water, will more and more find a valuable vent for the commodities which it brings from abroad, or manufactures at home. The *West* derives from the *East* supplies requisite to its growth and comfort . . . [and owes] the *secure* enjoyment of indispensable *outlets* for its own productions to the weight, influence, and future maritime strength of the Atlantic side of the union. . . .[10]

To the nationalists, American diversity was not an obstacle to union, but another incentive to it.

Additionally, there were certain dynamic factors in the economic and social substructure. Gradually, the economy of the country was beginning to knit together and to nationalize. Bray Hammond, the leading student of the history of banking in the United States, has observed that the three banks in existence when the Constitution was being framed—the Bank of North America in Philadelphia, the Bank of New York, and the Massachusetts Bank at Boston—did almost all their business with local merchants and depositors. It was not until after 1800 that these and other state banks began to do much business across state lines.[11] This reminder of the primitiveness of interstate economic intercourse is pertinent. Yet as the style of life in the states began to grow in complexity, there came to be greater and greater call for goods produced in or imported through other states.[12] To satisfy these demands, roads were being built, and the harbors of New York, Philadelphia, and Baltimore were dispatching more and more ships to ports on the North American mainland.

Another important spur to nationalization, and an evidence of its increasing attraction to certain spirits, was the speculation by wealthy men in western land. Several of the leading nationalists at the Convention—among them Washington, Mason, Gorham, and Gerry—owned large tracts beyond the coastal fringe.[13] The interest of these and others like them had moved the Congress of the Confederation to create a "national domain," so that these territories might be developed under the governance, not of the several states, but of the central government. The establishment of the national domain is cited by admirers of the Confederation as one of the great achievements of Congress during this period,[14] though from their standpoint it is an ironic one, since it strengthened the forces that demanded the replacement of the Articles of Confederation with a firmer instrument of national control.

In the final analysis, though, there was another factor more significant than these fragile hints and foretastes of the development of a national economy: the emergence of a genuine national political elite. However the case may be with modern "new nations," in the United States, political nationalization was far ahead of economic, cultural, and social nationalization. The central incubator of this elite was the national Congress, a place where, for more than a decade, leading men from the states had gathered to transact political business. To be sure, many delegates to Congress were determined to preserve the "sovereignty" of the states, to keep a firm foot on the brake as far as momentum toward national authority was concerned. The experience of the Confederation—dogged by interstate rivalries, resentments, and fears, and often powerless to discharge its responsibilities—was enough to discourage the patriotism of all but the most firmly committed and patient nationalists. But in the end, the simple fact of the existence of Congress as a convening ground for politicians concerned about the nation's welfare had drawn together an elite who had caught a vision of national destiny and who were sustained in this vision by the knowledge that other men in other states shared it. Thus, when the opportunity for a constitutional convention ripened in 1786 and 1787, Madison and Hamilton, John Rutledge, Oliver Ellsworth, Rufus King, and Gouverneur Morris knew of one another's existence and sympathies and were prepared to act.[15]

But if events and circumstances seemed to create an occasion suitable to the purposes of the nationalists, these same events conditioned the occasion and restricted the opportunities presented. On the matter of developing "nationality," for example, while it was true that the social and economic conditions for trust and confidence between the states were emerging, these same conditions created nearly equal pressures on the other side. The economic recovery in South Carolina made the leaders of that state confident that they could hold their own in national councils, but it must also have encouraged confidence that the state could go its own way if necessary. Certainly prosperity in New York State had had this effect on the thinking of its leaders. And if foreign "embarrassments" provoked a strong will to national union, they also increased suspicion among the states. Many Southerners believed that John Jay's willingness to concede American rights to navigate the lower Mississippi River reflected his inadequate solicitude for Southern and Western interests. New Englanders, for their part, could not see why some men wanted to risk war with powerful European nations in order to assert the right to carry a few boatloads of grain into the Gulf of Mexico, particularly when the alternative was to obtain favorable commercial relations with these nations. And while many men saw in Shays' Rebellion a demand for greater firmness in protecting the rights of property, others must have been apprehensive about the ways in which greater governmental force might be applied in future situations. Therefore, while the events and developments of the 1780's helped the demand for firmer national government, they also sowed suspicion between the states and sections and strengthened the insistence on carefully proscribed powers.

The understanding that national union had no chance of acceptance unless it commanded widespread, virtually unanimous support among leaders in the various states also conditioned the opportunity of 1787. At every critical juncture during the summer of that year, delegates were reminded that the solutions adopted would eventually have to run the gamut of ratification, and everyone knew that ratification, to be satisfactory, would eventually have to be unanimous. The visions of America's future that impelled the various delegates might be as different as New York City and Monticello, but no frame of government that failed to allow for both stood any chance of gaining the necessary consent of the American people in 1788.

Such, by 1787, was the setting. A widely dispersed group of experienced politicians, the energetic "young men of the Revolution," [16] had given up on the Articles of Confederation, but were committed, by sentiment and by calculation, to the cause of union among the American states, and were firm in their conviction that the union, to survive, required more powerful national government. Events seemed to play into the hands of these men in the late 1780's. But their opportunity was conditioned by the presence and determination of a counterelite, men who were genuinely fearful of centralized government, who tended to identify central authority with tyranny, and who feared that a more centralized constitution might gradually substitute Americans for King George and his advisers. In the view of these men, the states were the primary guardians of domestic happiness. No government that sought to preserve and foster happiness in America would want to interfere with the responsibility of state government to promote and protect the domestic happiness of its citizens.

When the Convention began its work, it was generally believed that the question of representation would divide the states according to size. The very terms of the issue—should representation be apportioned according to population or assigned to the states equally?—suggest that more populous states, the ones with most to gain by a change from the latter arrangement, would be pitted against less populous states, who would have most to lose. This impression is partially confirmed by the debate and votes in the Convention: Virginia, Pennsylvania, and Massachusetts, the three most populous states, contributed most of the support, in argument and in votes, to the drive for representation apportioned according to population; while New Jersey, Delaware, and Connecticut, three of the smallest states, led the opposition, insisting that the states remain equally represented in at least one branch of the legislature.

Yet there were significant deviations from this tidy picture. South Carolina, a state no more populous than Connecticut, provided staunch, unwavering support for the demand for proportioned representation. And the least populous state in the union, Georgia, stood on the same side, insisting that states be weighted

177

according to their relative populations. On the other side, New York, a huge and certainly a fast-growing state, insisted on states' equality in the legislative branch.

Close examination of the debates and votes reveals that the large-state–small-state explanation of the struggle that led to the Great Compromise of July 16, 1787, is superficial and misleading, leaving essential matters in the political situation of the Convention, and of the larger political setting, entirely out of account. It was James Madison who tried to get the Convention to consider a more substantial analysis of the stakes in the conflict. He repeatedly stressed that sectional considerations were more fundamental than the large-state–small-state dichotomy that mattered so much to the delegates from New York, New Jersey, and Delaware. He emphasized that the three most populous states in the union —Massachusetts, Pennsylvania, and Virginia—were divided, not drawn together, by their fundamental interests. In situation, in "manners, religion, and the other circumstances which sometimes beget affection between different communities," and in staple productions, he noted, "they were as dissimilar as any three other states in the union."

He admitted that every peculiar interest, whether in any class of citizens, or any description of states, ought to be secured as far as possible. . . . But he contended that the states were divided into different interests, not by their difference of size, but by other circumstances; the most material of which resulted partly from climate, but principally from the effects of their having or not having slaves. These two causes concurred in forming the great division of interests in the United States. It did not lie between the large and small states; it lay between the Northern and Southern.[17]

Later, in the Federalist Papers, he wrote that "in republican governments, the legislative authority necessarily predominates." Since "the principal task of modern legislation" was the regulation of property, it was on the substantial interests of the nation, not the size of the states, that the attention of delegates should focus in considering the composition of the legislature. A state's stake in a piece of legislation would be determined by its interests, its interests in large measure by its productions, and its productions by the effects of "having or not having slaves." Thus, "slavery and its consequences" drew the basic "line of discrimination" through the union's middle.[18]

He stressed the sectional analysis in part because it was strategically important for him, a Virginian, to counteract the impression that the effort to relate representation to population was a power play by the three largest states. Many Southern politicians were wary of the sometimes imperious Old Dominion, just as men in Connecticut and Rhode Island found the politicians of Massachusetts overbearing, and leaders in Delaware and New Jersey watched Pennsylvania and New York with a timorous eye. Unless these constellations of attitudes could be broken up, it would be impossible to revise the formula of representation, and consequently impossible to revamp the nation's constitution of government. So Madison consistently directed attention to substantial interests.

It should not come as a surprise to learn that his analysis had the greatest impact on the thinking of the Southerners present, for, in sectional terms, it was they who had the most to gain from the switch to proportional representation. Under the Confederation, each state had one vote in Congress. The five states south of the Mason-Dixon Line[19] had about 38 per cent of the representation in the old Congress. Even if representation in the new Congress was limited to free inhabitants, the South would have been entitled to 41 per cent of the seats in Congress—about twenty-six of sixty-four seats.

But no delegate seriously thought that the South would accept a constitution in which there would be no representation at all for slaves. However many protests there were against the idea of representation for slaves (or, more precisely, an increment to slave owners for the slaves they owned), nearly every national politician had by 1787 grown used to the fact that slaves, as wealth-producing elements in the body politic, had to be represented in some proportion to free men. When it came to specifying that proportion, most thought in terms of the federal ratio, counting five slaves as the equivalent of three free men; by this formula, the South taken as a whole would have been entitled to 47 per cent of the seats in Congress. A few of the delegates[20] thought slaves should be counted equally with free men. Since the Mason-

TABLE III. SOUTHERN SHARE OF CONGRESSIONAL REPRESENTATION,
UNDER VARIOUS SCHEMES

SCHEME	TOTAL UNITS	SOUTHERN SHARE	SOUTHERN PERCENTAGE
Articles of Confederation	13	5	38%
"Quotas of contribution" (1785)*	92¾	38½	41.3%
Total inhabitants (1790) (slaves equal to freemen)	3,929,000	1,962,000	49.9%
Free inhabitants (1790) (slaves not counted)	3,231,000	1,304,000	41%
Federal ratio (1790) (5 slaves equal to 3 free men)	3,651,000	1,700,000	46.5%
Actual apportionments:			
Senate in 1789	13	5	38%
in 1792	15	6	40%
in January 1820†	22	11	50%
House in 1789	65	29	44.6%
after census of 1790	105	47	44.8%
after census of 1820†	213	90	42.3%

* Adapted from Winton U. Solberg, ed., *The Federal Convention* (Indianapolis, Ind.: Bobbs-Merrill, 1958), pp. 407–408.

† In 1790 Delaware was usually considered a mid-Atlantic, not a Southern, state. By 1820, the basic division in the union was bipolar, and Delaware was grouped with the "slave-states," that is, with those which were not committed to abolition within their own jurisdiction.

Dixon Line divided the combined free and slave populations of America almost exactly in half,[21] the formula equating slaves with free men would have given the South almost 50 per cent of the seats in Congress. Thus any move in the direction of proportional representation would have increased the voting power of the South.

But more lay behind the Southern drive for weighted representation than is revealed by a static analysis of the situation as of 1790. Southern insistence on such representation was strongly reinforced by an expectation, frequently expressed by Northerners and Southerners alike, and never contradicted, that population was drifting in a "southwestwardly" direction.

The people are constantly swarming from the more to the less populous places [said Madison], from Europe to America, from the Northern and Middle parts of the United States to the Southern and Western. They go where land is cheaper, because there labor is dearer.[22]

Although estimates available to the delegates could show that Georgia had less than half the population of New Hampshire, and that South Carolina was smaller than Connecticut, these were not the calculations that guided them, particularly those from the South. With a view both to the present situation, where the Southern inhabitants of the union, composing half of the total population, lived in just five of the thirteen states, and to the future, where anticipated drifts of population were expected to add support for Southern interests, Southern delegates strongly favored a revision in the direction of proportional representation.

From the beginning of the Convention, in late May 1787, the delegates who intended to demand that representation be proportioned according to population had both the reigning "public philosophy" and the votes in the Convention on their side. The public philosophy, as it related to this question, was best summarized by James Wilson. "As all authority was derived from the people, equal numbers of people ought to have an equal number of representatives, and different numbers of people different numbers of representatives." [23] According to this view, the best way to insure that governmental policy would be responsive to the opinions and interests of the people was to put the power of lawmaking into the hands of men elected from districts that contained roughly the same number of people. Madison added that the new government would have to draw its support from the people, not from states as such. If this support was to be freely and reliably given, citizens of the most populous states would have to know that their voices in lawmaking were commensurate with their responsibility for its support.[24]

As far as Convention politics were concerned, those who believed that proportional representation should be introduced into the national government were supported by at least four of the Southern states (Maryland being the only doubtful one), plus Massachusetts and Pennsylvania. This gave them six, sometimes seven, votes, a preponderance strengthened by the fact that Rhode Island and New Hampshire were unrepresented while this question was being debated and decided, and by the contributions of the delegation from Connecticut, which contained men who were willing, even eager, to introduce this principle, properly counterbalanced, into the national government.

On May 29, Edmund Randolph, Governor of Virginia, presented to the Convention a series of resolutions drafted by the Virginia delegation. The second resolution went right to the heart of the matter: "Resolved . . . that the rights of suffrage in the national legislature ought to be proportioned to the quotas of contribution, or to the number of free inhabitants, as the one or the other rule may seem best in different cases." [25] The rest of the resolutions, fifteen in all, gave preliminary outlines of a constitutional structure that could, in the Virginians' view, be raised on the foundation of a national legislature whose representation was "proportioned."

As it turned out, Randolph's resolution on representation contained two major sources of controversy. Not only did it startle and provoke men committed to the notion that states, to maintain their "sovereignty," had to remain equal in the councils of the nation; it also invited an argument between those who wanted representation proportioned according to population and those who wanted to tie representation directly to wealth.

Though it was apparent that the proponents of proportional representation were dominant in the Convention,[26] by the middle of June it was equally clear that there was another faction which was determined to gain institutional guarantees for the preservation of states, and that this faction, though certainly a minority, would have to be satisfied if the Constitution was to obtain the necessary ratifications.[27] Once it was determined that there would be two houses in the national legislature, it seemed almost inevitable that one branch would reflect the ideas of the Virginians, while the other would reflect the determination to retain the states as distinct guardians of particular ways of life. This solution is sometimes called the "Great (or Connecticut) Compromise." It was hinted at by John Dickinson as early as June 2, proposed by Roger Sherman on June 11, and again by William Samuel Johnson and Oliver Ellsworth on June 29, and finally adopted on July 16. The only alternative to proportional representation acceptable to the small-state men was the "complete abolition of the state governments." Only so could Delaware and New Jersey be saved from their larger neighbors.[28] But of course the main proponents of weighted representation, the delegates from the South, would not listen seriously to this proposal. Therefore the Great Compromise provided the only satisfactory formula.

But if the argument that ended in the Great Compromise was cast in terms that obscured political reality and ended in the only possible way (if the Convention was to succeed in framing a constitution), the controversy over the basis for apportionment in the lower house was neither obscure in terms nor inevitable in outcome. It reflected the most serious differences of situation and opinion in the union, and its resolution was a matter for real negotiation. Involved in this dispute were the questions of the relationship of wealth to political right, the value of slavery to the political economy of the country, and the role of the West in America's future. In 1787, there were no more important questions.

The main debates on the terms of apportionment occurred during the second week in July. A committee chaired by Elbridge Gerry, of Massachusetts, was asked to frame, over the Fourth of July recess, a proposal that would break the deadlock of July 2, when the Convention had come to a full stop over the whole question of representation. Gerry's committee reported on July 5. Without dissent, it proposed that representation in the lower house be proportioned according to population, counting five slaves as three free men, that in the second branch each state have an equal vote, and that revenue and appropriation acts originate in the lower house and be passed or rejected by the upper house without alteration or amendment.[29]

The first clause was the one that absorbed the Convention's attention the ensuing week. In detail, it provided that each state be given one seat in the House of Representatives for each 40,000 inhabitants, with slaves being tallied according to the federal ratio. A dispute over this formula had been bubbling just beneath the surface throughout the month of June, and had threatened to erupt at least twice.[30] Each time, however, unity among proponents of proportional representation had been preferred, and the argument about the details of the ratio had been postponed until the principle of proportional representation itself had been established. Now, as the Convention moved to consider the first clause of the Gerry report, the issue had to be faced.

The argument over the federal ratio occurred in the context of a fundamental disagreement about the appropriate theoretical and practical basis for representation in a republican regime, a disagreement that derives from an ambiguity about what deserves, or needs, to be represented. Among the outspoken advocates of proportional representation at the Convention, there were two rather distinct approaches. One group, who can be called the "theoretical" republicans, developed the notion that all men are equally entitled to consent to the powers that rule them. "All men," as Wilson put it, "wherever placed, have equal rights, and are equally entitled to confidence." [31] Seeing the legislature as a mirror of society, this group argued that all members of society should be weighted equally in the attempt to construct a faithful mirror. No one, with the possible exception of Franklin, would have taken this position to its logical conclusion: insisting that women and blacks be permitted to vote. What they did insist upon was the general principle that representation be proportioned according to population, so that equal numbers of people, each choosing a single person to represent them, would have equal weight in the lawmaking process. Within the districts, different rules might obtain regarding the right to vote. Prudence dictated that the national government not try to standardize the qualifications for suffrage throughout the country. The important thing was the Constitutional guarantee that equal numbers of people have equal representation in the federal government.

The other approach, espoused by "realistic" republicans, developed a different, though perhaps equally fundamental, emphasis in the Lockean tradition: the notion that governments are instituted for the protection of property. It follows from this principle that control over the government should be given to those whose property most needs protection. Egalitarians might respond that all men have property that needs protection —property in their lives and their liberties, if not in estate. But realists regarded this view as romantic in origin and catastrophic in consequence. Certainly every man was entitled to his life and liberties. The question was how to erect a government that could be relied upon to protect these precious holdings, and to create and maintain an environment in which they would be worth holding. The proper answer was to entrust it to men with the greatest property, or "stake," in its stability and preservation. The greater a man's stake, the readier he would be to make sacrifices for the common safety. The greater his stake, the greater capacity he had shown for the management of affairs. The greater his stake, the more reason he had to insist that the government's energies be devoted to the protection of property, its just and true purpose, rather than to other purposes less compatible with human liberty.

In this view, the basic reason for the feebleness of the United States under the Articles was that men of property did not trust it. Puny, riotous little Rhode Island had the same share in the determination of policies as magnificent, serene South Carolina. This was unjust, for if the policies of the government led to conflicts with foreign nations, or to the collapse of the domestic economy, the suffering and loss would be wholly disproportionate. Furthermore, such calamities would be far less likely to occur if affairs were in the hands of those who had a demonstrated capacity to manage their own affairs and guide them toward prosperity. Therefore both justice and good policy demanded that weight in the government be assigned according to wealth.

South Carolinians were among the most prominent realistic republicans. Pierce Butler put their position this way: government "was instituted principally for the protection of property and was itself . . . supported by property." Property was "the great object of government; the great cause of war; the great means of carrying it on." Therefore, since "money was power . . . the states ought to have weight in the government in proportion to their wealth." [32]

But the South Carolinians were not alone. Rufus King gave the

New Englanders' version of the argument: "The number of inhabitants was not the proper index of ability and wealth. Property was the primary object of society. In fixing a ratio, this ought not to be excluded from the estimate." [33] Gouverneur Morris was another who "thought property ought to be taken into the estimate as well as the number of inhabitants." He was candid about his reasons.

He thought the rule of representation ought to be so fixed as to secure to the Atlantic states a prevalence in the national councils. The new states will know less of the public interest. . . . Provision ought therefore to be made to prevent the maritime states from hereafter being outvoted by them.[34]

In his mind, the issue of popular representation always raised the question of the safety of "maritime" interests in a nation dominated by farmers. Alluding to the expected drift of population in a southwestward direction, he drew the consequences from his point of view:

It has been said that North Carolina, South Carolina, and Georgia, only, will in a little time have a majority of the people in America. The consequence of such a transfer of power from the maritime to the interior and landed interest will . . . be . . . an oppression of commerce. . . . If the Southern states get the power into their hands, and be joined as they will be with the interior country, they will inevitably bring on a war with Spain for the Mississippi. . . .[35]

Curiously, despite Morris's identification of South Carolina as party to this plot against commerce, John Rutledge seems to have shared his apprehension.[36] The enthusiasm of the planter-merchants of Charleston for a revised and strengthened federal constitution stemmed in part from their fear that the yeomen of western South Carolina might seize control of the state government. To overcome this danger, they hoped to confide certain powers to the federal government, and, by allying themselves with merchants from the North, to exercise them in a way favorable to their interests.[37] The problem with this recourse was that it might open the way to even greater dangers. Hence, the strategy of Rutledge and the Pinckneys at the Convention was to work for a strong federal government, then confine it to the exercise of certain well-defined powers, mainly in the area of foreign commerce, defense, and finance.

This fissure in the ranks of those favoring a change to proportional representation is worth noting, because it foreshadowed a cleavage that reappeared in the next decade, in the form of a struggle between two political parties. The division in 1787 was between the group led by Madison and Wilson, who wanted representation to be based on numbers of inhabitants, and the group that included Butler, Rutledge, Morris, and King, who insisted that representation and taxation be based on a formula that included both wealth and population—Butler and Rutledge because they feared the West, Morris and King because they feared the agrarians in both South and West. The agreement between Morris, King, and the South Carolinians on this issue foreshadowed the Federalist alliance fashioned by Hamilton during the first few years under the Constitution. These men shared two basic political goals: the encouragement of American commerce, especially shipping, and the maintenance of political advantage over agricultural interests in the interior regions of their own states. Westward migration threatened both of these purposes and drove the nascent Federalists into one another's arms.

One concrete issue that was approached differently by theoretical and realistic republicans was the weight that should be given to slaves in the formula for apportionment. From the viewpoint of theoretical republicanism, slaves, not being constituent members of society, deserved no representation in the legislature at all.[38] Sometimes, however, they tried to argue that slaves, despite their bondage, partook to some degree of humanity, and were thus entitled to some degree of representation.[39] This rationale failed for two reasons: it was ridiculous in republican theory to try to put a fractional value on humanity, and the three-fifths compromise did not provide representation for slaves, but for slave owners. Notwithstanding its affront to their principles, most theoretical republicans accepted the three-fifths compromise in order to reach agreement on a formula for basing representation on population.

For realistic republicans, the problem was different. If numbers of people were to be accepted as a measure of wealth, the reason must be that where people were, there also would be productivity. But how was the productivity of a slave to be compared with the productivity of a free man? In 1783, when the question at issue was the capacity of states to contribute to the nation's treasury, it seemed to many Southerners that the productivity of slaves was not very great, while Northerners professed to believe that slaves performed prodigies of labor. Now, of course, the positions were reversed. Since the main factor at stake was weight in the formula of representation, Southern realists, especially the South Carolinians, wanted equal representation for their slaves, while Northerners began to insinuate that the "wealth" of the South had been greatly overestimated.[40] In these Northern eyes, slavery seemed a canceled asset: their labor produced national wealth, particularly in the form of staples for export, but their presence constituted a standing invitation to foreign intrigue and a proven weakness in times of invasion.

If the union was to survive, it was obvious that these positions would have to be compromised. The locus of compromise likewise was obvious. The federal ratio had by 1787 become "the language of all America," as Rufus King put it. This did not mean that slaves would be represented in the legislature at the ratio of three-fifths, but that a slave owner would gain a three-fifths increment in representation for each slave he owned. Thus, a slave owner who owned five slaves would have four units of representation, while his fellow countryman who owned five horses or five ships would have one. To many Northerners, this seemed a high price to pay for American union. Judge William Paterson, of New Jersey, and others noted that it would encourage the slave trade.[41] James Wilson feared that it would "disgust" the people of Pennsylvania. Rufus King worried that Northerners in their ratifying conventions would find it "intolerable," particularly in the context of other concessions to the South. And Gouverneur Morris, calling it "the most prominent feature in the aristocratic countenance of the proposed Constitution," predicted that Pennsylvanians would never accept it.[42] Yet once the decision had been made to tie representation to population, the federal ratio seemed to both theoretical and realistic republicans a natural compromise.

. . .

As soon as the Convention moved to consider the first clause of the Gerry Committee report—which provided that "each of the states *now in the Union* shall be allowed one member [in the lower house] for every 40,000 inhabitants," counting five slaves as three free men[43]—the difference between the two strands of republicanism came immediately into view. Gouverneur Morris spoke first, asking whether an apportionment based on numbers alone would produce a legislature that could be trusted to respect property. He doubted it, and his doubts hardened into conviction when he contemplated "that range of new states which would soon be formed in the West." [44] Rutledge shared the same fears. He proposed that the report be put aside, and moved that seats in Congress be allotted on the basis of "sums to be paid towards the general revenue by . . . each state respectively." Two Virginians, Mason and Randolph, warned that "unfavorable discriminations" against new states would alienate the inhabitants of the frontier from the new government. A vote was taken on Rutledge's substitute, and it received only one favorable vote, South Carolina's.[45]

The next morning Morris tried a new tack. He moved to recommit the first clause of the Gerry Committee report, and suggested that the new committee "absolutely fix the number for each state in the first instance, leaving the legislature at liberty to provide for changes in the relative importance of the states, and for the case of new states." [46] Supporting this motion, several delegates expressed the view that property—the "great," 'primary' object of society—was "the only just measure of representation," and that population figures should be tempered by estimates of wealth in apportioning representation.

Before the vote was taken on the motion, Charles Pinckney reminded the Convention of the difficulty of comparing the value of real estate and other property in the several states. Aside from any objections to Morris's suggestion from the viewpoint of the theoretical republicans, the political consideration he mentioned was a substantial obstacle to its realization as a basis for government in the American union. If representation was to be proportioned according to wealth, it would be necessary to agree on standards for measuring the comparative value of different kinds of property in different parts of the country. The same problem had dogged the effort to distribute the burden of taxation under the Articles of Confederation.

There was a significant difference between the problem that confronted the Congress of the Confederation and the proposal offered at Philadelphia by the realistic republicans. Article VIII of the Confederation dealt only with taxation, and so there was an unbalanced interest in underestimating the relative worth of a region. Some believed that the proposed clause in the new constitution could avoid that difficulty by tying both taxation and representation to the same census. Thus, the estimate of a state's wealth would determine its representation in Congress, which would encourage a high estimate, but would also determine its share of direct taxes, which would encourage a low estimate.

Against this argument, several delegates pointed out that direct taxes were not likely to loom very large in the finances of the new government.[47] Besides, linking the two considerations might remove the motive for biased estimates, but it did not make it much easier to construct fair ones. It would still be all but impossible to compare the value of a planter's mansion in South Carolina and a lawyer's residence in Boston, or of 200 acres planted with tobacco in Virginia and the same-sized plot producing wheat in Pennsylvania, or of a small "manufactory" in the Delaware Valley and a fleet of fishing boats based at Gloucester, Massachusetts. If the new government was saddled with the problem of making the assessments, it might never be able to surmount the difficulty that brought the government of the Confederation to its knees: the problem of raising a revenue. Even if the text of the Constitution included a formula for representation in the first House of Representatives—as it eventually did—the struggle to revise this apportionment every decade might well drain the authority of the federal government to the point where it would be impotent to govern the country.

When the vote was taken on Morris's motion, a strong majority favored commitment. A committee of five was accordingly appointed. Mason then suggested that the clause on suffrage in the Senate be given to this committee, too, but Randolph noted that

this would be unfair, since the committee "consisted of members
from states opposed to the wishes of the smaller states." [48] Indeed
it did. Chaired by Morris, of Pennsylvania, the committee contained a Virginian (Randolph), a South Carolinian (Rutledge),
and the two delegates from Massachusetts most firmly committed
to proportional representation (King and Gorham).[49] It should
also be noted that this committee contained a majority of men—
Morris, King, and Rutledge—who were strongly suspicious of the
West.

The committee reported on July 9. Its report consisted of two
parts. The first established an initial allotment of seats in the
lower house for each of the thirteen states. The second provided
that subsequent apportionments be made by Congress "upon the
principles of their wealth and number of inhabitants"—a deliberately vague formula.

A close examination of the report reveals that Morris had had
his way. It conforms exactly to the specifications he had outlined
earlier. The burden of explaining it fell to Nathaniel Gorham
who performed his duty faithfully but without enthusiasm. He
noted that, under a strictly numerical apportionment, ' the Western states . . . might . . . by degrees outvote the Atlantic." The
arrangement in the report obviated this objection: "The Atlantic
states, having the government in their own hands, may take care
of their own interest by dealing out the right of representation in
safe proportions to the Western states." [50]

Opening the consideration of the report, Morris and Rutledge
quickly moved that the first clause be postponed, in order to proceed directly to the more fundamental second clause. The vote on
this, which followed immediately, showed only New York and
New Jersey in the negative. Morris must have been happy and
proud of his coup. Sherman then moved that the first clause be
sent to a committee composed of a member from each state. Morris graciously seconded the motion, reinforcing the impression
that his real pride of paternity lay with the second clause.

Before this grand committee was chosen, several delegates took
the opportunity to indicate that they were not satisfied with the
principle of apportionment established by the quick vote just
taken. Randolph noted that "as the number was not to be

changed till the national legislature should please, a pretext would never be wanting to postpone alterations and keep the power in the hands of those possessed of it." [51] Although he had been a member of Morris's committee, he had apparently not realized the full implications of the formula. Further reflection (or, more likely, another, wiser, head) had cast light on the uses for which the Morris formula was intended once power was committed to the hands of the seaboard politicians. Now Randolph, in his rather ponderous way, was having second thoughts, and, before he was through, formulas born of his suspicion would prevail over Morris's deft stroke.

Another who saw the stakes involved in Morris's formula was Judge Paterson. Somewhat disingenuously, he called the rule for reapportionment "too vague." Gorham, in explaining the report had said that "the number of blacks and whites, with some regard to supposed wealth, was the general guide." Paterson now said that he "could regard negro slaves in no light but as property. They are no free agents, have no personal liberty, no faculty of acquiring property, but on the contrary, are themselves property, and like other property [are] entirely at the will of the master." He argued that according to "the true principles of representation," legislative assemblies were "an expedient" used when a body of citizens, too large to meet conveniently together, sent representatives as their "substitutes." Since slaves would not attend a meeting of citizens, they should not be represented in the nation's legislative assembly.

Though appealing in many respects, this argument was beside the point. The furthest thing from Rutledge's mind was to grant representation in the national legislature to slaves. What he did contend for was the principle that, inasmuch as slaves represented wealth, slave *owners* were entitled to an increment of representation for each slave they owned. Sherman understood this distinction. Later in the summer, when Morris and King complained that their constituents would never consent to the representation of slaves, he responded, "It was the freemen of the Southern states who were in fact to be represented according to the taxes paid by them. The negroes are only included in the estimates of taxes." [52]

Gerry understood, too. His response was to ask, if slave owners

192

deserved an increment for their property, why was he not entitled to one for his horses? There was invincible logic in his point, and he and several others (Wilson, King, Morris) had a lot of fun with it as the summer progressed.[53] But in the end, five of Rutledge's slaves counted the same as three of Gerry's constituents, and Gerry's horses counted for naught.

Responding "warmly" to Paterson's challenge, Butler "urged . . . the justice and necessity of regarding wealth in the apportionment of representation." King, wary lest a wedge be driven between the proponents of proportional representation, quickly acknowledged that the Southern states were "the richest," and said that "unless some respect were paid to their superior wealth," they would not join a union that promised "preferential distribution . . . and other advantages" to Northern commerce.[54] With these warning shots fired, an affirmative vote sent the initial allotment to a committee of eleven (one delegate from each state in attendance), with King as chairman.

The following morning, the committee reported a proposed allotment of seats in the First Congress. The ensuing scramble for increment exposed clearly the fact that the delegates thought in sectional terms. The difference between the Morris Committee report of July 9 and the King Committee report of July 10 was that the latter provided for nine additional seats—to a total of sixty-five—with five of the new seats going to Northern states (one each to New Hampshire, Massachusetts, Connecticut, New York, and New Jersey) and four to Southern states (two to Maryland, one each to Virginia and Georgia). This meant that the South, which had 45 per cent of the earlier allotment, got only 44 per cent with the increment—a difference that may seem trivial, but was not so regarded by Southerners, inasmuch as it represented movement in the wrong direction, from their standpoint.

Rutledge's assault on the report was a little devious. He moved that New Hampshire be reduced from three seats to two, and was seconded by Charles Cotesworth Pinckney, who then led the attack for the slaveholders. He predicted that, if the Southern states were so badly outnumbered in Congress, and if the regulation of commerce was turned over to the national government, Southerners would become "nothing more than overseers for the

Northern states." Hugh Williamson, of North Carolina, agreed, saying, "The Southern interest must be extremely endangered by the present arrangement. The Northern States are to have a majority in the first instance, and the means of perpetuating it." King leaped to the defense of his committee's report.

He was fully convinced that the question concerning a difference of interests did not lie where it had hitherto been discussed, between the great and small states, but between Southern and Eastern. For this reason he had been willing to yield something in the proportion of representatives for the security of the Southern. No principle would justify giving them a majority. They were brought as near an equality as was possible.

He hinted that other securities for slaveholders might be written into the Constitution, but said that no further ground could be yielded on the question of representation. Morris added that

[T]he Southern states have by the report more than their share of representation. Property ought to have its weight, but not all the weight. . . . [T]he possible revenue to be expected from the Southern states has been greatly overrated.[55]

He meant by his remark to suggest that the word "wealth," which the South Carolinians used as a euphemism for "slaves," was sometimes a misleading term in this connection. While he agreed that large holdings of slaves indicated great wealth on the rice flats near Charleston, he knew that the slaves who planted tobacco in the weary soil of Virginia and North Carolina were less certain symbols of wealth. Another reason for trusting South Carolinians, while fearing Virginians and North Carolinians, was that the nabobs of Charleston were often not only planters, but merchants as well.

Morris intended to convince the Southerners that nothing was to be gained from upsetting the King Committee agreement. In order to protect his victory of July 9, he knew that he had to prevent a sectional clash and restore a mood of trust and unanimity among the proponents of proportional representation. Despite his efforts, a series of motions followed whereby the Southern delegates sought to increase the representation of North Carolina, South Carolina, or Georgia. Each time, the three southernmost states voted "aye." Each time, they were outvoted by the states to the north. A final vote, 9 to 2, confirmed the King Committee apportionment, South Carolina and Georgia casting the negative votes.[56]

This unseemly scramble among the states was resolved only by the preponderant voting power of the North. Many wondered whether Congress could endure the strains that might attend a similar struggle in the future. If this contest had been preceded by months of bargaining for support, and if it had been conducted before public galleries, the wounds might have been deep and dangerous. George Mason put the point this way: "The greater the difficulty we find in fixing a proper rule of representation, the more unwilling ought we to be to throw the task from ourselves, on the general legislature." [57]

Randolph now indicated that his suspicions regarding Morris's formula were beginning to take shape. As an amendment to the provision that House seats be apportioned "upon the principles of their wealth and number of inhabitants," he moved that a "census and estimate" be taken regularly "to ascertain the alterations in the population and wealth of the several states," and "that the legislature arrange the representation accordingly." Morris's reaction was sharp and candid.

[He] opposed it as fettering the legislature too much. . . . He was always against such shackles on the legislature. He dwelt much on the danger of throwing such a preponderancy into the Western scale, suggesting that in time the Western people would outnumber the Atlantic states. He wished therefore to put it in the power of the latter to keep a majority of votes in their own hands.[58]

On this note, the Convention adjourned for the day, and Randolph and his friends went back to their rooms to consider their course of action.

It was by now clear that the fissure among the proponents of proportional representation could not be wished away. Morris's formula was *not* a way of papering over the fissure, but was in fact an instrument of his own position. Morris and his allies— King, Gerry, Butler, and Rutledge—were convinced that the destiny of the American nation lay in the direction of commercial development. To pursue this destiny, they believed, government should be committed to the property owners in the community. The only way to insure this commitment was to arrange for "property" to be represented proportionately. They were not dismayed by the suggestion that the wealth of various sections was impossible to compare. In their view, wealthy men knew how to assess wealth. Thus, if the government was committed to wealthy men (or wealthy, productive regions) in the first place, and if these men were not "shackled" with rigid reapportionment formulas, the government would remain safely in their hands.

Morris repeatedly stressed that his concern was for "the good of America." Nor did his concern end at the boundaries. "He came here as a representative of America; he flattered himself he came here in some degree as a representative of the whole human race." [59] These expressions were not cynical. Morris (and King and Rutledge) were convinced that the ship of state would move most smoothly for everyone if its sails were filled with the winds of commercial prosperity, and that prosperous men could guide the ship so that it would catch these winds.

Initially, Morris's group won its point. His committee's report left Congress free to regulate the representation that would be granted to new states already forming in the West, and to maintain at its own discretion a balance of Congressional power in favor of regions that respected commercial property, regardless of shifts in population. Once this had gained a footing, Morris's argument shifted in emphasis. He now began to stress that Congress ought not to be "shackled" by a rigid formula for reapportionment. As Madison pointed out, this argument was strange, coming from "a member who, on all occasions, had inculcated so strongly, the political depravity of men." Stranger still was the fact that delegates as canny as Sherman and Gorham were at first willing to accept the argument that it would be safe, as Sherman put it, "to choose wise and good men, and then confide in them." [60]

The Virginians—led now by Randolph and Mason, and joined by North Carolina's Williamson—were not so easily quieted, perhaps because they had more at stake than the New Englanders. Mason in a brilliant speech on July 11 exposed the implications of Morris's proposal. He did not object to the initial allotment of seats, even though it had been based upon conjecture. "According to the present population of America, the Northern part of it had a right to preponderate, and he could not deny it." What concerned him was that preponderance in Congress would not follow population unless "a revision from time to time, according to some permanent and precise standard" was written into the Constitution. "From the nature of man," he continued, borrowing one of Morris's own favorite principles, "we may be sure, that those who have power in their hands will not give it up while they can retain it." Applying this lesson to sectional politics, he said:

> If [after several decades] the Southern states . . . should have three-fourths of the people of America within their limits, the Northern will hold fast the majority of representatives. . . . The Southern states will complain, but they may complain from generation to generation without redress.

He went on to address himself directly to the supposed dangers "to the Atlantic interests from the new Western states." He argued that both justice and policy required the absence of distinctions between old and new states within the union. The issue was whether the inhabitants of these new regions were to become full citizens or rivals and enemies. He rejected the notion that frontier regions were inevitably poor, and thus hostile to prosperity. "He did not know but in time they would be both more numerous and more wealthy than their Atlantic brethren. The extent and fertility of their soil made this probable." [61]

This powerful speech, reinforced by Randolph's remarks following it, was enough to "convert" Sherman and Gorham, as both men later admitted. As Gorham put it, "If the Convention, who are comparatively so little biased by local views, are so much perplexed, how can it be expected that the legislature hereafter, under the full bias of those views, will be able to settle a standard?" [62]

One major contention of the Morris faction remained, and in this convention it could not be left unanswered. This was the argument that "the number of inhabitants was not a proper standard of wealth," and that a ratio based on population alone would be dangerous in a government with power over property. It was Madison who struck the decisive blow against this argument, by denying its premise.

It was said . . . that population and wealth were not measures of each other. He admitted that in different climates, under different forms of government, and in different stages of civilization, the inference was perfectly just. He would admit that in no situation, numbers of inhabitants were an accurate measure of wealth. He contended, however, that in the United States it was sufficiently so for the object in contemplation.

Morris had cited the varying wealth of different countries with nearly equal population in support of his view. Madison rejected the analogy.

[A]s the governments, the laws, and the manners of all [states] were nearly the same, and the intercourse between different parts perfectly free, population, industry, arts, and the value of labor would constantly tend to equalize themselves.* [63]

In effect, Madison was saying that it was not necessary for the Constitution to decide the central issue between theoretical and realistic republicans. Where internal intercourse was free, population would be drawn to wealth. A census of numbers would thus provide a reliable index of the distribution of wealth, and an apportionment based on such a census should satisfy both groups: those who thought that the legislature should be a mirror of the total population, and those who wanted it to have special ties to the most productive regions of the country.

As debate on the formula for representation reached its climax in the middle of July, a majority view emerged in favor of requiring that a census be taken regularly, and that Congress adjust representation accordingly. But before a formula could be agreed upon, the federal ratio, which had been overwhelmingly adopted on June 11, unexpectedly became a matter of controversy.

---

* Reading this thirty or forty years later, Madison must have wondered whether the sections had really been as "nearly the same" and intercourse as "perfectly free" as he had earlier thought. There can be little doubt, however, that the words he spoke in 1787 voiced the Convention's understanding.

On July 11, Randolph's rather vague proposal for a regular census was replaced by Williamson's more specific motion that representation be regulated according to the count of "the free white inhabitants and three-fifths of those of other descriptions." The South Carolinians immediately responded by moving that "blacks" be counted equally with whites. Defending the motion,

Mr. Butler insisted that the labor of a slave in South Carolina was as productive and valuable as that of a free man in Massachusetts, that, as wealth was the great means of defense and utility to the nation, they were equally valuable to it with free men, and that consequently an equal representation ought to be allowed for them . . .[64]

His argument was apparently not persuasive. The motion was defeated, by 3 to 7, with only Georgia and Delaware joining the nabobs from Charleston in support of it.

The expected approval of the federal ratio did not, however, immediately materialize. Perhaps Butler's greed had disturbed a delicate equilibrium in some minds. King predicted that the inclusion of blacks in the apportionment ratio "would excite great discontents among the states having no slaves." * Wilson questioned the principle on which the admission of slaves in the proportion of three-fifths could be explained. "Are they . . . citizens? Then why are they not admitted on an equality with white citizens? Are they . . . property? Then why is not other property admitted into the computation?" He went on to warn that "the tendency of the blending of the blacks with the whites" would "disgust" the people of Pennsylvania. And Morris announced that "he could never agree to give such an encouragement to the slave trade as would be given by allowing them a representation for their negroes." [65]

The vote was then taken, and it showed four states (Connecticut, Virginia, North Carolina, and Georgia) in the affirmative, with six states (Massachusetts, New Jersey Pennsylvania, Delaware, Maryland, and South Carolina) opposed. The federal ratio had been defeated by the union of delegates (from New Jersey,

---

* Both Williamson's motion and King's speech reflect the indifference of the framers to free Negroes. Both men appear to lump all "blacks" together, and to consider them under the category of "slaves." Free Negroes were simply not part of the structure of political society as perceived by the framers.

Delaware, and Maryland) opposed to any kind of proportional representation, those (from Massachusetts and Pennsylvania) who feared the growth of the South and the West, and those (from South Carolina) who would settle at this point for nothing less than full credit for their slaves as inhabitants.

Thus a convention that then lacked delegations from New Hampshire, Rhode Island, and New York was nevertheless temporarily able to deny any representation at all to slaves. But the true state of the matter was indicated by the fact that a vote on the Williamson motion, as amended—without any representation for slaves at all—was unable to draw a single affirmative vote. Wilson's comment about "the necessity of compromise" among the proponents of proportional representation had proved to be a shrewd one.

The following day, July 12, a compromise was struck. The debate began with an exchange of ultimatums between William R. Davie, of North Carolina, and Gouverneur Morris—Davie saying "he was sure that North Carolina would never confederate on any terms that did not rate [slaves] at least as three to five," and Morris responding that "the people of Pennsylvania will never agree to a representation of Negroes." General Charles Cotesworth Pinckney, annoyed by Morris's pronouncement, responded firmly that "property in slaves should not be exposed to danger under a government instituted for the protection of property."

To bridge the gap thus exposed, Ellsworth, Randolph, and Wilson framed a reapportionment formula that tied representation to direct taxation, and proportioned both to a population formula incorporating the federal ratio.[36] To some minds, this bit of legerdemain was crucial. It helped to undercut the objection that slaves were being represented in the national legislature, and it went part way toward meeting the complaint that slave owners were being rewarded for holding slaves.

The South Carolinians made a final effort to raise slaves to full equality in the ratio, but went down to defeat, gaining affirmative votes only from Dr. William Samuel Johnson, of Connecticut, two unnamed Pennsylvanians, and the delegation from Georgia. This cleared the way for a vote on the motion as a whole, which now prevailed, 6 to 2, with two states divided. New

Jersey and Delaware voted negatively, being opposed to *any* formula that apportioned representation. Massachusetts was now divided, presumably by the affirmative votes of Gorham and Strong, who did not share the fears of Gerry and King about the West. South Carolina, too, was split, probably by the acquiescence of the Pinckneys in the inevitable. And Pennsylvania and Maryland now voted affirmatively, overruling Morris's fears. The vote of July 12 thus marked a return to the consensus of June 11 regarding the federal ratio, except for the split delegations of Massachusetts and South Carolina and the departure of New York.

In retrospect, it seems all but inevitable that South Carolina's insistence on equal representation for slaves and Morris's counterultimatum on behalf of the people of Pennsylvania would be compromised, and that the federal ratio would provide the locus of agreement. In this sense, the crisis of July 11 was false, and the compromise of July 12 relatively minor.

Yet, in at least two ways, the settlement was momentous. It gave Constitutional sanction to the fact that the United States was composed of some persons who were "free" and others who were not. And it established the principle, new in republican theory, that a man who lived among slaves had a greater share in the election of representatives than the man who did not. With one stroke, despite the disclaimers of its advocates, it acknowledged slavery and rewarded slave owners. It is a measure of their adjustment to slavery that Americans in the eighteenth century found this settlement natural and just.

One important step remained: to decide whether the ratio of representation applied equally to new states forming in the West. An affirmative decision on this question was crucial to the strategy of the Virginians, who counted on the southerly and westwardly drift of population to reinforce and perpetuate a majority in the United States favorable to agrarian interests. Earlier, Mason had recommended equal treatment for the West on the grounds of justice and policy. Now Randolph, directly attacking the Morris formula adopted July 9, moved that the word "wealth" be eliminated from the formula altogether, and that the Constitution require Congress "to apportion the number of representatives . . . upon the principle of the number of inhabitants." The motion further specified that the ratio be applied "in case any of the states shall hereafter be divided or any two or more states united or new states created within the limits of the United States." [67]

The main effect of this motion was to apply the resolution of July 12 to the entire area of the United States without distinguishing seaboard from interior country or original states from new ones. To Gouverneur Morris, Randolph's resolution was a signal that the time for full candor had come. He had restrained his misgivings about Southern agrarianism while he enjoyed the co-operation of South Carolinians in the effort to have "wealth" included in the formula for apportionment. Now, by virtue of the federal ratio, it was assured that Southern wealth would be taken into account. But Northern wealth, which was chiefly maritime, or commercial, would be completely ignored in the distribution of representational weight if Randolph's motion passed.

Morris began his speech by referring again to the illogic of the federal ratio. Were Negroes "inhabitants" or "property"? If inhabitants, they ought to be included in their entire number; if property, then the word "wealth" should be retained, and applied to other forms of property. He went on to note that:

A distinction had been set up and urged between the Northern and Southern states. . . . Either this distinction is fictitious or real. If fictitious, let it be dismissed [along with all claims for preferential treatment, such as the federal ratio] and let us proceed with due confidence. If it be real, instead of attempting to blend incompatible things, let us at once take a friendly leave of each other.

He himself seemed to believe that the distinction was "real." To be sure, he called the doctrine of sectional conflict "heretical" and "groundless," but in the next breath he spoke of the distinction between the "maritime" and the "interior and landed" interest, saying that the consequence of a transfer of power to the latter would be "an oppression of commerce." He was not vague in specifying the form that this oppression might take "If the Southern states get the power into their hands, and be joined as they will with the interior country, they will inevitably bring on a war with Spain for the Mississippi. . . ." He concluded by insisting that it was not the Southern states alone that needed protection. "The Eastern states may claim it for their fishery, and for other objects, as the Southern states claim it for their peculiar objects. . . . There can be no end of demands for security if every particular interest is to be entitled to it." [38]

Butler reacted sharply: "The security the Southern states want is that their negroes may not be taken from them." [69] As the vote on Randolph's motion soon revealed, the South Carolinians had been converted to the view that their fundamental loyalties were Southern. The "property" that mattered most to them was slaves, because it was the most vulnerable and the most dangerous property in the nation, and the federal ratio was all the representation they could get for that property. However much they would have liked to promote the commercial position of Charleston—and they did much during this period to ally it with ports to the north in pursuit of policies favorable to trade—they knew that there was nothing more for slaveholders to gain by fighting, alongside Gouverneur Morris and Rufus King, for a formula that included "wealth." The fiasco of July 11, when the federal ratio was temporarily eliminated from the resolution on apportionment by the votes of the commercial coalition, carried a lesson the South Carolinians were not slow to appreciate: that their commercial allies were the strongest antislavery men in the union, not out of conviction so much as circumstance, and that, though they shared many aims with these fellow merchants, they had first to be certain that their slaves were safe before joining in pursuit of these other goals. Their allies in the defense of slavery were the agrarians of Virginia, North Carolina, and Georgia.

The vote on Randolph's motion was almost unanimous. Only Delaware was divided, perhaps by some delegate's stubborn fidelity to his credentials, which forbade the abandonment of states' equality in the legislature. [70] Despite Morris's impassioned protest, every other state was by now able to produce a majority in favor of compromise based on the federal ratio.

The following day, July 14, the Morris faction made one last effort to insure that control over the government would remain in the hands of men familiar and sympathetic with commercial interests. Elbridge Gerry was the spokesman. He moved that to secure the liberties of the states already confederated, the number of representatives in the first branch from the states which shall hereafter be established, shall never exceed the representatives from such of the thirteen United States as shall accede to this confederation.[71]

The vote on this motion drew the line between the sections about as sharply as any the Convention had considered. It was favored by New England and by Delaware and Maryland, states closed in on the west by others of the thirteen original states. But it was strenuously opposed by the four southernmost states, some of whose colonial charters gave them title to lands westward to the "South Sea," and whose claims now ran all the way to the Mississippi River. It was well known that the states of Kentucky and Tennessee were abuilding on the other side of the Appalachian Mountains, and that others were likely soon to arise to the west of South Carolina and Georgia. With population drifting southwestward, it was reasonable to suppose that these regions would become thickly populated and productive in the not-too-distant future, and would thus add considerable weight in the nation's councils to the regions from which they sprang.

Of course, there were new states building in the Old Northwest, too, between the Ohio River and the Great Lakes. Some men supposed that this region would add weight to Northern interests, thus counterbalancing the Southwest. But the fact is that no one quite knew what to make of this whole region west of the Appalachians. Roger Sherman, the former mayor of New Haven, stern and awkward, but confident in the future of his country, urged his fellow delegates to regard the future inhabitants of the West as children and grandchildren, and treat them with full equality. Yet no one knew whether to trust this vision or not. The presence of the West, politically empty in 1787, but pregnant with unforeseeable implications for the work of the Convention, introduced a large element of chance into the game of constitution making. Gerry's motion was an attempt to reduce the odds against the Easterners by placing a limit on the havoc of which the West would later be capable. Some men, concentrating perhaps on the agricultural production of North and South and seeing the Ohio River as an extension of the Mason-Dixon Line, might assume that the upper West would be an ally of the North in national legislation. But apparently most delegates, seeing the West, all of it, as agrarian, and forecasting that the North would pursue commercial and industrial lines of development, anticipated that the West would side with the South in defense of agrarian interests. The vote on Gerry's motion suggests that most delegates favored the latter view. New Englanders voted to set limits on Western influence in American politics; Southerners, in this case more confident of the future of the country, were willing to let nature take its course. The motion was defeated, 4 to 5, with one state divided.[72] The commercial men had come close to obtaining a provision that would almost certainly have doomed hopes for ratification by some Southern states.

The stage had finally been cleared for a vote on the Great Compromise. As it now stood, the compromise divided sixty-five seats among the thirteen original states for the first sitting of the House of Representatives; provided that representation be proportioned to direct taxation, and direct taxes to population, according to the federal ratio; required that both representation and direct taxation be adjusted regularly, in accordance with a census; gave each state an equal vote in the Senate; and provided that "money bills" originate in the House and be passed or rejected in the Senate, without alteration. It passed by a 5 to 4 margin, with one state divided.[73]

The Great Compromise on representation was fundamental.[74] It corrected the basic defect of the Confederation. It gave shape to the legislature, the central organ of republican government. It determined the weight of states in the selection of Presidents (the Electoral College was modeled on the representational scheme) and in the nomination (by the President) and ratification (by the Senate) of Supreme Court Justices. Now each state knew where it would stand in the new government. Now it was possible, as Madison put it, "to say what powers could be safely and properly vested in the government." [75]

The Southerners must, on balance, have been pleased with the new arrangement. Several (Madison, Rutledge, Washington, Mason, the Pinckneys) were leaders in the drive for energetic government. The possibility of erecting such a government was contingent for these men on the condition that the South should have more than five-thirteenths of the votes in the legislature. By the compromise, they received a 6-per-cent increment at the outset, plus a guarantee of adjustments as population drifted in their direction.

In the immediate aftermath of the Great Compromise, the most disgruntled Southerner was James Madison. In his view, the stubbornness of the Yankees had forced the Convention to dilute the most fundamental principle of republican government, and the result had been an unfair and impolitic discrimination against the interests of the agrarians, who composed a clear majority of population in the country. But as the Convention wore on, his mood mellowed. On August 29, as the Convention drew to a close, he offered what he described as a "pretty full view of the subject"—the situation of the South as it appeared under the proposed Constitution. Old George Mason and young Charles Pinckney were making a last-ditch effort to gain additional protection for Southern interests by inserting a clause that would have required two-thirds majorities for passage of commercial regulations, or, as they were then called, "navigation acts." Madison claimed that the additional security was unnecessary. Southern agriculture would be protected against the program of the commercial interests by the interplay of institutional arrangements and geographical factors: a bicameral legislature; the executive veto power; the sympathy of Connecticut and New Jersey, which were both "agricultural, not commercial states"; the interior interest of the most commercial states; and the promise of new states in the West, which would also be agrarian in their sympathies. Even if the commercial powers were abused, he said, the "disadvantage" would be temporary. It would serve mainly to induce Southerners to become more self-sufficient in matters of shipping and naval protection.[76]

So the South and the agrarian interest generally were in good shape, by Madison's reckoning. For other leaders of the section, it remained only to insure that the hand of the new government be restrained from touching slavery.

6

Slavery and the Constitutional

Revolution: The Debate over

Federal Powers

THE crisis that called the Federal Convention into being was
believed by the leading delegates to have been caused by a lack of
power and authority in the national government under the Articles of Confederation. The Articles prescribed that special, practically prohibitive majorities had to be gained for any significant
legislation. They directed that revenues be raised by requisitions
on the states, but failed to provide sufficient power to insure that
these requisitions were fulfilled, with the result that the national
treasury was in a perpetual state of collapse. The ultimate power
to enforce treaty obligations and to regulate commerce among the
states lay with the states themselves. On these crucial matters, the
Congress of the Confederation was reduced to exhortation, a device that had grown less effective and more contemptible with
increasingly frequent use.

It was primarily to reform this system of power, to give energy
to the national government, that the delegates had gathered in
Philadelphia during the hot summer of 1787. But many delegates
realized, and others soon discovered, that another, more fundamental defect needed attention first. James Madison remarked,
during debate on the question of representation, that "it would
be impossible to know what powers could be safely and properly
vested in the government before it was known, in what manner
the states were to be represented in it." [1] In a way, this question

207

of priorities had a chicken-and-egg quality. Many delegates believed that the question of powers should be tackled first. Without a clear definition of powers, they felt, the question of apportionment had an abstract quality, and would tend rather quickly to escalate into a struggle for survival. If the powers were defined, perhaps delegates would feel that less grave matters were at stake and would be willing to concede more. That, at any rate, was the thinking of many delegates who worried about the bitterness of the debates during June and the first two weeks of July. Madison and John Rutledge viewed the matter differently. In their view, the question of apportionment "involved the most fundamental points." Only when a state knew what weight it would have in the councils of the nation could it determine what powers to grant those councils. It was the Southern delegates who were most insistent on this point. As a matter of fact, the first straight sectional vote in the Convention's proceedings came on a motion by South Carolina's Pierce Butler, seconded by Madison, to settle the ratio of representation first, before considering legislative powers.[2]

The result of the struggle over representation in terms of anticipated sectional power in Congress was a standoff. The United States was to have no Prussia, no area with so much weight in the government that it could afford to ratify a constitution that gave legislative power in the form of a blank check. Under a government whose foundations were laid in the Great Compromise, each state, each section, each interest could look forward to a constant struggle for advantage, if not in some cases for survival. Yet despite the insistence of the South on settling the form of government first, before defining its substance, and despite the rather inconclusive result of the struggle over representation, the South moved with strength and boldness to the task of committing powers to the national authority.

This crucial point was sometimes obscured by later developments. But losing sight of it causes a misreading of certain episodes at the Convention. The central meaning of the Federal Convention, as several recent interpreters have pointed out, derives from the fact that the primary framers were striving to give increased energy to the national government. The Constitution, as it emerged from the Convention, was replete with checks and balances, devices that later proved useful to interests and forces that wanted to restrain the federal government from aggressive action. But most of these devices were granted reluctantly, and they suggest only part of the meaning of the Constitution in its contemporary setting. The central meaning of 1787 is best understood by setting the Constitution beside the Articles of Confederation. In this context, the Constitution stands revealed as a frame for vigorous, positive government, the leading framers as "young men of the Revolution," and the Convention itself as "a reform caucus in action." [3]

In the drama that produced the Constitution, Southern delegates were unmistakably prominent players. James Madison, the man whose leadership during the Convention earned him the title "Father of the Constitution," was a Southerner, a slave-owning Virginian who had been educated at the College of New Jersey, in Princeton, but who never in his long (eighty-five years) lifetime had a home other than his modest plantation in Orange County, in the Shenandoah Valley. John Rutledge, certainly a leading nationalist and chairman of the important Committee of Detail, which provided the first definition of legislative powers under the Constitution, was one of the wealthiest and best-established planters at the Convention, and deliberately represented the most candid slave owners, the rice planters of South Carolina's coastal flats. George Washington, whose presence contributed essential authority to the deliberations and who had always been a force for national prestige and integration, was an exceedingly rich man, whose fortune arose largely from the labor of slaves in and around Mount Vernon, Virginia. In fact, of the fifteen delegates whom Clinton Rossiter has termed either "principals" or "influentials," seven were planters.[4]

When the Convention turned to the definition of powers for the federal government, Southerners easily and naturally assumed a leading role, not just to be in a strategic position to defend "peculiar" interests, but also to perform as energetic architects of a governmental structure appropriate to a great nation. Thus, in the late stages of the Convention, when young Charles Pinckney moved that special majorities be required for the passage of bills affecting foreign commerce, it was old John Rutledge who scolded his excitable colleague, remarking that the Convention was "laying the foundation for a great empire" and ought to take an enlarged, permanent view.[5]

The South's enthusiastic participation in the nationalizing thrust of 1787 carried one portentous qualification: the national government could be as powerful as the vision of a great national empire demanded, *provided that it keep its hands off slavery.* The major premise of the Southern position was a desire for vigorous national government, but the crucial minor premise was that slavery was strictly a local matter, forever beyond the reach of national authority. No conclusion—no constitutional clause, no public policy or pronouncement—that failed to take this minor premise fully into account could ever be acceptable to the South.

The South's insistence on this point sprang from several sources. One was a sense of complete dependence on slavery. This dependence was acknowledged by Southerners many times during the Convention's proceedings, though perhaps never more candidly than when General Pinckney flatly stated that "South Carolina and Georgia cannot do without slaves." "The blacks are the laborers, the peasants of the Southern states," added his cousin, and fellow planter, Charles. In the South Carolinians' view, the Southern economy was totally dependent on the productivity of black laborers.[6]

Besides this, the determination of the Southerners to keep slavery out of the national political arena was reinforced by the feeling that people in the other sections were "prejudiced" against the institution, and might move in foolish ways to undermine it. They were convinced that slavery was essential to the peace of their social environment, and they suspected that those who lived where blacks were sparse could never understand this fact. This suspicion must have been fed by such remarks as the following, made by delegates from Connecticut: "the abolition of slavery seemed to be going on in the United States and . . . the good sense of the several states would probably by degrees complete it," and "As population increases, poor laborers will be so plenty [*sic*] as to render slaves useless. Slavery in time will not be a speck in our country." [7] These statements are sometimes taken as evidence that the framers looked forward confidently to the time when slavery would dissolve from the American social scene, and are thus seen as partial justification for the failure of the Convention to come to grips with the institution directly in 1787. But in the face of the candor of the South Carolinians, a better interpretation of their significance would seem to be that they reinforced the determination of the Southerners not to allow people so ignorant of the true situation of the South to obtain power to legislate over slavery at all.

There were, of course, other Southern delegates, particularly the Virginians, whose commitment to slavery was less enthusiastic. George Mason, for one, was deeply troubled by it. Author of Virginia's seminal Bill of Rights, which began with the assertion that "all men are naturally equal," he called the attention of the delegates to the tendency of slavery to weaken the nation's defenses against foreign foes, to corrupt the manners of masters, to discourage the migration into the South of free white laborers, and to stimulate avarice in "some of our Eastern brethren" who participated in the slave trade.[8] Madison too, could lament that "the mere distinction of color [had been] made, in the most enlightened period of time, a ground of the most oppressive dominion ever exercised by man over man." [9] Yet, despite these painful expressions of ambivalence toward slavery, there is no evidence that any Southerner departed from the determination to deprive the federal government of power to emancipate slaves. When Pierce Butler declared, "The security the Southern states want is that their Negroes may not be taken from them," he spoke for his entire section.[10]

Despite this absolute intransigence on the subject of power to abolish or regulate slavery, there was one related aspect of the question on which the mind of the South was divided: the slave trade. On this point, the South Carolinians were as adamant as on any other affecting slavery. Charles Pinckney stated, "In every proposed extension of the powers of the Congress, [South Carolina] has expressly and watchfully excepted that of meddling with the importation of negroes." His colleague Rutledge warned, "If the Convention thinks that North Carolina, South

Carolina, and Georgia will ever agree to the plan, unless their right to import slaves be untouched, the expectation is vain." [11] Here, though, the South Carolinians were unable to make their position stick, partly because the Marylanders and Virginians, overstocked with slaves already, opposed them on this point, and partly because the slave trade was conceived as a national question, affecting "the national happiness," the capacity for defense, and the relative political power of the great sectional interests. As Mason remarked, the slave trade "concerns not the importing states alone, but the whole union." [12]

The Convention's earliest consideration of the question of powers for the new government came in response to the sixth resolution of the Virginia Plan, which read as follows:

> Resolved . . . that the national legislature ought to be empowered to enjoy the legislative rights vested in Congress by the Confederation and moreover to legislate in all cases to which the separate states are incompetent, or in which the harmony of the United States may be interrupted by the exercise of individual legislation; to negative all laws passed by the several states, contravening in the opinion of the national legislature the articles of union; and to call forth the force of the union against any member of the union failing to fulfill its duty under the articles thereof.[13]

Two days after the introduction of the Virginia Plan, the Convention took up this resolution, and immediately the South Carolinians showed their anxiety. The first clause, amended to provide "for transferring all the legislative powers of the existing Congress" to the new Congress, passed without debate or dissent. But when the second clause was announced, Rutledge and Charles Pinckney "objected to the vagueness of the term *incompetent*" and asked for "an exact enumeration of the powers comprehended by this definition." Butler expressed "fear" that the Convention would reduce the states to impotence in its zeal to strengthen the national government.[14]

Edmund Randolph, the young Virginian who had introduced his delegation's draft, quickly assured the alarmed South Carolinians that "his" plan offered only general principles, and that he, too, was "entirely opposed" to giving "indefinite powers to the national legislature." Madison confessed his reluctance and doubts concerning the practicability of composing a list of powers, but he promised that an effort would be made. Significantly, the only delegate who found Madison's assurance inadequate, and who voted against the clause at this stage, was not a South Carolinian, but Connecticut's Roger Sherman.[15]

During these preliminary skirmishes, as the delegates felt their way toward an understanding of the issues before the Convention, a wide spectrum of opinion emerged on the question of the appropriate role of the states in the new national system. From the point of view of the developments being traced here, the important feature of this spectrum is that it was not defined along sectional lines. It did not pit Northern nationalizers against Southerners staunch for states' rights. If any generalization can be made, it might be that it was most often the Virginian Madison and the South Carolinian Charles Pinckney, with support from the Pennsylvanians and from a few small-state men from the mid-Atlantic region, who pleaded for generous endowments of power to the national government; while the leadership for states' rights fell to the Yankees from Connecticut.

The extreme nationalist position was sketched out by George Read, of Delaware, who frankly confessed that "he was against patching up the old federal system" and argued that "state attachments should be extinguished as much as possible." The "idea of distinct states . . . would be a perpetual source of discord. There can be no cure for this evil but in doing away states altogether and uniting them all into one great society." When it became obvious that the "evil" of state governments would persist, he joined those who pressed hard for the extension of federal authority into as many areas of government as possible. "He hoped," he said, "the objects of the general government would be much more numerous than seemed to be expected by some gentlemen, and that they would become more and more so." [16]

Though Read's nationalism was particularly marked, he was not alone in his wish to augment the power of the national government. Alexander Hamilton was another who asserted that the states as independent sovereignties "ought to be abolished." [17] Rufus King once referred contemptuously to the "phantom of

state sovereignty." He admitted that it was vain to talk of "annihi-
lating the states; but [he] thought that much of their power
ought to be taken from them." [18] And Judge David Brearly, of
New Jersey, proposed "that a map of the United States be spread
out, that all the existing boundaries be erased, and that a new
partition of the whole be made into thirteen equal parts." [19]

But these expressions of radical nationalism were rather eccentric. Most of the delegates recognized the need to divide authority
between federal and state governments in such a way as to preserve the states as guardians of distinct and differing ways of life.
This concern for states was by no means peculiar to Southerners.
As a matter of fact, the most sanguine statement of support for
state government came from Oliver Ellsworth, a future Senator
from Connecticut and Chief Justice of the Supreme Court.

What he wanted was domestic happiness. The national government
could not descend to the local objects on which this depended. It could
only embrace objects of a general nature. He turned his eyes therefore
for the preservation of his rights to the state governments. . . . His
happiness depended on their existence, as much as a new-born infant
on its mother for nourishment.[20]

Sherman agreed. "The objects of the union," he said, "were few."
He listed the chief among them: the conduct of foreign affairs,
including defense and tariff policies, and the settlement of disputes between the states. "These and perhaps a few lesser objects
alone rendered a confederation of the states necessary. All other
matters, civil and criminal, would be much better in the hands of
the states." [21]

It was Madison who responded to this narrow definition of national authority. He acknowledged that he

differed in thinking the objects mentioned to be all the principal ones
that required a national government. Those were certainly important
and necessary objects; but he combined with them the necessity of providing more effectually for the security of private rights, and a steady
dispensation of justice.[22]

An even more striking instance of aggressiveness by a Southerner came when Charles Pinckney, South Carolina's unpredict-
able young Turk, asked for and obtained a reconsideration of the

clause of the sixth resolution which gave to Congress the power to veto any state law it regarded as unconstitutional. He did not announce his reason for requesting the reconsideration, but delegates, remembering his earlier demand for "an exact enumeration" of legislative powers,[23] might have expected a move to curtail the power of Congress over the states. Imagine, then, their surprise when Pinckney opened the reconsideration by moving that "the national legislature should have authority to negative all laws which they should judge to be *improper*." [24] His explanation must have added to the consternation of such delegates as Ellsworth, Sherman, and Mason—to say nothing of his colleagues from South Carolina. The states, he said

> must be kept in due subordination to the nation. . . . [I]f the states were left to act of themselves in any case, it would be impossible to defend the national prerogatives, however extensive they might be on paper. . . . [U]nder the British government, the negative of the Crown had been found beneficial, and the *states* are more one nation now, than the *colonies* were then.[25]

Pinckney, who claimed that he was the youngest delegate to the Convention,[26] must have been the only man present too young to remember the vetoes of the King of England as a galling insult to colonial legislatures. This interference by an uncontrollable, distant sovereign had been one of the primary causes of the War for Independence, as Jefferson had indicated by placing these vetoes first in his list of "facts . . . submitted to a candid world."

Surely it was true, as Pinckney stated, that "the *states* [were] more one nation now, than the *colonies* were then." But since no one could be sure who would control the federal authority, few were willing that Congress should be empowered to determine whether or not state laws dealing with "local matters" were "improper." Hugh Williamson voiced a Southern perspective on the issue. He "was against giving a power that might restrain the states from regulating their internal police." But the concern was by no means uniquely Southern. Gerry insisted that "the states . . . have different interests and are ignorant of each other's interests. The negative therefore will be abused." [27]

The vote on Pinckney's proposal, while decisively negative,

showed that many delegates were prepared to go a long way in strengthening the central authority. The motion was defeated by the votes of seven states: Connecticut, New York, and New Jersey, from the North; Maryland, North Carolina, South Carolina, and Georgia, from the South. Delaware's voice was divided. But despite Gerry's premonitions, Massachusetts voted "aye," as did the other two large states, Pennsylvania and Virginia. The remarkable thing is that a proposal as strong as Pinckney's had such powerful backing in the second week of the Convention. This support, though not dominant for a proposal as unguarded as this, came from all sections and represented all major interests. While the vote on the motion indicated that the effort to divide authority between national and state governments would have to continue, it was apparent that there was broad intersectional support for a generous, if careful, augmentation of national powers.[28]

From late May through the middle of July, the attention of the delegates had focused on the question of the weight of states and persons in the representational scheme. Once this thorny issue had been settled, the Convention was at last ready to turn to a systematic consideration of the question of governmental powers. To expedite consideration, the Convention sent its various resolutions, including the amended sixth resolution of the Virginia Plan, to a Committee of Detail, so that a draft of the whole Constitution, including a list of enumerated powers, could be prepared.

A brief summary of the special concerns of the Southerners gives a better appreciation of the Southern triumph at this crucial stage in the Convention. The cornerstone of the Southern position was that slavery must be treated as a local institution beyond the power of Congress to regulate. On the slave trade, the mind of the South was divided. The Deep Southerners wanted it exempted altogether from federal regulation; men from the upper South wanted it stopped as soon as possible. In the area of foreign commerce generally, Southerners insisted that export taxes be prohibited to the federal government, and they sought to require special majorities for the enactment of regulations of maritime commerce. Because the Southern economy was based on the planting of staples, Southern statesmen were eager to prevent hostile majorities in Congress from inhibiting the export of tobacco, sugar, rice, and cotton, and from burdening the importation of the cheapest and best manufactured items.

Another issue of particular concern to the Southerners was the matter of foreign treaties. During the late stages of the Confederation, Southerners had feared that John Jay, the Secretary for Foreign Affairs, would negotiate a treaty with Spain that would yield American rights to navigate the Mississippi River past New Orleans in exchange for commercial privileges in trading with the Spanish Empire. Such a treaty would have been a boon to maritime interests in New England, but a crippling blow to settlers beyond the Appalachians, particularly those in the Ohio River Valley. On the eve of the Federal Convention, Madison had undercut Jay's project by inducing five states to vote in the Congress against a resolution authorizing Jay to compromise American rights in the lower Mississippi, if necessary, in order to gain other commercial advantages. The importance of this vote was that the opposition of five states would have been more than enough to defeat any proposed treaty under the Articles of Confederation, which required that nine of the thirteen states assent to treaties or alliances.[29] Now, at the Constitutional Convention, Southerners were determined that special majorities again be required for the ratification of treaties, in order to protect themselves in the future.

The Committee of Detail was appointed on July 24. It included five of the most active and influential framers: John Rutledge (Chairman), Edmund Randolph, James Wilson, Nathaniel Gorham, and Oliver Ellsworth.

The Convention could not have produced at this critical point an intersectional committee in whose hands the interests of slave owners would have been safer. The two Southerners, Rutledge and Randolph, were already on record as demanding a government of enumerated powers, and would, of course, be vigilant in defense of the whole range of Southern interests. Ellsworth had not yet publicly shown his hand on the question of slavery, but was soon to urge the Convention not to "intermeddle," not even with the slave trade. Wilson had earlier seconded Sherman's motion to prohibit Congress from interfering with the "internal police" of the states. Gorham, a former President of the Congress of the Confederation and Chairman of the Convention's Committee of the Whole, was a man experienced in accommodating national policy to the demands of states and sections.

The man on the committee with the strongest and most settled views regarding the extent of federal power was Rutledge. He was not a timid man, and his hopes for a strong and "permanent" Constitution have already been noted. But he always insisted that the powers of government be carefully bounded, so that South Carolinians could participate energetically in national affairs without fear that they were strengthening a hand that could one day be turned against them at their weakest point.

The report of the Committee of Detail was a monument to Southern craft and gall. It provided virtually everything that Southerners, especially Deep Southerners, wanted from the Convention: substantial (three-fifths) representation for their slaves, complete immunity for the slave trade and for slavery in general, prohibition of export taxes, and special majorities for navigation acts and treaties*—all this in addition to a government strengthened for defense and for prompt payment of its debts. Northerners, of course, would share in the general improvement in American affairs, but they faced the prospect of diminishing power in national councils (because of the slave trade and the

---

* Some scholars[30] include among the provisions won by the South clauses that looked forward to the use of federal force to quell slave insurrections. Power to call forth the militia to "suppress insurrections" is to be found in the fifteenth clause of Article I, Section 8, of the Constitution. In addition, Article IV, Section 4, guarantees that the United States shall protect any state "against domestic violence" if the legislature or governor of the state beckons. These clauses were included in the report of the Committee of Detail.[31] But debates surrounding the adoption of these provisions suggest that the delegates had in mind such disturbances as Shays' Rebellion and the turmoil in Rhode Island, and foresaw such future developments as the Whiskey Rebellion, rather than servile insurrections.[32] As to the latter, the attitude of Rutledge is significant. "He was not apprehensive of insurrections and would readily exempt the other states from the obligation to protect the Southern [states] against them." [33] It is difficult to imagine a South Carolinian so desperate as to want to call in the Massachusetts militia to suppress an uprising among the slaves. As a matter of fact, Southerners were usually, though not always, on the side of restricting the scope of these clauses dealing with domestic disturbances.[34]

expected drift of population) and of formidable obstacles in the path of favorable commercial regulations.

The Committee of Detail contained a majority of Northerners, but only Gorham among them seemed to understand what had happened or to object to it. Twice during the debate on the slave trade and navigation acts, he reminded the Convention that New England's main motive toward a stronger union was "commercial," that is, the hope that a united nation could make and enforce better commercial arrangements with foreign nations and among the states than any single state could by itself.[35] He knew that even if a majority of the Northern delegates could be brought to accept the arrangements struck by Rutledge's committee, a Constitution that followed the same pattern would stand little chance of being ratified by representatives of the merchants of Boston and Portsmouth and New York, or the farmers of the Connecticut, Hudson, or Delaware valleys.

One scholar suggests that the delegates found this report "very different from what most of them had . . . expected."[36] Certainly King and Morris were infuriated by the arrangements made to adjust the competing interests of North and South. King took his earliest opportunity to assail the report. Reacting to the vote affirming the federal ratio for representation, he stated that he had originally agreed to the inclusion of slaves in the hope that Southerners would then place full confidence in the federal government. The draft before them "put an end to all those hopes." The federal government, he said, had been given the task of defending against foreign invasion and against internal sedition. Slaves in the South increased both dangers, but slave owners were rewarded, and encouraged to increase their holdings through the slave trade, by an increment in representation. And now export taxes were not to be permitted.

If slaves are to be imported, shall not the exports produced by their labor supply a revenue, the better to enable the general government to defend their masters?—There was so much inequality and unreasonableness in all this, that the people of the Northern states could never be reconciled to it. . . .[37]

There was no abolitionism in King's speech, no sympathy or regard for blacks—just a calculated defense of sectional interest.

He demanded not emancipation, but export taxes, or else a limitation of the slave trade. But the Convention as a whole had no taste for an intersectional wrangle at this stage. Sherman gently suggested that, though the slave trade was "iniquitous," the clause on representation was no place to assault it, and Madison tried quickly to change the subject.

Morris, however, would not be silenced. Moving to limit representation to "free inhabitants," he admitted that he meant his motion as an assault on "domestic slavery." Throwing forbearance to the wind, he called slavery the "curse of heaven" on the Southern states, adding that "every step you take through the great regions of slaves presents a desert increasing, with the increasing proportion of these wretched beings." Referring to slaves as "his fellow creatures," he indicted Georgians and Carolinians for tearing them from their "dearest connections" in Africa and damning them to "the most cruel bondages," "in defiance of the most sacred laws of humanity." He went on to list the ways in which the Constitution as it then stood rewarded and encouraged slaveholders. "And what," he asked rhetorically, "is the proposed compensation to the Northern states for a sacrifice of every principle of right, of every impulse of humanity?" He concluded with a bold suggestion: "He would sooner submit himself to a tax for paying for all the negroes in the United States than saddle posterity with such a Constitution." [38]

This was a stirring speech, delivered by a man who was never delicate with the sensitivities of his Southern brethren. But as the sole expression of abolitionism at the Convention—which it was —it is surely a disappointment. Apart from the peroration, which seems almost whimsical in retrospect, and which died as a proposal with the sound of his voice, the speech points to no realistic, concrete steps that might be taken to eliminate slavery.

Close inspection of the speech and its context in the debate suggests that his purpose in delivering it was to force Southern concessions on navigation acts.* He seems—like Rufus King, who

---

* The fact that Morris's remark was rhetorical, rather than a serious proposal for compensated emancipation, can be seen by considering its cost. At the rate of $200 per slave,[39] the 700,000 slaves in America at the time were worth $140 million. The average expenditure per year for all functions of the federal government during its first decade under the Constitution was approximately $7

spoke before him—to have been genuinely shocked by the report of the Committee of Detail. Twice during the speech he concluded his rehearsal of provisions advantageous to the South by asking what compensations were to be made to the North.[40] When his rage was spent, Sherman again uttered a comforting word, Wilson described Morris's motion as "premature," and the Convention buried it under an avalanche of "nays." [41]

The Committee of Detail's basic intersectional arrangement did not come before the Convention until the third week of August. The first element to be reviewed was the prohibition on export taxes, a cardinal point for most Southerners. Several delegates, admitting that export taxes might be foolish for an agricultural country in time of peace, insisted that it would be even more foolish to proscribe this power permanently. Mason countered by arguing that export taxes would *never* be good for the staple-producing states, and that the only sure defense against them was to prohibit them in the Constitution. The balance of political power in the union convinced him that the South must not be prodigal with power to the federal government. "If we compare the states . . . the eight Northern states have an interest different from the five Southern states;—and have in one branch of the legislature thirty-six votes against twenty-nine, and in the other . . . eight against five." [42]

In 1787, at least, it appears that Mason's political arithmetic was less applicable to the question of export taxes than it was to other matters more peculiar to the Southern situation. Speeches by New Englanders Ellsworth, Sherman, and Gerry indicated that the carrying and planting states were united in opposition to export taxes, which were favored by the middle states. Madison, a nationalist at this point, rather than a spokesman for the interests of Virginia or the South, had earlier argued that taxes on exports

---

million. Adopting Morris's proposal would have meant trebling the national debt, and doubling the burden of taxation for at least ten years. And this would have been only the beginning of the burden—financial, social, and political—that would have fallen on the generation that undertook a program of compensated emancipation. Modern men may feel that the alternative was ultimately even more burdensome. But hindsight ought not to obscure the fact that the political problems raised by slavery were of an altogether unprecedented nature.

should be conceived by Southerners as a device for repaying Northerners, who would inevitably bear the greater part of the burden of national defense. Now he moved that, instead of prohibiting export taxes altogether, the Constitution require two-thirds majorities, but his motion was defeated, 5 to 6, with Connecticut joining the five Southern states in opposition. The vote to affirm the prohibition of export taxes was then taken, and was 7 to 4, with Massachusetts joining the carrier-planter alliance.[43] Thus did the Convention illustrate that in 1787 the South was far from isolated on matters of economic policy.

Apart from this victory on export taxes, the third week in August was a trying one for the delegates from the Deep South. By their zeal in protecting their "peculiar institution," it appeared that they might be losing this last, best hope for a strengthened federal union. It was during this period that the Convention wrestled with the questions of the slave trade and the navigation acts, problems that came to be related because they dealt with policies fundamental to the economic and social structure of society on both sides of the Mason-Dixon Line.

The draft submitted by the Committee of Detail had included the following clauses as the cornerstone of the intersectional arrangement:

Section 4. No tax or duty shall be laid . . . on the migration or importation of such persons as the several states shall think proper to admit; nor shall such migration or importation be prohibited.

Section 5. No capitation tax shall be laid, unless in proportion to the census hereinbefore directed to be taken.*

Section 6. No navigation act shall be laid, without the assent of two-thirds of the members present in each House.[45]

The assault on these provisions was initiated on August 21 by Luther Martin, of Maryland, who objected to the immunity of the slave trade from taxation or prohibition, arguing that the federal ratio encouraged the increase of slavery and ought to be strongly counteracted by obstacles to the importation of new slaves from Africa. It was necessary to prevent the increase of slavery, he insisted, not only because slavery weakened the South, but

---

* Slave owners wanted this provision, because they feared that a burdensome head tax might be imposed on their slaves by a Congress vindictive toward slave owners or bent on encouraging manumissions.[44]

also because it was "inconsistent with the principles of the Revolution."

These arguments were buffeted from both directions. From Rutledge came a stern rebuke. He disputed Martin's contention that the South was weakened by slavery, stating that he would "readily exempt the other states from the obligation" to quell servile insurrections. Nor did he admit the relevance of the principles of the Revolution. "Religion and humanity had nothing to do with this question. Interest alone is the governing principle with nations. The true question at present is whether the Southern states shall or shall not be parties to the union."

This was enough for Ellsworth. "[L]et every state import what it pleases," he pleaded. "The morality or wisdom of slavery are considerations belonging to the states themselves. What enriches a part enriches the whole, and the states are the best judges of their particular interests." [46]

The insistence of Rutledge and Ellsworth that "religion and humanity" and the "morality or wisdom of slavery" were not relevant to the debate at this point arose from their mutual determination that slavery not be permitted to pose a threat to the Convention's success. Slavery was the one institution on which the sections differed so sharply, in situation and—potentially, at least—in attitude, as to raise a serious obstacle to union. In every other case, there existed a consensual framework among the elements represented at the Convention, within which intersectional accommodations could be made. Even the struggle over representation, which had brought the Convention close to the brink of failure, was fundamentally a "contest for power' [47] rather than a dispute over principles. But in slavery, the Convention confronted an issue upon which the delegates, and the people they represented, might fatally differ if ever the debate was to center on the morality or the wisdom of the institution. It was not so much that there was a serious difference of opinion in 1787 about slavery—rather, that there was no agreement about it, no consensus, and, given the radical difference in circumstances, no real prospect of arriving at one. Indeed, a serious debate might expose and aggravate a cleavage that was still mostly latent.

Slavery, of course, was not the only institution that distinguished the sections. In forms of local government, in land and inheritance policies, in religious establishments, and in many other areas, each state and each section had its own laws and mores, and Southerners were not alone in being extremely jealous of the pretentions of outsiders to change their local patterns. There was general agreement in 1787, both inside the Convention and out, that the hand of the national government should be withheld from these "local matters."

Furthermore, no delegate to the Convention seems to have doubted that slavery was among these domestic institutions that ought to be left to the states. But what Rutledge and Ellsworth seemed not to understand was that, to some minds at least, there was a difference between slavery and the slave trade. Whereas slavery seemed to be rooted beyond the capacity of the constitution makers to eradicate, and whereas the nation had thus far been able to survive any weakness caused by it and had indeed found the institution and its fruits profitable for many elements in all sections, and whereas the institution seemed to pose no unacceptable threat to the balance of social, economic, and political forces in the union—on all these counts, the slave *trade* posed a different issue. Surely it would not be impossible to end the slave trade if the nation was determined to do so. Surely the slave trade, by introducing large numbers of "unseasoned savages" into the country, would add materially to the weaknesses attendant upon slavery. And surely under the federal ratio these new "persons" would disrupt the balance of forces within the union. Thus, to men like George Mason and John Dickinson, the slave trade seemed a national concern. As Dickinson put it, "The true question was whether the national happiness would be promoted or impeded by the importation [of slaves], and this question ought to be left to the national government, not to the states particularly interested." [48]

But if the national government undertook to deal with the importation of slaves, would it not inevitably confront issues having to do, not only with the ultimate prohibition of the trade, but also with its regulation in the meantime—conditions during the so-called "Middle Passage" and in the domestic slave markets? This "widening" of concerns, this reaching into sensitive areas, had a "threatening aspect," in Ellsworth's view. And if the slave trade ever came to be "considered in a moral light," the government might be called upon to emancipate the slaves. "If we do not agree [to make the slave trade completely immune from federal interference]," he warned, we will "lose two states . . . fly into a variety of shapes and directions, and most probably into several confederations, and not without bloodshed." [49]

Three considerations were urged by the Connecticut–Deep Southern axis against changing the arrangement submitted by Rutledge's committee. The first was that the summer was drawing to a close, the delegates were tired, and the nation was beginning to clamor for a look at their work. Introducing the debate on August 22, Sherman "urged on the Convention the necessity of dispatching its business." [50] King and Morris must have recalled somewhat bitterly that Sherman had admonished them on August 8 for their "premature" assault on the Rutledge Committee report. Now they were told that it was too late.

The second argument was that slavery was dying of its own accord, and that it was therefore foolhardy to risk the failure of the Convention, and civil war, in an attempt to end it now. It was at this point in the debate that Sherman and Ellsworth predicted that slavery would soon disappear from America. Several Southerners, too, uttered comforting words on this subject, but the assurances offered by the South Carolinians and Georgians differed slightly, but significantly, from those offered by New Englanders. Whereas the latter spoke of the "abolition of slavery," the hope held out by Charles Pinckney and Abraham Baldwin was specifically confined to the termination of the importation of slaves. And against both of these lullabies, the elder Pinckney candidly declared "that he did not think South Carolina would stop her importation of slaves in any short time, but only stop them occasionally, as she now does." [51] Nevertheless, the illusion that slavery, the slave trade, or both, was dying was apparently a key part of the rationalization of some Northerners for submitting to the demands of the Deep Southerners.

The ultimate appeal of the defenders of the Rutledge Committee report was that its clause on the slave trade was a necessary compromise.

Mr. Williamson . . . thought the Southern states could not be members of the union if the clause should be rejected, and that it was wrong to force anything down, not absolutely necessary, and which any state must disagree to.[52]

At this point, Rufus King re-entered the debate. He would agree to consider the clause "in a political light only." But he insisted that the three southernmost states were not the only ones to consider. If the slave trade was left untouched (the only "import" thus exempted from duty), and if the federal ratio was retained and export taxes prohibited, "great and equal opposition would be experienced" from the Northern states.[53] No one could expect such a Constitution to be ratified by state conventions in the North that would not be meeting in the intimidating presence of men like John Rutledge, Pierce Butler, and Charles Cotesworth Pinckney.

General Pinckney finally recognized the force of what King was saying and moved to send the clause dealing with the slave trade to a committee, "that slaves might be made liable to tax with other imports." Rutledge reacted sharply: "If the Convention thinks that North Carolina, South Carolina, and Georgia will ever agree to this plan, unless their right to import slaves be untouched, the expectation is in vain." But rather than allow the Convention to eliminate the clause, Rutledge seconded Pinckney's motion for commitment. Morris, delighted at this break in Southern intransigence, suggested that the intersectional "bargain" be widened to include navigation acts and export taxes, but Butler and Sherman drew the line at export taxes. A vote was taken, and showed an intersectional majority favoring commitment of the fourth, fifth, and sixth sections of the draft.[54]

The committee assigned to fashion the new intersection bargain was chaired by Governor William Livingston, of New Jersey, and was dominated by men who gave promise of being able to see the problem of the slave trade in a soundly commercial framework. Its report represented something of a recovery for the Northern commercial interests from the debacle they had suffered at the hands of the Committee of Detail. Instead of exempting the slave trade from taxes entirely, it allowed an impost "at a rate not exceeding the average of the duties laid on imports." Instead of making the trade perpetually immune from prohibition, it provided only that the slave trade "shall not be prohibited by the legislature prior to the year 1800." It left Section 5 intact, thus continuing the prohibition against a selective capitation tax. But instead of retaining the two-thirds majority for navigation acts, it eliminated Section 6 entirely, which meant that such acts could be passed, like other commercial regulations, by simple majorities in both houses of Congress.[55]

When, on August 25, this report was taken up, it quickly became apparent that an intersectional accommodation had been reached between the delegates from New England and those from the Deep South. General Pinckney, seconded by Gorham, moved to extend to 1808 the slave trade's immunity from prohibition. Despite a wail of anguish from Madison, the motion was carried by the three northernmost and the three southernmost states.[56]

Sherman and Madison now objected that the provision of a tax for the foreign slave trade admitted "into the Constitution the idea that there could be property in men." Sherman complained that so small a duty would never discourage the trade, but would merely raise a revenue for the government from a "nefarious" enterprise. Several other New Englanders announced, however, that they "considered [the tax] as the price" of allowing the slave trade to continue for twenty more years, and General Pinckney "admitted that it was so." Madison does not tell us why, or at whose initiative, but the tax was finally changed from "the average of the duties laid on imports" to "a tax . . . not exceeding ten dollars for each person." In this form, it passed.[57]

One other change made by Livingston's committee is worth remarking, though its significance is not altogether clear. Unlike the earlier version, this report guaranteed the slave trade from Congressional interference specifically for states "now existing." Was this meant to enable Congress to keep the slave trade, and thus slavery itself, out of the territories from the start of the new government? The clause deals with the "migration or importation" of "persons." Was this intended to refer to domestic as well as foreign slave trading?"[58] Was it thus implied that Congress was *not* enjoined, before 1800 (or 1808) or after, from outlawing the migration or importation of slaves into the territories?

Subsequent events indicate that this interpretation was not favored. There is no denying, however, that the language of the clause itself admits of this construction. And if this is what the committee, and the Convention, intended, there is support for those who, like Abraham Lincoln, believed that the framers produced a Constitution that looked forward, resolutely and practically, to the confinement of slavery within its present sphere and thus eventually to its elimination from the land.

That the inclusion of the words "now existing" mer no known resistance at the Convention, however, argues against this interpretation. The words were probably included to permit Congress to prohibit the slave trade into the Northwest Territory before 1808, as provided in the Northwest Ordinance, passed in Congress forty days before the Livingston Committee convened. The admission of the slaveholding states of Kentucky and Tennessee during the first decade under the Constitution, without an explicit challenge of their right to allow trade in slaves, fortifies the impression that the interpretation suggested above was not feared because it was not suspected by those in the founding generation who were watchful for the interests of slavery.

On August 28, two of the miscellaneous clauses toward the end of the Constitution came up for review, providing an occasion for the South Carolinians to seek further securities for their peculiar property. First, General Pinckney expressed dissatisfaction with the clause that guaranteed that "the citizens of each state shall be entitled to all privileges and immunities of the citizens in the several states." Madison's notes are scanty at this point, but the General seems to have wanted a specific guarantee that slaveholders could take their property into "free" territory without jeopardizing their claim to ownership. The vote affirmed the "privileges and immunities" clause without amendment, with South Carolina alone in dissent and Georgia divided.[59]

Second, Butler and Pinckney moved "to require fugitive slaves and servants to be delivered up like criminals." [60] The concept of the "fugitive slave" was introduced into American law during the summer of 1787, first in the Northwest Ordinance, then at the Federal Convention.[61] Its significance would be to give a nationwide sanction to the right to property in slaves. Thus slavery in one state could not be undermined by conditions or enactments in any other state. If the state of which the owner was a citizen recognized it as his right to own a slave, there would now be no place in the United States where the slave could escape. The federal government would guarantee the satisfaction of the master's claim.

The objections raised against Butler's motion were significant. Wilson complained only that the state obliged to return the slave would incur "public expense"—indicating that states preferred to commit the task of recovery to slave owners anxious for the return or replacement of their chattels, rather than retain for themselves the task of protecting their own citizens by distinguishing between fugitive slaves and free Negro residents. Sherman "saw no more propriety in the public seizing and surrendering a slave or servant than a horse." His usual Yankee prudence failed him at this point. It was the free Negro, more than the slave, who would be jeopardized by a fugitive-slave clause. And the difference between free Negroes and horses was that the owners of horses in the North would counteract horse thieves from outside the state, whereas free Negroes might not have anyone interested in preventing them from being dragged into slavery.[62]

Butler must have been delighted, even if he was not surprised, at this reaction. Withdrawing his motion, he promised to submit another version later, free of these objections. The following day he did so, and his proposal was accepted, without debate or dissent, in the following words:

If any person bound to service or labor in any of the United States shall escape into another state, he or she shall not be discharged from such service or labor, in consequence of any regulations subsisting in the state to which they escape, but shall be delivered up to the person justly claiming their services or labor.[63]

This was substantially the clause that finally appeared in Section 2 of Article IV, except that the Committee of Style changed the word "justly" to "legally" (thus narrowing the Constitutional sanction given to slavery), an adverb that was later removed, without replacement, to accommodate those who believed that the legality of slavery had a moral sanction and that the Constitution should not imply otherwise.[64]

It may be harsh to belabor Northern delegates for not foreseeing the abuses to which fugitive-slave acts were later put. Nevertheless, the casual way in which this clause—so full of peril to Negroes, both bond and free—was adopted tells volumes about the plight of black men in a nation governed by whites. The United States was a miserable place for Negroes, in part because, while Southerners were zealous to keep Negroes enslaved, Northerners cared only superficially, if at all, about the rights, welfare, and happiness of free Negroes. The careless language of the fugitive-slave clause reveals better than anything else in the Constitution that the fundamental problem for blacks in the union was that the government was in no way answerable to them, and white Americans in general did not hold them in just regard.

On August 29, the Convention returned to the last element in the Livingston Committee report, its elimination of the requirement of two-thirds majorities for navigation acts. Under the Confederation, the South had always resisted moves to give Congress power to enact commercial regulations. Southerners apparently feared that Northern merchants, supported by shipbuilders in the mid-Atlantic states, would grant themselves a monopoly of the American carrying trade, ignoring the interests of Southerners, as producers of staples, in transporting their products as cheaply as possible, regardless of the flag on the ship's mast.[65]

Charles Pinckney now spoke for those who shared this fear, and moved to reinstate the two-thirds requirement. He argued that his motion should be welcomed by everyone, since no single interest was dominant, and each should be happy to retain the means to defend itself. When Wilson retorted that the only way to secure "every peculiar interest" was to require unanimity, Mason admitted that, to the supporters of this motion, the Southern interest was primarily in view. "The Southern states are the *minority* in both houses. Is it to be expected that they will deliver themselves bound hand and foot to the Eastern states, and enable them to exclaim, in the words of Cromwell . . . 'the lord hath delivered them into our hands'?"[66]

During the debate, the embryo of the Hamiltonian Federalist party could be seen ranged in opposition to the Southern agrarians. All three of Pinckney's colleagues from South Carolina repudiated his motion. Rutledge urged the Convention to take an

enlarged, permanent view. Butler admitted that in many things
"the interests of [North and South are] as different as the interests of Russia and Turkey. Being notwithstanding desirous of
conciliating the affections of the Eastern states, he should vote
against requiring two-thirds instead of a majority." General
Pinckney tossed a bouquet to his "liberal and candid" brethren
from the East, noting "the interest the weak Southern states had
in being united with the strong Eastern states.' He admitted that
the concession on navigation acts was Southern *quid* for the
Northern *quo* on the slave trade, and he was confident that he
could reconcile his constituents to this "liberality" on the part of
the South.

Several delegates spoke for the Northern merchants, offering
the prospect of improved American ships, leading eventually to
cheaper transportation and a stronger naval defense for the whole
country. Gorham warned the Convention not to deprive New
Englanders of their end of the "bargain." The vote was then
taken, and showed seven states opposed to Pinckney's substitute,
with only four in favor. South Carolina joined the states north of
the Mason-Dixon Line, against Maryland, Virginia, North Carolina, and Georgia.[67] Once this motion had been rejected, the Convention, without further debate, completed the adoption of the
Livingston Committee report.

In the waning hours of the Convention, two incidents demonstrated Southern confidence that the Constitution was strong, as
they intended, but void of any threat to slavery. Commenting on
a proposed clause providing for the Constitution's amendment,
Rutledge stated emphatically that "he never could agree to give a
power by which the articles relating to slaves might be altered by
the states not interested in that property and prejudiced against
it." Following this statement in Madison's notes come these remarkable words:

In order to obviate this objection, these words were added . . . : "provided that no amendments which may be made prior to the year 1808
shall in any manner affect the fourth and fifth sections of the VII
article." [68]

In other words, there were only two clauses in the entire Constitution that were thought even to suggest a federal power over slavery: the one that protected the slave trade from federal regulation until 1808, and the one that prohibited selective capitation taxes. With these two provisions protected, Rutledge apparently felt that the slaveholders were safe under the Constitution, even in a union that might someday be dominated by states "prejudiced against" slavery.

The second incident concerned the slave interest only indirectly. On September 15, Roger Sherman "expressed his fears that three-fourths of the states might be brought to do things fatal to particular states," and moved to add to the amending clause a proviso "that no state shall without its consent be affected in its internal police, or deprived of its equal suffrage in the Senate." His motion was summarily defeated, drawing its three affirmative votes, not from the Carolinas and Georgia, but from Connecticut, New Jersey, and Delaware. Southern politicians of a later era would have been grateful if this clause had found its way into the Constitution, but their forefathers in Philadelphia were convinced that it was churlish to demand this additional security. Due to the "circulating murmurs of the small states," a guarantee of "equal suffrage in the Senate" was finally inserted, but the "internal police" proviso was allowed to fall, apparently because those who wanted these powers retained by the states could not foresee that the federal government would ever have occasion or desire to take them over.[69]

One cannot escape the feeling that a stronger, more deliberate stand against the slave trade or against the vagueness of the fugitive-slave clause, for example, might have called the bluff of the South Carolinians. During the main debates on the slave trade of August 21 and 22, the remarkable fact is that it was the delegates from Connecticut, Ellsworth and Sherman, who insisted most emphatically that the country would "lose two states" unless the report of the Committee of Detail was accepted as Rutledge had submitted it. When Sherman stated that it was "better to let the Southern states import slaves than to part with them, if they made that a sine qua non," [70] those who wanted to continue the trade must have felt reinforcement in the tendency to present their desires in the form of an ultimatum.

This shows the unequal tension that produced the Constitution's provisions on slavery: the clarity and determination of those with a direct interest versus the relative ignorance and unconcern of those without this direct interest. The reason the Convention was able to move against the slave trade was that there were many delegates who perceived that it threatened their interests: Virginians, who were already overstocked with slaves and knew from direct experience the dangers of a surplus; and Northerners, who could perceive the relationship between the slave trade and their relative weight in the government, via the federal ratio. With regard to other issues affecting slavery, there was no countervailence of interests among Southerners present and little sense of direct stake among the Northerners, and thus, no other move against slavery was taken, or even seriously contemplated.

On the question of the representation of states in Congress, many Northerners had shown themselves willing to take the Convention to the edge of collapse. One cannot help wondering what concessions could have been wrung from the slaveholders if a similar will had been shown to limit the power of slavery. Could slavery have been confined to "states now existing"? Could the rights of free Negroes have been defined and secured? Could the rights of owners who wished to emancipate their chattels have been established against state laws to the contrary? It is impossible to say, because the Convention never really broached these subjects. The most perceptive delegates acknowledged the power of slavery to cleave the union in two, but the Convention as a whole failed to regard this fact as a challenge to their moral and political imagination.

Most of the framers were either unperturbed about slavery or else completely resigned to its presence in America. None saw slavery as a sufficient moral or political evil to justify even a careful analysis of its effects, much less a stand against its continued existence. These men—who had shown themselves capable of the most imaginative political thinking and of the boldest political action on other issues—were willing to acquiesce in slavery for two reasons: because the suffering of Negroes did not sufficiently quicken their sympathies, and because they were unable to imagine a viable alternative. Because of these two defects of imagination, they were able to persuade themselves that the political realities of 1787 prevented them, not only from abolishing slavery outright, but from considering it carefully. Nevertheless, the presence of these unassimilated black neighbors would dog the pursuit of "a more perfect union" until the nation overcame its temptation to proceed as if the injustice of slavery could safely be ignored.

On September 17, 1787, George Washington, President of the Federal Convention, sent the completed Constitution to the Congress of the Confederation, along with a statement urging prompt ratification. His statement stressed the difficulties of fashioning a national constitution acceptable to all elements in the union. Differences among the states, in their "situation, extent, habits and particular interests," made the delegates reluctant to compromise each state's "independent sovereignty." Yet the conviction that "our prosperity, felicity, safety, perhaps even our national existence" depended upon the preservation of the union had induced them "to be less rigid on points of inferior magnitude than might otherwise have been expected." "The Constitution which we now present," he concluded, "is the result of a spirit of amity, and of that mutual deference and concession which the peculiarity of our political situation rendered indispensable." [71]

The Federal Convention had been conducted behind closed doors; the delegates had agreed not to discuss its proceedings with nondelegates.[72] In characterizing the Convention as a gathering of amiable, patriotic gentlemen, Washington had to some extent taken advantage of the public ignorance, but his purpose was not to enhance the reputation of the framers. Rather, he meant to cultivate, in Congress and in the ratifying conventions of the several states, a spirit of trust and "deference," without which the constitutional revolution could never have been consummated.

The Constitution was the creation of a group of the most nationally minded men in America. It emerged, in mid-September, the specific creation of a certain group of men, who had fashioned it through three and a half months of intense interaction and growth. Now this creation was to be cast into several different arenas: first, Congress; then, thirteen state ratifying conventions. Its elements would be scrutinized by men who would approach it from a great variety of perspectives. In most cases, this review would be conducted without an intimate awareness of the political processes that had led to certain features of the finished whole. Framers themselves would be on hand in many of the state conventions, and many would do their best to explain and justify the specific compromises. Others, of course, would try to turn feelings the other way. But it would be impossible even for these privileged witnesses to communicate a full appreciation of the play of forces that produced the ultimate text.

Washington's anxiety was understandable. He was acutely aware of the differences in situation and attitude throughout the union. He was aware that political leaders in many parts of the union were parochial men. He knew that not all men shared the conviction that a constitutional revolution was necessary to preserve the union. And he knew that a change of fundamental constitution was a most precarious and difficult undertaking. Men were being asked to commit their lives and destinies to an unknown and untried system of institutions, the specifications for which were necessarily sketchy and incomplete. Who could know how the powers committed to the federal government would be used? Who could know what elements would control the administration? Who could confidently anticipate the balance of forces in the legislature, or what the dominant elements would try to do with their power? The ratification of the Constitution would be a gamble for everyone. Much would depend on the attitude with which Congressmen and the delegates to ratifying conventions approached their task. Thus, Washington urged "deference," and several of the framers later echoed the plea to the ratifying conventions in the states.[73]

In light of these forebodings, one of the most remarkable features of the ratification process was the relative lack of controversy aroused by the arrangements in the Constitution affecting slavery. Consider the reception given to the federal ratio. Here was an issue that might have produced serious controversy, but never really did. Perhaps the subject, as framed in the Constitution, seemed too complicated. By tying both direct taxes and representation to a formula that included a fraction, the Constitution seemed to invite intricate calculation and facetious byplay between delegates, rather than serious consideration. In the Massachusetts convention, Rufus King noted that according to this formula the same taxes would be paid for five Negro children as for the governors of New Hampshire, Massachusetts, and Connecticut; to which another delegate replied that Massachusetts taxpayers, by this formula, were bound to pay the same amount of taxes for three helpless infants as Virginians were paying for five working Negroes. But these games were beside the point, and everyone knew it. Southerners had insisted on some increment in representation for their slaves; Northerners resisted full equality; and the federal ratio had become the "language of all America" for compromising the difference.[74]

Only once during the process of ratification did the federal ratio receive a thorough analysis: from James Madison, in number 54 of *The Federalist*. Here, for once, the difficulties of justifying the ratio were candidly confronted. Here, at last, the reasons for stepping around these difficulties were powerfully given.

Writing in a newspaper in New York City, Madison began by noting the difference between representation and taxation. In apportioning representation, one needed to bear in mind "the personal rights of the people." It was therefore appropriate to distribute units of representation according to the numbers of persons who possessed "personal rights," which would *exclude* slaves. Taxes, on the other hand, ought in justice to reflect wealth. Thus, if population was taken as the index of wealth, it was right in this case to *include* slaves, who were as productive, or nearly so, as free men. Thus, by strict logic, slaves, being productive property, but not free persons, ought to be included in the ratio for taxes but excluded for representation.

He then resorted to anonymous quotation (the only time in the *The Federalist* he used this curious device) to present the response of "our Southern brethren." Without discussing the propriety or morality of slavery, his mythical Southerner argued that, by the laws of Southern states, slaves were both property and persons. They were property in that their labor belonged, not to themselves, but to masters; they were "vendible"; and they were restrained in their liberty, and subject to physical punishment, according to "the capricious will" of another man. But they were also persons, in that the laws protected them in life and limb, and punished them for violence committed against others. Thus, slaves were regarded, at least in part, as members of society, moral persons, not as "part of the irrational creation," or as mere property. It was therefore altogether appropriate that the federal laws should follow the practice of the states in regarding slaves as human inhabitants, but "divested" of part of their humanity by servitude.

Madison ascribed one further argument to his mythical Southerner. "Government," he wrote, "is instituted no less for the protection of the property than of the persons of individuals." Experience was showing, however, that wealthy persons had great, if "imperceptible," influence over their neighbors. Thus, the evolving consensus of republican doctrine was that "the rights of property" would be adequately protected, even though "an opulent citizen [had] but a single vote in the choice of his representative, [because] the respect and consequence which he derives from his fortunate situation very frequently guide the votes of others to the objects of his choice." But a state, he went on, had no such influence over other states. Wealthy persons in one state were unlikely to be able to influence the selection of representatives from other states. If any group of wealthy people justly deserved special protection, it must be secured in the formula for apportionment.

The last argument was the crux of the matter. No one could translate the "mixed character" of slaves under Southern law into a fractional figure for comparison with free men, and no one ever really tried. The three-fifths figure was not a statistical measure of the degree of humanity that remained to the African enslaved. It was the point at which Americans had grown accustomed to compromising the difference between states with slaves and states without them. In 1783, Northerners had persuaded Southerners that it was fair to include slaves in the formula for taxation. In 1787, Southerners countered that the same argument worked two ways. Northerners might argue that the case was different now, but it was no use.

It would be twenty years before Northerners would begin to feel that they had yielded something substantial in 1787. Not a penny of revenue was ever collected under the formula of 1783; it had failed to gain the necessary unanimous ratification. Four years later, many Northerners reconciled themselves to the federal ratio by reflecting that it would govern direct taxes as well as representation. But, as several astute politicians had anticipated in 1787 and 1788, direct taxes never became an important source of revenue for the federal government. Tariffs and excises were easier to collect, and much less annoying to a predominantly agrarian population, as a brief experiment with direct taxes during the administration of John Adams amply demonstrated. The simple truth was that the Northern delegates were drilled into granting "representation for a species of property which they have not among them," as General Pinckney put it to the South Carolinians, and got nothing substantial in return.[75]

Besides the clause on apportionment, there were only two other clauses that referred specifically (though without using the word "slavery") to the institution: the clause on the slave trade and the fugitive-slave clause. People who were already sensitized to the issue spotted these and took offense. Joshua Atherton, of New Hampshire, for example, announced his intention to vote against ratification, saying with great feeling that he would not enter into covenant with "manstealers." And on the Southern side, Rawlins Lowndes, of South Carolina, who strenuously opposed ratification, said that Northerners insisted upon ending the slave trade because they had no slaves themselves and "therefore want to exclude us from this great advantage." "For his part," he added, "he thought this trade could be justified on the principles of religion, humanity and justice; for certainly to translate a set of human beings from a bad country to a better, was fulfilling every part of those principles." [76]

One other source of controversy in the South was the suggestion by Patrick Henry in Virginia that the "necessary and proper" clause implied a power to emancipate slaves if, for example, a majority of Congress found such an act necessary to the general defense. "Among ten thousand *implied powers* which [Congress] may assume," he said, "they may if we be engaged in war, liberate every one of your slaves, if they please." [77]

But these were exceptions, and in Henry's case, at least, they appeared to be the device of a man who had decided on other grounds to oppose the Constitution and who was using the attitudes of his neighbors toward slavery as part of an arsenal. Defenders of the Constitution, like Madison and Randolph in Virginia and General Pinckney in South Carolina, foiled these assaults rather easily, replying that no one in the Convention had ever suggested that slaves ought to be emancipated; that no sane Northerner would ever propose so calamitous a course; and that politics could not proceed unless men were willing to trust that their fellow covenanters were sane.[78]

In South Carolina, where suspicions arising from attitudes toward slavery were closest to the nerve of opposition, the Constitution was ratified rather handily. In other states, where the verdict was closer (New Hampshire, Massachusetts, New York, Pennsylvania, Virginia), opposition rested on various grounds.* Though information about these ratifying conventions is sketchy, it seems safe to conclude that the clauses affecting slavery nowhere constituted a serious threat to ratification.[80]

Yet despite this lack of serious controversy over slavery, a nationalist who could have attended each of the conventions might

---

* Despite the lack of controversy over clauses directly affecting slavery, the institution may ironically have influenced a feature that did constitute a serious obstacle to ratification in some states: the lack of a bill of rights. Even in South Carolina, opponents of ratification objected that there were no guarantees of liberty for the press. General Pinckney responded with the usual rather lame arguments: that the government had only enumerated powers, none of which constituted a danger to a free press; that a free press was "secured by all our state constitutions"; and that a list of explicitly protected rights might endanger any rights that were omitted. "Another reason," he added, "weighed particularly with the members from this state against the insertion of a bill of rights. Such bills generally begin with declaring that all men by nature are born free. Now, we should make that declaration with a very bad grace, when a large part of our property consists in men who are actually born slaves." The constitution of South Carolina was one of four (New Jersey, Georgia, and New York were the others) among the original thirteen that contained no bill of rights as such.[79]

well have come away from his experience with a deep sense of foreboding about the prospects for the American union. For the conventions, taken as a whole, did reveal an ominous cleavage in attitude and expectation with respect to slavery. The best illustration is a comparison of the reception given to the clause on the slave trade in Pennsylvania and in South Carolina.

In Pennsylvania, the burden of interpretation was assumed by James Wilson, who rose on December 3, 1787, to respond to the criticism that the Constitution left the government impotent to deal with "this reproachful trade" for twenty years. He pointed out, "Under the present confederation, the states may admit the importation of slaves as long as they please; but by this article, after the year 1808, the Congress will have power to prohibit such importation, notwithstanding the disposition of any state to the contrary." It missed the point to see this clause as a victory for slavery. He described it as, on the contrary, "laying the foundation for banishing slavery out of this country . . . [by] the same kind, gradual change which was pursued in Pennsylvania." [81] In a passage that would surely have raised eyebrows, if not muskets, in South Carolina, he went on to argue that "the new states which are to be formed will be under control of Congress in this particular, and slaves will never be introduced amongst them." He seemed to be referring to the power of Congress, contained in Article IV, Section 3, "to . . . make all needful rules and regulations respecting the territory or other property belonging to the United States." The exemption from Congressional interference with the "migration or importation" of slaves is specifically limited to "states now existing." He apparently concluded that the power of Congress over the territories included the power to prohibit the "migration" of slaves by land, as well as their importation from abroad by sea. [82]

In a letter written thirty years later, James Madison commented on Wilson's speech, asserting that it contained language "more vague and less consistent" than Wilson's usual mode of expression. He suggested that the reporter of the Pennsylvania convention might have been to blame. Certainly the Wilson that emerges from Madison's notes of the Federal Convention used a more cautious and accommodating style, particularly on the slavery issue, than the one reported from the Pennsylvania convention.

Laying aside the question of style, however, there is a difference, too, in the substance of Wilson's remarks on slavery at the two conventions, which may have arisen from the different political problems they presented. Whether his expression at the state convention was careful or not, he left the impression that the Federal Convention had dealt firmly with slavery, putting it on the road to extinction, and that Congress had power to keep slavery out of the territories. Madison later insisted that no power over the domestic movements of slaves was implied in the Constitution, and that Wilson's was the only attempt during the debates over ratification to advance this interpretation. Had this construction gained currency, Madison argued "it is easy to imagine the figure it would have made in many of the states, among the objections to the Constitution, and among the numerous amendments to it proposed by the state conventions, not one of which amendments refers to the clause in question. . . ." Not even Patrick Henry or George Mason, "among the multitude of their objections, and farfetched interpretations, ever hinted, in the debates on the 9th Section of Article I, at a power given by it, to prohibit an interior migration of any sort." [83]

Madison's point is a good one. Though the words of the Constitution are susceptible of the construction Wilson put on them, it is all but certain that they would not have been adopted by the Federal Convention if this interpretation had been hinted at or foreseen. Furthermore, if Southerners had learned of Wilson's construction before their ratifying conventions had met,* and if they had suspected that it contained a grain of justification, the conventions in Virginia and South Carolina would almost surely have refused to accept the Constitution. Maryland, too, might have withheld ratification, and Georgia would have tried hard to retract its (unanimous) approval. Since North Carolina held aloof on other grounds, the result of Wilson's speech, if it had been heard and believed in the South, might well have been to scuttle the Constitution.

Meanwhile, words being spoken in South Carolina would cer-

* Pennsylvania was the second state—Delaware being the first—to ratify.

241

tainly have given umbrage had they been heard in Pennsylvania. General Pinckney's problem was opposite from Wilson's. He had to convince his neighbors in Charleston that "considering all circumstances, we have made the best terms for the security of this specie of property [slaves] it was in our power to make." Noting that he and his colleagues "had to contend with the religious and political prejudices" of New England and Pennsylvania and with "the interested and inconsistent opinion of Virginia" (favorable to slavery, but opposed to importations from Africa), he justified Article I, Section 9 on the ground of necessity. He asserted his belief that "the nature of our climate, and the flat, swampy situation of our country, obliges us to cultivate our lands with Negroes," and he acknowledged that the need for black laborers was not declining. Without slaves, he said, "South Carolina would soon be a desert waste.* But he reported the basic Northern argument against the trade: that an increase in the number of slaves in the South would increase the nation's vulnerability at the same time that it augmented the South's influence in the government. Northerners felt that it was unfair to permit this process to continue indefinitely. Finally, he said, "after a great deal of difficulty," the Northern delegates promised "to restrain the religious and political prejudices" of their constituents if a date was set when the importation might be stopped altogether. By this arrangement South Carolina gained the right to "an unlimited importation of Negroes for twenty years" and the opportunity to resist the termination of the trade after 1808 by political means. Robert Barnwell, a leader in the fight for ratification, added his "opinion" that the economic interests of Northerners—their desire to transport the products of a vigorous Southern agriculture —would counteract their desire to prohibit the slave trade, even after the Constitutional moratorium had expired.[85]

A comparison of this defense of the clause on the slave trade with Wilson's remarks at the Pennsylvania convention suggests the existence of two completely different worlds of discourse on

---

* On this point, Rawlins Lowndes, who opposed ratification by South Carolina because he thought the Constitution rendered property in slaves precarious, stated, "Without negroes, this state would degenerate into one of the most contemptible in the union. . . . Negroes," he added, "are our wealth, our only natural resource. . . ."[84]

this issue. Despite the framers' efforts, the clause did not settle all questions affecting the slave trade, before or after 1808. It was not long before men were interpreting these ambiguities according to their own interests or commitments.

As the Constitution of 1787 was being ratified, the founders were satisfied that they had disposed of the issue of slavery to the satisfaction of everyone. Everyone, it seems, judged the Constitution in light of the Articles of Confederation, and nearly everyone found it superior.

Northerners exulted that the slave trade was finally under a sentence of death. Slavery had thus "received a mortal wound, and would die of consumption." Furthermore, power had been given to Congress to keep slavery out of the territories. Surely it was a blessing that an institution that had already "blackened half the plains of America" would now be restrained from spreading its contamination to the rest. Inasmuch as it would be wrong "to abolish slavery, by an act of Congress, in a moment, and so destroy what our Southern brethren consider property," the Constitution was to be saluted for doing the right thing: cordoning slavery into the South, setting a date when its supply could be cut off, and waiting for historical processes to work their miraculous cleansing effect.[86]

Southerners were equally pleased. Charles Cotesworth Pinckney assured the South Carolinians that the federal government could never "emancipate" slaves. In addition, the Constitution gave "much better security" than presently existed for owners whose slaves might escape across state lines.* As far as territories

---

* Compare Randolph at the Virginia ratifying convention: ". . . there was not a member of the Virginia delegation who had the smallest suspicion of the abolition of slavery." And Madison: "No power is given to the general government to interpose with respect to the property now held by the states."[87] It is possible that for Madison the word "now" was full of significance. His anxiety about slavery was profound. He was among those most vigilant to see that the word "slavery" was not included in the text of the Constitution. Perhaps the "Father of the Constitution" was trying to preserve the possibility that, should the national government's authority become firmly established and the commitment to slavery weaken, legislative action in the direction of abolition might someday be taken. But the evidence that he had such a thought in mind is extremely thin. And when, as a result of his struggle with Hamilton during the 1790's, he became a strict constructionist, and when

were concerned, there is no evidence that any Southerner anticipated the possibility of prohibiting slavery in territories controlled by the Southern states. Concerning the slave trade, opinions varied, but everyone seemed satisfied. Virginians looked
upon it as having been put under a sentence of death; Deep
Southerners, who "were now in want of hands to cultivate their
lands," saw an opportunity in the next twenty years to be "fully
supplied." Even then, there was no guarantee that the power to
abolish the trade could be exercised.[88]

And so most Southerners and Northerners entered into government under the Constitution convinced that they were better off
than they had been under the Articles, with regard to slavery as
well as most other things. Slavery had been confined to a cul-de-
sac, where it would be virtually unnecessary, as it would surely be
impolitic, for national politicians to handle it.

The framers had dealt with slavery by seeking, so far as possible, to take it out of the national political arena. They were unable in 1787 to settle the issue, one way or the other. They could
not establish straightforward Constitutional guarantees against
emancipation, as the South Carolinians desired, because many
Northerners, and perhaps some Southerners, would not permit it.
Nor could they give Congress power to regulate slavery in any
way, much less abolish it, because Southerners refused to yield
control over the institution. Realizing that it was utterly beyond
their power to fashion a national consensus on slavery, or to "govern" the issue in the absence of one, they had contented themselves with measures aimed at preventing friction over slavery between the states and sections. Thus, when it was decided to tie
representation to population, it became necessary to set a date
when the slave trade could be terminated, because of the relationship it now bore to the balance of political forces in the
union. And when Pierce Butler raised the question of escaped
slaves, the Convention was willing to oblige, because most Northerners were as reluctant for blacks to flee north as Southern slave
owners were to lose their property. The fugitive-slave clause, like

---

slavery's hold on the South tightened rather than weakened, his hope that
the federal government might or ought, in the foreseeable future, to legislate
against slavery faded rapidly.

the slave-trade clause, was intended to remove a potential sore point between the states.

It is possible that in steering clear of slavery in 1787, some framers may have had more in mind than the desire to avoid collision. Toward the end of the Convention, Gouverneur Morris proposed to "avoid the ambiguity" in the clause on the slave trade by amending it to read that the "importation of slaves into North Carolina, South Carolina and Georgia" could not be prohibited until 1808. But Madison remarked that it would be "wrong to admit in the Constitution the idea that there could be property in men." [89] To the end, Madison and others remained vigilant against any explicit reference to slavery. This linguistic fastidiousness may have represented a desire to save options for an uncertain future. If the Constitution withheld an explicit sanction from slavery, and if fate smiled on the young nation, it was possible that the future might miraculously present some way to remove the curse of slavery from America.

There is no evidence that any framer thought the Constitution contained power to abolish slavery. They all knew how the Deep Southerners felt, and however much some of them may have regretted the hold that slavery had on the South, they were all fully sympathetic with the determination of the Deep Southerners to resist abolition in the present circumstances. This was what Madison meant when he told the ratifying convention in Virginia that slave owners were safe under the Constitution, because it would be madness for the federal government to abolish slavery, and the Constitution represented a compact with sane and honorable men who would not commit mayhem on their fellow citizens.

But there was no guarantee that powers of emancipation were forever denied to the federal government. Patrick Henry was right, as Lincoln proved, when he argued that the power to abolish slavery might come to inhere in the power to wage war, and General Pinckney was wrong when he stated that the federal government was confined to powers "expressly" listed in the Constitution. If the framers had intended, as Pinckney said, to deny forever the power to abolish slavery, they could have included a clause to this effect in the Constitution. Export taxes were flatly and "expressly" prohibited. So was the granting of "titles of nobility." States were forbidden to enter into treaties or alliances with foreign powers. Sections 9 and 10 of Article I were full of such express prohibitions. But the power to emancipate slaves or to abolish or regulate slavery was not in that list.

The evidence there is permits the conclusion that the future, with respect to possible public action against slavery, was left open on purpose, at the insistence of such delegates as James Madison, Gouverneur Morris, and James Wilson. This speculation is important to an assessment of the political skill and intention of the framers. But as history actually developed, it was more important to the nation that the framers, as of 1787, agreed unanimously to place the institution of slavery, as it existed within the South, not "in the course of ultimate extinction," as Lincoln argued,[90] but beyond national regulation.

In so doing, they were inescapably giving a portentous hostage to fortune. The philosopher Thomas Hobbes said that the covenants upon which governments rest must be unfettered by reservations, that the covenanters must agree to yield all they possess, including their own lives, to the control of the sovereign power. Unless they do, they erect a "crazy building," one certain to fall around their ears as soon as the ground is disturbed by controversy.[91] Contrary to Hobbes, the founders of the American tradition taught that governments derive their authority from the consent of the governed, and that the governed, if they are wise, will limit the government to certain carefully defined and carefully enumerated powers. But experience has proved that Americans are also a pragmatic and flexible people, who have shown a remarkable capacity to amend their Constitution, the shrine of the federal government's "enumerated powers," by interpretation, according to circumstances.

The Americans who wrote and ratified the Constitution did not suspect that they were doing anything different with slavery from what was done with several other issues that were excluded from national politics. There were many institutions, many features of American life that the federal government was forbidden by the consensus of that time to touch. Slave owners were by no means unique in insisting on local control over local institutions.[92]

But the case of slavery *was* different. It was unique in the extent of its impact on national development, in its tendency to polarize the national community, and in its relevance to the fundamental principles of the government. Slavery pulled its proprietors in one direction, in terms of economic, social, and political development. The main currents of modernity pulled the rest of the country in another. When this tension began to bear on public policy, men who were affected by slavery only indirectly began to wish they could exercise some control over a factor so important to the nation. In reaction, the owners of slaves began to dread the desire of outsiders to interfere with an institution upon which their safety and prosperity seemed so intimately to depend, and their resistance to Constitutional evolution on this point stiffened. As the tensions produced by these contrary developments grew more and more intense, the determination of Northerners and the resistance of Southerners grew apace. Finally, in 1860 and 1861, the "crazy building" of 1787 fell to the ground, and over a half-million young men lost their lives in the crash.

7

Sectional Strains

in an Imperfect Union,

1789-1820

ALMOST as soon as the Constitution was ratified and went into effect, it was regarded as virtually sacred, providentially inspired to guide the infant republic, the hope of the world, to its destiny. Paradoxically, the union that produced it was seen as a perilous experiment, a brave and worthy, but certainly dangerous, exercise in putting diverse elements into the same container and hoping that the result would be social energy, not an explosion. By the end of the eighteenth century, the American union was a tenuous association of states and sections. The habit of thinking of these elements as a single nation was not yet a generation old. Even in the most nationalistic circles, it was still necessary to discuss the advantages and disadvantages of union, as compared with the alternative of two or three or thirteen or more confederacies.[1] And the ratification of the Constitution did not offer much respite from doubt and conflict among parties to the union.

In contrasting the framing of a constitution with the making of ordinary laws, care must be taken not to exaggerate the differences. Constitutions do not emerge from polite conversation among disinterested philosophers. There was plenty of hard bargaining between powerful interests during the summer of 1787.[2] Yet even if the Federal Convention is viewed as a political arena and the framers as human politicians, there are important differences between constitution making and the fashioning of ordinary public policy. A constitution is composed mostly of ground rules: an outline of the structure and composition of government, a description of functions for the various departments, a few imperative guidelines for policy. None of these rules is neutral, of course. In the Constitution of 1787, the bicameral legislature and the executive veto are conservative devices, increasing the opportunities to foil innovative measures. The prohibition against export taxes reflects the power of staple-producers in the Convention. But though these features certainly affect the content of public policy, they were included because they rested on a broad consensus among interests represented at the Convention and in the ratification process. Constitution making, in other words, is a consensual process, requiring virtually unanimous consent to be successful.

Lawmaking, on the other hand, is a more rough-and-ready exercise, in which slim majorities can more easily rule. It is one thing to agree that Congress shall draft tariff legislation; it is another to decide which items shall be taxed at 5 per cent and which at 8½ per cent. It is one thing to agree that the Executive shall negotiate and the Senate ratify treaties; it is another to decide when to negotiate and with whom, what to insist on, and what to do if the other side balks. In constitution making, success is a matter of finding a structure and process on which nearly everyone can agree, and of avoiding the appearance of favoring one interest over another. In making and applying laws, circumstances often force a choice between closely matched, contending elements in the body politic. The United States near the turn of the nineteenth century was fortunately able to agree on rules for conducting public business, but the actual conduct of that business brought intense conflict, which from time to time subjected the tender ligaments of the union to great strain.

Under the Federalists in the mid-1790's and especially in 1798, and under the Republicans in 1803–1804, 1807–1809, and 1812–1814, the reaction of the opposition to public policy took the form of doubts about the advantages of union and overt challenges to its continued existence. These tensions, under which the federal government operated during the first thirty years of its existence, help to explain the efforts of that government to cope with problems affecting slavery.

The most striking feature of life under the national government during the early national period was the saliency of foreign affairs.[3] After the First Congress (1789–1791), which was devoted mainly to the drafting of the Bill of Rights, the establishment of the federal judiciary and executive departments, and the passage of Hamilton's fiscal program, the leading events until the close of the War of 1812 were almost all related to foreign affairs. Washington's Neutrality Proclamation, Jay's Treaty, the XYZ affair and the "quasi-war" with France, the Louisiana Purchase, Jefferson's Embargo Act, and "Mr. Madison's War"—all these were directly in the field of foreign affairs. The program of direct taxes under President Adams, the Alien and Sedition Acts and the Virginia and Kentucky Resolutions, the "Burr Conspiracy" and the Hartford Convention—these were by-products of the nation's drive to establish an independent identity in a world at war.

The reason for the prominence of foreign affairs was that the United States was born just as France was throwing off its monarchy and seeking to impose its new-found vision of liberty, equality, and fraternity on the entire continent of Europe. The backbone of the will and capacity to resist French revolutionary energies lay across the English Channel. The titanic struggle between Britain and France, which raged from the mid-1790's until 1814, involved everyone having commercial relations with Europe, and that certainly included the United States.

The desire of early American statesmen to avoid "entanglement" with European politics is well known. This determination transcended party lines. Yet embroilment seemed unavoidable. The basic reason was not an inability to suppress imperial ambitions,[4] but the thrust of commercial enterprise. The idea that the United States could isolate itself from European politics stemmed partly from the notion that there could be commercial intercourse without political involvement,[5] but under the circumstances of the Napoleonic era, this proved to be an illusion.

Commercial intercourse with Europe and with European dominions in the Caribbean Sea was dictated by conditions in America. A Senate committee as late as 1816 pointed out that a ton of goods could be transported 3,000 miles from Europe to America for about nine dollars, but that the same sum of money would move a ton of goods only thirty miles through inland America. The following year, a month before the Erie Canal was authorized, a committee of the New York legislature reported that the cost of transportation from Buffalo to New York City was three times the value of wheat in New York City, six times that of corn, and twelve times that of oats. "Little wonder," concluded George Rogers Taylor, historian of American economic development, "that under such conditions foreign trade flourished while domestic commerce developed only very slowly." Never again, he added, would foreign commerce be "relatively so important a part of the whole American economy as in the period preceding the War of 1812." [6]

So, despite the efforts of statesmen who realized the perils of navigation in Europe's treacherous diplomatic seas, the infant republic inevitably became involved. And the involvement, perhaps just as inevitably, produced irritants in a system full of tension to begin with.

The strains first appeared under the severe impact of Hamilton's fiscal program. The assumption of state debts and the redemption of the foreign and domestic debt at par, coupled with the establishment of the first Bank of the United States, split Congress into groups that constituted the germ of the first party system, in which the "friends" of Washington's administration came to be known as the Federalists, and the opposition assumed the name Republicans.

Students of American political history differ in assigning a date for the emergence of parties under the Constitution.[7] In part, the dispute is a matter of definition. But if a party system can be defined as a fairly stable grouping of legislators into supporters of the administration and the opposition, then it seems possible to discern such a pattern in the American Congress by the early 1790's, perhaps as early as the beginning of the Third Congress (1793–1795). Joseph Charles, in his path-breaking study *The Origins of the American Party System,* is even more specific than that. He gives January 3, 1794, as the birth date.[8] On that day, James Madison introduced a set of resolutions that would have based American tariff regulations on reciprocity, whereby additional duties would have been imposed on items imported from nations "having no commercial treaty with the United States." The effect of these duties, he argued, would be to encourage negotiations toward fair commercial treaties. Failing that, Americans would be encouraged to develop sources of supply at home and to cultivate trade relations with other nations.[9] The resolutions were aimed at Great Britain, which had so far continued to treat the United States as a virtual colony, monopolizing its trade, yet disdaining to establish relations on the basis of a firm treaty.

These resolutions are indeed an appropriate symbol of the cleavage between Federalists and Republicans. The Federalists, led by men whose primary interests were commercial, were eager to co-operate with the leading commercial power in the Atlantic world and wary of twisting its tail. They were also disgusted with the excesses of the French Revolution, particularly after the execution of Louis XVI in January 1793. The Virginians, on the other hand, along with their political allies in Pennsylvania and New York, had bitter memories of the ravaging British Army during the Revolutionary War and deep resentment of their vassalage to British capital.[10] The passion of Jefferson and Madison for complete national independence amounted to an obsession, and was not compromised, as Hamilton's tended to be, by a desire to partake of the glories of international commerce. The preference of the Virginians for agrarian simplicity, mixed with modest town life and the peaceful cultivation of the human spirit, fitted nicely with their determination to separate themselves from the contamination of European politics. Jefferson had no special desire to identify America with the French Revolution. His wariness toward Citizen Genêt, which discomfited many French enthusiasts among the Republicans, was typical of his mistrust of European diplomats.[11] What made him seem partisan toward the French were his intense desire to wrench the United States loose from its symbiotic relationship with Great Britain and his readiness to encourage domestic political organization, much of which was directed, during the 1790's, against Washington's policies toward Great Britain (the Neutrality Proclamation and Jay's Treaty).[12]

Mixed with these differing perspectives on foreign and domestic policies was the still mostly latent, but ominous, difference of opinion over slavery. The cleavage on this issue did not follow party lines. Albert Gallatin, a Republican leader from Pennsylvania, probably held slavery in as much revulsion as any Yankee Federalist;[13] and, conversely, the Federalists from Charleston were as staunchly committed to slavery's immunity from federal regulation as were the Republicans from Virginia. Yet the centers of gravity of the Federalists and Republicans did tend to lie in the North and South, respectively, and during this first decade under the Constitution, there was a recurring counterpoint in Congressional debates that reflected this rough cleavage.

An interesting example occurred during the consideration of amendments to the Naturalization Act. The act of 1790 had been a liberal one. Some members of the First Congress had argued that American citizenship ought to be open to anyone who loved liberty and would obey good laws—including Roman Catholics and Jews, for example. Others had insisted that citizenship be made an achievement, a privilege, open to qualified people after a period of preparation and trial, since a republic depended heavily on the virtue of its citizens. From the tug between these polar conceptions emerged an act that extended citizenship to "all free white persons" * who, having resided here and shown good behavior for one year, expressed the intention of remaining here and took an oath of allegiance.[15]

By 1794, pressure was building to tighten these requirements, though men differed over the changes that ought to be made. Certain Federalists wanted to restrict immigration and naturalization. Theodore Sedgwick, noting that republican government depended upon "general intelligence and public virtue," argued that it was a mistake to think that as soon as an oppressed man set foot on republican soil, he was ready for self-government. He urged that the law be amended to require that an application for

---

* The restriction of naturalization to "free white persons" was retained through all the vacillations between liberality and xenophobia during this period.[14]

citizenship include an oath, sworn by two citizens, witnessing to the good moral character of the applicant.[16]

The debate took an ugly turn on New Year's Day of 1795 when William Branch Giles, a pugnacious Republican from Amelia County, Virginia, suggested that the main threat to republican government in the United States came, not from people whose habits were un-Puritan, but from men of wealth who sought to add the ornaments of nobility to their other instruments of oppression. To counteract the danger of aristocracy, he moved to add to the Naturalization Act a clause requiring aliens to renounce all claims to titles of nobility before taking the oath of allegiance.[17] The struggle that followed was extremely bitter, though mostly symbolic. It was animated more by feelings of hostility between Federalists and Republicans than by concern over the substantive issues raised by Giles's motion. European noblemen were not flocking to America; nor did the Republicans have anything substantial to fear in the aristocratic pretentions of some Federalists. The Constitution flatly forbade the American government from granting titles of nobility, and only a few Federalists chafed under the restriction.[18]

Nevertheless, Giles's motion, correctly interpreted as a taunt at the opposing party, aroused deep passions—so deep, in fact, that when Giles called for the yeas and nays on his motion, Federalist Samuel Dexter, of Massachusetts, responded by moving an amendment to the act that would have required aliens to renounce the possession of slaves, both at the time of applying for citizenship and for the future as well.[19] This motion hit Giles strongly. Stunned, he said that he was "sorry to see slavery made a jest of." Dexter's motion was "calculated to injure the property of gentlemen." He then launched into a defensive apology for slavery. He admitted that he "lamented and detested it; but from the existing state of the country, it was impossible at present to help it." Falling back upon a familiar rationalization, he gave it as his judgment that "The thing [slavery] was reducing as fast as could prudently be done." He sat down, wondering aloud why the Federalists had resorted to such an extraordinary measure to defeat his proposal.

Madison was less easily ruffled than his colleague. He, too, indulged in the premature rumor about slavery's death, noting that the importation of slaves was now prohibited virtually throughout the union. But he told the New Englanders that their continual agitation of the issue of slavery "had a dangerous tendency on the minds of these unfortunate people," inducing in them behavior that necessitated more severe discipline on the part of masters. Another Virginian, John Nicholas, chided Dexter for implying that slaveholders were unfit to be citizens or to hold public office in a republican government.[20]

After listening to this reaction, the Federalists moved to compromise. Sedgwick spoke the comforting word that "an abolition of slavery in this country would be the height of madness." Dexter offered to withdraw his motion if Giles would, too. Giles countered with an offer to withdraw his demand for a call of the roll on his amendment, but before an agreement could be reached, Congress adjourned for the day.

The next day, the Virginians apparently decided to stand and fight, and Dexter chose to accept the challenge. Robert Rutherford, of Virginia, warned that Dexter's amendment would alienate six to eight states of the union.[21] After a long and bitter exchange, the yeas and nays were taken on Dexter's motion. The result was defeat by a vote of 28 to 63. Of the twenty-eight Congressmen who voted to make slave owning a fault sufficient to disqualify a man from naturalization, twenty-seven were Northerners. Loyalty to the Federalist party, plus the chance to jab at his old foe, Giles, may have induced William Vans Murray, of Maryland, to support Dexter's motion. Significantly, the delegation from Pennsylvania gave only two votes for the motion, cast by arch-Federalists Thomas Hartley and James Armstrong while it threw nine votes the other way. Despite a well-established aversion to slavery, most of the Pennsylvanians disdained this gratuitous and profitless gesture, preferring to mollify, rather than exacerbate, the tensions between the sections.[22]

After the defeat of Dexter's maneuver, Giles's motion was quickly and decisively approved. The incident quickly passed, a brief reminder of the legitimacy of slave owning in republican America and the tremors produced by any challenge to it.

.   .   .

But the main business during these first years under the Constitution was foreign affairs, which has led Samuel Eliot Morison to suggest an analogy between these early national years and the period of the Cold War.[23] The counterpart of Communism in this analogy is the ideology of the French Revolution. Napoleon plays the part of Stalin, and the French Army, sweeping almost unimpeded through neighboring countries, constitutes the threat to the stability of Europe similar to that posed by the Red Army between 1944 and the early 1950's. It is the similarities in the American reaction to these European phenomena that are most striking. In both cases, some Americans found an imminent peril to the character and even the territory of the United States. In the earlier period many went so far as to fear an actual military invasion by the French, beginning in the South, where defenses were weak and "infatuation" with French libertarianism was most rampant.[24] In both eras the more typical apprehension was that the virus of revolution would infiltrate into high places in the government, the universities, and the churches, and, through "self-created" popular-front movements, infect "the masses." The response was a heightened suspicion of aliens and a deepening fear of sedition.

From the time, early in 1793, that France declared war on Britain, Spain, and Holland, American leaders struggled hard, but vainly, to eliminate the preoccupation with foreign affairs, a source of "discord and anarchy." [25] Yet it was the fate even of "separate and equal" nations in the Atlantic world to become embroiled in the French Revolution, notwithstanding proclamations of friendship to all belligerents.

Coincident with this evolving state of affairs was a hardening of lines of opposition between parties in the United States. While Washington held the Presidency, competition for influence on governmental policy was always kept within bounds countenanced by his magisterial presence. At the close of his second term, the mantle passed to John Adams, the distinguished but irascible leader of the Revolution, a far less commanding figure than Washington. His Federalist "running mate" in 1796 was South Carolinian Thomas Pinckney. But Pinckney did not win the Vice-Presidency. It went instead to Jefferson, who achieved it by gaining the second-highest number of votes for the Presidency. What happened was a failure of communication and discipline among Federalist electors. The votes for the leaders of the rival persuasions, Adams and Jefferson, were strictly along sectional lines. Adams was chosen by every elector in New England, New York, New Jersey, and Delaware; Jefferson was the choice of every elector in South Carolina, Georgia, Kentucky, and Tennessee, and all but one elector each in the large groups in North Carolina, Virginia, and Pennsylvania. The result was 71 votes for Adams, 68 for Jefferson. Each of the electors had a second vote, presumably for Vice-President, but, unfortunately for Pinckney, the second votes of the seventy-one Federalist electors were scattered, as sectional affinities overwhelmed weak party discipline. When eleven Federalist electors from New England deserted Pinckney and voted for Oliver Ellsworth, Pinckney's total fell well below Jefferson's.[26] The same loose party discipline affected the Republican electors, fifteen of whom in Virginia alone spurned the candidacy of Aaron Burr in favor of old Sam Adams, John's cousin, now Governor of Massachusetts.

Having beaten their rivals in both the executive and the legislative branches, the Federalists set out to govern with renewed confidence and vigor. The first task they faced was raising enough revenue to accomplish their purposes, particularly the floating of an adequate navy. But immediately upon addressing this issue, they ran into a series of nasty disputes touching on the explosive question of the status and government of slavery in the American national union.

One of the most important items on the agenda of the Convention of 1787 had been to devise means for raising national revenue. Slavery had affected the resolution of the issue in several ways. First, the Convention had determined that "direct" and capitation taxes must be apportioned as representation was, according to the federal ratio. This was to prevent Congress from adopting a scheme of taxation intended to destroy slavery, for the power to tax entailed the power to destroy, as everyone knew who could recall a scheme proposed by Robert Morris, the "financier" of the American Revolution. In 1782, he had suggested a tax of one dollar per one hundred acres of land per year, a tax that would have bypassed most yeomen in New England completely and sat lightly on farmers in the mid-Atlantic states, while falling heavily on many planters, whose operations depended upon the cultivation of vast holdings of land.[27] Second, the Convention had prohibited export taxes, which were seen as prejudicial against the producers of staples for export. This left, as primary sources of revenue, taxes on consumption (excises and tariffs), supplemented in times of special need by direct taxes, apportioned among the states according to the federal ratio.

This determination of the question of taxation had produced anxiety everywhere, but especially among the merchants of the North. As most knowledgeable observers had predicted in 1788, tariffs were to be the primary source of revenue during the early national period.[28] Because the transferral of this burden to consumers was inevitably imperfect, merchants believed themselves unjustly treated by the system, and it was not long before the Federalists, always sensitive to opinion among merchants, began to push for excises and direct taxes on land. The result of the ensuing forays into the pocketbooks of distillers, carriage makers, and farmers was depressing to Federalist political strength and disappointing from the standpoint of revenue.

The difficulties of the Federalists over excises are rather well known. Less familiar is the wrangle that attended the attempt to levy direct taxes. William L. Smith, Chairman of the House Committee on Ways and Means, submitted a report to Congress early in 1797 on the state of the nation's finances. Allowing $2.7 million for ongoing expenses (including about $2 million for the military), he calculated that the total national budget, including interest and payments on foreign and domestic loans, would be about $7.4 million per year before 1800, and up to $8.6 million per year for the first eight years after 1800. Current revenues, he reported, were about $6.2 million per year, $5.6 million of which came from imports. Subtracting probable revenues from projected budgets, he found that $1.2 million per year before 1800, and $2.3 million for each subsequent year, would have to be raised beyond existing revenues. Loans to meet these additional needs, he said, were not available on acceptable terms. All of this drove inevitably to the conclusion that new taxes would have to be enacted.

Smith, a Federalist from the port city of Charleston, suggested that the most appropriate new levy would be a direct tax on land, apportioned among the states according to their population— that is, the federal ratio. He then recommended an exception to the requirement that the new taxes be apportioned within each state strictly according to the value of the land. In certain areas of the country, he noted, wealth and the ability to pay taxes were most accurately and fairly measured, not in terms of the value of landholdings, but by the number of slaves available to cultivate the land. For purposes of apportioning taxes among inhabitants, the practice in most of these areas was to assess a head tax on each slave, payable by his master. This head tax was made to absorb most of the burden, leaving only a small amount to be raised by a straight tax on the value of land. Smith urged Congress, in drafting its law to lay a direct tax, to follow local practice in this regard.[29]

Most of the debate on Smith's report dealt with the general question of a direct tax on agriculture, a debate that pitted merchants against farmers. But on January 20, Congress discussed Smith's proposed exception to the principle that direct taxes be apportioned within the states according to the value of land. The debate showed almost no objection to his argument, supported as it was by Madison's assurance that the formula accorded with "the established usage of a very large tract of country." [30]

When two Representatives from Connecticut, Joshua Coit and Chauncey Goodrich, complained of the expense involved in enumerating the slaves, Richard Brent, of Virginia, speaking for the planters and reflecting the internal politics of his state, warned that inhabitants of the hills in the western sections of Southern states would "murmur" if landholdings were taxed, but not the slaves. So clearly did justice and habit support Smith's formula, he said, that Coit and Goodrich must have hidden motives for opposing it. Perhaps they sought to embarrass the South by refusing to accommodate national laws to its particular needs.[31]

When the vote was taken on Smith's proposed formula for the tax, it was accepted, 68 to 23.[32] Authorized by the House to prepare a bill, the Committee on Ways and Means two weeks later reported a bill to lay and collect direct taxes, but further action during the Fourth Congress was not taken. Congress apparently began to feel the heat of popular disapproval of direct taxes, and a package of indirect taxes was substituted for the time being.[33]

By mid-1798, during the second session of the Fifth Congress, military preparations against France had created a demand for revenue that could no longer be met from existing sources. Pressure for a direct tax on land and slaves was therefore renewed. The chairmanship of the House Committee on Ways and Means was now filled by Robert Goodloe Harper, also a Federalist, from South Carolina's Piedmont, a man particularly anxious to pursue a vigorous policy against France. During June 1798, he offered a draft bill to levy direct taxes. In the course of debate, this bill was divided into two proposals: to conduct an evaluation of landholdings and an enumeration of slaves, and to "lay and collect" the tax.[34]

The former was considered first. The issue it raised, as far as slavery was concerned, had to do with the kinds of slaves that were to be enumerated and taxed. The bill proposed to include all slaves between the ages of twelve and fifty. In terms of the distribution of the tax between planters and yeomen across the South, this was a generous proposal for planters to make. But for Virginia, where property in slaves was less reliable as a sign of great wealth, a tax based on this enumeration would mean that the planters, paying a fixed fee for all slaves included in this group, would absorb considerably more than their normal share of the total tax burden. To adjust the enumeration to Virginia's situation, Abraham Venable, a planter from the relatively depressed area of Prince Edward County, moved to exclude female slaves from the enumeration, and Thomas Claiborne, who represented the district next to Venable's in south-central Virginia, proposed to advance the minimum age of taxable slaves from twelve to sixteen.[35]

The result of these motions was that the House as a whole had to decide how taxes were to be apportioned within the Southern states. By favoring these motions, Congress would have reduced the burden on the planters who owned large numbers of slaves.

But such a course would nevertheless have hurt the slaveholding regime. Harper's original formula may have been a generous gesture from planters toward yeomen, but it was not prodigal. Planters in most areas of the South, apart from Virginia and Maryland, could well afford to shoulder a relatively large share of the taxes levied at that time. By assuming this burden, planters gained the gratitude of the yeomen and converted natural hostility and jealousy into support for the slaveholders. This was reminiscent of what Brent had meant in 1797 when he accused Coit and Goodrich of hidden motives for opposing the inclusion of slaves in the tax base. He suspected them of trying to stir up dissension between elements within the South, by pitting yeomen against planters.

Although the proposal of Coit and Goodrich to exclude slaves from the tax base entirely was mainly a political taunt, the motions of Venable and Claiborne offered the prospect of bringing more subtle pressures to bear. Congress, however, rejected this opportunity. Both motions were defeated on close votes—Venable's by 29 to 35, Claiborne's by 36 to 38. Siding with the South Carolinians against the Virginians, the Federalist-controlled Congress agreed to lay a heavier burden on the slave owners.

Unfortunately, since the roll was not called on either of these motions, it is impossible to tell exactly who voted against them. It seems reasonable to assume, though, that the question caused divisions within, rather than between, the two major sections. If there was division within the South (as there probably was, between the coast and the hills), the closeness of the totals suggests that the North was divided, too—perhaps along party lines.

This conclusion can be tested by comparing the results in the Senate, where the roll was called on three motions to reduce the number of slaves to be included in the enumeration. After Harper's proposal had passed the House unchanged with respect to its formula for enumerating slaves, it had gone to the Senate. When the formula for enumeration came up for discussion, Stevens T. Mason, of Virginia, moved to amend it by eliminating from the count all Negroes "incapable of labor." This description seems to have been purposely vague, perhaps to allow states some latitude in distributing the burden of the tax. The vote on the motion was 11 ayes to 8 nays.[36] Opposition came mainly from the North. Four New Englanders, two New Yorkers, and a Pennsylvanian, joined by John Brown, of Kentucky, preferred to keep the burden on the planters, while most of the Southerners voted for greater flexibility.

Brown responded by moving that the age limit be eliminated. The effect of this change would have been to increase the number of slaves subject to the tax by adding all those capable of labor, regardless of their age. The Senators from Virginia, North Carolina, and South Carolina who voted on this measure were opposed to it, and were joined in their opposition by Senators from New Hampshire, Rhode Island, and New Jersey. Supporting Brown were Senators from Massachusetts, New York, Pennsylvania, and Delaware. The delegations of Vermont, Connecticut, and Maryland were split. The result was defeat for the proposal, by a vote of 10 to 11.[37] The nearly even division among the Northerners permitted an enumeration that followed the Southern custom perfectly, laying a heavy tax on planters in the Deep South, but permitting officials in the upper South to modify the burden by eliminating slaves "incapable of labor." The bill for a valuation and enumeration then passed the Senate unanimously, differences between Senate and House were adjusted, and the act was signed into law on July 9, 1798.[38]

Having adopted a plan for enumeration, the House pressed on to consider the bill for laying and collecting the tax. The bill reported by Harper proposed that the tax apportioned to each state be assigned in three stages: a tax on homes, amounting to a percentage of each building's assessed value; a tax on slaves, of fifty cents each; and, if necessary, a tax on land, ad valorem, scaled to meet the remainder of the state's quota.

On June 29, 1798, the House debated the tax on slaves. Harper explained that the rate of fifty cents per slave would place a lower proportion of the total tax on South Carolina's slaveholders than they were accustomed to bear (taxes on slaves, he remarked, accounted for "most" of South Carolina's revenues),[39] but that the suggested figure represented a just compromise in a national tax law, in light of the situation in other parts of the country.

Venable disagreed. The owners of large holdings of slaves, he said, would already be paying more than their share, owing to the value of their homes. The suggested tax on slaves would mean that Virginia planters would pay almost all the federal taxes owed by the state, and, in their present straitened circumstances, this was inequitable. He suggested that the figure be reduced to twenty-five cents per slave. Gallatin took the opposite view. If, as they boasted, slave owners commanded the wealth of the South, he felt they could bear a levy of sixty-five cents per slave. Strenuously opposed by the Virginians, Gallatin's motion was quickly negatived.

A vote was then taken on Harper's suggestion, which was adopted.[40] Three days later the bill to lay and collect a direct tax on homes, slaves, and land was passed by 62 to 18, opposed only by the staunchest Republicans in the House. The bill went quickly to the Senate, where it was amended slightly, and passed. On July 14, 1798, President Adams signed it into law.[41]

This act demonstrates that routine legislative matters often gave to Congressmen from all sections both the opportunity and the responsibility to deal with slavery. Whether a Congressman wanted to overthrow slavery by setting Southerners at one another's throats, or preferred subtler pressures; whether he sought to maintain the existing balance and hope for history's gentle processes, or intended to strengthen the slave regime by every available means—whatever his feelings toward the South, he was called upon to vote on matters affecting slavery. Sometimes the impact on slavery was distant and indirect; sometimes the effect was more obvious. Often the issue was confused, and the best course, for those unsympathetic to slavery, was difficult to ascertain. Most Congressmen, from North and South, wished that the national government could have nothing to do with slavery. They were therefore reluctant to recognize that many measures necessary to the normal functioning of government inevitably had an impact on an institution threaded deeply into the fabric of national life. But their reluctance to accept this fact, and its corresponding responsibilities, could not and did not dissolve the reality. It only meant that the handling of slavery was usually indecisive and ineffective in the case of slavery's opponents, but alert and determined on the part of its defenders.

. . .

The experience with direct taxes was a nightmare for the Federalists. In fact, it was probably the leading cause of their defeat in 1800.[42] Yet the press of foreign affairs gave them little leisure to revise their thinking about methods of raising revenue in a primitive, agrarian economy. The French Directory, emboldened by dissension in the American body politic,[43] began to insult and spurn diplomatic overtures of the Adams administration. When relations broke down completely, Adams published the so-called XYZ correspondence, in which French emissaries demanded payments of money before opening negotiations for a treaty of commerce and amity. An undeclared naval war between French and American ships in the Caribbean added injury to the insults of Talleyrand,[44] and for a time it was nearly impossible to find a basis for sympathy between Americans and the French Republic.

The Federalists found this moment ripe for securing their advantage in the domestic political war with the Republicans. The Alien and Sedition Acts, conceived as barriers against "seditious" opposition to the government, nearly trebled the years of residence required for naturalization, authorized the President to order the removal of all aliens regarded as dangerous to the public peace and safety, and prescribed fines and imprisonment for citizens aiding or attempting "any insurrection, riot, unlawful assembly, or combination." [45]

It soon became apparent that the Federalists had overreached themselves with this legislation. The reaction, especially in areas of Republican strength and in the South generally, was strong and hostile. It came to sharpest focus in Kentucky and Virginia, where the state legislatures, under the indirect and secret prodding of Jefferson and Madison, enacted resolutions condemning the acts as unconstitutional. The term "unconstitutional" has become familiar to modern ears, but at a time when constitutional orthodoxy was considered the best hope for a shaky union, the charge of unconstitutionality had a frightening sound.[46] Relying on the theory that the federal union was based on a voluntary compact, the resolutions held that when the federal government exercised powers not specifically delegated to it by the Constitution, each state, which had voluntarily entered the union, had an equal right to consider "the mode and measure of redress." The initial ambiguity in specifying the appropriate response was apparently intentional. But when several Northern legislatures adopted language critical of the doctrines set forth in the resolutions, the Kentucky legislature replied that a "nullification . . . of all unauthorized acts . . . is the rightful remedy," [47] though the precise mode and agency of nullification were not specified. Many questions were left unanswered by the resolutions, probably deliberately, since they were written with an eye to the forthcoming Presidential campaign, by which the Jeffersonians hoped to be able to overthrow Federalist "oppression" without undermining the Constitutional system. [48]

It is difficult to measure the depth and strength of alienation from the union that underlay these resolutions. Historians still argue about the significance of Virginia's acts of preparation for defense in 1798 and 1799. Some see them simply as culminating a decade of effort to prepare Virginia for unforeseen eventualities; [49] others tie them more closely to the fears and disunionist tendencies produced by Federalist policy. Whatever the motives of the leading Virginians, there is abundant evidence that the controversies of 1798–1799 strained the union, and led Alexander Hamilton, if not the Virginians, to advocate the raising of armies to preserve "domestic tranquillity." "The years 1799 and 1800 passed without civil war," Stephen Kurtz has written, "because Adams was able [by opening negotiations with the French] to put an end to the threat of militarism in the Federalist ranks, and because Jefferson and Madison carefully warned their followers against taking an openly defiant attitude that might invite intervention." [50]

The year 1800 was decisive in American history, and, like many decisive moments, its outcome turned on a narrow axis. The leading event, the victory of Jefferson over Adams in the Presidential election, could easily have gone the other way.

Once Aaron Burr, the Republican Vice-Presidential candidate, had secured New York's twelve votes for Jefferson, it was apparent that the decision in the election depended on the results in South Carolina, and the competition for its eight electoral votes was keen. The political fortunes of that state, especially at the national level, had been in the hands of the Charleston Federalists since the Revolution, but the center of gravity was shifting. Power was drifting quite rapidly to the Piedmont and westward, where enterprising men were establishing large and productive new plantations.[51] These new planters, living inland, had less reason to seek a political alliance with New England's commercial Federalists, and every reason to feel drawn to the gentle agrarian from Virginia.

The politician most alert to these developments was the black sheep of the Pinckney family, Charles. An exchange of pamphlets between him and Henry De Saussure, of Charleston, illustrates the character of the emerging party cleavage. In an "Address to the Citizens of South Carolina," De Saussure lauded the restraint and courage of Washington and Adams, and urged a renewal of confidence in the latter. Jefferson, in turn, was ridiculed for his pusillanimous performance as Governor of Virginia in 1781, and criticized for intriguing against the government during the recent difficulties with France. Finally, De Saussure called pointed attention to the passage in Jefferson's *Notes on Virginia* which, he said, advocated the emancipation of slaves. In view of what was happening in Santo Domingo (where Toussaint L'Ouverture was leading a bloody rebellion of slaves against masters), it would be dangerous to place a man holding such doctrines in the Presidency. Pinckney's response was direct and sharp. Adams, he wrote, probably owned a good deal of commercial paper, which would account for his having signed into law a direct tax that shifted the burden of revenue from wealthy merchants to struggling farmers and planters. Why did the tax fall on slaves, but not on other holdings? Were planters and landholders obnoxious to the government? It was obviously in the interest of planters and farmers to replace Adams with Jefferson, a man

whose whole estate is exactly like that of your own planters, who owns two hundred negroes himself, and who, in order to remove all doubts upon the subject, has authorized his friends to declare as his assertion: "That the Constitution has not empowered the federal legislature to touch in the remotest degree the question respecting the condition or property of slaves in any of the states, and that any attempt of that sort would be unconstitutional and a usurpation of rights Congress do not possess." [52]

The political situation in South Carolina was as confused as it was crucial and pivotal. Some political leaders favored the elevation of General Pinckney over Adams; others would have preferred to unite Jefferson and General Pinckney on an all-Southern ticket. The main obstacle to these plans was the loyalty of Pinckney to Adams. When the General refused to accept election with Jefferson, the South Carolinians chose electors committed to Jefferson and Burr.[53] Thus the Republicans, with fifty-three electoral votes in the South and twenty in the North, beat the Federalists, who took nine votes in the South and fifty-six in the North.

This result, in turn, created its own crisis, inasmuch as it produced a tie between the two Republican candidates. Under the Constitution, such a tie was referred to the House of Representatives—in this case controlled by the lame-duck Federalists, to whom was thereby committed the choice between two Republicans for the Presidency. After considerable maneuvering, Hamilton's personal animosity for Burr compelled him to persuade a few Federalists to abandon the decision of the Federalist caucus to support Burr against the hated Jefferson. On the thirty-sixth ballot, the deadlock was broken in favor of Jefferson.

The year 1800 was important as a turning point for reasons other than the election of Jefferson. It was also the year of moving from Philadelphia, the capital since December 1790, to the District of Columbia, on the Potomac River between Maryland and Virginia. Henceforth, the capital of the United States would occupy this place in the upper South, a location that was little more than a swamp on November 17, 1800, when Congress convened there for the first time.

In many ways the move was symbolic. It signaled a shift of power away from such commercial centers as Philadelphia, Boston, and New York, where the Federalists held their diminishing sway, toward the South and the West, whose Republican leaders were more comfortable with the rising desire of the common man for a share in the nation's political power. The primitiveness of Washington in 1800, the difficulty of traveling from place to place within the city's limits, the remoteness from other centers of population, the relative absence of refinement and social grace, particularly noticeable after the splendor of the "Republican Court" —all of these features, however painful to the aristocrats who still occupied many positions in the federal government, were a more accurate reflection of life in the republic of which Washington was the capital than the atmosphere at the previous seats of government in New York City and Philadelphia had been.[54]

Washington quickly became, too, a more accurate reflection of the union's agony over slavery. In addition to its many slave owners, the "Washington community" included many men who opposed slavery and hated the continual reminders of its existence that came with life at a crossroads of the upper South. During the first twenty years of the nineteenth century, Washington became one of the leading centers of the domestic slave trade, despite an ordinance that made it illegal to bring Negroes into the city for sale. The sight, from the door of the Capitol, of "a procession of men, women and children, resembling that of a funeral . . . bound together in pairs, some with ropes, and some with *iron chains,*" on their way to be sold at auction, provoked Jesse Torrey, a visitor from the North, to write "one of the first effective pieces of anti-slavery propaganda in America." [55] Northerners might contend that the government of a free country should not conduct its business in the presence of a slave market, but the obvious answer was that this country included large areas where slavery was perfectly legal, and was governed under a Constitution that sanctioned the institution. What the Constitution permitted in the states, the government could not fairly prohibit at the capital. Indeed, it might be argued that the rulers of a nation that sanctioned slavery had no right to be free of its disgusting appearance.

Jefferson's victory had been close, but it was not the product of superficial or accidental causes.[56] The people were weary of war and the costs of war, exhausted by bitter controversy and prosecutions for sedition, and tired of the infighting between factions of the Federalist party. The prospect of fiscal retrenchment and gentle internal development under the mild Jefferson was attractive to almost everyone.

· · ·

Jefferson's Inaugural Address, delivered March 4, 180C, signaled the turn to a new era in American politics. In it, he stressed his determination to govern within Constitutional limits, to cut back the expenses of government, to preserve civil liberties, and to seek "peace, commerce, and honest friendship with all nations, entangling alliances with none." He concluded with the famous peroration "We are all Republicans, we are all Federalists," by which he meant that he hoped his election would be taken as the verdict of the American people, mandating a return to republican government within the limits of the federal Constitution, and obviating the need for further partisan conflict, at least for the foreseeable future.

The calm in the wake of Jefferson's inauguration seemed almost eerie to the Federalists, who expected a tidal wave of retribution from the "Jacobins." Fisher Ames spoke their mind when he wrote, in a letter to a friend:

The weather is mild since Jefferson was elected; but it is an unwholesome and treacherous softness, that seizes the windpipe like an assassin. Storms will succeed and find us relaxed. Is not this an emblem of the smooth hypocrisy with which his reign will begin, as well as of its inevitable rigor and agitation.[57]

The distribution of patronage by the Republicans, and the repeal of the Judiciary Act of 1801, which had created several judgeships filled by the lame-duck Adams, annoyed Federalist politicians, but in fact the reign of domestic tranquillity, coupled with relative calm in foreign relations, made the critics sound frantic and a bit silly during the first two years of Jefferson's administration.

The calm was broken, as far as New England's Federalists were concerned, early in 1803, when Jefferson bought the vast Louisiana country from Napoleon. With one stroke, he doubled the territory of the United States and neutralized the dangers to the nation posed by foreign domination of New Orleans and the west bank of the Mississippi River. To do it, he had had to jump over the bounds of the Constitution, which nowhere authorized anyone to acquire foreign territory and therefore established no procedures for the integration of such territory into the nation. But because the acquisition satisfied the longing of many Virginians to remove obstacles and threats to the development of the West, Jefferson had made the purchase without much hesitation, despite his commitment to strict Constitutional interpretation. Having done so, he now prepared to throw himself on the mercy of the nation, whose gratitude and confidence were forthcoming from nearly every quarter.

The only substantial pocket of disturbance over the purchase was in New England. Some of the Federalists there were becoming increasingly defensive about their place in the union. Convinced of the virtue of their own "steady habits," these men regarded the acquisition as auguring a decisive shift in the balance of power within the union.[58] Even in 1787, when the union reached only to the Mississippi River, New England merchants had been apprehensive about the effect of the expected southwestward drift of the center of population. Now a Southern President, who was the embodiment of the agrarian impulse and who had promised a return to strict Constitutional orthodoxy, had jumped the traces at the first temptation. The ground rules, the very framework of union, had been changed. The regime to which the states had consented in 1787 and 1788 had been reconstituted, without their consent. No one knew exactly what kind of people inhabited the region west of the Mississippi, but whoever they were and whatever their values, they were promised, by the treaty of acquisition, an equal voice in the union's government with people whose families had been tending their tidy farms in New England for two or three generations or more. If these people held slaves, their voice would be even greater. Living far from the Atlantic coast, they would have as little interest in policies conducive to commerce as the Piedmont Virginians and the trans-Appalachian Kentuckians. In 1787, under the impression that slavery was dying and in deference to the wealthy merchant-planters of Charleston, New Englanders had agreed to the federal ratio for augmenting the representation of slave owners. In 1800, this rule enabled Jefferson to triumph over Adams, and now Jefferson was adding a vast territory to the union, the most accessible parts of which seemed fit for cultivation only by slavery. By this means, the Republicans were cementing their hegemony over the union.

In the bright glare of Jefferson's diplomatic triumph, not many New Englanders in 1803 and 1804 adopted this attitude. Those who did, however, immediately began the search for remedies, a search that gained momentum with each succeeding crisis between 1803 and 1815. One obvious strategy was to press for the repeal of the federal ratio. A resolution to this effect passed the Massachusetts legislature in 1804, but was repudiated by every state in the union except Connecticut and Delaware.[59] Another obvious recourse was secession, but astute politicians knew that sentiment in New England was not ripe for so radical a course, that in fact the ligatures of union were growing stronger, and that if the erosion of old Yankee values was to be prevented, the work of redemption would have to begin first among the yeomen at home, many of whom were straying from the "ancient" faith.[60] The most feasible solution for the time being was one espied by Fisher Ames even before the purchase of Louisiana. "The Federalists," he said, "must entrench themselves in the state governments, and endeavor to make state justice and state power a shelter of the wise, and good, and rich, from the destroying rage of the southern jacobins."[61]

New England was not the only hornet's nest jarred by the passage of Louisiana from French to American hands. So vast a field, so remote from the government on the Atlantic coast, so full of adventurers and people naturally wary of Anglo-Saxons, inevitably spawned sentiments of questionable loyalty to the American federal union. The significance of the leading movement of this kind, the one associated with the name of Aaron Burr, is still a matter of dispute. But whether Burr was involved in an effort to establish a separate nation to the southwest or was attempting to lead an expedition to acquire Texas and Mexico for the United States,[62] the sensational disclosure of his plot in 1807, which involved the commanding general of the American Army, James Wilkinson, gave new evidence of the loose loyalties and frail channels of command in a union that now stretched two-thirds of the way across the continent.

. . .

During 1806, friction between France and England started again, and, inevitably, American maritime commerce began to feel the heat. When Britain tightened regulations against neutral shipping on the high seas, to cut off supplies to the French Army, Napoleon responded with a decree declaring the British Isles blockaded and ordering the confiscation of all vessels, under whatever flag, violating the blockade. When Britain countered by prohibiting commerce with any port from which the British flag was excluded, Napoleon declared that any ship that obeyed British regulations or submitted to British search would be considered British property by the French, and destroyed or confiscated, as the French pleased. It was in this maelstrom that Jefferson's policy of "peace, commerce and honest friendship with all nations" underwent its first serious test.

American attitudes toward this exchange of orders and decrees tended to vary according to pre-existing sympathies for Great Britain. Those who were inclined to drink toasts to the "World's last hope—Britain's fast-anchored Isle!" tended to believe that if Britain was compelled to yield, "our liberties and independence would fall a sacrifice," and it would soon be "time for us to prepare to be good and dutiful subjects to the French." [63] Such people could hardly find words to express their shock at Napoleon's decrees, or their hope that no obstacle would hinder the British in their effort to crush the pirate from Corsica. Those who hated Britain tended to focus, not on the balance of power in Europe, but on the impact of these regulations on American commerce. Inasmuch as the Royal Navy controlled the high seas, the Jefferson administration looked upon Britain as the primary threat to American interests.

To reduce suffering and to forestall military establishments, Jefferson devoutly believed that republics should search for an alternative to war as a way of coping with adversaries. Thus, when Britain failed to heed Secretary of State Madison's warning against continued ship seizures and impressment, Jefferson obtained from Congress the Non-Importation Act, proscribing a long list of goods normally acquired from England. Extremely unpopular with merchants in New England, the act had no noticeable effect on British commerce—except, perhaps, by inhibiting American competitors. British violations of American neutrality continued, culminating in an assault on the *Chesapeake,* in which three Americans were killed, eighteen wounded, and four alleged deserters from the Royal Navy, serving on the *Chesapeake,* were impressed.

American public opinion was outraged, and for a time the nation closed ranks around the administration, waiting for the President's response. Jefferson chose an embargo, prohibiting all land and sea commerce with foreign nations. The idea was to starve the Europeans into the realization of their dependence on American supply and thereby induce them to respect American rights. But the policy was a disastrous failure.

The effect in New England, especially, was devastating. Ports that normally buzzed with activity now languished; sailors walked the streets unemployed and surly; goods piled up on docks; perishables rotted; infant manufactories found no market for their products. In some respects, the situation was a mirror image of 1798–1799, when Southerners felt abandoned by a government that seemed to be provoking war unnecessarily with a naturally friendly European power, then taking measures to implement the policy (direct taxes on land and slaves) that weighed with particular gravity on precisely those interests least enthusiastic about pursuing the conflict. Now, in 1808, Jefferson's policies had led to conflict with Great Britain, and his way of coping with that conflict was to suspend the economy of New England.

This was an election year, and, just as Jefferson and Madison had been able to direct Republican resentment into electoral channels, so the Federalist leaders hoped to parlay resentment against the embargo into a victory over the Virginians. Madison was chosen by the Republicans to succeed Jefferson. The Federalists, in what has been described as the "first national nominating convention," considered joining with Eastern Republicans, many of whom were nearly as furious about the embargo as the Boston Federalists, and supporting Vice-President George Clinton. But the scheme did not work. Most Federalists regarded support for Clinton as an abandonment of principle, and decided instead to vote for electors pledged to Charles Cotesworth Pinckney and Rufus King. Despite the split in Republican ranks, Madison won.[64] The Federalists carried all of New England except Vermont, but outside New England, only Delaware and small portions of the electoral vote of Maryland and North Carolina.

The campaign produced no basic change in administration policy. The Presidential election was completed in December, and in January 1809 the Republicans passed the Enforcement Act, which tightened the administration of the embargo and imposed severe fines for violations. The response, especially in New England, was a new and perhaps even more threatening outburst of hostility against the federal government. In Newburyport, Massachusetts, a town meeting called on the state legislature to "interpose on our behalf" to end the embargo, which it described as a palpable violation of the Constitution. A newspaper in Boston termed the Constitution "a Treaty of Alliance and Confederation," and argued that "whenever its provisions are violated . . . it is no longer an effective instrument," and that under such circumstances, "any state is at liberty by the *spirit of that contract* to withdraw itself from the union." [65] The Governor of Connecticut, Jonathan Trumbull, in an address to his state legislature, declared that whenever the federal government exceeded its Constitutional authority, state legislatures must "interpose their protecting shield between the rights and liberties of the people and the assumed powers of the general government." [66] One concrete means of interposition adopted by governors in New England was the refusal to furnish militia for helping to enforce the embargo. New England thus went significantly farther than Kentucky and Virginia had gone in 1798–1799, specifying the agency (the legislature) responsible for interposition, and actually carrying out such acts. Later, Jefferson commented, rather bitterly, that he "felt the foundation of the government shaken under my feet by the New England townships." [67]

The administration finally realized the gravity of the situation. Just before turning over the reins of government to Madison, Jefferson signed the new Non-Intercourse Act, repealing the embargo and declaring that trade would be resumed with Britain and/or France as soon as either nation stopped violating the rights of Americans as neutrals. A few days after Jefferson thus signaled the defeat of his policy, he went to Monticello, leaving to

Madison the unenviable task of finding ways to implement a foreign policy that was as hazardous as it was idealistic in an international system dominated by men like Napoleon and the British Foreign Secretary, George Canning.

Once again, in 1812, the four-year rhythm brought affairs to a head. The Twelfth Congress, which came to Washington in 1811, contained a remarkable group of young legislators from the West and the South, notably Henry Clay, of Kentucky, and John C. Calhoun, of South Carolina. Dubbed "war hawks," these young nationalists were incensed by the treatment Americans had received at the hands of the European belligerents, and impatient with the suggestion that the United States was not strong enough to assert its rights against these giants. Staggered a bit by Gallatin's account of the costs of adequate defense,[68] they nevertheless pressed for a declaration of war, insisting that Britain was vulnerable in Canada, which could easily be taken as hostage, and at sea, where its commerce could be harassed by darting American privateers and armed merchant vessels. Besides asserting American rights, a war with Britain would punish its American allies, the Indians, whose terror might finally be eliminated from the western frontier if the British could be forced to stop agitation and supply of the savages.[69]

From the point of view of Federalists in New England, the declaration of war on June 18, 1812 was the ultimate madness. A republic virtually at war with itself, but practically naked of military or naval capacity, was declaring war on the most powerful nation, a nation presently occupied in turning back the challenge of a despot who threatened everything valuable in Western civilization. If Britain had committed crimes against American neutrality, these had been directed mostly at the interests of New England. If merchants in that section were inclined to forgive these insults, or at least postpone the demand for compensation until the pressure of Napoleon had been repulsed, why could not the rest of the country? Some in New England suspected that the war spirit derived from a desire for more territory, for Canada, or Florida, or perhaps both, to provide both Westerners and Southerners with counterbalancing incentives for the struggle. But to the eyes of the Federalists, expansion would only augment the forces that were already undermining the strength and vitality of the union, adding wild, unknown elements to a nation bursting with inharmonious variety.

At first, it was almost possible to regard the War of 1812 as a bad joke. The initial battles, particularly the American foray into Canada from Detroit, were disasters, and the assault on Montreal a fiasco. The only encouragement to the war-makers came from a series of naval victories. But the picture in general was bleak, and many were convinced that Madison's leadership had brought the country to the brink of collapse.

Again, as in 1800 and 1808, a Presidential election loomed, giving rise to hopes that Madison's policy could be repudiated by regular political processes. When a group of antiwar Republicans in New York nominated Governor DeWitt Clinton, a secret convention of Federalists agreed to throw their support behind him, too, and for a time realistic men seriously hoped that Madison would lose to a candidate committed to peace. But it was not to be. Madison won solidly in the West and South; Clinton won just as solidly in New England and the mid-Atlantic states, except in Vermont and Pennsylvania. When it was over, Madison had won by 128 to 89 electoral votes, with Pennsylvania's twenty-nine votes proving decisive. Running on a general ticket, Madison's electors in Pennsylvania won by a margin of about 20,000 popular votes.[70] Thus close the nation came to repudiating the Virginia dynasty and the policies that produced the War of 1812.

Madison's re-election meant that Yankee Federalists could look forward to four more years of government that seemed virtually alien to them. Many New Englanders had developed the habit of regarding the South, and particularly Virginia, as the author of their miseries.[71] Combining a rather selective recollection of peace and prosperity under Hamilton and Adams with a sense of diminishing power in the national government and of turmoil and hardship during Jefferson's second term, these men had their resentment fueled by a conviction that the federal ratio was unjust, and the whole national regime illegitimate. People were beginning to wonder aloud if the causes of the nation's malaise were "radical and permanent." If so, and if the cure (a revision in the formulas for representation) was impossible, perhaps separation was the only remedy. Shortly after the declaration of war on Britain, a minister in Byfield, Massachusetts, recommended that New England "proclaim an honorable neutrality; let the southern *heroes* fight their own battles, and guard . . . against the just vengeance of their lacerated slaves. . . ." Another, in Boston, admonished his congregation to "cut the connection" with the Southern states, "or so far alter the national constitution, as to ensure yourselves a due share in the government." Disunion, he said, was already virtually accomplished. It was time for New England to "take care of itself." [72]

In this spirit, New England settled down to see where the fortunes of war would carry. Mostly, they carried outside New England during 1813. A British blockade of the American coast concentrated on New York, Baltimore, and ports to the south, a focus suggested to British strategists by the desire to exploit the alienation between New England and the rest of the country. Hard battles took place near Detroit, around lakes Erie and Ontario, and along the way to Montreal, but the main result was to reduce to stalemate the American hope of driving the British from Canada.

As the year ended, the American command was hard-pressed for ideas. The only promising development—the arousal of Andrew Jackson and his Tennessee militia—was still not visible on the surface of events in the nation's capital. All Madison could see were the disaffection, the collapsing morale, and the incompetence of his field commanders and Department of War.

The climax of the war came in 1814. The year began with a renewal of the American embargo, imposed by Madison in response to information that agents in New England and New York were supplying food to British troops in Canada and off the coast. Despite strenuous efforts to enforce the law, it proved at once both ineffective and deeply aggravating, and within three months the President was asking Congress to dismantle the whole system of commercial restraint as a weapon of war.[73]

In April, Britain finally subdued Napoleon, thereby gaining freedom to concentrate on the war in America. The British were beginning to realize that their informants in New England had misled them about the extent of disunionist sentiment there. Not only were there many ordinary people who identified with the government out of simple patriotism, but the leading merchants themselves were bound to the union by ties of interest and sentiment.[74] Perhaps there was tinder in New England for a secessionist fire, but the strategy of favoritism was not bringing it to flame. And so the blockade was extended to New England, and punishing raids were conducted all along the coastline.

Meanwhile, Britain took the offensive elsewhere. There were three distinct parts to this campaign. One came down from Montreal through Lake Champlain, toward Albany and New York. Another swept up Chesapeake Bay, toward Washington and Baltimore. The third, begun late in the year, was aimed at New Orleans.[75]

The American cause was now at its lowest ebb, and the suffering fairly general. No longer was any section or segment of the union immune from the ravages and dislocations of war. The British blockade cut imports to the bone, and thus virtually eliminated the primary source of revenue. It also produced an artificial stimulus to the development of domestic manufacturing, causing speculation and inflation. In April the government, desperate for funds, authorized a loan of $25 million. Most of the nation's specie, however, was in banks in Boston, New York, and Philadelphia. When the leading merchant bankers of these cities decided not to pick up the loan, the government was forced to mortgage itself to foreign bankers.[76]

In New England, the difficulties of the federal government brought new strength and boldness to the outright disunionists, and considerable embarrassment to moderate Federalist leaders. Men like Harrison Gray Otis and George Cabot, who had played for years with the doctrine of interposition and the notion of Constitutional reform, and deplored the torpor of the general public in the face of oppression, were now rather startled by the popular clamor. The people had caught fire, or so it seemed from the rash of town meetings that dispatched resolutions to the state legislatures demanding protection against federal folly and oppression.[77]

The response of the Massachusetts General Court was to issue a call for a meeting of delegates from the states of New England to consider how they might better provide for their own defense, and "to take measures, if they shall think proper, for procuring a convention of delegates from all the United States, in order to revise the Constitution thereof, and more effectually to secure the support and attachment of all the people, by placing all upon the basis of fair representation." With this call, which resulted in the Hartford Convention of December 1814, the moderate Federalists hoped to keep control of popular sentiment, to divert it into non-revolutionary channels, and at the same time to communicate a sense of crisis to those outside New England who were inclined to take its loyalty for granted.[78]

Meeting at the Connecticut capital in December 1814, the convention held secret sessions for two weeks, then issued a set of resolutions, calling for, among other things, a series of Constitutional amendments that would have eliminated the federal ratio; required two-thirds majorities in both houses of Congress for declarations of war, restriction on foreign commerce, and the admission of new states; and limited Presidential tenure to one term. But, significantly, the convention issued no call for a nationwide convention to rewrite the Constitution, and, while it defended interposition by states in the case of "deliberate, dangerous, and palpable infractions of the Constitution," it warned against the temptation "to fly to open resistance upon every infraction of the Constitution." Given the mood of the constituents, the report can only be judged a moderate, and moderating, document.[79]

Otis was appointed by the Massachusetts legislature to lead a delegation to Washington to press these demands upon a government that was presumed to be helpless and unable to resist. When they arrived in the capital, however, the atmosphere was not what they had expected. In September the thrust from Canada toward the Hudson Valley had been stopped at Plattsburgh, on Lake Champlain. Almost simultaneously, the offensive in the mid-Atlantic, which had already burned through the nation's capital, was finally stopped at Baltimore. And while Otis was in Washington, news of Jackson's brilliant victory at New Orleans reached the East Coast.[80] Thus New England's drive for a change in the federal formula reached its culmination just as the fortunes of war and the prospects for peace were turning. The Americans had achieved little more than a stalemate, but by the end of 1814 a stalemate was highly favorable to their bargaining position in the peace talks at Ghent.

The reasons for the frustration of Britain's powerful forces, following their brilliant victory over Napoleon, reveal much about the capacity of the union to tolerate the kind of attitudes displayed by Virginians in 1798 and by New Englanders in 1814. The problem for English forces throughout the war was that America had no single focus or center of national vitality, no single point at which a decisive assault might be aimed. As the Duke of Wellington had remarked when proffered the British command in 1814, "I do not know where you could carry on . . . an operation which would be so injurious to the Americans as to force them to sue for peace. . . ." [81] Taking a leading American city (New York in 1776, Charleston in 1778, Washington in 1814) was like cutting a head off Hydra. The country had no single nerve center; as soon as one was severed, another cropped up somewhere else. The parts of the nation just seemed to hang together, without adhesive or hoops of any kind.

Modes of communication and transportation were so primitive that an army like the British was unable to maintain logistics on a scale to which it was accustomed and on which its technology depended. But the state of communications seemed perfectly appropriate to the stage of development of American forces. Men judging America by European standards might worry about the lack of a standing army, or a fully deployable navy, or a centralized banking and monetary system, or an efficient postal service. But in fact there was a nice fit between the technological capacities of the nation and the demands of its defense and mobilization. Had the framework been tighter and impulses more readily communicated, the nation would have been more vulnerable to disruption by foreign foes or domestic malcontents. But the looseness of structure rendered the disaffection of New England and the seditious tendencies in and around New Orleans relatively innocuous. The yoke of union was easy; the burden of nationalism light, even in time of war.

Thus, when the delegates to the Hartford Convention insisted that citizens of the states be protected against military conscription unauthorized by the Constitution, that the states assume primary responsibility for their own defense, and that they retain federal revenues collected within their jurisdictions for this purpose, they were in effect describing the approach actually taken by New England in the preceding three years, which the federal government had been powerless to stop. But in asking that these arrangements be written into the Constitution, they were trying to freeze Constitutional evolution just at the point when it was about to enter a new phase, toward tighter integration, greater central direction, firmer popular roots, and greater responsiveness to public opinion.

Once news of Jackson's victory and of the satisfying, if somewhat evasive, Peace of Ghent had arrived, the Hartford resolutions were abandoned as if they had never been drafted.

Among the important effects of the War of 1812 was the decision by policy makers in Britain to stabilize relations with the Americans, to allow the Royal Navy to be used as a shield to protect American maritime commerce and American independence from European politics. This decision, more than any taken in Washington or Boston, reduced the friction between New England and the rest of the republic. New Englanders, particularly some of the older ones, might regret the hold that Southerners, or "Northern men of Southern principles," had on the White House, but for many leading New Englanders this became a question of style rather than the substance of policy. As long as maritime commerce had smooth sailing and domestic industry enjoyed at least limited protection (the joint interest of the Pennsylvanians and Northwesterners in the latter cause helped to overcome the sense of isolation among New Englanders), the demands of union were not onerous to most New Englanders. Those who felt morally sensitive about slavery found the accommodations on this score morally repulsive, but it was the New Yorkers and Pennsylvanians who took the lead against the South on this question, at least during the Missouri crisis. During later struggles over slavery in the territories, the Hartford Convention and its flirtation with disunion became a favorite taunt of Southerners and probably had the effect of rendering men like Otis shy of taking a forthright stand on this issue. But with the collapse of

Otis's mission in early 1815, the notion of a separate Northern confederacy died forever as a viable political cause.

The Era of Good Feelings, usually identified with President James Monroe's administration, actually began early in 1815, while James Madison was still President. A good example of the bountiful sense of harmony that made American politics a relatively happy affair just after the Peace of Christmas Eve (as the Peace of Ghent was sometimes called), and of the factors that soon eroded this euphoria, can be seen by considering the tariff legislation of 1816 and 1820.

Tariffs have a dual aspect: they not only produce revenue, but they also regulate the flow of competition from foreign sources. With the end of the War of 1812, consumers whose appetites had gone unsatisfied for several years, owing to embargoes, blockades, and internal disruptions, now sought manufactured items with great intensity. This created a surge of interest in domestic manufacturing,[82] as well as a terrific impetus to foreign trade. Foreign merchants were as interested in the situation as Americans. The British saw the ambitions of American manufacturers as a threat to their own rapidly developing industrial capacity, and determined to strangle American enterprise in the cradle by flooding the American market with goods temporarily offered at a sacrifice. The American response was the tariff law of 1816, the first plainly and systematically protective impost in American history.[83]

The political circumstances of this law were remarkable. Twelve years later, a similarly protectionist piece of tariff legislation earned from Southerners the sobriquet "Tariff of Abominations." The Southern interest in cheap manufactured products and in a vigorous flow of commerce between Europe and America naturally made them favor "free trade" and oppose the high duties and restrictive shipping laws that were sought to foster the infant industries of Pennsylvania and New England. Yet in the Congressional debates and votes of 1816, leading Southerners were among the champions of protectionism. In this moment of fervent nationalism, and in order to liquidate the war debt, Deep Southerners heartily supported the program of imposts aimed at foiling the British attempt to snuff out American industry.[84] It is a curious fact about the War of 1812 that the burst of national feeling that often attends military adventures in a democracy did not come until after the war's conclusion. But when it came, it came with a rush, and carried the whole country with it.

By 1820, however, a portentous reaction had set in. Congressman Henry Baldwin, of protectionist Pennsylvania, who gave a crucial vote to the Southerners on the Missouri question in 1820, sought in the same year to extend and augment the duties adopted in 1816. His main arugment was that it was in the national interest to encourage the development of manufacturing capacity, in order to improve the nation's ability to make weapons and thus defend itself. This argument, which had been so powerful in 1816, proved to have little leverage by 1820. The fear of an imminent renewal of hostilities with Great Britain had ebbed by then, owing to an apparent change in British policy, and a series of diplomatic agreements had secured the national boundary as far west as the Rocky Mountains. Further evidence of a change in Britain's policy came in its mild reaction to General Andrew Jackson's summary execution of two British citizens accused of stimulating the Indians of Florida to commit atrocities against white settlers, and in its abandonment of Spain during the negotiations that led to the Spanish cession of Florida. And the policy of flooding American markets with underpriced goods had never really been implemented. Rarely has so disgraceful a military effort as the American performance during the War of 1812 produced so favorable a turn in a nation's international situation. By 1820, arguments based on the need to strengthen national defenses could not be heard above the sweet music of America's harmonious fit into the world fashioned at the Congress of Vienna.

Another factor conditioning the reception accorded to Baldwin's proposals was the Panic of 1819, which had had particularly grievous results for farmers, planters, and investors in land. Politically, the primary effect of the depression was to send each interest scrambling in retreat from the advanced positions of a confident and generous nationalism and to induce a defensive self-regard in each separate element in the national economy. Thus, the South Carolinians were forced to draw in their nationalist horns and promote policies more directly responsive to the hurting interests back home.

And of course contributing to the changed political atmosphere in 1820 was the controversy over Missouri. Whereas in 1816 it had been possible for nationally minded Southerners to adopt a grand view of sectional harmony, by 1820 a different mood prevailed. In 1816 the young war hawks had been riding high. They had enjoyed the disgrace of New England over the Hartford Convention, and felt that their policies and leadership had been vindicated by events and were supported by nearly universal popular acclaim. By 1820, however, the term "Era of Good Feelings" was becoming a bad joke.[85] Monroe's effort to convey the impression that he presided over a country in which political conflict was no longer necessary was beginning to look ridiculous, or pathetic, depending on one's point of view. Although he was re-elected in 1820 without declared opposition, it was apparent that his support was desperately thin and fragile, not the sort of base from which he could actually govern, even if he had been so disposed, which he was not.

In this atmosphere, Baldwin's vote for the Missouri Compromise was not enough to gain him the support he needed to carry the tariff revision. The effect of his defeat, in turn, was a serious augmentation of bitterness among Northerners against the prevailing tone of the national government. Many found, in the defeat of protectionism, further evidence that an unholy alliance of planters and backwoodsmen was bent on thwarting the development of American industry.[86]

In making the argument that the agreement to outlaw the slave trade in 1808 could perhaps not have been attained after 1787, Lewis Gray has noted the variety in the economies of most states at that time. Virginia, for example, was experiencing a severe depression in the value of its tobacco crop. Many planters, in consequence, were becoming interested in growing other commodities, and even in the development of home industries. The North was still predominantly committed to agriculture, although commercial activities occupied an increasing amount of its capital. A similar mixture obtained in South Carolina. The picture was one of fluidity and incipient development along any number of lines, all at once and throughout the country.[87] There seemed no reason to doubt that the nation's economy might grow as a single organism, each part contributing to the strength of the whole, no part needing to feel jealousy or fear in the face of good fortune in the other parts.

By 1820, however, patterns of serious sectional divergence were becoming unmistakably apparent. For a variety of reasons, manufacturing was beginning to flourish in Pennsylvania and New England, but was not taking any real foothold in the South. In part, the agrarian prejudices of men like Jefferson, Randolph, and John Taylor of Caroline were responsible. The difficulty of obtaining cheap power, the scarcity of raw materials, and such geographical factors as climate and dispersion added to the reluctance to commit resources to industrial enterprise. A fear of losing control over slaves if they were converted from planting to manufacturing employments and the absence of adequate white labor were additional factors of great importance.[88] By 1820 it was apparent that the South would face an uneven battle in the race to adjust to the demands of the Industrial Revolution. Southern politicians were thus determined to use their political leverage to cushion the impact of these developments on a society that was increasingly defensive toward outsiders.

This is not to say that the nation was on the verge of civil war in 1820. On the contrary, the most vigorous young politicians in the country, many of them from the New West, were still firmly committed to the union and confident that sectional tensions could be overcome.[89] Although the controversy over Missouri was intense and dangerous, there was no heart anywhere, yet, for open warfare over the question of slavery. Not enough Northerners perceived slavery and its socioeconomic and political consequences as an enemy.

The fugitive-slave law can be used to characterize the evolving attitude of national politicians toward slavery as a federal question.

By a quick maneuver late in the Federal Convention, Pierce Butler had gained the insertion of the fugitive-slave clause into the Constitution.[90] During its brief consideration of the clause, the Convention had determined that responsibility for retrieving escaped slaves should fall to the owner, rather than the state into which the escape was made. An owner of slaves in Virginia, for example, might pursue a fugitive into Pennsylvania, seize him, present a claim, and take the slave back to Virginia.

But to whom should the claim be presented? Could an owner employ an agent to make pursuit and lay claim? Would there be penalties against those obstructing the recovery? What protection would there be for freedmen against capture and enslavement under the pretense of their being fugitives? The Constitution left these questions unanswered. In 1793 Congress undertook to answer some of them.

Wasting little time, the legislators redeemed the promise of the Constitution by passing the Fugitive Act by substantial, intersectional majorities. The act provided that a master, or an agent authorized by him, could seize a runaway slave anywhere in the union and take him before any judge, federal or local. The judge was directed to satisfy himself as to the master's claim of ownership, then issue a certificate authorizing that the slave be taken back to his place of labor. A fine of $500 was imposed on anyone obstructing the recovery of runaways.[91]

This law, which ostensibly did no more than clarify a Constitutional provision, is nevertheless noteworthy, if only for its flaws. There were several. It failed to protect the rights and freedom of black citizens. Its machinery for retrieving fugitives was wholly inadequate to the purposes of aggrieved slave owners. It was severe in its treatment of people who might help slaves to escape, but it prescribed no penalties for those who sought to kidnap and re-enslave freed Negroes. And its administrative procedures were so cumbersome and so dependent on local opinion that it was a "dead letter" from the start in regions where public sympathies were hostile to slavery.[92]

Efforts to revise the act—both to strengthen and to limit it—were made from time to time during the founding period. In April 1796 Albert Gallatin presented a resolution from the legislature of Delaware. The burden of the statement was that Delaware had taken measures to prevent "future kidnapping of negroes and mulattoes," but that Congress would have to exercise its jurisdiction over territorial waters and over commerce across state lines if the practice was to be successfully prohibited. Gallatin moved that the standing committee on Commerce and Manufactures, chaired by Pennsylvanian John Swanwick, consider whether federal enactments were necessary to prevent the abuse described in the petition.

In December 1796 the committee delivered its report. Delaware's complaint was deemed valid and its request for federal legislation reasonable. The committee asked for instructions to bring in a bill that would prevent shipmasters from kidnapping Negroes in one state and selling them in another. The proposed method of regulation was to require ship captains to carry certificates listing the number of Negroes and mulattoes on board, with a description of their status—whether or not they were slaves.[93]

The debate provoked by this report is one of the strangest on record during the first twenty years under the Constitution. The Delaware legislature had asked for help in preventing kidnappers from stealing slaves out of its jurisdiction. In the absence of Delaware's Representative, the petition had been presented by a Congressman well known for his personal antipathy to slavery.[94] Now a Congressman from Quaker-heavy Philadelphia was asking permission to present a bill to meet the request from Delaware, and was supported by Samuel Sitgreaves, who also represented large numbers of Pennsylvania Quakers.

Southerners began to wonder why slavery's opponents were so interested in this bill to protect slave owners in Delaware. Maryland's William Vans Murray asked if it were known who these "kidnapped negroes" were. The answer was that the category as defined in the proposal included free Negroes who were being taken back into slavery, many of them to the West Indies. Immediately several Southerners advised that the question be dropped. Sponsors of the measure insisted that it would prevent the kidnapping of slaves as well as free Negroes, and they implored Congress to correct both abuses with one just law. Southerners nevertheless insisted that mischief would surely result if Congress began to legislate on this question. This bill, they said, was an "entering wedge." No one was kidnapping slaves from the Deep South. A law of this kind would only impose annoying regulations on commerce and create disturbing precedents that might encourage other attempts to meddle with domestic institutions. A motion that the whole subject be "postponed" was adopted by a vote of 46 to 30.[95]

The debate had been heated, ill-tempered, and full of sarcasm, marked by frequent accusations of bad faith and vicious intentions on both sides. When it was over, Murray, showing that Quakers were not the only ones unhappy with the Fugitive Act of 1793, proposed that $500 in damages be assessed against employers hiring a fugitive slave, payable to the slave's owner. Under present regulations, he said, owners were forced to prove that the employer hiring a Negro had known that he was a fugitive at the time of hiring. This was difficult and prevented the adequate enforcement of the act.[96] His motion was ordered to lie on the table.

About two weeks after disposing of the memorial from Delaware, Congress received a petition that rubbed salt into fresh wounds. The petition came from four Negroes manumitted by slave owners in North Carolina. According to the petition, their manumissions had been confirmed by the Superior Court of North Carolina, but now their liberty was threatened by retroactive state laws, which directed the re-enslavement of Negroes who had been freed for reasons other than "meritorious service." [97] They had fled from North Carolina, finding refuge first in Virginia, then in Pennsylvania. A claimant to their services in North Carolina had offered a ten-dollar reward if they were returned alive, and fifty dollars for proof that they had been killed. Addressing Congress as "fellow-rationals" and "fellow-men," they asked whether laws that restricted manumission so severely, and that operated *ex post facto* to deny freedom, did not show a "governmental defect," violating "fundamental principles of the Constitution." They assured Congress that they asked nothing unconstitutional, but were confident that Constitutional exertions would be salutary.[98]

The petition was presented on January 30, 1797. First to respond was Thomas Blount, of eastern North Carolina, who insisted that the petition be flatly and immediately rejected because these persons were slaves by North Carolina law and were thus not entitled to approach Congress. George Thacher, a Federalist from the Maine District of Massachusetts, was not impressed by this argument. These Negroes, he said, "certainly are free people," having been granted liberty by their owners, who alone had just claim to them. He insisted that the petition be referred to the committee instructed to consider amendments to the Fugitive Act. A law that permitted the capture of people like these, he said, was plainly defective. Joseph Varnum, a Republican from Massachusetts, reminded his colleagues that these men claimed to be free, and that color created no presumption to the contrary. (On this crucial point, of course, Varnum's principles were precisely at variance with those of his fellow Congressmen from the South.) "I hope," he said, "the House will take all possible care that freemen should not be made slaves; to be deprived of liberty is more important than to be deprived of property." He agreed with Blount that if these petitioners were in fact slaves, their petition ought to be rejected. But if they were freedmen, they were in danger of injury by the fugitive law. In any case, justice required that the petition be referred and that inquiries be made by a Congressional committee.[99]

These arguments provoked two kinds of response from the Southerners. The visceral reaction came from William L. Smith, an alert guardian of the slave interest, who remarked that this "dangerous" petition would make all Southerners "uncomfortable." Denouncing the request for amendments to the Fugitive Act, he argued, "These men are slaves and . . . not entitled to attention from this House. . . . This is a kind of property on which the House has no power to legislate." At this, Thacher jumped to his feet, noting that the question before Congress was whether or not to amend a law that already affected property in slaves. Obviously, he said, "this is a kind of property on which we are bound to legislate." [100] Madison spoke more effectively for the opposition. His basic argument was that the question presented in this petition was judicial rather than legislative. If these men had a legitimate claim to freedom, North Carolina's Court of Appeals would surely recognize it; if, on the other hand, the courts of North Carolina declared them to be slaves, then "the Constitution gives them no hopes of being heard here." * [101]

Two North Carolinians, Blount and Nathaniel Macon, supported him, promising that courts in North Carolina could be relied upon to render justice. Aaron Kitchell, of New Jersey, wondered why free men, if that was what they were, should have

* The petitioners had begun their plea by noting that "being of African descent . . . to you only, under God, can we apply with any hope of effect. . . ."[102]

to travel back to North Carolina to get justice. Nevertheless, a vote was taken on the motion to receive the petition and refer it to a committee for study. The count was 33 to 50 against any further consideration.

This curious debate, culminating in a decision to duck the issue presented by the manumitted slaves, reveals the impotence of the national government to handle controversies directly affecting the regulation of slavery. At stake was a clash between a slave owner's right to dispose of his property, reinforced by the claim of a group of Negroes to freedom, against the right of a state that sanctioned slavery to protect itself against the danger of free Negroes. Madison, arguing like a good Jeffersonian, claimed that this was a question for local authorities, to be decided by state courts interpreting state laws. Thacher urged that Congress assume the power, implied in the fugitive law, to make federal rules defining and delimiting the extent to which the disciplines of slavery were to apply throughout the nation. Though no honest man could have doubted the consequence of referring the question to the courts of North Carolina,* Madison's argument was preferred. Rather than give careful and deliberate consideration to an issue that reached deep into the heart of relations within the federal union, Congress chose to placate those who regarded any and all discussion of slavery as inflammatory.

Early in Jefferson's administration, Southern Congressmen discovered that the determination to avoid agitating the question of slavery was a weapon with two edges. Soon after the opening of the Seventh Congress, in December 1801, Joseph Nicholson, of Maryland, reported a bill directing that a fine of $500 be imposed on anyone "harboring, concealing or employing" a runaway slave. The bill defined a runaway as any black person who failed to show his employer a certificate of freedom signed by a justice of the peace or bearing a county seal. The bill would have compelled an employer who hired a Negro who was new to a region to publish a description of him in two newspapers within a month after hiring him.[104]

---

* The preamble to North Carolina's act for limiting manumissions spoke of "the evil and pernicious practice of freeing slaves." [103]

This was a remarkably harsh and arrogant bill. It sought to extend the principles and precautions of a slave regime throughout the nation. It would have made a pariah of every free Negro in New England and the mid-Atlantic states, as well as the South. It would have imposed a complicated and perpetual obligation upon people, many of whom were citizens, but few of whom were sophisticated in the carrying of documents. In addition, it would have imposed burdensome regulations on any Northern shopkeeper or millowner who chose to employ a Negro in any capacity. Congressmen of every political persuasion, including men never suspected of abolitionism or of radicalism on the racial issue, might well have objected to this bill.

Representatives from the South, however, leaped to Nicholson's support. Slave owners, they said, had long been injured by the practice among some groups in the North of assisting runaways to get employment in Eastern and mid-Atlantic states. Often, they said, when these Negroes were caught and returned, their meretricious tales of Northern hospitality led others to try to escape. The result was that masters were forced to exercise increasingly severe discipline to keep their property from disappearing. Thus, they said, Northerners concerned about the harshness of slavery ought to favor Nicholson's proposal. This argument was advanced by spokesmen for all shades of Southern opinion, from low-country Federalists to hill-country Republicans.

After the debate, a vote was taken on a motion to strike the penalties from the bill. The vote, on which no roll call was taken, resulted in a tie. Three days later, a roll-call vote on a motion to allow the bill to pass to a third reading resulted in defeat by 43 to 46.[105] The sectional breakdown was extremely sharp. Only six Republicans from New York, New Jersey, and Pennsylvania, plus a Federalist each from Vermont and Delaware voted with the South. The margin of victory for the opposition came from two North Carolina Federalists—Archibald Henderson, of Salisbury, in the west, and John Stanly, a Princeton-educated lawyer from New Bern, in the east.

If sectional discipline had prevailed with these two men, the South, with the connivance of a few Northern sympathizers, might have led the federal government to assist in imposing disci plines helpful to slavery throughout the country, all the while adamantly refusing to permit the passage of regulations safeguarding the liberty of Negro citizens in the North or to strengthen and enforce existing regulations against the slave trade. An unusual degree of solidarity among Northerners was barely sufficient to maintain the principle, against Southern challenge, that Congress should refrain from regulating the status of Negroes within the states.

Not until 1817 did Congress again confront a demand for revisions in the Fugitive Act of 1793. Then, once again, the impulse for reform came from the South, and its concern was for the rights of slave owners, not free blacks. The bill of 1817, of considerable importance to the holders of slave property, was introduced by a Virginian, James Pindall. It directed the seizure of any black suspected of being a fugitive and ordered his removal to the state granting the warrant for his arrest, there to stand trial as a runaway. Penalties were provided for state officials refusing to comply.

Southerners, still in the habit of expressing public regrets over the continued hold of slavery on Southern society, nevertheless insisted that the bill was necessary to cope with an increasingly serious problem. Northerners were divided. Some were opposed out of regard for the rights of free blacks or concern for the extension of federal supervision over state officials. But others expressed sympathy for the principle of the bill. The Constitution, they argued, required the rendition of fugitive slaves, and so did wise policy for the North. If the matter was made subject to trial by jury, as some had suggested, the decision "would in ninety-nine cases out of one hundred be in favor of the fugitives," and soon Northern cities would be "infested with the runaways from the South." [106]

A lot had happened since 1802, when Nicholson's bill had gone down to narrow defeat. Many Northerners had spent a decade and a half deploring the influence of slavery on American politics and asserting the responsibility of state officials to protect the rights of citizens from outside interference. But as the vote in the House (84 to 69 in favor of the amendments) revealed, these controversies about the nature of the union had had little effect on the attitude of most Northerners toward black people. Pindall's bill went to the Senate, which altered it in certain details, and it was eventually lost when the two houses were unable to iron out their differences.[107] Apparently the demand for firmer measures against fugitives was still not strong enough to surmount the hurdles of the legislative process.

The episode affords a clue to the nerve of Northern concern over slavery. That concern had more to do with the influence of slaveholding on the balance of power within the dominant white political culture than with a humanitarian concern for the place of black people in American life. There were some white politicians, of course, who were moved by compassion. But until the issue of slavery was joined on a point of central concern to contending forces directly represented in the political system, no black man in America could rest assured that he was safely beyond the reach of a system that held over 80 per cent of his race in bondage—not when a Congressman from Boston could defend a bill like that of 1817 by speaking of the danger of having his city "infested" with runaways.

It cannot be denied that the United States accomplished prodigies during these early years. Through luck and alert opportunism, the young republic managed to thwart Napoleon's intention of establishing French authority in New Orleans and to acquire the vast Louisiana Purchase, including most of the land from the Mississippi River to the Rocky Mountains. Despite an appearance of reckless bungling and feckless unco-ordination, it waged war for two and a half years with a formidable military power and escaped virtually unscathed. And despite the resistance of natives who were tough and sometimes desperately tenacious, it pushed the frontier westward with relentless, galloping momentum. It is sometimes implied that American development was achieved in the absence of obstacles, but in Napoleon, the British Navy and Army, and Indian warriors, the United States in the early nineteenth century faced foes that were cunning and powerful, and not always enthusiastic about the forces that were gathering and building and spreading out from the west coast of the Atlantic Ocean. Against external enemies, the new nation was anything but timid and weak.

When it came to dealing with entrenched domestic interests,

however, the American government was curiously impotent. It was perennially unable to raise revenue or float an adequate navy. Its bureaucracy was tiny and amateurish. Its national politicians tiptoed around the nation's capital constantly engaged in a ritual of self-effacement. The weakness of government in turn reflected deep divisions in the body politic. The nation was unable to decide where its sympathies lay or to pursue a prudent neutrality during the epic struggle between England and France. It could not achieve consensus about the definition and punishment of sedition. It teetered awkwardly on the brink of dissolution after a series of mortifying experiments with self-inflicted prohibitions of commerce. And, most profound of all, it was wracked by disagreement about the appropriate national attitude toward slavery. White Southerners, however ambivalent their feelings about enslavement as an abstract proposition, saw no viable alternative to slavery in the context of race relations in the American South. As far as Northerners were concerned, despite a growing awareness of the impact of slavery on the nation's life, they were unable to fashion and pursue a policy for setting the institution on the road to extinction, or even to craft laws to protect those few blacks who had wriggled loose from slavery and thus to begin to break the suffocating embrace of racial pride.

It was such a nation—bursting with energy but fearful of public authority, divided by fundamental circumstances but determined to perfect its union—that began the search for policies to regulate and, after 1808, to terminate the African slave trade.

8

The Attempt to End
the Importation of Slaves

THE foreign slave trade was one matter of fundamental importance to the system of slavery on which the federal government
had a clear mandate, under the Constitution, to act. Despite the
objections of the Deep Southerners, most of the framers had recognized that the slave trade would profoundly affect the make-up
and character of the nation, the balance of political forces within
the union, and its foreign relations. The threat of Deep Southerners to stay out of the union had won for them a Constitutional
guarantee that the trade would not be prohibited by the federal
government for twenty years, and that tariffs on the trade in the
meantime would not exceed ten dollars per slave. But apart from
these stated qualifications, the framers intended that Congress
should exercise its power over foreign commerce in such a way as
to prohibit the trade as soon as the twenty-year moratorium was
over. Despite this straightforward and apparently simple arrangement, however, the foreign slave trade was a source of bitter controversy throughout the early national period.

The roots of tension can be seen in the state laws that existed as
the Constitution went into effect. State laws on the slave trade
were important because the Constitution left it to the states to
prohibit the commerce, if they chose, before 1808
The state with the most deep-rooted hostility to the slave trade
was Virginia. Virginians hated it for several reasons. Perhaps
their deepest reason was moral. In a clause eliminated from the
Declaration of Independence at the insistence of Deep Southern-

ers, Thomas Jefferson had spoken the mind of the Old Dominion by calling the trade a "cruel war against human nature itself," and blaming it on the King. In their thinking about slavery, Virginians depended heavily on the idea that they were the unwilling victims of a system foisted on them by their heedless ancestors and by the policies of a brutish colonial government. The continuation of the slave trade after independence would make the crime unambiguously their own, and would also counteract the process by which Virginians hoped that slavery might gradually disappear—namely, by the dispersion of blacks across the land or by their return to Africa. Virginians worried, too, that the trade would increase the danger of "servile insurrections." For these reasons, the state legislature outlawed the trade into Virginia in 1778, and by 1787 Virginians were impatient for the day when they could end it once and for all, throughout the nation.

Most Northerners shared the Virginians' habit of deploring the trade, but the enactments of Northern legislatures reflect a different spirit. The Rhode Island law of 1774 illustrates the weakness of Northern legislation against the trade. After a stirring preamble, which related the desire to halt the trade to the Revolutionary concern for "personal liberty," the act seems almost cynical. It provided that "for the future, no negro or mulatto slave shall be brought into the colony," and it prescribed the penalty that was most likely to discourage traders: any slave illegally imported was to be "rendered immediately free." But then came a series of provisions indicating that the concern of the legislators was not primarily for the "personal liberty" of Africans at all, but for the welfare of Rhode Islanders engaged in the slave trade. "Any vessel belonging to this colony," it said, which had picked up slaves in Africa to sell in the West Indies, and which "could not" dispose of them there, might bring them to Rhode Island. For each slave so imported, a bond of one hundred pounds was to be posted with the treasurer of the colony. This bond would be forfeited unless the slaves were re-exported within one year, "if such Negro or mulatto be alive, and in a condition to be removed." Further to guard against an abuse of the law's intent, heavy penalties were provided for those who brought Negroes into Rhode Island with the purpose of freeing them.[1] This law

failed to address itself to the primary way in which Rhode Islanders were involved in the traffic between Africa and America.
Their state had ceased for many years to be a "consumer" of
slaves. Its relationship to slavery was as the "greatest slave-trader
in America." [2] Though the law made a great parade of prohibiting importation, it did so with a minimum of inconvenience to a
mainstay of the state's prosperity.[3]

New Jersey's law, passed twelve years later, displayed the same
cadence. It began by appealing to the "principles of justice and
humanity" against the "barbarous custom of bringing the unoffending African from his native country and connections into a
state of slavery," and noted the requirement of "sound policy"
that the increase of slavery be prevented, out of regard for "such
of the community as depend upon their labor for their daily subsistence." After this bold start, the act degenerated into a jumble
of legalisms and double negatives, the purport of which was that
slaves fresh from Africa were not to be imported into the state,
and that the importation of slaves "seasoned" elsewhere (in the
West Indies, for example) was to be discouraged by the imposition of a fine of twenty pounds. Settlers and travelers who
brought slaves with them were exempted.[4]

Despite these cynical provisions, it is nevertheless true that by
1787 every state from New England to Virginia had prohibited
African slaves from being introduced into its jurisdiction. What
gave these Northern exemptions significance was the situation in
the three southernmost states.

North Carolina was not so bad, from the prohibitionists' point
of view. The poor relation of the Carolinas had relatively few
slaves, by Southern standards, and employed them mainly in
planting tobacco, an enterprise that seemed to have found its
level toward the end of the eighteenth century.[5] By 1786 North
Carolina was ready to adopt a prohibitive duty, which went into
effect early in the following year. The duty was repealed in 1790,
but the legal trade in slaves was prohibited altogether in 1794.

The outlook in South Carolina was different. South Carolinians made it plain that they did not regard the slave trade as an
evil. At the Federal Convention, General Pinckney spoke the
mind of his state when he said "that the importation of slaves

would be for the interest of the whole union. The more slaves, the more produce to employ the carrying trade; the more consumption also, and the more of this, the more of revenue for the common treasury." [6] In the convention that ratified the Constitution for South Carolina, Rawlins Lowndes spoke even more forthrightly. The African trade, he said, "could be justified on the principles of religion, humanity, and justice; for certainly to translate a set of human beings from a bad country to a better, was fulfilling every part of these principles. . . . Without Negroes," he added, "this state would degenerate into one of the most contemptible in the union. . . . Negroes are our only wealth, our only natural resource." [7]

South Carolina had lost many slaves during the Revolutionary War.[8] In the postwar period, the desire to replace these losses and to participate in the expected boom had caused the slave trade to flourish. Duties imposed during the mid-1780's proved to be a source of considerable revenue to the state.[9] But when the rice market failed to revive as quickly as expected,[10] this continuing purchase of slaves had contributed to an upset in the state's balance of trade. By 1785 distressing economic conditions induced some of the planters to propose a temporary prohibition of slave importations. Opponents of the measure, led by John Rutledge and Thomas Pinckney, insisted that the trade in slaves was not a major contributor to the crisis, and that it would be foolish to divert Charleston's share of this profitable business to Savannah. These latter arguments prevailed in 1785, but when the economic picture failed to brighten during the next two years, the legislature decided, as part of its assault on the depression, to suspend the trade for three years. As General Pinckney emphasized at the Federal Convention, this act was considered a temporary regulation, rather than a permanent prohibition.[11] Supported by a phalanx of the most influential planters, including Charles Pinckney, David Ramsay, Edward Rutledge, and William Lowndes, the temporary prohibition was renewed every two or three years until 1803.[12]

In 1787 Georgia was the only state in the union that had not proscribed the foreign slave trade. Then, in 1793, its legislature responded to the insurrection in Santo Domingo by prohibiting the importation of slaves from the West Indies, the Bahamas, and Florida; and in 1798 the new state constitution outlawed any "future importation of slaves into this state from Africa or any foreign place." [13]

Thus, as government began under the Constitution, eight of the thirteen states (Connecticut, Rhode Island, New York, New Jersey, Delaware, Maryland, Virginia, and South Carolina) had made it a crime to import slaves as merchandise, two (Pennsylvania and North Carolina) had imposed prohibitive duties, and in two others (New Hampshire and Massachusetts) the abolition of slavery had obviated any enactments against the importation of slaves. Vermont and Kentucky outlawed the trade by the time they assumed statehood, and Tennessee in 1795 adopted North Carolina's prohibition. The Northwest Ordinance of 1787 made the trade illegal there, and Congress in 1798, at the suggestion of a representative from South Carolina, outlawed the importation of slaves from abroad into the Mississippi Territory. By the turn of the century, slaves could not legally be brought into the United States from any foreign place.

It was in part because of this situation at the state level that opponents of the slave trade had been willing to forgo federal prohibition for twenty years. In the meantime, they could express their disapproval by levying the ten-dollar tax—or so they thought.

Two weeks after the inauguration of Washington as first President, a Congressman from Virginia, Josiah Parker, moved that the nation's maiden tariff law be amended to include a ten-dollar tax on all slaves imported into the United States. Congress, he said, should go to the full limits of its power to discourage "this irrational and inhuman traffic." [14]

This straightforward proposal was met by some of the sharpest remarks heard by the First Congress. One South Carolinian warned that the proposal was "big with the most serious consequences." Another went so far as to say that nothing yet discussed by Congress "was so important to [South Carolina], and the welfare of the union, as the question now brought forward." [15]

General James Jackson, representing Georgia, next confronted

Congress with a question that may have seemed irrelevant to a debate on the slave trade, but in fact was fundamental to it: the status of slavery in the United States. Despite the fashion of the day, he said, he was opposed to the "liberty of slaves" under any circumstances. He insisted that free Negroes—he cited the situation in Maryland and Virginia—were a dangerous nuisance and a public burden. Besides, was Congress ready to talk about compensating slave owners for their property? The burden of compensation was obviously far beyond the powers of the young republic, but to entertain ideas that struck at slavery without confronting the problem of compensation was, in his view, to challenge the deepest principle of just government: the obligation to protect property.[16]

At this point, James Madison came to Parker's support. The Federal Convention, he recalled, had included the provision for taxing the foreign slave trade so that Congress before 1808 could express its disapproval of the trade. "It is to be hoped," he said, "that by expressing a national disapprobation of this trade, we may destroy it, and save ourselves from reproaches, and our posterity the imbecility ever attendant on a country filled with slaves." He recalled that the English had been drawn down on the South during the Revolutionary War by weaknesses stemming from slavery, and concluded that Parker's motion was in the best interests of the South, even if Deep Southerners did not recognize it.

The motion was opposed, however, not only by Deep Southerners, but also by representatives from New England. This alignment (the two ends of the union against the middle) seems ironic in view of the fact that the clause on which the motion was based had been part of a compromise drafted by a New England–Deep South coalition. But support for a tax on the slave trade had never been strong, not even at the Federal Convention. Many people who abhorred both slavery and the slave trade were reluctant to stain the statute books or fill the public treasury with gains gotten by this traffic. People who regarded the slave trade as a crime, rather than a business, were determined not to share in its proceeds.

Madison, feeling this sentiment, advised Parker to withdraw

his motion, in order to embody it in a separate bill. Parker accepted this advice, and on September 19, 1789 he reported a bill whose sole purpose was to impose the ten-dollar tax. His bill was read and immediately postponed "until the next session." Nothing further was said about the tax until 1804, when the reopening of the trade in South Carolina provoked the Eighth Congress to reconsider the question.

This opening "jostle" over Article I, Section 9 was both brief and fruitless, and in the broad context of the momentous debates and acts of the First Congress, it fades into almost total insignificance. In the context of developments on slavery, however, it is of considerable interest. For one thing, the brief exchange demonstrated the pain that was felt whenever this sensitive nerve received the slightest touch. Parker had moved no more than that a provision clearly authorized in the Constitution be enacted into law. The response of Congressmen from South Carolina and Georgia was as quick and violent as a bolt of lightning. When he sought to reinforce his argument by appealing to the Declaration of Independence, the stormy response heightened in intensity. Most notable was the speech of General Jackson, which contained many of the themes—slavery in America is better for the blacks than barbarism in Africa; freedom is debilitating to the Negro and dangerous to white society—that were heard later in defense of slavery as a "positive good."

Another characteristic feature of this debate was its brevity. If Americans had shared a common experience with slavery, it might have been unnecessary to discuss the culture and condition of slavery and speculate about the impact of a tax on the slave trade. But in fact they did not. To impose a tax on the slave trade raised difficult questions. Would such a tax imply complicity in the trade? Would the government come to depend on this revenue? Would the tax really reduce the number of Africans enslaved or imported into the United States? Was it politic or fair to tax a type of property owned by relatively few citizens? Did the failure to impose this tax represent a failure to go to the limits of the Constitution in opposing the growth of slavery? These questions were barely broached.

During the Constitutional Convention, it was easy to believe that the difficulty of framing a new government justified a refusal to enter into a divisive struggle over slavery. Now, during the First Congress, other, almost equally fundamental, tasks of founding—setting up the executive and judicial departments, deciding how to raise revenues and which debts to pay first, receiving Vermont and Kentucky into the union, framing the Bill of Rights—cried out for attention, and again the disposition to "postpone until the next session" asserted itself.

The political leaders of New England and South Carolina had another reason for wanting to avoid agitation on this issue. A Federalist coalition was just beginning to emerge. New Englanders and South Carolinians were finding that they had many legislative goals in common,[17] and they were reluctant now, as they had been in 1787, to let the Virginians disturb their plans. Only the Virginians showed any disposition to debate the question, and their tactical position was weakened by the fact that their motives, when it came to the slave trade, were suspect. Madison quickly decided that it was hopeless to force the issue at this point, and that the marginal gain against slavery, if the tax had been adopted, would not have justified the effort.

Congressional leaders and their lieutenants on the hustings were apparently quite frightened by the intensity of this initial bout with slavery, and there is evidence of attempts to restrain Quakers and other abolitionists from approaching Congress about the trade.[18] In February 1790, however, the pressure for Congressional action burst through the restraints. Thomas Fitzsimons, a wealthy merchant from Philadelphia and a member of the Constitutional Convention, presented a petition drafted by the Quaker Yearly Meeting of 1789. The petition was vigorous in its condemnation of the slave trade, calling it "abhorrent to common humanity and common honesty." But it was moderate and respectful in its request: that a "sincere and impartial inquiry" be made into the full extent of the power of Congress, under the Constitution, "to exercise justice and mercy" by regulating the slave trade.[19]

Several Southerners, including Fitzsimons's fellow framer Abraham Baldwin, of Georgia, urged that the ground so carefully laid in 1787 be not hastily or carelessly disturbed.

Mr. Baldwin was sorry the subject had ever been brought before Congress. . . . Gentlemen who had been present at the formation of this Constitution could not avoid the recollection of the pain and difficulty which the subject had caused in that body.[20]

But the next day, Baldwin's counsel of moderation was rejected by a man who had spent a lifetime probing the weaknesses of vulnerable establishments, and who, in the twilight of his career, had decided to take a crack at America's own peculiar institution. The man was Benjamin Franklin, who at the age of ninety had lent his name and vast prestige to the Pennsylvania Society for Promoting the Abolition of Slavery. As president of the society, he signed and submitted a petition that assailed slavery on the basis of the Christian religion and the "political creed of Americans," and urged Congress to "devise means" to remove this "inconsistency from the land of liberty." In particular, he urged that the slave trade be curbed, as far as Constitutionally possible. "Step to the very verge of the power vested in you," he counseled, "for discouraging every species of traffic in the persons of our fellow men." [21]

Representatives from South Carolina and Georgia were aghast. They leaped on Franklin's petition with fury. South Carolina's Thomas Tudor Tucker was emboldened by his rage to say that Franklin "ought to have known the Constitution better," and that the petition incited Congress to unconstitutional acts. Any attempt at emancipation, he warned, would lead to "civil war." His colleague William L. Smith recalled the difficulty of obtaining ratification in the Deep South, for fear of sentiments like Franklin's in the North. Insisting that "there is no point on which [Southerners] are more jealous and suspicious" than they were about slavery, he said that "the [Southern] states would never have entered into the Confederation, unless their property had been guaranteed to them, for such is the state of agriculture in that country, that without slaves it must be abandoned. . . . We look upon this [petition] as an attack upon the palladium of the property of our country; it is therefore our duty to oppose it by every means in our power." [22]

These speeches surprised and annoyed many Northerners. One Pennsylvanian announced that if he were a federal judge, he would go as far as he could to grant a claim of emancipation brought by any Negro slave. Elbridge Gerry, estimating that slaves now held in America were worth about $10 million,* suggested that Congress use proceeds from the sale of lands in the Northwest Territory as a source of funds for a program of compensated emancipation.[24]

Madison noted that the debate had taken a serious turn. He urged immediate referral, in hopes that a committee might quietly, and definitively, investigate the extent and limits of the powers of Congress over slavery and the slave trade, with an eye to laying this dangerous question to rest for the time being. Despite the threat by Aedanus Burke, of Charleston, that the mere commitment of these petitions would "blow the trumpet of sedition in the Southern states," Congress favored referral by 43 to 11. Seven who voted "nay" came from South Carolina and Georgia, two were Virginians, and one each came from Maryland and New York. Among those voting "aye" were eight members from Virginia and three from Maryland. The rest where Northerners.[25]

The committee appointed to consider the petitions is notable mainly for its lack of members from the Deep South.[26] Nevertheless, the report it submitted was signed by seven members of Congress, including Josiah Parker, who owned slaves himself and who represented the owners of over 12,000 slaves,[27] and who was re-elected to Congress for five terms following the submission of this report. Despite faults in the representativeness of the drafting committee, the report deserves attention as a statement of Constitutional interpretation acceptable to a considerable segment of Congress. As such, it serves as a measure of the subsequent reluctance of Northern Congressmen to "step to the very verge of the power vested" by the Constitution, according to their own reckoning.

The report proposed "to examine the powers vested in Congress, under the present Constitution, relating to the abolition of slavery." These bold words were followed by a clause avowing the lack of power in Congress to prohibit the slave trade until 1808.

---

* About fifteen dollars apiece, according to the census of 1790—an altogether unrealistic estimate, in light of the fact that slaves were worth about $300–$400 each at this time—a total closer to $200 million.[23]

The next clauses seemed to say that "by a fair construction of the Constitution," Congress was prohibited from passing an act of emancipation. But a close reading reveals that the Constitutional restraint on emancipation is held to apply only to "slaves who already are, or who may, within the period mentioned [before 1808], be imported, or born within, any of the said states." That is, the Constitution, by this interpretation, did not restrain Congress from emancipating slaves born in the United States after 1808.

Various "internal regulations" left by the Constitution to the states are then listed, including the instruction of slaves in morality and religion, rules governing their care and maintenance, marriage laws and family life, and provision for cases of "sickness, age, and infirmity." Significantly included in this catalogue of responsibilities left to the states is the "seizure, transportation, or sale of free Negroes." Apparently almost no one at this time felt that the federal government could prevent the "sale of free negroes." The fugitive-slave clause bade the federal government protect white citizens against the flight of slaves; but, by this interpretation, no agency of government was authorized to prevent the re-enslavement of black citizens.

After noting the power to lay the ten-dollar tax, the report went on to find that Article I, Section 9 was pregnant with implications of powers that had not been found by Southerners. Earlier, Baldwin had said that the clause on the slave trade had been "cautiously expressed and more punctiliously guarded than any other part" of the Constitution.[28] Notwithstanding this care, the committee found it full of holes, from the point of view of those bent on restraining the regulating hand of Congress for twenty years.

Congress have authority to [regulate], or (so far as it is or may be carried on by citizens of the United States, for supplying foreigners) to [interdict] the African trade, and to make provision for the humane treatment of slaves . . . while on the passage to the United States, or to foreign ports, so far as respects the citizens of the United States. . . . Congress have also authority to prohibit foreigners from fitting out vessels in any port of the United States, for transporting persons from Africa to any foreign port.[29]

The "discovery" of these powers should not have surprised anyone who had read Article I, Section 9 carefully and was willing to imagine how it might be construed by men resolutely opposed to slavery and the slave trade. The language of the clause and its position in the Constitution indicate that it was meant as a limitation on the power of Congress to regulate commerce.[30] It directed that the slave trade "shall not be *prohibited* by the Congress prior to" 1808. South Carolinians believed that the clause as a whole was intended as a complete catalogue of powers over the slave trade: power to tax for twenty years; then power to prohibit. But the committee found that a whole variety of regulations were permitted by the Constitution before 1808, so long as they did not prohibit the importation of slaves into states willing to admit them.

The report ended with a bow of gratitude to the memorialists, and a promise to pursue their "humane objects" to the limits of "justice, humanity, and good policy." But as soon as it had been read, William L. Smith, of South Carolina, rose to invoke the apocalypse. For Congress to adopt the report in its present form, he warned, "would excite tumults, seditions, and insurrections." But Connecticut's Roger Sherman, who at the Federal Convention and during the debate on the ten-dollar impost had been a valuable ally of the South Carolinians, called the report "prudent, humane, and judicious." Over the strenuous objections of Burke, Smith, and Jackson, the report was referred to the Committee of the Whole for debate.

It is unnecessary to trace in detail the debate that occurred between March 16 and 22. The attitudes expressed were epitomized by a brilliant exchange between Smith and Elias Boudinot, of New Jersey.

Smith's speech was the most thorough defense of slavery heard by Congress during the first twenty years of its existence under the Constitution. Slavery, he said, was a fit status for Negroes, who were by nature "indolent," "improvident, [and] averse to labor," but were nevertheless ideally suited to work on Southern plantations because of the nature of the work and their immunity to diseases that plagued white workers in the swamps of the Deep South. On the other hand, emancipation was bad policy for both

Negroes and whites. Negroes freed from the discipline of slavery never sought to improve themselves. Furthermore, when they congregated with slaves, they tended to boast, deceitfully, about the supposed advantages of freedom. Due to the volatile imagination of slaves, these contacts between slaves and freedmen created dangers that white society in the South could not and would not tolerate.

Smith argued that the advocates of emancipation had not faced the full implications of their position. Was it intended to grant the Negro full equality? This would result either in the sexual mixing of the races, with a resulting degeneration of white human beings,[31] or in eternal hostility between Negroes and whites, leading inevitably to the massacre and extirpation of one race or the other.

Nor was it, in Smith's opinion, either realistic or genuinely liberal to propose the removal of Negroes from America. Since Negroes themselves had no desire to leave, their freedom would be violated more by transporting them to a colony than by holding them in slavery, a condition in which most of them seemed to thrive and to be happy. Negroes returned to Africa would be either slaughtered or re-enslaved. Those shipped to colonies in the West, the Caribbean Islands, or Central America would be victimized by their incapacity for self-government and by their defenselessness against the Indians. "If, then, nothing but evil would result from emancipation, under the existing circumstances of the country, why should Congress stir at all in the business, or give any countenance to such dangerous applications."

Having dismissed the alternatives, he proceeded to present several positive arguments for slavery. He noted the classical precedents and the Scriptural basis of the system. He responded to the argument that slavery debased the mind and spirit of the South by pointing with pride to the culture and refined manners of Southerners, the softness of Southern women, and the valor of Southern men. He noted that South Carolina's prosperity depended on the labor of slaves, and that the nation as a whole, and especially Northern commercial interests, had a stake in the South's economic well-being.

He noted the claim that public opinion, even in the Deep

South, was opposed to slavery, accepting it only as a necessary but regrettable evil. He questioned the truth of this claim, pointing out that none of the petitions against slavery came from the Deep South.[32] In any case, slavery was thoroughly woven into the fabric of Southern society, and Southerners were convinced that it was bad policy from every point of view to try to remove it. If Northerners regarded slavery as a moral evil, he advised that they comfort themselves with the realization that all civilized countries must endure moral evils in order to exist.

Finally, he turned to his Constitutional argument. Northerners hate slavery; Southerners hate Quakers. In 1787–1788 Southerners decided that they could live in the same union with Quakers, in spite of their pacifism and meddlesome self-righteousness. At the same time, Northerners who regarded slavery as a source of weakness were coming to a parallel decision.

The best informed part of the citizens of the Northern states knew that slavery was so ingrafted into the policy of the Southern states, that it could not be eradicated without tearing up by the roots their happiness, tranquillity and prosperity; that if it were an evil, it was one for which there was no remedy, and, like wise men, they acquiesced in it.

Because of the danger of intersectional misunderstanding, said Smith, it was important that the Constitution be construed strictly. The framers had divided governmental responsibilities between federal and state authorities, and had wisely assigned power over slavery to the states. Instead of seeking ways to evade this arrangement, statesmen should honor it in letter and in spirit. If the federal government tried to usurp power over slavery, a struggle would surely ensue, and all wise property owners would recognize the cause of the slave owner as their own.

He concluded by registering his disapproval of the entire report, especially the clause commending the petitioners. Such expressions, he said, would only encourage reckless fanatics to continue their assault on the Constitution.[33]

It would be difficult to overestimate the importance of Smith's speech. It offers an unequaled insight into slavery and its prospects as seen by a keen Deep Southern observer in 1790. And of special interest is the fact that it was delivered before the outbreak of Toussaint's revolt and before the invention of the cotton gin. These two events, one or the other or both together, are often held responsible for arresting the decline of slavery in America. Smith's speech demonstrates that Deep Southerners were convinced of the dangers of emancipation before the uprising; and that slave owners in the Deep South had found slavery indispensable, and were proud of the uses they had made of it, long before Whitney's gin.

Most of the themes that later became familiar in the proslavery writings of the "positive-good" school can be found in Smith's presentation: that Negroes were better off in America than among savages in barbarian Africa; that Negroes developed best under the discipline of slavery and were innately unfit for the rigors of freedom; that only Negroes could cultivate the swamps of the Deep South; and that the whole union benefited from their labor. And there was no apology. The argument comparing Quakers and slavery as sources of weakness to the union suggests that the defense of slavery was assuming a less defensive tone, at least as presented by the South Carolinians. Northerners said they were proud of the Quakers; Southerners felt the same way about slavery.

Five days after this speech, on March 22, 1790, Elias Boudinot made a lengthy reply, which was remarkably moderate in tone, and in no way comparable as a forensic display. Boudinot rejected Smith's contention that the Scriptures sanctioned slavery, but he said that there was no disposition among Northern Congressmen to emancipate slaves in South Carolina. He insisted that he shared Smith's conviction about the impracticality of emancipation: "It would be inhumanity itself to turn these unhappy people loose to murder each other, or to perish for want of the necessaries of life." His strongest objection to Smith's speech was its appearance of "justifying this ungenerous traffic" in slaves. America's most fundamental commitment—and he quoted passages from the Declaration on the Necessity of Taking Up Arms, as well as the Declaration of Independence—was to the equality and liberty of men. Northerners had reconciled themselves to the necessity of slavery "under the existing circumstances"; and they had agreed not to prohibit the slave trade for twenty years. They had not, however, relinquished their right to consider whether there was Constitutional authority to control the increase of an institution that, in their judgment, violated the commitments and sapped the strength of the nation.[34]

During the course of debate in the Committee of the Whole, the report was gradually stripped of the clauses that gave the greatest offense to slave owners. The preamble, which had described the report as a consideration of "powers . . . relating to the abolition of slavery," was eliminated, as was the concluding clause expressing sympathy with "the humane objects of the memorialists." The implication of a possible future power of emancipation was converted into a categorical denial of such power. The enumeration of "internal regulations" that lay outside the authority of Congress became a brief denial of "authority to interfere . . . in the treatment of [slaves] within any of the states." The clause noting the power to lay a ten-dollar impost was stricken altogether. All that remained were a verbatim restatement of the first clause of Article I, Section 9 of the Constitution and an assertion of Congressional power "to restrain the citizens of the United States from . . . supplying foreigners with slaves," to regulate conditions during the passage from Africa to the United States, and "to prohibit foreigners from fitting out vessels in any port of the United States for transporting persons from Africa to any foreign port." [35]

Following a bitter debate on March 23, and by the margin of one vote, Congress decided to receive this emasculated report from its Committee of the Whole. A vote was then taken on a motion by Madison to enter both reports—the one received from the Select Committee as well—in the House *Journal*. The motion was adopted by a vote of 29 to 25. The eight representatives from the three southernmost states were unanimously opposed. Representatives from Maryland and Virginia, who had voted 11 to 3 in favor of the investigation by a special committee, now voted 6 to 9 against a permanent record. Eight Northerners (three from Massachusetts, two each from Connecticut and New York, and one from New Hampshire) added to the strength of the opposition.

Apparently, the debate left a bad taste in many mouths. The

motion for a permanent record was opposed, not only by Southerners, but by Representatives whose abhorrence of slavery and contempt for slave owners were deep and abiding—including George Thacher and Fisher Ames, of Massachusetts, and Jonathan Sturges and Jonathan Trumbull, of Connecticut. The amendments adopted by the Committee of the Whole seem to have alienated Northern support without gaining support among the Southerners. The changes may nevertheless have been justified, in the eyes of a conciliator like Madison, by the necessity of reassuring the South Carolinians and Georgians that the federal government was not hostile to their most fundamental interests.

The First Congress was dominated by men whose basic commitment was to the newly created Constitutional union. When these men saw the passions that were aroused, when they heard South Carolinians begin to express regret that they had strengthened a government that was now being used against them, and when they realized that a consensus could be gained only for marginal assaults on the slave trade, they apparently decided to put the issue to rest.

As for President Washington, his desire to avoid controversy over the slave trade was expressed in two letters to a friend, David Stuart, written shortly after the end of the debate in 1790. Describing the Quaker memorial as "mal-apropos," he called its introduction "an ill-judged piece of business" which had "occasioned a great waste of time." He rejoiced that the issue had "at length been put to sleep," and expressed hope that it would not be disturbed again until 1808.[36]

A frown from George Washington was hard to bear, even for a Quaker pursuing a righteous cause. Washington was determined to avoid issues that aroused "the spirit of party," whose "baneful effects" were particularly dangerous when reinforced by sectionalism. His anxiety was shared by the man who began life under the Constitution as the President's right-hand man and gradually emerged as the leader of the loyal opposition, James Madison. Having initially supported the investigation of Congressional powers over slavery and the slave trade, Madison quickly sensed that opinions were so profoundly divided that the mere discussion of them constituted a serious threat to the union. He consequently led the effort to scuttle the issue, helping to produce a "final decision . . . as favorable as the proprietors of this species of property could have expected." [37] Warned by this "harrowing experience," he refused a year later even to present a petition submitted by a constituent condemning the cruelty of the slave trade.[38]

After the bitterness of 1790, the Federalist administrations of Washington and Adams were not again seriously disturbed by agitation over the foreign slave trade. The issue occasionally flashed to the surface, but was readily dispatched, usually by the passage of symbolic legislation. For example, during the Second and Third Congresses, a spate of petitions was received from various "Quaker-inspired abolition societies," demanding that Congress do what it had said in 1790 it had the "authority" to do: prohibit American merchants from supplying slaves to foreigners —particularly plantation owners in the West Indies.[39] In March 1794, to pacify these pressures, Congress passed and President Washington signed what purported to be the nation's first law to limit the foreign slave trade—an act to prohibit "the slave trade from the United States to any foreign place or country." [40] It served mainly to prohibit the export of slaves from the United States, rather than to stop the involvement of Americans in the trade between Africa and the West Indies. Inasmuch as the United States was not a slave-exporting nation, it had virtually no effect.

With its passage, the legislative program of the most realistic opponents of the slave trade appeared to have been accomplished. The only power in the final report of 1790 not yet exercised was that of regulating conditions during the passage from Africa to America. Legislation on this subject would have been impossible to enforce, and an attempt to pass it would have been resisted by Northern merchants as well as Southern plantation owners. Besides, in 1794 the combined effect of state and federal laws on the slave trade meant that American ships could legally deliver slaves only from Africa directly to Georgia, and in 1798 even that point of entry was closed. From the point of view of the memorialists, there did not seem to be much more to do, except watch over the enforcement of existing laws and wait for 1808.

In 1798, however, a new factor entered the picture. A bill to set up territorial government in Mississippi caused certain New England ers to worry about the admission of slaves into this region. Southerners had no intention of permitting Congress to outlaw slavery there, but to quell the rising storm, South Carolina's Robert Goodloe Harper, floor manager of the territorial bill, added an amendment that made it illegal to import slaves into the territory from any place "without the limits of the United States." [41] It is worth noting that this amendment authorized the immediate emancipation of smuggled slaves—a remarkable provision in light of Southern resistance to the attempt to add a similar clause to the act terminating the trade in 1808. Southerners later argued that a provision requiring the release of smuggled slaves would make the prohibition unenforceable. If so, then the clause prohibiting the foreign trade into the Mississippi Territory was indeed merely a "peace-offering" to philanthropists, as South Carolinians later contended.[42]

So far, Federalist leaders in Congress had been successful in coping with what they regarded as premature pressure to outlaw the slave trade, but a petition presented on the second day of the nineteenth century constituted a dire challenge to their strategy. The petition was signed by a group of "free blacks" of Philadelphia, although the South Carolinians immediately detected the fine hand of the Quakers. The Negroes claimed that they were happy in the United States, but they lamented the hardships suffered by other Negroes, who were "equal objects of representation and attention with themselves or others under the Constitution." They noted the "degraded state and want of education" of most slaves. They specifically denied a desire for the immediate abolition of slavery. Instead, they pleaded for an end to the kidnapping and re-enslavement of free Negroes, for amendments to the act of 1794, and for "an amelioration of . . . [the] hard situation" of their brothers in slavery, to improve the prospect of eventual emancipation.[43] It takes a lively historical imagination to see this petition as anything but a mild, reasonable, almost ingratiating document. Perhaps its sponsor, Robert Waln, a Federalist Congressman from Philadelphia, also found the document innocuous.

Whatever he may have thought of it, however, John Rutledge,

Jr., a Federalist from the South Carolina Piedmont and son of the framer, found the petition dangerous and alarming. Unless Congress flatly repudiated this outburst of "new-fangled French philosophy," anarchy and insurrection would spread throughout the South. "I thank God" he said, that most Negroes in America are enslaved; "if they were not, dreadful would be the consequences." [44]

Waln, abashed by the assault, insisted that he was no advocate of emancipation and meant to commit only the parts dealing with kidnapping and the slave trade. Other Northerners rallied to his support. A few Republicans—including Gallatin and James Smilie, of western Pennsylvania—quietly defended the Negroes' right "to be heard." Smilie commented that "prudence" restrained him from speaking further about the lot of Negroes in America.[45]

Federalists, however, felt no such inhibitions. George Thacher denounced slavery as "a cancer of immense magnitude," and said that slaves constituted "700,000 enemies" within the American body politic. He noted that the "second man" in the United States government (Vice-President Jefferson) had authored a scheme for the elimination of slavery. Surely, he argued, it would not be improper or impolitic to study this and other, similar, proposals. The French, he admitted, had made many mistakes during their current revolution, but liberating their slaves had been a commendable step.

He could not possibly have uttered more inflammatory words in the hearing of men for whom Santo Domingo—the primary object of the French proclamation of abolition—represented the fires of Hell itself. Rutledge, insisting that calmness was not possible in the face of such dangerous lunacy, shouted:

[I]f driven to it, we will take care of ourselves. . . . Some of the states would never have adopted the federal form of government if it had not been secured to them that Congress would never legislate on the subject of slavery.[46]

John Brown, a Federalist from Rhode Island, tried to pour oil on the troubled Federalist waters. "No subject surely was so likely to cause a division of the states as that respecting slaves," he said. Northerners were no more interested than Southerners in encouraging slaves to flee from bondage, "to reside [in the North] as vagabonds and thieves." He held no slaves, but he respected the rights of property. And he rejected the notion that "700,000 enemies" constituted a danger to America. There are, he pointed out, "five million [whites] to withstand them; they can at any time subdue them." [47]

Samuel Goode, a Federalist from south-central Virginia, moved, as an amendment to referral, that the parts of the petition asking Congress to exceed its powers receive "the pointed disapprobation of the House." When he deleted the word "pointed," a record vote was taken. The motion was adopted, 85 to 1, the sole "nay" being cast by Thacher, who stubbornly insisted that the subject of emancipation should get a "full, free and deliberate discussion." [48]

The petition of the "free blacks" had been rejected, but the question of amendments to the act of 1794 remained. By mid-April 1800 a committee in the Senate reported a set of amendments. Their aim was to make it unlawful for American citizens or residents to participate in the slave trade to foreign ports, thus eliminating the device of foreign flags as a way of circumventing the act. The Senate passed the bill within five days, without a word of recorded debate.[49]

Debate in the House began as soon as the bill was received. Opposition came, appropriately enough, from Congressman John Brown, a man who had been hounded out of the slave trade by the Providence Abolition Society, of which his brother, Moses Brown, was a leading spirit.[50] He complained that Congress had been "drilled" into passing the act of 1794 "by certain persons who would not take no for an answer." He insisted that American self-exclusion from the trade did not spare a single Negro from slavery, since they were slaves in Africa and would be brought to the New World by European traders in any case. Besides, "Why should a heavy fine and imprisonment be made the penalty for carrying on a trade so advantageous?" America needed revenue. Why not open the trade and impose the ten-dollar tax on it? He noted that "distilleries and manufactories [were] all laying idle for want of an extended commerce." Why not stimulate the flow of American products by legalizing and encouraging a brisk triangular trade? It was foolhardy, in his opinion, to eschew this enterprise, particularly since Negro slaves "by the operation of the trade . . . bettered their condition." [51]

Rutledge joined the argument against the proposed changes, calling the bill "one of the most defective . . . ever before Congress." Since it was "impossible effectively to prevent" the trade, he said that merchants who wanted to compete with the British and Dutch ought not to be discouraged.

Despite the objections, the bill passed by a vote of 67 to 5. Once again Congress had passed a law to regulate the slave trade, but one that the government had neither capacity nor intention to enforce. To enforce it would have required an administration implacably hostile to the trade, and a navy as strong as Great Britain's. The act of 1800, which was supported by four Congressmen each from North and South Carolina, was a watchdog without fangs or voice, a comfort perhaps to those who did not think themselves seriously threatened, but no danger to its wily and determined foe.

The Seventh Congress, which convened in December 1801, was the first in which Republicans were in full control of the national government.[52] They had been swept to power by a nation weary of bitter division, especially over questions of foreign policy. The change in atmosphere was soon reflected in the handling of an issue that could easily have provoked explosive debate if it had been managed carelessly. In January 1803 residents of Wilmington, North Carolina, sent a memorial to Congress stating that Negroes and mulattoes from Guadeloupe, a French island in the Caribbean, having been emancipated by the French, had begun to enter the United States. These immigrants were mingling with American slaves, spreading dangerous ideas, and threatening the peace and safety of the South. The petitioners asked Congress to help the states prevent the admission of these dangerous "persons." [53]

The issue presented by this petition was certainly not as divisive as those that had faced the Federalists during the previous decade. The offenders were not American citizens or residents.

They were entering states that had plain, and plainly Constitutional, laws against their admission. Inhabitants of these states were asking the federal government, the nation's instrument in defense and foreign affairs, to assist them in excluding these unwanted intruders. An egalitarian might have found opportunity here to lament the vulnerability of slave states before a challenge of this kind. But under the circumstances, no one could doubt that West Indian Negroes might stir up trouble, and only a fanatic "citizen of the world" would have insisted on their right to do so.[54] So long as debate was confined to the specific issues presented by the petition, it might well remain polite, technical, and noncontroversial.

The petition was referred to a committee of Southerners, chaired by William Hill, a Federalist who represented Wilmington, North Carolina. On January 26 the committee reported a bill, introduced by the finding "That the system of policy . . . now pursued in the French colonial government of the West Indies, is fraught with danger to the peace and safety of the United States . . . [and] demands the prompt interference of the government of the United States." The bill imposed steep fines on the master or captain of a ship importing Negroes or mulattoes into any state that prohibited such importations by law.[55]

John Bacon, a Congressman from western Massachusetts, complained that the bill did not distinguish between various types of Negroes that might sail into a Southern port, and that it therefore discriminated against some American citizens in a way unknown and repugnant to "the radical principles and general tenor of the Constitution, which secures an equality of rights to our citizens at large." The "natural right" of shipowners to employ Negro seamen was jeopardized, because the bill would punish captains simply for sailing into ports with Negroes aboard. Bacon concluded that the bill, and the suspicions it would create, would further alienate the states from one another, "the interest[s] of whose citizens [were] so hostile to each other."[56]

The bill was recommitted and revised to meet Bacon's objection. When it returned to the floor, it was limited to Negroes or mulattoes who were not natives, citizens, or registered seamen of the United States.[57] In this shape, it quickly passed the House, then proceeded to the Senate. Within a week, it had completed its quick, noiseless passage and was on its way to the White House. Jefferson signed it into law on February 28, 1803. Thus a government powerless to prevent the importation of slaves where states saw fit to permit it enjoined its agents "vigilantly" to prevent the immigration of Negroes into states prohibiting their admission. Here was a law earnestly sanctioned by opinion in the South. It would be vigorously enforced there by federal officials.

The first eight years of the nineteenth century must have been an agonizing time for anyone seriously concerned about the importation of black slaves from Africa. By this time, evidence was accumulating that many Southerners, particularly Deep Southerners, were unrepentant about slavery, and that the disquiet of some sensitive men about the enslavement of Africans was no match for the powerful appetite of others for more and more slave labor.

To be sure, the states had erected legal obstacles in the path of the slave trade. Virginia and states to the north were maintaining their prohibitions against the entry of new slaves from abroad, and by 1800 the three southernmost states were excluding them as well. In the aftermath of the Constitutional Convention, several of the principal slave-trading states in the North had passed laws forbidding their citizens to participate in the slave trade anywhere in the world.[58] Unfortunately, however, these latter acts were impossible to enforce. Northern jurisdictions were remote from the points at which violations would be committed. The three Deep Southern states had periods, between 1790 and 1808, when the slave trade from Africa was legal. Georgia allowed it to continue until 1798. North Carolina repealed its prohibitive tariff in 1790 and permitted the trade to continue until 1794. South Carolina, which in 1792 had "deemed [it] inexpedient to increase the number of slaves within this state, in our present circumstances and situation," found the situation different by 1803 and reopened the trade for four years. In addition, smuggling into the Deep South was flagrant and widespread, according to the testimony of Congressmen on both sides of the issue.[59] Savannah and Charleston provided markets so lucrative, and so remote from Northern jurisdictions, that the enactments of 1787–1789 at the state level had little practical effect.[60]

The decision of South Carolina in 1803 not to renew its prohibition against the trade was a devastating blow to hopes for an early end to slavery and the slave trade. In December 1803 Governor James Richardson submitted a message to the legislature expressing his despair over enforcing the prohibition, which he declared to be "already nullified by the absence of public sanction." Noting that the only effective way to stop the smuggling of slaves was to provide for their emancipation, he called this "a remedy more mischievous than their introduction in servitude." [61] A legislative committee responded to the message by drafting a bill to repeal all acts against importation. Legislators anxious to extend the prohibition insisted that the presence of slaves on the open market would be an irresistible temptation to speculation, that it would cut in half the value of slave property, increase the volume and decrease the price of cotton, and augment the danger of servile revolts. But apparently most South Carolinians were more sanguine about the strength of the state's economy and society than the prohibitionists. The legislature favored repeal by a vote of 55 to 46.[62]

When the news reached Washington, in January 1804, Congressman David Bard, a Republican and former Presbyterian missionary who represented a district in south-central Pennsylvania, rose to say that he was appalled by this brazen act. "The morality, the interest, the peace, the safety, of individuals, and of the public" demanded an end to "this horrid traffic." Instead, he said, South Carolina had opened the floodgates once more and allowed "incalculable miseries" to pour into the country. To express the disapproval of Congress, and to discourage the trade, he moved that the ten-dollar tax on slaves be imposed immediately.

The debate on Bard's proposal opened with a somewhat apologetic defense of South Carolina's action by Thomas Lowndes, a Federalist from Charleston. Acknowledging that the actions of his state had provoked almost universal disgust, he pointed out that for several years "Eastern brethren" had been taking advantage of rivers that penetrated deeply into the heartland of South Carolina and had reaped great profits by ignoring the state's laws against the trade. The tax, he said, would be both unfair to South Carolina and impolitic for the nation. It would constitute a heavy and partial burden on Southern agriculture; he called this "my greatest objection to this tax." On the other hard, it would not be enough to discourage the trade; it would only produce stained revenue. He warned that, at a time when interest in the slave trade was being "strengthened by the immense accession of territory to the United States by the cession of Louisiana," it would be dangerous for the national government to derive large revenues from this source. It would come to depend on them and would be reluctant to yield them after 1808.* [63]

Responding to Lowndes, Bard admitted that Eastern shipping interests were guilty of smuggling, but he blamed South Carolina for rejecting the help of the national government, made available by the act against the Negroes from Guadeloupe. Calling the slave trade "self-evidently wrong," he said that Congress had an obligation to go to the limits of its power to preserve America's republican character. He noted that slaves were now worth about $400, which meant that a ten-dollar impost was a $2\frac{1}{2}$-per-cent tax—well within the capacity of planters made rich by the labor of slaves. [65]

Samuel Mitchill, of New York, described existing prohibitions against the slave trade as a nullity, and detailed the smuggling operations practiced, he said, up and down the East Coast. He estimated that 20,000 Negroes had been smuggled from "Guinea" into South Carolina and Georgia during the year before South Carolina repealed its prohibitions, and he supported the tax as a realistic means of regulating the traffic in slaves. [66]

Following this exchange, a resolution declaring that the House was in favor of the tax was strongly endorsed. The Ways and

* No one countered Lowndes's argument by suggesting that the shadow attaching to revenues from this source might be lifted if the money were used to purchase emancipations, or to educate free Negroes, or to finance colonization. Compare the cunning later shown by Peter Early, of Georgia. When Northerners objected to the forfeiture of smuggled slaves because the federal government would have to auction them off and thereby become a slave dealer, he suggested that the opprobrium might be lifted if the proceeds were used for "charitable purposes." [64] Often, it seemed that Southerners were simply more resourceful legislators than Northerners.

Means Committee, under the chairmanship of John Randolph (who had already indicated his opposition to the measure), was ordered to report a bill. The next day, Randolph submitted a draft bill. Lowndes immediately moved that it be postponed until December "to get rid of it altogether," as he candidly admitted. Citing "an official memoir" stating that the cultivation of Louisiana was going to "require the labor of slaves," he urged that the national government not share in the profits of this commerce. His colleague from South Carolina Benjamin Huger assured Congress that leading South Carolinians would work hard to reinstate the prohibition during the next session of the state legislature.

Lowndes's motion to postpone until December was defeated on a roll-call vote by 55 to 62. A subsequent motion to postpone until the middle of March was then adopted by a vote of 56 to 50. A bracketed note is inserted into the record at this point explaining that the postponement was granted to give the legislature of South Carolina a chance to forestall Congressional action by re-enacting its prohibition; but the postponement killed the bill for the Eighth Congress.[67]

There remained time before 1808 for Congress to agitate the question of the ten-dollar tax once more. In December 1805 James Sloan, of New Jersey, one of President Jefferson's chief lieutenants in the House of Representatives, moved that the tax be levied. On the prediction of Congressman David R. Williams, of South Carolina, that the legislature of South Carolina would "in all probability" reinstate the prohibition against the trade at its next session, Congress again postponed consideration, this time until after the first of the year.

By mid-January 1806 it was apparent that Williams's prediction had been erroneous, if not disingenuous. Sloan consequently called up his resolution, remarking that there was no reason why this commerce alone should be exempt from imposts. He was supported by his Republican colleague from New York Henry Southard, who called the tax "an expression of the national sentiment" of opposition to a trade that violated "the ties of nature and the principles of justice." [68]

But the measure was doomed. The keynote of the opposition was sounded by John Dawson, a Republican from Virginia. He called attention to the fact that Great Britain, under the threat of Napoleon's France, was hardening its policy toward neutral shipping, and that American commerce was suffering the effects. The crisis in foreign affairs was putting the pacific Jeffersonians to a severe test. He argued that this was a bad time to force an issue whose capacity for divisiveness was well known. It would be "more wise and more patriotic," he said,

to cherish the spirit of accommodation, and to unite all our efforts and wisdom in adopting those measures best calculated to vindicate our violated rights; and not to introduce subjects . . . which will excite one section of the continent, one portion of our fellow-citizens against another, thereby disturbing that harmony and union of councils so necessary for the good of the whole.[69]

Soon, men who had supported the bill in earlier tests began to raise hard questions. What, asked John Jackson, of Virginia, is to be done with slaves smuggled into the country and thus forfeited? He did not want the national government "to have anything to do" with the dirty business of disposing of them. Would the act apply to sailors who are slaves? asked Josiah Quincy. Would captains have to pay ten dollars for each Negro every time they sail into port? Following these damaging rhetorical questions, a motion to send the bill back to the Sloan Committee for amendments prevailed without a vote.

Time was running out. There was now only one month until adjournment, and many other issues clamored for the attention of a weary Congress. Sloan reported a bill amended to authorize the Secretary of the Treasury to seize Negroes smuggled into South Carolina and hire them out in another state "for a term of years." This solution was unsatisfactory to almost everyone. Even those who disapproved of the slave trade felt that releasing "raw" Africans into the land was worse than permitting the slave trade to continue.[70] As soon as the Representatives from the upper South had seen this amendment, the only question that remained was how to bury it.

The method chosen was indefinite postponement. A facetious

motion by Williams—that it be made the order of the day for the Fourth of July—failed, but the bill nevertheless faded below the horizon. A few days later, a committee on unfinished business was appointed; chaired by Early, it included John Randolph, of Virginia, and Jacob Crowninshield, of Massachusetts, among its five members. The tax on the slave trade lay dying, and this group could be relied upon to pass by on the other side.

Why did Congress fail ever to adopt this tax? Sanctioned by the Constitution, and promising rich rewards,[71] it was considered three times, and three times rejected.

A comparison of two votes taken in 1806 is suggestive of what happened and why. Spurred by the angry reaction to South Carolina's repeal of prohibitions against the trade, Congress initially cast a strong vote, 90 to 25, in favor of preparing legislation to levy the tax. At the Convention of 1787 and during the two previous attempts to enact the tax, New England had stood opposed. Now, however, only three New Englanders voted "nay." From the mid-Atlantic states, there was only a single vote against. Virginia, a long-standing foe of the foreign slave trade, returned a 13-to-4 vote in favor of the tax. The only sector showing strong opposition was the Deep South; South Carolina and Georgia voted unanimously against it.

But as time passed, indignation against South Carolina waned, and Southern resistance to the meddlesome hand of outsiders, particularly where slavery was concerned, reasserted itself. The Republican preference for mild, inoffensive government, reinforced by calls for national unity, helped to discourage the drive for the punitive tax. Thus, by February 5, when the abstract idea of a tax against the slave trade had been reduced to a bill, the motion for indefinite postponement was defeated by 42 to 68, indicating that the opposition was now almost twenty votes stronger than it had been two weeks earlier. Votes had been switched from support to opposition primarily in New England (three in New Hampshire and four in Connecticut) and in the antislave-trade South (two each in Virginia and North Carolina); in addition, several who had supported the resolution were not present to support the bill.

. . .

Those who were disappointed by the failure to levy the ten-dollar impost could console themselves that the year 1808 was at hand. In his annual message of December 2, 1806, President Thomas Jefferson called attention to this fact:

I congratulate you, fellow-citizens, on the approach of the period at which you may interpose your authority, constitutionally, to withdraw the citizens of the United States from all further participation in those violations of human rights which have so long continued on the unoffending inhabitants of Africa, and which the morality, the reputation, and the best interests of our country have long been eager to proscribe. Although no law you may pass can take prohibiting effect till the first day of the year one thousand eight hundred and eight, yet the intervening period is not too long to prevent, by timely notice, expeditions which cannot be completed before that day.[72]

In the House of Representatives, Jefferson's message was broken down into subject areas, each of which was referred to a select committee. The paragraph on the slave trade was referred to a committee chaired by Peter Early, the stern Republican, born in Virginia, educated at Princeton, now representing frontier Georgia, the man who had shown such *élan* in opposing the ten-dollar tax.

On December 15, 1806 the Early Committee reported a bill, which would have made it illegal to bring Negroes to the United States after December 31, 1807 with the intent of selling them as slaves. Persons preparing vessels for the slave trade would be fined $5,000, and their boats forfeited. Vessels equipped for the trade, found in American waters, would be forfeited, and the owners fined $10,000. Anyone buying a Negro who had been imported after the cutoff date would have to forfeit his property, and unless he could prove—the burden was on him, as it was on all persons to be prosecuted under this proposed act—that he had no way of knowing that the slave had been smuggled, he was to be fined $500. The same fine was to be assessed against the man who sold the smuggled property.

Early insisted that this was a strong bill. Given Southern goals for an act of this kind, there is no reason to question either his sincerity or his judgment. Under his bill, slaves seized by the government, like any other property taken by forfeit, would have been sold at auction—which would have made the United States government an accomplice in slavery. From Early's point of view, however, there was no reason to apologize for this provision The federal government had jurisdiction over a region where slavery was an integral and fully legitimate part of the social fabric. The government ought not to refuse to perform a task necessary to the well-being of that region just because citizens of another region had moral scruples against slavery. Laws, if they were to be obeyed and enforced, Early said, had to be attached to the passions and wishes of the people over whom they operated.[73] In his view, the bill reported by his committee would be welcomed in many parts of the South, and should be acceptable everywhere. Its penalties were stiff, but appropriate, and it laid no impossible demands on Southern society. It thus gave every reasonable promise of being effective as a bulwark against the slave trade, and that, he insisted, was the only valid criterion for an act of this kind.

The problem with his reasoning was that Congress was answerable to Northern constituents as well as Southern. Southerners expected the federal government to deal with slavery from a stance of moral neutrality, but many Northerners found such a stance impossible. From mid-December 1806 until February 1807, the House of Representatives was the scene of a public struggle in which each section sought to achieve provisions answerable to its own attitude toward slavery.

As soon as Early had finished reading the bill, James Sloan moved an amendment that would have given freedom, automatically, to Negroes smuggled into the country after January 1, 1808. If Southerners were as hostile as they said they were to the presence of free Negroes in their midst, he reasoned, no provision would be more likely to guarantee the co-operation of Southerners in enforcing the act.

Early responded sharply. The possibility of an effective law, he said, hung on the provisions for the "disposal" of Africans imported illegally. The only way to guarantee enforcement was to seize these slaves from the smugglers and sell them. Nothing else would work. No Southerner would inform on a smuggler if the consequence would be to release a freshly imported African into

Southern society. Southerners knew "from experience" that where Negroes existed in considerable numbers, they threatened to become "instruments of murder, theft, and conflagration." Slavery might be cruel, but it was the only way of insuring the safety of the white community against these dangers. To free slaves to run loose in the Deep South was "opposed to the principle of self-preservation and to the love of family," and would thrust "firebrands" into "the bosom of the country." [74]

Speaker Nathaniel Macon took a different tack. Sloan's amendment, said this gentle North Carolinian, would abandon persons who "understand nothing about the country," who do not even speak the language, to shift for themselves, and to be maintained and protected, if possible, at public expense. The only consequence was that "they must perish." Early agreed: "Not one of them would be left alive in a year." Joseph Clay, of Philadelphia, added the warning that these persons might end up in "the Eastern states." People there would be no more willing to receive these immigrants than were the Southerners. Sloan suggested that the difficulties raised by Early and Clay could be solved by shipping the Negroes back to Africa, but Macon responded that re-shipment was no act of benevolence for the Negroes. "If we set them loose and unarmed among nations who themselves pursue this traffic," he said, they would be either re-enslaved or massacred.[75]

After a long day of debate, Sloan's amendment came to a vote. It received only nineteen "ayes." Since it was clear that smuggling would occur mostly in the Southern states, and since Southerners were virtually unanimous in foreseeing that the emancipation of smuggled slaves would mean disaster, most Congressmen recognized that Sloan's proposal, as it stood, was unacceptable.

Yet many Northerners were still not reconciled to Early's measure. Barnabas Bidwell, a young Republican from Stockbridge, Massachusetts, suggested that the federal government turn the forfeited slaves over to the states, to be disposed of according to local regulations and customs. This, he said, would save the federal government from dirtying its hands with the business. But his proposal, which foreshadowed the eventual compromise, was met at this point by objections from all sides. Early ridiculed his squeamishness. The federal government, he said had been accepting forfeits and selling slaves for years to collect taxes and fines from planters who had no liquid capital. From Quincy and Sloan came a different kind of objection. Bidwell's proposal, they said, would leave these poor Africans—"the poor and needy, the dumb and the lame, and those who cannot plead their cause," as Sloan described them—in slavery. This would be both "cruel and dangerous," said Quincy, whereas the federal government, by retaining custody, would have an opportunity to be "prudent and humane."

To meet these objections, Bidwell finally moved that all property involved in the smuggling of slaves be forfeited, except "persons." The motion did not specify how the smuggled Negroes were to be handled. Bidwell's purpose was merely to establish the principle that the United States government would not be party to the enslavement of any more Africans.

Defending his amendment, Bidwell traced the process by which Africans were enslaved, from the viewpoint of American law. Negroes brought into the United States had been seized in Africa either by Europeans through brute force or by native princes as a result of bribes. In either case, Negroes dragged on board a slaver were no more the rightful property of the ship's captain than was a victim the property of a highwayman. Under Early's proposal, he continued, the United States government would seize these Negroes under forfeiture proceedings, and at that moment, for the first time, they would become lawful property. Prior to their arrival in the United States, no law, human or divine, made them property. After their arrival, the United States government, by receiving and selling them as stolen goods, would make their fetters legal. He concluded by distinguishing between this bill and the seizing and selling of Negroes to pay taxes and fines. In the latter situation, the Negroes were already legal property. In the former, the action of the United States government made them so.[76]

Once again, objections came from two quarters. First to respond were the Southerners. Smuggling, they said, was most likely to occur through the Spanish provinces, especially Florida. This traffic would not stop until planters knew that slaves smuggled across the border would be seized from them. Bidwell responded that he could not understand why emancipating smuggled slaves would not have the same effect as forfeiture. The first time the "immigrants" from Florida were released into Southern society, smugglers would lose not only their profits, but also their welcome among Southerners.[77]

The second response came in the form of a jewel of a speech by Josiah Quincy, later Mayor of Boston and president of Harvard University, now serving his first term in Congress. His felicitous speech stands virtually alone, among Congressional speeches by Northerners during this period, in its realism about slavery and its prudent counsel for dealing with the problem.

He began by commenting on Bidwell's account of the process by which Africans become slaves.

'The argument of my colleague is . . . [that black] persons are free by the law of nature—as free as any of us. The African prince who sold them was a usurper. The purchasers in Africa were trespassers against the law of nature. . . . Sir, the conclusions of the gentlemen are perfectly correct—his principles are solid. . . . Refer this question between the African prince and his subjects, and between the African and the importer, to five hundred juries in New England, and five hundred times a verdict would coincide with the principles and reasonings of my colleague.

But the real political issue concerned not the principles of juries in New England, but the facts of life in Africa and in the American South. The misfortune is, that, notwithstanding all these true and unquestionable principles, the African prince, at this day, does, and after our law passes, will sell his subjects. . . . But this is not the worst. A title in this description of persons is not only allowed in Africa, but is, and must be, after your law passes, in a large section of your own country. The gentlemen from that part of the United States tell you that they cannot be allowed to be free among them. The first law, self-preservation, forbids it.

This, said Quincy, is the "real, practical state of things" on which Congress ought to base its legislation. He then turned to the proposals advanced by his Northern colleagues as alternatives to forfeiture. It was "out of the question" to free the smuggled Africans into the South. Bidwell's suggestion that they be turned over to the Southern states for disposal was not much better, and was particularly inappropriate from those who claimed to abhor slavery. "Do not trust to others," he said. "You can be most certain this power will not be abused in your own hands "

He went on to argue that Congress ought not to shun forfeiture because it implied complicity in slavery, but ought to accept it and then make the most of it for the benefit of the Africans. "Are they not, after forfeiture, in your control? May you not do for them what is best for human beings in that condition . . . ?" He urged his colleagues to regard forfeiture, not as granting or confirming a title of ownership, but simply as guaranteeing that smugglers retained no color of title to their imports. He suggested that Africans brought under the government's control by forfeiture be bound out for a term of years as apprentices, as were orphans and children of the poor.

These Africans are as helpless, ignorant, and incompetent as . . . children, and the wisdom of national legislation certainly can, and I have no doubt will, devise means to make them useful members of society, without any infringement of the rights of man.

He emphasized that his proposals were only suggestions. The important thing was for Bidwell and his well-meaning friends to "descend from their high abstract grounds to the level of things in their actual state . . . such as have, do, and will exist, after your laws, and in spite of them." What was needed, he concluded, was "a little more practical good, and a little less theoretic impulse." [78]

Quincy's speech was not welcomed. Perhaps it was too brilliant, too clever to be really effective. Quincy, after all, was a cocky young Federalist in a legislature dominated by Republicans. Yet why did the Republicans refuse, or fail, to seize the opportunities inherent in the forfeiture scheme? Perhaps they were afraid that the assumption of responsibility for African "immigrants" would corrupt the purity and confound the simplicity of the federal government. Indeed, the task of converting Africans into "useful members of society" must have staggered the imaginations of politicians committed to Jefferson's philosophy of limited government. If the federal government could make them free men at a single stroke, that would be one thing. But if not—and no one denied that blacks directly from Africa would need help to adjust to life in America—it might be better to turn the problem over to the states and hope for the best.[79]

Smilie's response to Quincy—a reference to "the principles of 1776," a quotation from the Declaration of Independence, and a reiteration of the argument that Southern fears would help to execute the law—reveals that Quincy's argument had fallen on deaf ears.[80] Slavery's opponents were not appreciably more interested in grappling with the harder questions raised by abolition than were its defenders. Soon after Quincy had spoken, a vote was called on Bidwell's motion to strike the provision for forfeiture. The result was 36 in favor, 63 opposed.[81] Bidwell's vagueness on the eventual disposition of the imported Africans had attracted seventeen more votes than Sloan's proposal twelve days before, but the group that opposed the auctioning of smuggled slaves was still short of success.

On New Year's Eve 1806 the House began consideration of the second main issue lurking beneath the consensus that sought to prohibit the slave trade: the question of appropriate penalties—specifically, whether to assign a jail sentence or the death penalty to smugglers. Northerners argued that if Southerners were sincere in deprecating the trade and in blaming it on merchants from New England, they should be happy to join in punishing these outlaws with great severity.

But Peter Early did not agree. When he got to his feet on this last day of 1806, he was furious. What Northerners failed to understand was that there would be "no abhorrence" in the South for the crime of smuggling slaves. By prescribing the death penalty, Congress would eliminate any hope of getting informers and witnesses to testify against smugglers. Most Southerners would think that the offense was not "such an outrageous crime" as to justify the taking of a man's life. Those who felt differently would find that it cost more than their own lives were worth to bring suit or to bear witness against smugglers. To support his argument, he sought to characterize the Southern attitude toward slavery. Southerners "do not believe it immoral to hold human flesh in bondage." Twice before, during debates on the question

330

of forfeiture, he had referred to slavery as an "evil." * Now he explained what he meant, in terms that would be less easily misunderstood. Making what he called a "small distinction," he said, "Many [in the South] deprecate slavery as an evil—a political evil—but not as a crime." With mounting anger, he continued, "Reflecting men [in the South] apprehend, at some future day, evils, incalculable evils, from [slavery]; but it is a fact that few, very few, consider it as a crime. . . ." Then came the plainest assertion of all: "A large majority of people in the Southern states do not consider slavery as even an evil." [83]

Early's utterance is justly famous. It struck a stout blow against the myth by which Northerners justified and apologized for a policy of *laissez faire* where slavery was concerned. This myth was that slavery was dying, and that, inasmuch as Southerners hated it as much as Northerners and were in a better position to cope with the adjustments required by abolition, they ought to be trusted to preside over its demise without Northern "meddling." Early said that a "large majority" of Southerners did not consider slavery an evil, that only the reflecting minority thought it even a "political evil." When it came to social policies affecting slavery, reflecting men in Georgia thought about the blood bath in Santo Domingo. In light of that catastrophe, they were willing to admit that "at some future day, evils, incalculable evils" might fall on Georgia. Contrary to the wishes of the abolitionists, however, the lesson borne by the events in Santo Domingo, as far as planters were concerned, was that it was suicide to release Negroes from the discipline of slavery where there were enough Negroes to ravage the property and persons of their erstwhile masters. Thus when people who opposed slavery heard Southerners call the institution evil, it was a mistake for them to take comfort. The evils that Southerners found in slavery were such as to make remedies impossible. The prospect they most deeply feared was interracial warfare, and slavery, as they saw it, was the main bulwark against such a catastrophe.

Northerners quickly turned Early's remarks against the case he

* On the second occasion, however, he had gone on to add that the presence of freedmen in the midst of slaves was an "evil" far worse than slavery itself, foreshadowing the argument offered on December 31, 1806. [82]

was trying to make, pointing out that, far from demonstrating the inappropriateness of the death penalty, he had shown that *no* punishment could effectively stop the trade. If no Southerner would inform on, and no Southern jury convict, a smuggler, because smuggling would be regarded as a public service, then what was the use of framing an act to end the slave trade at all?

This was a searching question, and it was never answered. Early may have lost the debate—but he won the vote. On a roll call, sixty-three Congressmen favored the substitution of a ten-year jail sentence for capital punishment; fifty-three were opposed.[84]

When Congress reconvened in 1807, it was not long before the question of the disposal of smuggled slaves came back to haunt the deliberations. As the clause stood, smuggled slaves were to be forfeited to the United States, with the understanding that they would be sold at auction. The first indication that the opponents of this provision were not reconciled to defeat came on January 5, when Sloan moved, as a substitute, that slaves smuggled into the country be declared free and supplied with "food and raiment" until such time as they could be restored to freedom in Africa or "removed to states in which laws are congenial to their freedom," where they would be bound to service for a term of years and then unconditionally released.[85]

Here was a proposal that was hostile to the slave trade and to slavery itself. It was bold in its approach to the readjustments necessitated by the coexistence of slavery and emancipation. The support it attracted is thus one measure of the readiness in Congress to face the problem of absorbing freedmen into American society. When the vote was taken, three unidentified Congressmen rose in its favor.

The House was beginning to realize that it faced a serious legislative problem. This bill would have to have widespread support. Early had the votes to defeat Northern amendments, but many Northerners felt intensely about the question of forfeiture. When Bidwell moved that no person be sold as a slave by virtue of the act terminating the slave trade, it required the casting vote of Speaker Macon to break the tie and defeat the motion.[86] Early had won again, but no bill that was unsatisfactory to half the House of Representatives could possibly answer the demands of the situation. Opponents of the trade had waited twenty years for this bill. Their desire for one that promised to end the enslavement of Africans could not be ignored. And so, to break the impasse, the bill was recommitted, not to Early and his friends, but to a new "grand committee," composed of a member from each of the seventeen states.

A bill passed by the Senate provided the basis for discussion. Regrettably, from the time Senator Stephen Bradley, of Vermont, presented this bill * until the acceptance of the conference report at the end of February, the *Annals* for the Senate record neither a word of debate nor a vote on this subject. But although little is known of the process by which the Senate arrived at its decision, a fairly strong bill did emerge at the end of January. It provided that all Negroes forfeited to the United States be taken to a place designated by the President and employed there for a limited term as apprentices or servants, as might be "most beneficial for them, and most safe for the United States." It specified that the "place" chosen by the President be one where slavery was doomed to abolition, either immediately or gradually. And it also required the death penalty for smugglers.

Apparently this bill was acceptable to the House's "grand committee," for it was taken up when the House returned to the subject in February 1807. But if the Senate version gratified many Northerners, it infuriated Peter Early, who counterattacked fiercely. He warned that Southerners would resist an act of this kind "with their lives." He insisted that the South wanted "no civil wars, no rebellions, no insurrections, no resistance to the authority of the government," but that these calamities would surely come unless provisions threatening to the very fabric of Southern society were eliminated from the bill. He moved, as a substitute for the plan before the House, that Negroes smuggled into the country be delivered by United States marshals to state officials. The Negroes would then be disposed of in accordance with state laws.[88]

Smilie replied that the opponents of slavery would "not . . .

* Senator William Plumer, in his *Memorandum*, quotes Bradley as boasting that he had introduced "a bill to prohibit slavery," for which President Jefferson was receiving all the credit. Whether it was Plumer or Bradley who was responsible for misrepresenting this bill as an act of abolition the mistake was typical of a New Englander.[87]

be terrified by a threat of civil war." But the act as finally adopted nevertheless incorporated a version of Early's substitute. Somehow a majority of the House came to see his proposal as a way of accommodating Northern insistence that the federal government must not conduct slave auctions, with Southern determination that the federal government must not preside over a program of emancipation. Northerners settled for a technical victory; Southerners gained the substance. Once again Southern determination had outlasted Northern idealism.

The bill underwent two more changes before coming to a vote in the House. A motion to amend it by striking the death penalty was adopted, 67 to 48, and a substitute was inserted that defined smuggling as a "high misdemeanor" (instead of "felony") punishable by a fine of up to $10,000 and a prison sentence of from five to ten years.[89] Then, at the last moment, Early realized that the language of the bill about to be passed was susceptible of application to the domestic "coastwise" trade—from Baltimore to Savannah or Charleston to New Orleans. To forestall this construction, he insisted on a proviso that nothing in the act should forbid a ship captain from transporting any Negro not imported into the country contrary to the act. The House accepted the motion, apparently without dissent.[90]

The next day the bill to end the slave trade, as amended by the House, was read for the third time and passed by a roll-call vote of 113 to 5. Dissent came only from two Virginians and one man each from Vermont, New Hampshire, and South Carolina. The overwhelming majority of the House accepted it as an appropriate expression of disapproval for an enterprise that had troubled the conscience of the nation since its founding.

The bill was then sent to the Senate, which returned word that the House's amendments were acceptable except for Early's last-minute proviso exempting the coastwise trade. The Senate was convinced that the only way to stop smugglers from bringing contraband from Florida was to regulate the legitimate coastwise trade. This trade was consequently restricted by the Senate to large vessels (otherwise, detection would be difficult, and forfeiture would be no deterrent); and any vessel so engaged was required to have manifests drawn by the ship's captain and certified by the collector of the port, asserting that each "Negro mulatto, or person of color" on board had been imported into the United States prior to January 1, 1808.[91] In the Senate's view, the task of detecting smugglers would have been rendered impossible had Early's proviso stood.

When word of the Senate's demand reached the House, David R. Williams, one of the five who had voted against the House bill, moved that the House "insist" on its amendment. Only eleven members supported this motion. John Randolph leaped to his feet, threatening that the whole South would defy the law if the government sought to regulate the interstate slave trade, and that he personally would lead the way. He "would go with his own slaves," he said, "and be at the expense of asserting the rights of slaveholders." These words, spoken with blazing fury, resulted in the reconsideration and passage of Williams's motion. The House appointed managers to iron out the difference in conference with Senators.[92]

A week later, the bill returned from the conference. Apparently the Senate conferees, spared the withering fire of Randolph's wrath, had held firm, agreeing to permit slightly smaller vessels to engage in the coastwise trade, but insisting on the manifests and on outlawing the trade in vessels under forty tons.

When Early and Randolph saw the bill brought back by the House conferees, they were understandably furious. For the first time since the establishment of the government under the Constitution of 1787, the federal government was undertaking to regulate slavery "among" the Southern states. This was the kind of "entering-wedge" that Congressmen from the Deep South—William L. Smith in the First Congress, Robert Goodloe Harper and John Rutledge, Jr., in the Fifth and Sixth, and Peter Early in the Eighth and Ninth—had been at such pains to prevent. If the government could regulate the coastwise slave trade among the states, could it not regulate all interstate domestic slave trading? Southerners were convinced that slavery could endure without a legal *foreign* slave trade, but the transportation of slaves across state lines was considered crucial to the development of the South. If the government could regulate the domestic trade, it had the power of life and death over the entire system. In Randolph's view, it would "blow up the Constitution in ruins" if Congress were permitted to exercise this power. It would create the "pretext of universal emancipation."

He had rather lose the bill, he had rather lose all the bills of the session, he had rather lose every bill passed since the establishment of the government, than agree to the provision contained in this slave bill.[93]

Congressmen from the Deep South now began freely to predict evasion and nonenforcement. Early said that every provision in the bill was open to evasion and that the act would not prevent "the introduction of a single slave." Williams dismissed "the whole bill" as "not worth a single farthing." He said that the Southern members of Congress had been shouting "Florida! Florida!" for the past two months, but to no avail. Instead of accepting Southern suggestions in good faith, Congress was trying to prevent smuggling from Florida by a strategy that alienated Southerners. The result would be contempt for the whole effort at regulation.[94]

Despite these threats, the roll was solemnly called on a motion to accept the conference report. The result, 63 to 49 in favor of the act as it stood, was a better reflection of sentiment toward the act of 1807 than the earlier vote in favor of the House version. It revealed the persistence of a line through the middle of the union. Massachusetts returned thirteen votes in favor of the report, none opposed; New Jersey gave six "yeas," no "nays"; Pennsylvania showed thirteen in favor, only one opposed. From the South, on the other hand, Virginia returned one favorable vote, eighteen opposed; South Carolina and Georgia showed no "yeas," but five and three "nays," respectively. The act had almost no support at all where it was most likely to be violated. Only a fool could believe that it would stop the slave trade.

The second session of the Ninth Congress was drawing to a close, but Randolph fought desperately to repair the damage he saw in the act. In "an animated speech," he asked leave to present a bill to "explain" the section that imposed regulations on the coastwise slave trade. His resolution asserted that Congress had no intention of interfering with "the full, complete and absolute right of property of the owner or master of any slave . . . in and to such slave. . . ." It stated that no master was subject to penalties who transported slaves along the coast so long as the slaves had not been imported into the United States contrary to the act of 1807. This bill would have had the same effect as Early's proviso: stripping the regulations against the coasting trade of any capacity to prevent smuggling from Florida.[95]

Randolph, demanding immediate action in light of the impending adjournment, threatened that unless this "explanation" was enacted, the entire Virginia delegation would march to the White House and demand that Jefferson veto the act. But it was too late. Growing frantic as time ran out, he screamed that the House must act "today," but, by a vote of 60 to 49, his proposal was made the order of the day for "tomorrow." The failure to obtain immediate action, plus the certainty of great, probably insurmountable, resistance in the Senate, forced Randolph to see that his project was hopeless. His proposal died, without further agitation, when the session ended four days later.

On March 3, 1807, without having received the visitation threatened by Randolph, Jefferson signed the act into law. No doubt it gave him great satisfaction to do so. Yet, although nearly everyone in Congress insisted that he wanted a strong and effective law against the foreign trade, the result of nearly three months of labor was, as Ulrich B. Phillips has written, "a law which might be evaded with relative ease wherever public sanction was weak." [96]

Early's argument that Congress should let Southerners draft the bill, since it affected the South almost exclusively and would have to be enforced by Southerners, made sense in a way. But his speech of New Year's Eve, in which he stated that a "large majority" of Southerners did not regard slavery as an evil, forced the conclusion that Southerners could not be trusted to end the trade themselves. The situation must have seemed hopeless to sober men.

In terms of intersectional politics, the act of 1807 marked a turning point toward greater solidarity among Southerners on questions affecting slavery. In earlier legislative battles, when questions before the House dealt directly with the issue of the foreign slave trade, Southern opinion had been deeply divided.

During consideration of the act of 1807, a distinctly Southern position began to emerge. The South Carolinians and Georgians had reconciled themselves to legal termination of the African trade, but the questions still at issue—particularly the disposal of smuggled slaves and the regulation of the coastwise trade—affected the institution of domestic slavery itself. Thus the votes began to show a marked sectional cleavage. As the object of legislation moved closer to the institution of slavery itself, the resistance of the South stiffened and became increasingly monolithic.

The act of 1807 did not end the slave trade into the United States. As early as 1810, in his annual state of the union address, President James Madison told Congress that "American citizens are instrumental in carrying on a traffic in enslaved Africans, equally in violation of the laws of humanity and in defiance of those of their own country." He expressed confidence that the same "just, benevolent" motives that inspired the act of 1807 would induce Congress to search for new, more effective ways of "suppressing the evil." [97]

For a time during the War of 1812, the slave trade into the United States seems to have suffered from the British naval blockade. But after the war, the trade resumed, and between 1815 and 1820 it was estimated by Northerners and Southerners alike that over 10,000 blacks were being smuggled into the country annually, mostly through southern and southwestern borders. [98]

The traffic in slaves did not flow through loopholes in the law. The failure of the act of 1807 stemmed from political and administrative factors rather than legal defects. Evasion was made possible by the connivance of Deep Southerners, the smuggling skills of Northerners and Europeans, and the primitiveness of national governmental machinery.

The men who owned rich spreads on the coastal flats of South Carolina and Georgia were generally opposed to the African slave trade, but for rather narrow reasons. According to them, the primary danger arose from the temptation of parvenues to "speculate," buying more slaves than they could profitably manage, thus drawing the price of slaves beyond the reach of sensible men and draining off the assets of the state. Another danger was that the appetite for slaves might be met by lazy or rebellious blacks sent over by planters from the West Indies.[99] Fear of these "firebrands" was particularly keen after Toussaint had mounted his rebellion and successfully resisted Napoleon's efforts at quelling it.

Countering these fears were the voracious appetite and reckless courage of frontiersmen. As it became apparent that short-staple cotton could be profitably grown in the back country of Georgia and South Carolina, and as the territories of Alabama and Mississippi and then Louisiana and Arkansas began to open up, the ambition to get the forests and swamps cleared and the land broken to cultivation created a terrific demand for tractable labor. The fears of slave uprisings that haunted many Virginians and Charlestonians were more than offset by the drive to build an empire in the West.

If these differences between established planters and frontiersmen in the lower South had existed in isolation from the rest of the union, it is clear that the slave trade would have been regarded as a subject for *regulation,* rather than prohibition. As long as the ratio of white male adults to slaves remained high enough to insure communal defense, the main consideration of policy would have been to see that the slave trade did not threaten the "balance of payments" or the stability of credit adjustments within the state, and to prevent the dumping of "firebrands" from West Indian plantations. Measures directed specifically toward these ends might have gained widespread support in the Deep South, although, in the circumstances on the frontier, enforcement even of such regulations as these would have been extremely difficult for the state governments.

In assessing the weakness of Congressional legislation against the slave trade, it is important to keep these Southern attitudes in mind. They help to explain the reluctance to adopt the one measure that, if energetically enforced, might really have stopped the foreign slave trade: the immediate emancipation of Africans imported in violation of the act of 1807. This was the ultimate sanction, recognized as such by both abolitionist Congressmen and the Governor of South Carolina.[100] It would have deprived the purchaser of his purchase without reimbursement and, by releasing a freedman into the midst of a slave society, would have made public enemies of everyone involved in the importation. Yet this penalty was not imposed, because Southerners were unwilling to countenance the release of "unseasoned" Africans from white control.

Instead, the law of 1807 provided that Africans imported after January 1, 1808 be taken from their captors and delivered to officers of the state into which they had been imported for disposal according to that state's laws. In practice, this provision, when enforced at all, seems to have turned into an arrangement whereby slaves seized by a zealous national official (a customs collector or United States marshal) were delivered on demand to agents of the governor, then committed under bond to a planter (perhaps the same planter from whom they had been seized in the first place), whereupon the nominal bond was simply forfeited. In one recorded case, smuggled slaves seized by a United States marshal in Alabama were taken from his jurisdiction by a federal judge, who then appointed a group of his cronies as "guardians." These guardians then rented the slaves, making a nice profit for themselves and depriving the marshal of his own fair "pittance." [101] The records do not show whether the guardians were the original owners, or what eventually happened to the slaves. But it is obvious from this and other accounts that there were many ways around the law for men who were contemptuous of its restraints. Whether or not the laws redistributed benefits among particular white individuals, they did not prevent the enslavement of blacks.

And so, when peace restored the vigor of transoceanic commerce after 1815, a domestic market for the slave trade was readily available. Toward the end of the second decade of the nineteenth century, the Virginia dynasty in the White House sent several messages to Congress calling for more effective legislation against the slave trade.[102] Evidence was mounting that outlaws, some of them organized into virtual "confederacies of pirates," were operating in the Gulf of Mexico and on Amelia Island, off the northeast coast of Florida, and were pouring slaves through the southern borders of the union. In the face of this massive traffic, customs agents cried out for more and better-equipped "revenue cutters" to patrol the coast, while naval commanders pleaded for a more flexible force, including a fleet of boats small enough to ply the shallow coastline of the Gulf of Mexico. Particularly around New Orleans, the Mississippi River Delta was providing innumerable little avenues of access to inland areas.[103]

The American Navy at this time was a miserable floating monument to the conviction of the Jeffersonians that navies were both cause and effect of the twin evils of aristocracy and imperialism. Despite the embarrassments of the War of 1812, or perhaps because those embarrassments had not proved fatal, the Republicans remained reluctant to mount an adequate naval force. As a consequence, they had no ships to stop the slave trade.

Even if they had had greater naval power, it is doubtful that they would have used it to patrol the southern border in search of slave smugglers. The Jeffersonians would have been deeply reluctant to stir up the hornet's nest that would surely have been uncovered in a venture of this kind. Perhaps, if the Navy had been stronger, their own repugnance to the trade, reinforced by Northern hostility to it, would have driven the Virginians to more vigorous enforcement, but there is no evidence of really serious anxiety in the executive department between 1808 and 1820 over impotence to end the trade.

The act of 1807 was not totally without effect on the trade, however. This effect was felt on the coast of Africa. Great Britain, too, had outlawed the slave trade in 1807, but by an act that had teeth. It was straightforwardly interpreted by British courts and backed by the leading navy in the world. In 1809, British determination and power became a factor in American slave trading when a British Court of Admiralty, taking judicial notice of the act of 1807, sanctioned the seizure of a slaving ship flying the American flag. When that judgment was announced, the American flag disappeared for nearly two decades from the African coast.[104]

But the trade itself was less easily frightened off than the American flag. British power could prevent ships flying the American flag from engaging in the slave trade. Infuriating as it might be for Americans to see their laws enforced by a hostile foreign power, their government was as impotent to stay Britain's hand as it was reluctant to stand before the world as the champion of the slave trade. Under the circumstances, the easiest remedy for those engaging in the trade was to switch flags on slaving vessels, for Spain did not outlaw the trade until 1820, or Portugal until 1830. The procurement of Spanish or Portuguese "papers" and flags was a scandalously simple matter.[105] So long as these countries permitted the trade, it could not be stopped short of an act of war; and Britain, the only nation with the power to discipline them effectively, was allied with Spain against France during most of this period.

Conditions on the African coast were important, because most authorities agreed that it was there, alone, that the trade could be stopped.[106] A boat leaving America or Britain on a slaving mission could fairly easily disguise its purpose. It could obtain the necessary fraudulent papers near the African coast. And with the co-operation of smugglers, it was not difficult to dispose of the cargo. It was the operation in Africa that took time—to round up the Africans, dicker about the price, ferry them out to the trans-oceanic vessel, and secure them in their "floating dungeon." Sometimes this operation took days, or even weeks. Here was the best opportunity to foil the trade. But while there was a single slave-trading nation whose rights Britain respected, and while other nations withheld the "right of inspection" from the British Navy, smugglers would find the law a source of inconvenience rather than a serious obstacle.

Thus, when maritime commerce was possible at all, the carrying of new slaves to America continued despite the act of 1807. If the slave trade was truly to be stopped, it was obvious by 1817–1818 that new measures would have to be tried.

One suggestion was to reinforce the motives of informers. The act of 1807 had assigned a part of the fine assessed against smugglers as a reward for informing. The problem was that smugglers were often poor men themselves, unable to pay the fines assessed against them, which meant that informing, in addition to being dangerous, was also unprofitable. An amendment passed in 1818 provided that an informer would be entitled to half the value of a ship forfeited for participating in the trade,[107] which might have made informing fairly profitable. But according to a report submitted by the Treasury to a Congressional committee in 1819, not a single forfeiture for slave trading had ever been successfully prosecuted.[108] Apparently, Early had been right when he said that it would take more courage than most men had to force a prosecution for slave trading through a court in the Deep South.

Two other tacks were tried while Monroe was President. In 1819, responding to pressure from the distinguished leadership of the American Colonization Society, including Supreme Court Justice Bushrod Washington, nephew of the first President, and Speaker of the House Henry Clay,[109] Congress passed an act empowering the President to appoint an agent to reside in Africa. He was directed to establish a colony on the coast of Africa to which blacks smuggled to America might be "repatriated." This was a departure from the act of 1807, which had settled the problem of "disposal" by turning it over to the states. In 1817, a Congressional committee had considered various alternatives, including the possibility of establishing a reservation for freedmen on the frontier. This option was rejected because blacks were regarded as incapable of surviving alone on the frontier, and because it was foreseen that a society that included slaves might soon surround such a reservation, creating unacceptable hazards for slave owners. If smuggled blacks were to be spared from slavery, the committee concluded, there was no alternative but to return them to Africa, where there was every hope that they might be organized into civilized communities and develop into commercial partners for the United States.[110]

The committee expressed the hope that Britain might agree to "neutralize" Sierra Leone, its own experiment in repatriation, and accept slaves from the United States. But Britain was unwilling to abandon its responsibility for and control over Sierra Leone, and Americans were reluctant to contribute to a colony that promised to enrich only the British Empire. There seemed no alternative but for Americans to found a "colony" of their own.

In assessing the colonization project as it appeared in 1820, it must be said that the logic that rejected the alternatives to the scheme was stronger than the appreciation of the difficulties that confronted the colonizers. The memorials and Congressional reports that promoted the colonization effort showed idealism and genuine sympathy for black suffering, a deep sense of guilt about the wrecking impact of the slave trade upon African society, and a strong desire to do something to repair the damage. They take it for granted that slaves have profited from the "school of slavery," and they look forward confidently to the establishment of civilized, Christian communities on the west coast of Africa and to the dissemination of this civilizing influence throughout the "dark continent." The "colonizers" were not mean men, but they were provincial in their blueprint for Africa and they badly underestimated the challenge they faced. To make an impact on slavery in the United States and to "civilize" Africa, they would have had to command resources almost infinitely beyond those available during the heyday of the project, between 1820 and 1830.

The other approach tried during Monroe's tenure was to declare slave trading "piracy" and to assign the death penalty to those convicted of engaging in it. Not until Lincoln's first administration was any American put to death for engaging in the slave trade.[111] The act of 1820 was primarily symbolic. Its passage was heralded by lurid descriptions of the trade itself, cast in emotive language that began to appear for the first time in Congressional reports on the subject of slavery. In debates and reports before 1808, the trade had generally been analyzed in abstract terms and described by such words as "nefarious" and "detestable." Congressional reports leading to the act of 1820, however, described in detail the process by which blacks were kidnapped from their villages in Africa, dragged aboard wretched, ill-equipped ships, lashed in the hold of their "floating dungeons" "amidst the dead and the dying," and transported to a strange land, there to strain and sweat till death at last relieved their distress.[112] The romantic imagination of the nineteenth century was beginning to work on slavery and its effects. These assaults were matched by a defense of slavery that took on the same emotive character, producing an exchange that contributed greatly to the disruption of the arrangement of 1787, a settlement made possible in the first place by a tacit agreement to ignore concrete circumstances and confine attention to external relationships between the sections.

Serious men knew that calling slave traders "pirates" and making tentative gestures toward establishing a colony in Africa were not going to stop the smuggling of slaves into the southwestern frontier region. The only way to stop that, short of deploying a truly formidable naval force in the Gulf of Mexico, was to nip the commerce in Africa. There were two ways of doing that: to send American cruisers to the coast of Africa or to grant England a limited "right of inspection." The former course was undertaken, within the limits of American naval power, and not without some success. An American cruiser under the command of Stephen Trenchard reported a handful of seizures on the African coast in 1820.[113] But the American Navy was not equal to the task of stopping the trade entirely, and the facility with which flags and papers could be switched and substituted made it impossible to shut off the trade until all nations outlawed it and granted adequate powers of enforcement to the British Navy.

On the latter tactic, Monroe balked, paralyzed by the memory of the War of 1812 and its bitterness over impressment. In answer to a British request for permission to inspect ships suspected of engaging in the slave trade, he cited the tenderness of American opinion on this subject and presented objections, based on Constitutional interpretation, to the idea of delivering smugglers over to "mixed" tribunals (composed partly of foreign judges) for judgment.[114]

By 1820 it seemed apparent that, if it wanted to stop the African slave trade, the federal government would have to set aside these nationalistic sensitivities. A Congressional committee recommended that authority be given to the British Navy to police the African coast, an authority "limited in duration, or to continue at pleasure, for the sake of experiment . . . so restricted to vessels and seas . . . as not to be unacceptable." Inasmuch as the United States conducted almost no legitimate commerce with Africa, the committee suggested that little risk to legal American interests would be involved.[115]

But Monroe must have known that such an arrangement would have aroused great solicitude for shipping interests among the farmers and planters of the West and the South, reminiscent of the sensitivity of the war hawks for the interests of New England in 1812. Monroe, who always sought calm waters, knew where the fiercest winds in American politics came from. He was not likely to enter into arrangements that rendered him vulnerable to the charge that he had betrayed Jackson's victory at New Orleans. An effective prohibition of the slave trade required unprecedented action on the part of the federal government. Yet the slave trade touched too many raw nerves to be a stimulus to new departures, particularly for a nation trying desperately to preserve the façade of "good feelings."

It was too late to say "never again" to the slave trade. Yet the country was not ready to repent of the basic sin, which was racial slavery. Until the nation was willing to include black inhabitants in the promise of equality, it would not be able to prevent the introduction of black African slaves to America.

9

Slavery and Foreign Policy:

Two Cases

IF the argument that sectional differences over slavery helped to provoke and define sectional differences in attitude toward national policy is correct, an analysis of American diplomacy in the early years would show that sectional tensions arising from slavery were an important factor in the conduct of the young republic's foreign relations.[1] A full-scale study of this relationship cannot be attempted here. Instead, an analysis of two cases—the struggle over Jay's Treaty of 1795 and the conduct of relations with Santo Domingo under Adams and Jefferson—will illustrate the way in which slavery influenced foreign policy.

The need for a new treaty with Great Britain in the mid-1790's arose in part from violations of the Treaty of Paris, the treaty concluded in 1783 that proclaimed the success of the American Revolution. Among the arrangements established was a promise by Great Britain, in Article VII that its armies would depart from American shores without "carrying away any Negroes or other property of the American inhabitants."[2] This clause had been inserted at the suggestion of American negotiator Henry Laurens, apparently without controversy. Despite this clause, inspectors assigned by General Washington had seen British forces carry away considerable numbers of Negroes as they evacuated New York City in the spring of 1783. Washington's protest to the British commander, Sir Guy Carleton, had been of no avail. Carleton had contended that the Negroes who were boarding English ships had been promised freedom, and that he could not renege on that promise.[3]

The stage was thus set for a decade of controversy over the ambiguous language of Article VII. Were the Negroes who were "carried away" in 1783 the property of American citizens? If so, what ought Britain to do? Was it obliged to return the slaves or to compensate their owners? What effect did this alleged violation have on the rest of the treaty?

Informal negotiations for a new treaty with Great Britain began soon after the inauguration of George Washington. Leaders in the first administration, especially Alexander Hamilton, were anxious to resolve tensions and proceed to establish normal diplomatic and commercial relations with the mother country now that the passions of the struggle for independence were fading. Several obstacles stood in the way of this reconciliation. Both sides claimed that obligations accepted by the other in the Treaty of Paris had not been fulfilled. The British claimed that American courts had not enforced the payment of debts or prevented the confiscation of estates belonging to loyalists. Americans complained that the British Army had failed to evacuate forts in the western territories and had refused to return, or to pay compensation for, Negro slaves carried off at the end of the war. Hamilton and his friends hoped to settle these and other outstanding issues in order to pave the way for greater commercial co-operation between the two nations.

So long as Jefferson was Secretary of State in Washington's Cabinet—during his first term—little progress was made toward a new treaty. Jefferson did not share Hamilton's desire to reach an accommodation on the disputed points. His political sympathies went to England's continental rival, France, and to the agrarian element in American society, which made him cool to the prospect of improving commercial relations with Britain. Apparently, Britain, too, did not have much enthusiasm for a commercial treaty.[4]

One of Jefferson's primary instruments for warding off the accommodation with Britain was the issue of compensation for the stolen slaves.[5] Shortly after arriving in the United States, British Ambassador George Hammond submitted to Jefferson a summary of evidence intended to prove that the Treaty of 1783 had first been broken by the Americans. His abstract argued that Britain's retention of posts in the West was justified by prior infractions committed by Americans against the loyalists and British creditors.[6] Responding, Jefferson noted that British commanders had been informed of the ratification of the Treaty of Paris by April 1783, but that slaves had been carried off as late as May 8 of that year. Thus the "onus of original infraction" lay with Britain until compensation was made for the slaves. Jefferson responded also to other charges in Hammond's case, defending the competence and integrity of American courts and the good faith of American state legislatures. But the root of his argument was that the British Army under Sir Guy Carleton had first broken the treaty by removing slaves, and that Americans were justified in concluding that Britain did not intend to abide by its obligations. Since Britain had broken faith first, the United States was released from the performance of repugnant obligations, and would continue to withhold obedience until Britain had indicated readiness to make reparation for the stolen slaves.[7]

As long as Jefferson stood in Hamilton's path, and in the absence of eagerness for reconciliation on the part of Britain, the icy stalemate in Anglo-American relations persisted. But when Jefferson resigned from Washington's Cabinet, a new opportunity was presented. His successor, Edmund Randolph, was unable to offset Hamilton's influence within the administration. When relations with Britain became critical during 1794, several Federalist Senators suggested to the President that a special envoy be sent to England. When Hamilton himself urged that Chief Justice John Jay be selected for the mission, Washington decided to act.

As chief negotiator for the Americans, Jay differed from Jefferson in two fundamental respects: he longed for an Anglo-American reconciliation, and he had no heart for the issue of the stolen slaves. His Anglophilia was well known and long-standing. As for the claims of the slave owners, he had demonstrated his attitude in a report made in 1786, while he was serving as Secretary for Foreign Affairs under the old Continental Congress, a report that went far to form the attitude of Southerners toward him.

In 1785 John Adams, then America's Minister to Great Britain, had demanded Britain's withdrawal from American soil, particularly from the Western forts. England's answer, signed by the Marquis of Carmarthen, had consisted of a long list of acts passed by American state legislatures allegedly in violation of the Treaty of 1783. Carmarthen had argued that until English debts were recovered in accordance with Articles IV through VI of the Treaty of Paris, the British Army would not comply with the stipulations of Article VII.

Congress transmitted Carmarthen's note to Jay, instructing him to prepare an answer. Jay's response, delivered as a report to Congress on October 13, 1786, was careful and detailed.[8] On the question of alleged violations by state legislation, he agreed that nearly all the acts cited were in fact at variance with the treaty, but he urged Congress to remind Britain, and the state legislatures, that Article IX of the Articles of Confederation gave to Congress "the sole and exclusive right and power" to enter into treaties. He urged Congress to pass a general act repealing all laws (without naming any of them specifically) that violated America's obligations under duly ratified treaties.[9]

He then came to the question whether American reluctance to perform obligations under the treaty was justified by prior infractions on Britain's part. There is "no doubt," he said, that Article VII, promising the withdrawal of the British without "carrying away any Negroes," had been violated from the start. But it was important to distinguish between three classes of Negroes held by the British at the close of hostilities. The first, those stolen by the British Army during the course of the war, must be regarded as "booty." If these slaves were regarded by both sides as property, then Americans, under the rules of war, could not insist that they be returned. On whether men can be so totally "degraded" as to become property in the full sense, "opinions are unfortunately various, even in countries professing Christianity and respect for the rights of mankind." [10] Nevertheless, Jay concluded, our laws do assert that men may have property in other men, and so we have no ground of complaint against their retaining slaves snatched as "booty." *

---

* Apparently this class included the bulk of the slaves lost during the war. Jefferson reported that Virginia lost 30,000 slaves during Cornwallis's invasion. David Ramsay, South Carolina's contemporary historian, estimated that his state lost 25,000 Negroes during the war, valued at over $12 million. Most Southerners, with varying grace, accepted these losses as part of the price of independence, knowing that they had no chance of being compensated for most of them.[11]

The second class of Negroes held by the British comprised slaves that were behind British lines at the cessation of hostilities but who remained American property because British authorities had made no effort to change their status by law or pronouncement. American owners, said Jay, were entitled by the treaty to keep these slaves, or to get them back now that the war was over.

The third class included Negroes who had responded to British proclamations promising freedom and protection to those who fled from their masters and who remained in British camps at the war's end. Since these Negroes were not captured, but had surrendered and were received into British lines as friends and refugees, rather than as slaves, the titles of their masters were never extinguished. By agreeing to Article VII, Britain had undertaken to leave these Negroes in America. Yet Washington's inspectors had witnessed the departure of many.

Jay noted the argument of certain Britons (notably Sir Guy Carleton) that the promise of protection* to slaves who fled relieved Britain of the obligation to leave them behind as mere American property. He indicated his sympathy for this British position, but noted that Britain had nevertheless agreed to Article VII. This raised two questions: how far a covenant could obligate a nation to do wrong, and how far a covenant might be modified to permit the mitigation of an evil. By following the letter of Article VII—that is, by returning slaves "to their former bondage, and to the severities to which such slaves are usually subjected"—Britain would be doing great wrong to the Negroes. By totally ignoring this clause, Britain would be doing "great wrong to their masters." The only way to do justice both to the Negroes and to their former masters was for Britain to pay compensation for these slaves.

As a matter of practical diplomacy, Jay's analysis had much to recommend it. Negroes taken in 1783 probably could not have been recovered by 1786 in any case. Compensation was thus the best settlement the owners could expect to achieve. Jay's argument—that Britain had obligated itself to account for these slaves by agreeing to Article VII and that British spokesmen had re-

* The obligation to "protect" these slaves seems in most cases to have been assumed by plantation owners in the West Indies.

peatedly acknowledged this obligation (by holding that its performance was contingent upon American fulfillment of other articles)—was as powerful and realistic as could be made under the circumstances.

From the Southern point of view, Jay's report was wholly unacceptable. It was full of gratuitous insults against slavery. It frankly confessed the author's sympathy for Britain's stand on this issue, rather than the position of those whose agent he had agreed to be.* By calling it "unfortunate" that nations professing Christianity and acknowledging human rights nevertheless allowed men to be held in bondage, and by calling attention to the "severities" of slavery, Jay had rubbed raw nerves. Thus, when Washington asked Jay to seek a new treaty with England in 1794, Southerners were immediately on their guard. Jay was not only the author of the report of 1786; he was also past president of the New York Society for the Abolition of Slavery, and the man who had been willing, during negotiations with Spanish Minister Gardoqui in 1785, to barter America's right to navigate the full length of the Mississippi River. The faction he represented was most earnest in its desire for an accommodation with Britain, and quite free of dependence on slavery. He had every reason to want a treaty with Britain, and no desire to let "the Negro question" embarrass the negotiations unduly. It was not paranoia that led most Southerners to fear the worst from Jay's mission.

Because the negotiations between Jay and Lord Grenville were conducted for the most part orally, comparatively little is known of the processes. Jay's reports to Secretary Randolph[13] do indicate that the question of the Negro slaves came up early and often and was a principal source of difficulty. During these discussions, Jay relied on the position he had worked out in 1786 to support his claim that the British Army, by taking Negroes away in April and May of 1783, had committed the "first aggression" against the treaty. Grenville countered by arguing that slaves who had entered British lines at any time prior to the war's end were subject to British authority by the rules of war. The language of Article

* Compare, for example, the attitude and performance of John Quincy Adams, who hated slavery, but who, as Secretary of State under James Monroe, forthrightly served the interests of his Southern constituents.[12]

VII, in Grenville's view, did not require that Negroes who were
no longer the property of Americans be left in America. To interpret the article as requiring British generals to renege on their
promise of freedom and protection to the Negroes was to make
the treaty "odious," and thus not strictly binding.[14]

Neither Jay nor Grenville wanted the negotiations to bog
down on this issue, which was regarded as secondary by both of
them. The impending showdown between France and Britain
made both the British and the Federalists eager to compose their
differences. As agreements were reached on the other outstanding
issues, the question of "first aggression" against the Treaty of
1783 began to fade in significance, and hence in usefulness and
interest to Jay. Grenville apparently sensed that Jay would sign a
treaty that omitted any mention of compensation for slaves; Jay
decided that the failure to "agree about the Negroes" was not a
"good reason for breaking up the negotiations." [15] Accordingly,
the treaty signed on November 19, 1794 contained no mention of
the slaves at all.

The reaction of most Southerners—and many Northerners—to
Jay's Treaty was one of disgust and anger. Southern Anglophobia
was traceable in large part to confiscations of slaves during the
war.[16] Jay's failure to gain a promise of compensation for these
depredations became a major ground of opposition. In addition,
Article XII of the treaty, which renounced America's right to
carry the South's primary staples (cotton and sugar) anywhere in
the world, enraged many Southerners. Historian Edward Channing has pointed out that exports of these staples from the United
States before 1793 had been "trifling." [17] Planters were thinking
not of the past, however, but of the future. Jay's willingness to
agree that America's exports of these staples should be subject to
the supervision of the British Empire confirmed the impression of
the planters that the envoy was careless of their interests.[18]

By the time President Washington transmitted the treaty to the
Senate, which met in special session to consider ratification in
June 1795, Southern resistance had begun to stiffen. Rumors,
provoked partly by Jay's political affiliations, partly by his record
of indifference and hostility toward Southern interests, had condemned the accord before its stipulations were precisely known.

The document placed in the hands of the Senate on June 8 did nothing to soften this hostility. Southern Senators, with two or three Northern Republican allies, felt that their worst fears had been realized.

The first move of the antitreaty bloc was to try to rescind the rule of secrecy that governed the Senate's consideration of treaties. Pierce Butler, a leader of the opposition, was convinced that it could not be ratified if its contents became known to the public. Secrecy was maintained, however, by a vote of 20 to 9.[19]

The first week of debate convinced even the treaty's sponsors that Article XII had been a mistake. Planters were not the only ones to take offense; merchants and shippers, too, resented the attempt of the British, with Jay's acquiescence, to inhibit the development of American commerce. When the motion to ratify the treaty was made on June 17, it included a "condition" that Article XII be suspended.

As a consequence of this maneuver, the grounds of opposition narrowed. As stated in a motion by New York's Senator Aaron Burr, the primary objections were that the treaty was unequal, that it would tie American commerce too closely to the British Empire, and that it would enable Britain to dictate American foreign policy toward third parties. The motion was in the form of a list of revisions to be sought through "further friendly negotiations." Prominent in the list was a demand that "the value of the Negroes . . . carried away, contrary to the 7th article of the Treaty of 1783 . . . be paid for by the British government." [20]

Burr's motion for renegotiation was lost on June 23, by a vote of 10 to 20, which foreshadowed the decision on ratification. The motion amounted to a total repudiation of the treaty. It attracted the support of those who would refuse to ratify, but it drew no other backing. Thus the vote, showing a two-thirds majority against Burr, indicated that an all-out assault on the treaty could not succeed in the Senate.

South Carolina's Senators—Federalist Jacob Read and Republican Pierce Butler—had divided on Burr's motion, Read opposing, Butler supporting it. On the day following the defeat of Burr's proposal, these two planters co-sponsored an amendment to the motion of ratification. Their motion was to add a condition that ratification be delayed until Britain had agreed to a procedure for compensating owners of slaves lost in 1733. Read was an ardent Federalist, always anxious to stand in good stead with the Eastern establishment of his party. Yet his motion on this occasion must have stirred up a hornet's nest among the Federalists. Though the debate is not recorded, the upshot of it was that Read agreed to withdraw his motion "in order," as the Senate *Journal* reports, "to introduce a motion drawn up with more consideration on the same subject." [21]

Straightway, Read's motion was renewed by two Republican Senators, John Brown, of Kentucky, and James Jackson, of Georgia. Both had indicated by their votes on Burr's motion that their opposition to the treaty was thorough. As opponents, they may have felt that the issue of compensation represented their best hope of preventing ratification.* The vote, taken on June 24, showed how near they came to success. The motion to make ratification conditional was rejected by only 12 to 15. Federalists Humphrey Marshall, of Kentucky, and Read changed sides, voting on this occasion with the antitreaty forces. James Gunn, of Georgia, and Richard Potts, of Maryland, were the only Southerners voting to ratify the treaty before slave owners were compensated.

The Senate proceeded to vote on the motion for ratification. By a bare two-thirds majority of 20 to 10, the treaty, minus Article XII, was ratified. The opposition came mostly from the South, though three Republican votes from the North brought the opposition within one vote of success. Three votes from the South, cast by Federalists Marshall, Read, and Gunn, were crucial to ratification.[22]

Thus, the commercial men from the East had gotten their treaty despite the opposition of those in the North who hated Britain almost as much as they hated Hamilton. Because of this opposition, ratification depended upon the support of the South's wealthiest planters, who were drawn by ties of interest and cul-

---

* Brown was not always sympathetic with slave owners, as he demonstrated by his votes during the consideration of an ordinance for Louisiana. In this case, he apparently felt that Jay had shown a defective regard for the just expectations of one section of the country, and an excess of zeal for reconciliation between the mercantile interests of the two countries.

tural affinity into an alliance, both political and commercial, with merchants in the East and in England. Though these Southern votes obscured the sectional cleavage, the appearance was deceptive. Read, a staunch supporter of the treaty, acknowledged that his colleague Pierce Butler, who bitterly opposed ratification, was a better reflection of opinion in the lower South. Read, who described himself during the controversy as a "Senator for the Union," was defeated for re-election in 1800 and never recovered, politically, from the odium of having supported Jay's Treaty.[23]

Controversy over the treaty did not end with ratification by the Senate. As soon as the terms became known to the public,* a storm of protest arose from a number of quarters.[25] Secretary of State Randolph, in letters to Jay written after the close of negotiations with Grenville, averred that he was "extremely afraid" that "some quarters of the union [would] suppose themselves neglected" by the failure to gain compensation for the stolen slaves.[26] During the months following the publication of the treaty, the furor rising from these "neglected" elements caused Washington to hesitate before completing ratification by adding his signature. The discovery of a document suggesting Randolph's complicity in a French plot produced Randolph's resignation. Washington then signed the treaty, which had been opposed, within his administration, only by Randolph.[27]

Though the administration stood united, the political forces Randolph represented had been neither silenced nor effectively answered. The latter task was undertaken by Hamilton, who wrote a series of essays under the pseudonym "Camillus" during the closing months of 1795. In the third and fifth essays, he dealt specifically with objections based on the demand for compensation for Negroes taken in 1783. Admitting that the "seduction" of Negroes from their masters was "infamous," he insisted that it would have compounded the fault to surrender them after promising them liberty. Following Grenville's line of argument, he contended that British negotiators in 1783 could not have meant to guarantee such a surrender. Since it would be "odious" to as-

* Senator Stevens T. Mason, of Virginia, in violation of the Senate's rule of secrecy, had given a copy of the treaty to Benjamin Franklin Bache, editor of the *Aurora,* who printed it on June 29.[24]

sume that the British meant to renege on their promise of freedom to the Negroes, it was incumbent on interpreters of the treaty to search for another construction. Article VII, upon which the claim for compensation was based, constituted Britain's promise not to lure any more Negroes from their masters while evacuating. This promise had been kept. Americans who demanded compensation for Negroes who had escaped during the course of the war were exceeding their rights under the Treaty of Paris.[28]

The "collosus" of the Federalists[29] also argued that Jay's Treaty promised great benefits to the United States. The two most important were Britain's promises to evacuate the western posts and to compensate for spoliation of American commerce during the war between England and France. He denounced as "hot-heads" those who would sacrifice these gains by holding out for the least important object of the negotiations, compensations to slave owners.[30]

The response to these arguments came during debates in the House of Representatives in April 1796. Republican leaders there claimed a Constitutional right to pass independent judgment on treaties, insofar as they required laws and appropriations to be carried into effect. But when the House asked Washington for papers relating to Jay's negotiations, the President refused, on the ground that the House, which lacked authority to ratify treaties, had no legitimate reason to see these documents unless it was preparing to impeach the President. Provoked by this insulting response, the House adopted two resolutions offered by Thomas Blount. They asserted that the House of Representatives had independent responsibility to consider—to pass or to reject—laws designed to give effect to treaties ratified by the Senate and signed by the President. Having so resolved, the House proceeded to consider a resolution for carrying the treaty into effect, giving Republicans an opportunity to respond to the arguments of Hamilton and Grenville.[31]

The assault was led by James Madison. His critique of the treaty was thorough, but, among the many faults he found, the failure to demand satisfaction for slaves taken away in 1783 was given prominent attention. He denounced Jay for his "very ex-

traordinary abandonment of the compensation due for the Negroes." He pointed out that British negotiators before Grenville,
even those who refused to recognize an obligation to return the
Negroes to bondage, had never questioned America's right, under
the treaty, to compensation. But even if British officials had not
uniformly accepted responsibility for taking the slaves, Jay had
no business surrendering the claim. By yielding, he was admitting
that Britain had a better right to interpret the disputed clause
than did the United States. To the argument that Jay's success on
other issues compensated for his failure on the question of the
slaves, Madison responded that advantages gained by the
commercial interests would not defray the losses suffered by
planters.[32]

Virginian John Nicholas then recalled that Laurens had inserted the clause forbidding the evacuation of slaves in order partially to relieve the planters, who owed to British merchants most
of the debts sanctioned by the Treaty of Paris. He charged that
the ratification of a treaty confirming debts owed to the British,*
while ignoring those owed to American slave owners, constituted
a severe injustice to the South.[33]

The Federalist position on the Negroes taken by the British
was stated by James Hillhouse, of Connecticut. He argued that
the American case was ambiguous at best. The Treaty of 1783
prevented the removal of "any Negroes or other property of the
American inhabitants." But he cited the authority of Vattel (and
Jefferson) to the effect that the factual situation at the time of a
treaty's ratification constitutes the law unless the treaty stipulates
to the contrary. American negotiators, he said, tried to gain the
restoration of all Negroes taken during the war; the British
sought the restoration of all Tory estates. Both had to yield. There
had been a conflict in construction from the start, and whenever
there existed legitimate ground for difference in interpretation,
the presumption of the law ought always to favor liberty, regardless of "complexion." So long as the door was open to the British

---

* Article VI submitted the question of "debts . . . contracted before the
peace" to a binational commission empowered to ascertain the amount of the
debts; the government of the United States was obliged to guarantee that
awards made by the commission be honored by the American debtors.

to construe the article in such a way as to justify the emancipation of slaves, it would have been wrong for them to fail to do so.

To buttress his argument, Hillhouse cited the analogy of American seamen held captive by the Barbary pirates. If these Americans escaped to France, would we think that the French had an obligation to return them to bondage in Africa?

So far as principle is concerned, what difference does it make whether the citizens of the United States are carried into slavery in Africa, or the inhabitants of Africa are brought into slavery in the United States? He knew of no principle that made a difference between the natural rights of a white or black man. . . .

He went on to say that all men, black as well as white, are born free and equal; "a man's complexion [does not] increase or diminish his natural rights." But if the slavery of black men in America is not justified by natural right, and if the language of the treaty permits the construction advanced by the British, then Americans had no ground to insist upon a contrary interpretation.[34]

As the debate came to a close, Speaker Jonathan Dayton, of New Jersey, had the last word, contending that if the House refused the appropriations necessary to carry the treaty into effect, it would be mocking the Constitution's allocation of the treaty-making power to the President and the Senate. A series of votes were then taken: first on a motion calling it "expedient" to make the necessary appropriation; then on a motion declaring the treaty "objectionable"; finally on a motion for carrying the treaty into effect. On the first two, tie votes of 49 to 49 were broken in favor of the treaty by Dayton. On the motion to carry the treaty into effect, a favorable majority of 51 to 48 was found.[35] In each case, the majority came almost entirely from the North. Only two South Carolinians, one North Carolinian, and one Virginian, all of them strong Federalists, voted to give effect to the treaty. A Constitutional crisis of the first magnitude—the House refusing to implement a treaty duly negotiated and ratified—was thus narrowly averted.

The issue of British responsibility for slaves evacuated in 1788 was only one objection to Jay's Treaty. By itself, it could not have stirred up the furor that developed in 1795 and 1796. But as it happened, the resentment of the slave owners lent powerful reinforcement to the offense taken by farmers and tradesmen against the empire building of the Eastern Federalists.

The cast of the argument between Madison and Hillhouse was such as to create sympathy for the slave owners, even among those who held no slaves. Madison argued that the American right to compensation was based upon an agreement reached in 1783 and reinforced by ten years of acceptance by both sides. Hillhouse took a position against this established American right, countering the claim of legal right with a plea for abstract justice. Madison refused to argue the question of slavery's standing in natural law. He assumed that the Negroes taken in 1783 were beyond recovery. Their freedom was not really the issue. What he demanded was that Britain honor its undertaking of 1783. If Britain felt an obligation to the Negroes not to return them to their masters, that was its business. What it did with the Negroes, however, did not, in Madison's view, dissolve obligations under the treaty.

To a man disposed to dislike the treaty anyway, this must have seemed a powerful argument. Hamilton had justified the surrender of compensation by pointing to the advantages gained by Jay on other matters, and by insisting that all would have been lost if Jay had remained adamant on the slaves. Those who were less satisfied than Hamilton with Jay's work were correspondingly less disposed to be forgiving for failure on the question of compensation.

The major political consequence of Jay's Treaty was the alienation of the South from the Federalist persuasion. Many Southerners, particularly the South Carolinians, had found themselves in sympathy with Hamilton on most issues that provoked a division of opinion during the Presidency of George Washington. Now these same Southerners stood by like unrequited lovers as Federalist leaders from the North abandoned the rights and interests of their Southern colleagues, without remorse or apology, and then justified the betrayal by reference to the natural rights of black men. The disgust felt by a man like John Rutledge was so great that he sacrificed his appointment as Chief Justice of the Supreme Court by his criticism of the work of Jay, his predecessor on the court. According to Associate Supreme Court Justice James Iredell, himself a Federalist from North Carolina, "the sentiments *publicly* expressed by Mr. John Rutledge . . . were shared by almost every other man south of the Potomac, even by those personally friendly to Mr. Jay and staunch Federalists.'[36]

The struggle over Jay's Treaty resulted in a setback for the opponents of slavery. By obtaining a treaty that abandoned compensation, they had freed no slaves. Nor had they chosen a propitious occasion for instructing Southerners on the universality of natural rights. What they had done was to demonstrate to most Southerners that the Hamiltonian wing of the Federalist party was so hostile to slavery that it ought not to be trusted with the management of the nation's affairs.

From the Federalists' point of view, the willingness of Southerners to scuttle the treaty because compensation for slaves was not included provoked doubt as to the viability of the union.[37] When, in the end, the House voted to grant the appropriations, the talk of disunion subsided among the Northerners, and Republican leaders chose to organize for a political assault on the Presidency rather than secede. The crisis of the mid-1790's gradually eased, but not before the most dangerous fissure in the union had been exposed for a brief but frightening moment.

In the struggle over Jay's Treaty, the interests of slave owners were surrendered by the Federalists. But in the nation's relations with Santo Domingo, slave owners, after a disappointing start under President John Adams, finally gained control over American policy under the Republican administration of Thomas Jefferson. Despite these differences, however there is a basic similarity between the two cases: in both, in the pull and haul over the rights and exigencies of slavery in the field of foreign policy, the national interest was allowed to suffer.

The importance of Santo Domingo in world trade at the time of the founding of the United States is suggested by the fact that in 1783 one-third of the foreign trade of France passed through the ports of this precious colony. The chief staple was sugar, grown on huge plantations owned and managed by white Europeans, but worked by black African slaves. In 1790 Santo Domingo's population consisted of 32,000 whites, plus 24,000 freedmen (mostly mulattoes), and 480,000 slaves (mostly African-born).[38] By comparison, the three states of Virginia, North Carolina, and South Carolina had about the same number of Negroes as Santo Domingo, but over twenty-seven times as many whites. In the three southernmost states, whites outnumbered Negroes by nearly two to one; in Santo Domingo, Negroes outnumbered whites by more than fifteen to one. These statistics indicate Santo Domingo's dual aspect: commercial gold, but social dynamite.

In 1791 the dynamite exploded. For months that dragged on into years, the island was convulsed by awful conflicts between slaves desperate for their freedom and masters fighting for control of the island, and ultimately for their lives. Both sides fought with "inhuman ferocity," [39] but the blacks were victorious. The French commissioner on the island was forced in 1793 to announce the emancipation of all slaves. The following year the French Convention in Paris made it official by declaring the emancipation of all slaves within the French Empire.[40]

The revolution had a profound effect in the United States. Planters feared that their own slaves might follow the example of the Negroes of Santo Domingo, and that American statesmen, particularly the Francophiles, might respond to such a cataclysm by decreeing emancipation, as the French Convention had done.[41] Nor were planters alone in fearing that the example of Santo Domingo might provoke a rebellion of slaves in the United States. Proposals to abolish slavery in the Mississippi Territory and to liberate slaves smuggled into the United States were rejected by large Congressional majorities partially because of the widespread fear of causing Santo Domingo's "horrid scenes" to be reproduced on American soil. Many scholars are convinced that the revolution in the Caribbean was at least as important as the invention of the cotton gin in reversing the tide that seemed to be running against slavery in the upper South at the end of the eighteenth century.[42]

The initial reaction of most Americans to the revolt of the slaves in Santo Domingo was to sympathize with the French colonials. According to Treasury Department reports in 1790, the

French West Indies ranked second only to Great Britain in terms of the value of its trade with the United States.[43] The uprising of 1791 threatened to disrupt this lucrative commerce. Thus the interest of Northern merchants coincided with the emotions of Southern planters in dictating a policy of support for the maintenance of French authority.

After 1793, when they had won their freedom, the Negroes, under the captaincy of ex-slave Toussaint L'Ouverture, vied with French agents, represented by a mulatto, Andre Rigaud, for control of the island. Toward the end of 1793, a third factor entered the picture, when the British, at war with France, occupied part of Santo Domingo.[44]

As these developments unfolded, American policy toward Santo Domingo underwent a series of shifts. The basic urges of the merchants and the planters remained the same as they had been before 1793: the merchants wanted a stable trading partner; the planters wanted the Negroes brought under control. After 1793 they began to produce pressure in opposite directions, as far as American policy in the Caribbean was concerned.

Officially, the policy of the American government was one of neutrality, of refusal to interfere with commerce to any belligerent. Under this policy, American merchants brought supplies, arms, and ammunition indiscriminately to the natives under Toussaint and to the French and British forces, depending only on which could pay the highest price.[45] But as the war between the European powers increased in bitterness, American commerce to one became the prey of the other. Desire for pacification in the Caribbean grew.

In the dispute between France and Britain, the sympathy of the Federalist administrations of Washington and Adams lay with Britain, a predilection that led to the negotiation and ratification of Jay's Treaty. In the French view, by signing this treaty the United States had violated the principles of neutrality. The French Directory declared that British colonies in the West Indies were in a state of siege, and ordered the capture of all vessels carrying provisions to them. Relations between France and the United States steadily worsened, until, at the end of 1796, the French suspended diplomatic relations.[46]

The policies of the Federalists had thus caused America's lot in the Caribbean to be cast with the British. But the British were unable to maintain their occupation of Santo Domingo. During 1795–1796 alone, 12,000 of the 18,000 British troops on the island died of yellow fever.[47] By the summer of 1798 General Thomas Maitland, commander of the British forces, had decided to evacuate. He found Toussaint, now the dominant leader among the Negroes, eager to negotiate and to grant honorable terms to the withdrawing British forces. In return for a promise not to attack Santo Domingo "during the entire duration of the present war" with France, Maitland gained Toussaint's "most solemn and positive" promise not to allow his troops to be used in any attack on the British island of Jamaica. In addition, Maitland promised that the British Navy would not interfere with cruisers bringing provisions to Santo Domingo.[48]

The result of the British withdrawal was that Toussaint became America's man in Santo Domingo. The Adams administration—under the prodding of Hamilton, and with the sometimes reluctant acquiescence of the President—despised France more than it feared Toussaint. To be sure, the idea of dealing with a black head of state took some getting used to. Rufus King, America's Minister to Great Britain at the time, acknowledged that *"the example upon our slaves in the Southern states"* constituted a real danger. He expressed anxiety lest the Negroes become pirates and begin to prey on Carribbean commerce. The United States, he said, did not want to encourage the emergence of a "new Barbary [pirate] power." [49] But Lord Grenville, the British Foreign Minister, assured King that the British, who had their own colonies in the West Indies, shared these fears. The result of these mutual dispositions was the "King-Grenville doctrine," whereby Britain and the United States shared in the commerce with Santo Domingo and at the same time agreed to avoid any actions that would tend to recognize Toussaint's regime as an independent nation.[50]

The attitude of Southerners toward this policy tended to split along party lines. Although the administration intended not to encourage Toussaint's dream of nationhood for Santo Domingo, the policy adopted in 1798 clearly strengthened his hand in dealing with the French. Southern Federalists like Thomas Pinckney

were able to face this prospect without flinching. "[S]hould the
independence of the island take place," said Pinckney in the
House in 1799, "the event would be more advantageous to the
Southern States than if it remained under the dominion of
France." His colleague Robert Goodloe Harper agreed. To support his opinion, he said there was evidence that France was sending secret black agents among the slaves of South Carolina to
incite an insurrection. He credited Toussaint with counteracting
French designs and preventing an invasion from Santo Domingo
for that purpose.[51]

Republicans Samuel Smith, of Maryland, and Virginia's John
Nicholas, on the other hand, opposed commerce with Toussaint
on the ground that it would place the United States on the same
footing as the revolters with regard to France, and would amount
at least to *de facto* recognition of the independence of Toussaint
and his government.[52] So Southern Federalists supported the administration's policy, and Southern Republicans opposed it.

In a letter to Rufus King dated March 12, 1799, Secretary of
State Timothy Pickering acknowledged his doubt that Toussaint
could establish a viable regime on Santo Domingo; "the blacks,"
he wrote, "are too ignorant." Yet he insisted that the United
States ought to trade with them.

[T]here will not, and ought not to be, any inducements to withdraw
the blacks from the cultivation of the island to navigation; and confined
to their own island they will not be dangerous neighbors. Nothing is
more clear than, if left to themselves, that the blacks of St. Domingo
will be incomparably less dangerous than if they remain the subjects
of France.[53]

This attitude stood behind American policy toward Santo Domingo until the turn of the century. In fact, by 1800 the United
States was ready to extend to Toussaint, not just trade and supplies, but outright military aid. In March 1800 Toussaint's army
besieged the port city of Jacmel, a stronghold of forces under the
command of Rigaud. To head off Toussaint's plan to impose a
blockade with ships of his own, and to open a French-controlled
port to American commerce, the United States sent ships to blockade and bombard the forts of Jacmel, an action that constituted

"the first armed intervention by the United States in a foreign civil war." [54] Toussaint gained a decisive victory. Later, he expressed profound gratitude to the American Consul General, Edward Stevens, acknowledging that the American Navy had "contributed not a little to the success" of the siege.

Toward the end of his term as President, John Adams decided that the "quasi-war" with France should be brought to an end. To the dismay of the Hamiltonians in his Cabinet, he appointed a commission of three to treat with France.[55] In the fall of 1800 the negotiations bore fruit in the Treaty of Morfontaine, which released the United States from the defensive alliance of 1778 and composed the most important differences between the two nations.

For Toussaint, the treaty was a calamity. It eliminated America's most important reason for helping him and opened the prospect that France, rejuvenated under the leadership of Napoleon and Talleyrand, might seek to reimpose its authority over Santo Domingo. The danger was compounded when Napoleon, by the secret Treaty of San Ildefonso (October 1, 1800), gained the retrocession of Louisiana from Spain to France. Soon his design became clear: to establish a new French colonial empire in the New World, with the sugar plantations of Santo Domingo as a centerpiece and Louisiana as a prime source of supplies.[56]

On March 4, 1801 primary responsibility for American policy toward Santo Domingo passed from John Adams to Thomas Jefferson. With his background and because his support came mainly from the South, Jefferson naturally regarded Toussaint warily. When Louis A. Pichon, the French Chargé d'affaires in Washington, told him of Napoleon's plan to restore French authority in Santo Domingo, Jefferson responded that the United States could not help but wish him success, for two reasons: because Toussaint's example was a menace to slavery in the United States, and because Santo Domingo was becoming a base for pirates in the Caribbean.[57]

On the other hand, when rumors of the retrocession of Louisiana to France began to filter across to Washington in the spring of 1801, Jefferson was not slow to appreciate the significance of the development. Earlier, before he had learned of Napoleon's acquisition of Louisiana, he had led Pichon to believe that the United States would "reduce Toussaint to starvation" by suspending trade in co-operation with the French attempt to reconquer Santo Domingo. But when a French expeditionary force under the command of Napoleon's brother-in-law, Victor Leclerc, arrived in Santo Domingo in the early spring of 1802, it found American merchants engaging in a brisk trade with the Negroes. Pichon addressed a complaint to Secretary of State Madison, arguing that Toussaint's resistance to France was a defiance to all white civilization, and that all nations holding slaves had an interest in seeing this resistance broken. Madison responded that the American government had no obligation or intention to impose an embargo. It was up to France to enforce its own blockade. American merchants, he said, knew of France's attempt to stop their commerce, and knew, too, that the government of the United States would not protect them in their efforts to run the French blockade. He refused to contribute more to the French effort to stop the commerce.

Jefferson himself, in an interview with Pichon, described his predicament. As President, he explained, he had no power to interdict the commerce with Santo Domingo. Only Congress could take such action. And if the question were raised in Congress, he continued, there would be angry debate between representatives of the various groups interested in Santo Domingo. Congressmen would argue about the capacities of Negroes, the morality of dealing with them as commercial equals, and the prospect of an independent Negro republic in the Caribbean. Such a discussion would provoke the passions of American slaves. It would also give opportunity to those most resentful of interference with American commerce to fan the flames of patriotism and force the Navy to protect them. He concluded that the question ought not to be put to Congress. The best course for France, he advised, was to strengthen its blockade and hasten the reconquest.[58]

Jefferson was not wholly candid in this interview. His main reason for winking at the American commerce went deeper than his reluctance to exert executive authority or to stir up a hornet's nest in Congress. His eye was on New Orleans. Perhaps no problem in foreign affairs was more important to him than the "Mississippi question." Until America's right to navigate down the Mississippi to the Gulf of Mexico was placed beyond the vicissitudes of European politics, the union would be subject to continual harassment. Since France controlled New Orleans, Jefferson decided that his best policy for the time being was one of "wary neutrality." [59] He would permit American commerce to strengthen Toussaint's resistance until a crisis in Europe forced Napoleon to abandon his adventure in the New World. But he would avoid an open break with Napoleon, to keep alive the possibility of obtaining New Orleans peacefully.*

Rarely has a rather casually conceived policy borne such sweet fruit. Many of the factors that led to success were beyond Jefferson's control: the epidemic of yellow fever that claimed Leclerc himself and decimated the French force;† the brilliance and courage of Toussaint, and the persistence of Dessalines and Christophe after Toussaint had succumbed to Napoleon's treachery;[63] and the renewal of hostilities in Europe in the spring of 1803.[64] These developments may have been fortuitous, but Jefferson moved swiftly to take advantage of his opportunity. When Napoleon decided to quit in Santo Domingo and to sell, not just New Orleans, but the whole of Louisiana, he abruptly set aside his Constitutional scruples and accepted the offer.

Henry Adams has written, about the relationship between France's failure in Santo Domingo and America's acquisition of Louisiana, that "the prejudice of race alone blinded the American people to the debt they owed to the desperate courage of 500,000 Haitian Negroes who would not be enslaved." [65] There was a temptation to be grateful, not to the Negroes of Santo Domingo, but to France and Napoleon. Jefferson himself had no

---

* There is a temptation to make Jefferson's policy seem more conscious, more explicit than it really was. He certainly did not foresee that it would lead to the acquisition of Louisiana. He could not have counted on the dramatic suddenness and totality of Napoleon's decision, early in 1803, to abandon his New World empire and concentrate on Europe. Nevertheless, there is evidence that he knew the reconquest of Santo Domingo by France would be a demanding, if not impossible, task,[60] and that, by 1802, he was beginning to see the connection between Santo Domingo and the Mississippi question.[61]

† When the French, after a year and a half of struggle against the Negroes and the fever, evacuated in November 1803, only 8,000 survivors remained out of an original force of over 43,000 veteran troops.[62]

romantic illusions. He knew that Napoleon felt no tenderness for the United States, but had sold Louisiana to strengthen the Americans against Britain in the New World and to free the French Army to concentrate on Europe. Nor did Jefferson fear the prospect of a Negro republic in the Caribbean. In the period immediately following France's withdrawal from Santo Domingo, he seems to have discounted the apprehensions of slave owners that the success of the Haitian Negroes would provoke uprisings by slaves in the United States. Instead, he apparently shared the desire of merchants to take advantage of the new possibilities for trade.[66]

Soon after the French withdrew, the Negroes of Santo Domingo, under the command of Jean-Jacques Dessalines, proclaimed independence.[67] France refused to recognize the claim, preferring to regard the Negroes as rebels whose resistance would be broken as soon as French forces were free from peril in Europe. In the meantime, France called on all friendly nations to respect a French quarantine of the island.

At first, the Americans ignored this request. Merchants were determined to enjoy the lucrative trade. France was impotent to stop them. The position of the administration was that the United States had a right to trade with a nation that had established its independence *de facto*. In response to complaints from Pichon, Madison insisted that, even if Haiti were still a French colony, the American government had no obligation to stop its merchants.[68] There is no doubt that the administration was under pressure from Southern slave owners to discourage the intercourse.[69] Opposition arose from fear that the rebellion might prove contagious, reinforced by alarm that Santo Domingo might become a nation of pirates (this being a concern felt mostly by slave owners *on behalf of* merchants, rather than by the merchants themselves). Nevertheless, Jefferson's judgment that the Caribbean revolution was not an immediate danger to the slaveholding states, coupled with his concern that American merchants, rather than British, reap the profits of trade,[70] led him at first to restrain the Southern opposition and to permit the commerce.

During the course of 1804 another element entered the picture:

America's interest in "the Floridas." The Floridas at the time were a Spanish possession, but an object of great desire on the part of those (Southerners and Westerners) who were strongest in the Republican administration.[71] A letter of instruction from Secretary of State Madison to Robert Livingston, the American Minister in Paris, written March 31, 1804, indicates that the questions of trade with Santo Domingo and the acquisition of the Floridas came to be related in the eyes of the administration. Napoleon's influence with Spain was well known. Madison began his letter by presenting the American claim to "the Floridas" and suggesting that it was in France's interest to have Spain transfer them to the United States, "as the only effectual security against their falling into the hands of Great Britain." He then moved directly to a defense of the American right to trade. He never specifically related the two subjects, but it seems clear that the American hope for French support in the acquisition of Florida was one reason for the policies of 1805–1806 toward Santo Domingo.

Throughout the latter half of 1804 the volume of American trade with Santo Domingo increased, as did the intensity of French diplomatic protests. The French were incensed at rumors of a public subscription in Philadelphia to pay the cost of arming the American merchant marine. Pichon complained of "private war" against France and urged the American government to prohibit and punish these "illegal acts." Early in 1805 Congress in part obliged by passing a law that forced the owners of armed merchantmen to post bond equal to twice the value of their ship as a guarantee that arms would be used only in self-defense and not sold in the West Indies.[72]

The act of 1805 failed to satisfy the French purpose. American commerce continued to run through the French blockade. A convoy of twelve ships returned to New York on May 18, 1805 after a successful voyage to Santo Domingo, and a banquet celebrating the achievement was held aboard one of them, an armed merchantman named the *Indostan*. In the presence of numerous public officials, including Rufus King and Edward Livingston, brother of the former American minister to France, toasts were drunk to

The commerce of the US! May its sails be unfurled in every sea and as free as the winds which fill them.

The government of Haiti, founded on the only legitimate basis cf all authority: the people's choice! May it be as durable as its principles are pure.[73]

Infuriated by the continuing American commerce and by these public insults, the French renewed the pressure on Jefferson. Probing a vulnerable point in the administration's armor, Talleyrand instructed the new French Ambassador, Louis Turreau, to appeal to America's racial prejudice. In his letter to Turreau of July 5, 1805, he urged him to emphasize that

The existence of an armed Negro people, occupying places that they have despoiled by the most criminal acts, is a horrible spectacle for all the white nations; all of them should feel that, by allowing them to continue in that state, they are sparing incendiaries and assassins.[74]

Turreau's protest to Madison, delivered on October 14, 1805, described "the rebels of Santo Domingo" as "the reproach and refuse of nature," and called the American commerce with them "ignoble and criminal." He enclosed a letter from Talleyrand demanding that the United States government interdict "every private adventure . . . destined to the ports of Santo Domingo occupied by the rebels." [75]

At first, Jefferson resisted France's bullying. There were still over 500 American vessels employed in trade with Santo Domingo.[76] The owners of these ships constituted a powerful interest. The shock of the initial strike for emancipation and independence in Santo Domingo had been weathered without disrupting slavery in the American South. Furthermore, the internal difficulties faced by the rulers of Santo Domingo were keeping them fully occupied and impotent to initiate guerrilla activities in the American South or to commit piracy against American commerce.

Nevertheless, pressures were mounting against the President's policy of *laissez faire*. These became manifest in mid-December 1805, when Senator George Logan, a Republican leader from Pennsylvania, asked leave to bring in a bill to suspend all American commerce with Santo Domingo.[77] Both Britain and France, he said, viewed Santo Domingo as a threat to their West Indian holdings and had asked the American government to prohibit merchants from sending arms and supplies to the Negro rebels.

He maintained that the act of 1803 had proved inadequate and unenforceable. Stronger measures were urgently needed. Calling attention to the racial aspect, he asked:

[I]s it sound policy to cherish the black population of Santo Domingo whilst we have a similar population in our Southern states, in which, should an insurrection take place, the government of the United States is bound to render effectual aid to our fellow-citizens in that part of the union? [78]

Both the "immediate honor and future peace of the United States" were at stake. He urged quick action to suspend all support for the rebellious Negroes.

His motion was not well received. John Quincy Adams complained that the French and British protests cited by Logan had been received before the passage of the act of 1805. Senator Mitchill noted that the American Revolution had been fought in part to free this country from Europe's attempt to dictate our commercial policy. He argued that American merchants had a perfect right to trade with Santo Domingo. [79] James Jackson presented the planter's point of view. When peace came to Europe, "it must and will then become the interest of every nation of Europe, having colonies in the West Indies, to extirpate this horde or ship them off to some other place." Americans, by trading with the Negroes, became "their allies—their supporters and protectors." If we continued this trade in defiance of French authority, when France returned, it would expect the United States to grant "asylum" to Negroes who refused to return to slavery. Hillhouse ridiculed this argument, terming it a "bugbear." Jackson replied that it was easy enough for "the honorable gentlemen from Connecticut . . . safe and remote from the scene of action," to term his fears a "bugbear." As for himself, he did not hesitate to admit that the "horrid scenes" of Santo Domingo frightened him, as they did most other Southerners.

The exchange, as usual where slavery was concerned, was bitter, but the result for the time being was stalemate. The best Logan could achieve was a resolution asking the President to submit "documents and papers . . . relative to complaints by the government of France." [80]

On January 3, 1806, a week after the adoption of Logan's resolution, Turreau wrote to Madison demanding an answer to his protest of October 14. A week later, "surprised" by the intensity of French feeling,[81] Jefferson succumbed to the pressure and laid the diplomatic correspondence before Congress. When Logan, a few days later, resubmitted his motion for a bill "to suspend commercial intercourse" between the United States and Santo Domingo, only the badly outnumbered Federalists were opposed.[32]

Now that the President had signaled his acquiescence, action on the bill proceeded swiftly. A draft prepared by Logan was considered, then amended, then sent back to a committee chaired by Abraham Baldwin. Baldwin, a Georgian, had faithfully served the interests of slaveholders throughout a long and often distinguished public career. His committee added amendments to the bill that stiffened the penalties and narrowed the definition of "emergencies" justifying exemptions.[83]

But before a vote on the bill was taken, Samuel White, a Federalist from Delaware, set forth the objections of his party. "The people of Santo Domingo are fighting to preserve not only their independence as a community, but their liberty as individuals." Americans, having engaged in a similar struggle not many years before, ought readily to sympathize with these oppressed people, who had undertaken "to take their stand among the nations of the world." But instead of extending sympathy, the proponents of this bill sought "to starve the people of Santo Domingo into submission to their enemies." He did not want to be misunderstood; he deprecated "as sincerely as any man" the prospect that Negroes from Santo Domingo might come to the United States, "either as friends or enemies." But that, he said, was not the real issue. Americans incurred no obligation to receive these people as citizens by trading with them. On the contrary, by conducting their international commerce for them, American merchants were preventing them from developing a navy of their own and were thus helping to confine them to the island of Santo Domingo. Was it not better policy, he asked, to continue to trade with the island, profiting from the commerce and at the same time forestalling the development of pirates in the Caribbean? Americans had every right in international law to engage in this trade. The only explanation for this bill, he said, was a craven desire to anticipate and serve the wishes of France, unable alone to enforce its Caribbean policy. In his view, America's heritage and national self-respect coincided with commercial interests and with the canons of international law to demand the defeat of Logan's bill.[84]

The Republicans did not pause to answer White's speech, but proceeded directly to the vote, passing the embargo by 21 to 8. Again, only the Federalists were opposed—five from New England, two from Delaware, and one from North Carolina.[85]

Consideration by the House was even quicker. An attempt was made to pass the embargo the day it was received from the Senate. The only serious controversy arose over a suggestion to remove the one-year limit contained in the Senate bill. Several Republican leaders urged that the limit be struck, but were defeated when Peter Early, noting that the measure was already long overdue, called for an end to quibbling about details. The Republican steamroller did pause long enough to allow the Federalists to raise a brief cry of anguish. Samuel Dana, of Connecticut, conjured up the specter of "a black Algiers," warning that these "rude, untutored sons of nature, fired with the full force of the *lex talionis*," would be driven to piracy. His colleague John Cotton Smith complained that the measure had been "dictated by the government of France." Republicans responded by describing the bill as "an act of justice." John Eppes, of Virginia, the President's nephew, asked whether anyone in the House meant to argue that the Negroes of Santo Domingo were legitimately free. "In such a case, he will cover himself with detestation, [defending] a system that would bring immediate and horrible destruction on the fairest portion of America."

When the vote was taken, the Senate version passed, 93 to 26, without amendment.[86] Three days later, February 28, 1806, Jefferson signed into law an act that, according to Henry Adams,

violated the principles of international law, sacrificed the interests of Northern commerce, strained the powers of the Constitution, as formerly construed by the party of State-rights, and, taken in all its relations, might claim distinction among the most disgraceful statutes ever enacted by the United States government.[87]

Why did Jefferson sign this act? Until January 1806 he seems to have sided with the merchants against the planters, at least to the point of showing a kind of "salutary neglect" toward the trade of Yankees with Santo Domingo. But then he changed sides, signaling the switch by forwarding the French protests to Congress. There seem to have been two reasons, both stemming from a desire to accommodate France. First, his perennial quarrel with Britain was becoming more and more intense. British impressment of American sailors and spoliations against commerce made him sympathetic toward Britain's foes. Second, he wanted Florida, and he thought Napoleon held the key. In a letter to General John Armstrong, the American Minister in Paris, he noted that among the "inducements" Armstrong could use "to produce favorable dispositions" in France toward the American acquisition of Florida was the embargo against Santo Domingo.[88]

One historian calls Jefferson Machiavellian for trying to obtain Florida by starving the Haitians.[89] But would Machiavelli have approved a policy whereby a leader voluntarily yielded a favor to a "prince" like Napoleon without the semblance of a guarantee that the prize he sought would be delivered in return? The embargo against Santo Domingo was continued, by annual renewal, until 1810, but the Floridas were not obtained until Napoleon's influence on American affairs had been neutralized by his European foes.[90] The blunt fact is that there was no good reason to suspend trade with Santo Domingo in 1806.

Santo Domingo was "the first Latin American colony to win independence, the second nation in the Western world to separate from the European mother country." [91] As such, and as a natural trading partner for American merchants, it might have become an ally and friend, an associate in the task of exhibiting to the Old World the benefits of republican liberty. But it was also "the first Negro state in modern times . . . the only state to found its independence upon a revolution of slaves." [92] In this guise, it was anathema to half of the union and, at best, an anomaly to the rest.

While the Northern half of the union governed the nation's affairs, coexistence, sometimes even co-operation, was possible between the two countries. When the Southerners gained command, fate decreed that the administration should depend for the realization of its fondest wish (the acquisition of New Orleans) upon the determination of Negroes to be free and independent of their white rulers. But as soon as the wish for Louisiana had been satisfied, antipathy rooted in fear was allowed to have its sway.

At its founding, the United States was, in part, a nation of slaveholders. In the conduct of national affairs, the federal government was responsible under the Constitution for the protection of property, including property in slaves. Officials of the federal government, particularly in the field of foreign affairs, were thus bound in duty to protect slave owners against assaults on their human property. Yet the Federalists in the mid-1790's, while negotiating and ratifying Jay's Treaty, allowed themselves to be distracted from this responsibility by the combined effects of their bad conscience about slavery and their determination to serve other interests. Against the treaty, slaveholders could justly complain that the Federalist administration had sacrificed their rights. To the extent that doubt about the right of slavery led Jay to yield on the question of compensation, the treaty was truly unfair to the South.

Events during the following decade showed that attitudes toward slavery could jeopardize the nation's interest in the opposite direction as well. To justify the embargo against Santo Domingo, administration leaders in Congress relied mainly on fear that the rebellion on the island might spread to America, either by the contagion of example or by the work of Negro guerrillas and pirates. To forestall this threat, they insisted on a total quarantine. They hoped, too, that their policy would help the United States to acquire the Floridas.

The Federalists responded that the quarantine would not bring about the collapse of Haitian independence, but would only encourage the Negroes to become self-reliant, and that yielding to Napoleon's demands in the Caribbean brought the Floridas no closer. On both these points, the Federalists were vindicated. The policy of the Republicans was not based upon a realistic appraisal of danger and prospects. Santo Domingo was a terrifying spectacle, and useful when slave owners needed a "parade of horrors" to frighten those who had little understanding of conditions in Santo Domingo or in the American South, or of the differences between the two. But in 1806 Santo Domingo posed no real danger to the United States. Besides, New England merchants hated to lose trade valued at $4 million a year[93] simply because planters who controlled the administration were determined to obliterate all evidence that blacks might gain their liberty by fighting for it.

Slavery's role in foreign policy reflected the fact that almost no one in the union was comfortable with the institution. The bad conscience of Northerners and the fears of Southerners gave opportunities that men like Grenville and Napoleon were quick to seize and exploit. Until the union resolved this tension, it would continue to give a valuable hostage to the fortunes of international politics.

10

Slavery and the Territories from the Northwest Ordinance to the Missouri Compromise

THE refrain that Congress had no power under the Constitution to legislate on the question of slavery has been frequently encountered. The foreign slave trade and the problem of fugitives across state lines were explicit exceptions, but these were external to the institution of slavery itself. According to prevalent doctrine, the Constitution assigned to Congress a specific list of powers. Control over slavery within the states was not included. The nation's vast extent, the variety of practice and experience with slavery in different regions, and a deep-seated preference for mild government induced the framers to "reserve" control over slavery to the states. Southerners, and many Northerners as well, were convinced that the consummation of a "more perfect union" depended on the willingness of politicians at the national level to abide by this determination.

By 1787, when the Constitution was framed, Congress had already assumed responsibility for a great expanse of land northwest of the Ohio River. Within a few years after 1787, as deeds of cession were completed by Virginia, North Carolina, South Carolina, and Georgia, Congress gained control over several sizable tracts south of the Ohio River. Then, soon after the turn of the century, the United States doubled in size by acquiring Louisiana. Under the Constitution these territorial holdings were to be governed by Congress until they could be settled and organized as new states.

Yet herein lay an enormous difficulty. One great task of government at that time was to deal with slavery, either by providing regulations (slave codes and codes for "free blacks") or by prohibiting it. How did the framers expect Congress to discharge this Constitutional responsibility, even before the Louisiana Purchase, without getting involved in controversies over slavery? The answer tells much about the framers' handling of the problem of slavery and their expectations for Congressional responsibility in this area of policy.[1]

Soon after the Revolutionary War was over, Congress began trying to establish government in the transmontane territory of the United States. Several factors made this responsibility difficult to discharge. Leaders from the original settlements along the coast disagreed on the impact these frontier regions would or should be allowed to have on national politics. Many who thought the impact would be beneficial wanted to carve the territory into relatively large districts, set minimal population standards for districts applying to become states, and admit new states quickly, on the basis of equality with the original states. They were opposed on each of these points by men who regarded the unknown quantity to the west with apprehension.[2] Moreover, politicians were anxious to write laws for the West that would mold it in a likeness they knew and admired, or, in some cases, dreamed about. New Englanders, for example, hoped to encourage the development of a region full of tidy villages, each gathered around a scrubbed Congregational church. Many Southerners had a different image, in which large landholdings, worked by slaves, were the prominent feature.

During the years immediately following the war, these conflicting pictures competed for the minds and votes of the delegates in Congress. The effort to establish "temporary government of the western territory" led to a report in March 1784 by a committee chaired by Thomas Jefferson. It contained a proviso to the effect that there should be "neither slavery nor involuntary servitude" in any part of the western territory after 1800.[3] A month later, Richard Dobbs Spaight, of North Carolina, moved that these words be struck. On matters of this kind, the Articles of Confederation required that a majority, seven states, be recorded in favor. On April 19, 1784, of the ten states "present" in Congress at the time, six—New Hampshire, Massachusetts, Rhode Island, Connecticut, New York, Pennsylvania—voted "aye"; three—Maryland, Virginia (Jefferson was outvoted by Samuel Hardy and John F. Mercer), and South Carolina—voted 'nay"; one—North Carolina—was divided.[4] The result was a disappointing defeat for Jefferson and his friends, who had fallen just one vote short of including the ban on slavery in America's first ordinance for the West. If New Jersey had had a full delegation on that day (Samuel Dick voted "aye," but the Articles required that a state have two delegates in Congress to have its vote counted), if William Grayson or James Madison had been in the Virginia delegation instead of Hardy or Mercer, or if Delaware had been present, the story might have been different.

Such speculations led Rufus King to try again in 1785. On March 16, he gained an 8-to-3 victory* for a motion to commit a proposition differing from Jefferson's only in instituting the ban immediately, rather than in 1800. On April 6, his committee submitted a draft resolve reintroducing the delay until 1800, and adding a fugitive-slave clause[6]—the first appearance on the national scene of this clause.[7] Despite these modifications, he was unable to bring the issue to a vote, and the matter was set aside until 1787.

The appearance, from these incidents, that the Continental Congress came close to banning slavery from the entire western territory of the United States is misleading. The most significant consequence of Jefferson's effort came late in 1784, when the North Carolina legislature repealed the act ceding its territory west of the Appalachians to the federal government.[8] In fact, the federal government did not in the mid-1780's have undisputed title to any of the western territory. Before Virginia and South Carolina would enact, and North Carolina re-enact, clear and realistic deeds of cession, they were waiting to be satisfied that Congress would exercise its governance in a fashion acceptable to prospective Southern settlers. Northerners, many of whom were not enthusiastic about the West, fearing an alliance between

---

* The vote was strictly along sectional lines: New Hampshire, Massachusetts, Rhode Island, Connecticut, New York, New Jersey, Pennsylvania, and Maryland against Virginia, North Carolina, and South Carolina.[5]

Southern and Western agriculture against the mercantile East, were doubly determined to prevent the rise of a slave empire in the West. Thus the sentiment of the country had clearly been overreached. The result was stalemate for a Congress virtually impotent anyway to impose its will on contrarily determined states.

The stalemate persisted until 1787. Efforts to frame an ordinance for the West foundered on the inability of Congress to agree on terms for the admission of new states. Pressure to resolve the issue increased as several groups petitioned for permission to migrate westward and establish settlements.

Finally, on July 9, 1787, a new committee was appointed to draft an ordinance for the West. Within two days, a draft bill of "An Ordinance for the Government of the Territory Northwest of the River Ohio" had been distilled from earlier versions.[9] It outlined a governmental structure headed by a federally appointed governor, and including, once the population in the territory reached "five thousand free male inhabitants," a general assembly and a legislative council. It went on to outline "the fundamental principles of civil and religious liberty, which form the basis whereon these republics, their laws and constitutions, are erected." This list of "fundamental principles" came in the form of five "articles of compact," outlining the prospective state boundaries,* and guaranteeing such things as religious liberty, trial by jury, and the "encouragement" of education.

The draft was read a second time on July 12. The following day saw the hasty climax of an issue that had been agitated for nearly a decade. With William Grayson presiding, Nathan Dane, of Massachusetts, moved that a sixth "article of compact," banning slavery in the Northwest Territory, be added. To quiet Southern alarm, he incorporated into his amendment a clause proposed by Rufus King in 1785 providing that slaves escaping into the territory might be reclaimed by their owners. Without a murmur, Dane's amendment was accepted. Then the ordinance

---

* All these arrangements, and particularly the boundaries, were subject to the consent of Virginia, which had not yet enacted a satisfactory act of cession, and to the future judgment of Congress, which had discretion to form three, four, or five states out of the territory.

as a whole was brought to a vote and passed by the unanimous assent of the eight states present. The only individual who voted "nay" was Abraham Yates; he was overruled by his colleagues from New York Melancton Smith and John Haring.[10]

A consideration of the limits of the ordinance explains why a Congress dominated by Southerners—half of the eight states that voted on July 13 were Southern, nine of the eighteen individual delegates were Southerners, and the presiding officer was a Virginian—suddenly resolved this complicated issue in a way apparently inimical to Southern interests.[11] Previous drafts—Jefferson's ordinance of 1784, King's amendment of 1785, and a draft ordinance submitted by James Monroe in 1786[12]—had been directed at the entire western territory of the United States, and had thus invited the sectional collision that blocked them. The version of July 1787 sidestepped that collision by confining itself to the territory northwest of the Ohio River—that is, the region lying west of the mid-Atlantic states. The region west of Virginia, the Carolinas, and Georgia was tacitly set aside for future consideration.

In lending its support to the drafting and adoption of this ordinance for the Northwest, including its antislavery amendment, the South was not resigning itself to defeat. There were advantages in the arrangement finally adopted by Congress. For one thing, the South was by no means ready to concede that the Northwest would be its foe in national politics. Without slaves, settlers in the Northwest would be unlikely to grow indigo and tobacco, and would thus not be in direct competition with Southern planters.[13] But as farmers, they would be natural allies of Southern agrarians against the commercial men from the East.* By supporting a plan that encouraged rapid settlement, Southerners in Congress were hastening the day when these yeomen would add to the agrarian interest in the union.[15]

Additionally, acceptance may have arisen from the relationship between the question of territorial government and another issue

* Dane, encouraged by the thought that a company of New Englanders would get the first jump, saw in the West a potential ally for "Eastern politics," but few New England Federalists shared his optimism on this score. Jefferson anticipated a struggle for influence between the sections, with the outcome depending on which was settled first—the banks of the Ohio, by Southern yeomen, or the shores of the Great Lakes, by Yankees.[14]

with which it became "much entangled"—the struggle for the right of Americans to navigate the full length of the Mississippi River.[16] The interests of the sections on the latter question varied sharply, at times so seriously as to endanger the union. With the achievement of independence, the United States found itself confronted by Spain, a nation that was a potential partner in trade, valuable particularly because of its American colonies, and yet, by its control over the mouth of the Mississippi River, one that had power to inhibit the development of the West by preventing the flow of commerce into the Gulf of Mexico. Many Easterners were willing to exchange the right to navigate the Mississippi for commercial access to the Spanish Empire. Most Southerners, who were closer both geographically and in terms of interests to the western settlements, were prepared to fight, if necessary, for the right to navigate through New Orleans.

Negotiations for a treaty with Spain continued throughout the mid-1780's. Under the Articles of Confederation, the assent of nine states was required to ratify a treaty, and so both sections seemed relatively safe against an unfavorable bargain. But in August 1786 the instructions of Congress to John Jay, the Secretary for Foreign Affairs, included an authorization to see what advantages could be gained if the United States yielded its right to navigate the lower Mississippi for a term of twenty years. The vote affirming these instructions showed seven Northern states aligned against the five Southern states.[17] The outcome infuriated Southerners, who recognized that their determination to open the Mississippi River to American commerce was not shared by Jay and the majority of Congress. It also disappointed Easterners, who knew that seven states could not ratify a commercial treaty. The stalemate was serious enough to stimulate speculations about dividing the union into separate confederacies.[18]

Madison returned to Congress early in 1787 and straightway sought to undercut Jay's instructions. His motive, in part, was to reassure Southerners, many of whom had been frightened, on the eve of the Constitutional Convention, by Patrick Henry's warning not to augment the power of a government that treated vital Southern interests so lightly. Jay, in a report to Congress, admitted that he and the Spanish Ambassador had reached tenta-

tive agreement to ban American commerce from the lower Mississippi for the duration of the proposed treaty. Madison, implying
that Jay had yielded American rights unnecessarily, suggested,
first, that the negotiations with Spain be transferred to Madrid
and entrusted to Jefferson; then, after Jay objected bitterly to
this, that the instructions of August 1786 be rescinded. Six states
—New Jersey, Pennsylvania, Delaware, Virginia, North Carolina,
and Georgia—supported the latter proposal, one short of the
number needed to annul the instructions legally, but enough to
demonstrate that no treaty could be ratified if it sacrificed American claims to the navigation of the Mississippi.[19]

Jay, realizing that he could not negotiate on the basis of instructions having only the flimsiest legal sanction, asked for new
instructions. A committee to draft new orders was appointed,
having a majority of Southerners among its five members. On
July 4, 1787, the committee reported a set of instructions that
included an affirmation of America's right to navigate the length
of the Mississippi River. There the matter lay while the Congress
of the Confederation moved through its last days. Finally, in September 1788, the whole question of the treaty with Spain was referred to the new government, with a declaration of opinion in
favor of the report of July 4.[20]

Before the tide turned in favor of the Southern position on the
Mississippi question, Northerners hoped, and Southerners feared,
that Spanish interference with trade down the Mississippi would
eventually force western commerce up through the Great Lakes
and down the Hudson River. This flow would tend to tie the
West to the Northeast. But by mid-1787 there were indications
that Americans would fight, if necessary, rather than yield their
claim to navigate past New Orleans. If the Mississippi basin were
open to Americans, trade from the Northwest and from the territory southwest of the Ohio River would be expected to flow
south, thus helping to link the new settlements to the Southeastern states. Once this disposition to assert American rights became manifest, especially in the pivotal state of Pennsylvania,
Southerners thought they had good reason to favor the early admission of new states from the Northwest regardless of the standing of slavery in them.

Perhaps the most important reason for Southern support for the ordinance was that its passage signaled the end of the attempt to prohibit slavery south of the Ohio River. Timothy Pickering, in a letter to Rufus King, expressed the view that stood behind earlier efforts to include antislavery provisions as amendments to ordinances drafted for the whole western territory:

To suffer the continuance of slaves till they can be gradually emancipated, in states already overrun by them, may be pardonable because unavoidable without hazarding greater evils; but to introduce them into countries where none already exist . . . can never be forgiven.[21]

By agreeing in 1787 to separate the western territory at the Ohio River, Northerners were virtually conceding defeat in the effort to apply this doctrine south of the river. The desire of many Southerners to proceed with the settlement of the West was the best source of leverage for Northerners seeking to influence the territorial ordinances. By permitting Dane's amendment to pass, Southerners had demonstrated that their desire to see states organized in the West was stronger than their hope that slaveholders might move north of the Ohio. But by confining the ordinance to the Northwest, while leaving the areas that became Kentucky in 1792 and Tennessee in 1796 under the control of their parent states to the east in 1787,[22] Northerners were effectively leaving the territory south of the Ohio River open to slaveowning settlers from the states adjacent to it.

North Carolina passed a new act of cession in 1789, this time specifically providing that Congress could make no laws emancipating slaves in the ceded territory. Congress quickly accepted this grant, including its qualification. In the same year, Virginia ceded all claims to land northwest of the Ohio River, then consented that the district of Kentucky be erected into an independent state. To govern the territories thus committed to its keeping, Congress passed the Southwest Ordinance, applying the ordinance of 1787 to "the territory of the United States south of the river Ohio," but specifically omitting the prohibition of slavery.[23]

Throughout the period during which Kentucky and Tennessee were evolving through territorial status into full statehood, no effort was made to abolish slavery there by federal enactment.

Between February 1791 and June 1792 Kentucky was subject to the Southwest Ordinance of 1790. When it entered the union, the constitution of 1792 went into effect, giving slavery full legal status and depriving the state's legislature of "power to pass laws for the emancipation of slaves without the consent of their owners." [24] When the admission of Tennessee was being considered during the Fourth Congress, there was an effort by some Deep Southerners in the Senate to postpone action until it could be divided into more than one state, thereby giving Southern interests a greater increment of power in the Senate and the Electoral College. But the attempt was foiled by pressure from the House,[25] and Tennessee, already firmly committed to slavery, was admitted to the union in 1796.

No evidence has been found to indicate that Northerners made a specific bargain in 1787, gaining the antislavery provision in the Northwest Ordinance in exchange for a promise not to interfere with slavery south of the Ohio River. Indeed, no such explicit bargain was necessary. Slavery had already been introduced into the territory south of the river, and the Southern states that had claim to these areas had clearly indicated their determination to hold on until they could gain assurances that Congress would not try to abolish slavery there. Northerners were confronted, in the applications of Kentucky and Tennessee for statehood, by a *fait accompli*. By stalling in the hopes of overthrowing slavery in these regions, Congress would only have alienated these frontiersmen, whose attachment to the government on the East Coast was sometimes tenuous to begin with.

Yet by dividing the western territory at the Ohio River, Congress was in effect extending the Mason-Dixon Line to the Mississippi River. It was with an eye to this understanding that Southerners later argued that Congress had no power to legislate on the subject of slavery, even though the Constitution appeared to give plenary powers over the territories.

During the first decade under the Constitution, this tacit understanding was challenged in Congress only once. This came in 1798, while the Fifth Congress was considering an act "authorizing the establishment of a government in the Mississippi Territory."

In some respects, the Mississippi Territory was like the North-west Territory: it was the object of incomplete cessions and com-peting claims by several states; and Congress had to frame an ordinance of government before these legal matters were finally adjusted. Thus Congress had greater responsibility to provide government in Mississippi (as it had had in the Northwest) than in Kentucky and Tennessee—although the latitude it had had in the Northwest was restricted in Mississippi by the fact that 5,000 "souls" had already settled there by 1798.[26]

The bill to provide government in Mississippi was debated in the House during March 1798. The main issue arose from the anxiety of the Georgia delegation lest the act prejudice the claims of Georgians in the territory. Robert Goodloe Harper, the bill's manager, assured them that it would not. Nevertheless, the Geor-gians, noting that this was "the last instance in which this ques-tion of cession could be presented to Congress," pleaded that the act to establish government be delayed until negotiations with Georgia over conflicting claims could be completed. Harper op-posed any delay:

[T]hese people are at the distance of six hundred miles from the ordi-nary jurisdiction of the government of Georgia, which distance is a con-tinued desert, in which are several nations of Indians. It cannot be expected, therefore, that the state of Georgia will or can extend her gov-ernment thither. So that one of our most valuable frontiers will be left in an unprotected and disorderly state.[27]

The issue was compromised by the addition of language guaran-teeing that the passage of the ordinance would not affect any claims to land in the territory.

This routine and relatively amicable discussion suddenly be-came embittered when George Thacher, a Yankee Federalist, moved that slavery be prohibited in the Mississippi Territory. As it stood, the draft ordinance authorized the President to establish in Mississippi a government "in all respects similar to that now exercised in the territory northwest of the Ohio, excepting and excluding the last article of the ordinance made . . . by the late Congresss." [28] Thacher's motion was that the "'excepting clause,'" prohibiting slavery, be struck. He ascribed his motion to a con-cern for "the rights of man." [29] In the context of the Fifth Congress, there was a certain irony in the fact that these words fell from a man whose party was urging the passage of laws redefining the crime of sedition. The irony was not unintentional. Thacher and his Federalist friends had been subjected to sharp criticism by opponents who felt that the proposed alien and sedition laws showed a defective regard for the principles of republican government.* Much of this abuse had come from Southern Republicans, especially the Virginians. Now Thacher was trying to turn the tables, confronting Republicans with a motion based on the argument that slavery violated the "rights of man."

If Thacher expected to embarrass and divide the Republicans with his motion, the debate that followed must have been a disappointment to him. In the first place, it was not the Republicans from Virginia, but the Federalists from South Carolina, who took greatest offense. For Harper, the salient human right where slavery was concerned was the right of property. He pointed out that Thacher's motion would be "a decree of banishment to all the [white] persons settled there, and of exclusion to all those intending to go there." The second salvo came, not from a Virginian, but from a Boston Federalist, Harrison Gray Otis, who welcomed the chance to show that there were Northerners, loyal Federalists, who would not

interfere with the Southern states as to the species of property in question. . . . He thought it was not the business of those who had nothing to do with that kind of property to interfere with that right; and he really wished that the gentlemen who held slaves might not be deprived of the means of keeping them in order.

* A fine example of the way in which Federalists used slave ownership to parry the thrusts of the Virginians came in a speech by James Bayard, of Delaware, during a debate on "foreign intercourse": "Sir, when I look around this hall and observe how parties are composed; when I see some men who come from a land of real equality, many of whom have been educated in laborious employment, and none of whom can boast of but a few paternal acres, and find that they are called aristocrats, while, on the other hand, men who can count in their train a hundred slaves, whose large domains, like feudal baronies, are peopled with the humblest vassals, are styled democrats, I am astonished that the weakest of mankind can be imposed on by such an abuse of words. I know that this is a delicate subject . . . but when I see these high-priests of liberty so zealously proclaiming freedom on one hand, while on the other they are rivetting the chains of slavery, I cannot forbear tearing aside the veil which conceals the truth from the world." [39]

Thomas Hartley, another Federalist, remarked that he had considered making a motion similar to Thacher's, but had decided against it, and would now vote against the proposal. "He found it would interfere with, and be a serious attack on, the property of" settlers already in the Mississippi Territory.[31]

The only speakers who came to Thacher's defense were two Republicans from the North, Joseph Varnum and Albert Gallatin. Varnum took the good Republican ground that "where there was a disposition to retain a part of our species in slavery, there could not be a proper respect for the rights of mankind." He noted that the normal rebuttal to abolitionist proposals was to plead that it was unsafe to emancipate Negroes on account of their great numbers in certain sections. Now Congress had an opportunity to act before slaves had been taken into Mississippi in great numbers. "He hoped, therefore, Congress would have so much respect for the rights of humanity as not to legalize the existence of slavery any further than it at present exists."[32]

Gallatin devoted his speech to a rebuttal of various objections that had been, or could be, made to Thacher's proposal. He insisted that the amendment need have no effect on "the peace, tranquillity or property of any other state." Stressing the urgency of adopting the prohibition, he contended that this was the last chance Congress would have to prevent the spread of slavery into the Southwest. He argued:

[I]f this amendment is rejected, we establish slavery for the country, not only during its temporary government, but for all the time it is a state; for by the constant admission of slaves, the number will increase . . . and when the territory shall become a state, the interest of the holder will be such as to procure a constitution which shall admit of slavery, and it will be thereby made permanent.

He pleaded that the amendment was not only timely, but Constitutional. Earlier the argument had been made that it would strike at the property of Georgians living in the Mississippi Territory, before the claims of Georgia had been finally adjudicated. Responding to this argument, he observed that Congress had decided to assume responsibility for governing Mississippi, and that one of the tasks of government was to decide what to do with slavery. "Was there any more reason," he asked, "for excepting this jurisdiction [that is, over slavery] than any other?" [33]

Unfortunately for Thacher's amendment, the short answer to Gallatin's question was "yes." There was widespread agreement, fully shared by Southerners, that effective government should be established in the territory west of Georgia, and that legal niceties regarding the claims of Georgia should not prevent the dispatch of this business. Southerners interested in promoting the settlement of this "valuable frontier" were leaders among those who sought to disregard the objections raised by Georgians. But it is not hard to imagine what effect the adoption of Thacher's motion would have had on this disposition.

Southerners had various motives for wanting to establish government in Mississippi. South Carolinians and Georgians looked upon the area as a vast and rich opportunity for plantation agriculture. Harper, who represented the piedmont region of South Carolina, clearly expressed the eagerness of his constituents to expand their operations southwestward when he responded rather impatiently to the objections of the Georgians.

To Virginians, Mississippi bore a slightly different aspect. Debt-laden tobacco planters in the Old Dominion were overinvested in slaves and may have seen Mississippi as a market for their surplus. In addition, many still hoped that conditions might one day permit an emancipation of slaves. The principal factor weighing against it was their density, which made the presence of free Negroes extremely dangerous. Several Virginians in Congress spoke for this opinion when they urged that Thacher's motion be rejected so that slavery might be thinned out over a wider area, and thus made both more humane in its discipline and less compelling in its hold on Southern society.[34]

Thus Virginians and Deep Southerners shared the expectation and determination that the new territory be open to slavery. If Thacher's motion had been adopted, there can be little doubt that Southerners would have retreated behind the defense offered by Georgia's incomplete cession and insisted that the United States could not govern in a way so inimical to the interests of a state before that state had fully yielded its jurisdiction.

The vote on Thacher's motion showed twelve supporters.

There was no roll call, but the debate indicated that sympathy for the proposal came from a few Northerners, of both parties, who wanted to take advantage of this "last chance" to contain slavery and perhaps to show that the South could be cultivated without slaves.

This debate shows that the compromise of 1787, extending the Mason-Dixon Line to the Mississippi River via the Ohio River, was widely accepted at least until the turn of the century. The prevailing argument in 1798 was that the application of Article VI of the Northwest Ordinance to the Mississippi Territory would be "a decree of banishment to all the persons settled there, and of exclusion to all those intending to go there." Just as the Northwest Territory "belonged" rightfully to men from New England and the mid-Atlantic states, so Mississippi "belonged" to Southerners. Following this reasoning, it was thought unfair to lay conditions on the settlement of Mississippi that would make it impossible for Southerners to settle there into a familiar way of life.

Another significant item emerging from this debate was Gallatin's point on the question of Congressional jurisdiction over national territory, that the Constitutional power to provide government in the territories included the power to regulate or abolish slavery. His argument, as applied to Mississippi, was overcome by the contention that national jurisdiction in this case was limited by the lingering claims of Georgia. This left the implication that where no state had a claim Congressional authority over territories was plenary. Perhaps Gallatin's doctrine went unchallenged because few men foresaw any further application, since the Mississippi Territory in 1798 was the last remaining region under national control, apart from the Northwest, for which the decision to exclude slavery had already been made.

Nevertheless, Gallatin's doctrine had solid foundation in the language of the Constitution. Though few men in 1787 or 1798 could foresee the event, it was not long before Congress, legislating for a newly acquired territory, had to decide which course to adopt: to extend the Mason-Dixon Line, across the Mississippi and on west; to let nature and "popular sovereignty" take their course; or, through the vigorous exercise of its Constitutional authority over territories, to restrict slavery to the area east of the Mississippi River.

Despite Thacher's last-minute effort, Congressional governance over territories held during the eighteenth century was exercised in accordance with the compromise of 1787. At the beginning of the nineteenth century, however, a series of unexpected developments created a Constitutional problem that had not been anticipated in 1787.

The main development was the startling decision of Napoleon, following the disastrous failure of his army to suppress the revolt in Santo Domingo, to dismantle France's American empire. The result was the sale of Louisiana to America, a transaction that doubled the size of the United States.

Napoleon's offer raised Constitutional and political problems that were especially serious for a President and party that had won popular support on the basis of a promise to exercise only those powers of government specifically set forth in the Constitution. Nowhere in the Constitution was the power to acquire or receive territory vouchsafed either to the President, Congress, or a combination of the two. Nowhere was power given to lay down rules for the assimilation of new territory into the union. To get a fair idea of Republican orthodoxy on these questions, one need only imagine the reaction in Virginia if John Adams and the Federalists had bought Canada from Great Britain in 1798 and then begun to lay off this acquisition into states.

But 1803 was another year, and Republicans in power were different from Republicans in opposition. The desire to gain control over the mouth of the Mississippi had been a guiding star of policy for leaders of Jefferson's administration ever since the recognition of American independence. When Napoleon made his offer, Jefferson moved quickly to seize the opportunity, knowing that what had been impetuously offered might be abruptly withdrawn. The American ministers in Paris, Robert R. Livingston and James Monroe, signed the treaty of cession on May 2, 1803, less than a month after Napoleon had informed his ministers that he intended to sell Louisiana to "those republicans whose friendship I seek." [35]

Throughout the summer of 1803, Jefferson considered various ways of redeeming the dangerous Constitutional precedents thereby established, and of limiting the impact of those further acts necessary to conclude the treaty with France and establish government in the territory. He summarized his thinking in a letter written in August to Senator John Breckinridge, of Kentucky. Congress, he said,

must . . . appeal to *the nation* for an additional article to the Constitution. . . . The Constitution has made no provision for our holding foreign territory, still less for incorporating foreign nations into our union. The Executive, in seizing the fugitive occurrence which so much advances the good of their country, have done an act beyond the Constitution. The Legislature, in casting behind them metaphysical subtleties and risking themselves like faithful servants, must ratify and pay for it, and throw themselves on their country for doing for them unauthorized what we know they would have done for themselves had they been in a situation to do it.[36]

The vistas of Constitutional interpretation opened by this passage must have haunted Jefferson as long as he lived.

He issued a call for a special meeting of Congress to consider the ratification of the treaty. As time for the special session drew near, Republican leaders in Congress, not wanting to give Napoleon an excuse to withdraw his offer, determined to act with as little public debate as possible, particularly over Constitutional difficulties. Jefferson expressed his anxiety over this course in a letter to Senator Wilson Cary Nicholas, of Virginia:

I had rather ask an enlargement of power from the nation, where it is found necessary, than to assume it by a construction which would make our powers boundless. Our peculiar security is in the possession of a written Constitution. Let us not make it a blank paper by construction. . . .

Having put his fears on record, he then told Nicholas that if Republicans in Congress felt differently, he would "acquiesce with satisfaction, confiding that the good sense of our country will correct the evil of construction when it shall produce ill effects." [37]

The dilemma posed by the peculiar opportunity to buy Louisiana was a serious one for the Republicans, especially for Southern

Republicans. They were "strict constructionists," because of their preference for government that was mild and familiar, limited and local. Those in the South had a special reason for wanting to restrain the federal government from involvement in domestic affairs: the fear that slavery might be overthrown or subjected to inimical regulation by a government dominated by people who had no slaves and relatively few Negro neighbors. Southerners who found "peculiar security . . . in the possession cf a written Constitution" were especially determined to maintain and fortify Constitutional safeguards against the encroachments of federal power.

On the other hand, the acquisition of New Orleans had long been "the chief ambition of Southern statesmen in foreign affairs." [38] Jefferson recognized that the purchase of New Orleans required the violation of some of his deepest political principles: strict construction, the reduction of the national debt, perhaps even the avoidance of entanglements with Great Britain. Yet he was willing to lay these considerations aside for New Orleans alone.

Secretary of State Madison admitted to John Quincy Adams, then a Senator from Massachusetts, that "the Constitution had not provided for such a case as this," but urged that the matter be judged by the "magnitude of the object." [39] By leaping at Napoleon's offer, the Jeffersonians opted for a continental nation, confident that they were carrying out the will of "the nation," that the people would gratefully maintain them in office, and that they would be able to assimilate the newly acquired territory into the Constitutional union without depriving the original states of the liberties they expected under mild Republican rule.

Thus, the exigencies of dealing with an impetuous dictator, plus the widespread confidence enjoyed by the administration, induced the Republicans to proceed without waiting for the sanction of a Constitutional amendment. Jefferson greeted the special session of the Eighth Congress on October 17, 1803 with a message that outlined the advantages to the United States under the proposed treaty: full control over the Mississippi River, acquisition of a territory of almost unimaginable fertility, and a broader area "for the blessings of freedom and equal laws." He bade the Senate ratify the treaty, and the House appropriate funds for the purchase.[40]

Both houses quickly moved to comply. Meeting in a secret session, the Senate quickly ratified the treaty, then proceeded to authorize the President to "take possession" of the territory. A slim majority of New Englanders—two Senators each from Massachusetts, New Hampshire, and Connecticut—was opposed. The rest of the Senate (including two men each from Vermont and Rhode Island) was in favor of proceeding to assert American control over Louisiana.[41] In the House, John Randolph's motion committing the House to frame provisions carrying the treaty into effect was also approved overwhelmingly, despite considerable opposition from New England. Massachusetts voted against the treaty, 9 to 6, and Connecticut cast all five of its votes in the negative. Sentiment west and south of New England, however, solidly supported the initiative taken by the administration. Pennsylvania gave all seventeen of its votes to the motion. Outside of New England, only one Congressman from Maryland and four from Virginia indicated disapproval.[42]

The opposition of New Englanders in both houses stemmed from several sources. Some thought it a mistake to extend the territory of the United States so far. One of the dogmas of Whig orthodoxy was that republics could not exceed a certain size without trenching into the liberties of citizens. Breckinridge denounced this as "an old and hackneyed argument," [43] but to men like Timothy Pickering, of Massachusetts, and Uriah Tracy, of Connecticut, it still served as a ground of opposition to the purchase. More serious was the feeling among Federalists that Jefferson was right in believing that the acquisition of Louisiana would seal the triumph of the Republicans over the Federalists "forever," even in New England, unless drastic steps were taken. Gouverneur Morris found some satisfaction in the fact that the Republicans had secured their triumph by strengthening the Presidency more than Federalists, even in Washington's day, had dared to do. But the dominant feeling among New England Federalists was one of desperation. When they considered the impact of "this new, immense, unbounded world" on the contours of American politics, they foresaw that "thick-skinned beasts [would] crowd Congress Hall—buffaloes from the head of the Missouri and alligators from the Red River." [44] Sensing that their power in the union had been dealt a mortal wound, a few High Federalists went so far as to begin to broach publicly the idea of a Northern secession.[45]

Few even among the Federalists went to the extreme of advocating disunion, however. Most of them knew that they were impotent to arrest the momentum of expansion. Instead, they occupied themselves with suggestions for reconciling the acquisition with the Constitution. They urged that the newly acquired territory be regarded as a colony and governed as part of an American empire. Republicans countered by citing the treaty of purchase, Article III of which promised that "the inhabitants [meaning, of course, the *white* inhabitants] of the ceded territory shall be incorporated into the union, and admitted, as soon as possible, according to the principles of the Federal Constitution, to the enjoyment of all the rights, advantages, and immunities of citizens." When the Federalists argued that this article rendered the treaty unconstitutional, Republicans responded by characterizing the situation as unique and insisting that unless the (white) inhabitants of Louisiana were welcomed as citizens and equal partners in the union,* all American territory west of the Appalachians would be likely to secede.[47]

The bill to provide temporary government in Louisiana originated in the Senate in December 1803. The occasion was momentous. Led by John Breckinridge—who in 1798 had sponsored the Kentucky Resolutions, drafted by Jefferson as a protest against the Alien and Sedition Acts on the ground that the central government was assuming powers not delegated by the Constitution—Republicans now found themselves venturing far beyond the conscious intentions, not to say the wildest dreams, of the framers. They proceeded, as Senator Nicholas, of Virginia, explained, on the authority of Article IV, Section 3, of the Constitution which

---

* Jefferson's intentions on this were indicated in the draft of a Constitutional amendment submitted to his Cabinet in August 1803: "Louisiana as ceded by France to the United States is made a part of the United States. Its white inhabitants shall be citizens, and stand, as to their rights and obligations, on the same footing with other citizens of the United States in analogous situations." [46]

said: "The Congress shall have Power to dispose of and make all needful Rules and Regulations respecting the Territory or other Property belonging to the United States." This did seem to provide ample authority, now that the territory had been purchased and possessed.[48]

As the debate in the Senate developed during the early months of 1804, two issues emerged as primary. One was slavery; the other, the question whether the legislature of the territory should be appointed by the President or elected by inhabitants of the territory.

On the latter question, the Senate tended toward firmer control by the federal government, whereas the House hoped as quickly as possible to hand responsibility over to the inhabitants. The issue persisted until it became the final obstacle to the passage of the ordinance, being resolved only when the House yielded to a recalcitrant Senate with the understanding that the question would be reviewed before the ordinance was renewed during the Ninth Congress.[49]

On the question of slavery, Congress found itself in the position, unprecedented during its brief history under the Constitution, of determining whether slavery should be lawful in a given region or not. Ever since the First Congress convened, it had been the fixed policy of Southerners to oppose even the consideration by Congress of any scheme to regulate slavery anywhere. Cries of "entering-wedge" and "dangerous meddling" met every proposal to this effect. Even Southerners who felt that slavery was "evil" and who believed that the South would never be happy until it had eliminated slavery (and Negroes) from its midst were convinced that the South had to handle the problem itself, because Northerners lacked the understanding and experience necessary to proceed wisely in this area. In 1804, however, this whole orthodoxy had to be modified under the necessity of framing an ordinance for Louisiana.

The attempt to regulate slavery there began on January 25, 1804, when Federalist Senator James Hillhouse moved to outlaw the foreign slave trade into the territory. The motion succeeded by a vote of 21 to 6. The Senators from Vermont, who voted with the minority, explained that "no law [could] prevent or destroy" the slave trade while South Carolina, which had recently re-opened its ports to the trade, permitted it to continue. The response of those who favored the prohibition was that Congress should make every possible effort to prevent "another Santo Domingo." [50]

Hillhouse then moved to exclude from Louisiana slaves imported into the United States since 1798, the year the last of the original states, Georgia, outlawed the foreign traffic in slaves. This provision was intended primarily as a rebuke to South Carolina. In the absence of the South Carolinians, who were not present in the Senate until early February, the Senate adopted the motion by 21 to 7.[51]

So far, the Senate had exercised only its powers over commerce. The fact that the prohibitions would apply to a territory, rather than to "any of the states now existing," meant that the Constitutional suspension of power over the slave trade until 1308 did not apply. Furthermore, in outlawing the slave trade, the Senate was exercising powers made familiar by the regulations of 1794 and 1800, by the prohibition of the foreign slave trade into the Mississippi Territory, and by anticipations of the general prohibition in 1808. If these had been the only regulations of slavery in Louisiana, Southerners concerned about precedent-setting federal legislation affecting slavery might have breathed easily.

But this was not all. The debate over the ordinance also produced two attempts to weaken or prohibit slavery itself in Louisiana. The first came on January 30, on a motion by Hillhouse to add a proviso to the ordinance that no slave brought into the territory could be held in bondage for more than a year. The proposed amendment, like Article VI of the Northwest Ordinance, included a clause guaranteeing the return of fugitive slaves.[52]

The motion was momentous. A decision to exclude slavery from all territory west of the Mississippi River would have had the most far-reaching consequences, not only for the territory itself, but also for the balance of political forces within the union. If the Federalists and their Northern Republican colleagues had succeeded in passing this motion, and had gotten President Jefferson to sign it, American history would have taken a different course.

But no such decision was taken. By a vote of 11 to 17, the motion was defeated. Again, the two Senators from Massachusetts voted in opposition to Hillhouse. John Quincy Adams explained his vote rather lamely by arguing that the Senate was "proceeding with too much haste upon such an important question." [53] He did not explain why he was unwilling to slow the Republicans down, as he and two other Senators (his colleague Pickering and Federalist Samuel White, for example) could have done by switching their votes; nor did he acknowledge that the Senate was deciding this "important question" by default, just as much as they would have by adopting the proposed amendment. So the decision was made to allow slavery to continue in Louisiana under American rule virtually as it had under Spanish and French rule.*

One final effort to regulate the institution within Louisiana took the form of a motion to restrict slavery to bona fide settlers. The purpose was to discourage professional traders from using Louisiana as a market for the most "vicious" slaves from the Old South, and to make sure, at least legally, that every slave who entered the southwestern frontier was the responsibility of a genuine settler. [55]

The vote on this motion, on February 1, was 18 to 11 in favor. The roll call revealed a divided mind in the South, which split its votes exactly in half, but considerable determination among the Yankees that slavery be kept under close control. The Virginians opposed the restriction, because they represented men who owned surplus slaves and coveted this market, although few of them had any intention of migrating themselves "amongst the Indians and alligators." Thomas Sumter, of South Carolina, and Georgia's General Jackson supported the provision, because of their concern that slavery remain a stable institution, and perhaps also in

---

* On November 14, 1803 Jefferson sent Congress a "Description of Louisiana," which included—in addition to details about geography, Indians, hurricanes, and local customs—a "Digest of the Laws of Louisiana" and several censuses. The leading census, which underestimated the population, but gave a fairly accurate idea of the proportion of whites, "free people of color," and slaves, said that, in 1785, there were 14,000 whites, 1,300 free Negroes, and 16,500 slaves. In the Digest of Laws was a section entitled "Police of Slaves," containing an outline of a slave code which was adopted, for the most part, into the code of the territory, and which has been called "one of the most comprehensive and severe" codes of the entire antebellum period. [54]

retaliation for remarks by Virginians when South Carolina reopened the African slave trade in 1803.[56]

On February 18, the Senate passed the Louisiana Ordinance by a vote of 20 to 5. A solid phalanx from west and south of the Hudson River acted for a young nation impatient to extend its sway over this vast treasure.[57]

The measure now went before the House. After a brief controversy over the mode of selecting the first territorial legislature, the House brought its version to a vote. Again, despite resistance from Yankee Federalists, and despite four "nays" and an unusually large number of abstentions among the Virginians, an overwhelming majority supported the ordinance. On March 26, 1804, President Jefferson added his signature, and the ordinance became law.

In enacting the Louisiana Ordinance of 1804, Congress moved for the first time decisively beyond the concrete expectations of the framers, and it did so, ironically enough, at the behest of Southerners. The purchase and assimilation of Louisiana forced Southerners, particularly Southern Republicans, to abandon many cherished notions. Their consent to national legislation regulating slavery was a prime example. By a twist of circumstance, it fell to Yankees John Quincy Adams and Timothy Pickering to argue that it was wrong for Congress "to legislate at all" on a matter of this kind. In addition, the ordinance governing slavery and the slave trade, as well as numerous other domestic institutions, bore the name (the "Breckinridge Bill") of a leader who first gained fame as a spokesman for "strict construction" during the Constitutional crisis of 1798. The arrangement struck by the framers and restored, so they thought, by the Republicans in 1800 was shattered in 1803–1804. How long the original settlement could have succeeded in compromising the differences between the sections, had it not been for the Louisiana Purchase, cannot be known. What many seemed to sense in 1804 was that the American union had been reconstituted by the acquisition of Louisiana. The balance of political power between the sections had been disturbed, and before it could be stabilized, a new generation of politicians would have to reconsider the place of slavery in the greatly expanded republic.

. . .

Later in 1804, the tacit arrangement of 1787 was again threatened in a way apparently unanticipated by the framers of the Constitution. The challenge came when James Sloan proposed a scheme of gradual emancipation for the District of Columbia. His motion provoked a brief but extremely bitter debate. When it came to a vote, it was defeated by 31 to 77, owing to solid Southern opposition and the ambivalence of Northerners, especially Northern Republicans.[58]

The proposal to abolish slavery in the District was not a clear test for the compromise of 1787. The issue posed was almost wholly moral. The slaves in question were mostly domestic servants. The fate of plantation agriculture and the balance of power between the sections—the main concerns affected by the compromise of 1787—were not at stake. But in a more fundamental sense, the compromise *was* at stake. The words of the Constitution gave Congress ample power to abolish slavery in the seat of the federal government,* just as the words of the Constitution gave Congress full authority to prohibit slavery in the Mississippi Territory. But ever since Congressman William L. Smiths speech in 1790, Southerners had insisted that they had ratified the Constitution with the understanding that the federal government would not tamper with slavery in any way. With increasing boldness, they had asserted that any attempt to modify the Constitution as they understood it (interpreting all ambiguities in favor of slavery's presumed right to exist and to spread into areas south of the Ohio River) would lead to a dissolution of the union. They had established this point, not by arguments drawn from the text of the Constitution, but by appeal to the spirit of 1787, and through the use of threats, ultimatums, and advancing precedents.

The resistance to Sloan's proposal followed in this train. Southerners argued that nothing less than the Constitutional union was at stake. If Congress abolished slavery in the District of Columbia, the property of Southerners would never again be secure.

* Article I, Section 8: "The Congress shall have power . . . to exercise exclusive legislation in all cases whatsoever, over such district (not exceeding ten miles square) as may . . . become the seat of the government of the United States. . . ."

In the end, the spirit of the compromise of 1787 prevailed. Congress voted not to exercise its full Constitutional powers, but to abide by the understanding that the federal government must not attempt to regulate slavery. It might also be said that by permitting slavery in the District, Congress was merely accepting a consequence of permitting it in the South, for if John Randolph could own slaves in Roanoke, it was probably wrong to forbid him to bring them to the nation's capital. On the contrary, having them in the nation's capital might serve to keep the problem in front of Congressmen who were all too eager to believe that the South could be quarantined, that the rest of the nation could isolate itself from the infection of slavery.

What made the position of the Jeffersonians difficult in legislating for the Louisiana Territory was that the purchase and the assumption of authority in the territory required a wrenching stretch in Constitutional interpretation, whereas the establishment there of society and government amenable to Southern interests depended upon a reversion to "strict construction" in its purest form.[59] The Missouri controversy of 1820, which brought this home to many Southerners, was thus an important turning point in the nation's constitutional development.[60]

During the Constitutional Convention, it had been a cardinal assumption on all sides that population was drifting in a southwestward direction. By 1820, it was clear that this assumption, as understood in 1787, had been false. The center of population was moving west, but it was not moving south. In the 1780's some Southerners had believed that it would be enough for population to move westward. That alone would counteract the dominance of politicians like Alexander Hamilton, Rufus King, and John Jay, and throw the balance toward agrarian interests. Others believed that the effect of this migration would depend on where the migrants had come from. If they came from the South, they would appreciate the South's peculiar situation and might be relied upon as allies when Southern interests were at stake. If they were native Yankees or New Yorkers, they might carry notions hostile to the South. Confident that logistics favored a swift migration from Kentucky and Virginia into the lower Northwest, this latter group of Southerners, too, supported the Northwest Ordinance in 1787, though perhaps more cautiously than those who regarded the matter strictly in terms of agrarian versus commercial interests.

By the second decade of the nineteenth century, it was obvious that factors other than place of origin had to be taken into account. The most attractive areas of the Northwest might be immediately adjacent to the South, but men who had grown used to farming with the use of slaves were unwilling to sell their slaves, or free them, in order to move across the Ohio River. Many Southern frontiersmen did, of course, move into southern Ohio, Indiana, and Illinois, and they later had a powerful effect on the political affiliations of the Northwest during the Missouri controversy. But the prospects in the Northwest seemed uncertain to most Southerners. Wherever the Northwesterner might have come from, his social circumstances in his new home, at least with respect to the proportion of blacks in his midst, were more similar to those in the East than in the South. By 1820 blacks constituted about 1 per cent of the total population of the Northwest, but about 32 per cent in the four states (Kentucky, Tennessee, Mississippi, Alabama) of the old Southwest. For a generation or two, native Southerners in the Northwest might remember the peculiar opportunities and dangers of life in a slave society, but as these memories faded, and as Northwesterners settled into other patterns of development, there could be no assurance that they would remain sympathetic to Southern interests. From the Southern viewpoint, the only man absolutely trustworthy to respect the requirements of slavery was a man who lived in the midst of large numbers of blacks. Increasingly, Northwesterners failed to meet this test of sympathy.[61]

As Southerners contemplated the territory bought from France, this experience with territorial development east of the Mississippi River shaped their outlook. The most inviting parts of the territory, at least for the present, were adjacent to the South. Both logistics and climate were encouraging to the view that this region would ally itself with Southern interests. But the prospect depended on the opportunity to take slaves into the territory and, of course, to keep the ones that were already there.

TABLE IV. NEGROES AND SLAVERY IN THE WEST, 1790–1820

REGIONS	NEGROES AS % OF TOTAL POPULATION	SLAVES AS % OF NEGROES
Northwest (Ohio, Indiana, Illinois, Michigan Territory)		
1790	..	..
1800	1.2%	21.2%
1810	1.3%	12.4%
1820	1.0%	14.3%
Southwest (Kentucky, Tennessee, Alabama, Mississippi, Louisiana, Missouri, Arkansas Territory)		
1790	14.9%	97.0%
1800	17.5%	97.9%
1810	23.7%	94.0%
1820	26.7%	95.4%

SELECTED STATES

Indiana

1790	..	..
1800	5.3%	45.3%
1810	2.6%	37.6%
1820	1.0%	13.3%

Kentucky

1790	17.0%	99.0%
1800	18.6%	98.2%
1810	20.2%	97.9%
1820	22.9%	97.8%

Mississippi

1790	..	..
1800	41.5%	95.0%
1810	42.9%	98.6%
1820	44.1%	98.6%

Missouri

1790	..	..
1800	..	..
1810	17.4%	83.2%
1820	15.9%	96.7%

SOURCE: U.S. Bureau of the Census, *Negro Population, 1790–1915* (Washington: Government Printing Office, 1918), pp. 45, 51, 57.

Southerners were not alone in viewing the territory west of the Mississippi with anxiety. Northerners were pleased that population seemed to be drifting due west, rather than southward, but they were increasingly appalled at how little difference it made in Congress and in the Electoral College. During the second decade of the nineteenth century, the so-called "free states" held a preponderance of 56 per cent of the seats in the House of Representatives, and there was every indication that this percentage was growing, as immigrants swarmed into New York and Pennsylvania and settlements sprang up throughout the region north of the Ohio River. Yet ever since the admission of Tennessee in 1796, the "slave states" had held an equality of seats or occasionally, for short periods, just two seats short of an equality in the Senate. Furthermore, because the South was virtually monolithic on certain crucial issues, and because Northern representatives were divided between the Federalist and Republican persuasion, and the Northern Republicans themselves into various factions, it often seemed that the South governed the nation.

These Northern difficulties in national politics were due, in part, to the divisions among Northerners; in part, to the political skill of leading Southerners, whose interests, being relatively simple, were simpler to assert and defend. But in the minds of Northern politicians, to whom these explanations were not flattering, another factor loomed larger: the federal ratio, which counted five slaves as three free men for apportioning representation in Congress and in the Electoral College.[62] Some Northerners argued that, had it not been for the federal ratio, John Adams would have been re-elected President in 1800, and it would have been he, rather than Jefferson, who would have inherited the political windfall of Louisiana. Or, they argued, without the representation of slaves, DeWitt Clinton might have beaten James Madison in 1812, in which case the war begun in June of that year would almost certainly have ended sooner, before the desperate New Englanders had been driven to gather at Hartford to draft amendments to the Constitution. There was really no point in wondering what the North might have done had it not been for the federal ratio, for without it there would have been no union under the Constitution. The primary significance of such

405

speculations was that they symbolized the growing alienation between North and South.

There were several other factors reinforcing the Northern desire to curb the expansion of slavery across the Mississippi. One was the accumulating evidence that the slave trade, which had been outlawed in 1808, had by no means been stopped. As the evidence poured in, in the form of reports by customs collectors and United States attorneys in Southern districts and in testimony by Deep Southern Congressmen, the attitude of Northerners toward slavery began to shift. Oliver Ellsworth could say at the Constitutional Convention of 1787 that Northerners ought not to "intermeddle" with slavery because it soon would not be a "speck" in the nation. James Wilson could predict at the Pennsylvania ratifying convention of 1788 that when the slave trade was outlawed in 1808, slavery would vanish from the South by the same gradual process that removed it from the Quaker State. But by 1818 the slave trade had been outlawed for ten years, and Northerners had certainly not "intermeddled" with slavery. Yet the institution was still growing. Planters in the newly settled regions of Alabama, Mississippi, and Louisiana were showing great zeal and determination in applying slave labor to the cultivation of cotton and sugar. Meanwhile, the evidence of slave smuggling undercut the argument of the Virginians that the "diffusion" of slavery into the territories would permit less harsh discipline and encourage the consideration of plans for gradual emancipation. There was no doubt that slavery was spreading westward across the land, but there was no reason to believe that attitudes toward the institution or its black victims were softening in South Carolina or Georgia, or even in Virginia.

A second factor contributing to Northern concern was the Adams-Onís Treaty with Spain, signed at Washington in 1819. In this treaty, the United States renounced all claims to Texas, but gained clear title to Florida. Apparently the arrangement was unpopular in both North and South. Southerners who regarded Texas as the southern half of the trans-Mississippi territory were sorry to see it renounced, especially by a Secretary of State from Massachusetts. Northerners feared that Florida would only add weight to the forces that regularly overwhelmed them in the Senate. There was some talk of an effort to amend the treaty by prohibiting slavery in the newly acquired territory, but in light of geographical considerations, the effort was seen by most politicians as quixotic. There were already nearly as many blacks as whites in Florida, and no serious man could have supposed that President Monroe would direct the American Army in Florida, under the command of General Andrew Jackson, to abolish slavery there. The plainest effect of the treaty was to add at least one slave state to the union.[63]

A final factor in accounting for the different atmosphere in 1819 was the rise of "benevolence" as a social force throughout the North, especially in New York and New England. The sons of Federalists, for whom public careers were no longer promising, were turning to nongovernmental endeavors. Thwarted in the attempt to govern by public enactment, they took to private exhortation and organization. Bible societies, missionary alliances, prison-reform leagues, societies for "uplifting and civilizing" the Indians, and of course abolition and manumission societies began to sweep through the North and upper South.[64] Networks of communication developed between these reformers, so that when the Missouri controversy emerged in Congress, there was a group in the North ready to mobilize sentiment behind Congressmen who opposed the expansion of slavery, and to bring pressure to bear on Congressmen who at first misread the significance of the controversy.[65] The dominant mood of the country was very different from that of 1787. Instead of anxiety to promote the union, there was restlessness under its constraints. This unrest, fueled by the passion for benevolence, made it more difficult to calculate the advantages of union through toleration, more tempting to invoke the apocalypse as the alternative to reform.

The prospective state of Missouri lay almost wholly north of the latitude of the Ohio River where it joined the Mississippi, but there were already 10,000 Negroes there, about one-sixth of the total population. It could safely be assumed that Missouri, left to its own devices, would enter the union as a slave state. Nevertheless, when the bill directing the people of Missouri to form a state government came before Congress, James Tallmadge, of New York, moved to amend it by adding the provision that the further introduction of slavery . . . be prohibited . . . and that all children of slaves, born within the said state after the admission thereof into the union, shall be free, but may be held in service until the age of twenty-five years.[66]

This amendment was not without precedent. In 1798 Thacher had tried to prohibit slavery in the Mississippi Territory, and in 1804 Hillhouse had offered a similar amendment with respect to the entire Louisiana Territory. More recently, Tallmadge himself had sought vainly to make the admission of Illinois in 1818 explicitly contingent on a promise never to admit slavery.[67] Still, the announcement of his notion, on a Saturday afternoon, February 13, 1819, provoked what the official House reporter called "an interesting and pretty wild debate."

The debate addressed itself to both Constitutional and political considerations. The supporters of the amendment were led by John W. Taylor, of New York, in the absence of Tallmadge, who was ill when the debate began. John Quincy Adams, then Secretary of State, thought that the "free side of the question" offered an invitation to eloquence unrivaled since the development of human speech,[68] but if this was true, then Taylor and his supporters were either unequal to the occasion or else judged its requirements differently from Adams. Rarely did they reach for eloquence, and when they did, they often stumbled into traps which Southern debaters were quick to spring.

Taylor's basic argument was that the power of Congress to admit new states was discretionary. If Congress had power to deny admission to the union, surely it had power to set conditions for such admission. The precedent had been set in 1812, when Congress conditioned the admission of Louisiana on that state's acceptance of trial by jury, republicanism as a constitutional standard, and the use of English as the official language, among other things.[69]

Southerners responded sharply to this Constitutional argument. The most important reply came from Philip Barbour, of Virginia, who argued that Missouri was already a mature political community, applying for admission to the union as the sovereign equal of the thirteen original states and their eight younger sisters. The regulation of slavery was municipal legislation. Over a territory, Congress might have jurisdiction to enact such laws, but over a state, it did not. To insist that Missouri abolish slavery before entering the union was to invite it to join as a cripple, giving away part of its sovereignty at the outset.[70]

Underlying this debate was a conflict over the meaning of the fundamental principles of the regime, and it was no coincidence that it produced the first extended consideration by Congress of the meaning of the Declaration of Independence and the relationship between the Declaration and the Constitution. The Northern position was straightforward: the doctrines of the Declaration were basic commitments, providing substance for the "republican form" of government guaranteed to every state by Article IV, Section 4 of the Constitution. In framing the Constitution, the equalitarian thrust of republicanism against slavery had been set aside in deference to the predicament of the Southern states, where slavery was already entrenched beyond uprooting. But in legislating for the territories, where social patterns were not yet set, Congress should consider itself bound by the standards of republicanism, by which slavery could not be justified.

Some Southerners responded that the Declaration, a "fanfaronade of metaphysical abstractions," had no standing in American law. Others insisted that their plea for the admission of Missouri without restriction as to slavery was based precisely on the doctrines of the Declaration. What Missourians sought, they said, was "the right of self-government." As self-governing men, they had the same right to fashion their social environment as men of Virginia, whose right under the Constitution to own slaves had not been questioned.

The Southern argument applied the doctrine of equality to white men, and insisted that whites in Missouri were equal to those in other parts of the country. The Northern position rested on the assumption that blacks were equal to whites, an argument useful when setting conditions on the admission of a slave state, but embarrassing when seen in the light of actual practice in the Northern states. It is difficult to avoid the feeling that the Southern position, though paradoxical, had firmer roots in the prevailing public opinion toward Negroes in 1820. John Tyler, the future President from Virginia, in suggesting to restrictionists that they direct their arguments against slavery to the Missourians and let *them* decide, appealed to this opinion, and in so doing anticipated the doctrine that came to be known as "popular sovereignty." [71]

On the question of policy, the differences were equally profound. Northerners expressed a desire to save Missouri from the agony bemoaned throughout the South. Southerners often said that they regarded slavery as an evil, but that they could not abolish it under present circumstances without committing suicide. Northerners argued that Congress was now in the position of those who had saddled Virginia with slavery. Unless the prohibition were enacted now, future generations of Missourians would be in the same miserable position as the Virginians, and might well blame the Fifteenth Congress for their plight. Taylor compared the clean, well-kept farms of southern Pennsylvania with the decadent tobacco plantations of northern Maryland. The difference he ascribed to slavery. He hoped that his sons, who might want someday to migrate westward, would find Missouri more like Pennsylvania than Maryland.

Southerners met these arguments head on, some of them showing a candid approval of slavery that did not usually characterize intersectional discourse on this subject. Charles Pinckney, the only framer then serving in Congress, gave a long, forceful statement of the position of South Carolinians. Slavery, he said, was a great blessing to blacks and masters alike, providing the former with a far better life than could be expected in Africa or as freedmen in America, and supplying the latter with laborers of almost incalculable value. Emancipationists were the "greatest enemies" of black men. Louis McLane, of Delaware, later Secretary of the Treasury and of State in Jackson's Cabinet, declared that emancipation in the South was now "utterly impracticable," and gradual abolition "almost hopeless." The best that one could do for blacks was "to meliorate their sufferings, and soften the rigors of their servitude" by diffusing the institution more widely across the country, and hope thereby to make it less formidable to whites, and consequently less rigorous for blacks. Barbour added that the question of slavery in Missouri would determine whether

Southerners could migrate into the area. If slavery was permitted, Northerners might still come as merchants; but if slavery was prohibited, most Southerners would not feel at home there.[72]

Several Northerners, citing the teachings of Thomas Malthus, noted that the population of Africa had not diminished, despite the slave trade, because the land and the uses made of it could sustain a certain population, and the removal of some of the population was quickly compensated for by a jump in growth rates. Diffusion, they argued, would stimulate the market for slaves, encourage smugglers, and drive the price of slaves up. It would be better, they said, to confine slavery to its present extent, let prices drop as the land burned out, encourage individual emancipations, then establish a reservation to which freed blacks could be sent.

This plan suffered from two political weaknesses: Southerners who owned the most slaves were opposed to any plan that threatened their livelihood and way of life; and Northerners were far more concerned to halt the spread of slavery's influence than to wrestle with the institution itself. Another problem was that there was no coherent statement or co-ordinated support in Congress for any realistic plan to abolish slavery. One man would cite Malthus; another would discuss the effects of diffusion on the slave trade; still another would suggest the idea of a reservation for freed blacks. No one seemed to be organizing the antislavery forces behind a defensible position. Consequently, when the delegate from Missouri accused Northerners of wanting to keep blacks penned up in one corner of the union, using slave owners as keepers of the pen, Northerners had no confident rebuttal. At one point, Clay ridiculed the "Negrophobia" of Northerners. Indeed, the reluctance of the restrictionists to face the problem of slavery in its citadel greatly weakened their demand that slavery not be allowed to pollute the western territories.[73]

The most important features of the debate were its ferocity and the readiness with which debaters resorted to threats of disunion and civil war. Thomas W. Cobb, of Georgia, accused Tallmadge of kindling "a fire which all the waters of the ocean could not extinguish. It can be extinguished," he said, "only in blood." Calling attention to blacks in the galleries, a Virginian shouted that Northerners were stirring up insurrection by their careless remarks about the immorality of slavery. He compared such Northerners to Arbuthnot and Ambrister, British citizens whom Andrew Jackson had arrested in Florida, tried by court-martial, and summarily executed for fomenting trouble among the Indians. Northerners, he said, who encouraged blacks to regard slavery as wrong deserved no better fate.[74]

To these strong words, Tallmadge responded that if blood were required to quench the fire kindled by his motion, he would not hesitate to contribute his own. Jefferson called the restrictionist movement "a mere party trick," "not a moral question, but one merely of power." But he was mistaken. Despite their reluctance to embrace all the implications of their own position, it was obvious that many Northerners took the controversy over Missouri seriously. Their mood is best reflected in a speech by Arthur Livermore, of New Hampshire, which came as close to the eloquence anticipated by Adams as any given during the debate. As the House approached the vote on the amendment, Livermore outlined its significance.

An opportunity is now presented, if not to diminish, at least to prevent the growth of a sin which sits heavy on the soul of every one of us. By embracing this opportunity, we may retrieve the national character and, in some degree, our own. But if we suffer it to pass unimproved, let us at least be consistent, and declare that our Constitution was made to impose slavery, and not to establish liberty. Let us no longer tell idle tales about the gradual abolition of slavery; away with colonization societies, if their design is only to rid us of free blacks and turbulent slaves; have done also with bible societies, whose views are to extend to Africa and the East Indies, while they overlook the deplorable condition of their sable brethren within their own borders; make no more laws to prohibit the importation of slaves, for the world must see that the object of such laws is alone to prevent the glutting of a prodigious market for the flesh and blood of man, which we are about to establish in the West, and to enhance the price of sturdy wretches, reared like cattle and horses for sale on our own plantations.[75]

When the roll was called, the House voted to outlaw slavery in Missouri. The clause that prohibited the "further introduction" of slavery into Missouri passed by 87 to 76; the clause that required gradual abolition prevailed by 82 to 78.[76] The votes were strictly along sectional lines except for a handful of Northerners, most of them Republicans, in opposition. Not a single Representative from south of the Mason-Dixon Line supported the first clause; Samuel Smith, of Baltimore, was alone among Southerners in supporting the second. The sectional line had been drawn taut, and Southerners were discovering that they were outnumbered in the House so badly that ten defections in the North were not enough to work the Southern will.

But all was not lost for the South. The measure passed by the House still faced consideration by the Senate, not to mention the possibility of a veto by President Monroe. In 1819 it was the Senate that came to the South's rescue. There, by votes of 16 to 22 and 7 to 31, the two clauses of Tallmadge's amendment were defeated.[77] The two houses were now deadlocked. As the session drew to a close, the Fifteenth Congress resigned itself to failure, for the time being, on the question of admitting Missouri to the union. Members could now go home to test the sentiment of their constituents on this explosive new issue.[78]

Three events intervened, before the second Missouri debate, to change the political context and sharpen the issues posed by the controversy. One was the admission of Alabama to the union. No effort was made to force the Alabamians to "exclude" slavery. It was surrounded by slave states, and the census of 1820 showed that there were already over 40,000 blacks in the state, one-third of the total population. Tallmadge himself, noting that contacts between slaves and free blacks, where blacks were so numerous, could only produce "servile war," disavowed any intention of seeking to undermine slavery there. Consequently, the act to admit Alabama passed through Congress quickly and without controversy, and in 1819 Alabama entered the union as the twenty-second state, and the eleventh slave state.[79]

The second intervening event was the establishment of territorial government in Arkansas. The Arkansas Territory, comprising most of the present states of Arkansas and Oklahoma, lay across the river from Mississippi and Tennessee, and already included about 1,600 slaves, about 11 per cent of the population.

But the total population of the territory, according to the census of 1820, was only about 14,000 people. Those who regarded the question of slavery's expansion as a matter of principle, rather than of geography or climate, might yet regard Arkansas as a virtual *tabula rasa* and want to prevent the smudge of slavery while there was still time. On February 17, 1819 Taylor offered the expected motion.

As a matter of fact, the main principle that inspired Northern pressure against slavery in Missouri was more properly applied to Arkansas: that slavery, which might be tolerated east of the Mississippi River because men could not conceive of a way to eliminate it, ought certainly to be excluded from areas where it had not yet taken root. There were far fewer slaves in Arkansas than in Missouri. Apparently, however, a few Northern Congressmen —just enough to turn the balance—saw the issue strictly in terms of political power within the union, and felt that Arkansas belonged to the South. When the roll was called on Taylor's motion, it was defeated, although by the surprisingly close vote of 87 to 89. Southerners voted in a bloc; Northerners, by a margin of 87 to 16, wanted to restrict slavery from Arkansas.[80]

In the Senate, the outcome of the attempt to exclude slavery from Arkansas depended upon the Northwesterners. Twelve Northerners voted for restriction; fifteen Southerners voted against it. This left the decision in the hands of the six Senators from Ohio, Indiana, and Illinois. The men from Ohio and Indiana divided their votes, but the Senators from Illinois, Jesse Thomas and Ninian Edwards, voted with the Southerners, which made the count 14 to 19 against restriction.[81] And so the decision was made to permit Arkansas to become a territory and to develop as nature, the zeal of planters, and the stamina of blacks gave opportunity.

The third factor affecting the tactical situation in 1820 was the application of Maine for admission as a state separate from Massachusetts. There were eleven free states and eleven slave states in the union after the admission of Alabama. The admission of Maine and Missouri as free and slave states, respectively, would preserve the political balance in the Senate. In many minds— Henry Clay's, for one—the cases of Maine and Missouri seemed "equivalent," and deserved to be considered together.[82]

A bill to accept Maine's application passed through the House on January 3, 1820, but when it reached the Senate, where the disposition to compromise was strong, the Maine and Missouri bills were joined into a single piece of legislation. The vote on this was close: 23 to 21. The roll call showed that the linking of these measures was predominantly a Southern proposition. Every Senator from south of the Mason-Dixon Line voted to link the applications; all the Northerners except two from Illinois and one from Indiana were opposed.[83]

Jesse Thomas now added an amendment to the bill that slavery be "forever prohibited" in all the territory ceded by France that lay west and north of Missouri. This amendment, the central feature of the Missouri Compromise, was adopted by a vote of 34 to 10. Later the same day (February 17, 1820), by a vote of 24 to 20, the combined Maine-Missouri bill, including the Thomas proviso, passed to its final consideration, and on the following day was adopted without a roll-call vote.[84]

The Senate debate was not officially recorded in detail, but it has left its mark in history nonetheless. This was the occasion when Rufus King entered the fray with a startling assault on the moral and philosophical justification for slavery, an attack unprecedented in Congressional debate for the absolute terms in which slavery was condemned. His speeches assumed added importance when they were published in pamphlet form and distributed around the country—into the hands, among others, of Denmark Vesey, a free Negro who lived in Charleston and whose ambition to become the Toussaint L'Ouverture of the American South was beginning to move beyond the stage of private fantasy.[85] The speeches were remarkable for their candor in assailing the political influence of slavery and in expressing determination to curb that influence, but most of all for their direct assault on the legitimacy of slavery itself. In deference to the predicament of Southerners, most Northern politicians, when performing on the national stage, tended to skirt the question of slavery's right to exist, and to deal with it as a fact. In King's mind, however, the Missouri controversy forced a confrontation of the issue at a different level. Where slavery's presence was already formidable, there might be excuse for simply regretting its evils and hoping against hope for deliverance sometime in the future. But when the question concerned the extension of the practice where it did not now exist in intimidating scope, it was necessary for legislators to confront the question whether men had any right to enslave other men. They did not, said King, and since the extenuating demand of self-preservation was not present, Congress was bound in duty to the "law of nature, which is the law of God . . . and is paramount to all human control," to forbid the entry of slavery into territory under its governance, and to require every new state formed from the territory purchased from France to purge itself of this crippling, immoral institution before entering the union.[86]

The votes on February 17 were crucial ones in the Senate. As already indicated, the linking of the Maine and Missouri applications was basically a Southern idea. Even more significant is the fact that the Thomas proviso was also favored by a majority of Southern Senators. It was this element of the Missouri Compromise that was declared unconstitutional by Chief Justice Roger B. Taney, of Maryland, in the Dred Scott case of 1857. Yet in 1820 the salient concern of most Southerners was the preservation of political balance between the slaveholding and nonslaveholding sections of the union. Thomas's proviso made sense to them as an extension of the Mason-Dixon Line westward through the Louisiana Purchase. Consequently, the Senators from the Southwestern states of Kentucky, Tennessee, Alabama, Mississippi, and Louisiana voted 9 to 1 in favor of the exclusion of slavery north of thirty-six degrees, thirty minutes of latitude.

The pure states'-rights Jeffersonians from Virginia, the Carolinas, and Georgia were strenuously opposed to the Thomas proviso, on the ground that the federal government ought not to legislate over the internal relations of its citizens.[87] Conviction on this point was truly fanatical in Virginia, where John Randolph, Judge Spencer Roane, Thomas Ritchie, editor of the influential Richmond *Enquirer,* and the sage of Monticello himself kept public concern at a fever pitch. Jefferson's confidence lay in an arrangement whereby Southerners offered a litany of regret for the existence of slavery, Northerners extended their sympathy and understanding, and both agreed to leave it to the South to work out measures by which the "evil" would be eradicated

gently, by "insensible," "imperceptible" stages. Jefferson, especially in his twilight years, believed that the possibility of union,
if it existed at all, depended on an almost reverent regard for this
liturgy. It was for this reason that the Missouri controversy
sounded to him like "the knell of the union." It signaled an ambition on the part of Northerners to have a part in framing policy
for dealing with slavery. He knew that leading Southerners
would never tolerate such an assertion of national authority, and
he rightly discerned the emergence of "a geographical line, coin-
ciding with a marked principle, moral and political," which
could "never be obliterated." [88]

Despite the opposition of the Jeffersonians, the compromise as
a whole passed through the Senate, producing almost a straight
sectional vote. The only favorable Northern votes were cast by
the Senators from Illinois and by two New Englanders. One of
the New Englanders was a Democrat from New Hampshire who
viewed the whole controversy as an attempt by Federalists to
drive a sectional wedge through the Republican party, add
Northern Republican strength to their own, and thus recover national dominance by exploiting the issue of slavery.[89] There were
two Southern votes against the compromise, those of Nathaniel
Macon and William Smith, two of the purest "Old Republicans"
in Washington. The rest of the South was as "dough-faced" as
the Northern Republicans in the House who later earned Randolph's contempt by supporting the compromise. They believed
that their best hope of getting Missouri admitted as a slave state
lay in granting the Thomas proviso, and they preferred compromise to an extension of the crisis. To achieve these ends, they
were willing to lend their support to the proposition that Congress had power to "prohibit" slavery "forever" from a part of the
territory of the United States.

And so the Missouri Compromise, in virtually its final form,
passed through the Senate. In the Senate itself, the Thomas proviso might not have been necessary to win admission for Missouri,
but the House was already showing signs of a tougher attitude
toward slavery in Missouri. The leadership there, particularly the
Southerners, hoped that the Thomas amendment would win
enough support to carry the admission of Missouri through the

House. But the struggle was far from over. As a matter of fact, knowledgeable men still feared that the nation's legislative process would be tied in a knot by the disagreement between the houses over Missouri.

While the Senate was adopting its amendments, the House was wrestling with a Missouri bill of its own. At the end of February, the Maine bill as amended by the Senate (to include the Missouri bill, plus the Thomas proviso) came back to the House, but was immediately rejected, by the decisive majority of 93 to 72. Then the House passed its own Missouri bill, incorporating an amendment proposed by John W. Taylor, requiring the Missourians to provide for the abolition of slavery in their first state constitution. The vote for passage of the amended bill was 91 to 82.[90]

Thus, by the end of February, the deadlock was complete. The Senate insisted on linking the Maine and Missouri bills, enabling the Missourians to adopt a constitution that permitted slavery, and prohibiting slavery north of thirty-six degrees, thirty minutes latitude, excepting Missouri. On each of these points, the House was solidly opposed. The putative states of Maine and Missouri stood at the door, the Missourians at least with ill-disguised impatience, full of threats to take their fate into their own hands. Meanwhile, the legislative process had ground to a halt. Among the consequences was the inability of Congress to respond to the panic that had gripped the nation's economy since 1819.[91]

The issue of slavery was at last out in the open, and few men were so strong, or so oblivious to danger, as not to be frightened by the spectacle. The determination of national politicians throughout the founding period to avoid a direct confrontation over slavery had collapsed, succumbing to the accumulated pressures in the North for a response to Southern domination over national policy and personnel. The sections were now more aware of themselves as sections than ever before in the nation's history. The vast acquisition beyond the Mississippi River was breaching the compromise of 1787. Madison's line of discrimination was at last coming to the surface. Congress was in severe crisis, stupefied by threats of violence and disunion that came with regularity now from both ends of the union.

Congressmen began to look ahead to the consequences should they enact a restriction of slavery from Missouri. What if the Missourians resisted by force? asked John Tyler. Would the government send an army to coerce them? Did anyone believe 'that Southern bayonets will ever be plunged in Southern hearts"? John Quincy Adams, Secretary of State in Monroe's Cabinet, gave a Congressman from New Hampshire what the latter took to be the administration's view: that the government was powerless to enforce a restriction against slavery on Missouri, that Missouri would be supported by half the states in the union in resistance to federal authority, and that the Senate compromise should be adopted as offering the best hope to curb the expansion of slavery *beyond* Missouri. Congressman John Holmes, who represented the Maine District of Massachusetts and was therefore understandably anxious to expedite the compromise, predicted that if Missouri's application was not honored without humiliating conditions, it would retire to sulk, and might return one day, allied with Mexico, in a different frame of mind toward the United States.[92]

Despite the growing talk of secession, the nation's leading politicians were still committed to the union. Early in March, at the suggestion of Senator Thomas and with the hearty concurrence of Speaker Henry Clay, a conference was arranged between the houses. Clay managed to send to the conference an intersectional group of Representatives anxious to compose the quarrel. On March 2 the unanimous recommendations of the conference committee were announced: that the Senate withdraw its amendments to the Maine bill (namely, its own Missouri bill); that both houses strike the restriction against slavery from the House's Missouri bill; and that both houses add the Thomas proviso to the Missouri bill. Defending the arrangement in the House, Charles Kinsey, of New Jersey, demonstrated that Northerners were finally flinching in the face of Southern defiance. If they rejected this compromise, he said, "the moral cement of our body politic" would dissolve, the ligaments of union would be torn asunder. This was "the only alternative," the last chance to save the union.[93] The moderate restrictionists were agreeing to permit Missouri to frame a constitution that recognized slavery; the moderate expansionists were agreeing to draw a line beyond which slavery could not go.

There was substantial opposition to every part of the compromise, but the votes showed that Clay had found a way to get over the difficulty. A crucial part of his strategy was that, as the conference report stood, the House never had to vote on the whole package. Instead, votes were taken on the proposed changes in the House's own Missouri bill—namely, that the Taylor amendment be stricken and the Thomas proviso added to it. If these propositions had been presented to the House together, there would have been enough votes against the package to defeat it. But the crucial vote in the House came on the recommendation that the Taylor amendment, which required Missouri to abolish slavery, be stricken. It had earlier passed the House by 93 to 72. On one of the most dramatic occasions in American Congressional history, the House now adopted the recommendation to strike the amendment by 90 to 87.[94] The South gave not a single vote against the recommendation; fourteen Northerners (the "doughfaces") also voted affirmatively.

The drama of the occasion was reflected in the deathbed wish of Congressman David Walker, of Kentucky, who asked that, if he lived long enough, his friends carry him to the House chamber so that he could spend his last breath on an "aye" for Missouri. The last debater for the Southern side was Charles F. Mercer, of Virginia, who fainted midway through his speech but remained in the chamber to cast his vote in the affirmative. Four Northerners, enough to change the outcome, were absent when the vote was taken. One later explained to his constituents in Connecticut that the length of the session had so fatigued him that he finally slipped out for supper, confident that Mercer's speech would give him time to get back before the vote. The Hartford *Courant* compared Mercer's determination, staying to vote even after he had fainted, with their Representative's foolish mistake.[95] Indeed, the comparison did offer a kind of parable.

The acceptance of defeat by the House meant that Clay's efforts had succeeded. Once again Congress had exercised its jurisdiction over territories and over the admission of states without breaking up over the question of slavery. It had done so by extending the line of discrimination virtually to the Rocky Mountains. The Virginians, who bitterly denounced the compromise, had nevertheless won an important point. Congress, in this coda

to the Constitutional Convention of 1787, had reached the same
conclusion as its illustrious predecessor: it would not assert power
to regulate slavery where it already existed; it would merely draw
a line between the sections, keep slavery from crossing north of
the line, and leave it to the planters to manage affairs south of the
line.

The Missouri Compromise provides a fitting close to the founding of the American political system, because it reveals both the
strengths and the ultimate weakness of that system. The main
strength lies in the capacity to distract attention from insoluble
problems and to transvalue moral questions into more tractable
forms. Slavery itself was ungovernable, so far as the national government was concerned. Those who held slaves were unwilling to
permit those who held no slaves to share in managing the institution. There was no consensus, no trust between members of the
union, where slavery was concerned. Instead, a strong consensus
supported the view that the federal government should avoid regulating slavery wherever possible.

But when Missouri presented itself for admission, and when a
bill was introduced to establish territorial government in the unorganized parts of the West, it seemed that the question could no
longer be avoided. Southerners, led by the Virginians, insisted
that the federal government need do no more than admit Missouri, which was already as mature a community as many of the
thirteen original states had been in 1787, and then sketch out the
structure of government in the rest of the Louisiana Purchase,
allowing the people there to decide which domestic institutions
they wanted. In a way, such a solution would have been consistent with the approach of the Constitutional Convention of 1787:
leave it to the states and localities to decide whether they wanted
slavery or not.

By 1820 there was substantial opinion (dominant, as it turned
out, in the House of Representatives, and thus in a position to
demand an accommodation) that slavery was wrong, that its influence in the republic was baneful, and that the federal government should therefore search out every prudent opportunity to
stem its growth and undercut its influence. This opinion, repre-

sented most forcefully by Rufus King, was reinforced by the feeling that slaveholders had greater weight in the government than they deserved by republican principles.

The difference between the Virginians and King was thus partly political, but fundamentally moral. The government staggered and reeled while the issue was cast in this form. But at this point, the thoroughly American political genius of Henry Clay went to work. First, he suggested that Maine and Missouri were "equivalent" and might form the basis of a bargain. Still, King's group was not reconciled. So he took up the Thomas proviso as a way of transvaluing the dispute. If men could be made to see the issue in terms of parcels of real estate, rather than absolute moral principles, the skills of the broker could be brought to bear. In the first test, when the issue of slavery in Missouri was presented by itself, the restrictionists had won by nine votes. But when it was joined with the prospect of prohibiting slavery in the northern part of the Louisiana Purchase, and when the alternative was to alienate the affection of Missourians, not to mention their allies east of the Mississippi River, the compromise slipped through the House of Representatives.

Clay and the compromisers were able to succeed because they framed the issue in its most superficial and immediate terms. The deeper and more permanent dimension of the problem was the question of how white Americans were going to come to terms with black Americans.[96] Southerners talked of the need to diffuse slavery across the country, so that they could contemplate emancipation without confronting the prospect of suicide. Northerners insisted on confining the black scourge of slavery to its present limits. The premise of both arguments was that blacks had no permanent, stable place in equalitarian America except as slaves in regions where white men refused to work.

To many Southerners, especially those in the five states of the Old South, the program of the restrictionists looked like an attempt by the commercial and industrial elites of the North to cordon off the southeastern quarter of the union, lock slave owners and blacks into that sector, then seize control of the national government to force-feed the development of cities and industries throughout the remaining portions of the union. It was the

Jeffersonian vision that seemed in peril. Politically, Rufus King was regarded by many old allies of Jefferson as a cunning, ambitious politician, bent on gaining the Presidency and willing to risk the union, willing to disturb the very foundations of its stability, to achieve his selfish purposes. According to this conception, he was still the candidate of the Federalists, as he had been in 1816, when he received only 15 per cent of the Electoral College vote against Monroe. Not willing to abide by that result, King and the Federalists had found in the Missouri controversy a wedge to divide the Northern and Southern adherents of the Jeffersonian ideal. By raising the problem of slavery to first place on the public agenda, the enemies of Republicanism hoped to get back into the White House.[97]

Republicans north and south believed that this was the ambition of King and his allies. To thwart it, they knew they had to get the public mind off slavery. In the end, there were enough Northern Republicans who saw the problem this way to enable the compromise to pass. Their hope was to preserve and extend the alliance that had produced the Virginia dynasty in the White House—elevating to the Presidency, not necessarily native Virginians, but men who espoused the Jeffersonian principles of limited national government, agrarianism, and state particularism.[98]

11

Slavery and National Integration

IN 1787 and 1788, when the Constitution of the United States was framed and ratified, optimism about the prospects of the American union inspired the thinking of the ablest minds. The struggle over ratification had been intense and the outcome seriously in doubt, but when it was over, it seemed, as Woodrow Wilson once put it, that the opponents of ratification had been not only defeated, but also convinced.[1] In the early political infighting, men who had been the staunchest supporters of the Constitution during the ratification process tried to brand their opponents as enemies of the Constitution, but it was soon apparent that the charge would not stick. After 1790 there were virtually no anti-Constitutionalists anywhere in the union. From that time forward, politicians contended, not for, or against, the Constitution, but for the title of most faithful interpreter of its meaning. Patriotism came to be wholly identified with the Constitution.

Underlying this broad Constitutional consensus, however, was a corrosive legacy from the colonial period. One-fifth of the "non-aboriginal" population of the nation was locked in a caste system that found no stable place in the Constitution. To get the Constitution ratified, all explicit mention of this system had to be avoided, and its anomalous existence was forced to depend on elaborate circumlocutions and tacit understandings. Meanwhile, much of the nation's wealth was being wrung from the sweat of black faces, and social relations in large parts of the country depended on an institution that violated the nation's deepest commitments.

The refusal to receive black people into the American body politic dogged the pursuit of a "more perfect union" from the beginning of the nation's existence. By failing to come to grips with the caste system, delegates to the Constitutional Convention permitted the seeds of civil war to take root in the soil of American democracy. In the early national period, 1790–1820, the danger of intersectional conflict over slavery was sometimes lost to view, but it was always ominously present just beneath the surface of events. A comparison of the situation in 1790 with that in 1820 illustrates that slavery's potential to cleave the union, not generally recognized at the beginning, was becoming ever more difficult to ignore by the end of the second decade of the nineteenth century.

In 1790 concern about slavery was actively felt by few politicians, and among private men by only a few highly sensitive souls, most of them Southerners.[2] The prevailing view was that slavery was evil, but that there was nothing that could be done about it, at least not for the time being. It seemed irrational to be paralyzed by sensitivity to a situation that was irremediable. It seemed wiser to proceed toward national development, and trust that in the fullness of time a way would be found to remove the stain of slavery. Slavery surely violated the laws of nature and of nature's God, but by and by an appropriate way to right this ancient, inherited wrong would be revealed. In the meantime, sensible men would concern themselves with developing the nation's economic, military, and political potential.

The vast majority of Americans was satisfied that the framers had fashioned a federal government that could move on with a minimum of interruption from the vexatious question of slavery. They had fixed a formula for representation that seemed fair to most men, and was not yet an object of criticism even among those Northern Federalists most resentful of Southern "republicanism."[3] The framers had also set a date, eighteen years hence, when the foreign slave trade could be outlawed, and they had provided for the possibility that slaves might try to flee their bondage and descend upon states where slavery was illegal and Negroes unwanted. They had thus set tidy legal barriers around the system, and confined it for the most part to a region whose leaders seemed, at least for the benefit of outsiders, confident of their control of the situation.

The institution was under sentence of death throughout New England and badly stricken in most of the mid-Atlantic region. As for its condition in the South, little was reliably known, which left men free to believe what they wanted to believe. But inasmuch as the African slave trade had been outlawed by most of the states, men seemed justified in believing that the period of slavery's dynamic growth was over, that the institution might now stabilize and go, soon, into the decline for which men everywhere ostensibly longed.

In 1790 the nation's economy was quite primitive, particularly in terms of intersectional integration. Those who concerned themselves with the prospects for growth, however, were inclined to foresee a rosy future, in which the diverse elements would pull together and, by complementing one another, produce a powerful and harmonious union. The Constitution had created an encouraging governmental environment, producing the conditions for a national market and for an improvement in international trade. The developing economy in turn would lend strength and incentive to the Constitutional union. The fact that the produce of plantations worked by slaves constituted an integral part of this rather dazzling picture did not interfere much with the enthusiasm of its beholders. As Oliver Ellsworth had remarked at the Constitutional Convention, "Let us not intermeddle. What enriches a part, enriches the whole." [4]

The First Congress (1789–1791) had many basic tasks to perform. There were the executive departments and federal courts to establish, and the debt to fund. Hamilton's program for the latter aroused controversy that sometimes had sectional overtones, but the prevailing mood was to avoid explicit reference to such considerations. Whenever allusions were made to sectional factors, elaborate apologies were offered and promises made to transcend this demeaning concern whenever possible in the future.[5]

The seat of government in 1790, New York City, was a place where Negroes already played a prominent part, many of them as free men, in the life of the city. Though blacks there were the victims of severe racial discrimination, and relations between the races were often tense and occasionally violent, it was already apparent that blacks were a permanent feature and an active force to be reckoned with by political leaders.[6] Not until the end of the decade was New York State to commit itself to gradual emancipation, but by 1790 the atmosphere in the nation's temporary capital and the attitude of some of its leading men toward slavery and racial discrimination constituted a new world for Congressmen and Cabinet members who came from the South, and an environment at least mildly encouraging to slavery's opponents.

The political and civic atmosphere in Washington in 1820 was in marked and significant contrast to the one that prevailed in New York three decades earlier. There was only one "leading issue" in the nation's capital in 1820—the Missouri controversy—and slavery was in no way peripheral to it. Because of the long and bitter debates on this question, and because few men honestly believed that the Missouri Compromise would dispose of the issue for good, it was no longer possible to assume that the Constitutional settlement of 1787 had removed slavery from the national political arena. Indeed, not only was it patently impossible to avoid a direct confrontation over slavery in the territories, but the experience of government during the preceding three decades had shown that the tidy arrangements established in 1787 had themselves become matters of continuing, bitter controversy. In 1820 the federal ratio was no longer an active point of contention, at least as applied to states east of the Mississippi River.[7] Complaint about that feature of the Constitution had been discredited by its prominent place in the agenda of the Hartford Convention of 1814–1815, now a memory acutely embarrassing to the politicians who had sponsored it. Instead, the focus of attack had shifted to the extension of the ratio to slave states across the Mississippi River—but on that point, the Missouri debates revealed a deeply divided public mind. Likewise, the task of terminating the slave trade had proved not to be the cut-and-dried matter that men in 1790 had thought it would be. In addition, a new source of concern, the interstate slave trade, was beginning to claim the attention of the nation, and was particularly nettlesome for a government situated at a crossroads of the flourishing traffic. Although the Virginians fiercely insisted that Congress could not lay a hand on this trade, most Northern politicians could see no Constitutional barrier to federal legislation on the subject. When Chief Justice John Marshall, himself a Virginian and owner of slaves, announced the Supreme Court's decision in the cases of *Cohens* v. *Virginia* (1821) and *Gibbons* v. *Ogden* (1824),[8] those who opposed the federal regulation of the domestic slave trade must have felt the noose tightening.

As for the institution of slavery itself, it was obviously thriving. Perceptions of trends seen in 1790 had proved reliable for the region north of Maryland. Slavery was all but dead everywhere except in Delaware, and though a struggle loomed in Illinois, the opponents of slavery were gathering strength and were to withstand the challenge.[9] But the projection of these trends into the upper South had proved deceptive. Having made the mistake of regarding slavery primarily as a tool in the economy, many Northerners had jumped from the incontrovertible premise that tobacco was a sick industry to the mistaken conclusion that slavery would gradually disappear from the Old Dominion, where tobacco had been virtually the only productive industry. But slavery's role in society there was far more than economic. By 1820 the miserable Virginians faced equally loathsome alternatives: staggering along with plantation agriculture, despite its disheartening prospects, or converting the state into a slave-breeding and export farm, a recourse that disgusted these humane men. Many succumbed to the latter alternative, but Jefferson's revulsion against degrading Negroes to the status of cattle forced him to adopt the former course, with the result given in the following report made by a visitor to Monticello not long after Jefferson's death:

I beheld nothing but ruin and change, rotting terraces, broken cabins, the lawn ploughed up, and cattle wandering among Italian mouldering vases, and the place seemed the true representative of the fallen fortunes of the great man and his family. He died in want; almost his last words were that if he lived much longer a negro hut must be his dwelling.[10]

What the prognosis of 1790 had failed to take into account was what Jefferson had warned in 1784: that slavery could not be abolished, and would not fade away, until some provision was made for the removal of the erstwhile slaves from the country. In their desperate condition, many Virginians yielded to the temptation of making an industry out of removal.[11] It would be a mistake to underestimate the psychic cost of this recourse for sensitive and proud Virginians, caught in a predicament from which their racial prejudice and a 200-year legacy of racial antipathy permitted them no honorable escape. The frenzied John Ranolph; the brilliant but arid Spencer Roane; his mercurial cousin, Thomas Ritchie; the despondent, almost morose, Thomas Jefferson; the miserably weakened James Madison; the impotent, trivial James Monroe—these were the remnants of the brilliant Virginia dynasty, the residue after the polluting stream of slavery had worked its disabling effect on one of the most remarkable political congregations of human history.[12] Despite the decrepit condition of plantation agriculture in the upper South, and despite their participation in the domestic slave trade, Virginians in 1820 were no closer to emancipation from slavery than they had been in 1790.

In the Deep South, the situation was little different from what it had been in 1790, so far as the commitment to slavery was concerned, though there was a difference in that the condition was now more widely known. In the meantime, the cotton gin had been developed, a discovery that poured new fuel on a fire that was already burning brightly across the region. The prospects thereby engendered had induced the South Carolinans to brook the wrath of the rest of the country by opening the African slave trade between 1803 and 1807, an act that had finally wrenched many minds loose from the comforting illusion that slavery was disappearing even in the Carolinas and Georgia.

Basically, the problem of slavery was different in two critical respects by 1820: it was no longer possible to believe that it was passing out of existence by gentle evolutionary processes, and it had clearly become a sectional phenomenon. Nevertheless, Jefferson was only superficially right when he wrote that the Missouri crisis exposed the coincidence of a geographical line and a moral principle. There *was* a sectional difference in outlook toward slavery. The North held a view toward the institution that the South was not free to adopt—namely, that inasmuch as slavery violated the nation's fundamental commitments and sense of right, it ought to be eliminated from the country. But there was a still more fundamental principle, over which the sections were not divided, and it was this that gave the issue its recalcitrance— namely, the refusal of Americans generally to consider the only ultimately stable alternative to slavery, racial integration. Here was a moral principle that knew no geographical line in America. Its pervasiveness made the North eager to acquiesce in the self-imposed isolation of the South, and it led eventually both to the Civil War and to the agony of the ensuing adjustments.

The presence of slavery exacted terrible costs, but its positive contributions to the founding of the country must also be taken into account. If, in assessing the American experience with slavery, one asks only how good men could tolerate and perpetuate an evil institution, the significance of the experience is apt to be missed. Slavery was hard to eradicate in part because it was not an unmitigated evil.

On the positive side, the availability of large drafts of slave labor encouraged the rapid and successful development of vast regions of the nation that would otherwise, in all probability, have long remained barren of settlement and cultivation. By the time of the founding period, planters had already sent their slaves into the swamps and forests of the coastland South and cleared and cultivated some of the most productive soil on the continent. Between 1790 and 1820, the push of this development surmounted the Appalachian Mountains, moved strongly into Kentucky and central Tennessee, and produced areas of settlement in central Alabama, along the lower Mississippi Delta, and around St. Louis, Missouri.[13] And already planters were casting jealous eyes toward the flats of Arkansas and the jungles of north Florida. Southerners often argued that it would be impossible to cultivate these regions without black slaves, that only Negroes could withstand the heat and disease and still work productively there. Modern historians have noted that blacks suffered greatly from the dangers and discomforts of life and work in these tropical climates, but were not free to complain or to choose a more amenable environment.[14] But though it was owing as much to the avarice and appalling brutality of white men as to the stamina of blacks that these forbidding regions were brought under cultivation, it is nevertheless true that slavery greatly encouraged and hastened the development of the southernmost regions of the United States.

The achievement of these planters and black slaves was to turn these jungles and swamps into productive fields, thereby extending the "nerves" of effective communication to the farthest reaches of the nation's territory, keeping the pressure of development on the frontier and strengthening it against foreign intrigue or domestic disaffection. As a result, in terms of the technological capabilities available in the late eighteenth and early nineteenth centuries, the extent of the republic under the harness of the Constitution was vast almost beyond comprehension.

The commitment of the most dynamic Southerners to development and cultivation through the use of slave labor contributed in another way, too, to the pioneering thrust westward. Under the Constitution of 1787, the weight of representation was tied to population in one house of Congress, to statehood in the other, and to a combination of these factors in the Electoral College. This meant that there were high political stakes attached to the race westward. From the beginning, men in both sections but especially Southerners, were aware that the West was a crucial arena of competition. Whether the basic sectional cleavage was conceived in terms of agrarianism versus commerce and manufacturing or more directly in terms of slavery versus nonslavery, the sense of urgency and of the stakes involved in the competition was keen among the most alert leaders along the seaboard. It is difficult to measure the effect of this sense of competition on the decisions of individuals considering a move westward, but there is plenty of evidence that lawmakers at the nation's capital were anxious to encourage migrations from their own sections by shaping the West to the habits and aspirations of their constituents.[15]

Historians of economic development in the United States suggest another vital contribution of slavery to the integration, development, and enrichment of the country as a whole. The beginning of the nineteenth century was a time when technological discoveries were enabling men to use natural and cultivated resources in new and extremely productive ways. The adaptation of steam power and spinning machines to the production of cotton cloth was an example. The use of these techniques created a terrific demand for raw cotton, which in turn stimulated a demand for the services of merchants and sailors who could bring raw cotton to the makers of cloth, and the clothes and other finished products to market. The purveyors of these mercantile services realized a great profit from this trade, which constituted, according to one leading authority, nearly 40 per cent of the entire American export trade between 1815 and 1819.[16] Despite a spurt of growth in the textile industry in New England on the eve of the War of 1812,[17] much cotton was still shipped to Great Britain. This resulted in a considerable balance of trade in favor of the United States. Much of the earnings from this commerce returned to New England, New York, and Pennsylvania, where they were invested in manufacturing enterprises. Economic historians state quite flatly that industrial growth is the key to economic development, and that the presence of investment capital is the key to industrial growth.[18] In this case, profits from the cultivation and export of cotton contributed substantially to the accumulation of the margin of capital with which American industry and the American economy as a whole gathered steam for its future growth.

Thus, the slave labor of blacks was an integral part of the process by which the American industrial economy got started. Agriculture is often the sick sister of an economy that is straining toward the development of a manufacturing capacity, but in the American case, the existence of slavery made agriculture not only a viable industry itself, but also the one that produced a substantial part of the capital essential to the development of the rest of the economy. Assuming that the investors in the manufacturing enterprises of the North knew where their capital was coming from, it is perhaps possible to understand why Northern capitalists were not always in the vanguard of the abolitionist train.

The cotton gin, by encouraging sectional specialization, produced a substantial increase in the interdependence of the nation's economy.[19] Economic intercourse between the sections during the period of the Confederation (1781–1788) had been minimal. The change that had occurred by 1820 should not be overestimated. The American economy was still extremely primitive, and the amount of interstate and intersectional commerce was still quite small. But the potential was beginning to be seen. One effect of this interdependence was felt in the nation's political life. Politicians who represented men with money to invest were not so oblivious of their own interest as to mount an assault on the modes of Southern agricultural production. Thus, many Northern debaters during the Missouri controversy were careful to specify that they had no desire to abolish slavery where it was already deeply entrenched.[20] Like the British Army in 1780, Northerners were limited in what they could do to punish the South by their desire not to wreck a productive vine.

In terms of specifically political development, slavery and its consequences strengthened the resistance to governmental centralization. Sometimes slavery's influence in this regard is deemed negative. But, as Tocqueville pointed out, republican government—that is, government responsive to its citizens—must have strong and relatively independent local centers. Particularly in a large country, the more initiative shifts to the central government, the more oligarchical that government inevitably becomes. Oligarchy sooner or later threatens liberty, and the undermining of liberty is the end of republicanism.

The tendency of modern theorists of national development has been to favor an approach that is more self-conscious, more deliberate in its over-all allocation of resources than the American process was, and to look to the central government to take the lead in this process. The wastefulness and inefficiency of the American process are regarded as unfortunate and unnecessary, and in any case impossible where nature and fortune are less prodigal than in the American case. Recently, however, theorists have begun to recognize that democracy is not an efficient form of government, and that a concern for efficiency is often inimical to democracy. Modern Americans who sense the threat that centralized national power poses to a healthy popular participation in public affairs are more sympathetic to the notion, which used to be of concern only to political conservatives, that the price of democracy may be a willingness to reject the deceptive promises of centralized planning.

As conservatives, who have preached this doctrine for a long time, will attest, it is difficult to persuade people that the pursuit of efficient development threatens democracy, and that the game is not worth the candle. In the American case, however, persuasion on this point was easier. The sectional cleavage produced by slavery was enough to convince many leading Americans in the first half of the nineteenth century to restrain the federal hand from directing the process of national development. There were other factors, of course—among them, the innate resistance of agrarian people to commercial and industrial modernization and the political potency of this conservatism in a country overwhelmingly rural and agricultural; and the animus against political power and authority in a country that was born in a struggle against "grasping power." [21] But the aggressiveness of *state* governments in fostering economic development suggests that a doctrinaire attitude of *laissez faire* was not pervasive in the American political system.[22] It is often suggested that Americans were reluctant to grant authority to the federal government lest the effect of the American Revolution be simply to replace the despot in London with "one hundred seventy-three despots" at home, as Jefferson once put it.[23] But it seems unlikely that this attitude, which was undoubtedly strong at the time of the Revolution, could have persisted indefinitely unless it was powerfully reinforced by impulses other than the memory of the oppression that produced the Revolution. Tensions related to slavery were prominent among the forces that maintained the resolve to develop the country without strong direction from Washington. Had it not been for the sectional cleavage produced by slavery, the forces pressing for centralization might well have prevailed early in the nineteenth century.[24]

These, then, were the contributions of slavery to American economic and political development. None amounts to a justification of the institution, but they do help to explain how the founders were reconciled to its continued existence. There were other factors, too, that reinforced slavery against abolition—factors having to do, not with the advantages of the continued toleration of slavery, but with the difficulty of removing it.

The main stumbling block to the elimination of slavery was the belief among most white Americans that the races were incompatible except in circumstances that insured the perpetual subservience of blacks. In regions where blacks were sparsely settled, social control did not require great vigilance, and emancipation involved only a simple act of manumission. But for Southerners, two acts were required: manumission and transportation. Slavery was regarded by most Southern whites as essential to their self-preservation in the midst of large numbers of blacks. "What is practicable must often control what is pure theory," wrote Jefferson in 1802, "and the habits of the governed determine in a great degree what is practicable." Blacks set free from slavery would resent the inhibitions that remained after emancipation; whites would continue to behave in ways expressive of their deeply ingrained contempt. Such attitudes could not be wished away, and they made abolition almost unthinkable for most Southerners.[25]

Another part of the problem was financial. The South had an enormous investment in slavery. Plantation agriculture was virtually the only productive industry in the entire region. The investment in black labor alone was reckoned in the hundreds of millions of dollars, at a time when the national budget for a year was about $10 or $20 million.[26] It was sometimes proposed that the vast national domain be committed to assisting emancipation, the income from the sale of the land being used to support a program of gradual emancipation and, if necessary, a program of recolonization of the blacks on the coast of Africa or on an island in the Caribbean.[27] But apart from the objection that most slave owners did not want to sell their slaves because they could not imagine conducting their plantations without them, there was a strictly economic objection. Land in the West was often bought with money borrowed from banks or earned in industries that derived capital funds from the transoceanic traffic in cotton, sugar, and tobacco. Thus much of the capital that carried migration westward came either directly or indirectly from the earnings of slavery. If, somehow, the political will could have been found to overthrow slavery and to transport the blacks, a prolific source of capital would have dried up. The irony of the economic situation was that the primary source of the capital needed to liquidate the investment in slavery was slavery itself.

Therefore, in the United States, a political system "exquisitely" sensitive to the elements of which it was composed[28] and whose structure, both formal and informal, was geared to frustrate rather than facilitate public action at the national level,[29] could not be expected to produce forthright action to end slavery, particularly when the group with the most immediate interest in overthrowing slavery was itself completely unrepresented in the system.

Some analysts of American development argue that sectional loyalties prevented the accumulation of political power at the center of the system, and thereby delayed the full realization of American nationality.[30] These analysts of modernization, in assessing the early national period, deplore the fact that political power, particularly at the national level, was regarded as anathema.[31] When indicating how power might have been used had Congressmen been willing to use it forthrightly, they point to such plans as Albert Gallatin's $20-million scheme for internal improvements, set forth in 1808, or to the programs of John Quincy Adams, contained in his messages to Congress. They also deplore the nation's impotence in the face of threatening actions by England and France during the first two decades of the nineteenth century.

The best answer to these points is that, whether owing to the prodigality of nature or the distraction of our foes, the nation survived these trials and muddled through to a pace of development that is the envy of modern nations seeking the path to social and economic prosperity. In fact, it was not the failure to float a formidable navy or the inability to develop an intricate system of canals and roads that brought the nation to crisis, but simply and precisely the failure to come to grips with slavery. Given the nation's circumstances in 1820, its geographical isolation and the energy of its people, it was, on balance, an advantage to commit the task of internal improvement to states and localities. It was in failing to confront slavery that the American republic made its most catastrophic blunder.

The strength of the American system of government lies in its responsiveness. The system has been stable throughout most of the country's history because its legitimacy has been sustained by the belief that the government is not an autonomous agency pursuing purposes of its own, but an instrument of the popular will. Periods of instability have come when sectors of the polity have thought that the federal government was proceeding in a way heedless of their interests and demands; as when the farmers of western Pennsylvania mounted resistance to an excise tax on whisky, which they regarded as discriminatory, and New England grew restive under the Jeffersonian embargo and Mr. Madison's War. But such episodes have been rare because the tendency of the government is rather not to act at all than to act recklessly in defiance of feelings intensely held in the constituency.

An essential component of success in such a system is a low moral temperature in the underlying political culture.[32] A government more likely not to act than to act must preside over a people who tend to look to their own energies and exertions for secular fulfillment. Tocqueville has provided the classic treatment of this element in the American political culture. He noted that the energies of Americans were consumed by commercial enterprise; that their religious practices held out no compelling vision of beatitude, but, rather, counseled patience and thrift and a narrowly focused concentration on the development of God's bounty; that the controlling moral value, equality, was conceived in political and material terms, and, while generous in its inclusiveness where whites were concerned, had little revolutionary leverage in a society where popular energies had abundant outlet in private enterprise and local association. Such a political culture, operating in an abundant natural setting, seemed well adapted to a governmental system designed to frustrate rather than facilitate public action.

It is tempting, when looking at the early national period, to conclude that the system and its culture were perfectly well suited to the nation's circumstances.[33] From this perspective, the Civil War appears as a disturbing footnote, but forces no fundamental revision of the thesis. One of two approaches is taken to explain what happened. At one time, there was a tendency to hold that the conflict between the states was produced by fanatics who drove the sections to extremes, rendering a political solution impossible. The implication was that, except for this unwarranted intrusion of moral fervor on both sides, the conflict could have been transcended, or repressed, and the problem solved by rational, political means. Earlier, and recently, a different explanation has been preferred: that slavery, being the one institution that challenged the moral basis of American democracy, presented a problem unique in American history, the one problem that merited and required a moral approach; that the country floundered until Abraham Lincoln was able to cast the issue in an appropriate framework and force a confrontation on those terms; that the problem so cast was unamenable to political solution that a military struggle was necessary to restore the moral basis upon which the system depended; and that once the war had been won by the side committed to the fundamental principles of the Declaration and the Constitution, the way was cleared for a return to politics according to the intention of the framers—that is, politics where the moral basis is assumed, rather than contended over, and where the public agenda is devoted primarily to questions of economic regulation.[34]

The trouble with both these views is their tendency to focus on slavery as the basic issue, which it was not. The basic issue was relations between the races, and it is because of reluctance to confront this issue squarely that American democracy has been unable to solve its greatest and continuing crisis by political means.[35] The attempt to abolish slavery without coming to terms with the racial question has been continually abortive. Though conflict between the sections over dominance in the territories forced an oblique assault on slavery,[36] the agonizing ordeal of Reconstruction and the long century of bitterness that followed demonstrate the superficiality of the result, signified by the Thirteenth Amendment.

The problem with slavery was that it was morally wrong, that its fruits, upon which so many people depended for their livelihood, were corrupt and tainted, and that everyone who took the moral commitments of the government seriously knew that slavery was at variance with those commitments. The national community was thus divided and distracted and living in a poisoned atmosphere as long as slavery existed. The real reason that slavery had to be abolished was not that it inhibited development, but that as long as it existed the morality of the government was corrupt and idealistic men could not commit themselves to its purposes, particularly when events made it impossible to ignore slavery's malignant presence.

One manifestation of the moral pollution produced by slavery was the proliferation of myths by which politicians and other citizens made their accommodation to slavery: that slavery was dying by degrees; that Congress would have power to abolish slavery itself after 1808, and that the act of 1808 against the African slave trade might fairly be called a "Slave Abolition Act," as it was by many Congressmen; that it was possible to conduct the nation's business without touching slavery in any except certain carefully specified ways; that slavery was somehow an appropriate status for Africans, inasmuch as they were naturally indolent, improvident, and spasmodically vicious when free, but capable of great productivity and loyalty when harnessed to the disciplines of slavery.

Corresponding to these myths was a set of public policies that grew up during the early national period to keep alive the belief that there were ways to reduce slavery's hold short of abolishing it and undertaking a reorientation in race relations. Colonization was one of these, a program whose only excuse was the desperation that provoked it. No more was the money forthcoming than were Africans interested in making the trip or Americans capable of securing a place in Africa fit for their habitation.[37]

Another fantastic public policy was the one called "diffusion." Its proponents argued that if slavery could not be abolished because slaves were too densely settled in certain areas, slave owners should be enabled and encouraged to spread their holdings over a wider area, and then it would be possible to talk sensibly about schemes of emancipation. Rarely have men fallen prey to greater nonsense than did the proponents of diffusion. It was societies of men, not acres of geography, that would have to consider emancipation. If a given area was opened to development by owners of slaves, there was no reason to suppose that elements in a society that depended on slavery would not move into the new area in roughly the same proportion in which they had earlier existed together.

In fact, the early settlement patterns in Tennessee and Ken-

tucky suggest that whites without slaves or with only small holdings of slaves were more likely to move across the mountains from
Virginia than were planters who owned large numbers of slaves.
Between 1790 and 1810, the population of Kentucky rose from
73,000 to over 400,000, and the proportion of blacks rose from 17
per cent to about 23 per cent. Meanwhile, the population of Virginia was growing, too, from about 750,000 in 1790 to close to one
million by 1810. According to the diffusion theory, these growth
figures, at least in Virginia, should have been attended by a drop
in the ratio of blacks in the population as a whole, but in fact the
ratio rose from 40.9 per cent to 43.4.[38]

In seeking to explain these figures, Northern Congressmen
spoke of the doctrines of Malthus, who taught that population
expands to consume the available produce. Assuming that the net
reproductive capacities of the races were about equivalent, there
was no reason, taking all things into consideration, to assume that
the ratio of blacks in the total population would be affected by
the dissemination of people across acres of land. The number of
blacks in any given county might decline, but on balance the
ratio of blacks would probably not—and, in fact, did not—decline, throughout the antebellum period.

The prospect of diffusion—the promise that it would increase
the chances for emancipation by evolutionary means—was a
snare and a delusion. The only way for blacks to be more generally diffused throughout the population was either to lure whites
into areas of heavy black concentration, to which the masses of
white men were not attracted at that time, for reasons which slave
owners must not have found hard to understand; or to send
blacks into states where slavery was already outlawed. Several
schemes for accomplishing the latter purpose were proposed during this period. Congressman James Smilie suggested that the
slave trade from Africa might be stopped by seizing all slaves illegally imported after 1808, removing them to free states, and
equipping them for gradual assimilation into these Northern
communities. Another scheme was to encourage citizens of free
states to purchase slaves to labor for a term of years and then set
them free.[39] But there was no enthusiasm anywhere for any of
these ideas. Racial prejudice was general throughout the land, as
Leon Litwack's *North of Slavery* has made abundantly clear.[40]

Northerners were nearly as reluctant to share in the task of overcoming racial discrimination as most Southerners were to give up a valuable, fundamental resource, a system of labor without which the rest of their productive process, as constituted, would be utterly inoperable.

The intersectional dialogue in Congress on diffusion illustrates the refusal to face squarely the problem that lay at the root of the sectional cleavage and demonstrates its effect. Southerners asserted that the territories should be opened to slavery so that the institution could be diffused across a greater area and thus made less dangerous and easier to cope with. Jefferson once described slavery as a wolf which Southerners held by the ears, dangerous to hold, but even more dangerous to release. The implication of the diffusion theory was that slavery could somehow be domesticated sponded with another image. Slavery was a virulent disease, like by being spread out over a wider territory. Northerners resmallpox. It was no cure for such a plague to allow it to spread. It would be best to quarantine it and let it play itself out.

This was in many ways an apt image for the Northern outlook on slavery. But Southerners were well aware that slavery carried the seeds of annihilation for their region. The specter of Santo Domingo was ever quick in their imagination. In these circumstances, the Northern barb could only be taken by them as hostile, and as evidence that they would have to cope with the danger alone. This being the case, they naturally determined to fight for survival with every means at their command, including the political power to gain as much breathing space as possible in the territories.

Most Northerners regarded slavery as primarily and fundamentally a Southern problem. They blamed Southerners for their reliance on slave labor, and they were full of judgments about the effects of this reliance on Southern mores. Some were inclined to be generous with sympathy and to agree, for public policy's sake, not to "meddle" with slavery. Those more hostile took every opportunity to gain political advantage from the South's defensive posture. But the common denominator for Northerners was the view that slavery was a Southern problem for which they need feel no responsibility.

In this context, it was natural for Southerners to reciprocate the view that slavery was their own business. The institution, by the end of the eighteenth century, was thoroughly integral to the Southern way of life. Economically and socially, Southerners regarded it as necessary. Their mode of production depended on slave labor; the stability of their communities depended on the disciplines of slavery.[41] At the same time, they knew that slavery was wrong, and many of them were candid in admitting that they wished the institution had never taken root in America. They were even willing to agree, many of them, that abolition would be a blessing if it could be accomplished safely and beneficially. But disentangling the commitment to slavery and making the adjustments that emancipation would require were jobs that could not be accomplished quickly or neatly. The weakness of the bands of union with the Northern states and the detached attitude of Northerners toward their predicament suggested that it would be foolish for them to rely on outside help in a matter on which their survival seemed so plainly to depend.

Though Southerners were willing to admit that slavery posed a potential danger, they were confident that they could handle it for the time being and the foreseeable future.[42] And when they arose in Congress to insist that slavery was their problem and that Northern meddling produced only peril for every inhabitant of the Southern region, black as well as white, there were always Northerners quick to agree. Encouraging blacks to strive for freedom would only induce them to flee north, either as fugitives or as manumitted freedmen, since Southern society was so hostile to the presence of free blacks. During the Congressional debates of the founding period, this point was apparently never answered by a frank espousal of the desire to welcome blacks into Northern communities.

David Potter has suggested the need to specify more carefully than is often done the source of the sectional conflict in mid-nineteenth-century America.[43] He notes the inadequacy of the most familiar explanations: the abstractness and formalism of the states'-rights-versus-nationalism approach; the failure of theories based on the assumption of conflict between societies whose economies are fundamentally antagonistic to explain the violence of the American rupture, and the healing of the breach after the war; and the failure of a strictly moral interpretation to acknowledge the racial prejudice of Northerners. He suggests a different line of interpretation: that the sectional controversy produced violent conflict when one party to the controversy came finally to believe that the very lives of its people would be jeopardized if it accepted political defeat.

The sectional conflict was extraordinary because of the racial element. Had the struggle been confined to questions of tariffs and subsidies and international relations and the normal affairs of politics, the South could have accepted occasional defeats, or even a long series of defeats, without coming to the conclusion that it was better to fight than to accept any more losses. But in the circumstances of Lincoln's victory in 1860, the South believed that it was decisively outnumbered and confronted by the prospect of a government unalterably hostile to policies upon which its survival depended. In Southern eyes, Lincoln led a party committed to the overthrow of slavery without regard for the consequences, and no assurances from him could, by 1860, placate Southern fears.

The stability of a state depends in large measure on the government's record of dealing with past crises. It accumulates strength as it demonstrates that it can handle problems in a manner that gives satisfaction to most citizens and is tolerable to the overwhelming majority.[44] Potter's thesis suggests that the federal government had failed, as of 1860, to persuade the South of its capacity to deal with the intersectional differences over slavery. Yet because the normal course of government inevitably raised questions affecting slavery, it was impossible, with the best will in the world, to satisfy the Southern demand that the federal government restrain its hand from slavery completely.

During most of the early national period, politicians from the South or those fully sympathetic to the Southern position on slavery were in command of the government. The result was that, during this period, the government grew steadily in stability, accumulating a record of dealing satisfactorily with most matters in which the sections were in conflict. Most of the restiveness that did exist was found in New England, where certain nervous leaders feared that the nation was falling into the grip of reckless agrarians and fanatic Francophiles and pursuing policies that threatened to undermine the commercial prosperity of New England. There were other flare-ups of secessionism, too, especially in the West, where the ambitions of separatists were encouraged by the remoteness of the seaboard government (it took a full five weeks, in good weather, to travel from New York to the Mississippi River at the turn of the nineteenth century[45]) and the proximity of Spanish intrigue. But apart from a brief flirtation with nullification during the alien-and-sedition controversy of 1798 and the invocations of Armageddon by South Carolinians and John Randolph whenever they felt that Congressional legislation was moving too close to the institution of domestic slavery, the deepest threats to the union came, between 1789 and 1819, from outside the South.

Although the seeds of the sectional clash of 1860 were in the soil at the nation's founding, it was not until the Missouri controversy of 1820 that the conflict appeared at the surface of American politics. During this crisis, the South saw for the first time the possibility that it might one day be outnumbered in all branches of the federal government. It saw that there were issues on which the federal government could not possibly evade action on the subject of slavery. It saw, too, that on the territorial issue, at least, the Constitution contained no real barrier to action inimical to slavery. Reflection revealed further that such Cassandras as Patrick Henry and Rawlins Lowndes had been basically correct in 1788, during the ratification debates, when they argued that the war powers, for example, might one day be construed to give the federal government power to regulate or abolish slavery. The only barriers to such action in 1820—the political power of the South and the memory of the spirit of the compact made in 1787—could not be relied upon to last forever. Because the Missouri controversy brought these points to the attention of Southern leaders, it is justly seen as the first clear step on the road that led to the Civil War.

The irony is that the storm came just two or three years after the period of greatest calm in the history of the republic. Henry Adams ended his account of the administrations of Jefferson and

Madison by picturing the United States as riding the crest of a wave of democratic nationalism. The young nation, impelled by the energy and ambition and confidence of young leaders from the South and West, had emerged remarkably victorious from a war with the world's greatest military power. A secessionist movement in New England had been disgraced, and the Democratic-Republican party appeared to be virtually unopposed at the nation's capital. The young men who had led the nation into the war were now eager to embark on a program of internal development, whose purpose was to tie the nation's sections into a single, strong, flexible unit, thus fulfilling the "ancient" dream of leading statesmen in both political parties. Only a small Constitutional cloud obscured the light in 1816, and there seemed no opponents of the plan to wipe that obstruction away by granting a more generous interpretation to the original text or by amendment, whichever seemed the most propitious course.[46]

The Constitutional problem, however, was more serious than it looked. Older hands still controlled the rudder in the executive branch, and a rain of vetoes began to descend on the bright hopes of Clay and Calhoun. Then the Panic of 1819 took the steam out of the economic enthusiasms of 1816, the government fell to haggling over the enforcement of the law of 1807 against the slave trade, and the question of slavery in the territories thoroughly doused the vision of harmony and good feeling that followed Jackson's victory at New Orleans. Briefly, the euphoria of victory had made it possible to forget the divisive fact of slavery, but as soon as the government returned to the business of regulating the affairs of the nation, the cleavage in the nation's spirit reappeared.

In 1787, the South had taken a leap of faith. Knowing the danger of allowing alien hands to intrude on the regulation of slavery, but believing that it was possible to frame a constitution that could provide general government without touching domestic slavery, the South determined to enter a constitutional union with nonslaveholders. But this decision was premised upon a whole series of misjudgments. Southern leaders underestimated the effect of slavery on their own economic and social development, and overestimated the drift of population, wealth, and power in their direction. They mistakenly trusted in their own ability to control the evolution of Constitutional interpretation. They gave themselves to the view that slavery was a Southern problem, and that, if it was not destined to last forever, it could be eliminated by gradual, if not easy, stages. In their situation, such errors of anticipation were fatal.

But so, in the long run, were the errors of Northerners. It reflected a colossal failure of moral and political wisdom for Northerners to persuade themselves that the subculture of slavery could be isolated indefinitely. There would be no escape for any American from the consequences of the sins of discrimination and exploitation committed by whites against blacks. And the problem that began in the founding period could not be settled until the American people, the whole American people, undertook the work of reconciliation to which their Declaration of Independence committed them from the outset.

Short Titles and Abbreviations
Used in the Notes

Notes

Index

Short Titles and Abbreviations
Used in the Notes

Annals: The Debates and Proceedings in the Congress of the United States (Washington: Gales and Seaton, 1834–). Citations also give the number of the Congress, the number of the Session, and the date of the speech or vote cited.

Bailyn, *Pamphlets:* Bernard Bailyn, ed., *Pamphlets of the American Revolution, 1750–1776,* vol. 1 (Cambridge: Harvard University Press, Belknap Press, 1965).

Burnett, *Letters:* Edmund C. Burnett, ed., *Letters of Members of the Continental Congress,* 8 vols. (Washington: Carnegie Institution, 1921–1936).

Farrand, *Records:* Max Farrand, ed., *The Records of the Federal Convention of 1787,* 4 vols. (New Haven, Conn.: Yale University Press, 1911, 1937).

Force, *American Archives:* Peter Force, comp., *American Archives,* 9 vols. (Washington: M. St. Clair Clarke and Peter Force, 1837–1853).

JCC: Journals of the Continental Congress, 1774–1789 (Washington: Government Printing Office, 1904–1937). The figures that follow the abbreviation are volume and page numbers.

Jensen, *Documents:* Merrill Jensen, ed., *English Historical Documents,* vol. 9, *American Colonial Documents to 1776* (London: Eyre and Spottiswoode, 1955).

Notes

INTRODUCTION

1. Few people in the country were prepared to act on a radical interpretation of the Declaration of Independence as far as equality for blacks was concerned, but, at the same time, open hostility to the Declaration, even among Southerners, was not common. During the debates over Missouri, however, Southern impatience with the Declaration, as applied to the blacks, did burst into the open. See Glover Moore, *The Missouri Controversy, 1819–1821* (Lexington: University of Kentucky Press, 1953), pp. 308–309.

2. For a good introduction to the scholarly literature addressed to the question of the relationship between slavery and Southern economic and social development, see Harold D. Woodman, ed., *Slavery and the Southern Economy* (New York: Harcourt, Brace & World, 1966), pt. 4.

3. A slave named Gabriel Prosser did succeed in organizing an uprising around Richmond, Virginia, in 1800 but it was exposed before the blood of any whites was shed. The main results of the "rebellion" seem to have been the execution of every Negro suspected of involvement in the plot and the strenuous tightening of security against "servile insurrections" in Virginia and throughout the South. For an account and bibliographical references, see Winthrop D. Jordan, *White Over Black* (Chapel Hill: University of North Carolina Press, 1968), pp. 393–394.

   It is extremely difficult to assess the resistance to slavery by slaves themselves. The interest of slave owners and Southern editors in picturing their chattels as contented, plus fear that uprisings might prove contagious, made them generally reluctant to be candid about the extent of resistance among their slaves. On the other hand, when they did feel free to talk about it, as in letters among themselves, Southerners often showed exaggerated fears of the "savages" they had enslaved. Coupled with the illiteracy cf most slaves, these attitudes make it nearly impossible to recover a reliable picture of this aspect of American Negro slavery. Among the most important attempts to surmount these obstacles are John Hope Franklin, *From Slavery to Freedom,* 2nd ed. (New York: Alfred A. Knopf, 1964), pp. 204–212; Kenneth Stampp, *The Peculiar Institution* (New York: Alfred A. Knopf, Vintage Books, 1956), pp. 86–140; Jordan, *op. cit.,* pp. 391–399; and Herbert Apteker, *American Negro Slave Revolts* (New York: Columbia University Press, 1943). Marion J. Russell, "American Slave Discontent in the Records of the High Courts," *Journal of Negro History,* 31 (1946), 411–434, draws on Helen Catterall, ed., *Judicial Cases Concerning American Slavery and the Negro,* 5 vols. (Washington: Carnegie Institution, 1926–1937).

4. My guess is that Jefferson was more deeply troubled about slavery and its implications for the future of America than any other public man of his generation. On the relationship between Jefferson and Sally Hemings, see Pearl M. Graham, "Thomas Jefferson and Sally Hemings," *Journal of Negro History,* 46 (1961), 89–103.

5. Franklin, *op. cit.,* p. 209.

6. See *The Methodology of the Social Sciences* (Glencoe, Ill.: The Free Press, 1949), pp. 182–185. See also the use of Weber's insight in Joseph LaPalombara and Myron Weiner, eds., *Political Parties and Political Development* (Princeton, N.J.: Princeton University Press, 1966), pp. 20 ff.

7. "The Shape of American Politics," *A Commentary Report* (New York: Commentary Magazine, 1967), p. 3.

CHAPTER 1

1. This account of the status of slavery in seventeenth-century America is based almost entirely on secondary literature. It provides merely a sketch of the institution and its place in American society, which may serve as background for the study of policy that follows. Readers who want to delve more deeply into the institution of slavery as such may consult the following works: for the most comprehensive history of the "black experience" in America in a single volume, John Hope Franklin, *From Slavery to Freedom,* 2nd ed. (New York: Alfred A. Knopf, 1964); for a description of the slave trade, its origins in Africa, the Middle Passage across the Atlantic, and the settlement in America, James Pope-Hennessy, *Sins*

of the Fathers (New York: Alfred A. Knopf, 1963); for an account of the institution itself from an "abolitionist" point of view, Kenneth Stampp, *The Peculiar Institution* (New York: Alfred A. Knopf, Vintage Books, 1964), and from a more sympathetic observer, Ulrich B. Phillips, *American Negro Slavery* (New York: D. Appleton and Co., 1918); for an interpretive essay full of suggestive insights, Stanley M. Elkins, *Slavery: A Problem in American Institutional and Intellectual Life* (New York: Grosset & Dunlap, Grosset's Universal Library, 1963); for discussions of evolving attitudes toward the idea of slavery, David Brion Davis, *The Problem of Slavery in Western Culture* (Ithaca, N.Y.: Cornell University Press, 1966), and Winthrop D. Jordan, *White Over Black* (Chapel Hill: University of North Carolina Press, 1968); for a portrait of slavery drawn by a gifted modern novelist, William Styron, *The Confessions of Nat Turner* (New York: Random House, 1967); and for important critical reflections on Styron's work, John Henrik Clarke, ed., *William Styron's Nat Turner: Ten Black Writers Respond* (Boston: Beacon Press 1968). Treatments of special topics will be indicated in subsequent notes. Suggestions for further reading will be found in the first chapter of Elkins's book, and in the footnotes in Davis's book.

2. The phrase "unthinking decision" is taken from Jordan, *op. cit.*, chap. 2.

3. Davis, *op. cit.*, chap. 2, discusses similarities and differences between American and previous forms of slavery. He emphasizes what he calls the "patterns of continuity," but he does not ignore the differences stemming from the factor of race in the American version.

4. Jordan, *op. cit.*, p. 74.

5. The Oxford dictionary definition is quoted from *ibid.*, p. 7. Davis *op. cit.*, pp. 281–288, discusses the question of the origin of racial prejudice as it bears on the founding of slavery in America.

6. So important was this element of religious prejudice in the rationale of slavery that there was concern lest the baptism of Negroes might render them ineligible for slavery. The question was resolved by a series of statutes in the colonies which declared that baptism in no way affected the status of a slave. See Jordan, *op. cit.*, p. 92, and Davis, *op. cit.*, pp. 101–102.

7. Jordan, *op. cit.*, pp. 24–28. Jordan speaks mainly in terms of the first contacts of white men with Africans in Africa. Although the accounts of merchants in Africa are not directly apropos, they do

help us to imagine what the reactions of men in Virginia and Massachusetts must have been. Elkins, *op. cit.,* pp. 98–103, has described the passage of Africans to America, aboard the ghastly slave ships, as a profound trauma that produced complete disorientation in the victim, destroying his memory, breaking his spirit, and dropping him into new circumstances, completely isolated from familiar neighbors and surroundings that could reinforce previous habits. Recently, Elkins's thesis has been subjected to severe criticism by those who argue that the shock of transplantation did not obliterate the African heritage of its victims. (See *Civil War History,* vol. 8 [December 1967], especially the articles by Eugene Genovese, George Fredrickson, and Christopher Lasch.) It is not time yet to attempt a balanced verdict on this debate; the search for African survivals must be pressed further. It is enough to note here that the Africans who came to America seemed alien and savage to their owners and that this strangeness constituted part of the rationale for enslavement.

8. "Epidemiology and the Slave Trade," *Political Science Quarterly,* 83 (1968), 190–216.

9. The migration of white servants to colonial America is described by Abbot E. Smith, *Colonists in Bondage* (Chapel Hill: University of North Carolina Press, 1947).

10. For an account of "concerted action by bound servants" to protest rough treatment, see Richard B. Morris, *Government and Labor in Early America* (New York: Columbia University Press, 1946), pp. 167–182 *et passim.*

11. This old guess, made by Henry C. Carey in 1853, in *The Slave Trade, Domestic and Foreign* (Philadelphia: A. Hart, 1853), p. 18, is often cited by modern authors, and is probably as accurate as any.

12. Lewis C. Gray, *History of Agriculture in the Southern United States to 1860* (Washington: Carnegie Institution, 1933), vol. 1, pp. 356–359.

13. Alexis de Tocqueville, *Democracy in America,* ed. Phillips Bradley (New York: Alfred A. Knopf, Vintage Books, 1945), vol. 1, pp. 347, 368–369.

14. John Locke, *Two Treatises of Government,* ed. Peter Laslett (New York: New American Library, Mentor Book, 1965), pp. 433 ff.; see also Davis, *op. cit.,* pp. 118–120.

15. Jordan, *op. cit.,* pp. 69–70.

16. *Ibid.,* p. 88; Smith, *op. cit.,* pp. 153 ff.

17. Smith, *op. cit.*, p. 171. It is a mistake to draw the contrast between white and black servitude too sharply. White servants in colonial America suffered greatly, both during their passage to the New World and in subsequent labors for their new masters. Besides Smith's book, see Marcus W. Jernegan, *Laboring and Dependent Classes in Colonial America, 1607–1783* (Chicago: University of Chicago Press, 1931), pp. 50 ff.; and Gottlieb Mittelberger, *Journey to Pennsylvania*, eds. and trans. Oscar Handlin and John Clive (Cambridge: Harvard University Press, Belknap Press, 1960). The difference, however, was that the need for labor, combined with environing social attitudes, drove toward increased opportunity and freedom for enterprising white workers, but toward ever harsher treatment for black slaves. For a discussion of these differences see Davis, *op. cit.*, pp. 245 ff.

18. There were several ways in which Africans became slaves to Europeans, only one of which was by losing in battle to other Africans. Criminals were sold as punishment. Famine forced some men to deliver themselves into bondage. Some were kidnapped by Europeans or by native gangs. A few had been slaves to Africans—though Africans were apparently reluctant to sell their own slaves. Elkins, *op. cit.*, p. 98 n.

19. See Winthrop D. Jordan, "The Influence of the West Indies on the Origins of New England Slavery," *William and Mary Quarterly*, 3rd ser., 18 (1961), 243–250.

20. For a summary of the motives behind the "English colonial intention," see Samuel Eliot Morison, *The Oxford History of the American People* (New York: Oxford University Press, 1965), pp. 48–49.

21. Gray, *op. cit.*, vol. 1, pp. 362–364.

22. See Franklin's "Observations Concerning the Increase of Mankind," in Leonard W. Labaree, ed., *The Papers of Benjamin Franklin* (New Haven, Conn.: Yale University Press, 1959–), vol. 4, pp. 229–231.

23. Richard C. Wade, *Slavery in the Cities: The South, 1820–1860* (New York: Oxford University Press, 1964), pp. 243–280.

24. There were, of course, scattered exceptions to these generalizations. A law passed in 1809 in New York, for example, permitted slaves to own property (see Edgar McManus, *A History of Negro Slavery in New York* [Syracuse, N.Y.: Syracuse University Press, 1966], p. 178), and there were occasions when slaves were permitted to bear arms. But these exceptions do not detract seriously from Davis's conclusion that, "Given the wide range of differences in colonial

societies, the surprising fact [about the slave codes] is their underlying similarity" (*op. cit.*, p. 248; cf. pp. 248–261). For a summary of slave codes in the antebellum South, see Stampp, *op. cit.*, chap. 5.

25. W. J. Cash, *The Mind of the South* (New York: Alfred A. Knopf, Vintage Books, 1941, 1960), pp. 87–89.
26. Davis, *op. cit.*, p. 259.
27. The other two were Kentucky and the Indian Territory (now Oklahoma).
28. Arthur Zilversmit, *The First Emancipation: The Abolition of Slavery in the North* (Chicago: University of Chicago Press, 1967), pp. 113–115.
29. Quoted in *ibid.*, p. 114. Abolition in Massachusetts affords interesting comparisons to the parallel process in Great Britain, where slavery was abolished by Somerset's Case in 1772. Lord Mansfield, Chief Justice of Great Britain, reluctantly decreed that, in the absence of positive law to the contrary, slavery was "so odious" that it could not be established by any "reasons, moral or political," in Great Britain itself. Mansfield's decision resulted in uncompensated emancipation for an estimated 14,000 Negroes living in Britain (Ruth Anna Fischer, "Granville Sharp and Lord Mansfield," *Journal of Negro History*, 28 [1943], 381–389), at a time when there were only slightly more than 4,000 Negroes in Massachusetts.
30. Zilversmit, *op. cit.*, p. 115 n.
31. Merrill Jensen, *The New Nation* (1950; reprint ed., New York: Alfred A. Knopf, Vintage Books, 1965), p. 135. On John Adams, see Lorenzo J. Greene, *The Negro in Colonial New England, 1620–1776* (New York: Columbia University Press, 1942), pp. 113, 322. For evidence of "concerted action by white workmen against Negro artisans," see Morris, *op. cit.*, pp. 182–188.
32. Zilversmit, *op. cit.*, p. 116.
33. Elisha P. Douglass, *Rebels and Democrats* (Chapel Hill: University of North Carolina Press, 1955), chaps. 12–14.
34. The idea was not new in 1780, however. Anthony Benezet and other Quakers had advanced various schemes for gradual emancipation before the outbreak of the Revolution. See Mary S. Locke, *Anti-Slavery in America . . . 1619–1808* (1901; reprint ed., Gloucester, Mass.: Peter Smith, 1965), pp. 31–32.
35. Zilversmit, *op. cit.*, pp. 127–129.
36. *Ibid.*, pp. 131–137.
37. *Op. cit.*, vol. 1, pp. 386–387.

38. For an account of the effect of Negro votes in several close elections, see Dixon Ryan Fox, "The Negro Vote in Old New York," *Political Science Quarterly*, 32 (1917), 252–275.

39. Other pockets of concentration were in southern Rhode Island and southeastern Connecticut, and in York County, Pennsylvania. But each of these areas lay in states that were overwhelmingly white, and they were unable to swing enough weight politically to stall the coming of emancipation more than a few years.

40. Zilversmit, *op. cit.*, p. 162; see also McManus, *op. cit.*, chap. 3 and pp. 197–200.

41. McManus, *op. cit.*, pp. 122–126 *et seq.*

42. This account of abolition in New York is based primarily on Zilversmit, *op. cit.*, chaps. 6 and 7; and McManus, *op. cit.*, chaps. 8 and 9.

43. Zilversmit, *op. cit.*, p. 161.

44. In 1798, Jay wrote, "I purchase slaves, and manumit them at proper ages, and when their faithful services shall have afforded a reasonable retribution." Quoted by Zilversmit, *op. cit.*, p. 167 n.

45. *Ibid.*, pp. 165–166.

46. *Ibid.*, p. 177.

47. Quoted in *ibid.*, p. 209.

48. McManus, *op. cit.*, p. 178.

49. *Op. cit.*, vol. 1, pp. 390, 397.

50. Leon Litwack, *North of Slavery: The Negro in the Free States 1790–1860* (Chicago: University of Chicago Press, 1961), chap. 2 *et passim*.

51. Ulrich B. Phillips calls this "the central theme of Southern history" (*The Course of the South to Secession*, ed. E. M. Coulter [1939; reprint ed., Gloucester, Mass.: Peter Smith, 1953], p. 152). My only objection to Phillips's argument is that this resolve is not really distinctive to the South, at least not in the period before 1860 If the South seemed more firmly committed to racial purity during these years, it was only because Southerners knew the threat of amalgamation more intimately. An interesting corollary of Phillips's "central theme" occurs in the "Address to Six [Indian] Nations," dated July 13, 1775, by the Continental Congress. In an effort to persuade the Indians to remain neutral during the impending struggle with Great Britain, Congress wrote "We [Americans and British] are brothers . . . one blood. . . . This is a family quarrel between us and Old England. You Indians are not concerned in it." *JCC* 2:182.

52. Jordan, *White Over Black*, chap. 2, pp. 66–82.

53. Kenneth M. Stampp, "The Historian and Southern Negro Slavery," *American Historical Review,* 57 (1952), 621.
54. Gray, *op. cit.,* vol. 1, pp. 21–22, 37, and chap. 12.
55. Herbert S. Klein, *Slavery in the Americas: A Comparative Study of Cuba and Virginia* (Chicago: University of Chicago Press, 1967), pp. 142–151.
56. Stampp, "The Historian and Southern Negro Slavery," p. 623.
57. Beni Perley Poore, comp., *The Federal and State Constitutions, Colonial Charters, and Other Organic Laws of the United States* (Washington: Government Printing Office, 1878), pt. 2, p. 1408.
58. Jordan, *White Over Black,* pp. 84–85.
59. Jensen, *op. cit.,* p. 177.
60. *Ibid.,* pp. 324 ff.; Gray, *op. cit.,* vol. 1, pp. 301 ff.
61. *Op. cit.,* vol. 1, p. 372 n.
62. See, for example, *The Federalist* (especially numbers 41, 53, and 56), in which Madison suggests that the economy of the nation was gradually "assimilating," with each section showing greater internal variety. At the Federal Convention Madison indicated that he welcomed this development in the South. Farrand, *Records,* vol. 2, pp. 451–452; cf. vol. 3, pp. 518–521. See also Irving Brant, *James Madison* (Indianapolis, Ind.: Bobbs-Merrill Co., 1941–1961), vol. 3, pp. 389–400; Thomas P. Abernethy, *The South in the New Nation, 1789–1819* (Baton Rouge: Louisiana State University Press, 1961), p. 328.
63. The South was, of course, not devoid of industry. For an account of the use of Negroes in Southern industry, see Robert Starobin, "Race Relation in Old South Industries," in Allen Weinstein and Frank Otto Gatell, eds., *American Negro Slavery: A Modern Reader* (New York: Oxford University Press, 1968), pp. 299–309; George R. Taylor, *The Transportation Revolution, 1815–1860* (New York: Rinehart and Co., 1951), pp. 292–294, and works cited there.
64. Robert R. Russel, "The General Effects of Slavery Upon Southern Economic Progress," *Journal of Southern History,* 4 (1938), 34–54. See also Russel, *Economic Aspects of Southern Sectionalism, 1840–1861* (Urbana: University of Illinois Press, 1924); Harold D. Woodman, "The Profitability of Slavery: A Historical Perennial," *Journal of Southern History,* 29 (1963), 303–325, esp. n. 52; and Woodman, ed., *Slavery and the Southern Economy* (New York: Harcourt, Brace & World, 1966), pt. 4.
65. I use the term "fragment" here in deliberate reference to the anal-

ysis of Louis Hartz in *The Founding of New Societies* (New York: Harcourt, Brace & World, 1964), pp. 58–63 *et passim*. My analysis of the "unfolding" of the Southern fragment of British liberalism differs somewhat from his. I agree with him that it is misleading to call the American South "feudal," but it seems to me no less misleading to insist that it was "bourgeois" or capitalistic. I think it best to concentrate more concretely on the reasons for Southern failure to fit either of these familiar categories, the foremost of which is the factor of racial separation.

66. Clement Eaton, *The Growth of Southern Civilization* (New York: Harper & Brothers, Harper Torchbooks, 1961), chap. 4.
67. In *The Revolution of American Conservatism* (New York: Harper & Row, 1965), pp. 227–412.
68. Eaton, *op. cit.,* pp. 9–10, 18–24; Douglass, *op. cit.,* chap. 3. Fletcher M. Green, in "Democracy in the Old South," *Journal of Southern History,* 12 (1946), 3–23, argued that "the history of the Southern state constitutions and governments from 1776 to 1860 reveals a progressive expansion in the application of the doctrine of political equality," and that, by 1860, "the aristocratic planter class had been shorn of its . . . political power." But Green's measures of political democracy—qualifications for the suffrage, proportion of voters in the total adult population, and the struggle between political parties—are all formal standards. *All other things being equal,* if everyone votes, and the choice is between competitive parties, politics tends to be more democratic. But students of politics have learned that it is necessary to look into social and economic factors, and to study actual public policies, before making judgments about the democratic responsiveness of political regimes. V. O. Key, especially in his study *Southern Politics in State and Nation* (New York: Alfred A. Knopf, 1949), has been a primary source of instruction on this crucial point. For a critique of Green's article, see Carl N. Degler, ed., *Pivotal Interpretations of American History* (New York: Harper & Row, Harper Torchbooks, 1966), vol. 1, pp. 184–187.
69. Starobin, *op. cit.,* p. 300.
70. Wade, *op. cit.,* p. 262.
71. Charles Grier Sellers, Jr., "The Travail of Slavery," in Sellers, ed., *The Southerner as American* (Chapel Hill: University of North Carolina Press, 1960), pp. 40–71.
72. It is also often noted that as late as 1827, 106 of the 130 known abolition societies in the United States were located in the South-

ern states. Stephen B. Weeks, "Anti-Slavery Sentiment in the South," *Publications of the Southern Historical Association, 2* (April 1898), 88–89.

73. Gray, *op. cit.*, vol. 1, p. 525; Henry W. Farnam, *Chapters in the History of Social Legislation in the United States to 1860* (Washington: Carnegie Institution, 1938), pp. 200, 208, 406. Thomas R. Dew commented, on the debate over emancipation in the Virginia Assembly in 1831–1832, "Never before had the subject of emancipation been seriously discussed in any of the legislatures of our Southern slave-holding country." (Quoted in James C. Ballagh, *A History of Slavery in Virginia* [Baltimore: Johns Hopkins Press, 1902], p. 137.) I would add that the discussion in 1831–1832 was not "serious," either, in the sense that it grappled with a feasible plan for abolition. For a critical analysis of various schemes for emancipation advanced in eighteenth-century Virginia, see Robert McColley, *Slavery and Jeffersonian Virginia* (Urbana: University of Illinois Press, 1964), chaps. 6 and 7.

74. Ballagh, *op. cit.*, p. 130. See also McColley, *op. cit.*, pp. 115–116.

75. U.S. Bureau of the Census, *Historical Statistics of the United States: Colonial Times to 1957* (Washington: Government Printing Office, 1960), p. 719. On the unsympathetic feeling of most blacks toward "removal" to Africa, see Louis R. Mehlinger, "The Attitude of the Free Negro toward African Colonization," *Journal of Negro History*, 1 (1916), 276–301. On the general question of colonization, see Philip J. Staudenraus, *The African Colonization Movement, 1816–1865* (New York: Columbia University Press, 1961), and Jordan, *White Over Black*, pp. 542–569.

76. Perhaps the leading exponent of this position—its "mentor," so to speak—was Abraham Lincoln. See his "reply" to Senator Stephen Douglas in their third debate, at Jonesboro, Illinois September 15, 1858; and his "rejoinder" in the sixth debate, at Quincy, Illinois, October 13, 1858. (Robert W. Johannsen, ed., *The Lincoln-Douglas Debates of 1858* [New York: Oxford University Press, 1965], pp. 132, 277–278.

77. Jensen (*op. cit.*, p. 236) notes that "a cotton gin was in common use long before Eli Whitney made his improvements in 1793." If Whitney's contribution must be dramatized, let it stand as a symbol of intersectional complicity in the sin of slavery. Whitney was a tutor from Connecticut studying law in Georgia when he learned of the need to find a way to separate seeds from short-staple cotton. His device was conceived on a plantation belong-

ing to the widow of General Nathanael Greene, of Rhode Island, the distinguished veteran of the Revolutionary War whose plantation was the gift of a grateful nation.

78. Jean-Jacques Rousseau, "A Discourse on the Origin of Inequality," in *The Social Contract and Discourses,* trans. G.D.H. Cole (New York: E. P. Dutton and Co., 1950), p. 251.

79. *Op. cit.,* vol. 1, p. 6.

80. S. E. Morison and H. S. Commager, *The Growth of the American Republic* (New York: Oxford University Press, 1937), vol. 1, p. 82.

CHAPTER 2

1. Charles Francis Adams, ed., *The Works of John Adams* (Boston: Little, Brown and Co., 1850–1856), vol. 3, p. 452.

2. See his letter to Dr. Jeremy Belknap, March 21, 1795, in *Collections of the Massachusetts Historical Society,* 5th ser., vol. 3, p. 40.

3. For a sympathetic review of humanitarian reforms during this period, see Merrill Jensen, *The New Nation* (1950; reprint ed., New York: Alfred A. Knopf, Vintage Books, 1965), chap. 6. This account puts the problem of slavery in proper perspective, as far as the priorities of idealists of that time were concerned. See pp. 134–136.

4. David Brion Davis, *The Problem of Slavery in Western Culture* (Ithaca, N.Y.: Cornell University Press, 1966), p. 24. The opening chapter gives a dynamic, developmental interpretation of "the American dilemma." From the beginning, Davis argues, America's destiny has been intertwined with Negro slavery. What he calls "the meaning of America"—the effort to plant a just republic in the wilderness, beyond the reach of the Old World's contamination—has been dogged and compromised by the willingness of Americans to sacrifice the lives and labors of Negroes to their dream. For Davis, this is no incident or accident, but lies at the heart of the American experience.

5. *Ibid.,* pp. 9, 154–156.

6. David Duncan Wallace, *The Life of Henry Laurens* (New York: G. P. Putnam's Sons, 1915), pp. 88–89. For a portrait of life among the slaves in colonial South Carolina, see Carl Bridenbaugh, *Myths and Realities* (New York: Atheneum Publishers, 1963), chap. 2.

7. Daniel Boorstin, *The Americans: The Colonial Experience* (New York: Alfred A. Knopf, Vintage Books, 1958), pp. 101–102.

8. Charles Sydnor, *American Revolutionaries in the Making* (New York: Free Press of Glencoe, 1965), p. 42 and p. 120, n. 40. According to Sydnor, an "average" justice of the peace, who was an important official in colonial Virginia, held twenty-five slaves, thirteen of them over twelve years of age, and employed them on 903 acres of land (*ibid.*, pp. 64–65).

9. Letter of March 30, 1757. Jensen, *Documents,* pp. 494–495.

10. Davis, *op. cit.,* pp. 154–155.

11. The figure for Boston is estimated from Evarts B. Greene and Virginia D. Harrington, *American Population Before the Federal Census of 1790* (New York: Columbia University Press, 1932), pp. 22, 30, 46. The figure for Connecticut is from U.S. Bureau of the Census, *Historical Statistics of the United States: Colonial Times to 1957* (Washington: Government Printing Office, 1960), p. 756.

12. William V. Wells cited a number of advertisements and announcements from issues of the Boston *Gazette* in the spring of 1761 in *The Life and Public Services of Samuel Adams* (Boston: Little, Brown and Co., 1865), vol. 3, pp. 185–187. George Moore printed several similar advertisements from issues of the *Independent Chronicle* and the *Continental Journal*, two Boston newspapers, in his *Notes on the History of Slavery in Massachusetts* (New York: D. Appleton and Co., 1866), pp. 178–179.

13. For descriptions of the so-called "triangular trade," see James Pope-Hennessy, *Sins of the Fathers* (New York: Alfred A. Knopf, 1968), chap. 2; Lorenzo J. Greene, *The Negro in Colonial New England, 1620–1776* (New York: Columbia University Press, 1942), pp. 24–25; Eric Williams, *Capitalism and Slavery* (Chapel Hill: University of North Carolina Press, 1944); Bernhard Knollenberg, *Origin of the American Revolution* (New York: Macmillan Co., 1960), pp. 146–147; and Clinton L. Rossiter, *Seedtime of the Republic* (New York: Harcourt, Brace and Co., 1953), pp. 66–67, 80–81.

14. Bailyn, *Pamphlets,* vol. 1, pp. 368–370, 513–514.

15. I use the term in the sense defined by Theodore Lowi, in "The Public Philosophy: Interest-Group Liberalism," *American Political Science Review,* 61 (March 1967), 5–24. He defines a "public philosophy" as "any set of principles and criteria above and beyond the reach of government and statesmen by which the decisions of government are guided and justified" (p. 5).

16. This slogan is better for the American Revolution as a whole than

"no taxation without representation." As Bailyn notes, the issue of taxation and representation was "a mere incident" in the constitutional struggle between Britain and America. On the question of representation, colonial opinion vacillated for a while, but by the time of the Stamp Act Congress of 1765 had settled on the position that American representation in Parliament was impracticable. From that point forward, the constitutional issue broadened and deepened. See Bernard Bailyn, *The Ideological Origins of the American Revolution* (Cambridge: Harvard University Press, Belknap Press, 1967), p. 162.

17. On the Sons of Liberty, see H. Morais, "The Sons of Liberty in New York," in R. B. Morris, ed., *The Era of the American Revolution* (New York: Harper & Row, Harper Torchbooks, 1965), pp. 269–289.

18. For a provocative discussion of the notion of "inalienability," see Staughton Lynd, *Intellectual Origins of American Radicalism* (New York: Pantheon Books, 1968), chap. 2.

19. See section 125 of the Second Treatise, in John Locke's *Two Treatises of Government,* ed. Peter Laslett (New York: New American Library, Mentor Book, 1965), p. 396.

20. Bailyn, *Pamphlets,* vol. 1, pp. 63–66. For an example of the colonial "philosophy of history," see John Dickinson's "Letters from a Farmer in Pennsylvania" (1767–1768), Letter IX, in Forrest McDonald, ed., *Empire and Nation* (Englewood Cliffs, N.J.: Prentice-Hall, 1962), pp. 50–58.

21. The wealthiest planters in Virginia and South Carolina apparently studied the English aristocracy with an eye to "transplanting" their way of life to America. But the irrelevance of the model soon forced them either to abandon the effort or to resort to caricature. For a portrait of Virginians as "transplanters," see Boorstin, *op. cit.,* bk. 1, pt. 4.

22. Bailyn, *Pamphlets,* vol. 1, p. 507.

23. See Hopkins's pamphlet, entitled "The Rights of Colonies Examined" (1765), in Bailyn, *Pamphlets,* vol. 1, pp. 507, 516–517. Hopkins quotes Algernon Sidney's definitions: ". . . liberty solely consists in an independency upon the will of another; and by the name of slave we understand a man who can neither dispose of his person or goods, but enjoys all at the will of his master." See also John Dickinson, who quotes Montesquieu to the same effect, in "The Late Regulations" (1765), in *ibid.,* p. 671 n.

24. As Otis said in "The Rights of the British Colonies Asserted and

Proved" (1764), ". . . in a state of nature, no man can take my property from me without my consent; if he does, he deprives me of my liberty and makes me a slave. If such a proceeding is a breech of the law of nature, no law of society can make it just" (Bailyn, *Pamphlets,* vol. 1, p. 447).

25. Edmund S. Morgan has written that "The Americans fought England because Parliament threatened the security of property." See his "The American Revolution: Revisions in Need of Revising," in E. S. Morgan, ed., *The American Revolution: Two Centuries of Interpretation* (Englewood Cliffs, N.J.: Prentice-Hall, 1965), p. 176.

26. Morais, *op. cit.,* pp. 277 ff.

27. Otis quotes and paraphrases Locke's *Second Treatise,* chaps. 9 and 13 (*op. cit.,* pp. 395–399, 412–420), to this effect, in the introduction to "The Rights of the British Colonies Asserted and Proved" (Bailyn, *Pamphlets,* vol. 1, pp. 434–435).

28. Bailyn, *Ideological Origins,* pp. 152 ff.; Alfred de Grazia, *Public and Republic* (New York: Alfred A. Knopf, 1951), p. 56.

29. For an effort to explain this system to the colonials, see the letter of Jared Ingersoll to Thomas Fitch, in Edmund S. Morgan, ed., *Prologue to Revolution* (Chapel Hill: University of North Carolina Press, 1959), pp. 29–34. For an illuminating analysis of trends and contemporary interpretations, see Bailyn, *Ideological Origins,* pp. 161–174.

30. This definition was offered by Thomas Whately, chief draftsman of the Stamp Act and member of the Grenville and North ministries, in his essay entitled "The Regulations Lately Made" (1765) (Bailyn, *Pamphlets,* vol. 1, p. 602).

31. Bailyn, *Pamphlets,* vol. 1, p. 611.

32. Rossiter, *op. cit.,* p. 15.

33. McDonald, *op. cit.,* p. 44. (Emphasis in original.)

34. Morgan, *Prologue,* pp. 9, 12.

35. Bailyn, *Pamphlets,* vol. 1, p. 632. (Emphasis in original.)

36. Morgan, *Prologue,* pp. 118–119. Pitt, in many respects the outstanding champion of the colonies in Parliament, would not have followed Dickinson all the way on this point. As he said in Parliament, in connection with the proposed Declaratory Act of 1766, "The Commons of America, represented in their several assemblies, have ever been in possession of . . . this, their constitutional right, of giving and granting their own money. They would have been slaves if they had not enjoyed it. At the same time, this

kingdom, as the supreme governing and legislative power, has always bound the colonies by her laws, by her regulations, and restrictions in trade, in navigation, in manufactures, in everything, except that of taking their money out of their pockets without their consent" (*ibid.*, p. 136). The distance between this formulation and the statement of even so conservative a colonist as James Duane, of New York, is a measure of the widening gulf between the colonies and Great Britain in the third quarter of the eighteenth century.

37. Burnett, *Letters*, vol. 1, p. 26. On Duane's role in the First Continental Congress, see the *Dictionary of American Biography* (New York: Charles Scribner's Sons, 1930), vol. 5, p. 465.
38. Jensen, *Documents*, pp. 604–606.
39. *Ibid.*, pp. 592–604. For an account of these two Regulator movements, see John R. Alden, *The South in the Revolution, 1763–1789* (Baton Rouge: Louisiana State University Press, 1957), chap. 9.
40. Bailyn, *Pamphlets*, vol. 1, p. 664.
41. *Ibid.*, p. 296.
42. Parliament, as a matter of policy, never entertained petitions on the subject of taxes, but the colonists regarded their petitions on the constitutional theory of taxation as being of a different order.
43. See Locke's *Second Treatise*, chap. 4 (*op. cit.*, pp. 324–326). For an analysis, see Davis, *op. cit.*, pp. 118–121, and sources cited therein. It should be noted that Locke's formula is not wholly satisfactory to owners of Negro slaves. It does not justify the passing of slavery from one generation to the next.
44. Bailyn, *Pamphlets*, vol. 1, p. 319 and p. 710, n. 27. For a portrait of Bland as an "American aristocrat," see Rossiter, *op. cit.*, pp. 247–280. Bland's attitude toward slavery and the milieu of colonial Virginia are illuminated by the following episode recounted by Thomas Jefferson: "In the first or second session of the legislature after I became a member, I drew to this subject the attention of Col. Bland, one of the oldest, ablest, and most respected members, and he undertook to move for certain moderate extensions of the protection of the laws to these people. . . . [In the ensuing debate,] he was denounced as an enemy of his country, and was treated with the grossest indecorum" (quoted in Rossiter, *op. cit.*, p. 249).
45. Otis knew Locke's arguments on slavery, too, of course, but the only one he cited was the one in which Locke holds that no man may voluntarily make himself a slave, since all men's rights are

inalienable. Thus, the man who violates another's property and loses all his rights as a consequence has not freely handed over his liberty. Rather, his life, and his life alone, has been spared at the sufferance of the conqueror. See Otis's citations and quotations in Bailyn, *Pamphlets,* vol. 1, pp. 434–435, 444, 456; cf. pp. 477–478 n.

46. Quoted by Bailyn, *Ideological Origins,* p. 93.
47. Bailyn, *Pamphlets,* vol. 1, pp. 213, 204–211.
48. Morgan, *Prologue,* pp. 114–116; Jensen, *Documents,* pp. 673, 710 ff., 774.
49. The Boston Massacre climaxed a melee between a squad of British troops near the State House and a mob of Bostonians who gathered nightly to taunt the Redcoats. On the evening of March 5, 1770, the frightened soldiers, pushed off balance by the surging mob, fired a fusillade into the crowd, killing three men, among them a freed black named Crispus Attucks, and fatally wounding two others. Though John Adams led a successful effort to have most of the soldiers acquitted of crime, Bostonians regarded the so-called massacre as the inevitable result of stationing a standing army in the midst of a city, and rang the changes on the episode at every opportunity. For a fine account, see Catherine Drinker Bowen, *John Adams and the American Revolution* (New York: Grosset & Dunlap, 1949), chaps. 20–22.
50. Jensen, *Documents,* pp. 758, 759.
51. *Ibid.,* pp. 843–847.
52. See Hopkins, in Bailyn, *Pamphlets,* vol. 1, p. 516.
53. Morgan, *Prologue,* p. 141.
54. Rossiter, *op. cit.,* p. 80.
55. L. A. Harper estimates that mercantilism cost the colonies upward of $3 million per year, comparable to about half of the national budget during the early years of George Washington's administration. See his essay "The Effect of the Navigation Acts on the Thirteen Colonies," in Morris, *op. cit.,* p. 37. There was, of course, some smuggling. Rossiter (*op. cit.,* p. 81) calls the Molasses Act of 1733, intended to restrict colonial trade with the foreign sugar islands in the Caribbean, "the most flagrantly disregarded law between the Seventh Commandment and the Volstead Act." But most of the navigation acts were well enforced, and obeyed.
56. Historians disagree as to whether the Revolutionary controversies began in 1765 or earlier. Bernhard Knollenberg, for example, in his notable study of the period (*op. cit.*), sees the origin of the American Revolution in the agitations of 1759–1766.

57. This is L. H. Gipson's name for the war known to Americans as the French and Indian War. For an explanation of the title and its significance, see Gipson, "The American Revolution as an Aftermath of the Great War for the Empire, 1754–1762," in Morgan, *American Revolution,* pp. 147–165.

58. The term "nationality," as used here, is defined by Karl Deutsch in *Nationalism and Social Communication,* 2nd ed. (Cambridge: M.I.T. Press, 1966), pp. 104–105.

59. The image is Burke's, quoted in Rossiter, *op. cit.,* pp. 8, 84.

60. For an interesting attempt to measure these developments statistically, see Richard L. Merritt, "Nation-Building in America: The Colonial Years," in Karl Deutsch and William Foltz, eds., *Nation-Building* (New York: Atherton Press, 1966), pp. 56–72.

61. In his letter to Pitt of December 1765, John Dickinson warned that the colonists were coming to regard the long-standing prohibition on manufacturing in the colonies with resentment. Earlier they had not objected to it, partly because they had almost no capacity to manufacture things for themselves. Dickinson, who wanted more keenly than most Americans to preserve the connection between Britain and the colonies, nevertheless told Pitt that if Parliament interfered at all in their "internal government," the colonists would think they had been reduced to "a state of slavery" (Morgan, *Prologue,* pp. 118–119).

62. For the text of the King's Proclamation, see Jensen, *Documents,* pp. 850–851.

63. "Letters from a Farmer in Pennsylvania," Letter XII, in McDonald, *op. cit.,* p. 81.

64. Davis, *op. cit.,* p. 119.

65. Davis's book is the best guide to these accumulating pressures; see pp. 411–421, 427–433. He concludes (pp. 488–489): "By the early 1770's a large number of moralists, poets, intellectuals, and reformers had come to regard American slavery as an unmitigated evil. In Britain, France, and the North American colonies there were forces in motion that would lead to organized movements to abolish the African trade and the entire institutional framework which permitted human beings to be treated as things. Although slavery was nearly as old as human history, this was something new to the world." Without disputing Davis's over-all conclusion, I argue that few political leaders in the American colonies contributed intentionally to these emerging "forces."

66. Jensen, *Documents,* pp. 491–499; Samuel Sewall, "The Selling of Joseph" (Boston: Bartholomew Green and John Allen, 1700); Ben-

jamin Lay, "All Slave-Keepers That Keep the Innocent in Bondage, Apostates . . ." (Philadelphia: "Printed for the author" by Benjamin Franklin, 1737). See also Lawrence W. Towner, "The Sewall-Saffin Dialogue on Slavery," *William and Mary Quarterly*, 3rd ser., 21 (1964), 40–52.

67. Leonard W. Labaree, ed., *The Papers of Benjamin Franklin* (New Haven, Conn.: Yale University Press, 1959–), vol. 4, pp. 229–231; Carl Van Doren, *Benjamin Franklin* (New York: Garden City Publishing Co., 1941), p. 216.

68. There are grounds for believing that Franklin was a relatively old man before he began to overcome his racial prejudice. See Davis, *op. cit.,* p. 426. For Henry's observation about the impracticability of transporting Negroes back to Africa, see his letter to Robert Pleasants, January 18, 1773, in H. S. Commager and R. B. Morris, eds., *The Spirit of 'Seventy-Six* (Indianapolis, Ind.: Bobbs-Merrill, 1958), vol. 1, p. 402.

69. Davis, *op. cit.,* pp. 426–427, 431 *et passim.*

70. Bailyn, *Pamphlets,* vol. 1, pp. 438–440.

71. *Ibid.,* p. 409.

72. *Ibid.,* pp. 546–552. A portent of the comparative future usefulness of Otis and his fellow Bostonian John Adams to the cause of Revolutionary nationalism came during the controversy over the writs of assistance in 1761. In attacking these writs, lawyer Otis based his plea on the inalienable rights of man, and explicitly related his argument to the case of Negro slaves. Fifty-seven years after the event, John Adams, who had been twenty-six years old at the time, could still recall his own reaction. "Young as I was, and ignorant as I was, I shuddered at the doctrine he taught; and I have all my life shuddered, and still shudder, at the consequences that may be drawn from such premises. . . . I adore the ideal of gradual abolition! but who shall decide how slowly these abolitions shall be made?" (Quoted by Louis Hartz in "Otis and Anti-Slavery Doctrine," *New England Quarterly,* 12 [1939], 745).

73. Mary S. Locke, *Anti-Slavery in America . . . 1619–1808* (1901; reprint ed., Gloucester, Mass.: Peter Smith, 1965), pp. 21–40; Carl Bridenbaugh, *Cities in Revolt* (1955; reprint ed., New York: G. P. Putnam's Sons, Capricorn Books, 1964), pp. 353–354; Thomas Edward Drake, *Quakers and Slavery in America* (New Haven, Conn.: Yale University Press, 1950).

74. Locke, *op. cit.,* p. 60.

75. "A Forensic Dispute on the Legality of Enslaving the Africans"

(Boston: John Boyle, 1773), pp. 4, 12, 14, 27–28, 31, 24, 20–21, 35, 39–45, 46.

76. For further elaboration of this argument, see Carl Becker, *The Declaration of Independence* (New York: Alfred A. Knopf, Vintage Books, 1958), pp. 212 ff.

77. (Norwich, Conn.: Spooner, 1776), pp. 61, 50, 51. See also David S. Lovejoy, "Samuel Hopkins: Religion, Slavery and the Revolution," *New England Quarterly*, 40 (1967), 227–243.

78. Arthur Zilversmit, *The First Emancipation: The Abolition of Slavery in the North* (Chicago: University of Chicago Press, 1967), pp. 125–137. The Reverend William Gordon, later author of a multivolume history of the American Revolution, in 1776 published a plan for the gradual emancipation of slaves. But George Moore (*op. cit.*, p. 180) points out that the first, last, and only direct attack on Negro slavery ever made in the Massachusetts legislature did not come until 1777. It failed, being tabled without a vote. No other colony came close to acting during the Revolutionary War directly against slavery.

79. W. E. B. DuBois, *The Suppression of the African Slave-Trade to the United States of America, 1638–1870* (New York: Longmans, Green and Co., 1904), pp. 15, 25–26, 37–38, 41–42. Davis (*op. cit.*, p. 142) concludes that "there is little evidence, prior to the great conflict between Britain and her colonies, that restrictive duties implied a hostility to slavery itself."

80. This was apparently what happened in Massachusetts, where Governor Thomas Hutchinson was forced to veto three separate acts aimed at preventing the importation of slaves, one in 1771 and two in 1774 (Locke, *op. cit.*, pp. 69–71). No doubt Samuel Adams and his fellow legislators were motivated in part by the desire to embarrass the detested Governor. One side effect, however—especially significant in Virginia, where a similar drama between Assembly and royal governor was played out—was to identify the slave trade with British supervision and intrusion, and its prohibition with patriotism, thus making it easier to outlaw the trade once and for all when the colonies assumed responsibility for their own affairs.

81. *JCC* 1:32–38.

82. Force, *American Archives*, 4th ser., vol. 1, pp. 600, 530. For similar resolves, see pp. 494 (Prince George County), 523 (Culpepper), 616 (Hanover), 641 (Princess Anne). The Culpepper Resolves noted that the slave trade was "injurious" to the colony because

469

it "obstructs the population of it with freemen and useful manufacturers."

83. Moore, *op. cit.*, pp. 144–147.

84. Quoted by Davis, *op. cit.*, p. 3.

85. The South Carolinians, most of whom had no intention of quitting
the slave trade permanently, lacked either the heart or the power,
in 1774, to insist that the second article of the Association be stated
less extravagantly. They had already gained the exemption of rice
from the Association (for a sensible and fair explanation of this
triumph of South Carolinian politics, see Alden, *ob. cit.*, p. 178),
and they must have been reluctant to push their demands any further than necessary. By 1776, at the Second Continental Congress,
they were able to force a revision of the language, so that now
Congress undertook simply to see that "no slaves be imported into
any of the thirteen united colonies" (*JCC* 2:122). The promise of
future discontinuation and the quarantine against all who were
"concerned" in the trade had been stricken.

86. This argument seems to fly in the face of Bailyn's discussion of the
"contagion of liberty," but it need not. He shows that the relevance
of the Revolutionary ideology to chattel slavery was too obvious to
be missed, and he quotes many sermons and tracts that make the
connection explicitly (*Ideological Origins*, pp. 232–245). What he
does not show (it is superfluous to his point, but of the essence
here) is that *political* leaders stressed this linkage. My point is that
political leaders—with only a few exceptions, none of them de-
structive of the argument—abstained from criticizing chattel slavery and, above all, from trying to act against it.

87. Otis, for his intemperate, sometimes downright insane, reaction
to criticism; Rush, for his involvement in the "cabal" against General Washington in the winter of 1778. Rush later recovered some
influence at the state level. He served ably in the Pennsylvania
convention that ratified the Constitution. From 1797 to 1813, he
was treasurer of the U.S. Mint. But, for the most part, after the
Conway Cabal he was an extinct volcano as far as national politics
was concerned, and devoted most of his energy to the practice of
medicine.

88. In 1770, Franklin apparently wrote a pamphlet entitled "A Conversation Between an Englishman, a Scotchman, and an American
on the Subject of Slavery," in which the American is put to the embarrassment of apologizing for the enslavement of Negroes in
America. No doubt the pamphlet reflected conversational situations in which Franklin found himself during his sojourn abroad.

Such exchanges must have strengthened his animus against slavery. See Van Doren, *op. cit.,* pp. 393–394.

89. Henry's letter is printed in Commager and Morris, *op. cit.,* vol. 1, p. 402.

90. In 1763, Laurens had taken the position that slavery was bad for the moral development of young white men, but argued that the economy and safe government required it and that individuals were helpless to break its hold. He blamed South Carolina's "northern neighbors" for entailing it on his region. By 1776, like most patriotic Southerners, he had shifted the blame solely to Great Britain. Portions of his correspondence bearing on these issues are reproduced in Wallace, *op. cit.,* pp. 444–446.

91. Quoted in Locke, *op. cit.,* pp. 69–70.

92. *Ibid.,* p. 70. See also Moore, *op. cit.,* pp. 136, 124–147.

93. Wells, *op. cit.,* p. 185.

94. Paul Leicester Ford, ed., *The Works of Thomas Jefferson* (New York: G. P. Putnam's Sons, 1904–1905), vol. 1, p. 7. The fact that there is no record in the *Journal* by itself casts no doubt on the reliability of Jefferson's memory. Legislative journals were by no means a complete record of business in those days.

95. Quoted, with commentary, in Carl Becker, *op. cit.,* pp. 212–213 *et seq.* (Italics in original.)

96. Burnett, *Letters,* vol. 1, p. 516 n.

97. *Ibid.,* p. 515.

98. Benjamin Quarles, *The Negro in the American Revolution* (Chapel Hill: University of North Carolina Press, 1961), p. 42.

99. Bailyn, *Pamphlets,* vol. 1, p. 635.

100. *Ibid.,* p. 435. The best study of the roots of these attitudes is Winthrop D. Jordan, *White Over Black* (Chapel Hill: University of North Carolina Press, 1968), pts. 1–3.

101. The "invisibility" of blacks extended beyond politics, too. Jordan (*op. cit.,* p. 340) notes that David Ramsay, a contemporary historian of the Revolution in South Carolina, "discoursed on the contributions to South Carolina made by the Scots, Swiss, Irish, Germans, New Englanders and Dutch—all without mentioning even the presence, much less the importance, of African Negroes in his state."

102. Jensen, *Documents,* p. 867; Locke, *op. cit.,* p. 2. Defending the Constitution of 1787 in South Carolina, Charles Cotesworth Pinckney noted that he and his fellow delegates from South Carolina had opposed the insertion of a bill of rights in the main body of the Constitution. "Such bills generally begin with declaring that

all men are by nature born free," he said. South Carolinians "should make that declaration with a very bad grace, when a large part of our property consists in men who are actually born slaves." Farrand, *Records,* vol. 3, p. 256.

103. The best portrait of political life in Virginia at the time of the Revolution is by Charles Sydnor (*op. cit.*). He shows, without specifically trying, that Negroes were simply nowhere to be found in the political arena except as objects of taxation and regulation.

104. *The American Revolution Considered as a Social Movement* (Princeton, N.J.: Princeton University Press, 1926). See also Frederick B. Tolles, "The American Revolution Considered as a Social Movement: A Re-evaluation," *American Historical Review,* 60 (1954), 1–12. Tolles concludes that despite thirty years of whittling, "the 'Jameson thesis' is still sound." Nevertheless, what Jameson posits as rhetorical questions ("How could men who were engaged in a great and inspiring struggle for liberty fail to perceive the inconsistency between their professions and endeavors in that contest and their actions with respect to their bondsmen? How could they fail to see the application of their doctrines respecting the rights of man to the black men who were held among them in bondage far more reprehensible than that to which they indignantly proclaimed themselves to have been subjected by the King of Great Britain?"), I see as real questions, demanding straightforward answers. Jameson cites the rise of anti-slavery societies and the comment of Patrick Henry (cited in this chapter) as evidence of "substantial progress" against slavery, due to the influence of the Revolution. A similar approach, stressing the "contagion" of Revolutionary doctrines, can be found in Louis Hartz, *Economic Policy and Democratic Thought: Pennsylvania, 1776–1860* (Cambridge: Harvard University Press, 1948), pp. 181–186; and in Hartz, "Otis and Anti-Slavery Doctrine," pp. 745–747. But what seems to me to need explaining is not the impact of Revolutionary ideas on slavery in Pennsylvania and Massachusetts, but the virtual impotence of those ideas with respect to slavery in New York, Virginia, and South Carolina, where substantial numbers of blacks confronted the white community.

105. See the speech by Joseph Warren, in Jensen, *Documents,* pp. 753–759; Benjamin Church, "Liberty and Property Vindicated," in Bailyn, *Pamphlets,* vol. 1, pp. 588–597; the resolutions of the Sons of Liberty, in Morgan, *Prologue,* pp. 114–118.

106. Jensen, *Documents,* pp. 776–777.

107. *Ibid.*, pp. 816–818.
108. Bailyn, *Pamphlets*, vol. 1, p. 232.
109. See, for an arresting example, the passage on "the poor African" in "A Letter to the People of Pennsylvania" (1760), probably written by Joseph Galloway, in Bailyn, *Pamphlets*, vol. 1, p. 271. The writings of the Quakers, especially Benezet's essay on Guinea (see Jordan, *op. cit.*, p. 286), provide more familiar examples.
110. *Op. cit.*, chap. 13.
111. Anthony Benezet took this dimension of the problem seriously. He devoted considerable space in his pamphlets to the question of fair compensation to owners who would free their slaves. See, for a good example, his sixteen-page pamphlet *Brief Considerations on Slavery, and the Expediency of Its Abolition* (Burlington, Vt.: Isaac Collins, 1773).
112. Letter to Hezekiah Niles, February 13, 1818, in C. F. Adams, *op. cit.*, vol. 10, p. 283.
113. Bailyn, *Pamphlets*, vol. 1, p. 676 n.
114. *Ibid.*, pp. 439–440. On the last page of his pamphlet, Otis adds this remarkable "P.S.": "I now recollect that I have been credibly informed that the British sugar colonists are humane towards their slaves in comparison with the others. Therefore in page 29 [the page of his pamphlet on which the passage quoted above appeared], let it be read, foreign sugar islanders. . . ." Perhaps the qualification was added in the hope that the British islanders might join the mainlanders in resistance to Parliament's taxes. Knollenberg (*op. cit.*, p. 11) notes that, although the island planters had as good reason as the mainlanders to object to the Stamp Act they remained silent. Outnumbered seven to one by their slaves and in constant fear and danger of an insurrection, they submitted quietly to regulations, because they were "utterly dependent on the continued protection of the British army and navy."
115. For other evidence of hostile feelings, especially of New Englanders, against the "sugar islands," see Oxenbridge Thacher, "The Sentiments of a British American" (1764), in Bailyn, *Pamphlets*, vol. 1, p. 452; and Davis, *op. cit.*, p. 442, where John Adams's opinions are quoted.
116. Jensen, *Documents*, p. 876; cf. pp. 711–713, 858–859 *et passim*.
117. As it was, Georgia delayed joining the Association for several months, objecting, among other things, to the clause banning the slave trade. See Kenneth Coleman, *The American Revolution in Georgia, 1763–1789* (Athens: University of Georgia Press, 1958), chap. 3.

118. Jefferson's preparation of his response to Marbois and his effort to control distribution are recounted in the Introduction to *Notes on the State of Virginia,* ed. Thomas Perkins Abernethy (New York: Harper & Row, Harper Torchbooks, 1964); and by Dumas Malone, in *Jefferson and His Time* (Boston: Little, Brown and Co., 1948–), vol. 1, pp. 373–375; vol. 2, pp. 94–98, 104–106.

119. *Notes,* pp. 131–132. There follows this remarkable comment: "The bill reported by the revisers does not itself contain this proposition; but an amendment containing it was prepared, to be offered to the legislature whenever the bill should be taken up . . ." (*ibid.,* p. 132). In other words, Jefferson's inclusion of this proposition in the list of proposed revisions was unnecessary, almost gratuitous, and so, of course, was the extended digression that follows.

120. *Ibid.,* p. 132. For an account of Jefferson's leading role in the preparation of the revisions, and of the place of the scheme for emancipation in those revisions, see Malone, *op. cit.,* vol. 1, pp. 261–264.

121. *Notes,* pp. 133–137.

122. *Ibid.,* pp. 137–138.

123. *Ibid.,* pp. 138–139.

124. *Ibid.,* p. 156. The exclamation point, an unusual device for Jefferson, and the recurrent invocation of miracles and supernatural intervention in these passages reflect Jefferson's great anxiety concerning slavery. In a passage in his *Autobiography,* written in 1821, he wrote, "Nothing is more certainly written in the book of fate than that these people are to be free. Nor is it less certain," he added, "that the two races, equally free, cannot live in the same government." Quoted by Malone, *op. cit.,* vol. 1, p. 268.

125. Quoted by Jordan, *op. cit.,* p. 442, from a pamphlet by Clement Clarke Moore, published in New York during the 1804 Presidential campaign. Jordan's book, pp. 429–481, contains a suggestive analysis and critique of Jefferson's ideas on the subject of race.

126. See chap. 6, an analysis of "Gentlemen's Opinions on Race and Freedom," in Robert McColley, *Slavery and Jeffersonian Virginia* (Urbana: University of Illinois Press, 1964). A fascinating exception came from Jefferson himself. In a letter to Edward Bancroft written from Paris, January 26, 1788, he declares his intention to try an "experiment," importing "as many Germans as I have grown slaves," and settling them on "farms of fifty acres each, intermingled. I have no doubt but that they will be good citizens" (Andrew A. Lipscomb, ed., *The Writings of Thomas Jefferson* [Washington: Jefferson Memorial Association, 1903], vol. 19, pp. 42–43).

127. Two good expressions of Jefferson's view that fundamental reforms can be accomplished only gradually come in letters to the Reverend Charles Clay (January 27, 1790) and to Joel Barlow (December 10, 1807). (Ford, *op. cit.,* vol. 6, pp. 39–40; vol. 10, pp. 529–530).

128. Letter to Chastellux, June 7, 1785, in Julian P. Boyd, ed., *The Papers of Thomas Jefferson* (Princeton, N.J.: Princeton University Press, 1953), vol. 8, p. 184.

129. Letter to Dr. Richard Price, August 7, 1785 (Boyd, *op. cit.,* vol. 8, p. 357). The point in providing copies for the students at the college in Williamsburg was to set off a train of thought among leaders of the "rising generation," to which Jefferson looked, rather than to his own generation, for "these great reformations," abolition and Constitutional reform. It is not clear when the promised copies arrived in Williamsburg, but the president of the college, James Madison's namesake and uncle, and George Wythe, the leading tutor at the college, were eager for the *Notes,* "judiciously distributed among our young men," to work their enlightening effect (Malone, *op. cit.,* vol. 2, p. 97).

130. Reproduced in facsimile following p. 246 in Boyd, *op. cit.,* vol. 8.

131. Malone, *op. cit.,* vol. 2, pp. 104–105.

132. Abernethy, *op. cit.,* p. xv.

133. Congressman W. L. Smith, of Charleston (Jordan, *op. cit.,* p. 452).

134. John Harold Wolfe, *Jeffersonian Democracy in South Carolina* (Chapel Hill: University of North Carolina Press, 1940), p. 152.

135. Jordan, *op. cit.,* pp. 347, 551.

136. Ford, *op. cit.,* vol. 8, pp. 335–336.

137. Letter to John Holmes, April 22, 1820 (*ibid.,* vol. 12, pp. 158–160).

138. Letter to John Adams, December 10, 1790 (*ibid.,* vol. 12, p. 151).

CHAPTER 3

1. These estimates are based on tables in U.S. Bureau of the Census, *Historical Statistics of the United States: Colonial Times to 1957* (Washington: Government Printing Office, 1960), p. 756; and Evarts B. Greene and Virginia D. Harrington, *American Population Before the Federal Census of 1790* (New York: Columbia University Press, 1932), pp. 141–142, 177–179.

2. Martin did not mention, though it would have been pertinent, a militia law passed by North Carolina in 1768, which directed that overseers responsible for six or more slaves be fined if they joined a muster. Benjamin Quarles, *The Negro in the American Revolution* (Chapel Hill: University of North Carolina Press,

p. 8 n. It will be obvious in the notes to this chapter that I have relied heavily on Quarles's judicious, thorough book.

3. It is not clear which three colonies Lord North meant. Surely he intended Georgia and South Carolina. In terms of the proportion of Negroes in its midst, Virginia ranked second only to South Carolina, and ought surely to have been included in this category. But if North meant Virginia, then the King's enthusiastic response, coupled with the suggestion that the assault ought to begin with North Carolina, seems curious. Perhaps the King meant that North Carolina, with its numerous loyalists, should be subdued first, and that the army might then proceed easily to restore British authority in the three neighboring colonies. For North's memorandum and King George's response, see Sir John W. Fortescue, ed., *The Correspondence of King George the Third from 1760 to December 1783* (London: Macmillan and Co., 1927–1928), vol. 3, pp. 265–270. For a summary of British strategic thinking behind the Charleston expedition of 1776, see Piers Mackesy, *The War for America, 1775–1783* (Cambridge: Harvard University Press, 1964), pp. 43–44. Paul Smith focuses on the role of loyalism in British planning for this campaign, in *Loyalists and Redcoats* (Chapel Hill: University of North Carolina Press, 1964), pp. 20–22.

4. For an account of the Southern campaign of 1776 told from the viewpoint of the British commander, Sir Henry Clinton, see William Willcox's Introduction to *The American Rebellion: Sir Henry Clinton's Narrative* (New Haven, Conn.: Yale University Press, 1954), pp. xix–xxi. The South Carolinian perspective is set forth in Edward McCrady, *The History of South Carolina in the Revolution, 1775–1783* (New York: Macmillan Co., 1902), vol. 1, chap. 7.

5. Mackesy, *op. cit.*, p. 158, in paraphrase of Jenkinson's memorandum. It is doubtful whether the King would have been impressed with Jenkinson's commercial argument. In a remarkable note to Lord North in June 1779, the monarch had responded to those who were arguing that the war was costing too much. It was a mistake, he wrote, to count the cost of a war of this kind in currency. In economic terms, war always impoverished the state and enriched individuals. But this, he insisted, was the "tradesman's scale," wholly inappropriate as a measure when the integrity of the empire itself was at stake. If the American colonies succeeded in asserting their independence, "the West Indies must follow them." Ireland would be next, and soon England would be poor, isolated,

depopulated (by the flight of merchants to more hospitable climes), and alone. From this point of view, the commercial value of New England to the empire was almost beside the point. For the King's memorandum, see Fortescue, *op. cit.,* vol. 4, pp. 350–351.

6. In July 1775, Congress had sent an address to six Indian nations in which, with a combination of paternalistic advice and dire warnings, they sought to persuade the Indians to remain aloof from the war. *JCC* 2:178–183. This address, and many of similar tenor that followed, did not succeed in neutralizing the Indian threat.

7. Smith, *op. cit.,* p. 25. John R. Alden warns us not to assume that all highlanders were loyalists. Many recognized that British authorities served them no better than the Americans, and believed that their best chance for fair treatment lay in struggling for political advantage within an independent state (*The South in the Revolution, 1763–1789* [Baton Rouge: Louisiana State University Press, 1957], chap. 9).

8. Jonathan Boucher, "A Letter from a Virginian to the Members of the Congress" (New York[?]: no publisher, 1774), pp. 28–29.

9. Dunmore's proclamation was not the first evidence he had given of a willingness to exploit the vulnerability of Virginians before their slaves. He warned in early 1775 that if he were injured or insulted in any way personally, he would respond by declaring freedom for the slaves. So, at any rate, John Adams had heard. See Charles Francis Adams, ed., *The Works of John Adams* (Boston: Little, Brown and Co., 1850–1856), vol. 2, p. 458. In April of that year, he had directed British marines to remove gunpowder from the public magazine at Williamsburg, leaving the Virginians exposed before the possibility of slave uprisings. He explained his act by referring to rumors of servile insurrections in a nearby county. He had removed the powder, he said, to a place of security, aboard H.M.S. *Fowey* in the James River. Peyton Randolph, supported by the knowledge that 600 troops of light horse were awaiting instructions at Fredericksburg, told the Governor that Virginians were confident that they could keep their slaves under control if he would return the powder to its proper place. The affair was smoothed over without an armed clash, though it left a bad taste in the mouths of the Virginians, who did not respond amiably when outsiders trifled with their control over the slaves. The documents relevant to this early clash between Dunmore and the Virginians can be found in Force, *American Archives,* 4th ser., vol. 2, pp. 371–372, 426, 465. A narrative account is given by Douglas

Southall Freeman, *George Washington* (New York: Charles Scribner's Sons, 1948–1957), vol. 3, pp. 411–415.

10. Quarles, *op. cit.*, p. 20 n, from Rutledge's letter to Ralph Izard, December 8, 1775. Dunmore's proclamation is in Force, *American Archives,* 4th ser., vol. 3, p. 1385.

11. Washington believed that the South's geography was the primary factor in its vulnerability. Writing to Governor Thomas Jefferson after the Old Dominion had sustained some punishing blows in the winter of 1781, he noted that the penetration of waterways deep into Virginia invited raiders to hit and run, plundering as they came. Nevertheless, he urged Jefferson to continue to supply men to the Continental forces working against Cornwallis in the Carolinas. The British raids, he wrote, were intended to distract Virginia from this essential supply function. Since Virginia had no way to defend itself against the assaults, the best bet was to bring pressure on Cornwallis and keep him from marching the main British force into southern Virginia. Washington's letter is in John C. Fitzpatrick, ed., *The Writings of George Washington* (Washington: Government Printing Office, 1931–1944), vol. 21, pp. 191–192. For an account of the campaign in Virginia, see Dumas Malone, *Jefferson and His Time* (Boston: Little, Brown and Co., 1948–), vol. 1, chaps. 22 and 23.

12. General Horatio Gates, quoted in George Billias, ed., *George Washington's Generals* (New York: William Morrow and Co., 1964), p. 100.

13. Smith, *op. cit.*, pp. 89–90. See also Malone, *op. cit.*, vol. 1, chaps. 22 and 23, and John C. Miller, *Triumph of Freedom, 1775–1783* (Boston: Little, Brown and Co., 1948), chap. 24, where the South is called the "soft underbelly" of the American defenses.

14. Edmund Burke, *Selected Writings and Speeches,* ed. Peter Stanlis (Garden City, N.Y.: Doubleday & Co., Anchor Books, 1963), p. 160.

15. Malone, *op. cit.*, vol. 1, pp. 342–343.

16. Adams, *op. cit.*, vol. 2, p. 458.

17. Fortescue, *op. cit.*, vol. 4, p. vii.

18. In 1775, before the issuance of Dunmore's proclamation, a group of merchants in London had petitioned the King, expressing indignation at reports that slaves were being incited against "our American brethren." See Force, *American Archives,* 4th ser., vol. 3, p. 1011.

19. Kenneth Coleman, *The American Revolution in Georgia, 1763–1789* (Athens: University of Georgia Press, 1958), p. 171.

20. Quoted by Lorenzo Greene, in "Some Observations on the Black Regiment of Rhode Island in the American Revolution," *Journal of Negro History*, 37 (1952), 154. For evidence of Northern sensitivities on this subject, see the letter from John Adams to General William Heath, October 5, 1775, in Burnett, *Letters*, vol. 1, p. 217.

21. Howard H. Peckham, *The War for Independence* (Chicago: University of Chicago Press, 1958), pp. 136–137.

22. Anticipating this development, Lord Amherst had warned the King against British involvement in a land war in America. He believed that a naval blockade, conducted out of a relatively few garrisons (Halifax, Boston, New York, Charleston, East Florida), could break the back of the American rebellion. For a summary of Amherst's counsel, see Fortescue, *op. cit.*, vol. 3, p. xiii; vol. 4, pp. 14–15.

23. Smith, *op. cit.*, pp. 86–88, 154, 160; Willcox, *op. cit.*, pp. xxxviii ff.

24. Smith, *op. cit.*, pp. 128–129, 140–141. See also McCrady, *op. cit.*, vol. 1, chaps. 25 *et seq.*

25. See Smith, *op. cit.*, pp. 102–104, 127–128, 147 *et passim.*

26. In early 1782, after Yorktown, he was still recommending to Clinton that 10,000 Negroes be armed and put under the command of white officers for an assault on Charleston. A letter advising him to relay his plan to Sir Guy Carleton, the new commander in chief in America, arrived after Dunmore had departed for England, and the plan died. For an account, see Quarles, *op. cit.*, pp. 150–151.

27. Burke, *op. cit.*, p. 167.

28. American harassment prevented the effective implementation of the plantation scheme, but Negroes were successfully used as carpenters, teamsters, smiths, and in other laboring tasks. See Quarles, *op. cit.*, pp. 137–140.

29. Force, *American Archives*, 4th ser., vol. 3, p. 1335; R. W. Gibbes, ed., *Documentary History of the American Revolution* (Columbia, S.C.: Banner Steam-Power Press, 1835), vol. 3, pp. 140–141.

30. For a summary of these and other American reactions, see Quarles, *op. cit.*, chap. 7.

31. Fitzpatrick, *op. cit.*, vol. 4, p. 167; General Lee, quoted by Quarles, *op. cit.*, p. 122.

32. Lorenzo J. Greene, *The Negro in Colonial New England, 1620–1776* (New York: Columbia University Press, 1942), pp. 126–128, 186–190.

33. Burnett, *Letters*, vol. 1, p. 207. If John Adams was among those who opposed Rutledge's motion, it was not because he was proud of the Negroes in the Massachusetts Line. In a letter to General

William Heath, October 5, 1775, he expressed his sympathy with the view that Congress should not be asked to pay salaries to boys, old men, Negroes, and others "unsuitable for service" (*ibid.,* p. 217).

34. Fitzpatrick, *op. cit.,* vol. 4, p. 8 n.; Force, *American Archives,* 4th ser., vol. 3, p. 1161.

35. Fitzpatrick, *op. cit.,* vol. 4, pp. 195, 195 n. According to Freeman (*op. cit.,* vol. 3, p. 586), Washington's communiqué to Congress was not completely candid. The reversal in policy was dictated, in part at least, by the fact that the Continental Army was dissolving, owing to the expiration of enlistments at the end of 1775, and Washington needed soldiers, regardless of their hue.

36. The most notable exception, curiously enough, was Virginia, which permitted free Negroes to render military service throughout the war. Quarles, *op. cit.,* pp. 14–18; cf. p. 183.

37. Lorenzo Greene, "Some Observations . . . ," pp. 148–150.

38. The text of the protest is in George W. Williams, *History of the Negro Race in America from 1619 to 1880* (New York: G. P. Putnam's Sons, 1882), vol. 1, pp. 348–349.

39. Lorenzo Greene, "Some Observations . . . ," pp. 169–172.

40. Connecticut legalized the substitution of slaves for masters in 1777. New Hampshire permitted slaves and free Negroes to be "unobtrusively filtered into the state levies," and Massachusetts, after winking at Negro enlistments for several months, gave specific legal sanction to the practice in 1778. New York and Maryland, too, yielded to the mounting pressure for troops and authorized the enlistment of slaves. For a summary of these and similar enactments, and the controversy surrounding their adoption, see Quarles, *op. cit.,* pp. 52–58.

41. For examples of opinions of this sort, see the letter of Alexander Hamilton to John Jay, then President of the Congress, written March 14, 1779, and the note by the Reverend Samuel Hopkins, pastor of the First Congregational Church at Newport. Both can be found in Williams, *op. cit.,* vol. 1, pp. 354–355, 388. Also see "Antibiastes," *Observations of the Slaves and the Indentured Servants, Inlisted in the Army and in the Navy of the United States* (Philadelphia: Styner and Cist, 1777).

42. Quoted in Quarles, *op. cit.,* p. 57.

43. *Ibid.,* pp. 85–87, 94–102. Quarles notes that in the unsuccessful allied siege of Savannah, Negroes from Santo Domingo fought valiantly with the French. Henri Christophe, later a fighter with Toussaint L'Ouverture against Napoleon's army and, after the

death of Toussaint, King of Haiti, was among those who came to Savannah with the French Navy. Apart from the engagements in which the "black battalion" from Rhode Island took part, the siege of Savannah marked "the only action [of the war] in which a Negro unit was identifiable as such . . ." (*ibid.*, p. 82).

44. Williams, *op. cit.*, vol. 1, pp. 354–356.

45. The resolutions appear in *ibid.*, p. 356. A convenient summary of the whole episode is in Quarles, *op. cit.*, pp. 60–67. For the relationship of the Laurenses over this episode, see David Duncan Wallace, *The Life of Henry Laurens* (New York: G. P. Putnam's Sons, 1915), pp. 448–452.

46. See the letter of David Ramsay to W. H. Drayton, in Gibbes, *op. cit.*, vol. 2, p. 121.

47. Wallace, *op. cit.*, p. 450. For other evidence of this reaction see Gibbes, *op. cit.*, vol. 2, p. 121.

48. A delegate to Congress from New Hampshire, William Whipple, gave evidence that Northerners, too, looked upon the proposal in this light. In a letter written the day before Congress adopted the plan, he wrote, "This [project] will I suppose lay a foundation for the emancipation of those poor wretches in that country, and I hope be the means of dispensing the blessings of freedom to all the human race in America." Burnett, *Letters*, vol. 4, p. 122.

49. See Laurens's letter to his father, January 14, 1778, quoted in Quarles, *op. cit.*, p. 63.

50. *Ibid.*, p. 58. When the British threatened Charleston late in 1779, many leaders wanted to send a flag of truce, with an offer that South Carolina would remain neutral during the rest of the war. They were motivated in part by indignation at the refusal of Congress to send a greater proportion of the Continental Army southward to defend Charleston, a city they regarded as the linchpin of American nationalism in the three southernmost states. See *ibid.*, p. 64; Wallace, *op. cit.*, p. 450; Gibbes, *op. cit.*, vol. 2, p. 122.

51. U.S. Bureau of the Census, *op. cit.*, p. 756.

52. Laurens's letter of May 19, 1782, is in Jared Sparks, ed., *Correspondence of the American Revolution* (Boston: Little, Brown and Co., 1853), vol. 3, p. 506; Washington's reply, July 10, 1782, is in Fitzpatrick, *op. cit.*, vol. 24, pp. 421–422.

53. Fitzpatrick, *op. cit.*, vol. 12, pp. 327–328; vol. 14, pp. 147–149; vol. 22, p. 14. For an account of his evolving attitudes toward slavery, see Paul F. Boller, Jr., "Washington, the Quakers, and Slavery," *Journal of Negro History*, 46 (1961), 83–89.

54. According to John C. Miller (*op. cit.*, p. 509), there was an average

of fifty Negroes per battalion in Washington's army in the late 1770's. Seven hundred ex-slaves fought at Monmouth Courthouse, New Jersey.

55. Fitzpatrick, *op. cit.,* vol. 10, p. 401. Lafayette once told Washington, "Nothing but a treaty of alliance with the Negroes can find us dragoon horses, and it is by this means the enemy have so formidable a cavalry" (Quarles, *op. cit.,* p. 141).

56. British leaders were indeed thinking along those lines toward the end of the war. Such a settlement would have left much of the territory they regarded as most valuable in their hands—namely, New York City and the plantations in the low country of the Deep South. See Fortescue, *op. cit.,* vol. 5, pp. 375–376. Southerners in Congress realized the danger of the doctrine of *uti possidetis* to their region. A committee chaired by John Mathews, of South Carolina, sent a "circular letter" to the states in June 1781 urging great exertions so that American negotiators could use the "firm and decided language" of "free, sovereign, and independent states" at the bargaining table (*JCC* 20:587).

57. Quarles, *op. cit.,* pp. 66–67; Wallace, *op. cit.,* p. 452; Miller, *op. cit.,* p. 510.

58. Wallace, *op. cit.,* p. 489.

59. This effort had begun while the war was still in progress. Raids were conducted into British camps to seize fugitives and to steal slaves who belonged to British officials and loyalists, and attempts were made to deal with British commanders for the return of runaway slaves. See Quarles, *op. cit.,* pp. 131–133.

60. Fitzpatrick, *op. cit.,* vol. 23, pp. 202, 262, 264–265. In the articles of capitulation signed at Yorktown on October 18, 1781, the British agreed that American "property" would be subject to recovery. But it soon appeared that the Americans needed a similar undertaking from their French allies. Repeated attempts to win French co-operation in the return of slaves purloined by French officers were met with Gallic bafflement (Quarles, *op. cit.,* p. 162). Cf. Fitzpatrick, *op. cit.,* vol. 23, pp. 488–491. The frustration created "a very ill humor" in many influential planters, and may have contributed to the antipathy later shown by many Southerners, especially Deep Southerners, toward the French, or "Jacobins," as they called them. At any rate, the incident showed that the British did not have a monopoly on disregard for American feelings toward slavery.

61. For the carefully wrought "Instructions" to the negotiators, see

JCC 20:651–655. For Madison's notes on the sectional considerations underlying the negotiations, see *JCC* 23:873–874.

62. Quoted in Wallace, *op. cit.,* p. 403. For the text of the treaty, see *JCC* 24:249.

63. In July, the British had left Savannah, taking 5,500 Negro slaves with them. Most of them belonged to a few wealthy loyalists. At one point, ten families of whites left with 1,568 Negroes, bound for Jamaica. Coleman, *op. cit.,* pp. 145–146. Since few of these 5,500 Negroes seem to have belonged to patriots, the evacuation from Savannah never became a focal point in the ensuing controversy.

64. Quarles, *op. cit.,* pp. 165–167, 173.

65. Miller (*op. cit.,* p. 508) notes that a Southern command often meant a small fortune to British officers willing to go into the slave trade on the side.

66. Another motive often mentioned by the British can be dismissed as either disingenuous or rooted in ignorance—namely, a reluctance to return slaves to the wrath of their masters. What tempered the severity of a harsh master was his concern for the health of his property, a motive that would protect most of the fugitives, as it did other slaves who earned their masters' suspicion and fear.

67. Fitzpatrick, *op. cit.,* vol. 26, pp. 274–275, 364–365, 370. On the whole episode of the evacuation from New York, see Quarles, *op. cit.,* pp. 167–172.

68. Egbert Benson's memorandum recording the substance of the conference between Washington and Carleton is in Fitzpatrick *op. cit.,* vol. 26, pp. 402–406.

69. To his own plantation steward, Washington wrote that the Negroes taken from Mount Vernon had departed for Nova Scotia (*ibid.,* pp. 401–402, 406–407).

70. Both are quoted by Williams, *op. cit.,* vol. 1, pp. 358–359, 355 n. The loss of slaves was, of course, not the only factor causing distress in the Deep South. The cultivation of rice in Georgia, for example, depended on a complex system of canals for irrigation. When these were destroyed during the war, Georgia's annual export of 20,000 barrels of rice was completely stopped. A major effort, lasting several years, was required to restore these canals to good working order (Coleman, *op. cit.,* pp. 170–171).

71. Jefferson estimated that nine-tenths of the slaves lost in Virginia, including thirty that were taken from Monticello, had died of smallpox and putrid fever (Williams, *op. cit.,* vol. 1, pp. 358–359).

72. *JCC* 25:964–967.
73. For example, see the instructions for American ministers in Europe, drafted by Thomas Jefferson and adopted April 15, 1784, in *JCC* 27:368; also, the instructions to the Minister in Great Britain, March 7, 1785, in *JCC* 28:123; a resolution directing the Secretary for Foreign Affairs, John Jay, to submit to the governors of the states lists of the Negroes, belonging to citizens, who were carried off by the British, adopted August 9, 1786, in *JCC* 31:508; a summary report by Jay, presented October 13, 1786, in *JCC* 31:863–875; and the resolution directing the Minister in London, John Adams, to seek the agreement of Great Britain for a bilateral commission to establish the value of slaves borne off in 1783 and to arrange for compensation, adopted July 20, 1787, in *JCC* 32:378–379.
74. Quarles, *op. cit.,* pp. 171, 173–174.
75. A Congressional committee composed of three Southern delegates submitted a report in 1780 noting that, according to Adams's reports from London, Britain had apparently decided to concentrate its fire on the South and urging that American defenses be massed to meet this assault. The report was "read," and on January 1, 1781, "recommitted" (*JCC* 18:1078). A good reflection of Southern sentiment on this issue is McCrady, *op. cit.* See also Richard Barry, *Mr. Rutledge of South Carolina* (New York: Duell, Sloan & Pearce, 1942), chap. 6.
76. Fitzpatrick, *op. cit.,* vol. 26, pp. 297–300.
77. Quoted by Dwight Lowell Dumond, *Antislavery Origins of the Civil War in the United States* (Ann Arbor: University of Michigan Press, 1939, 1959), p. 9. Though Washington did, in his will, grant freedom to his slaves, during his lifetime he always insisted that the problem should be dealt with, not by individuals, but by the legislature, which alone could provide for the necessary adjustments on a statewide basis. It must be admitted that there was realistic wisdom in this position.

CHAPTER 4

1. See the letter of Edward Rutledge to John Jay, June 8, 1776, and the opinion of John Dickinson, given in debate, July 1, 1776, both printed in Jensen, *Documents,* pp. 868, 875–877.
2. "What reasonable social and political order could conceivably be built and maintained where authority was questioned before it was

obeyed . . . ?" This, according to Bernard Bailyn, was the question posed by the "articulate defenders of the status quo" in the wake of the American Revolution (*The Ideological Origins of the American Revolution* [Cambridge: Harvard University Press, Belknap Press, 1967], pp. 318–319).

3. See Rupert Emerson, *From Empire to Nation* (Cambridge: Harvard University Press, 1960), pp. 100, 102 *et passim*.

4. This statement is most often made by those who seek to understand America by comparing it with Europe. See, especially, Louis Hartz, *The Liberal Tradition in America* (New York: Harcourt, Brace and Co., 1955). Hartz's book adopts as its theme Tocqueville's remark that "The great advantage of the Americans is that they have arrived at a state of democracy without having to endure a democratic revolution; and that they are born equal, instead of becoming so."

5. See Jefferson's letter to Richard H. Lee, written in 1825, quoted by Gilbert Chinard, *Thomas Jefferson* (Ann Arbor: University of Michigan Press, 1939), p. 72.

6. These developments are ably summarized in Merrill Jensen, *The New Nation* (1950; reprint ed., New York: Alfred A. Knopf, Vintage Books, 1965), chaps. 5 and 6. See also J. Franklin Jameson, *The American Revolution Considered as a Social Movement* (Princeton, N.J.: Princeton University Press, 1926), and Elisha P. Douglass, *Rebels and Democrats* (Chapel Hill: University of North Carolina Press, 1955), chap. 16. On the economic policies of the states, see Louis Hartz, *Economic Policy and Democratic Thought: Pennsylvania, 1776–1860* (Cambridge: Harvard University Press, 1948), and Oscar and Mary Handlin, *Commonwealth: A Study of the Role of Government in the American Economy: Massachusetts, 1774–1861* (New York: New York University Press, 1947).

7. The best account of the impact of the Revolutionary ideology on slavery in the Old Dominion is by Robert McColley, *Slavery and Jeffersonian Virginia* (Urbana: University of Illinois Press, 1964), pp. 81–90 *et passim*. See also Dumas Malone, *Jefferson and His Time* (Boston: Little, Brown and Co., 1948–), vol. 1, pp. 367 ff.

8. *JCC* 1:113. Also, *JCC* 2:68–70, *JCC* 3:204–205, and *JCC* 1:122. On October 21, 1774, Congress ordered the preparation of "letters to the colonies of St. John's, Nova-Scotia, Georgia, East and West Florida, who have not deputies to represent them in this [First Continental] Congress" (*JCC* 1:101). See also Article XI of the

Confederation, which provided that "Canada acceding to this confederation . . . shall be admitted into and entitled to all the advantages of this union. . . ."

9. *JCC* 5:689–690. Jensen, *Documents,* p. 90, quotes the *Pennsylvania
Gazette* of October 5, 1785, to the effect that the United States had
become an "asylum" for the indigent and oppressed, crushed to
earth by the lawless hand of European despotism. For a discussion
of the Great Seal and its origins, see Winthrop D. Jordan, *White
Over Black* (Chapel Hill: University of North Carolina Press,
1968), p. 337 n.

10. *JCC* 10:405–409. The draft originally submitted to Congress by
Francis Dana, of Massachusetts, offered to admit the Hessian deserters "into the full enjoyment of all the rights, liberties, privileges, and immunities of free and natural born subjects of these
states." Congress, deleting this passage, was apparently not ready
to assume jurisdiction over the question of naturalization.

11. *JCC* 27:453–464.

12. *JCC* 28: 118–120, 136–139, 159–162, 183–184.

13. Braxton's letter is in Jensen, *Documents,* pp. 865–866. See also
pp. 858–859. Galloway's Plan of Union, and his address defending
it, are in *JCC* 1:43–51. Anderson's pamphlet, published in Edin-
burgh in 1776, is referred to by John R. Alden, in *The South in
the Revolution, 1763–1789* (Baton Rouge: Louisiana State University Press, 1957), p. 190.

14. See note 1, chapter 4.

15. The references to Great Britain hold steady during this period,
while the rest of the world falls almost entirely from view.

16. Richard L. Merritt, *Symbols of American Community, 1735–1775*
(New Haven, Conn.: Yale University Press, 1966), pp. 54–59 *et
passim;* see also Merritt's essay "Nation-Building in America: The
Colonial Years," in Karl Deutsch and William J. Foltz, eds., *Nation-Building* (New York: Atherton Press, 1966).

17. Chinard, *op. cit.,* pp. 78–79, 87–88.

18. For a summary of these meetings, see Jensen, *Documents,* pp. 730–
732.

19. Charles M. Andrews, *The Colonial Period* (New York: Henry
Holt and Co., 1912), chap. 9.

20. Edmund S. Morgan, *The Birth of the Republic* (Chicago: University of Chicago Press, 1956), p. 101.

21. Jensen, *Documents,* pp. 826–827.

22. Alden, *op. cit.,* p. 172.

23. Richard Barry, *Mr. Rutledge of South Carolina* (New York: Duell, Sloan & Pearce, 1942), pp. 103–106.

24. These estimates are from Evarts B. Greene and Virginia D. Harrington, *American Population Before the Federal Census of 1790* (New York: Columbia University Press, 1932), pp. 102, 178. The differences between New York City and Charleston are further revealed by the fact that Charleston's population of about 10,000 was just over half black, of whom all but twenty-four, according to one source, were slaves; whereas in New York City only one person in seven was black.

25. "Journal of Josiah Quincy, Junior," *Massachusetts Historical Society Proceedings,* 49 (1916), 454–457. (Emphasis in original.)

26. For Deane's reactions, see Burnett, *Letters,* vol. 1, p. 4. See also pp. 11, 18, 28–29. For Adams's comments, see pp. 114, 67, 195, 368 n., 81.

27. Opinions among historians vary as to the strength of the idea of union in 1776. Claude H. Van Tyne has written that the war was carried on by "thirteen independent states which were temporarily acting together in the business of acquiring their individual independence" (*The American Revolution* [New York: Harper and Brothers, 1905], p. 182). But E. S. Morgan has written (*op. cit.,* p. 103), "By 1776 the consciousness that they belonged together had grown so strong that . . . it did not even occur to the colonists that they might establish thirteen separate governments and go their different ways." Actually, both may be right. The years of the war were a turning point, when "thirteen independent states" began to realize that they "belonged together," and needed to find a permanent basis for "acting together."

28. Douglas Southall Freeman, *George Washington* (New York: Charles Scribner's Sons, 1948–1957), vol. 3, p. 388.

29. To Horatio Gates, March 23, 1776, in Burnett, *Letters,* vol. 1, pp. 405–406. Adams added "land speculators" to his list of those reluctant to permit the establishment of a union based on popular principles.

30. Burnett, *Letters,* vol. 1, pp. 259–260; Benjamin Quarles, *The Negro in the American Revolution* (Chapel Hill: University of North Carolina Press, 1961), p. 47.

31. June 29, 1776, in Burnett, *Letters,* vol. 1, pp. 517–518. See also the letter of Carter Braxton to Langdon Carter, April 14, 1776, in *ibid.,* vol. 1, pp. 420–421, wherein Braxton complains about Yankees who invoke "their darling democracy."

32. *JCC* 6:1087–1093.

33. Burnett, *Letters,* vol. 2, p. 514.

34. Merrill Jensen, *The Articles of Confederation* (Madison: University of Wisconsin Press, 1963), pp. 249–253. Though I have made an independent, indeed prior, study of the sources, I cannot and do not want to deny that my understanding of the framing of the Articles is enriched from having studied Jensen's *The Articles of Confederation.* It will be obvious that his "good" men are often "bad" men in my account, and vice versa. But his work has taught me to appreciate the ambiguities of the "critical period."

35. Franklin's draft, dated July 21, 1775, is in *JCC* 2:195–199.

36. *JCC* 6:1105.

37. *JCC* 9:849.

38. Jensen, *Articles,* p. 256.

39. *JCC* 2:221–222. Franklin's proposal had provided that taxes be apportioned according to the number of "male polls" in each colony. The term "poll" as then used meant white men between the ages of sixteen and sixty, and Negroes of *both* sexes between those ages (Greene and Harrington, *op. cit.,* p. xxiii). By introducing the qualifying adjective "male," Franklin was reducing the burden on the Southern states. But his proposal would have meant the inclusion of Negroes at the same value as whites. Since this formula would have resulted in a tax burden greater than the South intended to accept, his proposal on taxation had no more chance of acceptance than his proposal for representation.

40. The delegates from North Carolina, a state widely believed to be both populous and poor, entered a caveat at this point. See John Adams's notes on the debates (Charles Francis Adams, ed., *The Works of John Adams* [Boston: Little, Brown and Co., 1850–1856], vol. 2, p. 498), and a letter by delegate Cornelius Harnett, dated November 30, 1777, in Burnett, *Letters,* vol. 2, p. 578.

41. This account of the debate over the clause on taxation is drawn from notes taken by Jefferson and John Adams, printed in *JCC* 6:1102–1106 and 1079–1082.

42. Burnett, *Letters,* vol. 2, p. 564.

43. *Ibid.,* p. 541.

44. Forrest McDonald, *E Pluribus Unum* (Boston, Mass.: Houghton Mifflin Co., 1965), pp. 10–11. Historians say that conflicting claims in the West represented one of the most serious obstacles to union during the first decade after 1776. See Andrews, *op. cit.,* chap. 1; Jensen, *New Nation,* pp. 8–11; Jensen, *Articles,* pp. 150–160.

45. Morgan, *op. cit.,* pp. 109–113. See also Merrill Jensen, "Cession of the Old Northwest," *Mississippi Valley Historical Review,* 23 (1936–1937), pp. 27–48.
46. Jensen, *New Nation,* p. 350.
47. *JCC* 9:932–934.
48. *JCC* 11:637–640, 647–656.
49. The only serious threat of amending the Articles was Maryland's proposal that they specifically include a limitation of Virginia's massive land claims. The proposal was defeated, 5 to 6, with one state divided. The result was Maryland's refusal to ratify until 1781, after Virginia had indicated its willingness to cede these claims of its own accord.
50. The word quoted is used by Howard H. Peckham in *The War for Independence* (Chicago: University of Chicago Press, 1958), p. 84.
51. See Madison's notes, in *JCC* 25:845 ff.
52. See the draft of a circular letter to the states, deemed too candid to be sent, in *JCC* 22:132–135, 149–150 (3/15 and 3/26/1782).
53. *JCC* 23:798–809.
54. *JCC* 24:294–311.
55. *JCC* 25:926.
56. *JCC* 24:112.
57. *JCC* 25:948.
58. Three years later, a committee report on the response of the states to the proposed amendment of 1783 stated that the main opposition to the three-fifths ratio was from the North, where it was believed that the ratio was too low, that slaves ought to be counted the equal of white men. See *JCC* 30:106.
59. *JCC* 25:948–949; cf. *JCC* 24:214–216.
60. *JCC* 25:951–952; cf. *JCC* 24:223–224.
61. *JCC* 24:277–283.
62. *JCC* 24:293.
63. *JCC* 30:102–108.
64. *JCC* 31:619.
65. *JCC* 24:287.
66. For examples of these proposals to regulate foreign commerce, see *JCC* 24:188–191 (1783); *JCC* 26:321 ff. (1784); *JCC* 28:201–205, 419 ff. (1785); *JCC* 31:494–499 (1786).
67. *JCC* 31:703. See *JCC* 30:93–94 for other exemptions.
68. Jensen, *New Nation,* pp. 403–405.
69. *JCC* 28:204.

70. Quoted in Jensen, *New Nation,* p. 406.
71. For examples of talk about separate confederacies, see John R. Alden, *The First South* (Baton Rouge: Louisiana State University Press, 1961), pp. 30–31, 61–62, 72, 115.
72. Jensen, *New Nation,* pp. 350–359.
73. *Ibid.,* pp. 347–421. The classical statements of the opposite argument are Madison's "Vices of the Political System of the United States," notes written in April 1787, as he prepared for the Constitutional Convention (Gaillard Hunt, ed., *The Writings of James Madison* [New York: G. P. Putnam's Sons, 1900–1910]. vol. 2, pp. 361–369); and *The Federalist,* number 7, by Alexander Hamilton.
74. William McCord, *The Springtime of Freedom* (New York: Oxford University Press, 1965), p. 279. See also Joseph La Palombara, ed., *Bureaucracy and Political Development* (Princeton, N.J.: Princeton University Press, 1963), pp. ix, 4; A. F. K. Organski, *The Stages of Political Development* (New York: Alfred A. Knopf, 1967), p. 7; Paul Sigmund, ed., *The Ideologies of the Developing Nations* (New York: Frederick A. Praeger, 1963), p. 40.
75. McCord, *op. cit.,* p. 249 n., is a perfect example. See also La Palombara, *op. cit.,* p. 4. The best attempts to compare American development with other cases are Louis Hartz, *The Founding of New Societies* (New York: Harcourt, Brace & World, 1964); Seymour M. Lipset, *The First New Nation* (New York: Basic Books, 1963); Samuel Huntington, *Political Order in Changing Societies* (New Haven, Conn.: Yale University Press, 1968), chaps. 1 and 2.
76. See chapter 8, below, for important qualifications to this generalization.
77. Douglass, *op. cit.,* p. 322.
78. Hannah Arendt, *On Revolution* (New York: Viking Press, 1963), pp. 16–17, 62–66, and chap. 6.
79. This brief account of the early years of the federal bureaucracy is based on Jensen, *New Nation,* pp. 360–374.
80. Hamilton's enthusiastic attitude toward governmental sponsorship of industrial development is seen in this Report, written in 1791. (Alexander Hamilton, *Papers on Public Credit, Commerce, and Finance,* ed. Samuel McKee, Jr. [Indianapolis, Ind.: Bobbs-Merrill Co., 1957], especially pp. 204 ff).
81. See Staughton Lynd's essay "Slavery and the Founding Fathers," in Melvin Drimmer, ed., *Black History* (New York: Doubleday and Co., 1968), pp. 117–131.

CHAPTER 5

1. For a brilliant analysis of these two stages in the emergence of nations, see Hannah Arendt, *On Revolution* (New York: Viking Press, 1963), pp. 140–141, 206 *et passim*.

2. See Lincoln's speech at the Young Men's Lyceum at Springfield (1838), in Roy P. Basler, ed., *The Collected Works of Abraham Lincoln* (New Brunswick, N.J.: Rutgers University Press, 1953), vol. 1, p. 109.

3. One recent book that takes this uncertainty seriously is Forrest McDonald's *E Pluribus Unum*, which is called *The Formation of the American Republic, 1776–1790* in its paperback version (Baltimore: Penguin Books, 1965).

4. It is a useful corrective for people who tend to see the late 1780's as the "critical period of American history" to read Benjamin Franklin's assessment of economic conditions in the late Confederation period, "Comfort for America, or Remarks on Her Real Situation, Interests, and Policy," published in *The American Museum,* 1 (1787), 6–7, excerpts from which are conveniently available in David M. Potter and Thomas G. Manning, eds., *Nationalism and Sectionalism in America, 1775–1877* (New York: Henry Holt and Co., 1949), pp. 44–45. Franklin was no political ally of Richard Henry Lee or George Clinton, but his essay does suggest that these men were not alone in the attempt to deflate the sense of crisis that Madison, Hamilton, and others were trying to build.

5. Gaillard Hunt, ed., *The Writings of James Madison* (New York: G. P. Putnam's Sons, 1900–1910), vol. 2, p. 319. See also the references in Jackson T. Main, *The Antifederalists* (Chapel Hill: University of North Carolina Press, 1961), app. A.

6. Quoted by John R. Alden in *The First South* (Baton Rouge: Louisiana State University Press, 1961), p. 72.

7. Clinton Rossiter, *1787: The Grand Convention* (New York: Macmillan Co., 1966), pp. 72–73.

8. For example, see *The Federalist,* number 5, by John Jay, and numbers 15 and 22, by Hamilton; and the exchanges between Gunning Bedford and the leading nationalizers at the Federal Convention, in Farrand, *Records,* vol. 1, pp. 492–493, 514, 528, 530, 535. For a general analysis, see Hans Kohn, *American Nationalism* (New York: Collier Books, 1957), chap. 3.

9. *Cui Bono?* (1781), pp. 118–119, quoted in Potter and Manning, *op. cit.,* p. 24.

10. John C. Fitzpatrick, ed., *The Writings of George Washington* (Washington: Government Printing Office, 1931–1944), vol. 35, pp. 218–233. (Washington's emphasis.) It is perhaps anachronistic to cite the Farewell Address, presented in 1796, to illustrate a sentiment ascribed to 1787. I use it because it was the clearest and most detailed call to national union in the early national period, and was produced by the joint labors of three of the leading framers.

11. *Banks and Politics in America* (Princeton, N.J.: Princeton University Press, 1957), pp. 77, 87–88.

12. The strain this put on states that lacked good harbors is reflected in Madison's remark: "New Jersey, placed between Philadelphia and New York, was likened to a cask tapped at both ends; and North Carolina, between Virginia and South Carolina, to a patient bleeding at both arms." Quoted in *ibid.*, p. 89.

13. Rossiter, *op. cit.*, p. 143.

14. Merrill Jensen, *The New Nation* (New York: Alfred A. Knopf, Vintage Books, 1950), pp. 350–359.

15. In *Nationalism and Social Communication*, 2nd ed. (Cambridge: M.I.T. Press, 1966), p. 33, Karl Deutsch presents a schematic diagram of the early American political elite, which is suggestive of the phenomenon described here, even if it is deficient in its preoccupation with leaders from the mid-Atlantic states. (Remarkably, Deutsch's diagram contains not one name from the five Southern states.) One good indication of the strength of this national political network can be seen in Burnett, *Letters.* Many of these letters reflect, of course, the tensions in the union, rather than the strengthening bonds. Still, the mere fact that political communication throughout the union was so widespread and so frequent is in some ways more significant than the content of particular letters. A good discussion of the role of this national political elite in the founding is in John P. Roche, "The Founding Fathers: A Reform Caucus in Action," *American Political Science Review*, 55 (1961), 799–816.

16. Stanley Elkins and Eric McKittrick, "The Founding Fathers: Young Men of the Revolution," *Political Science Quarterly*, 76 (1961), 181.

17. Farrand, *Records,* vol. 1, pp. 447, 486.

18. *The Federalist*, numbers 51 and 10; Farrand, *Records*, vol. 2, p. 10.

19. Accepting this line as the sectional boundary was the almost universal practice in the late eighteenth century. John R. Alden in the first chapter of *The First South* presents both contemporary

evidence in support of this usage and a few dissenting opinions by those who would have excluded Maryland, or added Delaware.

20. Charles Pinckney, of South Carolina, and Dr. William Samuel Johnson, of Connecticut, were two who expressed this view (Farrand, *Records,* vol. 1, pp. 593, 596).

21. The census of 1790 found 1,967,000 human beings north of Maryland, and 1,962,000 in Maryland and to the south.

22. Farrand, *Records,* vol. 1, pp. 585–586. See also pp. 571, 578 *et passim*. Delegates who made this point did not differentiate between South and West, presumably because population in either area would be "agrarian," and would be opposed to politics in the "mercantile" East. On this point see Staughton Lynd, "The Compromise of 1787," chap. 8 in *Class Conflict, Slavery, and the United States Constitution* (Indianapolis, Ind.: Bobbs-Merrill Co., 1967), pp. 190–191.

23. Farrand, *Records,* vol. 1, p. 179.

24. For a summary discussion of these points, see the speeches of Madison and Wilson on July 14, 1787 in Farrand, *Records,* vol. 2, pp. 8–11.

25. Farrand, *Records,* vol. 1, p. 20.

26. See Farrand, *Records,* vol. 1, pp. 200 and 202 for the key votes.

27. Madison, during the summer of 1787 at any rate, would have disagreed with this analysis. He apparently felt that the proponents of proportional representation could proceed, by themselves if necessary, to frame a constitution, get it ratified in the more populous states, and then wait while the smaller states gradually fell into line, as political realities would dictate that they must. See Farrand, *Records,* vol. 2, pp. 19–20. But it seems clear that Madison underestimated the determination of men like Paterson, Sherman, and George Clinton, and also the appeal that their ideas and loyalties had for men like Baldwin, Gerry, and perhaps even Randolph himself.

28. Farrand, *Records,* vol. 1, pp. 177, 202; see also Madison's letter to Thomas Jefferson, dated October 24, 1737, in *ibid.,* vol. 3, p. 135.

29. Farrand, *Records,* vol. 1, p. 526. The last clause, which Gerry once described as the "cornerstone of the accommodation" (Farrand, *Records,* vol. 2, p. 5), was a concession to those who believed that wealth was insecure except where it was represented, and that "money bills" could therefore be safely entrusted only to a body whose representation was proportioned either to wealth or to pop-

ulation, since numbers of people were thought, where migration was unimpeded, to reflect wealth.

30. Farrand, *Records,* vol. 1, pp. 169, 196.

31. Farrand, *Records,* vol. 1, p. 605.

32. Farrand, *Records,* vol. 1, pp. 542, 581, 196. Cf. Wilson on this point: "He could not agree that property was the sole or the primary object of government and society. The cultivation and improvement of the human mind was the most noble object. With respect to this object, as well as to other *personal* rights, numbers were surely the natural and precise measure of representation" (*loc. cit.;* original emphasis).

33. Farrand, *Records,* vol. 1, p. 541.

34. Farrand, *Records,* vol. 1, pp. 533–534.

35. Farrand, *Records,* vol. 1, pp. 604–605.

36. Farrand, *Records,* vol. 1, p. 534.

37. Ulrich B. Phillips, "The South Carolina Federalists," *American Historical Review,* 14 (1909), 529–543, 731–743, esp. 540–543.

38. Farrand, *Records,* vol. 1, p. 561.

39. Perhaps the most thorough expression of this rationale is found in *The Federalist,* number 54, by Madison. It was also advanced by W. R. Davie at the North Carolina ratifying convention in July 1788: "as rational beings," said Davie, slaves "had a right of representation" (Farrand, *Records,* vol. 3, p. 343).

40. Farrand, *Records,* vol. 2, p. 222.

41. Farrand, *Records,* vol. 1, p. 561; vol. 2, p. 364.

42. Farrand, *Records,* vol. 1, pp. 583, 586–587; vol. 2, p. 222.

43. Farrand, *Records,* vol. 1, p. 526. (Emphasis added.)

44. Farrand, *Records,* vol. 1, p. 533.

45. Farrand, *Records,* vol. 1, p. 534.

46. Farrand, *Records,* vol. 1, p. 540.

47. Farrand, *Records,* vol. 2, pp. 6 (Rufus King), 223 (Gouverneur Morris). See also *The Federalist,* number 12, by Alexander Hamilton.

48. Farrand, *Records,* vol. 1, p. 543.

49. These were the two who split the Massachusetts vote on July 16, by voting against the Great Compromise.

50. Farrand, *Records,* vol. 1, p. 560.

51. Farrand, *Records,* vol. 1, p. 561.

52. Farrand, *Records,* vol. 2, p. 223.

53. Farrand, *Records,* vol. 1, p. 201; cf. p. 587; vol. 2, pp. 220–223.

54. Farrand, *Records,* vol. 1, p. 562.

55. Farrand, *Records,* vol. 1, pp. 566–567.
56. Farrand, *Records,* vol. 1, p. 570.
57. Farrand, *Records,* vol. 1, p. 578.
58. Farrand, *Records,* vol. 1, p. 571.
59. Farrand, *Records,* vol. 1, pp. 593, 529; cf. 552.
60. Farrand, *Records,* vol. 1, pp. 578, 559–560.
61. Farrand, *Records,* vol. 1, pp. 578–579.
62. Farrand, *Records,* vol. 1, p. 583.
63. Farrand, *Records,* vol. 1, p. 585. For Morris's remark see *ibid.,* p. 582.
64. Farrand, *Records,* vol. 1, pp. 580–581.
65. Farrand, *Records,* vol. 1, pp. 586–588.
66. Farrand, *Records,* vol. 1, p. 594. Later, when John Dickinson and James Wilson tried to remove the phrase "and direct taxes" from the clause governing representation, Gouverneur Morris responded that the phrase had been inserted "in order to exclude the *appearance* of counting the Negroes in the representation" (Farrand, *Records,* vol. 1, p. 607; emphasis added).
67. Farrand, *Records,* vol. 1, p. 603.
68. Farrand, *Records,* vol. 1, p. 604–605.
69. Farrand, *Records,* vol. 1, p. 605.
70. See the credentials of the Delaware delegation, in Farrand, *Records,* vol. 1, pp. 4, 37.
71. Farrand, *Records,* vol. 2, p. 1.
72. Farrand, *Records,* vol. 2, p. 3. Massachusetts, Connecticut, Delaware, and Maryland were affirmative; Pennsylvania divided and New Jersey, Virginia, the Carolinas, and Georgia were opposed.
73. The vote showed Massachusetts divided (Gerry and Strong preferring compromise to failure); Pennsylvania, Virginia, South Carolina, and Georgia voting negatively; and Connecticut, New Jersey, Delaware, Maryland, and North Carolina in the affirmative. In light of a sectional analysis, the deviating votes were cast by Maryland and North Carolina. Maryland's vote was probably influenced by jealousy of Southern neighbors. It was the one slave-heavy state without a direct stake in the development of the West. Furthermore, Baltimore gave it ties of interest with the commercial states to the North. On balance, the delegates from Maryland were probably delighted with the compromise, which gave them an increment for their slaves in one house, and equality with Virginia in the other.

   Tallying North Carolina's vote, Madison noted that Richard

Dobbs Spaight voted "no." This implies that Hugh Williamson, William R. Davie, Alexander Martin, and William Blount voted "yes," if they were present at all (and two of them must have been, to outvote Spaight). None of these men had been expansive during the debate about his attitude toward the compromise. Some switching had apparently occurred, though, between the "full stop" of July 2 and the first vote on the Gerry Committee proposals of July 6 and 7. Williamson had remarked, after the equal division of July 2, "If we do not concede on both sides, our business must soon be at an end." Davie, as a member of the Gerry Committee, had seen how difficult it was to settle this question, and when his view on representation for slaves prevailed after the exchange of ultimatums with Morris on July 12, he may have decided to throw his support solidly behind the compromise.

74. Forty years later, James Madison wrote to Martin Van Buren that "the *threatening contest* in the Convention of 1787 did not, as you supposed, turn on the degree of power to be granted to the federal government, but on the rule by which the states should be represented and vote in the government . . ." (Farrand, *Records*, vol. 3, p. 477; emphasis in original).

75. Farrand, *Records*, vol. 1, p. 551.

76. Farrand, *Records*, vol. 1, pp. 451–452.

CHAPTER 6

1. Farrand, *Records*, vol. 1, p. 551.

2. On its first offering, this motion was defeated when six Northern states overpowered the five states to the south. But following a day of desultory debate, Rutledge moved it again. This time the motion prevailed without objection (Farrand, *Records*, vol. 1, pp. 407–408, 436). The fact that this was the first straight sectional vote was called to my attention by Staughton Lynd. See his *Class Conflict, Slavery, and the United States Constitution* (Indianapolis, Ind.: Bobbs-Merrill Co., 1967), p. 161.

3. Stanley Elkins and Eric McKittrick, "The Founding Fathers: Young Men of the Revolution," *Political Science Quarterly*, 76 (1961), 181; and John P. Roche, "The Founding Fathers: A Reform Caucus in Action," *American Political Science Review*, 55 (1961), 799.

4. The planters were Madison, Washington, Rutledge, the two Pinckneys, Mason, and Randolph; the nonplanters, Gouverneur Morris,

Wilson, Franklin, Sherman, King, Ellsworth, Gorham, and Gerry. See Clinton Rossiter, *1787: The Grand Convention* (New York: Macmillan Co., 1966), pp. 247–250.

5. Farrand, *Records,* vol. 2, p. 452.
6. Farrand, *Records,* vol. 2, p. 371; *ibid.,* vol. 1, p. 595.
7. Farrand, *Records,* vol. 2, pp. 369–370, 371.
8. Farrand, *Records,* vol. 2, p. 370.
9. Farrand, *Records,* vol. 1, p. 135.
10. Farrand, *Records,* vol. 1, p. 605. Cf. General Pinckney's warning to the Committee of Detail "to insert some security to the Southern states against an emancipation of slaves" in their draft of the Constitution (Farrand, *Records,* vol. 2. p. 95).
11. Farrand, *Records,* vol. 2, pp. 364, 373.
12. Farrand, *Records,* vol. 2, p. 370; cf. Dickinson (p. 372), King (p. 373), and Gorham (p. 374).
13. Farrand, *Records,* vol. 1, p. 21.
14. Farrand, *Records,* vol. 1, p. 53. (Original emphasis.)
15. Farrand, *Records,* vol. 1, pp. 53–54.
16. Farrand, *Records,* vol. 1, pp. 136, 202, 570.
17. See his speech of June 18 (Farrand, *Records,* vol. 1, pp. 282–311), and especially his comment thereon the following afternoon (p. 323).
18. Farrand, *Records,* vol. 1, pp. 489, 324. (Original emphasis.)
19. Farrand, *Records,* vol. 1, p. 177.
20. Farrand, *Records,* vol. 1, p. 492.
21. Farrand, *Records,* vol. 1, p. 133.
22. Farrand, *Records,* vol. 1, p. 134.
23. Farrand, *Records,* vol. 1, p. 53.
24. Farrand, *Records,* vol. 1, p. 164. (Emphasis added.)
25. Farrand, *Records,* vol. 1, p. 164. (Original emphasis.)
26. His claim was inaccurate. Jonathan Dayton, of New Jersey, who was three years younger than Pinckney, joined the Convention June 21 (Rossiter, *op. cit.,* pp. 132–133, 100).
27. Farrand, *Records,* vol. 1, pp. 165, 166.
28. The boldness of Southerners generally, and of Pinckney in particular, continued to the end of the Convention. On August 23, as the Convention drew to a close, Pinckney moved to give Congress power to veto state laws "interferring in the opinion of the legislature with the general interests and harmony of the union." The motion to send the proposal to a committee for further consideration was defeated, 5 to 6, with Maryland and Virginia in the affir-

mative, and North Carolina, South Carolina, and Georgia opposed (Farrand, *Records,* vol. 2, pp. 390–391).

29. Irving Brant, *James Madison* (Indianapolis, Ind.: Bobbs-Merrill Co., 1941–1961), vol. 2, pp. 403–407.
30. See, for example, Lynd, *op. cit.,* pp. 153–154; cf. the speech of Gouverneur Morris on August 8 (Farrand, *Records,* vol. 2, pp. 221–222).
31. Farrand, *Records,* vol. 2, pp. 168, 174.
32. Farrand, *Records,* vol. 2, pp. 330–333, 384–389.
33. Farrand, *Records,* vol. 2, p. 64.
34. Farrand, *Records,* vol. 2, pp. 317–318, 387, 467.
35. Farrand, *Records,* vol. 2, pp. 374, 453.
36. Carl Van Doren, *The Great Rehearsal* (New York: Viking Press, 1948), p. 140.
37. Farrand, *Records,* vol. 2, p. 220.
38. Farrand, *Records,* vol. 2, pp. 222–223.
39. See the graph between pp. 371 and 372 in Ulrich B. Phillips, *American Negro Slavery* (New York: D. Appleton and Co., 1918).
40. The impression that the speech of August 8 was basically a tactical maneuver is reinforced by Morris's readiness two weeks later to foresee a "bargain among the Northern and Southern states" when General Pinckney moved to commit the clause regarding the slave trade (Farrand, *Records,* vol. 2, p. 374).
41. Farrand, *Records,* vol. 2, p. 223.
42. Farrand, *Records,* vol. 2, pp. 361–362.
43. Farrand, *Records,* vol. 2, pp. 363–364; cf. pp. 306–307.
44. See the "recollection" of William Paterson, of New Jersey, who, as a Supreme Court Justice writing in the case of *Hylton* v. *United States* (1796), said that "the principal purpose of the provision [against capitation taxes] had been to allay the fear of the Southern states lest their Negroes and land should be subjected to a specific tax." Cited from 3 Dallas 171, 177, by Edward S. Corwin, ed., *The Constitution of the United States of America: Analysis and Interpretation* (Washington: Government Printing Office, 1952, 1964), p. 367.
45. Farrand, *Records,* vol. 2, p. 183.
46. Farrand, *Records,* vol. 2, p. 364. Cf. General Pinckney's comment: "He contended that the importation of slaves would be for the interest of the whole union. The more slaves, the more produce to employ the carrying trade; the more consumption also, and the more of this, the more of revenue for the common treasury" (*ibid.,* p. 371).

47. Alexander Hamilton, in Farrand, *Records,* vol. 1, p. 466.
48. Farrand, *Records,* vol. 2, p. 372.
49. Farrand, *Records,* vol. 2, pp. 371, 375.
50. Farrand, *Records,* vol. 2, p. 370.
51. Farrand, *Records,* vol. 2, pp. 364–365, 371–374.
52. Farrand, *Records,* vol. 2, p. 375. Cf. Charles Pinckney (p. 364), C. C. Pinckney (p. 372), Baldwin (p. 372), and Rutledge (p. 373).
53. Farrand, *Records,* vol. 2, p. 373.
54. Farrand, *Records,* vol. 2, pp. 374–375.
55. For a list of committee members, see Farrand, *Records,* vol. 2, p. 375; for its report, *ibid.,* p. 400.
56. Farrand, *Records,* vol. 2, p. 415. "Twenty years [1788–1808] will produce all the mischief that can be apprehended from the liberty to import slaves," said Madison. "So long a term will be more dishonorable to the national character than to say nothing about it in the Constitution."
57. Farrand, *Records,* vol. 2, pp. 416–417. The tax had been proposed earlier by General Pinckney, Rufus King, and Luther Martin (*ibid.,* pp. 373, 364, respectively), before being adopted by Livingston's committee.
58. This became a hot question during the debates over the Missouri Compromise. As is so often the case, it is difficult to tell exactly what the framers did intend by the term "migration or importation." Wilson in 1787 apparently thought the word "migration" referred to interstate commerce in slaves (Farrand, *Records,* vol. 3, p. 161). But Madison, in number 42 of *The Federalist,* implies that the word refers to migrations of whites from abroad; in 1820, he was certain that the term referred "exclusively . . . to migration and importation, *into the U.S.*" (Farrand, *Records,* vol. 3, p. 439; Madison's emphasis).
59. Farrand, *Records,* vol. 3, p. 443.
60. Farrand, *Records,* vol. 2, p. 443.
61. The idea had first seen daylight as one of Rufus King's proposed amendments to the ordinance for the Western Territory, offered in 1785.
62. Farrand, *Records,* vol. 2, p. 443.
63. Farrand, *Records,* vol. 2, pp. 453–454.
64. Farrand, *Records,* vol. 2, p. 628. Historian George Bancroft has pointed out that by this clause the laws that sealed the bondage of slaves were made for the first time to extend to the limits of American jurisdiction (*History of the United States* [New York: D. Appleton Co., 1885], vol. 6, pp. 308–310).

65. As General Pinckney once put the point rather graphically, what Southerners feared was that if Northerners got control of Congress "and the regulation of trade is given to the general government, they will be nothing more than overseers for the Northern states" (Farrand, *Records,* vol. 1, p. 567).
66. Farrand, *Records,* vol. 2, p. 451. (Original emphasis.)
67. Farrand, *Records,* vol. 2, pp. 449–453.
68. Farrand, *Records,* vol. 2, p. 559.
69. Farrand, *Records,* vol. 2, pp. 629, 630.
70. Farrand, *Records,* vol. 2, p. 374.
71. Farrand, *Records,* vol. 2, pp. 666–667.
72. Farrand, *Records,* vol. 1, p. 15. See Rossiter, *op. cit.,* pp. 167–169, for a discussion of the so-called "secrecy rule."
73. Farrand, *Records,* vol. 3, pp. 250–256; see also *The Federalist,* number 49, by Madison, and number 85, by Hamilton.
74. Jonathan Elliot, ed., *The Debates in the Several State Conventions, on the Adoption of the Federal Constitution* (Philadelphia, Pa.: J. B. Lippincott Co., 1876), vol. 2, pp. 36–37, 39.
75. *Ibid.,* vol. 4, p. 283. In 1803, Rufus King remarked that "had it been foreseen that we could raise a revenue to the extent we have done, from indirect taxes, the representation of slaves would never have been admitted . . ." (Farrand, *Records,* vol. 3, p. 400). But it *was* foreseen, by King's ally, Gouverneur Morris, during the debate on representation (Farrand, *Records,* vol. 2, p. 223). Additional evidence of awareness among framers that most revenues would arise from indirect taxes can be found in *The Federalist,* number 12, by Hamilton. See also Albert F. Simpson, "The Political Significance of Slave Representation, 1787–1821," *Journal of Southern History,* 7 (1941), 316–320.
76. Elliot, *op. cit.,* vol. 2, pp. 203–204; vol. 4, p. 272.
77. *Ibid.,* vol. 3, pp. 589–590. (Original emphasis.)
78. *Ibid.,* vol. 3, pp. 458, 622; vol. 4, pp. 284–285.
79. Pinckney's speech is in Farrand, *Records,* vol. 3, p. 256. On the bills of rights in the state constitutions, see Robert A. Rutland, *The Birth of the Bill of Rights, 1776–1791* (New York: Collier Books, 1962), pp. 71–72.
80. Even in North Carolina, where ratification was first defeated, then granted, in November 1789, attitudes toward slavery seemed not to be a decisive factor.
81. Farrand, *Records,* vol. 3, p. 161.
82. Farrand, *Records,* vol. 3, p. 161. Southerners understood the word

"migration" to refer only to the voluntary movements of free whites. See, for example, the speech by James Iredell, of North Carolina, in Elliot, *op. cit.*, vol. 4, p. 102.

83. Farrand, *Records,* vol. 3, p. 437.

84. Elliot, *op. cit.*, vol. 2, p. 272.

85. *Ibid.*, vol. 2, pp. 283–286.

86. William Dawes, of Massachusetts, and Thomas Tredwell, of New York, *ibid.*, vol. 2, pp. 40, 403.

87. Farrand, *Records,* vol. 3, pp. 334, 325.

88. Elliot, *op. cit.*, vol. 4, pp. 100, 286.

89. Farrand, *Records,* vol. 2, pp. 415–417. Four days later, the fugitive-slave clause was introduced. This clause came closest to acknowledging the existence of slavery in America. As originally proposed by Pierce Butler, it would have required "fugitive slaves and servants to be delivered up like criminals" (*ibid.,* p. 443). As adopted August 29, it provided for the return of "any person bound to service or labor" (*ibid.,* pp. 453–454); as revised by the Committee of Style, it spoke of persons "legally held to service or labor" (*ibid.,* p. 601); and on September 15, the next to last day of the Convention, the word "legally" was eliminated (*ibid.,* p. 628). Evident throughout is an attempt to avoid an explicit reference to slavery, and to narrow the Constitutional sanction for it.

90. See Robert W. Johannsen, ed., *The Lincoln-Douglas Debates of 1858* (New York: Oxford University Press, 1965), pp. 55, 132–133, 277–278.

91. Thomas Hobbes, *Leviathan,* pt. 2, chap. 29, "Of Those Things That Weaken or Tend to the Dissolution of a Commonwealth."

92. Hamilton in *The Federalist,* number 36, describes the "New England states" as being the "most tenacious of their rights."

CHAPTER 7

1. At the Federal Convention, for example, some of the leading nationalists (sometimes as a debater's ploy, but at other times with apparent sincerity) openly countenanced the possibility of subdivisions. See Farrand, *Records,* vol. 1, pp. 482 (James Wilson), 532 (Elbridge Gerry), 593, 604 (Gouverneur Morris), 595–596 (Rufus King); vol. 2, p. 4 (Luther Martin). And see also *The Federalist,* number 13, where Hamilton discusses the viability of two or three confederacies, instead of the United States. For a general discussion of the concept of "union" see Paul C. Nagel, *One Nation Indivisi-*

ble: The Union in American Thought, 1776–1861 (New York: Oxford University Press, 1964).

2. The classic analysis along these lines is Charles A. Beard, *An Economic Interpretation of the Constitution of the United States* (New York: Macmillan Co., 1962).

3. Samuel Eliot Morison estimates, for example, that "nineteen twentieths of the congressional business" between 1797 and 1801 "concerned the French Revolution, directly or indirectly" (*Harrison Gray Otis, 1765–1848: The Urbane Federalist* [Boston: Houghton Mifflin Co., 1969], p. 97; see also p. 91).

4. Imperial ambitions on America's part ought not to be totally discounted, however, as William Appleman Williams makes clear in his article "The Age of Mercantilism: An Interpretation of American Political Economy, 1763–1828," *William and Mary Quarterly Review,* 3rd ser., 15 (1958), 419–437. American pressure on the Indians and on Spanish and British boundaries in America was certainly one source of the foreign entanglements that constituted so divisive a force in early national politics.

5. See Alexander De Conde, *Entangling Alliance: Politics and Diplomacy Under George Washington* (Durham, N.C.: Duke University Press, 1958), pp. 5–7, and sources cited there, especially Felix Gilbert, "The 'New Diplomacy' of the Eighteenth Century," *World Politics,* 4 (1951), 1–38. For a refutation of the notion that there could be commercial intercourse without political involvement, see *The Federalist,* numbers 5 and 34, by Hamilton.

6. *The Transportation Revolution, 1815–1860* (New York: Rinehart and Co., 1951), pp. 132–133, 176.

7. The best general analysis of the first party system is William Nisbet Chambers, *Political Parties in a New Nation: The American Experience, 1776–1809* (New York: Oxford University Press, 1963). For an emphasis on ideological aspects, see Joseph Charles, *The Origins of the American Party System* (New York: Harper and Brothers, Harper Torchbooks, 1961). Wilfred E. Binkley, *American Political Parties: Their Natural History* (New York: Alfred A. Knopf, 1963), assays a description of the rival coalitions in terms of interest groups. Chambers's book includes a useful bibliographical essay.

8. *Op. cit.,* p. 95.

9. *Annals,* 3rd Cong., 1st Sess., 1/3/1794, pp. 155–158. In the light of Jefferson's trouble with the Non-Intercourse Acts (1806, 1809) and the embargo (1808), one wonders if Madison's approach

might not have forestalled grievous difficulties and achieved important purposes without the bloodshed and suffering subsequently required. It is more likely, however, that the same factors that led to Jefferson's problems (Britain's contemptuous attitude toward the American government, the extent of American trade with Great Britain, the desire of merchants to participate in this trade on almost any terms, and the primitiveness of domestic manufacturing capacities) lay behind the defeat of Madison's program in 1794. On the "British connection" in American foreign trade, see Curtis P. Nettels, *The Emergence of a National Economy, 1775-1815* (New York: Holt, Rinehart and Winston, 1962), pp. 230 ff.

10. Eugene Link cites debts owed to British creditors as an important factor in turning the South toward "republicanism" (*Democratic-Republican Societies, 1790-1800* [New York: Columbia University Press, 1942], p. 53).

11. Dumas Malone, *Jefferson and His Time,* (Boston: Little, Brown and Co., 1948-), vol. 3, chap. 6, esp. pp. 102-105.

12. Link, *op. cit.,* p. 205 *et passim.*

13. In 1793, Gallatin prepared a committee report in the Pennsylvania legislature which declared that "slavery is inconsistent with every principle of humanity, justice and right, and repugnant to the spirit and express letter of the constitution of this commonwealth," and ought therefore to be abolished straightway. He regarded the uprising in Santo Domingo as "the just punishment" for the "crimes" of slavery, and "the natural consequence of slavery." In national politics, Gallatin was a strict unionist, determined to respect what he regarded as the "compact" of the Constitution, not to agitate against slavery, and to abide by such explicit guarantees as the federal ratio and the fugitive slave law. But he believed in construing these Constitutional guarantees as narrowly as possible. He did not feel obliged to extend the federal ratio to new territories, and argued that to do so required the unanimous consent of the original contracting parties—that is, the states in the original territory of the United States. See Henry Adams, *Albert Gallatin* (Philadelphia: J. P. Lippincott, 1879), pp. 86, 109-110, 671-675.

14. In addition to the Naturalization Act of 1790, see the acts of 1794 (*Annals*, 3rd Cong., 1st Sess., 1/29/1795, p. 1497), 1802 (*Annals* 7th Cong., 1st Sess., 4/14/1802, p. 1329 ff.), and 1804 (*Annals,* 8th Cong., 1st Sess., 3/26/1804, p. 1303). See also F. G. Franklin,

"Legislative History of Naturalization, 1776–1795," American Historical Association *Annual Report for 1901*, vol. 1, pp. 301–317.

15. For the debate, see *Annals*, 1st Cong., 2nd Sess., 2/3/1790, pp. 1109–1125.
16. *Annals*, 3rd Cong., 2nd Sess., 12/22/1794, pp. 1005–1009.
17. *Annals*, 3rd Cong., 2nd Sess., 1/1/1795, p. 1033.
18. Article I, Section 9, Clause 8. Modern tastes are startled by the conceits of John Adams and others in Washington's administration. See Claude Bowers, *Jefferson and Hamilton: The Struggle for Democracy in America* (Boston: Houghton Mifflin & Co., 1966), chap. 1. These somewhat ludicrous pretentions are best understood as reflections of anxiety for the dignity and authority of the fledgling national government. Time would tell that titles and the trappings of royalty were counterproductive, however, in terms of the quest for legitimate public authority in America, at least during the nineteenth century.
19. *Annals*, 3rd Cong., 2nd Sess., 1/1/1795, p. 1039.
20. *Annals*, 3rd Cong., 2nd Sess., 1/1/1795, pp. 1039–1040.
21. *Annals*, 3rd Cong., 2nd Sess., 1/2/1795, p. 1042.
22. *Annals*, 3rd Cong., 2nd Sess., 1/2/1795, p. 1057.
23. *Op. cit.*, p. 91.
24. *Ibid.*, pp. 102–105. Morison writes that "by the middle of 1798, most Federalists, from Washington down, believed that the French Directory intended to invade the United States via Hispaniola, raise a slave insurrection in the South, and seek to set up a vassal republic west of the Alleghenies or south of the Potomac" (p. 103). For a Southern Federalist expression of this fear, see Robert Goodloe Harper, *Observations on the Dispute Between the United States and France* (Philadelphia: Thomas Bradford, 1797).
25. The quoted phrase is from Washington's message to Congress, December 5, 1793, communicating "certain correspondences" with French Minister Edmond Genêt; printed in *American State Papers: Foreign Relations* (Washington: Gales and Seaton, 1832–1861), vol. 1, p. 141.
26. Stephen Kurtz provides a thorough account of politics within the various states in *The Presidency of John Adams* (New York: A. S. Barnes, 1957), chaps. 7 and 8. See also his tables, arranged sectionally, on pp. 412–414. Another useful analysis is Manning J. Dauer, *The Adams Federalists* (Baltimore: Johns Hopkins Press, 1953), chap. 6.
27. The tendency of such a tax to encourage land redistribution was

openly avowed and defended by Morris in his report of July 29, 1782. For an analysis, see Stuart Bruchey, *The Roots of American Economic Growth, 1607–1861* (New York: Harper & Row, Harper Torchbooks, 1968), pp. 102–106.

28. See, for example, *The Federalist,* numbers 12 and 41, by Hamilton. "Customs" collections provided over 80 per cent of the receipts during most years between 1789 and 1820. See U.S. Bureau of the Census, *Historical Statistics of the United States· Colonial Times to 1957* (Washington: Government Printing Office, 1960), p. 712. One item of import not found on the tariff schedules was slaves, owing to the resistance of the merchants from New England and the Deep Southern planters. See chap. 9.

29. *Annals,* 4th Cong., 2nd Sess., 1/12/1797, pp. 1845–1852.

30. *Annals,* 4th Cong., 2nd Sess., 1/20/1797, p. 1932.

31. *Annals,* 4th Cong., 2nd Sess., 1/20/1797, pp. 1939–1941.

32. *Annals,* 4th Cong., 2nd Sess., 1/20/1797, p. 1941. The nays came from opponents of direct taxes in any form.

33. *Annals,* 4th Cong., 2nd Sess., 2/25/1797, pp. 2239–2290.

34. *Annals,* 5th Cong., 2nd Sess., 6/5/1798, p. 1869.

35. *Annals,* 5th Cong., 2nd Sess., 6/11/1798, p. 1893.

36. *Annals,* 5th Cong., 2nd Sess., 6/30/1798, p. 595.

37. *Annals,* 5th Cong., 2nd Sess., 6/30/1798, p. 595.

38. *Annals,* 5th Cong., 2nd Sess., 7/9/1798, Appendix, pp. 3763, 3770.

39. *Annals,* 5th Cong., 2nd Sess., 6/29/1798, p. 2053.

40. *Annals,* 5th Cong., 2nd Sess., 6/29/1798, p. 2059. The vote on this motion was not recorded.

41. *Annals,* 5th Cong., 2nd Sess., 7/2/1798, 7/14/1798, pp. 2066, 3777–3785.

42. Kurtz, *op. cit.,* pp. 361–365.

43. Kurtz (*op. cit.,* pp. 114–117, 127–132, 189) attributes this boldness partly to the near-success of French interference in the Presidential election of 1796 in Pennsylvania.

44. An arrangement with Great Britain provided that the Royal Navy protect transatlantic shipping, while American ships guard the merchants of the two nations in the Caribbean. Samuel Eliot Morison, *The Oxford History of the American People* (New York: Oxford University Press, 1965), p. 350. It was in carrying out its end of the bargain, scouring the Caribbean for French picaroons, that the American Navy encountered several battles in this curious "quasi-war." Many Republicans regarded the French as justified by Jay's Treaty in their spoliations.

45. The most thorough study of these acts, their origins and administration, is James Morton Smith, *Freedom's Fetters* (Ithaca, N.Y.: Cornell University Press, 1956). They are defended by Morison, in *Otis*, pp. 118–121.

46. When Jefferson had used the same term in counseling Washington to veto the First Bank of the United States in 1791, Fisher Ames charged that the tendency to cry "unconstitutional" was a "vice that has grown inveterate with indulgence" (S. E. Morison, "Squire Ames and Doctor Ames," *New England Quarterly*, 1 [1928], 13).

47. New Englanders in 1798 believed that the adoption of this view would have rendered the Constitution inoperable. See James Truslow Adams, *New England in the Republic, 1776–1850* (Boston: Little, Brown and Co., 1926), p. 224. By 1814, the positions of Virginia and Massachusetts (bearing this time on the state-militia question) would be precisely reversed, and with a vengeance. See Morison, *Otis*, p. 370 *et passim*.

48. This aspect of the Resolutions' significance is stressed in Adrienne Koch and Harry Ammon, "The Virginia and Kentucky Resolutions: An Episode in Jefferson's and Madison's Defense of Civil Liberties," *William and Mary Quarterly Review*, 3rd ser., 5 (April 1948), 145–176.

49. Philip G. Davidson, "Virginia and the Alien and Sedition Laws," *American Historical Review*, 36 (January 1931), 336–342.

50. *Op. cit.*, p. 358.

51. The leading exposition of these trends is Ulrich B. Phillips, "The South Carolina Federalists," *American Historical Review*, 14 (1909), 529–543, 731–743. It is usefully supplemented by a book that focuses on the other side: John Harold Wolfe, *Jeffersonian Democracy in South Carolina* (Chapel Hill: University of North Carolina Press, 1940).

52. These pamphlets are quoted and analyzed in Wolfe, *op. cit.*, pp. 149–152.

53. Wolfe, *op. cit.*, chap. 6; Morison, *Otis*, chap. 9; Dauer, *op. cit.*, chap. 16.

54. A rich account of the feel of life in Washington is provided by Constance McLaughlin Green, *Washington: Village and Capital, 1800–1878* (Princeton, N.J.: Princeton University Press, 1962), chaps. 1–3. Another recent study, which focuses more sharply on the political processes among national politicians, is James S. Young, *The Washington Community, 1800–1828* (New York: Columbia University Press, 1966).

55. Green, *op. cit.*, p. 96, quoting Jesse Torrey, *A Portraiture of Domestic Slavery in the United States*, pp. 33–34 (Torrey's emphasis). See also pp. 52–55 of Mrs. Green's book, where Edward Coles, "President Madison's charming young secretary," is said to have "reminded Madison of the effect upon foreign ministers [not to say politicians from Boston, New York, and Philadelphia] of 'such a revolting sight' on the streets of the nation's capital—'gangs of Negroes, some in chains, on their way to a Southern market.'"
56. Morison, *Otis*, pp. 174–175.
57. Quoted in William A. Robinson, *Jeffersonian Democracy in New England* (New Haven, Conn.: Yale University Press, 1916), p. 76.
58. Henry Adams, ed., *Documents Relating to New-England Federalism, 1800–1815* (Boston: Little, Brown and Co., 1877), pp. 352–356. For a carefully documented analysis of attitudes in New England during this period, see James M. Banner, Jr., *To the Hartford Convention* (New York: Alfred A. Knopf, 1970), chap. 3.
59. Morison, *Otis*, p. 270.
60. H. Adams, *Documents*, pp. 346, 361, 363.
61. Quoted by Morison, *Otis*, p. 268. "With these words," he adds, "Ames struck the keynote of the policy followed for the next twelve years by his native state."
62. The most thorough effort to sort out the tangled threads of this episode is Thomas P. Abernethy, *The Burr Conspiracy* (New York: Oxford University Press, 1954). He writes, "There was no strong national spirit in the early Transmontane West; it was a period of tumult and separatist intrigues—the Spanish conspiracies, the Blount conspiracy, the Genêt affair, and finally the Burr conspiracy" (p. vii).
63. Morison, *Otis*, pp. 313, 105.
64. The most interesting aspects of this election are covered in Morison, *Otis*, pp. 257–260 (the "first national nominating convention"); and Harry Ammon, "James Monroe and the Election of 1808 in Virginia," *William and Mary Quarterly Review*, 3rd ser., 20 (1963), 33–56.
65. Quoted by Banner, *op. cit.*, pp. 300–301, from Benjamin W. Labaree, *Patriots and Partisans* (Cambridge: Harvard University Press, 1962), pp. 166–168, and the Boston *Columbian Sentinel*, September 10, 1808 (original emphasis). Banner notes that the doctrine of interposition was widely held in New England between 1808 and 1815, and is best understood as a moderate alternative to disunion for people who saw themselves greatly abused by the federal gov-

ernment. It was, he says, a threat, rather than a carefully detailed plan of resistance (*op. cit.*, p. 119).

66. Quoted in Richard B. Morris, ed., *Encyclopedia of American History*, rev. ed. (New York: Harper and Brothers, 1961), p. 137.

67. Quoted by Morison, *Otis*, p. 310.

68. Irving Brant, *James Madison* (Indianapolis, Ind.: Bobbs-Merrill Co., 1941–1961), vol. 5, pp. 402–403.

69. The historians' debate on the causes of the War of 1812 is summarized by Harry L. Coles, *The War of 1812* (Chicago: University of Chicago Press, 1965), pp. 27–37. Excerpts from the leading articles on the subject are available in Bradford Perkins, ed., *The Causes of the War of 1812* (New York: Holt, Rinehart and Winston, 1962). Additional source materials are in G. R. Taylor, ed., *The War of 1812* (Lexington, Mass.: D. C. Heath, 1963).

70. Charles O. Paullin, *Atlas of the Historical Geography of the United States* (Washington: Carnegie Institution, 1932), p. 94. He reports, quoting the newspaper *Aurora* (November 20, 1812), that the Federalist margin in counties they carried was 2,819, and the Republican margin in their counties 23,641, leaving a statewide margin of 20,822 for the Republicans. Unfortunately, the total statewide vote is not given.

71. The Boston Federalists, who had close, personal friends in Charleston, always specified Virginia, with its transmontane political allies, as the culprit. Some hoped to realize a reunion of the "good old thirteen states," separated from the post-1790 additions—confident that Virginia could be controlled under these circumstances, as it had been in the 1790's. See Morison, *Otis*, pp. 259, 264; Banner, *op. cit.*, pp. 166–169. These feelings were a reflection of Western impulses to pull free of the union—both of them, however, flying in the face of powerful currents in the direction of democratic nationalism.

72. Banner, *op. cit.*, p. 307. The clergymen were Elijah Parish, of Byfield, and John S. J. Gardiner, of Boston.

73. The only protest, ironically enough, came from a few New Englanders, who feared that the removal of "protection" would expose their infant domestic industries to overwhelming competition (Morris, *op. cit.*, p. 148a).

74. Robert A. East, "Economic Development and New England Federalism," *New England Quarterly*, 10 (1937), 430–446.

75. The precise purpose of the drive on New Orleans, inaugurated after the change of the British bargaining position at Ghent that

led to peace, is still unclear. A recent analyst suggests that had New Orleans been captured, the British might have dragged their feet about abandoning it, waiting to see if anything was to be gained from encouraging the ambivalence of the Creoles and other non-Anglo-Saxons toward the union (Coles, *op. cit.*, pp. 233–236).

76. Brant, *op. cit.*, vol. 6, pp. 258–259; Bray Hammond, *Banks and Politics in America* (Princeton, N.J.: Princeton University Press, 1957), pp. 227–230; Nettels, *op. cit.*, pp. 331–335; Morison, *Otis*, pp. 341–342.

77. A close-up account of the atmosphere in Newburyport, Massachusetts, is in Labaree, *op. cit.*, chap. 8, "The Brink of Secession." Newburyport, "along with other New England towns, was ready for revolution by the end of 1814 . . ." (p. 196). For evidence that even in this crisis, much of New England was loyal to Madison, see Robinson, *op. cit.*, pp. 157–158 *et passim*.

78. Banner, *op. cit.*, pp. 314–324. The recoil of the Federalist merchants, when the people were finally aroused, is reminiscent of the reaction of the merchants on the eve of the Revolutionary War, as chronicled by Arthur M. Schlesinger, Sr., in *The Colonial Merchants and the American Revolution, 1763–1776* (New York: Columbia University Press, 1917).

79. Quotations from Banner, *op. cit.*, pp. 337–343. The report itself is in Theodore Dwight, *History of the Hartford Convention* (New York: N. and J. White, 1833), pp. 352–379.

80. A helpful chronology of the fast-moving events of early 1815, including Otis's mission, Jackson's victory, and the arrival of the peace treaty at New York, and finally at Washington, can be found in Morison, *Otis*, p. 542.

81. Quoted by Coles, *op. cit.*, p. 152.

82. Samuel Rezneck, "Industrial Consciousness in America, 1760–1830," *Journal of Economic and Business History*, 4 (August 1932), pp. 784–811.

83. For an analysis of tariff legislation during the Fourteenth Congress, see Norris W. Preyer, "Southern Support of the Tariff of 1816—a Reappraisal," *Journal of Southern History*, 25 (1959), 306–322; and William W. Freehling, *Prelude to Civil War: The Nullification Controversy in South Carolina, 1816–1836* (New York: Harper & Row, 1966). Freehling's book, especially chaps. 2 and 4, provides a brilliant analysis of the tariff issue in the politics of South Carolina during this period.

84. Preyer (*op. cit.*, pp. 306–309) warns against drawing the contrast

between 1816 and 1818 too sharply. The South Carolinians were not reckless in 1816. They voted against duties on imported woolen and cotton goods, and made it plain that they favored the protection of industry, not in their home state, where they opposed the development of manufacturing, but in the North, where it might be safely and expediently developed to serve the national interest. That the tariff of 1816 was a revenue-raiser as well as a protector can be seen from the receipts it produced. For 1816 they were over $36 million, more than twice as high as they had ever been before in the nation's history (U.S. Bureau of the Census, *op. cit.*, p. 712).

85. The best general account of the era is George Dangerfield's brilliantly written book *The Era of Good Feelings* (New York: Harcourt, Brace and Co., 1952). See also chaps. 3 and 4 of the same author's *The Awakening of American Nationalism, 1815–1828* (New York: Harper & Row, Harper Torchbooks, 1965).

86. Of course, there were Northerners who took the opposite view: that people interested in the development of manufacturing were pushing the nation in the wrong direction, and that the best hope of holding the proper course lay in an alliance of Southern planters, Western farmers, and Eastern mechanics and artisans. Martin Van Buren was the chief organizer of those in the North who saw the issue this way. See R. H. Brown's article "The Missouri Crisis, Slavery, and the Politics of Jacksonianism," *The South Atlantic Quarterly,* 65 (1966), 55–72.

87. Lewis C. Gray, *History of Agriculture in the Southern United States to 1860* (Washington: Carnegie Institution, 1933), vol. 1, p. 613 *et passim.* There are several good indications in *The Federalist* of the direction "Publius" expected development to take. Hamilton claimed that it was our destiny to be a commercial people (number 11) and said this meant we would need a strong navy (numbers 11, 24, 34). He added that future trends would favor industry over agriculture (number 41). Madison agreed that America would witness a trend toward industry (number 56), and he looked forward, too, to an increase in interstate commerce (number 53). These forecasts were fundamental to the argument of *The Federalist* for a vigorous national government, capable of raising revenues, protecting enterprises, and regulating a national market. I find no division between Hamiltonian and Madisonian elements in the mind of "Publius" on these points.

88. S. Sydney Bradford, "The Negro Ironworker in Ante Bellum Virginia," *Journal of Southern History,* 25 (1959), 194–206, is a recent summary of the reasons why "slave labor brought neither satisfac-

tion nor progress to Virginia's ironworkers and their industry."
Richard Wade's analysis of the "Vesey plot" in Charleston, 1822,
sets forth the background of fear that inhibited Southern willingness to experiment with the use of slave labor in urban, industrial
settings ("The Vesey Plot: A Reconsideration,' *Journal of Southern History,* 30 [1964], 143–161).

89. In arguing for his "Bonus Bill," which would have created a permanent fund for internal improvements from the bonuses and
dividends earned by the government's stock in the Bank of the
United States, John Calhoun dismissed Constitutional objections
almost out of hand, noting that he was no "refiner." He cited the
Louisiana Purchase as a precedent (*Annals,* 14th Cong., 2nd Sess.,
2/4/1817, pp. 855–857). Indeed, his bold performance calls to
mind John Randolph's strong defense of Jefferson's decision to lay
aside Constitutional scruples in buying Louisiana from Napoleon.
In 1817, as in 1803, it was a Federalist (Timothy Pickering, of
Massachusetts, in both cases) who tried to insist that the government abide by a strict construction of the list of enumerated powers. As the last act of his Presidency, old James Madison, whose
memory of the uses to which a flexible writ of authority might be
put was longer and more varied than Calhoun's, vetoed the young
Congressman's pet project, stating that to base such an act on the
"general welfare" clause "would be contrary to the established and
consistent rules of interpretation, as rendering the special and careful enumeration of powers which follow the clause nugatory and
improper."

90. The fugitive-slave question, especially during these early years,
needs a good modern treatment. The only comprehensive one currently available is Marion G. McDougall, *Fugitive Slaves (1619–
1865)* (Boston: Ginn and Co., 1891). For a legal history of the
problem in the state of Ohio, see William Cox Cochran, *The Western Reserve and the Fugitive Slave Law* (Cleveland: Western Reserve Historical Society, 1920), pp. 9–77. For a discerning analysis
of the impact of British law on the handling of the fugitive question in America, see Jerome Nadelhaft, "The Somersett Case and
Slavery: Myth, Reality and Repercussions," *Journal of Negro History,* 51 (1966), 193–208.

91. *Annals,* 2nd Cong., 2nd Sess., 2/12/1793, pp. 1414, 1415.

92. Warren Choate Shaw, *The Fugitive Slave Issue in Massachusetts
Politics, 1780–1837* (abstract of doctoral dissertation) (Urbana:
University of Illinois, 1938), p. 7.

93. *Annals,* 4th Cong., 2nd Sess., 12/29/1796, p. 1730.

94. H. Adams, *Gallatin*, pp. 671–674.

95. *Annals*, 4th Cong., 2nd Sess., 12/29/1796, pp. 1730–1737.

96. *Annals*, 4th Cong., 2nd Sess., 12/29/1796, pp. 1740–1741.

97. For a description of North Carolina's laws on this subject, see Henry W. Farnam, *Chapters in the History of Social Legislation in the United States to 1860* (Washington: Carnegie Institution, 1938), pp. 198–199, 379–381.

98. *Annals*, 4th Cong., 2nd Sess., 1/30/1797, pp. 2015–2018.

99. *Annals*, 4th Cong., 2nd Sess., 1/30/1797, pp. 2018–2019, 2023.

100. *Annals*, 4th Cong., 2nd Sess., 1/30/1797, pp. 2021–2022.

101. *Annals*, 4th Cong., 2nd Sess., 1/30/1797, p. 2020.

102. *Annals*, 4th Cong., 2nd Sess., 1/30/1797, p. 2015.

103. Farnam, *op. cit.*, p. 199.

104. *Annals*, 7th Cong., 1st Sess., 12/18/1801, 1/15/1802, pp. 336, 423.

105. *Annals*, 7th Cong., 1st Sess., 1/18/1802, p. 425.

106. *Annals*, 15th Cong., 1st Sess., 1/27–30/1818, pp. 819, 827–831, 837–840; McDougall, *op. cit.*, pp. 21–22.

107. *Annals*, 15th Cong., 1st Sess., 3/12–13/1818, 4/10/1818, pp. 262, 1339, 1716.

CHAPTER 8

1. W. E. B. DuBois, *The Suppression of the African Slave-Trade to the United States of America, 1638–1870* (New York: Longmans, Green and Co., 1904), pp. 222–223.

2. *Ibid.*, p. 34. DuBois quotes the judgment of Samuel Hopkins to the same effect. See Elizabeth Donnan, ed., *Documents Illustrative of the History of the Slave Trade to America* (Washington: Carnegie Institution, 1930–1935), vol. 3, pp. 277–404, for abundant evidence of the involvement of Rhode Islanders in the slave trade throughout the early national period.

3. Cf. an enactment of 1774 in Connecticut, which called "the increase of slaves . . . injurious to the poor and inconvenient" (DuBois, *op. cit.*, p. 37). Another indication of the spirit in which these acts were adopted comes from the fact that settlers were often excepted from the prohibition against importing new slaves. The enactments of Virginia and Maryland were specific on this point, as was Rhode Island's. The provisions adopted by Connecticut and Delaware were not to apply to those who brought slaves with them, without intending to sell them (*ibid.*, pp. 222–225).

4. *Ibid.*, pp. 227–228.

5. Ulrich B. Phillips, *American Negro Slavery* (New York: D. Appleton and Co., 1918), p. 205: "Tobacco was losing in the east what it gained in the west. . . ." See also Lewis C Gray, *History of Agriculture in the Southern United States to 1860* (Washington: Carnegie Institution, 1933), vol. 2, pp. 605 ff., 752–759.

6. Farrand, *Records,* vol. 2, p. 371.

7. Jonathan Elliot, ed., *The Debates in the Several State Conventions, on the Adoption of the Federal Constitution* (Philadelphia: J. B. Lippincott Co., 1876), vol. 4, p. 272.

8. Twenty-five thousand, according to some sources; for example, DuBois, *op. cit.,* p. 11.

9. *Loc. cit.*

10. Gray, *op. cit.,* vol. 2, p. 610.

11. Farrand, *Records,* vol. 2, p. 373.

12. Phillips, *op. cit.,* p. 135. Excerpts from the debates of 1785 and 1787 are printed in Donnan, *op. cit.,* vol. 4, pp. 430–489, 492–494.

13. Phillips, *op. cit.,* pp. 132–133; DuBois, *op. cit ,* p. 239.

14. *Annals,* 1st Cong., 1st Sess., 5/13/1789, p. 336. The ten-dollar tax would have been at the rate of about 3 per cent, which would have been quite low by the standards of the tariff of 1789. Rates in that law averaged 8½ per cent for the listed articles and 5 per cent for all other goods.

15. *Annals,* 1st Cong., 1st Sess., 5/13/1789, pp. 336, 337.

16. *Annals,* 1st Cong., 1st Sess., 5/13/1789, pp. 336–337.

17. For a perceptive account of these common interests, see Ulrich B. Phillips, "The South Carolina Federalists," *American Historical Review,* 14 (1909), 530; also, Manning J. Dauer, *The Adams Federalists* (Baltimore: Johns Hopkins Press, 1953), pp. 10–15.

18. See a letter from Tench Coxe to Madison, dated March 31, 1790, in Farrand, *Records,* vol. 3, p. 361.

19. *Annals,* 1st Cong., 2nd Sess., 2/11/1790, pp. 1182–1183.

20. *Loc. cit.*

21. *Annals,* 1st Cong., 2nd Sess., 2/12/1790, pp. 1197–1198.

22. *Annals,* 1st Cong., 2nd Sess., 2/12/1790, pp. 1198–1199.

23. Phillips, *American Negro Slavery,* pp. 370–371.

24. *Annals,* 1st. Cong., 2nd Sess., 2/12/1790, p. 1204.

25. *Annals,* 1st. Cong., 2nd Sess., 2/12/1790, p. 1205. The *Annals* gives the total as 43 to 14, but only eleven names are listed as voting negatively in the roll call.

26. Three of its members were New Englanders, three were from mid-Atlantic states, and one was from Virginia. DuBois (*op. cit.,* p. 78)

observed that the Deep South's boycott made this committee's report "a sort of official manifesto on the aims of Northern antislavery politics." Thomas Edward Drake states that the report was based on "a memorandum prepared for the committee by Warner Mifflin," a Quaker from Delaware who, with the rest of his wealthy family, earned the contempt of slave owners in the Deep South by emancipating a large number of slaves at the time of the Revolutionary War (*Quakers and Slavery in America* [New Haven, Conn.: Yale University Press, 1950], p. 105).

27. Dauer (*op. cit.*, pp. 274, 292, 332) indicates that Parker represented Norfolk, Princess Anne, and Isle of Wight counties. Evarts B. Greene and Virginia D. Harrington record that in 1790 these counties contained 5,345, 3,202, and 3,867 slaves, respectively (*American Population Before the Federal Census of 1790* [New York: Columbia University Press, 1932], pp. 154–155).

28. *Annals*, 1st Cong., 2nd Sess., 2/12/1790, pp. 1200–1201.

29. *Annals*, 1st. Cong., 2nd Sess., 2/12/1790, p. 1466. The bracketed words in the first paragraph quoted were interchanged in the original—owing to a "clerical error," according to DuBois (*op. cit.*, p. 79 n.).

30. Cf. Edmund Randolph's speech at the Virginia ratifying convention, in Farrand, *Records*, vol. 3, p. 334.

31. Smith noted that even the Quakers, for all their liberality, were generally opposed to miscegenation. *Annals*, 1st Cong., 2nd Sess., 3/17/1790, p. 1455. Cf. Drake, *op. cit.*, p. 121, where Smith's argument is confirmed.

32. Although abolitionist petitions were received from Maryland and Virginia during the Second Congress, it remained true, at least until 1808, that no petition against slavery was received by Congress from sources south of Virginia. See DuBois, *op. cit.*, p. 80; Drake, *op. cit.*, p. 107; *Annals*, 2nd Cong., 1st Sess., 12/8/1791, pp. 241 ff.

33. *Annals*, 1st Cong., 2nd Sess., 3/17/1790, pp. 1453–1464. There is an excellent biography of Smith, by George C. Rogers, Jr., *Evolution of a Federalist: William Loughton Smith of Charleston (1758–1812)* (Columbia: University of South Carolina Press, 1952).

34. *Annals*, 1st Cong., 2nd Sess., 3/22/1790, pp. 1466–1471 On Boudinot's subsequent career as an abolitionist, see Glover Moore, *The Missouri Controversy, 1819–1821* (Lexington: University of Kentucky Press, 1953), pp. 68–73.

35. For the "Report of the Select Committee" and the "Report of the

Committee of the Whole," in parallel columns, see DuBois, *op. cit.,* pp. 78–80.

36. Washington's letters dated March 28 and June 15, 1790 are in John C. Fitzpatrick, ed., *The Writings of George Washington* (Washington: Government Printing Office, 1931–1944), vol. 31, pp. 30, 52. Washington did not mention Franklin's sponsorship of the parallel memorial.

37. *Ibid.,* p. 52.

38. Irving Brant, *James Madison* (Indianapolis, Ind.: Bobbs-Merrill Co., 1941–1961), vol. 3, pp. 309, 493 n. 6.

39. Drake, *op. cit.,* p. 107.

40. *Annals,* 3rd Cong., 1st Sess., 3/22/1794, pp. 1425–1426.

41. *Annals,* 5th Cong., 2nd Sess., 3/23/1798, pp. 1306–1313. See chap. 11 for a full discussion of this episode.

42. John Rutledge, Jr., in *Annals,* 6th Cong., 1st Sess., 4/28/1800, p. 689.

43. *Annals,* 6th Cong., 1st. Sess., 1/2/1800, p. 229.

44. *Annals,* 6th Cong., 1st. Sess., 1/2/1800, p. 230. Rutledge's intimate friend, Harrison Gray Otis, added that, since the petition had been subscribed to by illiterates "incapable of digesting the principles of it," it must have been ghostwritten. He deplored the imprudence of those who had induced the blacks to sign it. "It would teach them the art of assembling together, debating, and the like, and would soon, if encouraged, extend from one end of the union to the other"—perhaps even to Boston itself. Thacher retorted that if anything was "new-fangled," it was to deny rights to men because they were illiterate (*ibid.,* pp. 231–233). Thacher was called to order for his remark.

45. *Annals,* 6th Cong., 1st Sess., 1/2/1800, pp. 237–238.

46. *Annals,* 6th Cong., 1st Sess., 1/3/1800, pp. 240–242.

47. *Annals,* 6th Cong., 1st Sess., 1/2/1800, pp. 232–233.

48. *Annals,* 6th Cong., 1st Sess., 1/3/1800, pp. 243, 244–245.

49. *Annals,* 6th Cong., 1st. Sess., 4/14/1800, p. 159; 4/18/1800, p. 164; 5/5/1800, p. 173; 5/7/1800, p. 175.

50. On Brown's career as a slave trader, see Drake, *op. cit.,* p. 111 n.; and Elizabeth Donnan, *op. cit.,* vol. 3, pp. 341, 348 n., 383 n. See also the biography by Mack Thompson, *Moses Brown, Reluctant Reformer* (Chapel Hill: University of North Carolina Press, 1962).

51. *Annals,* 6th Cong., 1st Sess., 4/26/1800, pp. 686–687.

52. Joseph Charles, *The Origins of the American Party System* (New

York: Harper and Brothers, Harper Torchbooks, 1961), p. 94; Dauer, *op. cit.*, p. 297.

53. *Annals,* 7th Cong., 2nd Sess., 1/17/1803, pp. 385–386.

54. For a discussion of the "absolute" power of Congress "to exclude aliens from the United States and to prescribe the terms and conditions on which they come in," see Edward S. Corwin, ed., *The Constitution of the United States of America: Analysis and Interpretation* (Washington: Government Printing Office, 1952, 1964), pp. 303–306.

55. *Annals,* 7th Cong., 2nd Sess., 1/26/1803, p. 424.

56. *Annals,* 7th Cong., 2nd Sess., 2/7/1803, p. 469.

57. *Annals,* 7th Cong., 2nd Sess., 2/28/1803, pp. 1564–1565, for the text of the act.

58. Rhode Island in 1787; Massachusetts, Pennsylvania, and Connecticut in 1788; and Delaware in 1789 (DuBois, *op. cit.,* pp. 229, 230–234). Significantly, New York and New Hampshire abstained.

59. See a speech by Representative Samuel Mitchill, an opponent of slavery, from New York City, in *Annals,* 8th Cong., 1st Sess., 2/14/1804, pp. 998–1000; and a comment by Senator James Jackson, a rice planter and slave owner from Georgia, reported in William Plumer, *Memorandum of Proceedings in the United States Senate, 1803–1807,* ed. Everett Somerville Brown (New York: Macmillan Co., 1923), p. 120.

60. Proof of the ineffectiveness of these laws comes from the returns of the Customs House in Charleston for the years (1803–1807) when the slave trade into that port was legal. Of the 202 slave ships that stopped to make deliveries during the four years, 88 were consigned to natives of Rhode Island. Ships owned by Northern capital brought almost 9,000 slaves from Africa to Charleston during this period. Elizabeth Donnan (*op. cit.,* vol. 4, p. 505 n.) demonstrates the incompleteness of the Customs House report on which these figures are based, and asserts that it contains "many mistakes." The errors, however, are on the side of underinclusiveness. Donnan's own reports of "Negroes Imported into South Carolina," compiled from the Charleston *Courier,* support the conclusion that owners and captains of vessels from Rhode Island were heavily engaged in the slave trade that entered Charleston between 1804 and 1807 (*ibid.,* pp. 504, 508, 513 and 521).

61. Phillips, *American Negro Slavery,* p. 136; Donnan, *op. cit.,* vol. 4, pp. 500–501.

62. Phillips, *American Negro Slavery,* pp. 136–138.

63. *Annals,* 8th Cong., 1st Sess., 2/14/1804, pp. 891–983.
64. *Annals,* 9th Cong., 2nd Sess., 1/8/1807, p. 273.
65. *Annals,* 8th Cong., 1st Sess., 2/14/1804, pp. 994–997.
66. *Annals,* 8th Cong., 1st. Sess., 2/14/1804, pp. 998–1010.
67. *Annals,* 8th Cong., 1st. Sess., 2/17/1804, p. 1024.
68. *Annals,* 9th Cong., 1st. Sess., 1/20/1806, pp. 348–349.
69. *Annals,* 9th Cong., 1st. Sess., 1/22/1806, pp. 372–373.
70. *Annals,* 9th Cong., 1st. Sess., 2/14/1806, p. 466.
71. Elizabeth Donnan (*op. cit.,* vol. 4, pp. 513–521) estimates that nearly 30,000 slaves were legally brought into Charleston during 1806–1807. Thus, if Congress had adopted the ten-dollar tax in 1806, almost $300,000 in additional revenue would have been forthcoming.
72. Printed in *Annals,* 9th Cong., 2nd Sess., 12/2/1806, p. 14.
73. *Annals,* 9th Cong., 2nd Sess., 12/17/1806, pp. 173–174.
74. *Annals,* 9th Cong., 2nd Sess., 12/17/1806, pp. 173–174.
75. *Annals,* 9th Cong., 2nd Sess., 12/17/1806, pp. 172–173, 174, 176–177.
76. *Annals,* 9th Cong., 2nd Sess., 12/23/1806, pp. 200–202.
77. *Annals,* 9th Cong., 2nd Sess., 12/29/1806, pp. 220–221.
78. *Annals,* 9th Cong., 2nd Sess., 12/29/1806, pp. 221–224.
79. Louis Hartz, comparing the problem of emancipation in egalitarian and hierarchical societies, suggests that the former face a more difficult prospect, inasmuch as there are no intermediary statuses between enslavement and freedom. Thus, once abolition is declared, the egalitarian society is under pressure to accept the freedman as fully equal to all other citizens—equal in rights and in responsibilities for self-support (*The Founding of New Societies* [New York: Harcourt, Brace & World, 1964], p. 17). The distinction here can easily be exaggerated, but it does help to explain the difficulty of the Ninth Congress in conceiving a place in an individualistic, egalitarian society for free men who were not really able to shift for themselves.
80. *Annals,* 9th Cong., 2nd Sess., 12/29/1806, p. 226.
81. *Annals,* 9th Cong., 2nd Sess., 12/29/1806, p. 228.
82. *Annals,* 9th Cong., 2nd Sess., 12/29/1806, p. 174; see also *ibid.,* 12/17/1806, p. 169.
83. *Annals,* 9th Cong., 2nd Sess., 12/31/1806, p. 238.
84. *Annals,* 9th Cong., 2nd Sess., 12/31/1806, p. 243.
85. *Annals,* 9th Cong., 2nd Sess., 1/5/1807, p. 254.
86. *Annals,* 9th Cong., 2nd Sess., 1/7/1807, pp. 264–265.

87. Plumer, *op. cit.*, p. 574.
88. *Annals,* 9th Cong., 2nd Sess., 2/9/1807, pp. 477–478.
89. *Annals,* 9th Cong., 2nd Sess., 2/12/1807, p. 483.
90. *Annals,* 9th Cong., 2nd Sess., 2/12/1807, p. 484.
91. See section 9 of the Act, in *Annals,* 9th Cong., 2nd Sess., 3/2/1807, pp. 1269–1270.
92. *Annals,* 9th Cong., 2nd Sess., 2/18/1807, p. 528.
93. *Annals,* 9th Cong., 2nd Sess., 2/26/1807, p. 626.
94. *Annals,* 9th Cong., 2nd Sess., 2/26/1807, p. 626.
95. *Annals,* 9th Cong., 2nd Sess., 2/27/1807, pp. 636–637.
96. Phillips, *American Negro Slavery,* p. 147.
97. Printed in *Annals,* 11th Cong., 3rd Sess., 12/5/1810, p. 14.
98. For a summary of the evidence, see DuBois, *op. cit.,* pp. 110–117.
99. House Document 42 (16th Cong., 1st Sess., 1/20/1820) contains a memorandum from Treasury Secretary William Crawford, who was a Georgian, stating that people in "the eastern section of the Southern states" feared for their rights, their peace and tranquillity, because of the introduction of West Indian insurrectionists among their blacks.
100. Cf. the motion of Congressman James Sloan, of New Jersey (*Annals,* 9th Cong., 2nd Sess., 12/17/1806, p. 174), and the message of Governor James Richardson (Donnan, *op. cit.,* vol. 4, pp. 500–501). See also Robert Goodloe Harper's amendment to the ordinance for the Mississippi Territory (*Annals,* 5th Cong., 2nd Sess., 3/26/1798, p. 1313).
101. For numerous examples of ways in which the act of 1807 was evaded, see the report of Secretary Crawford to the House of Representatives, dated January 13, 1820, and including statements by the customs collectors of the ports of Savannah, New Orleans, and Mobile, among others; and a statement by Crawford in answer to a direct question from Congress, that "no particular instructions" had ever been given by the Secretary of the Treasury for enforcing any of the acts against the slave trade. (*Annals,* 16th Cong., 1st Sess., pp. 904–910.) For the Alabama case, see House Document 107, 15th Cong., 2nd Sess., 1/13/1820.
102. See Madison's last annual message, December 3, 1816 (*Annals,* 14th Cong., 2nd Sess., pp. 11–17), and Monroe's message of November 16, 1818 (*Annals,* 15th Cong., 2nd Sess., pp. 11–18).
103. House Documents 84 and 107, 15th Cong., 2nd Sess.: the former, a collection of documents from the Navy Department, including correspondence between the department and naval commanders in the Gulf of Mexico; the latter, a collection of reports from cus-

toms collectors to the Secretary of the Treasury including one in which Collector Addin Lewis, of Mobile, begs for a revenue cutter to send against the pirates. Such a cutter, he said, "would render more important services to the country, than any cutter employed on the Atlantic coast." See also the report of Secretary Crawford to the 16th Congress (*Annals*, 16th Cong., 1st Sess., 1/13/1820, pp. 904–910), in which Collector McIntosh, of Brunswick, Georgia, writes that "African and West Indian negroes are almost daily introduced into Georgia for sale or settlement, or passing through it to the territories of the United States for similar purposes." And see House Document 36 (16th Cong., 1st Sess.), for further communications illustrating the flow of slaves through "numerous inlets to the westward [of New Orleans], where the people are but too much disposed to render them every possible assistance."

104. H. R. Report 59 (16th Cong., 2nd Sess.). This report, with its appendixes, which include an extended exchange between Lord Castlereagh and the African Society of London on the state of the trade as of 1820, is by far the best public treatment of the subject during the early national period. It shows a quality and range of research all too often unavailable to American Congressmen who were responsible for governing a country in which slavery was so important a factor. For a study of the role of the British Navy in suppressing the African slave trade, see Christopher Lloyd, *The Navy and the Slave Trade* (London: Frank Cass and Co., 1968), especially chap. 4.

105. H. R. Report 59 (16th Cong., 2nd Sess.), pp. 26–30 *et passim;* see also Madison's message of December 18.6 (*Annals*, 14th Cong., 2nd Sess., pp. 14–15).

106. See, for example, H. R. Report 97 (16th Cong., 1st Sess.); also, H. R. Report 59 (16th Cong., 2nd Sess.), pp. 6–7, *et passim*. For a powerful, modern description of the slave trade in operation see James Pope-Hennessy, *Sins of the Fathers* (New York: Alfred A. Knopf, 1968).

107. *Annals,* 15th Cong., 1st. Sess., 4/20/1818, p. 2571.

108. House Document 107 (15th Cong., 2nd Sess.), p. 5.

109. See the Memorial of the American Colonization Society, signed by Justice Washington (*Annals,* 14th Cong., 2nd Sess., 1/14/1817, pp. 481–483), an eloquent statement of the purposes and program of the society.

110. For the report of the Select Committee on the African Slave Trade, chaired by Timothy Pickering, which endorsed the colonization

scheme, see *Annals,* 14th Cong., 2nd Sess., 2/11/1817, pp. 939–941. For a general account, see Philip J. Staudenraus, *The African Colonization Movement 1816–1865* (New York: Columbia University Press, 1961).

111. DuBois, *op. cit.,* p. 191.
112. See, for example, H. R. Report 97 (16th Cong., 1st Sess.), dated May 8, 1820. The publications of private citizens and abolition societies had sometimes shown a similar sensitivity to the horrors of the trade, but earlier public documents had eschewed such affecting language.
113. Trenchard's report is included in the appendix to H. R. Report 59 (16th Cong., 2nd Sess.).
114. Monroe's arguments are presented in *ibid.,* pp. 5–6.
115. *Ibid.,* pp. 7–8.

CHAPTER 9

1. Doris A. Graber, *Public Opinion, the President and Foreign Policy: Four Case Studies from the Formative Years* (New York: Holt, Rinehart and Winston, 1968), focuses on Adams's policy during the quasi-war with France, Jefferson's acquisition of Louisiana, Madison's conduct of the War of 1812, and Monroe's Doctrine for the Americas. It sets forth the broad background of public opinion and foreign policy against which the specific episodes of this chapter occurred.
2. Samuel Flagg Bemis, *Jay's Treaty: A Study in Commerce and Diplomacy* (New York: Macmillan Co., 1923), pp. 448–449.
3. Frederic Austin Ogg, "Jay's Treaty and the Slavery Interests of the United States," American Historical Association *Annual Report for 1901,* vol. 1, p. 275.
4. Bemis, *op. cit.,* p. 130.
5. *Ibid.,* pp. 129–139.
6. *Ibid.,* pp. 132–133.
7. *Ibid.,* pp. 135, 270.
8. *JCC* 31:781–874.
9. *JCC* 31:781–782, 783–797.
10. *JCC* 31:863.
11. Ogg, *op. cit.,* p. 276.
12. Samuel Flagg Bemis, *John Quincy Adams and the Foundation of American Foreign Policy* (New York: Alfred A. Knopf, 1949), pp. 415–416 *et passim.*

13. *American State Papers: Foreign Relations* (Washington: Gales and Seaton, 1832–1861), vol. 1, pp. 476–518.

14. Ogg, *op. cit.*, pp. 280, 285. The merits of this controversy over the interpretation of Article VII are analyzed in Ogg's article. His conclusion, in brief, is that a strict reading of the treaty's language permits the British interpretation, but that the American position represented the intentions of the treaty's framers and the understanding of its leading American and British interpreters between 1783 and 1794 (*ibid.*, pp. 295–298).

15. Jay to Randolph, February 6, 1795, in *American State Papers. Foreign Relations,* vol. 1, p. 518.

16. Ogg, *op. cit.*, p. 284. For a general account of the objections to the treaty, see Irving Brant, *James Madison* (Indianapolis, Ind.: Bobbs-Merrill Co., 1941–1961), vol. 3, pp. 424–426, 437–438. For evidence that the issue of compensation was a leading source of opposition to the treaty, see W. R. Riddell, "Jay's Treaty and the Negro," *Journal of Negro History,* 13 (1928), 137; and A. G. Lindsay, "Diplomatic Relations Between the United States and Great Britain, 1788–1828, Concerning the Negro," *Journal of Negro History,* 5 (1920), 406. John Harold Wolfe, *Jeffersonian Democracy in South Carolina* (Chapel Hill: University of North Carolina Press, 1940), pp. 82–92, shows that there were extremely deep feelings on the issue in the lower South.

17. Edward Channing, *A History of the United States* (New York: Macmillan Co., 1905–1925), vol. 4, p. 142. See the tables at p. 143 n.

18. Bemis, *Jay's Treaty,* p. 355.

19. On the effects of secrecy, see Brant, *op. cit.*, vol. 3, p. 425.

20. *Annals,* 3rd Cong., 1st Sess., 6/22/1795, p. 860.

21. *Annals,* 3rd Cong., 1st Sess., 6/24/1795, p. 861. The next day, following ratification, Senator Read co-sponsored a motion instructing the President to begin negotiations for compensation, subsequent to the negotiations involving the elimination of Article 12 from the treaty. The motion was defeated, 14 to 15, by a vote that broke mostly along sectional lines. See *ibid.*, p. 865.

22. *Annals,* 3rd Cong., 1st Sess., 6/23/1795, p. 861.

23. Wolfe, *op. cit.*, pp. 85–86, 89, 157, 164; George C. Rogers, Jr., *Evolution of a Federalist: William Loughton Smith of Charleston (1758–1812)* (Columbia: University of South Carolina Press, 1962), pp. 277–281.

24. Joseph Charles, *The Origins of the American Party System* (New

York: Harper and Brothers, Harper Torchbooks, 1961), p. 105.
25. Brant, *op. cit.*, vol. 3, p. 426; Charles, *op. cit.*, pp. 104–108.
26. *American State Papers: Foreign Relations*, vol. 1, p. 509.
27. The debate over Randolph's conduct continues to this day. Cf. Brant, *op. cit.*, vol. 3, pp. 426–428, with Samuel Eliot Morison's account in *The Oxford History of the American People* (New York: Oxford University Press, 1965), pp. 344–345. For a less partisan review of the evidence, see Leonard D. White, *The Federalists: A Study in Administrative History* (New York: Macmillan Co., 1961), pp. 170–171.
28. Henry Cabot Lodge, ed., *The Works of Alexander Hamilton* (New York: G. P. Putnam's Sons, 1904), vol. 5, pp. 214–220.
29. So called by Jefferson himself. See Jefferson's letter to Madison, September 21, 1795, in Paul Leicester Ford, ed., *The Works of Thomas Jefferson* (New York: G. P. Putnam's Sons, 1904), vol. 8, p. 192.
30. Lodge, *op. cit.*, vol. 5, pp. 238–244.
31. *Annals,* 4th Cong., 1st Sess., 4/1/1796, pp. 771–772, 782–783. The resolutions offered by Blount, which were "drawn by Madison," according to Brant (*op. cit.*, vol. 3, p. 436), passed by a vote of 57 to 35.
32. *Annals,* 4th Cong., 1st Sess., 4/15/1796, p. 977. On the centrality of the question of compensation among the treaty's opponents, see the speech by John Williams, of New York, who noted: "The great objection against the Treaty was, that payment for the Negroes which were carried away by the British . . . was not provided for" (*ibid.,* 4/19/1796, p. 1070).
33. *Annals,* 4th Cong., 1st Sess., 4/16/1796, pp. 1005–1015.
34. *Annals,* 4th Cong., 1st Sess., 4/19/1796, pp. 1078–1085.
35. *Annals,* 4th Cong., 1st Sess., 4/30/1796, p. 1291.
36. Quoted in Charles, *op. cit.,* p. 117. (Iredell's emphasis.)
37. *Ibid.,* pp. 113–114.
38. Ludwell Lee Montague, *Haiti and the United States, 1714–1938* (Durham, N.C.: Duke University Press, 1940), p. 6.
39. *Loc. cit.*
40. Rayford Logan, *The Diplomatic Relations of the United States with Haiti, 1776–1891* (Chapel Hill: University of North Carolina Press, 1941), p. 41.
41. A remarkable letter (dated August 28, 1797) from Thomas Jefferson to St. George Tucker, the Virginia emancipationist and a good friend of Jefferson's, shows his reaction to the insurrection in Santo

Domingo. He expressed the hope that Toussaint's rebellion would goad Americans into considering serious programs for eliminating slavery, and perhaps even provide "an answer to the difficult question, whither shall the colored emigrants go?" He thought it imperative that some such program begin immediately; "the revolutionary storm, now sweeping the globe, will [soon] be upon us," and it was vital that "we make timely provisions to give it an easy passage over our land" (Ford, *op. cit.*, vol. 8, p. 335).

42. John Hope Franklin, *From Slavery to Freedom*, 2nd ed. (New York: Alfred A. Knopf, 1964), pp. 148–150; Ulrich B. Phillips, *American Negro Slavery* (New York: D. Appleton and Co., 1918), p. 131; W. E. B. DuBois, *The Suppression of the African Slave-Trade to the United States of America, 1638–1870* (New York: Longmans, Green and Co., 1904), p. 70; and W. D. Jordan, *White Over Black* (Chapel Hill: University of North Carolina Press, 1968), pp. 375–386. For a suggestion of the impact of the revolution in Santo Domingo even on relatively remote areas of the South, see Edward W. Phifer, "Slavery in Microcosm: Burke County, North Carolina," in Allen Weinstein and F. O. Gatell, eds., *American Negro Slavery: A Reader* (New York: Oxford University Press, 1968), p. 85.

43. *American State Papers: Commerce and Navigation* (Washington: Gales and Seaton, 1832–1861), vol. 1, pp. 34, 330 *et passim*. See also Richard B. Morris, ed., *Encyclopedia of American History*, rev. ed. (New York: Harper & Row, 1961), p. 514.

44. For a powerfully written analysis of the revolution in Haiti, see C. L. R. James, *The Black Jacobins: Toussaint L'Ouverture and the San Domingo Revolution*, 2nd ed. (New York: Alfred A. Knopf, Vintage Books, 1963).

45. Logan, *op. cit.*, p. 53. Louis Guillaume Otto, France's minister to Britain, stated that in 1797 American merchants had "more than six hundred ships engaged in the trade with Santo Domingo alone" (*ibid.*, p. 60).

46. *Ibid.*, p. 59.

47. Montague, *op. cit.*, p. 7 n.

48. Logan (*op. cit.*, pp. 65–66) presents a translation of the L'Ouverture-Maitland Convention.

49. Quoted in *ibid.*, p. 70. (King's emphasis.)

50. *Ibid.*, pp. 69–71. For the similar views of President Adams and Secretary of the Treasury Oliver Wolcott, see *ibid.*, pp. 85–86.

51. *Annals*, 5th Cong., 2nd Sess., 1/23/1799, p. 2766.

52. *Annals,* 5th Cong., 2nd Sess., 1/23/1799, pp. 2757–2758, 2760.
53. Quoted in Logan, *op. cit.,* pp. 83–84.
54. *Ibid.,* p. 103.
55. Manning J. Dauer, *The Adams Federalists* (Baltimore: Johns Hopkins Press, 1953), pp. 230–232.
56. Logan, *op. cit.,* pp. 112–113, 119–123; Montague, *op. cit.,* p. 41.
57. Logan, *op. cit.,* p. 121.
58. *Ibid.,* pp. 130–131.
59. Montague, *op. cit.,* p. 42.
60. Logan, *op. cit.,* p. 128.
61. Henry Adams, *History of the United States During the Administrations of Thomas Jefferson and James Madison* (New York: Charles Scribner's Sons, 1889–1901), vol. 1, p. 406.
62. Montague, *op. cit.,* p. 9.
63. For a brilliant account of the demise of Leclerc's expedition, see Adams, *op. cit.,* vol. 2, pp. 18–21.
64. Logan, *op. cit.,* p. 143. For a somewhat different interpretation, see William M. Sloane, "The World Aspects of the Louisiana Purchase," American Historical Association *Annual Report for 1903,* vol. 9, p. 513, where Napoleon's decision to quit in Santo Domingo is traced to Britain's decision to oppose him in Europe.
65. Adams, *op. cit.,* vol. 2, p. 21.
66. Logan, *op. cit.,* p. 154.
67. *Ibid.,* p. 150.
68. Gaillard Hunt, ed., *The Writings of James Madison* (New York: G. P. Putnam's Sons, 1900–1910), vol. 7, pp. 123–140. There were harassments by French privateers operating out of Guadeloupe and Cuba, but the merchants armed their ships and overcame the annoyance (Logan, *op. cit.,* p. 168).
69. For evidence of the intensity of this feeling, see the debates in the House on the bill to suspend commerce with Santo Domingo, in *Annals,* 9th Cong., 1st Sess., 2/24/1806, pp. 497–499, and 2/25/1806, pp. 510–516.
70. William Plumer, *Memorandum of Proceedings in the United States Senate, 1803–1807,* ed. Everett Somerville Brown (New York: Macmillan Co., 1923), p. 545.
71. Adams, *op. cit.,* vol. 3, pp. 22–23.
72. Logan, *op. cit.,* pp. 159–162.
73. Quoted in *ibid.,* p. 173, from the New York *Evening Post,* June 13, 1805.
74. *Ibid.,* p. 172.

75. *Ibid.,* p. 176.
76. *Ibid.,* p. 180.
77. *Annals,* 9th Cong., 1st Sess., 12/18/1805, p. 21. In his *Memoirs,* Adams quotes Logan as saying that "his only object was to have power to tell the French government that we have prohibited the trade. . . ." The context suggests that many Republicans viewed the question of commerce with Santo Domingo in light of their desire to win Napoleon's support for the purchase of the Floridas. See J. Q. Adams, *Memoirs: Comprising Portions of His Diary from 1795 to 1848,* ed. Charles Francis Adams (Philadelphia: J. B. Lippincott Co., 1874–1877), vol. I, pp. 383, 386.
78. *Annals,* 9th Cong., 1st Sess., 12/20/1805, p. 29.
79. *Annals,* 9th Cong., 1st Sess., 12/20/1805, pp. 29–30, 31–36.
80. *Annals,* 9th Cong., 1st Sess., 12/24 and 12/27/1805, pp. 37, 42–43.
81. Plumer, *op. cit.,* p. 545.
82. *Annals,* 9th Cong., 1st Sess., 1/16/1806, p. 52.
83. *Annals,* 9th Cong., 1st Sess., 2/18/1806, p. 114.
84. *Annals,* 9th Cong., 1st Sess., 2/20/1806, pp. 124–126. Another summary of the Federalist case against Jefferson's policy toward Santo Domingo can be found in Plumer, *op. cit.,* pp. 186–189.
85. *Annals,* 9th Cong., 1st Sess., 2/20/1806, p. 138.
86. *Annals,* 9th Cong., 1st Sess., 2/25/1806, pp. 493, 512–516.
87. H. Adams, *op. cit.,* vol. 3, p. 142.
88. Logan, *op. cit.,* p. 179.
89. Charles Tansill, *The United States and Santo Domingo, 1798–1873* (Baltimore: Johns Hopkins Press, 1938), p. 109.
90. West Florida was occupied by American forces in 1810; East Florida, in 1819.
91. Logan, *op. cit.,* p. 151.
92. *Ibid.,* p. 112.
93. *Ibid.,* p. 180.

CHAPTER 10

1. Staughton Lynd finds this answer central to what he calls the "compromise of 1787." He uses it to refer jointly to the Northwest Ordinance and the Great Compromise of the Federal Convention, both of which were concluded in mid-July 1787. I would like to acknowledge my debt to Mr. Lynd for many of the ideas upon which this chapter rests. Several of his essays on the subject of slavery in the early national period are in *Class Conflict, Slavery,*

and the United States Constitution (Indianapolis, Inc.: Bobbs-Merrill Co., 1967), pt. 2.

2. For an account of these attitudes, see George Bancroft's *History of the United States of America* (New York: D. Appleton and Co., 1885), vol. 6, pp. 277–291.

3. *JCC* 26:119. Jefferson was not among those Southerners who preferred the Southern plantation system to the New England village as a model for the West.

4. *JCC* 26:247.

5. *JCC* 28:165.

6. *JCC* 28:239.

7. Burnett, *Letters,* vol. 8, p. 622, n. 5.

8. Francis Newton Thorpe, ed., *The Federal and State Constitutions, Colonial Charters, and Other Organic Laws of the States, Territories, and Colonies Now and Heretofore Forming the United States of America* (Washington: Government Printing Office, 1909), vol. 6, p. 3409 n. See also Lynd, *op. cit.,* pp. 192–193, where the acts of the North Carolina legislature bearing on this point are quoted.

9. *JCC* 32:313–320.

10. *JCC* 32:343.

11. See B. A. Hinsdale's *The Old Northwest* (New York: T. Mac-Coun, 1888), chap. 15, for a further account of ironies and coincidences involved in the enactment of this legislation.

12. *JCC* 26:118–120, *JCC* 28:164, and *JCC* 32:281 ff.

13. This point is made in a letter from Grayson to Monroe, in Burnett, *Letters,* vol. 8, p. 632.

14. Lynd, *op cit.,* pp. 190–191 *et passim.*

15. It should be noted that Southerners were not all agrarians. As became apparent during the debate on representation at the Constitutional Convention, the leading South Carolinians were not agrarians in the usual sense of that term, and were in fact deeply suspicious of the whole western territory. For them, the best reason to support the Northwest Ordinance was the one cited last in this list of "reasons": that it signaled an end to the effort to abolish slavery south of the Ohio River by federal enactment.

16. Arthur Preston Whitaker, *The Mississippi Question, 1795–1803* (New York: D. Appleton-Century Co., 1934), pp. 151–154; Edmund Cody Burnett, *The Continental Congress* (New York: Macmillan Co., 1941), pp. 651–653. The term quoted is from Burnett, *op. cit.,* p. 653.

17. *JCC* 31:604–607.

18. See, for example, the letter of James Monroe to Governor Patrick Henry, in Burnett, *Letters*, vol. 8, p. 424. For a Northern version, see Theodore Sedgwick's letter to Caleb Strong, in *ibid.*, pp. 413–414.

19. *JCC* 32:184–204, 219, 289–290. See also Irving Brant, *James Madison* (Indianapolis, Ind.: Bobbs-Merrill Co. 1941–1961), vol. 2, pp. 403–407.

20. *JCC* 32:277, 292, 299–300; *JCC* 34:319, 530–535.

21. Quoted by Ulrich B. Phillips, *American Negro Slavery* (New York: D. Appleton and Co., 1918), p. 127.

22. Kentucky and Tennessee remained under the control of Virginia and North Carolina until satisfactory terms of cession could be arranged with the federal government. For Kentucky, see Thorpe, *op. cit.*, vol. 3, p. 1263 n.; for Tennessee, *ibid.*, vol. 6, p. 3409 n.

23. *Ibid.*, vol. 6, pp. 3409–3413; vol. 3, p. 1272.

24. *Ibid.*, vol. 3, pp. 1263, 1272.

25. *Annals*, 4th Cong., 1st Sess., 5/16/1796, p 92; 5/28 and 30/1796, pp. 1473–1474.

26. This estimate was given by Congressman Robert Goodloe Harper, of South Carolina, in *Annals*, 5th Cong., 2nd Sess., 3/20/1798, p. 1283.

27. *Annals*, 5th Cong., 2nd Sess., 3/23, 3/20/1798, pp. 1304, 1283.

28. *Annals*, 5th Cong., 2nd Sess., 4/17/1798, p. 3720.

29. *Annals*, 5th Cong., 2nd Sess., 3/23/1798, p. 1311.

30. *Annals*, 5th Cong., 2nd Sess., 3/5/1798, p. 1229.

31. *Annals*, 5th Cong., 2nd Sess., 3/23/1798, pp. 1306, 1308, 1309.

32. *Annals*, 5th Cong., 2nd Sess., 3/23/1798, pp. 1306–1307.

33. *Annals*, 5th Cong., 2nd Sess., 3/23/1798, pp. 1309–1310.

34. *Annals*, 5th Cong., 2nd Sess., 3/23/1798, pp. 1308–1309, 1310.

35. Quoted in Henry Adams, *History of the United States During the Administrations of Thomas Jefferson and James Madison* (New York: Charles Scribner's Sons, 1889–1901), vol. 2, pp. 26–27.

36. Quoted in *ibid.*, pp. 34–35. (Jefferson's emphasis.)

37. Quoted in *ibid.*, pp. 90–91.

38. *Ibid.*, p. 81.

39. J. Q. Adams, *Memoirs: Comprising Portions of His Diary from 1795 to 1848*, ed. Charles Francis Adams, (Philadelphia: J. B. Lippincott Co., 1874–1877), vol. 1, p. 267. Irving Brant (*op. cit.*, vol. 4, pp. 141–145) traces Jefferson's vacillations on the need for a Constitutional amendment.

40. *Annals*, 8th Cong., 1st Sess., 10/17/1803, pp. 11–15.

41. On the ratification, see Samuel Flagg Bemis, *John Quincy Adams and the Foundation of American Foreign Policy* (New York: Alfred A. Knopf, 1949), pp. 119–121. For the second vote, see *Annals,* 8th Cong., 1st Sess., 10/26/1803, p. 26.
42. *Annals,* 8th Cong., 1st Sess., 10/25/1803, pp. 488–489.
43. *Annals,* 8th Cong., 1st Sess., 11/3/1803, p. 60.
44. *Annals,* 8th Cong., 1st Sess., 11/2/1803, pp. 31–35. The last item is from a letter by Josiah Quincy to Oliver Wolcott, quoted in Brant, *op. cit.,* vol. 4, p. 151. On the apprehensions of Federalists regarding the impact of the Louisiana Purchase on the fate of their party, see David Hackett Fischer, *The Revolution of American Conservatism: The Federalist Party in the Era of Jeffersonian Democracy* (New York: Harper & Row, 1965), pp. 175–176.
45. On opposition in New England to the Louisiana Purchase, see James M. Banner, Jr., *To the Hartford Convention* (New York: Alfred A. Knopf, 1970), pp. 111–114; and James Truslow Adams, *New England in the Republic, 1776–1850* (Boston: Little, Brown and Co., 1926), pp. 235–239. The *locus classicus* of Yankee opposition to expansionism under the Jeffersonians is the speech by Josiah Quincy on January 14, 1811, against the admission of Louisiana to the union. At the eleventh hour, he sought to "postpone" the admission of Louisiana until the original states could consider a Constitutional amendment authorizing Congress to admit new states from territory not belonging to the United States at the time of the ratification of the Constitution. "When you throw the weight of Louisiana into the scale," he declared, "you destroy the political equipoise contemplated at the time of forming the contract." When you do that, he argued, you dissolve the moral obligation that binds the states to the union. He concluded that if Congress admitted Louisiana, "as it will be the right of all [states], so it will be the duty of some, definitely to prepare for a separation, amicably, if they can, violently if they must" (*Annals,* 11th Cong., 3rd Sess., pp. 525, 540).
46. Quoted in Henry Adams, *op. cit.,* vol. 2, p. 87.
47. *Annals,* 8th Cong., 1st Sess., 11/3/1803, pp. 54, 65. For the text of the treaty, see Thorpe, *op. cit.,* vol. 3, pp. 1359–1362. For details of the acquisition of Louisiana, see James K. Hosmer, *The History of the Louisiana Purchase* (New York: D. Appleton and Co., 1902).
48. For a discussion of "Constitutional Doctrines with Regard to Slavery in Territories," see the article of that title by Robert R. Russel in

Journal of Southern History, 32 (1966), 466–486. Russel points out that, apart from some letters written by James Madison during the Missouri controversy, it was not until 1840 that any substantial opinion developed that Congress might not have the *Constitutional authority* to "exclude slavery from a territory, or legalize it there, or continue in effect the laws on the subject that had been in effect there prior to the annexation . . . or delegate to the territorial legislature the power to legislate in regard to slavery" (p. 468). The choice between these alternatives was thus a matter of *political power,* rather than Constitutional authority.

49. *Annals,* 8th Cong., 1st Sess., 3/23/1804, pp. 1229–1230.
50. *Annals,* 8th Cong., 1st Sess., 1/26/1804, pp. 240–241. See also William Plumer, *Memorandum of Proceedings in the United States Senate, 1803–1807,* ed. Everett Somerville Brown (New York: Macmillan Co., 1923), pp. 115, 120–121. Plumer's notes, like J. Q. Adams's *Memoirs,* are a useful supplement to the records in the *Annals,* which are extremely spare during these early years.
51. *Annals,* 8th Cong., 1st Sess., 1/30/1804, p. 242; Plumer, *op. cit.,* p. 124.
52. *Annals,* 8th Cong., 1st Sess., 1/30/1804, pp. 241–242.
53. Quoted in Bemis, *op. cit.,* p. 122.
54. Henry W. Farnam, *Chapters in the History of Social Legislation in the United States to 1860* (Washington: Carnegie Institution, 1938), p. 185. For Jefferson's "Description," see *Annals,* 8th Cong., 1st Sess., 11/14/1803, Appendix, pp. 1498–1578.
55. Plumer, *op. cit.,* pp. 119, 127, 131.
56. *Annals,* 8th Cong., 1st Sess., 2/1/1804, p. 244; Plumer, *op. cit.,* p. 130.
57. *Annals,* 8th Cong., 1st Sess., 2/18/1804, p. 256.
58. *Annals,* 8th Cong., 2nd Sess., 1/18/1805, pp. 995–996. On the situation of blacks in Washington, see Constance M. Green, *The Secret City: A History of Race Relations in the Nation's Capital* (Princeton, N.J.: Princeton University Press, 1967), chap. 1.
59. The same dilemma is apparent in Chief Justice Roger B. Taney's "Opinion of the Court" in the Dred Scott case. Taney asks "by what provision of the Constitution the present Federal Government, under its delegated and restricted powers, is authorized to acquire territory outside of the original limits of the United States," and answers that there is "certainly no power given by the Constitution of the Federal Government . . . to enlarge its territorial limits in any way." But he goes on to say, "We do not

mean, however, to question the power of Congress in this respect." Congress has the power to admit new states, and "in the construction of this power by all the departments of the government," it also has the power to "authorize the acquisition of territory," with the intention of admitting new states from the territory, "as soon as its population and situation would entitle it to admission."

In exercising this temporary governance, however, Congress once again returned to the principle of strict construction. "The principle on which our governments [*sic*] rest, and upon which alone they continue to exist, is the union of states, sovereign and independent within their own limits in their internal and domestic concerns, and bound together as one people by a general government, possessing certain enumerated and restricted powers, delegated to it by the people of the several states. . . ." Congress, in exercising its authority over territories, is bound to adhere to this list of enumerated powers, and to respect any limitations on the exercise of power set, for example, in the Bill of Rights. Taney concluded that the Fifth Amendment guarantee against the taking of property "without due process of law" made the Thomas proviso in the Missouri Compromise unconstitutional (*Dred Scott v. John F. A. Sanford*, 19 Howard 393, 426–432, 436–437, 446–452, 454). See note 87 for the development of Taney's argument on this last point.

Taney further took the position that the Constitutional power "to dispose of and make all needful rules and regulations" for the territories had "no bearing on the present controversy," that is, on the constitutionality of the Missouri Compromise. The clause "was a special provision for a known and particular territory," not a writ to acquire and integrate new territory into the United States. If this argument is accepted, then the ordinances for the Orleans, Louisiana, Arkansas, and Missouri territories, as well as all territorial ordinances that followed them, were based on "implication" from the power to admit new states, and it is difficult to see a valid *Constitutional* reason for rejecting the Northwest Ordinance as a precedent—unless one was persuaded by Taney's argument concerning the Fifth Amendment. See note 87. If the Fifth Amendment argument is rejected, then it would seem a question of *political* power whether the Northwest, or Southwest, Ordinance be adopted as the controlling precedent in a given case.

60. Glover Moore suggests that the Missouri debates of 1819–1821 produced a virtual about-face in Southern opinion toward Constitu-

tional construction. "From 1801–1819," he writes, "with their own party in power and Virginians holding the Presidency, Southern Congressmen had shown a more nationalistic view than formerly. The Missouri Controversy sent them scampering back to the old strict constructionist, state rights standard" (*The Missouri Controversy, 1819–1821* [Lexington: University of Kentucky Press, 1953], p. 119).

61. In accounting for the failure of slavery to take root north of the Ohio River, Eugene H. Berwanger emphasizes the racial prejudice of settlers there. Many efforts were undertaken, especially by land speculators, to "disenthrall" (William Henry Harrison's word) Illinois from Article VI of the Northwest Ordinance. They were foiled, not by sympathy for Negroes, but by determination not to saddle the state with a huge black population, and with an institution fit only for agriculture. See chap. 1 of Berwanger's *The Frontier Against Slavery* (Urbana: University of Illinois Press, 1967).

62. On attitudes in New England toward the three-fifths clause, see James M. Banner, Jr., *To the Hartford Convention* (New York: Alfred A. Knopf, 1970), pp. 101–104.

63. Moore, *op. cit.,* pp. 343–346. For an analysis of the Adams-Onís Treaty, see Samuel Flagg Bemis, *op. cit.,* chaps. 15 and 16.

64. Moore, *op. cit.,* chap. 3. Moore's book provides an excellent account of the Missouri controversy. My interpretation differs at points from Moore's, but it is one great virtue of his book that it provides abundant evidence for the reader who wants to form conclusions of his own.

65. The outburst of organized public pressure during the winter of 1819–1820 does not seem to have had much effect on the vote in Congress on the Missouri question. Tallmadge's motion of February 1819, to prohibit the further introduction of slavery into Missouri, carried by nine votes. The agitation in New York and New England intervened. Then, in March 1820, the House adopted a bill for admitting Missouri on condition that it outlaw slavery—again by nine votes. The pressure does seem to have aroused Senator Harrison Gray Otis, of Massachusetts, from the traumatic aftermath of the Hartford Convention. His vote switched sides between the first and second consideration of the measure. But otherwise, the agitation was practically without effect on the voting in Congress. Its primary significance was that it signaled a change in the atmosphere of intersectional relations between the 1780's

and the 1820's, a stiffening in the Northern will to do something about the influence of slavery in the republic. On Otis's remarkable reversal, see Samuel Eliot Morison, *Harrison Gray Otis, 1765–1848* (Boston: Houghton Mifflin Co., 1969), p. 426.

66. *Annals,* 15th Cong., 2nd Sess., 2/13/1819, p. 1166.
67. Tallmadge's Illinois amendment and the debate and the vote that defeated the motion are in *Annals,* 15th Cong., 1st Sess., 11/23/1818, pp. 306–311.
68. J. Q. Adams, *op. cit.,* vol. 4, p. 492.
69. *Annals,* 15th Cong., 2nd Sess., 2/15/1819, pp. 1170–1179; cf. *ibid.,* 11th Cong., 3rd Sess., 1/15/1811, pp. 577–579. The Constitution provided that "new states *may* be admitted by the Congress into this union" (Article IV, Section 3; emphasis added).
70. The Constitutional position of the Southerners was most ably put by Barbour (*Annals,* 15th Cong., 2nd Sess., 2/15/1819, pp. 1186–1191) and John Scott, delegate from Missouri (*ibid.,* 2/16/1819, pp. 1195–1203). The next year (1820), when the issue before Congress would concern the right to prohibit slavery in the unorganized part of the Louisiana Purchase west and north of Missouri, Southerners would argue that Congress had no power to enact municipal legislation even over the territories. See *ibid.,* 16th Cong., 1st Sess., 2/14/1820, pp. 1326–1327 (Charles Pinckney), and 2/17/1820, pp. 1385–1391 (John Tyler).
71. Northerners who alluded to the Declaration were Timothy Fuller, of Massachusetts (*Annals,* 15th Cong., 2nd Sess., 2/15/1819, pp. 1179–1182), and Taylor, of New York (*ibid.,* p. 1173); Southerners critical of the appeal were Ben Hardin, of Kentucky (*ibid.,* 16th Cong., 1st Sess., 2/4/1820, p. 1074), Louis McLane, of Delaware (*ibid.,* 2/7/1820, pp. 1154–1155), and John Tyler, of Virginia (*ibid.,* 2/17/1820, p. 1384); among Southerners who anticipated "popular sovereignty" were Senators James Barbour, of Virginia, and Richard M. Johnson, of Kentucky (*ibid.,* 1/14 and 2/1/1820, pp. 104, 348–349). See also Felix Walker, of North Carolina (*ibid.,* 15th Cong., 2nd Sess., 2/17/1819, pp. 1226–1227). On this question generally, see Philip F. Detweiler, "Congressional Debate on Slavery and the Declaration of Independence, 1819–1821," *American Historical Review,* 63 (1958), 598–616.
72. *Annals,* 15th Cong., 2nd Sess., 2/17 and 2/15/1819, pp. 1233–1234, 1186–1189. See also Robert Reid, of Georgia (*ibid.,* pp. 1032–1033), and Charles Pinckney, of South Carolina (*ibid.,* 16th Cong., 1st Sess., 2/14/1820, pp. 1324–1327).

73. For speeches setting forth the idea of diffusion, see Clay (*Annals,* 15th Cong., 2nd Sess., 2/15/1819, pp. 1174–1175), P. P. Barbour (*ibid.,* pp. 1189–1190), and Tyler (*ibid.,* 16th Cong., 1st Sess., 2/17/1820, p. 1391). For criticism of the idea, see Taylor (*ibid.,* 15th Cong., 2nd Sess., 2/15/1819, p. 1175), Joseph Hemphill, of Pennsylvania (*ibid.,* 16th Cong., 1st Sess., 2/5/1820, pp. 1132–1133), Ezra Gross, of New York (*ibid.,* 2/11/1820, pp. 1245–1246), and William Plumer, Jr., of New Hampshire (*ibid.,* 2/21/1820, p. 1431).

74. *Annals,* 16th Cong., 1st Sess., 2/9 and 2/21/1820, pp. 1203–1205, 1437; *ibid.,* 15th Cong., 2nd Sess., 3/2 and 2/16/1819, pp. 1437, 1205.

75. Tallmadge's address is in *Annals,* 15th Cong., 2nd Sess., 2/16/1819, pp. 1203–1214; Livermore's in *ibid.,* 2/15/1819, pp. 1191–1193. For Jefferson's assessment, see Paul Leicester Ford, ed., *The Works of Thomas Jefferson* (New York: G. P. Putnam's Sons, 1904–1905), vol. 10, p. 165 (letter to Charles Pinckney, September 30, 1820) and p. 191 (letter to Lafayette, December 26, 1820).

76. *Annals,* 15th Cong., 2nd Sess., 2/16/1819, pp. 1214–1215.

77. *Annals,* 15th Cong., 2nd Sess., 2/27/1819, p. 1273. This first Senate debate on the question of statehood for Missouri was not recorded in the *Annals.* It was apparently dominated, however, by Rufus King, a man whose authority in a chamber controlled by Republicans was vitiated by the fact that he had been the last Federalist candidate for President, in 1316. Texts left by King suggest that his arguments were similar to Taylor's in the House. See Moore, *op. cit.,* pp. 55–59.

78. Early in 1820, several Northern town meetings and state legislatures adopted resolutions supporting Tallmadge's amendment. Several are printed in *Annals,* 16th Cong., 1st Sess., pp. 69–72, 234–235 *et passim.* The Kentucky legislature sent a petition to Congress pleading for respect for the right of Missourians to self-government, and demanding admission without restrictions (*ibid.,* pp. 235–236).

79. *Annals,* 15th Cong., 2nd Sess., 2/16/1819, p. 1203; *ibid.,* 16th Cong., 1st Sess., 12/6/1820, pp. 11, 20, 71C.

80. *Annals,* 15th Cong., 2nd Sess., 2/19/1819, pp. 1273–1274. For the debate, see *ibid.,* pp. 1222–1236.

81. *Annals,* 15th Cong., 2nd Sess., 3/1/1819, p. 274.

82. *Annals,* 16th Cong., 1st Sess., 12/30/1819, pp. 831–832. Advocates of Maine's early admission argued that it was unfair to link the two

issues. The merits of Maine's application were questioned by no one, and besides, Massachusetts, in agreeing to separation, had set a deadline (March 4, 1820), after which Maine would revert to its former status if it had not yet been admitted to the union. Arguing in favor of linking the applications, Senator Edward Lloyd, of Maryland, asked rhetorically if Northerners believed it would be Constitutional to compel Maine to permit slavery as a condition of admission. He apparently assumed the answer was no, and that the analogy would undermine the effort to prohibit slavery in Missouri. Northerners could have responded, however, that it would not be unconstitutional to make the stipulation—just unwise, and politically impossible. For the Senate debate, see *ibid.*, 1/13 and 1/14/1820, pp. 85–118. Lloyd's question is on p. 93.

83. *Annals,* 16th Cong., 1st Sess., 1/3 and 2/16/1820, pp. 849, 424. Earlier in this session, a Senate committee had linked the Senate versions of the Maine and Missouri bills, and had been sustained by a vote of 25 to 18. The vote referred to here (23 to 21) was on a motion to join the House's Maine bill to the Missouri bill currently before the Senate. The margin in the Senate narrowed in the interval, but the Southerners and Northwesterners were still in command.

84. *Annals,* 16th Cong., 1st Sess., 2/17/1820, pp. 426–427, 428.

85. King's influence on Vesey is noted by Joseph Lofton, *Insurrection in South Carolina* (Yellow Springs, O.: Antioch Press, 1964), pp. 128–130. For a judicious account of the Vesey conspiracy, see William W. Freehling, *Prelude to Civil War: The Nullification Controversy in South Carolina, 1816–1836* (New York: Harper & Row, 1966), pp. 53–61. For grounds of doubt that any conspiracy existed at all, see Richard Wade, "The Vesey Plot: A Reconsideration," *Journal of Southern History,* 30 (1964), 143–161.

86. According to Senator William Smith, of South Carolina, King added that "all laws or compacts imposing any such condition [i.e., slavery] upon any human being are absolutely void," which would have meant that slavery even in the Old South was without legal sanction. But elsewhere in his speeches, King specifically noted that he had not raised the issue in connection with the applications of Mississippi or Alabama for statehood, because they had been created out of states where slavery was already legal and well entrenched. For an analysis of King's speeches, see Robert Ernst, *Rufus King: American Federalist* (Chapel Hill: University of North Carolina Press, 1968), pp. 370–375.

87. It was a version of this argument that Taney used in 1857 (*Dred Scott v. Sanford,* 19 Howard 426–432, 436, 437) to declare the Missouri Compromise unconstitutional. Taney admitted that Congress had power to "make all needful rules and regulations" for the territories, but he insisted that this power was not plenary, that it was limited by the Constitution. Congress, he said, could not establish a religion in the territories, or forbid trial by jury, and it could not take property without "due process of law." He concluded that the Thomas proviso (and presumably Article VI of the Northwest Ordinance, and perhaps even the laws of the Northern states for gradual abolition) violated the Fifth Amendment of the Constitution, and was therefore unconstitutional.

   As Edward S. Corwin has pointed out, such a doctrine, taken to its logical conclusion, would proscribe virtually all legislation, inasmuch as most laws set conditions on the holding and transfer of property. If the passing of a law regulating the movement of property across state or territorial lines was not "due process," then the governments of the United States (including the state governments, which also were bound by their constitutions to "due process") were impotent to regulate property holders at all. See Corwin, "The Dred Scott Decision in the Light of Contemporary Legal Doctrines," *American Historical Review,* 17 (1911), 52–69.

88. For a summary of "public opinion in the slaveholding states," see Moore, *op. cit.,* chap. 7, especially pp. 231–257, which focuses on opinions in the Old Dominion. For Jefferson's reflections, see Ford, *op. cit.,* vol. 12, pp. 150–206, esp. pp. 158–159 (letter to John Holmes, April 22, 1820).

89. Moore, *op. cit.,* p. 108.

90. *Annals,* 16th Cong., 1st Sess., 2/23 and 3/1, 1820, pp. 1455–1457, 1572, 1573.

91. Congressman Charles Kinsey, of New Jersey, pleading for support for the compromise, noted that the wheels of government had ground to a halt. It was imperative, he said, for Congress to clear the decks and begin to deal with the depression (*Annals,* 16th Cong., 1st Sess., 3/2/1820, p. 1582). For an account of "The Panic of 1819," see George Dangerfield, *The Awakening of American Nationalism, 1815–1828* (New York: Harper & Row, Harper Torchbooks, 1965), chap. 3.

92. *Annals,* 16th Cong., 1st Sess., 2/17 and 2/23, 1820, pp. 1394, 1462. For a report on the conversation with Adams, see the letters

of Congressman William Plumer, Jr., published in *The Missouri Compromises and Presidential Politics, 1820–1825,* ed. E. S. Brown (St. Louis: Missouri Historical Society, 1926), pp. 15–17. Holmes's speech is in *Annals,* 16th Cong., 1st Sess., 1/27/1820, pp. 966–990.

93. *Annals,* 16th Cong., 1st Sess., 3/2/1820, pp. 1576–1583. See also Plumer, *op. cit.,* pp. 14–15, where Plumer bewails the tendency of Northerners to flinch in the war of nerves with the South.

94. *Annals,* 16th Cong., 1st Sess., 3/2/1820, pp. 1586–1587. This is the vote depicted by Charles O. Paullin, in *Atlas of the Historical Geography of the United States* (Washington: Carnegie Institution, 1932), plate 113D. It was the vote that made the Missouri Compromise possible.

95. Moore, *op. cit.,* pp. 100, 101, 104–105.

96. The following year (1821), a second dispute arose over Missouri. Many Northerners took exception to a clause in the Missouri state constitution which forbade free Negroes and mulattoes from entering the state, on the ground that this clause abridged the "privileges and immunities" of citizens of the United States. The controversy produced another genuine crisis for the union. The Senate, reflecting Southern opinion, voted to admit Missouri on the understanding that it was already a state and that the clause excluding free Negroes and mulattoes was no more subject to Congressional review than similar clauses in the constitutions of other slave states. The House, on the other hand, held that the clause violated the federal Constitution, and that until it was eliminated Missouri could not enter the union. This time it was even harder to ignore that race relations and the status of the blacks in America lay at the root of the controversy.

If the issue had been pushed in its literal sense, it would have been even more threatening than the one the year before. The issue at stake was whether or not black Americans had any rights under the Constitution—a question that Northerners, for ideological consistency and because it would make little practical difference for them, wanted to answer in the affirmative, but that Southerners, for reasons of self-preservation, thought they needed to answer in the negative. If Congress had insisted on thrashing the issue out in these terms, an explosion would have been virtually inevitable. Instead, a search began for a formula of evasion. Finally, in February 1821, Henry Clay produced one. Missouri would be admitted to the union on "the fundamental condition" that the clause forbidding the entry of free Negroes and mulattoes "never be construed" to authorize the exclusion of citizens from the enjoyment of privileges and immunities guaranteed by the Constitution of the United States. Clay's resolution stipulated that Missouri's admission would be officially proclaimed by the President, without further Congressional action, as soon as the state's legislature promised never to pass any law discriminating against the citizens of another state.

The resolution passed the House by 87 to 81. On its face, the second Missouri Compromise looked like a victory for equal rights, and a rebuke to slavery. But the vote suggests a different meaning. All eighty-one votes against Clay's resolution came from the "free states." Sixty-nine of the favorable votes came from the South. Most of its Southern opponents were purists, like John Randolph, who objected on principle even to this mild implication that a state's prerogatives were subject to national review. But most of the South was willing to see the compromise for what it was: a symbolic appeasement of sensitive Northern consciences. It was not long before this assessment was borne out. In its very act of compliance, the Missouri legislature pointedly noted that it had no authority to bind the future inhabitants of the state and their elected representatives in the manner demanded by Congress. For an account of this second Missouri Compromise, see Moore, *op. cit.*, pp. 271–273; also F. H. Hodder, "Sidelights on the Missouri Compromise," American Historical Association *Annual Report for 1909,* pp. 158–161.

97. King's recent biographer, Robert Ernst (*op. cit.,* pp. 373–374), says that King was motivated, not by personal ambition, but by a desire to rally Northerners against Southern domination of the federal government.

98. For an analysis of this aspect of the Missouri controversy, focusing on the role of Martin Van Buren, see R. H. Brown, "The Missouri Crisis, Slavery, and the Politics of Jacksonianism," *The South Atlantic Quarterly,* 65 (1966), 55–72.

CHAPTER 11

1. Woodrow Wilson, *Congressional Government* (New York: Meridian Books, 1956), p. 26.

2. Alice D. Adams, *The Neglected Period of Anti-Slavery in America, 1808–1831* (Boston: Ginn and Co., 1908), pp. 57, 62 *et passim.*

3. Albert F. Simpson, "The Political Significance of Slave Representation, 1787–1821," *Journal of Southern History,* 7 (1941), 320. Representative Elias Boudinot, of New Jersey, an alert critic of slavery's impact throughout a career that began during the Revolution and continued through the Missouri controversy, noted that under the permanent apportionment of 1790 the South would have twelve representatives for its slaves (*Annals,* 2nd Cong., 1st Sess., 11/21 and 12/12/1791, pp. 203, 244.

4. Farrand, *Records,* vol. 2, pp. 364, 370.

5. George Rogers Taylor, ed., *Hamilton and the National Debt* (Boston: D. C. Heath and Co., 1950), pp. 3–4, 40–53.

6. Soon in New York there would be great interest in the question of the effect of black votes upon the competition between the parties, and much discussion between Federalist patricians and the rough-hewn sons of Tammany about the reliance of the Federalists on these sometimes pivotal votes. See Dixon Ryan Fox, "The Negro Vote in Old New York," *Political Science Quarterly,* 32 (1917), 252–275.

7. Simpson, *op. cit.,* pp. 334–342.

8. In the case of *Cohens* v. *Virginia* (6 Wheaton 264), Marshall firmly declared that the decisions of state courts were subject to review by the national Supreme Court, and based his opinion on the "supremacy clause" in Article VI of the Constitution. In *Gibbons* v. *Ogden* (9 Wheaton 1), his opinion argued that the commerce clause in the Constitution gave Congress jurisdiction over "every species of commercial intercourse," and that the Congressional power "does not stop at the jurisdiction lines of the several states," but includes all commerce not wholly intrastate in operation. Though the opinion did not, of course, comment on the interstate slave trade, Marshall's doctrines would seem to have implied that Congress had Constitutional power to regulate the interstate traffic in slaves.

9. For an introduction to the struggle over slavery in the Northwest, see Eugene H. Berwanger, *The Frontier Against Slavery* (Urbana: University of Illinois Press, 1967), pp. 7–29.

10. Quoted by James S. Young, *The Washington Community, 1800–1828* (New York: Columbia University Press, 1966), p. 58, from Margaret Bayard Smith, *The First Forty Years of Washington Society,* ed. Gaillard Hunt (New York: Charles Scribner's Sons, 1906), pp. 382–383.

11. For an account of the emergence of the domestic slave trade in the

upper South, see Frederic Bancroft, *Slave-Trading in the Old South* (Baltimore: J. H. Furst Co., 1931), chaps. 1–3.

12. A brilliant analysis of the struggle produced by bondage to slavery in Southern souls is Charles Grier Sellers, Jr., "The Travail of Slavery," in Sellers, ed., *The Southerner as American* (Chapel Hill: University of North Carolina Press, 1960), pp. 40–71.

13. Charles O. Paullin, *Atlas of the Historical Geography of the United States* (Washington: Carnegie Institution, 1932), plates 67B–67E, 76B–76E.

14. Kenneth Stampp, *The Peculiar Institution* (New York: Alfred A. Knopf, Vintage Books, 1956), pp. 295–307.

15. See chapter 10.

16. Douglass C. North, *The Economic Growth of the United States, 1790–1860* (New York: W. W. Norton & Co., 1966), pp. 67–69, 179 *et passim.* "Cotton," writes North (p. 68), "was the most important proximate cause of expansion" in the American economy between 1815 and 1860.

17. *Ibid.,* p. 56.

18. Stuart Bruchey, *The Roots of American Economic Growth, 1607–1861* (New York: Harper & Row, Harper Torchbooks, 1968), p. 14.

19. *Ibid.,* pp. 157–158.

20. There were, of course, other reasons for this assertion, two important ones being respect for the settlement of 1787 regarding the area east of the Mississippi River, and sympathy for white men whose communities were permeated with sullen black slaves.

21. Young, *op. cit.,* chap. 3. "A second characteristic of the Washington community, no less distinctive than the bleakness of its physical setting, was the pronounced antipathy of the governing group toward their community, their disparaging perceptions of their vocation, and their restiveness in their role as power-holders" (*ibid.,* p. 49).

22. Recently, a group of studies on the role of state governments in fostering development has forced a fundamental revision of the theory that Americans of the founding generation were committed to doctrines of *laissez faire.* See Louis Hartz, *Economic Policy and Democratic Thought: Pennsylvania, 1776–1860* (Cambridge: Harvard University Press, 1948); Oscar and Mary F. Handlin, *Commonwealth: A Study of the Role of Government in the American Economy: Massachusetts, 1774–1861* (New York: New York University Press, 1947); and Milton S. Heath, *Constructive Liberalism: The Role of the State in Economic Development in Georgia to*

1860 (Cambridge: Harvard University Press, 1954). Bruchey (*op. cit.*, pp. 114–122) makes the provocative suggestion that Jefferson, whose strong personal preference for agrarian society is well known, held out the promise of federal aid to internal improvement (via Gallatin's report and his own sixth and eighth annual messages), because he wanted most desperately to recapture American hearts for republicanism and believed that, since the people wanted these improvements, he had better yield to them—or, at least, *seem* to. For an analysis of Gallatin's report, see Carter Goodrich, "National Planning of Internal Improvements," *Political Science Quarterly*, 63 (1948), 18–23. In another article ("The Revulsion Against Internal Improvements," *Journal of Economic History*, 10 [November 1950], 145–169), Goodrich says that a widespread reaction against public sponsorship of internal improvements did not come until after the mid-nineteenth century.

23. Query XIII of the *Notes on the State of Virginia*, ed. Thomas Perkins Abernethy (New York: Harper & Row, Harper Torchbooks, 1964).

24. For a forceful, perhaps an extreme statement of this viewpoint, see chap. 1 of Brooks Adams's introduction to Henry Adams, *The Declaration of the Democratic Dogma* (Gloucester, Mass.: Peter Smith, 1949), pp. 13–35, wherein the younger grandson depicts John Quincy Adams as a successor to George Washington in his vision of a tightly integrated, highly developed national economy, and as a man driven to tragic defeat by the crippling divisiveness of slavery.

25. Southerners also noted, what was no doubt true, that most Northerners who were calling for policies inimical to slavery had no greater desire to live on an intimate and equal basis with blacks than most Southerners did. Jefferson's comment is quoted by Bruchey, *op. cit.*, p. 117.

26. U.S. Bureau of the Census, *Historical Statistics of the United States: Colonial Times to 1957* (Washington: Government Printing Office, 1960), p. 719. For four years during the War of 1812, total expenditures rose to over $30 million, but otherwise the total between 1800 and 1820 was between $8 million and $22 million. By 1820, there were a million and a half slaves in the South, and "prime field hands" sold for nearly $1,000 at New Orleans (U. B. Phillips, *Life and Labor in the Old South* [New York: D. Appleton Co., 1935], p. 177). Not all the slaves were "prime field hands," of course, but the estimate here, that the investment in slaves would go to nine figures, seems safe enough. During the Con-

gressional debate over the admission of Missouri, South Carolinian Charles Pinckney estimated the value of slaves in the United
States at $600 million, and noted that the availability of slaves
made land values in the South much higher than they would
otherwise have been (*Annals,* 16th Cong., 1st Sess., 2/14/1820,
p. 1329).

27. Plate 57B in Paullin's *Atlas* gives an idea of the amount of land
available for sale by the federal land offices in 1810. Even at $1.25
per acre (the price under the Land Act of 1820), this land could
have yielded a considerable start toward the purchase price of
emancipations, had Congress been so disposed. For a recent account of the land question, see Malcolm J. Rohrbough, *The Land
Office Business: The Settlement and Administration of American
Public Lands, 1789–1837* (New York: Oxford University Press,
1968).

28. Young, *op. cit.,* pp. 97–100, 152.

29. For an analysis of the Constitutional structure and its tendency
to "deadlock," see James MacGregor Burns, *The Deadlock of
Democracy* (Englewood Cliffs, N.J.: Prentice-Hall, 1963), pp. 17–
23, 204–279.

30. Without ascribing this view to Karl Deutsch, it can be seen that
it might follow from the models and theories set forth in his
books on national development, particularly *Nationalism and
Social Communication,* 2nd ed. (Cambridge: M.I.T. Press, 1966),
a book full of suggestive insight into the process of national
development. Chap. 6, "National Assimilation or Differentiation:
Some Quantitative Relationships," suggests that nations with unassimilated elements (the Negroes and the South, both, in the
American case) are confronted with potential conflict. Thus, while
sectionalism carries a definite advantage (the impulse to rely on
local initiative in planning and development), it also presents the
danger of open, violent conflict.

31. Young, *op. cit.,* is a good example of this tendency. On p. 250 he
calls the new nation "thrice handicapped": by the remoteness and
isolation of the government from its citizens; by the internal
organization of the government, which amplified the separate and
rival interests of which the nation was composed by reflecting them
perfectly in the nation's capital; and by the negative attitude of
the rulers themselves toward power, which "stifled the impulse
toward that statecraft which seems essential for the effective management of conflict. . . ."

32. One provocative statement of this point is Robert Lane's *Political*

Ideology (New York: Free Press, 1962), esp. pp. 321–345, which suggests a relationship between "low-tension morality and low-tension politics" in America. For a theoretical analysis, see Reinhold Niebuhr, *The Children of Light and the Children of Darkness* (New York: Charles Scribner's Sons, 1944), chap. 4; and Hannah Arendt, *On Revolution* (New York: Viking Press, 1965), chap. 2, esp. pp. 65–68.

33. As William Nisbet Chambers, for example, argues, it cannot be denied that, despite the occasional bitterness of political dialogue during this period, conflict between the Federalists and Republicans was for the most part peaceable and the regime remarkably stable during what he calls "the first American party system." See his essay "Parties and Nation-Building in America," in *Political Parties and National Development,* eds. Joseph La Palombara and Myron Weiner (Princeton, N.J.: Princeton University Press, 1966), pp. 104–106. See also the more extended treatment in his *Political Parties in a New Nation: The American Experience, 1776–1809* (New York: Oxford University Press, 1963), esp. pp. 96–99.

34. These two strands, with variations, are identified and brilliantly analyzed by David Potter in *The South and the Sectional Conflict* (Baton Rouge: Louisiana State University Press, 1968), chap. 4.

35. Robert Dahl calls the place of the Negro in American society "the single most concrete, persistent and explosive issue" from the founding to the present. See his essay, chap. 2, in Dahl, ed., *Political Oppositions in Western Democracies* (New Haven, Conn.: Yale University Press, 1966), p. 49.

36. Ulrich B. Phillips used to insist that the South made a strategic error in allowing the sectional conflict to focus on slavery, on which it was easily isolated and put on the defensive. If the South had been willing to abolish the institution of slavery, and rest its social institutions simply and candidly on the concept of white supremacy, it might even have been possible to gain a national consensus in support of the "central theme" of their view, that the United States was a white man's country (*The Course of the South to Secession,* ed. E. M. Coulter [Gloucester, Mass.: Peter Smith, 1958], pp. 124–126, 151 ff.). Phillips may be right in suggesting that no section had a monopoly on racial prejudice, but the uniqueness of the Southern situation with regard to the black presence would nevertheless have isolated the Southerners as surely on the proposition of modifying the nation's commitment to human equality as it did on altering the nation's commitment

to human liberty. It is doubtless true that an openness toward including blacks in the promise of equality was possible for Northerners only because the question was basically abstract and moral for them, but never so for Southerners. Still, if Southerners had found a way to maintain a plantation regime based on a caste system and still keep whites supreme, the effect, politically, would have been to augment the Southern share of political power in the national government by two-fifths of the black population, without changing the basic conflict between the Northern and the Southern social systems. One possible effect might have been to force the North to a more profound understanding of the stakes of the struggle of 1861–1865, but it seems unlikely that the struggle itself could have been averted by such a change in Southern strategy.

37. For an astute analysis of these myths, including their modern counterparts, see Theodore Draper, "The Fantasy of Black Nationalism," *Commentary*, 48 (September 1969), 27–54.

38. The figures and ratios are neatly summarized in A. D. Adams, *op. cit.*, pp. 3–7.

39. *Ibid.*, p. 39.

40. The subtitle of Litwack's book is *The Negro in the Free States, 1790–1860* (Chicago: University of Chicago Press, 1961).

41. As U. B. Phillips summarized the Southern view, "Slavery was instituted not merely to provide control of labor but also as a system of racial adjustment and social order" (*Course of the South to Secession,* p. 152).

42. Perhaps if the blacks had been able to mount a serious resistance movement, and the South had been driven to seek Northern aid, a sense of national responsibility might have developed—though where this would have left the blacks is frightening to contemplate. But inasmuch as Southern police forces were able to cope with the threat of black insurrection, leaders in both sections were happy to leave the problem to state and local control.

43. Potter, *op. cit.*, pp. 72–81.

44. This point is emphasized, and related to a larger theory of the relationship between government and opposition, by Dahl, *op. cit.*, pp. 359–367.

45. Paullin, *op. cit.*, plate 138A. Stagecoach routes were limited to a perimeter bounded by Boston, Bennington, and Albany on the north, the Alleghenies on the west, and Richmond on the south (*op. cit.*, p. 133).

46. Goodrich, *op. cit.*, pp. 23–36.

Index